Tricks of the Visual Basic™ 4 Gurus

Tricks of the
Visual Basic™ 4
Gurus

James E. Bettone,
Dwayne R. Gifford,
et al.

SAMS
PUBLISHING

201 West 103rd Street
Indianapolis, IN 46290

This is to my lovely, patient, understanding, and gorgeous wife, Helaina and to Chanel, both of whom patiently and gently guided me, cheered me on, put up with my bad moods, and kept me on track. Without their loving support and guidance, it would not have been possible for me to write this book. I can never thank you both enough.

-James E. Bettone

To my hearts and souls, Iris my most beautiful wife, Kevin, Michelle, and Jason, my lovely children. Without their love and support it would have been impossible to have completed this book.

-Dwayne Gifford

Copyright© 1996 by Sams Publishing

Publisher and President:	*Richard K. Swadley*
Acquisitions Manager:	*Greg Wiegand*
Development Manager:	*Dean Miller*
Managing Editor:	*Cindy Morrow*
Marketing Manager:	*John Pierce*
Assistant Marketing Manager:	*Kristina Perry*

Acquisitions Editors
Brad Jones, Sharon Cox

Development Editor
Anthony Amico

Software Development Specialist
Steve Straiger

Production Editor
Tonya R. Simpson

Copy Editors
Fran Blauw, Anne Owen, Greg Horman, Anna Huff, Joe Williams, Kim Hannel, Marla Reece

Technical Reviewers
Stephen Tallon
Ricardo Birmele

Editorial Coordinator
Bill Whitmer

Technical Edit Coordinator
Lynette Quinn

Resource Coordinator
Deborah Frisby

Formatter
Frank Sinclair

Editorial Assistants
Carol Ackerman, Andi Richter, Rhonda Tinch-Mize

Cover Designer
Tim Amrhein

Book Designer
Alyssa Yesh

Copy Writer
Peter Fuller

Production Team Supervisor
Brad Chinn

Production
Stephen Adams, Carol Bowers, Michael Brumitt, Tim Griffin, Jason Hand, Daniel Harris, Paula Lowell, Casey Price, Laura Robbins, Bobbi Satterfield, Andrew Stone, Susan Van Ness, Jeff Yesh, Mark Walchle

Overview

Contents

Acknowledgments

I would like to thank everyone who made it possible for Dwayne and me to write this book. A book of this caliber on such a broad topic as this would not have been possible for one individual, let alone two. I would like to personally thank all the authors who contributed so much of their time and knowledge to help make this book the *Top Gun* of Visual Basic books.

It would not have been possible for me to spend so much time and energy on this book without the loving support and understanding from my family, Helaina, Chanel, and of course, my "other" children, Garfield, Diamonds, Tazzy, and Pearl.

I would also like to acknowledge these people whose help and guidance made it possible for me to be where I am today: Riley Carrier, SFC, Hank Gawlik, SFC, Mark Boland, Gibson (Hey, Mon!), Robert Brown, Mike Seerden, Chris (did Bob bring doughnuts?), Curt Doolittle, Lyle Hazel (Lame Dude!), John Norwood (thanks for everything), Jim Meyer (Baa! Baa!), and Shawn Oberst (what was that clue?).

For all you "C" guys: So, BASIC isn't a real language, eh? <heh! heh!>

—*James E. Bettone*

It would be impossible for just one or two people to write this top notch of a book. I would like to thank the great authors who helped James and me write this book.

I would like to thank Brenda McGee for writing such a great Biography for me. Also I would like to thank Rob Schoedel for his help on "The Jet Database Engine" and "Cross-Platform Development." Finally, I would like to thank some very good friends for helping throughout my professional career: Amrik Bhogal, Allen Nieman, Aaron Carta, Robert Altinger, and Craig Longman.

I can never say enough about the love that I receive from my wife, Iris, and my three children, Kevin, Michelle, and Jason. If it were not for them it would have been impossible for me to have completed this book on time.

—*Dwayne Gifford*

About the Authors

James Bettone is a Software Developer for CEGELEC ESCA Corporation in Kirkland, Washington. In addition to organizing and authoring this book, he has also contributed to *Access 95 Unleashed*. He has been working with Microsoft Visual Basic and Microsoft Access since their initial release and has developed a variety of applications for the last ten years. He is currently developing software products for the utility industry at CEGELEC ESCA and currently resides in Everett, Washington with his wife, Helaina, foster child Chanel, and two dogs and two cats, Diamonds, Tazzy, Garfield, and Pearl, respectively.

Dwayne Gifford has been a developer/analyst in Access, Excel, SQL Server, and Visual Basic for the past five years. He has been a professional trainer in Access, Excel, Visual Basic, and Microsoft Project. In addition to organizing and writing *Tricks of the Visual Basic 4 Gurus* and *Access 95 Unleashed*, he has contributed to *Office95 Unleashed*. He has chosen topics that are important in that the reader can gain a general to extensive knowledge of the powers of these Microsoft applications. You will find his writing style to be clear and easy to follow. He is currently a Lead Systems Analyst for Excel Data Corporation on contract to Microsoft, where he supports the operations of their largest internal systems. He can be contacted at a-dwayg@microsoft.com.

Dan Clark is a Senior Consultant for Financial Data Systems Incorporated and is currently under contract with Microsoft's Information Technology Group. He specializes in analysis, design, and development of client/server database systems using a wide variety of tools, including Microsoft SQL Server, Visual Basic, and Access. Clark's computer industry career spans 20 years in a wide variety of technical and management positions with major U.S. companies including: Peat, Marwick, Mitchell & Company (now KMPG), Digital Equipment Corporation, and Texas Instruments. Since 1990, as a consultant, he has developed systems in Massachusetts, New Hampshire, Texas, and Washington state for many major corporations including: Fidelity Investments, Lotus Development, Digital Equipment Corporation, First Data Corporation, and the University of Massachusetts Medical Center. Currently he is focusing on the development of Internet-enabled data warehouse and decision support systems. He can be reached at danc@halcyon.com.

Ken Felder graduated from the University of North Carolina in Chapel Hill with degrees in Physics and English. His first job was as a technical writer for a small software company, where he discovered that he loved the industry and hated the job. He went on to become a professional developer for three or four years. In various software companies and at various times, he has also done UI and API design, marketing, sales, and occasionally, management. He currently works at Microsoft as the Program Manager for Visual SourceSafe.

Ken lives in Redmond, Washington with his wife, daughter, and fetus. His spare time is mostly spent searching for higher truth in Hindu, Buddhist, and Zen practices. No luck so far.

Bryce Ferguson is one of a vanishing breed, a native of Washington state. Once intent on a professional music career as an orchestral trombonist, he studied trombone at the University of Washington, after which he quickly came to his senses and opted to seek out a real job. He worked with fellow RDO guru Brad, working on GIS and demographic data projects. During that time he undertook programming studies at the University of Hard Knocks where he graduated with a DVB (Doctor of Visual Basic). When not furiously hammering out VB code, he freelances as a semi-professional trombonist to keep in shape just in case VB doesn't last. He currently resides in Redmond, Washington with his lovely wife and two marvelous children.

Frank Font started using Visual Basic when version 1.0 first came out and hasn't stopped using it since. He works in the Washington, DC area and is in the process of completing a masters degree in AI. He is blessed with a lovely wife and two young sons. Frank was a co-author of *Visual Basic 4 Unleashed* and a contributer to *Visual Basic 4 Developer's Guide*, both by Sams Publishing.

Delane Hewitt has been working with Visual Basic since its initial Beta. His primary interests are client/server computing, man-machine interfaces, and applications of virtual reality, for which he also holds advanced degrees. He enjoys the Pacific Northwest outdoors and all aspects of the Internet. He is currently a Program Manager for the upcoming Microsoft Internet Studio project. Delane can be contacted at `delaneh@microsoft.com`.

A. Nicklas Malik is the President of Malik Information Services, a Seattle-based consulting and training firm. He is a consultant, designer, author, and instructor specializing in enterprise database management, client/server development, user interface design, and artificial intelligence. He is a recognized expert in Visual Basic and is a recipient of the prestigious Microsoft MVP award for his contribution to Visual Basic on CompuServe. He can be reached at `76055.2722@compuserve.com`.

Merrill Mayer is a software developer for BEST Consulting in Kirkland, Washington. She has been working with Microsoft Visual Basic and Access for several years, developing a variety of business applications. She is currently a consultant/developer for Microsoft's Information Technology Group.

Brad Midstokke has been a consultant with BEST Consulting for over two years, specializing in C/C++, VB, and SQL Server applications design and development. A reformed carpenter, he's been perfecting his craft as a programmer since the IBM PC was a newfangled thing. In the past he designed, co-developed, and acted as project manager for several versions of a significant Geographic Information Systems application. He also led the team that designed the data management engine for a data selection and retrieval application. Current projects have him migrating large applications from VBSQL to RDO. He lives in Bothell, Washington with his bride, son, and twin daughters.

Michael Murphy has been employed at Microsoft for the past three years and is currently the Production Manager for Licensing and Sales Programs. He has produced tools that are used worldwide by Microsoft customers and employees in support of the licensing business. The applications he has written and supported utilize the full suite of Microsoft products, including Visual Basic, Access, and SQL Server.

Shawn Oberst is a Development Lead for Microsoft's Information Technology Group. As a Development Lead, he is responsible for all technical aspects of product development and project management. As an architect and developer within ITG's Reusable Technology Group, he specializes in the application of OLE/COM technologies to building *n*-tier client/server applications. With degrees in both Information Systems and Computer Science, he believes his greatest strength is in the practical application of computer science concepts to real-life business problems. He is an expert in information systems, object-oriented technologies, language design, CASE tools, and video game development. He has the strange distinction of having built production applications in thirteen different formal programming languages and twenty-three different applications languages. He can be reached at ShawnOb@Microsoft.Com.

Christopher Rotberg is a graduate of California State Polytechnic Pomona where he studied Finance and Economics. He is currently on assignment at Microsoft in Redmond, Washington, developing business applications for ITG. Chris programs in Visual Basic, Access, Excel, and is currently moving into Visual C++. This is his first writing project and he hopes to improve his writing skills on future projects. He credits his accomplishments to his parents, wife Billie, and his sons Dominic and Nicholas, who put up with his long hours and constant studying.

Introduction

By James E. Bettone

Welcome to *Tricks of the Visual Basic 4 Gurus*, which covers the latest release of Visual Basic, version 4.0. It also covers the tips and tricks to programming Visual Basic 4.0, specifically 32-bit development in Windows 95.

Visual Basic is finally being recognized as a "real" programming language, even by hard-core C developers. There are many new and powerful features of this new release that make it hard to ignore this fact. In this book, you learn how to use the new, powerful features of Visual Basic 4 to develop object-oriented applications, design and develop applications using the three-tier services model, deploy application components across a remote network, use the latest in database programming techniques, and much more.

We authors have tried to stay true to the original intent of this book, which is to provide tips and tricks from Visual Basic gurus and show you how the gurus do it. You will find that each chapter has a plethora of examples, sample illustrations, and, of course, tips and tricks. Not only do we explain *what* it is we're doing and *how* we're doing it, we also provide working sample code.

In any case, find the topic that you are interested in, start reading, and jump into the sample code provided. Eventually, even you can be a guru!

Good luck,

James E. Bettone

Conventions Used in This Book

The following typographic conventions are used in this book:

- Code lines, commands, statements, variables, and any text you type or see on the screen appears in a `computer` typeface.

- Placeholders in syntax descriptions appear in an *`italic computer`* typeface. Replace the placeholders with the actual filename, parameter, or whatever element it represents.

- *Italics* highlight technical terms when they first appear in the text and are sometimes used to emphasize important points.

- A special icon ➡ is used before a line of code that is really a continuation of the preceding line. Sometimes a line of code is too long to fit as a single line in the book, given the book's limited width. If you see the ➡ before a line of code, remember that you should interpret the "line" as part of the line immediately before it.

Extending
Visual Basic

P A R T

1

Visual Basic Naming Conventions

by Michael Murphy

CHAPTER 1

This chapter describes the importance of standardizing your code by using Visual Basic naming conventions, gives you a list of those conventions, and shows you how to use them in your project. This chapter also briefly discusses how these naming conventions are used throughout the book.

An Overview of Naming Conventions

Imagine reading this book without punctuation, capitalization, or any other standard formatting. The author's points would be hard to understand and would allow a lot of room for interpretation. Using standard formatting enables the author to communicate more effectively. The idea behind Visual Basic naming conventions is the same: Write your code so that others can easily understand it.

There are many Visual Basic naming conventions in use today. *Hungarian notation,* named in honor of legendary Microsoft programmer Charles Simonyi, is a widely used convention used not only in Visual Basic, but also in many other languages such as C/C++, FORTRAN, and so on. You will find it mentioned in Microsoft product documentation, trade journals, and many other publications. This chapter focuses on the use of Hungarian notation as the naming standard.

Hungarian notation is pretty simple; use a lowercase letter(s) to denote the data type of the variable and separate the prefix from the body of the variable by using a capital letter. As you can see from the following example, applying naming conventions to the code helps the developer read and understand code:

Before applying Hungarian notation:

```
Private Sub Command1_Click()
    Dim x As Long, y As Currency
    x = CLng(InputBox("Please enter the number of shares."))
    y = CCur(InputBox("Please enter the current share price."))
    MsgBox "The total amount of this transation is: " & x * y
End Sub
```

Now, apply the naming convention:

```
Private Sub cmdCalculatePrice_Click()
    Dim lngShares As Long, curPrice As Currency
    lngShares = CLng(InputBox("Please enter the number of shares."))
    curPrice = CCur(InputBox("Please enter the current share price."))
    MsgBox "The total amount of this transation is: " & lngShares * curPrice
    End Sub
```

This notation has evolved over the years to adapt to changes in programming techniques and to allow for flexibility. It is discussed in more detail in the following sections.

Although Hungarian notation is viewed as a "standard," you will find many variations of it. If you use Windows API calls, for example, you will find a different version of Hungarian used in the Windows SDK than the one listed in this chapter. The important thing to remember about a naming convention is that you need to adopt one and stick to it.

Why Use Naming Conventions?

Using standard naming conventions in your Visual Basic project is very important. These naming standards are especially important on larger projects and projects with more than one developer. Using naming standards in your project will improve the overall success of your project by doing the following:

- Reducing the number of bugs by eliminating much of the ambiguity of your source code.
- Reducing errors caused by a data type mismatch. These errors are caused when you are trying to assign a value that is not compatible with the receiving data type. For example, assigning a string value of "one" into an integer data type would cause a type mismatch error (runtime error 13). Because Hungarian notation describes the use and data type of the variable, you are less likely to have errors caused by a data type mismatch.
- Reducing maintenance costs and time because the code is in a standardized format that is easier to read and understand.
- Increasing code reusability. If you use naming standards for all your projects, you should be able to easily incorporate code segments from other projects.

Applying Naming Conventions to Your Code

The following sections show you how to apply Visual Basic naming conventions to your variables, objects, database objects, constants, menus, and third-party controls.

Variable Naming Conventions

If you declare your variables using Hungarian notation, you should be able to simply look at the variable and know the scope, data type, and intended purpose of the variable. By placing lowercase prefix values (scope and type) and beginning the body of the variable with an uppercase letter, the variable should be easy to read. Use the following structure when you declare variables:

scope type Body

Table 1.1 explains the elements of this structure. Note that the bold characters in the Example column are used to highlight the part described.

Table 1.1. The naming structure of variables.

Part	Description	Example
scope	Describes the scope of the variable	**m**strCompanyName
type	Describes the data type of the variable	m**str**CompanyName
Body	Describes the variable	mstr**CompanyName**

Defining Scope

The *scope* of a variable is the level at which the variable is visible. A variable declared in a function is visible only in that function, for example. Procedures also can declare variables as *arguments*. It is useful to denote these types of variables according to their usage. Table 1.2 illustrates the use of the scope prefix.

Table 1.2. Defining scope and usage.

Prefix	Description
g	Global
m	Local to the module or form
(none)	Local to the procedure (nonstatic)
st	Static variable
r	Variable passed by reference
v	Variable passed by value

> You should try to declare variables with the smallest possible scope. Global variables add complexity and make maintenance and reusability more difficult.

Defining the Data Type

The *type* segment of the naming convention enables you to easily identify the data type of the variable. Table 1.3 defines Visual Basic variable prefixes. You should use these prefixes with all variable declarations.

Table 1.3. Using Visual Basic variable prefixes.

Prefix	Data Type	Example
bln	Boolean	blnAnswer
byt	byte	bytAge
cur	currency	curPayment
dat	date	datBirthDay
dbl	double	dblHeight
int	integer	intCounter
lng	long	lngRecordCount
obj	object	objListBox
sng	single	sngWeight
str	string	strFirstName
udt	user defined	udtTask
vnt	variant	vntInfo

Defining the Body

The body of a variable should use mixed case and should clearly describe the variable. The first letter of the body should begin with a capital letter. Other words that make up the body also should begin with a capital letter. If you have a variable that will contain information about someone's name, for example, you can use *FirstName* or *LastName* as the body of the variable. Capitalizing the beginning of each word in the body makes it easier to read.

You also should be as descriptive as possible in the body of the variable. You could have abbreviated *FirstName* to *Fname*, for example, but you should not abbreviate unless it is necessary due to the 40-character limit in Visual Basic.

Object Naming Conventions

Applying Hungarian notation to objects is quite easy. All you need to do is add a prefix (in lowercase), and then describe the object in the body. Use the following structure when you name objects:

prefix Body

The *Visual Basic Programmer's Guide* contains a list of common object types along with the associated prefix.

Database Object Naming Conventions

Again, follow the same Hungarian structure when you name database objects.

prefix Body

Table 1.4 lists these objects and their prefixes.

Table 1.4. Database object prefixes.

Prefix	Object Type	Example
db	Database	dbProject
ds	Dynaset	dsCustomer
fd	Field	fdCompanyName
fdc	Field collection	fdcLicense
ix	Index	ixCustomerID
ixc	Index collection	ixcContact
qd	QueryDef	qdSales
ss	Snapshot	ssCountry
tb	Table	tbAccount
td	TableDef	tdChannel

Naming Conventions for Constants

The naming convention for constants is slightly different than those for variables. As you can see from the following structure, it looks the same:

scope type BODY

The only difference in naming a constant is that you use all uppercase letters in the body. Also, you should use the underscore (_) character between words. If you use this convention for your constants, constants are easily distinguishable from variables, as you can see from these examples:

```
gstrAPPLICATON_NAME
mintTASK_LIST
```

Menu Naming Conventions

Naming conventions for menu controls also are handled slightly differently than other objects because of the way they are accessed. You should use the mnu prefix along with *Body*. The *Body* should indicate the level of nesting. Look at the following examples:

```
mnuFile
   mnuFileOpen
   mnuFileClose
   mnuFileExit
mnuEdit
   mnuEditCut
   mnuEditCopy
   mnuEditPaste
```

When the menu convention is used, all members of a particular menu group are listed next to each other in the Code and Property windows. This makes menu objects very easy to find, as you can see from Figure 1.1.

Figure 1.1.
Menu objects.

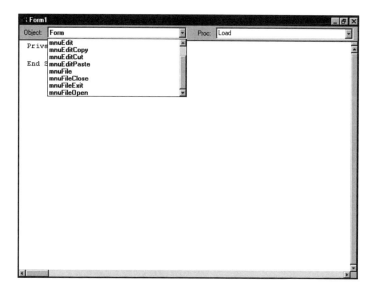

Third-Party Controls

Naming conventions for third-party controls are much like naming conventions for a standard object. The only difference is the addition of a company name prefix in the structure. When you use the company name prefix, you can use the first letter (in lowercase) to represent the company name, or simply use "o" for other.

prefix   company name prefix   Body

Summary

Naming conventions should play an important role in your Visual Basic projects. Using the conventions provided in this chapter should help you increase your project's success by reducing bugs caused by data-type mismatches and ambiguity, reducing maintenance costs, making your variables easy to read and understand, and improving the reusability of your code. Although there are many variations of Hungarian notation in use today, it is important that you adopt one as your standard and use it. These naming standards are used throughout the book.

Windows 95 Common Controls

by James E. Bettone

CHAPTER 2

The release of Windows 95 introduced an entirely new and powerful set of controls native to Windows 95 and Win32 operating systems, such as NT 3.51 with the enhanced Win95 interface. These controls are used throughout Windows 95, much as previous versions of Windows used the common dialog box.

In this chapter, you learn how to implement solutions through Visual Basic using these powerful sets of controls, which usually are referred to as the *Windows 95 common controls*. You also will learn how to take advantage of the new object-oriented features common to all OLE Custom Controls or OCXs—specifically, the object-oriented features of the Windows 95 common controls.

An Overview of the Common Controls

If you have ever installed or used Windows 95 or even NT with the Windows 95 interface, you will notice a new "look and feel" to the environment. And if you're even a little sharper, you will have noticed some similarities between the different dialog boxes throughout the operating system. These controls are used heavily throughout the operating system to provide that common look and feel.

Windows 95 introduces a new set of eight common controls that replaces the common dialog box interface used in earlier versions of Windows. Table 2.1 lists these new controls, and the sections throughout this chapter explain how to use these controls.

Table 2.1. The Windows 95 common controls.

Control	Function
ImageList	Stores images such as bitmaps and icons
TreeView	An enhanced hierarchical control similar to the Outline control
ListView	An enhanced listbox
ToolBar	A toolbar control
ProgressBar	Displays progress for lengthy operations
StatusBar	A control used to display various kinds of status data
TabStrip	A tabbed container control
Slider	A slider control

The Object-Oriented Aspects of the Windows 95 Controls

All the Windows 95 common controls are object-oriented and, to some degree, so is any control that is an OCX. The object-oriented aspects of these controls make them powerful, easy to use, and flexible. Almost all the common controls have some type of collection or properties that return objects. This chapter assumes that you already have a basic grasp of object-oriented objects. To fully understand concepts such as objects, collections, and classes, see Chapter 7, "Object-Oriented Concepts."

Keys and Indexes

All the Windows 95 common controls support the use of keys and indexes. *Indexes* are numeric base indexes on items in a collection, whereas *keys* are textual indexes on items in a collection. If a key is not specified for a certain object, the Key property is ignored; however, if a key is set for an object, both the key and the index can be used to access that object (in most cases). You cannot set the key to a numeric value; it automatically is typecast (or forced) into a numeric data type, and, if this succeeds, the key you specified returns an Invalid Key error. Keys must be all text or a combination of text and numerals—they can never contain just numerals.

The ImageList Control

The ImageList control contains a collection of images called List Images, each of which can be manipulated or referred to simply by using its index or key. This control is meant to be used in conjunction with other controls similar to the Image or PictureBox controls. See Figure 2.1 for an example of the ImageList control.

Figure 2.1.
The ImageList control.

All the common controls use images and have properties that specify an ImageList control. This makes it simple to use images of varying sizes, to use color or black-and-white images, and to load images from disk into your application. You can use the ImageList control, for example, to store a set of large and small images to be used with the Toolbar or TreeView control so that a user can switch back and forth between the two sizes at runtime. An image list can load either bitmaps or icons or a combination of both. The number of images that the control can hold is limited by memory.

Although you can load images into the ImageList control, you should be aware that the first image loaded sets the size for the rest of the images. If the other images are of a different size than the first image, they are all resized (and dithered) to the size of the first image. You'll notice this because the images will have a hazy look to them if they are not the same size as the first image in the image list.

Adding Images

You can add images to the image list at design time by clicking the Custom property and selecting the General tab. You can also right-click on the ImageList and Select properties. This will bring up the Properties dialog box, which you can use to insert images or remove images from the image list. You can also access properties for keys and indexes in this dialog box. For an example of the Custom Property screen of the image list, Figure 2.2 shows the General tab of the ImageList Control Properties dialog box.

Figure 2.2.
The General tab of the ImageList Control Properties screen.

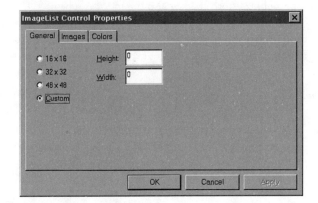

The Key property enables you to set a textual index for each image in the image list. As is the case with all the Windows 95 Custom Controls, the Key property cannot be a number of any type or a string containing just numbers; instead, it must contain all text or a combination of text and numbers. I will continually reiterate this throughout the chapter because this is a common mistake when using the Common Controls and this property.

Although the key can be any length, the longer the key, the slower it takes to access the image associated with it. This is true for all the common controls that support the Key properties. Consider this example:

```
' This is Bad
Set objImage = frmImageList.imgMyImageList.ListImages("This
➡is my unique key")
```

```
      ' This is Best
      Set objImage = frmImageList.imgMyImageList.ListImages("R1")
```
In short, you should keep the length of the key to a minimum. Also, keep in mind that the key is case-sensitive.

Manipulating Images at Runtime

Although images in an image list can be populated at design time, you might want to load images dynamically during runtime using the Add method of the ListImages collection. Each image list has a ListImages collection that contains ListImage objects (ListImages is a collection of ListImage objects). Each ListImage object represents an image in the image list. To add images to an image list at runtime, you can invoke the Add method and pass a pointer to an image, optionally passing in a key. The following example shows the different parameters of the Add method:

```
ImageList1.Add([index], [key], picture)
```

The Add method has three parameters: Index (optional), Key (optional), and Picture, as shown in the following example:

```
Dim objImage as ListImage

' Adds an image with a key of "James.ICO"
' and adds the image "C:\James.ICO" to the ListImages collection
➥of imgMyImageList
Set objImage = frmImageList.imgMyImageList.ListImages.Add
➥ (,"James.ICO",LoadPicture("C:\James.ICO"))
```

Manipulating Images

The ImageList control also has several methods that enable the developer to manipulate and render images. If you have ever tried to manipulate images with the Windows API (in Visual Basic 3.0), you probably remember how difficult, cryptic, and frustrating it can be for someone not familiar with that API. These methods make it much easier and less complicated to accomplish the same set of tasks. Table 2.2 lists the methods you can use to manipulate images.

Table 2.2. ImageList **image-manipulation methods.**

Method	Control	Description
Overlay	ImageList	Enables you to combine two separate images into one image
Draw	ListImages	Enables you to draw an image onto another image
ExtractIcon	ListImages	Converts an image to an icon

Using the `Overlay` Method

You can use the `Overlay` method to combine two separate images into one single image. Use this method with the `MaskColor` property to determine which color of the overlying image will be transparent. This method has two parameters: `Image1` and `Image2` (`Image2` is overlaid onto `Image1`). Consider the following example:

```
' Clears the contents of a Picture Box
picPicture.Picture = LoadPicture()

' Set the maskcolor to black
imgMyImageList.MaskColor = BLACK

' Overlays Rain.icon with Litening.ico, Pretty Cool, HUH?
picPicture.Picture = imgMyImageList.Overlay("rain.ico", "litening.ico")
```

`MaskColor` is the color that will be removed from `Image2`, making it appear transparent (so that you can see `Image1`). The default mask color is usually black. You can change this at design time or runtime. At design time, click the `Customize` property, and select the Colors tab. From the Property dialog's PropertyName list, select MaskColor. Select a color by clicking it or selecting it from the SystemColor drop-down list. Usually, you'll want to set this to the background color of the overlying bitmap.

Using the `Draw` Method

You can use the `Draw` method to draw or manipulate a single image and create a whole new separate image. You can stretch the image, create a highlight, or create a selected look for the image. Although most of these are done for you automatically by the other controls, there might be times when you need to manipulate images separate from the other common controls. The following example shows the `Draw` method:

```
' Set MaskColor to red, which will become transparent.
imgMyImageList.MaskColor = vbRed

' Draw the image with red (MaskColor) the transparent color.
imgMyImageList.ListImages(1).Draw picPicture.hDC,
➥lImageX, lImageY, imlTransparent
```

Using the `ExtractIcon` Method

You can use the `ExtractIcon` method to create icons from bitmaps. To do this using code in previous versions of Visual Basic, you had to have an intimate knowledge of the API and how bitmaps and icons work. The `ExtractIcon` method simplifies all this greatly. Simply execute this method from a `ListImage` object and—*viola!*—an icon is created. Consider this example which uses the first image in an image list (which happens to be a bitmap) and creates an icon from it:

```
' Creates an Icon from the first image in the ImageList.
frmImageList.MousePointer = imgMyImageList.ListImages(1).ExtractIcon
```

Tricks for Using `ImageList`

■ Store all application images in image lists. *Image lists* are lightweight (low-cost) controls (resource-wise, that is). Almost all applications use icons and bitmaps. The image list enables you to store these with the application without requiring that you first move to a directory external from the application.

■ Store icons or bitmaps of varying sizes in image lists. When you use the `ToolBar` control, you might want to have the capability to switch between small and large icons. The `ImageList` control enables the developer to store different sets of icons or bitmaps. You could dynamically resize the images at runtime, but this can create a dithered or hazy look to the icons.

■ Use the image list to manipulate images at runtime. The methods mentioned here make it simple and easy to manipulate images without the use of the API.

For examples of the `Draw`, `Overlay`, and `ExtractIcon` methods, see the `ImageList` example on the CD-ROM included with this book.

The `TreeView` Control

Do you remember the `Outline` control from Visual Basic 3.0? If you take that control one step into the future, you will get the `TreeView` control (see Figure 2.3). It is similar to the old `Outline` control because it specializes in the display and navigation of hierarchies. This is the control used in the Windows 95 Explorer (actually, most of the common controls are used throughout all of Windows 95) to represent the disk/file directory structure. If you want to have something a little bit different, however, the control allows for this. A complete set of properties, methods, and events is available to give you complete control over every aspect of `TreeView`.

Figure 2.3.
The `TreeView` control.

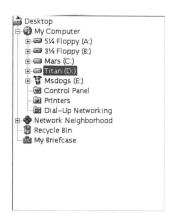

Using the Nodes Collection

The TreeView control manages its hierarchy via the Node objects and Nodes collection. A *node* is a point in the tree view hierarchy, and the *collection* is all the nodes in a tree view. If you look at Explorer (the left side is the tree view), for example, you can see that all the different directories are represented by various folder icons. Each folder or directory is a node and is represented by a folder in the tree view.

When a user clicks on a node in the tree view, it returns a Node object. The Node object represents that item in the TreeView that the user clicked; you can use it to learn anything you want to about that item, including where the node is in relation to the top-level node or root node, what its parent node is, or what and how many child nodes it possesses. Figure 2.4 shows an example of the hierarchical nature of the Node object/Nodes collection.

Figure 2.4.
The TreeView control's Node/Nodes collection hierarchy.

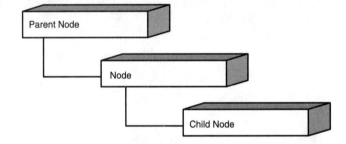

Setting the Events

Although the TreeView control possesses a complete set of events to control and monitor user interaction, there really are only three events that need special attention and *must* have code inside them: the Collapse, Expand, and NodeClick events. The Expand and Collapse events are pretty self-explanatory: They fire off or trigger when the user expands or collapses (opens or closes) a node. The NodeClick event occurs when a user clicks on a node but doesn't expand or collapse the node. In all these events, you are passed a *node object*, which is an object that represents the node on which the user clicked.

When you use TreeView, you usually will want it to load dynamically rather than all at once. Although this can be done (you will see an example of how to do this later), it can be somewhat slow (we all know how users don't like to wait). The NodeClick and Expand events are where you dynamically load the TreeView. This spreads the cost of loading the TreeView throughout the application rather than loading it all at once while the application is loading.

Using TreeView Properties

A few properties are quite useful and deserve special attention. Table 2.3 shows a list of the properties to remember when you use TreeView.

Table 2.3. Important properties of `TreeView`.

Method	Control	Description
HideSelection	TreeView	Hides the user's selection when the focus is lost
SelectedItem	TreeView	Returns an object that is the selected item
Image	Nodes	Specifies which image to display
ExpandedImage	Nodes	Specifies which image to display when expanded
SelectedImage	Nodes	Specifies which image to display when selected

The `HideSelection` property is common between both the `TreeView` and the `ListView`, and they both function in the same manner. This property, which defaults to `True`, causes whatever is selected to become "hidden" when the control loses focus. It might look like your selected items have become unselected, but actually they still are selected and can be accessed via the `SelectedItem` property. If you want to always show what is selected, regardless of which control the user clicks (a menu item, for example), you should set this property to `False`.

The `SelectedItem` property returns an object that represents the currently selected item (by you or a user).

Using the `EnsureVisible` Method

Use the `EnsureVisible` method when you want to make sure that an item is visible in the tree view (and the list view). This is a method of the `Node/Nodes` object. For the tree view, this sets the `SelectedItem` and `Selected` flag of the item to `True` and then repositions the item to ensure that it is visible. The following example sets the `Selected` property and illustrates how to use the `EnsureVisible` method.

```
' Select Item but might not be visible
TreeView1.Nodes(1).Selected = True

' This will both Select it and ensure it is visible
TreeView1.Nodes(1).EnsureVisible = True
```

Clearing a Tree View

You can remove the nodes of a tree view one item at a time or all at once. The `Clear` method removes everything from the tree view's `Node` collection, whereas `Remove` only removes one item at a time. The following example shows how to `Remove` a node of a tree view and how to `Clear` the entire tree view of nodes.

```
' This will get rid of the first Item
TreeView1.Nodes.Remove TreeView1.Nodes(1).Index

' This will clear the whole thing
TreeView1.Nodes.Clear
```

Editing the Text at Runtime

The tree view supports editing of text at runtime via the `StartLabelEdit` method. When this method is invoked, it will enable the user to edit the text label of the currently selected node. For more information on this feature, refer to the `ListView` control, Editing Text at runtime. This method reacts the same across both `TreeView` and `ListView` controls.

> **Tricks for Using `TreeView`**
>
> ■ If you are implementing a tree view into your application by itself, you only have to place code in the `Expand` and `Collapse` events and then use the `NodeClick` event to populate a `ListView` or other controls (if you have them).
>
> ■ If you want to find out whether the `SelectedItem` object is valid, use `Is Nothing` in an `If` statement, as in this example:
>
> ```
> If tvwTreeView.SelectedItem Is Nothing Then...
> ```
>
> ■ If you have a lot of data to place into the `TreeView` control, consider populating it gradually, as the user navigates through the control. This can be done by only populating the tree view with the nodes the user sees. As the user expands the nodes, add the additional nodes via the `Expand` event of the `TreeView`.

The `ListView` Control

The `ListView` control is a specialized type of listbox with some enhanced features that make it a pretty unique and useful control. With the listbox from Visual Basic 3.0, you could display information only in one way: in columns. With the `ListView` control, you can display information in three ways: in columns, icons, or both. This is the control used at the right side of Windows 95 Explorer that displays files and directory information. Figure 2.5 shows a sample of a list view.

Using `ListItems`

Each item in the list view is represented by a `ListItem` object, and each `ListItem` object belongs to the `ListItems` collection. This is similar in function to the `List(n)` property (in the listbox) in previous versions of Visual Basic, except that now it is in an object-oriented format.

Figure 2.5.
The list view.

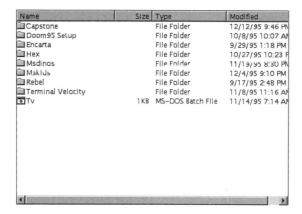

Using the `ColumnHeader` Object

The `ColumnHeader` object represents each column in the list view's Report view and can be viewed only from there. You can add columns to the list view at design time and runtime using the `Add` method of the `ColumnHeader` collection. There is always one column in the list view that is the actual list item. Any additional columns are considered subitems and are referred to by the `SubItems` property of the `ListItems` collection. If you have a list view with two columns (the first being the list item and the next being the subitem), for example, you can retrieve or set the value of the column using the following method:

```
' The second column
ListView1.ListItems(1).SubItems(2)
```

You also can add `ColumnHeaders` at runtime using the `Add` method. You can set most of the properties you need to while adding the column (as a parameter). Consider the following example, which shows how to add a column at runtime:

```
Dim colNewColumnHeader as ColumnHeader

' First Parameter is Index (Optional)
' Next is Key (Optional)
' Next is the Text Heading of the Column (Optional)
' Next is the Width of the Column (Optional)
' Next is the Alignment of the Column (Optional)
Set colNewColumnHeader = ListView1.ColumnHeaders.Add(,"R101", "Attributes",
➥(me.Textwidth("Attributes"))

' No Parameters
Set colNewColumnHeader = ListView1.ColumnHeaders.Add()
colNewColumnHeader.Text = "Attributes"
colNewColumnHeader.Width = Me.TextWidth(colNewColumnHeader.Text)
```

Notice that if parameters are left out (in this example, the Index parameter), a comma is still used to represent that parameter which you want to pass to the Add method. You only need to do this when there are other parameters after that parameter. If there are no parameters, you should follow the second example and pass in no parameters at all. Because the Add method returns an object (that points to the newly added ColumnHeader), you can set the properties off that returned object.

Using the SelectedItem Property

The SelectedItem property returns a ListItem object to the item the user selected or the currently selected item.

> Setting the Selected property of a ListItem object does not set the SelectedItem object. To work around this, set the SelectedItem object/property directly instead of setting the Selected property to True, as shown in this example:
>
> ```
> ' Doesn't Work
> ListView1.ListItems(1).Selected = True
>
> ' This Works
> ListView1.SelectedItem = ListView1.ListItems(1)
> ```

Using the View Property

You use the View property to specify which view to use to display the information contained in the list view. Table 2.4 lists the four available views.

Table 2.4. List view views.

View	Description
Icon	Program Manager type view with large icons (see Figure 2.6)
Small Icons	Program Manager type view with small icons
List	Listbox type view with small icons
Report	Detail view with columns of data using small icons

Like most of the other common controls, the ListView gets its images from an ImageList control. Two property settings actually exist for ImageLists: the Icon and SmallIcon properties. The Icon property points to an image list containing the large icons that ListView displays in Icon view. The small icon images are used by the remaining views.

Figure 2.6.
The Icon view of
`ListView.`

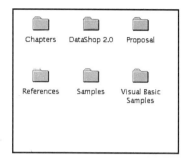

Using the `Ghosted` Property

The `Ghosted` property is a really slick property. When set, it gives that item a dimmed or "ghosted" look, as you can see by the "Dogs" entry in Figure 2.7. This is similar to what happens in Explorer when you cut an item and then paste it to the Clipboard. The item that is cut has a dimmed, ghost-like look to it.

Figure 2.7.
A "ghosted" list item.

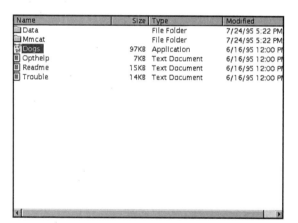

Using the `ItemClick` Event

The `ListView` has all the common set of events that almost all controls support, as well as a couple of special events. One of these events is the `ItemClick` event. This event triggers after a user clicks an item in the list view. The event returns a `ListItem` object that is a reference to the item the user selected.

Using the `FindItem` Method

One of the most useful methods of the `ListView` is the `FindItem` method. This method enables you to programmatically search through the contents of the list view—the text, the tag, or the subitems of the `ListItems` collection. This method is useful if the list view contains a large amount of data that you must search through, or if you want to find out whether an item already exists in the list view. This method returns an object (a `ListItem` object). Simply check whether this object is valid for success or failure, as shown in this example:

```
Dim lstFoundListItem As Object

' Start Search
' The First Parameter is the Text to look for
' The next is what to look in to find the Text
' The next is where to start (what index)
' The next what type of match
Set lstFoundListItem = ListView1.FindItem("ME", lvwTEXT, , lvwWholeWord)

' This Works
If Not (lstFoundListItem Is Nothing) Then
    ' Found or Already in List
Else
    ' Not Found or Not in List
End If
```

Using the `EnsureVisible` Method

The `EnsureVisible` method is similar to the `TreeView` method; it ensures that an item is selected and visible to a user. It sets the `SelectedItem` and `Selected` properties appropriately and moves the item so that it is visible to the user. Consider the following example:

```
' Select Item but might not be visible
TreeView1.Nodes(1).Selected = True

' This will both Select it and ensure it is visible
TreeView1.Nodes(1).EnsureVisible = True
```

Clearing a List View

The `ListView` control also supports both the `Clear` and `Remove` methods. The `Clear` method removes everything inside the list view, whereas the `Remove` method removes only the specified items from the list view. Both these methods are methods of the `ListItems` collection, not the `ListItem` object. Consider this example, which shows how to remove a specific list item and clear all list items from a list view:

```
' This will get rid of the first Item
ListView1.ListItems.Remove ListView1.ListItems(1).Index

' This will clear the whole thing
ListView1.ListItems.Clear
```

Editing the Text at Runtime

The list view also supports editing of text at runtime. Most of the time, you invoke these edits by double-clicking an item (this depends on the `LabelEdits` property setting of Automatic, Default, or Manual). If you want to programmatically start the editing process, you can invoke the `StartLabelEdit` method of `ListView`. This is similar to the user double-clicking an item. After the user presses Enter, an `AfterLabelEdit` event triggers (a `BeforeLabelEdit` event also triggers before the `LabelEdit` event), and this is where you place the code to actually make the change and save it. Figure 2.8 shows what this Edit mode looks like.

Figure 2.8.
An item in Edit mode.

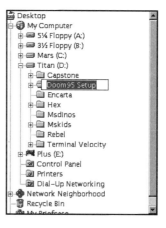

Tricks for Using `ListView`

- Use the `ItemClick` and `Double_Click` events for most of the processing for this control. The user is either going to select an item by clicking or double-clicking an icon in the list view.

- Remember that setting the `Selected` property to `True` does not set the `SelectedItem` object. If you want to set the `Selected` property for a list item, set the `SelectedItem` directly.

- Use `ImageList` to manage the large and small icons. Use the `ImageList` control to store different size bitmaps and icons and plug them into the list view's Normal and Small Images properties (on the Custom tab).

The ToolBar Control

The ToolBar control provides an easy way to implement toolbars in your application. It provides such features as *ToolTips* (floating Help), button groups, and toggle buttons. With this control, you can add buttons at runtime as well as customize which buttons are displayed to the user at runtime. You can find this control throughout Windows 95. For an example of the ToolBar control, see Figure 2.9.

Figure 2.9.
The ToolBar control.

Usually, a toolbar will have buttons that match items in the application's menu. Each button provides a graphical interface to the most frequently used functions or commands (usually from the menu).

Using the Button Object and Buttons Collection

Each button on the toolbar is represented by a Button object in the Buttons collection. With each Button object, you can optionally set the image/text for that button, the caption, and the ToolTip text.

To program the toolbar, you need to insert code behind or in the ButtonClick event. When this event fires off, you are passed a Button object. You can use this on a Select Case statement to process the proper button by checking its Index or Key property, as this example shows:

```
Select Case Button.Index
    Case 1 ' First Button
    Case 2 ' Second Button
End Select
```

Using the Style Property

You can control how the buttons in the toolbar react by setting the Style property. You also can set hidden buttons (which is how you place spaces between buttons) or a ButtonGroup type button. Table 2.5 lists the settings for this property.

Table 2.5. The Button object's Style property.

Style	Constant	Description
Regular button	tbrDefault	A regular pushbutton.
Toggle button	tbrCheck	Acts like a toggle switch.

Style	Constant	Description
Group of buttons	tbrButtonGroup	Only one button can be pressed in one button group, and it remains pressed until another button is pressed.
Hidden button	tbrSeparator	A hidden button you can use to separate other buttons (provides a space of eight pixels).
Placeholder	tbrPlaceholder	Serves as a placeholder for another control, such as a drop-down combo box. You can set the width of this button.

Adding Controls to the Toolbar

You can use the ToolBar control to add other controls to the toolbar. You do this by placing a button on the toolbar and assigning a style of PlaceHolder. Size the button to the size and width of the control and then place the control on the toolbar. Figure 2.10 shows an example of a toolbar with different styles of buttons such as PlaceHolder, Group, Check, and Default.

Figure 2.10.
A sample toolbar.

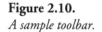 

Adding Buttons

You can use the toolbar to programmatically add and delete buttons with the Add and Remove methods of the Button object. The Add method offers settings for the button's caption, image, style, and key.

Customizing the Toolbar

You can use the ToolBar control to customize the toolbar at runtime. The user can simply double-click the toolbar to invoke the Toolbar Control Properties dialog box, which enables the user to hide, display, or even rearrange buttons on the toolbar (see Figure 2.11). The AllowCustomize property of the toolbar enables or disables this functionality, and the SaveToolbar and RestoreToolbar methods save and restore the toolbar. You use the Change event of the toolbar to place the code that actually invokes the SaveToolbar/RestoreToolbar methods. Figure 2.11 shows the customize dialog of the toolbar available at design time only.

Figure 2.11.
The Toolbar Control Properties dialog box, in which you customize your toolbar.

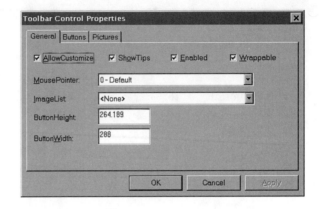

Creating ToolTips

Another neat feature of the toolbar is the built-in functionality of ToolTips. *ToolTips* are the little Help windows that appear when you place the mouse cursor over a toolbar button. The ToolBar control automatically supports this functionality; all you need to do is specify what text to display.

You use two properties to set up ToolTips: the ShowTips property of the ToolBar control and the Description property of the Button object. After you specify these settings, a description is displayed when the user places the mouse cursor over the button.

Tricks for Using ListView

- ■ Use the Button_Click event to manage the different buttons in the toolbar. Better yet, place all code in a Select Case statement based on the key or index of the buttons.

- ■ Use the ImageList control to manage toolbars of different sizes. You might have two image lists containing identical images but of different sizes, for example. You can use the appropriate image sizes from the image list so that the toolbar's buttons are resized automatically when the user wants to change the size of the toolbar.

The ProgressBar Control

You use the ProgressBar control to show the progress of lengthy or processor-intensive operations. It does this by completely filling a rectangle from left to right. See Figure 2.12 for an example of the ProgressBar control.

Figure 2.12.
The ProgressBar
control.

The ProgressBar control monitors an operation's progress toward completion. It functions like the Gauge control, but without the same precision.

The ProgressBar control is fairly easy to use. It generally is used to approximate the progress toward completion. You need to set three properties in order for the ProgressBar control to work properly. These properties are the Min and Max properties, which control the minimum and maximum values of the progress bar, and the Value property, which determines how much of the progress bar to fill at any given time. The progress bar displays only an approximation of the Value property based on the control's size.

The StatusBar Control

You use the StatusBar control to display information to a user or various types of status data. The status bar can have up to 16 panels, which can be controlled by the developer. See Figure 2.13 for an example of the StatusBar control.

Figure 2.13.
The StatusBar *control.*

Using the StatusBar Control

A StatusBar control consists of panels called *panel objects,* which can contain text or even a picture. You can control the appearance of the panels within the StatusBar control by setting certain properties. The Width and Bevel properties control the width and look of the status bar, and the Alignment property controls the alignment of text or pictures. Table 2.6 lists the seven styles of properties you can use.

Table 2.6. Style property values.

Style	Function
sbrText	Displays text
sbrCaps	Displays the status of the Caps Lock key
sbrNum	Displays the status of the Num Lock key
sbrIns	Displays the status of the Insert key

continues

Table 2.6. continued

Style	Function
sbrScroll	Displays the status of the Scroll Lock key
sbrTime	Displays the time using the system format specified in the International settings of the Control Panel
sbrDate	Displays the date in system format specified in the International settings of the Control Panel

At design time, you can customize the appearance of the status bar via the Customize property (by using the Panel Properties dialog box). This dialog box enables you to add and remove panels, set captions, and set pictures or text. Figure 2.14 shows a sample status bar.

Figure 2.14.
A sample status bar.

The TabStrip Control

The TabStrip control gives you the power to provide that Windows 95 tabbed dialog box look and feel to your applications. With the TabStrip control, you can define multiple dialog boxes or tabs for the same area of a screen within your application. Figure 2.15 shows a tabbed dialog box created with a TabStrip control.

Figure 2.15.
A tabbed dialog box created with the TabStrip control.

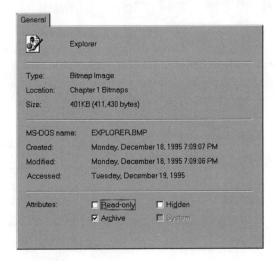

The `Slider` Control

A `Slider` control contains a sliding marker and some optional tick marks that form a dimensionless scale, as shown in Figure 2.16. This control is useful when you want to give your users an easy way to set values, all the while allowing them to have a feel for the magnitude of how much they are moving the control. You can use the `Slider` control to select which track to play on a CD, for example, or even where to play within that track.

Figure 2.16.
The Slider *control.*

Summary

In this chapter, you learned how to use the Windows 95 common controls, learned about the different common controls and some tips to use these controls to implement solutions and jazz up any application. With this powerful set of controls, you will be able to do things with your application that previously were very difficult to accomplish. You now know how to give your applications a familiar look and feel. You're on your way to becoming a common controls guru!

Creating a Good Interface

by James E. Bettone and A. Nicklas Malik

CHAPTER 3

I was talking to a friend the other day about the new program she had written. She was proud of its user interface—but I wasn't terribly impressed. It prevented me from entering duplicate information (completely discarding my input), its online help was poor, and I got tired of having to close one window and open another before I could perform an action. I couldn't imagine how novice users would manage it, yet my friend didn't see anything wrong.

I know many Visual Basic programmers who have the same kind of interface "blind spot." They believe that they design good interfaces, but really, how do they know? What is the difference between a "good" and a "bad" interface? Does Visual Basic really make interface design easy?

Actually, Visual Basic only makes it easy to *construct* a user interface and to put code behind it. It does not make user interface design any easier. Good design implies that you have a method, not just a tool. A good designer knows how to structure the interface and how to tell when it is set up correctly.

What follows is a four-step process that you can use to evaluate the user interfaces of your programs. This method can expose problems in an interface early in the development process, when it is the least expensive to repair, and well before the users get the chance to complain. This chapter also covers design standards and issues for building good Windows 95 interfaces.

Step One: Understanding the Application

Designing a user interface is really an extension of overall program design. This means that you first have to decide what actions the user will need to perform. This is kind of like creating an informal function point analysis. In practical terms, here's how you do it.

Make a list of every different "action" that the user might want to perform. For example, if you were designing a word processor, your list would look something like this:

- Open a document
- Save a document
- Enter text
- Underline some text
- Change the current font
- Print one or more pages

And so on. Notice that this list does not include "select some text." The act of selecting text is a method contrived to accomplish other actions. It has no inherent value.

Keep in mind that the user can perform these actions in any order. Nothing in your program should require that core tasks be performed in a certain order. Some actions obviously precede others, such as opening a file before printing it. But, for the sake of the evaluation, ignore these requirements and focus on the actions themselves.

Step Two: Creating the Strawman

The next step is to put together an interface to work from. Slap together some forms, add the menus, put some controls on the forms, and put in only the code needed to load and unload every dialog and child window. This is your "interface strawman," a skeleton of the interface design that you will evaluate and sharpen. If the interface needs data elements in order to make sense, hard-code three or four lines to a text box or listbox, as needed. Don't worry about 3-D panels, color-coded selections, or any other visual details; they're not important at this point.

Don't write the real code yet. Once you do, you encase the interface in cement, and you first need to make sure you've got it right. Of course, if you are evaluating an existing program, you don't have the leisure of destroying a strawman. While this doesn't make a difference to the evaluation process, functional systems are considerably more difficult to retrofit than a strawman is.

Step Three: The Tools of Evaluation

The third step is at the heart of the issue: deciding whether or not your interface will actually make your program easy and efficient to use. Will feature X make your program better, or just waste your time? How can you improve the user interaction? Note that I am discussing the user *interaction*, not the overall user *interface*. Fine tuning this conversation between the computer and the user can make the difference between users experiencing ultra-fast productivity and head-pounding frustration.

Four criteria affect the foundation of the user interaction:

- Appearance
- Availability
- Responsiveness
- Reversibility

When evaluating your application, you'll be comparing it to other commercial-level applications on the basis of the preceding criteria.

Appearance

An appropriate appearance helps your users determine where they are in a process and what the next step should be. Some examples of appearance features include the following:

- Filenames in the title bar
- Cue cards
- Status messages and panels

- Well-organized menus
- Tool tips
- Carefully chosen default actions (that is, what happens when the user presses Enter)

Users of applications that have a high appearance value rarely feel lost or confused about what they should do next. While expert users often look on these features as "fluff," the novice and intermediate users of your program will appreciate them.

Availability

Availability measures the number of user actions that can be performed during or immediately after any other action. For example, when we say that the Print Document action is "very available," we mean that the user can print a document during or after most other actions—such as after entering text, doing a spell check, or creating a table. You'd be surprised how many applications do not enable the user to perform basic functions except at specific times.

Responsiveness

Responsiveness refers to the amount of work a user must do to perform the action itself. In a highly responsive application, even the most complicated actions can be accomplished through the use of well-selected default values. Some examples of responsive features include

- Wizards
- Toolbars
- Shortcut keys
- Customizable option settings
- Drag-and-drop functionality

The Print button on a Microsoft Word 6.0 toolbar shows good responsiveness. Normally, when you select the Print option from a menu, you have already selected, by default, the printer, page format, page layout, margins, paper tray, and print quality. In addition, the common Print dialog box includes pre-selected options such as "print one copy" and "print all pages." But the Word 6.0 toolbar goes one step further, and—with the click of a single button—prints the document.

Poor responsiveness occurs when the user has to maneuver through a nested menu or, even worse, has to exit one dialog and enter another in order to perform the desired action. Highly responsive applications appeal to expert and frequent users; however, attempts to make applications more friendly to novice users don't have to result in unresponsive applications.

Reversibility

The fourth criterion, reversibility, is the program's capacity for tolerating user mistakes. This measurement is familiar to most programmers. In this context, the ability to undo includes more than simply being able to reinsert deleted text. Users must also be able to cancel lengthy operations after they have begun. In general, an action is undo-able if the user can readily stop or reverse the effects of an action within a few seconds after its initiation.

In those cases in which the user will not be able to reverse an operation, the program should warn the user before the operation begins. This warning can be in a pop-up message box or can be a textual description printed on the dialog. A good example of reversibility is prompting the user before exiting an application where some editing has not yet been saved. Other reversibility features include being able to cancel a print operation, killing a window that is taking a long time to appear, or halting a long series of calculations.

Making the Grade

Evaluating the interface is not a difficult process, but it is a little tedious. The rewards, however, are well worth the effort. If you have any doubts about this method, walk through the entire process once for any application. The flaws and compromises in the user interface design will stand out.

First, make a chart with three columns, labeled Action, Criteria, and Evaluation. In the Action column, write each of the actions that the user can perform. Then evaluate that action as a complete process. The action begins when the user decides to perform it, and it ends when the action has been performed. The entire process should be viewed as a whole, including every mouse click and every keystroke. See Table 3.1 for an example evaluation.

Table 3.1. Sample "interface report card" for three of the actions in the Windows 3.1 Notepad applet.

Action	Criteria	Evaluation
Open a file	Appearance	Average. The assumed interaction is create a new file, not open existing file. However, use of the common dialog and standard menus helps to further the process.
	Availability	Excellent. Files can be opened at any time, except during a print operation.
	Responsiveness	Above average. Good defaults in the File Open dialog window.

continues

Table 3.1. continued

Action	Criteria	Evaluation
	Reversibility	Above average. Cancel button provided in File Open dialog. In addition, the user is prompted to save the current file before the new one is opened.
Denote text file as a TimeLog	Appearance	Poor. Described in online help only. No example given. Unusual and confusing notation (easily confused with file extension).
	Availability	Poor. Flagging an existing file as a TimeLog file only takes effect the next time the file is opened. Also, the .LOG string can appear in only one location in the file.
	Responsiveness	Below average. The following sequence is used: Move to top of document, enter the string `.LOG`. Effect is seen the next time file is opened.
	Reversibility	Below average. In addition to the fact that the automatic insertion of the timestamp cannot be undone, the operation of removing the .LOG string from the first line is undocumented, unusual, and counter-intuitive.
Insert timestamp	Appearance	Average. Cryptic menu entry "Time/Date" provides no clue to the actual operation. Well-described in online help. No help provided for changing timestamp format.
	Availability	Excellent. Timestamp can be added at any time.
	Responsiveness	Excellent. Hot key (F5) has immediate response. Good default format (from control panel).
	Reversibility	Poor. Inserting a timestamp cannot be undone, and its use wipes out the previous undo buffer.

Grading Appearance

To get a good grade for appearance, the interface must clearly show what task the user is in the process of performing, and it should prominently present the most common "next step" operations. Consider the most extreme case: that the user has stopped half-way through an operation before leaving for an extended vacation. When the user returns, the application is still running. Can the user tell what action to perform next? If so, you have an above-average appearance value.

Grading Availability

To earn high marks in availability, the action has to be available to the user during or immediately after most of the other actions. This means that the user does not have to go to any special lengths to begin the action. Thus, if a user has started to enter information for an invoice and then realizes that the customer is not in the customer table, the user should be able to enter the new customer and print a record for the paper files without quitting the process of entering the invoice. In this case, the Enter New Customer and Print Customer Details actions would be considered available. If these actions are available during a majority of other actions as well, the interface would deserve higher marks.

Grading Responsiveness

Evaluating responsiveness is basically a matter of counting keystrokes and mouse-strokes. The better your defaults are, the quicker the interaction will proceed. However, to decide if an action *should* be highly responsive, you have to consider who will be using it. Not every button will be pressed by every user, especially if you have a menu that is visible only to "power" users. Novice users are often more comfortable when being asked for more information.

Expert users expect your application to "know" what they are doing. Therefore, when a dialog appears to an expert user, the default values in it should reflect the actions that the user has taken in the past.

As a general rule, an action cannot be considered responsive if it requires more than two or three keystrokes and/or mouse clicks. Good default values are the key. Remember that a screen that appears with blank fields still has default values: empty strings. The only advantage of using empty strings for default values occurs when the user wants to routinely change the default. In this case, they don't have to delete the old text first. A good alternative is to highlight the entire contents of the field when the focus shifts to it. This way, if the user wants to enter a new value, he or she simply types it in.

Grading Reversibility

Reversibility is the most difficult criterion to meet for most applications. To understand where Reversibility is needed, you have to first find every place where the user is paying a penalty by performing an action. This ranges from the obvious (exiting without saving data) to the subtle (beginning a process that might take 90 seconds to complete). Not all penalties are in the form of lost data; some are in the form of lost time or distractions.

Determining all of the penalties that your program will assess on a user requires that you consider things from the user's point of view. Your user is generally not interested in the neat features of your application, nor in how difficult it was to do some special trick. The user has a job to do, and your program is a tool for accomplishing it. Anything that gets in the way of that job is a penalty.

For all of your penalties, assign protections. Provide ways to recover lost data. Make the users declare that they want to discard their work. Ask them to click two buttons to overwrite files or tables. Put bold warnings next to any buttons that they should think twice about before clicking. Flash the text or title bar, beep the speaker, or, on multimedia systems, speak a warning via the sound card. (But be polite; no one wants their computer calling them an idiot.) Most of these things can be placed directly into your interface strawman to see how they affect the interaction.

Don't overdo it, however. Remember that each of these protections is, in itself, a penalty. I find few things more annoying than having an application beep at me for doing what I intended to do. For example, Word 6.0 beeps if I am at the bottom of my document and I press the down-arrow. Why? Was I going to pay a penalty for clicking that key? If not, why penalize me by beeping?

As a general rule, the best reversibility features start after an action is done. The worst inform the end users of things they already knew.

When you are evaluating your strawman interface, actually use the application the same way that a novice would use it. Then try again, using the application the same way that an expert would use it. Try to understand the difference, and cater to both with different features. Aim the best appearance features at novice users and the most responsive features at the expert users.

Step Four: Refining the Interface

After you do the evaluation, determine what you can do to raise your grades. Change the interface, move controls, re-label menu items, add prompts, and so on. Then re-evaluate. Don't think of it as trial-and-error. Think of it as "prototype and refine."

Just as a good developer can always get better at coding, a good interface designer gets better at designing the interface. After a dozen times of following this process, you will have embedded it into your design thinking. This whole process will go very quickly, and the results will be better programs and more productive users.

Designing for Windows 95

Visual Basic 4.0 inherently supports the Windows 95 interface by directly supporting it within its design environment and in its custom controls. Designing a Windows 95 interface is already partially accomplished when using Visual Basic 4.0, and thus half of the battle for a good, polished interface is already won. Earlier in this chapter, you learned important design guidelines that in general lead to a user-friendly interface. This section covers the additional steps to creating a good visual interface from within Visual Basic 4.0, above and beyond what is already done automatically for us.

Designing a Form

When you are designing forms, be they non-MDI or MDI, there are some basic considerations to remember. The following are some general guidelines to follow.

Modal Versus Modeless

This is the question of the day. Generally, modal dialog boxes limit the interaction of a user unless he or she responds to the dialog box. Of course, this goes against the fundamental Windows design standard that says "The user is in control," because the user isn't in control when a modal dialog box is displayed—the application is. So the rule of thumb is to use dialog boxes only when absolutely necessary. (Message boxes are OK.)

Using Icons

Setting an icon for a form will do a number of things. Using a good icon is as important as setting one in the first place. Setting the `Icon` property of a form does a number of things, such as the following:

- Sets the icon to display when the form is minimized
- Sets the icon to display in the taskbar (assuming `ShowInTask` is set to `True`)
- Sets the icon to display in the title bar

Before compiling your application, make sure that all the icon properties for each and every form (dialog boxes, message boxes, and forms) are set to the proper icon. Don't ever use the default.

Other Form Considerations

There are a few other things to remember when you are designing forms. One of the most under-used properties is the `ShowInTask` property. This property determines if there will be an icon button displayed in the taskbar of the desktop. In general, dialog boxes or modal forms should never have this property set to `True`. Only *main* forms should have this set to `True`.

Another design consideration is the use of the `BorderStyle` and `ControlBox` properties. The `BorderStyle` property of a form designates what and how the form will look when displayed, and the control box is the small box located in the left corner of the form in the title bar. The following table lists what type of form uses which particular border style and control box.

Form Type	Styles	Control Box
Modal dialog box	3 or 4	Usually False
Main forms	2	True

Figure 3.1 shows a correct example of a generic non-modal form.

Figure 3.1.
An example of a generic non-modal form.

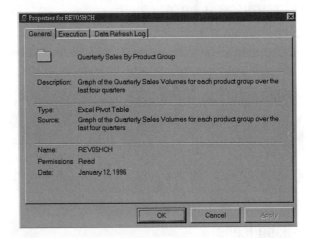

Message Boxes and Other Modal Dialog Boxes

When you are using messages boxes, it is important to remember to use the proper type of message box with the proper icon displayed, as shown in Table 3.2. Try not to overuse the *critical* icon when displaying information. If you use the critical icon all the time when you display messages, the user becomes anesthetized to the critical icon and ignores its importance in a real situation. So use your best judgment and only use the critical icon if necessary.

Table 3.2. Message box icons.

Icon	Description
vbCritical	Displays the Critical Message icon.
vbQuestion	Displays the Warning Query icon.
vbExclamation	Displays the Warning Message icon.
vbInformation	Displays the Information Message icon.

Context-Sensitive Menus

Context-sensitive menus are special types of menus that pop up in place when the user has right-clicked on an object in a form such as a text box or listbox. These are special types of menus that directly relate to the object on which the user has right-clicked. These types of menus have a certain structure that you should follow when you are designing your menus. Generally, the following is the structure:

- The default action should be in **bold**.
- The menus should be grouped together in a specific order. Operations that are specific to that object should be listed first, followed by the edit functions such as Cut, Copy, and Paste, and then the more generic items such as Properties or Delete.
- The last item in the menu should always be a Property menu if appropriate.

For an example of a context-sensitive menu, see Figure 3.2.

Figure 3.2.
An example of a context-sensitive menu.

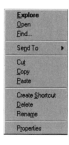

WhatsThisHelp

WhatsThisHelp is a new user-friendly feature of Windows 95. Basically, a user can either select a WhatsThisHelp icon from the toolbar or title bar or can right-click on the menu item and select the WhatsThisHelp menu. WhatsThisHelp displays help that is specific and tailored to the particular item or object on which the user right-clicked. This is almost like building a high-level tutorial right into your application; the user can go from field to field or from object to object, selecting WhatsThisHelp to figure out what every field and object on the screen does. How's that for user friendly?

See Figure 3.3 for an example of WhatsThisHelp.

Figure 3.3.
An example of WhatsThisHelp.

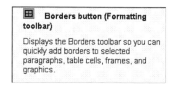

Summary

If the methods described in this chapter are used effectively, they will help you design an effective, user-friendly interface. The criteria for judging your interface can be expressed in a single sentence: "Can the users tell what to do, and can they do it whenever they want, with minimal interference and without penalties?" Sounds like Utopia, doesn't it? Aim high.

Optimizing Reports/Crystal Reports

by Daniel Clark

CHAPTER 4

What does "optimizing reports" mean? To define this, first we have to define "reports"; then we can define "optimizing."

In general, a *report* is a means of presenting business information to a user.

Optimizing reports in the context of this chapter means

- providing the data that the user wants
- in the form that he or she wants it
- at a speed that is acceptable
- with data that is consistent and accurate
- with a system that is easy to use

The types of systems and number of issues that can fit within this definition are extremely broad. Solutions range from simple reports run directly against a single-user, desktop, operational database to highly advanced, analytical systems that give the user an optimized reporting server, high-speed data retrieval and distribution mechanisms, and a wide range of desktop analysis tools.

This chapter limits the discussion to the mid-range of these solutions—producing structured ("canned") reports from client/server systems, which is a major need that many developers face. Although the term *report* can include graphical representations of data, this discussion is confined to reports in the more traditional sense—nongraphical tabular representations or form representations of the data. Using the architecture and methodology presented here, you can extend your system by adding modules of functionality or replacing current modules.

The most effective way to meet your goals is to use a *modular reporting system. Modular* means that it is comprised of components. *System* means that the components are integrated; each component is optimized for its role in the overall system solution. It enables the user to modify the output of the system on the fly. If designed properly, one report file will appear to be multiple reports, with different sets of data, displayed in different formats.

Unfortunately, the number of paths to creating a reporting system are many and varied. Very few books address the complex issues that you encounter. Many focus on the features of a single product and do not discuss architecture. The examples in these books are relatively simple, whereas the problems are complex. Most examples use desktop databases as the data source and imply that the solutions are extensible. Reality is that large, multiuser, network server-based databases present unique problems with very few documented solutions. Reality is that optimized solutions should have the capacity to be extended to more advanced systems as the needs of the user grow.

You see many avenues to approach your development problems. Which way is best? What are the bottlenecks? Where are the dead ends? What is the right way to do it?

The goal of this chapter is to give you the direction and answers you need to create a robust, expandable, professional-quality "optimized" reporting system for a client/server system. The tools used in the demonstration examples and discussions are Visual Basic (VB), Crystal Reports, and the Microsoft SQL Server DBMS. Rather than tell you all of the things that you *can* do with these tools, this chapter focuses on the key things that you *should* do (and should not do). The ideas presented can be extrapolated to other front-end development tools, report writers, and databases.

> Build the foundation—don't go for the quick fix. There is always a temptation to get a quick hit—to give the users what they want quickly, knowing you can always add to it later. Don't do it! Build the proper foundation.

Of special importance: All of the examples in this chapter were developed using Crystal Reports Pro version 4.5.1.1 (hereafter referred to as "CRW Pro"). The CRW Pro software modules that are included in VB 4.0 are custom 16- and 32-bit versions of Crystal Reports version 3.0. Although these are useful tools to learn the basics of creating reports, they lack many components necessary to create a robust system.

CRW Pro is the newer, higher-end, professional version of Crystal Reports. CRW Pro includes developer necessities such as CRW Print Engine documentation and declarations, 99 (versus 44) direct Print Engine functions, report drill-down features, and a more fully featured OLE control. The enhanced user interface includes an undo button, a data search feature, an auto arrange button, and visual table linking (for faster prototyping). Using CRW Pro is strongly recommended.

One final note: When you create a reporting system, the most important element is the database and the methods that you use to retrieve data from it. The finest, easiest-to-use user interface and the slickest-looking reports are of little value if the data in the report is inaccurate or the report takes too long to print. Remember the political slogan in a recent American presidential campaign: "It's the economy, stupid!" To paraphrase that slogan, the most important issue is, "It's the database, stupid!" Spend most of your time on the database.

What Are Reports?

Reports are mechanisms for producing business information in a format that is meaningful to the user. Why so specific a statement about something that should be obvious? The reason is to focus on two key phrases, "business information" and "meaningful to the user." With reports, we transform operational data into meaningful business information. We make it relevant to the user. We provide business-specific context, derive additional data, interpret, and extract significance from seemingly disconnected bits of operational data.

Reports are categorized in two ways: the type of reports and how they are produced.

There are two types of reports: operational reports and management reports. *Operational reports* provide the details of the day-to-day operations of the business: "What orders did we process today?" "Mr. Jones called; we need a list of all of his invoices for the last two months." Users of these reports tend to be administrative and clerical staff and their immediate managers. *Management reports* provide an understanding of the state of the business and predict where it is going: "What were the average sales per month for the last 12 months?" "What is the growth rate of orders?" Users of these reports are usually management and executives.

Reports are produced in two ways: canned reports and *ad-hoc* reports. In *canned reports*, the data source, selection criteria, sorting, grouping, and formatting are relatively structured and controlled. This type of report provides the business measurement baseline. *Ad-hoc reports* enable users to choose the data that they want to see and how they want to see it.

Although it is to be covered more in-depth later, in "Analysis: A Few Words," you should be aware now that establishing the type of reports and how they are produced early in the project is critical. Determining the primary goals of the project will have a significant effect on the design and effectiveness of the solution. Each of the report types and methodologies is appropriate in a particular situation.

Reporting Systems

Reporting systems or subsystems (depending on your viewpoint) are mechanisms to control the production of reports. Although every reporting system can be somewhat different, successful reporting systems address the users' reporting needs in a focused, consistent way. A reporting system provides the user with a controlled, stable environment in which to work. A well-designed reporting system can also provide a significant increase in performance. Each component of a reporting system can be optimized to perform its role in the best and fastest way. It enables managers to ensure that their reporting system users retrieve consistent data from the system with minimal effort and training.

Reporting System Architecture

Although the end result of a reporting system is retrieving and displaying business data, the focus of the developer should be on creating an effective architecture for reporting that meets the customer's needs. Rather than focusing on the production of individual reports, the architecture-based approach builds a structure that is robust and expandable.

An effective design for a reporting system uses the best-of-breed approach to development. The system is broken into components, and the best tools and design are chosen for each component. As the system grows, additional components can be added and new development tools can be used.

In concept, a reporting system is very simple. It is useful in three ways:

- A place to store the data
- A mechanism to retrieve the data that the user needs
- A way to display, print, or further analyze the data

To keep within the scope of this chapter, let's reword this to focus on a client/server reporting system that produces structured reports. More concretely, these three components are

- Data storage—A server-based database-management system appropriate to the application.
- Retrieval mechanism—This includes a user interface to capture user-entered report parameters and a control system to execute database queries and control report creation.
- Data output—A report format file used to display or print the report.

System Design

The next sections discuss the process and details of building the system. Before diving into the process, look at how the system fits together. (See Figure 4.1.)

Figure 4.1.
The reporting system architecture.

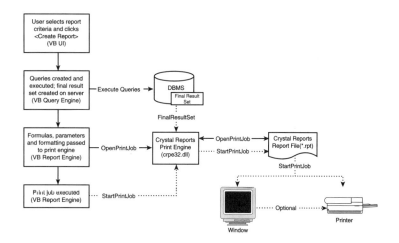

As illustrated in Figure 4.1, here is how the process works:

1. After starting the reporting system, the user chooses a report to run and selects report-specific parameters (row selection, sort, number of copies, and so on).
2. When the user is ready to run the report, he or she clicks Create Report.
3. A set of functions passes user-selected parameters to a data structure that holds them for future use.

4. Using the user-selected report parameters, the front end creates SQL queries and executes them on the database server. The output of these queries is a user-specific final result set table or view that will be called by the report Print Engine.

5. Report print procedures open the print job (that is, they start the CRW Pro Print Engine) for the selected report. During the Open Print Job phase, the Print Engine ensures that a report file exists for the selected report. Then the Print Engine functions pass formulas and formatting to the Print Engine. Finally, the location of the user-specific final result set is passed to the Print Engine.

6. Print Engine procedures execute the print job. The CRW Pro Print Engine queries the server, retrieves the final result set, and passes the result set to the CRW Pro report file. The formatted report is either displayed or sent directly to a printer using the report file format.

The concept is relatively simple. Performing most of the work on the server and passing parameters to the report file maximizes report speed and minimizes the number of unique form layouts that need to be developed. Design goals include maximum performance and flexibility, minimum coding, and maximum code reuse.

Development Process Overview

Here is a quick review of the process for developing a reporting system. The details are discussed in the following sections.

1. Analyze customer needs—The primary objective here is to define the number and type of reports and the characteristics of each report. Especially important is to define the report data that the user wants to see.

2. Find the data—Perform a data-sources analysis to determine where and how you get the data for the reports. Estimate the size of the production system, the size of the result set for each report, and the size and nature of the source data.

3. Evaluate data sources—Decide if it is feasible to access the operational system(s) directly for the data. If feasible, consider optimizing it; then continue to step 4. If not feasible, determine the cost and the possibility of developing more robust data sources, such as a reporting database or a reporting server.

4. Create a prototype report—Develop a prototype report to test the process and learn your system's idiosyncrasies. Choose a relatively easy report to begin with. Using the customer requirements and data-source analysis, create a report result set table or view using hand-coded queries executed using a SQL query tool such as Microsoft ISQL/W. With the result set as your data source, develop a report format for the selected report (in this case, it will be a CRW Pro .RPT file). Review the just-created prototype report with your customer to get feedback.

5. Create the front end—In the context of this chapter, you will be using Visual Basic. Create the user interface (UI) VB form based on the requirements documentation.

Next, create the user-interface report parameter structures. Finally, create the print control procedures. Without passing parameters to the report, test-run the report from VB to ensure that the basic Print Engine functions are working correctly.

6. Create report parameter procedures—Create VB functions to pass parameters to the report. These functions pass CRW Pro formulas, sorting and grouping parameters, and the result-set location. Again, test to ensure that the system functions correctly.

7. Create database query procedures—Develop VB procedures that create and execute database queries. These queries will retrieve the data and generate a final, user-specific result set on the server. Procedures include report-specific and utility procedures. Spend time optimizing the database queries that these procedures create.

8. Return to step 4 and repeat the process for the rest of the reports. Note that you might have to re-visit the "analyze customer needs" and "find the data" phases.

Experience has shown that this process works. You might want to make some changes to fit your needs. You might even be tempted to skip a step or two. For example, you might want to skip over the data-analysis phase and jump directly into the fun stuff—creating the report and the user interface. Don't do it. Your customer might be thrilled to see a pretty UI and a spiffy report format in just a few days. However, the first time the customer sees incorrectly calculated data, or data from the wrong data source, he or she will lose confidence in the system. From there it's a long, uphill climb.

Analysis: A Few Words

As with any project, the first step in creating a reporting system project is analysis. Optimizing reports starts with good analysis. Analyzing (and designing) a reporting system is different from traditional development. In traditional development, one of the first tasks is to determine the customer's business processes, find out what they want to do, and finally build the system. The end result is a system that produces and manages data.

With a reporting system, your starting point is the end result of the operational system: the data. In this case, data is divided into two types: the data the user wants to see on the report and the sources of that data. Between the two is the data retrieval, the data manipulation to process the raw source data to final result-set data, and the formatting algorithms that display the data.

Like determining users' operational system needs, many times it is difficult to determine the users' exact reporting needs because they don't know them. Unlike the operational portion of systems, when you can observe a manual process to help determine user needs, reporting needs are based on the business. Don't assume that the users understand their business; this understanding grows with each new report. Plan on multiple report prototypes, many revisions to your requirements documentation, and several additional reports.

Analysis: Defining Report Data

The first step in defining report data is to define the data the users want to see on the reports. At this stage, you need to determine (to the best extent possible) five kinds of report parameters:

- Data Elements—What elements of data will be reported? Be specific. For example, "Sales" is not enough. "Store Sales," "Book Sales," and "Regional Sales" might refer to completely different concepts.

- Sorting—How does the user want the data sorted? What is the hierarchy from top to bottom?

- Summarization and Grouping—At what point will the rows be grouped on the report, with summary information for each group? Which columns will be summarized?

- Row Selection—Row-selection parameters limit the selection of rows that will appear on the report. What criteria will be used to select a subset of rows?

- Row and Column Computing Algorithms—Are some rows and columns in the report computed? How are they computed—what are the algorithms? What rows and columns are used in the computation? At what grouping level will they be computed?

Capturing these elements helps determine what will appear on the reports and how it will be retrieved and processed. Capturing and stabilizing user requirements for reporting systems can be very frustrating. Often users do not truly understand their business, especially if their current business-reporting system is manual. They want something, but they're not sure what that is. Furthermore, several customers might have differing opinions. For example, you might find yourself in a room with several customers discussing requirements. Just when you think you have the report specs nailed down, the customers start arguing with each other about the sort hierarchy.

Here are some methods for capturing valuable information and focusing attention on the vital issues:

- Use a Report Data form. While discussing each report with the user, use a form titled "Report Data" to capture the user requirements. The Y axis of the form is divided into sections that match the sections of the target report, including page header and footer, group headers and footers (one for each group), and a detail section. The X axis of the form includes four columns: Data Item, Description, Column Source, and Mechanism.

  The Data Item column contains a name for each field in the report. The corresponding entry in the Description column defines the Data Item. The Column Source column contains the actual or likely table and column name source of the data. The Mechanism column entry is the algorithm that you use to query the source. Entries in Mechanism can include any brief queries, joins to other tables, or SQL or CRW Pro formulas used to retrieve or derive the data item.

A sample form is included as part of RptSpec.Doc—a Word version 7.0 document on the CD-ROM that accompanies this book. You can use this document as a template to create your own Reporting System Functional Specifications form.

■ Use current reports. Ask the users for old, manually created or computer-generated reports to stimulate conversation. If these are not available, find reports from other departments. Even if the report does not look anything like what they want, you can gain useful tidbits. For example, "It doesn't look anything like what we want, but I do like the header, and we need to sum on sales, and the page number should be on the left…"

■ Create prototype reports. After you get an initial idea of what the users want, mock up a report (even if you have to use a word processor) and revisit them to further clarify their needs.

Expect to make several trips to the user refining these needs. Make sure that you talk to the users who will *use* the report! Analysts, superiors, and subordinates will not understand some of the subtleties. Hours spent now will save days or weeks of effort later.

Here is an example of what can happen when you talk to the wrong person. While on contract to develop a reporting system, the author got the reporting specifications from the customer project manager (not the end user). After the entire reporting system was finished and within one week of project finish, the end user stopped by to review the reports. For the most important report, the user said, "NO! We don't want locations across the top with one row for each quarter; we want quarters across the top, with one row for each location!" Because the algorithm to compute the data was very complex, it would have taken another four days to rewrite the report. The project manager decided it was out of scope and shelved the report. The good news was that the report specifications were detailed and approved, so there were no repercussions for the author. The bad news was that the customer paid for an important report and did not get it!

Data-Source Analysis

After you have defined the data to be included in the report, you need to know where and how you will get it. As mentioned before, part of the definition for an optimized report is that the data be *consistent and accurate*. Let's say you are retrieving data from multiple systems, consolidating it into one data source, and reporting on it. Even if your report represents the data in the resulting database accurately, your report could be very false and misleading. Does the data from multiple systems have the same definition? Does it have the same domain? Is it measured the same way? Therefore, you need to examine your data carefully.

■ Nature of the data. What is the data? Where does it come from? What are the definitions of the tables and columns? What is the domain of the data (the range of values in each column)? Does it change often or rarely?

■ Size of the data. What is the expected size of the data? Is the system a small, departmental system with a few thousand rows of data created each year? Or is it a large divisional or enterprise-level system that generates millions of rows each year? How many tables? How many columns?

■ Source of the data. Where does the data reside? In an operational system? In a reporting server? Is some form of reporting server in the plans? Does the data come from one system or multiple systems? What types of systems does the data come from? Is the data accessible?

■ How reports query data. What do the report queries look like? How many tables are joined together? Can the queries use appropriate indexes? Are the indexes optimized for reports?

■ An additional point to consider. Where do you stand in the development cycle? Can you affect the design of the operational system? If you determine that the data sources are not optimal, can you change the plans?

Significant complications stem from the answers to these questions, some or all of which you have to address. Major issues can include the following:

■ Data not accessible. By far the biggest problem developers face is that the data is not in a form that is readily accessible or usable. If you are lucky, all of the data is in a modern client/server database. Many times, however, the data will be in a mainframe database, multiple client-server databases (from different manufacturers, yet), or in multiple spreadsheets on the desks of multiple users. If luck has really forsaken you, it will be a combination of all of these. Moving this data from multiple sources into a single, common source is your first priority.

■ Data not available. Another major problem is that some of the data is not available; either it was not captured at the source or it was summarized prior to being entered into a database. This is a particularly vexing problem because the cost of capturing the data might be higher than its value to the customer. Should you find this problem, first assess the cost and difficulty of gaining access to the data and then communicate the situation to the customer immediately.

■ Data in operational database. The data might be in a highly normalized database. This is good news in that at least you have access to the data. It can be bad news if the database is highly normalized, is very large, and/or is accessed by a large number of users. The issue becomes critical if large, complex reports pull data from multiple tables. A highly normalized state is considered good design for operational databases. Because it typically requires multiple, complex joins to get the data that you want, however, it can destroy reporting-query performance.

■ Reporting system viewed as an afterthought. Unfortunately, many project managers, development managers, and developers have little or no reporting-system experience. More often than not, development projects are well under way before anyone realizes that the system has reporting requirements. They will grab any developer who happens to be free, hand him or her a limited set of specs, and say, "Go create some reports."

The nature, size, sources, and uses of data have the greatest impact on the performance and success of your reporting system. No other single factor will affect your optimization efforts more than these issues.

Choosing the Optimal Data Source

Choosing the optimal data source might seem simple because of environmental constraints. For example, you perceive that you are limited to operational systems. Time is short. Budgets are limited. You have no choice. Your perceptions might be real; you might be operating under severe constraints. But you need to know the impact of these environmental constraints.

See Table 4.1 for a comparison between reporting systems and operational systems.

Table 4.1. Reporting and operational system differences.

System Characteristics	Operational	Reporting
Query Types	Select, Insert, Update, Delete	Select
Transaction Volume	High	Low
Number of rows impacted	Few	Many
Optimal database design	Highly normalized with many long, narrow (few columns) tables	Highly denormalized with few short, wide tables
Acceptable query performance	Seconds	Minutes to hours

If you have a small number of simple reports in a smaller, relatively simple database, reporting directly from the operational system might produce acceptable results. In fact, in cases where the user needs real-time status reports, you will be forced to report directly from the operational system. As the size and complexity of your operational system grows, as the number and type of data sources grow, and/or as the complexity of the uses of data grows, the difficulty in achieving acceptable reporting results increases dramatically.

To optimize reporting database performance, you need to consider several options. First, try to ensure that all data for each report is in one database. Then consider these alternatives:

- Optimize the operational database for reporting.
- Create permanent reporting tables within your current operational system.
- Create a clone of the operational database that is somewhat report-optimized.
- Create a fully optimized reporting server.

Optimizing Operational Databases for Reporting

Trying to optimize an operational database structure is the first solution many developers try. Unfortunately, this solution will work only up to a point. As you can see from Table 4.1, reporting systems and operational systems place different types of stresses on a database. It is extremely difficult to create one database that produces optimal results for both types of system.

To illustrate this point, let's look at optimizing the use of indexes. One way to speed up reports is to increase the number of indexes on tables that are used for report queries. To do this, simply determine the specific tables and columns used in report queries and create an index on those columns. (For more information on general techniques, see the section titled "General System-Optimizing Techniques," later in this chapter.)

What will happen? For SELECT queries (used by reports), the database's query optimizer uses these indexes instead of performing table scans; thus, query performance increases. The downside is that each extra index has to be maintained. When a row is inserted (or updated, if you are updating an indexed column), each index is updated. This means that insert and update operations will be slower. As the system grows larger, users will start complaining about how long it takes to enter new data or edit existing data in the operational system.

Now you see the double-edged sword of trying to optimize an operational database for reports. If you optimize for one need, you might de-optimize for the other. It is difficult to generalize about this issue, but the best advice is to make changes carefully and expect a suboptimal solution.

Permanent Reporting Tables

Another way to optimize reporting database performance that meets with some success is the use of permanent reporting tables within your current operational system. With this solution, the developer creates a set of tables that are optimized to meet the needs of specific reports. At some off-hour time, such as at night, a batch file runs to load or update these tables.

The design of these tables is highly denormalized. They have large numbers of columns and relatively few rows. Many times the data is aggregated and timestamped for a period. Many or most of the columns will be indexed, with the indexes optimized for SELECT queries.

When report queries are run against these tables, the queries have few or no joins. The database query optimizer will have an index to use for every selection parameter in the WHERE clause.

The downside is that the overall database is still not optimized for a reporting system. For example, the temporary database might not be optimal. Further, you still have two different types of users using one database on one server. One large report can severely impact the other users.

Report-Optimized Operational Database Clone

Another alternative is to create a partially report-optimized clone of the operational database. For this method, you create an exact copy of the operational database on a reporting server. (An easy way is to dump the operational database and restore it to the reporting server.) Then, by running a script, you drop and re-create operational system indexes that are optimized for reporting. In addition, you create new indexes that would be used by report queries. The database server's temporary database can be optimized for reports (typically made larger). Finally, you can run scripts to create reporting tables (similar to the solution in the previous section).

There are several benefits of this solution, including improved report performance and minimal impact on the operational system. Also, the implementation is relatively easy.

Unfortunately, there are some problems with it as well. The major problem is that you are misusing an administrative procedure whose primary purpose is to protect the data. You are performing operations on all of the rows in all of the tables every time you restore. You never leverage the existence of your older data; the restore process wipes out all previous data (as you would expect it to). Restoring the database might take some time. Worse, you will be restoring all of the rows in all of the tables. As time goes on and the operational database gets larger, the full dump-and-restore process takes longer. If you want to optimize the indexes, you need to drop and rebuild the current indexes and create new reporting indexes from scratch. This takes additional time. At its extreme, you might reach a point where there is no time to run the dump-and-restore process.

Fully Optimized Reporting Server

Arguably the optimal solution, but also the most difficult and expensive, is a fully optimized reporting server. This is a special database, on a different server, that is optimized for reporting. Sometimes these systems are referred to as "data warehouses" or "data marts." The data is loaded from the operational system to the reporting database regularly. The frequency of loads depends on the reporting requirements. Data loads normally take place at night or in other off-hours periods.

Tables are optimized for reporting. Reporting-optimized tables are denormalized and typically have many columns. The combination of the denormalization and the number of columns drastically reduces the need for joins. The tables contain summarized and computed data. In many cases the summarized or computed data is *time-stamped* (data for a time period). For example, an operational database might have the sales price per unit and the unit count. The reporting database would have both of these columns and the result of multiplying them—the sales revenue for that transaction (price per unit times the quantity). While the operational database would have the individual sales transactions, the reporting database could have a table whose data was the weekly sum of sales transactions for each store.

Typically, reporting servers have few or no updates or deletes. Data is inserted for new time periods—"Sales data for week ending 1/31/96." You should use database optimization techniques (listed later in "General System-Optimizing Techniques").

A fully optimized reporting server can improve reporting query performance tenfold (or more). Here is one simple example. During one project, the author developed a query to calculate total revenue by product from a sales transaction table of 375,000 rows. The calculation was complex and included joining five tables and multiplying the sales list price by the sales count and a country multiplier. The result was then further processed. This query took about 31 minutes at its fastest. After summarizing the data into two aggregated, summary tables with less than 1,500 rows and then using the summary data for joins, the query took 17 seconds!

Developing a reporting server is not for the timid. Detailed analysis must be performed to determine reporting requirements. This includes defining the appropriate schema, aggregation criteria, and time periods for the summarization. One of the challenges is getting management to fund another server specifically for reporting.

The topic of data warehouses and reporting servers is explored in depth by W.H. Inmon in his book *Building the Data Warehouse*.

General System-Optimizing Techniques

Optimizing a reporting database system is important to report performance. Although some techniques (such as adding memory) will improve performance in operational and reporting systems alike, many techniques (such as optimizing indexes for reports) can degrade operational system performance. The following are several methods of improving reporting database performance. Before using them, check your database vendor's documentation to ensure that they are right for your system.

- Optimize report queries. Optimizing report queries can have an extremely positive impact on reporting performance. Although a well-written query might not have much impact on a poorly designed reporting database system, the opposite is worse. A poorly written reporting query can bring the fastest, best-designed reporting database system to a complete halt. For more details on optimizing report queries, refer to the section "Optimizing Queries," later in the chapter.

- Get More Memory. One of the cheapest ways to improve performance of a database server is to buy more memory and then allocate appropriate memory to the database. Different databases and operating systems require different allocation algorithms. Refer to your database documentation for specifics.

- Index Report Columns. Where possible, create an index on every column used for report-selection criteria or for table joins. The query optimizer will try to use these indexes instead of performing table scans. In general, using indexes with fewer columns in each index rather than using larger, compound indexes will be faster. Also, try to create clustered indexes on the most-used columns; they are faster than non-clustered indexes in a reporting database. If you must use an operational system for reporting, avoid over-indexing because each extra index has to be maintained. When a row is inserted (or updated, if you are updating an indexed column), the index is updated. This means that insert and update operations will be slower.

- Optimize indexes for reports. Indexes can be modified to improve read-only performance. In Microsoft SQL Server, for example, you will want to increase the index fill factor to 100. This forces the server to use 100 percent of the index page, enabling queries to process fewer data pages. Again, if the index is used by an operational system, what is optimal for read-only performance might be suboptimal for operational-system performance.

- Modify the temporary database. Reporting queries typically make use of sorting, grouping, and aggregate functions. All of these place a heavy load on the temporary database (`tempdb` in Microsoft SQL Server). Increasing the size of the temporary database and placing it in memory (if you have enough system memory) can improve server performance.

The Prototype Report

For your first, prototype report, choose an easy one. In this context, "easy" means that it will have data from a limited number of tables, no (or at most only one) group section, and relatively simple formatting. Hopefully you can find one that has few joins and returns a limited number of rows. Your goal here is to choose a "guinea pig" report to create the system from front (user interface) to back (CRW Pro report file).

After you select the report, review the requirements that the customer gave you and the data-source analysis. Create one or more queries that will generate a final result set. This final result set could be a table or a view. Execute the queries using a SQL query tool such as Microsoft ISQL/W.

Ensure that the query generates a final result set with all required report columns. Recheck the query to make absolutely sure that the data comes from the correct source tables and columns. Do not add extra row-selection, sorting, or grouping parameters to the query; keep it minimal.

If necessary, add dummy WHERE criteria to return a limited number of rows. Three to four pages of report data are usually enough to enable you to create and debug a CRW Pro report file (the next step). It is very difficult to create a report if your query returns 40 pages of data. At the opposite end of the spectrum, if the query returns only 10 rows of data you might not be able to spot data or formatting idiosyncrasies in the report.

Now you are ready to create the report file (and you thought that was the first step). Because CRW Pro's user interface is quite easy to use, we will not describe the report creation process in depth.

Before you create a report, you will need to create an ODBC DSN (in the Control Panel) that points to your database. If you want to use the example reporting system, you need to create a DSN that points to any SQL Server pubs database.

The following is a brief description of the report-creation process:

1. Open Crystal Reports Pro.
2. Click on the Create a New Report button.
3. Choose a Report Expert from the Create New Report dialog box. (For this exercise, click the Custom>>> button. You will notice that the dialog box has expanded at the bottom.)
4. In the expanded portion of the dialog box, notice a new row of buttons. Click the SQL/ODBC button. A dialog box pops up with a list of DSNs. Select the appropriate DSN and click OK. A login dialog box pops up. Enter a valid Login ID and Password, and then click OK.
5. If the login is successful, the Choose SQL Table dialog box pops up. Select the table or view that you created with your query (earlier in this section) and click OK.
6. The Insert Database Field dialog box pops up. Select the columns you need and place them in the report. Add appropriate page and report field labels and then click the Preview tab.
7. The report queries the data from your table and displays it in the preview window.
8. Continue working on the report to refine it to the approximate format that the user requires. You might not want to spend significant time making it absolutely perfect at this point. After reviewing it with the customer, he or she will probably want changes.

After you create your first report, sit down with the customer and review the report. This will be their first chance to see a live report. After reviewing the report, make the necessary changes and modify the functional specifications.

The Front End

The reporting system *front end* is composed of four parts:

■ User interface (UI). The UI captures report and report-output parameters and initiates the start of the report.

■ Database query procedures. Database query procedures that dynamically create report-specific result sets based on the user-entered report parameters.

- Report parameter procedures. Report parameter procedures pass parameters to the report. Parameters include user-selected sorting and grouping criteria, report formulas, and report formatting.
- Print control procedures. Print control procedures are utility functions that execute the print job and determine how it will be displayed (window or printer), the number of copies that will be printed, the status of the report, and the definition of optional window positions.

The User Interface

The user interface should capture all of the user-entered report parameters in one place. Typically, users want to choose a report to print and have the system display only the appropriate parameters for that report. Figure 4.2 displays the characteristics of an appropriate user interface. Note that each report can have different parameters that are appropriate for that report. As the user selects another tab, he or she sees only those parameter controls that are appropriate for that report.

Figure 4.2.

A reporting-system user interface.

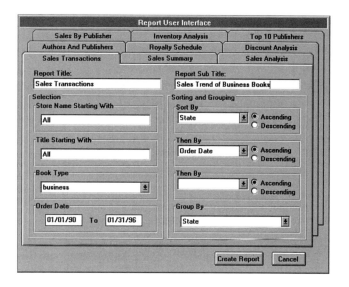

As with any other system, it is very useful to use metaphors with which the user is familiar. For reports, the tab metaphor (implemented in the example application using the Sheridan ssTab control) is appropriate because the user can select a tab and see all of the parameters for that report displayed. This is intuitively obvious to the user and is consistent with newer Windows interface standards. Note the sort controls from Figure 4.2; they are very similar to the sort controls from Microsoft Excel. Because many users are familiar with Excel, the probability increases that the user will understand their meaning and use quickly.

Use a tab control container on the user interface, but don't place individual controls in it. Start with invisible panels; place logical groups of controls in the panels. Then, place all of the panels on top of the tab control and set the position, visibility, and enabled properties as the user changes reports. This will reduce resource requirements and increase speed.

Report Parameters

Reports, especially structured ("canned") reports, typically use five kinds of report parameters: row-selection, sorting, grouping, formatting, and output parameters. These parameters, which are described in the following list, are used in report database queries, are passed to the report files, and control the process of producing the report.

■ Row Selection. Row-selection parameters limit the selection of rows that will appear on the report. Notice from Figure 4.2 that the user has selected the Sales Transactions report. For that report, the user specified that he wants all stores ("Store Name Starting With"), all book titles ("Title Starting With"), but only the business book type ("Book Type"). Also, the user has selected a range of order dates ("Order Date") from 01/01/90 to 01/31/96.

■ Sorting. Sorting refers to the order in which the rows will appear. As noted previously, the controls are similar to Microsoft Excel's sorting controls. In this case, the user wants to sort by State first, and then by Book Title.

■ Grouping. Grouping refers to how the rows will be categorized on the report, with summary information for the group and possibly page breaks. In Figure 4.2, the user has chosen to group the data by State. This means that the report will have a summary section for each state. A summary section provides a place for aggregate information, such as a count of rows or sum of sales for that state. If the user had chosen to group by Book Title, there would be a break for each title and the summary section would aggregate information by book title; for example, as a count of rows for each Book Title or sum of sales for each Book Title. Note that CRW Pro automatically sorts data first by the group hierarchy. Then, after sorting by the group hierarcy, it sorts by the user-selected sort criteria.

■ Formatting. Formatting information controls how the report will look. Typical formatting includes dynamic title and subtitle, print date and time, and the selected report criteria (always a good idea). In a more complex report, you might need to set other report labels dynamically, such as report-column headers.

■ Output. After the user selects a report and its details, he needs the capability to select where he wants the output to go—to the screen or a printer. If output goes to the printer, the user needs to be able to select a printer and number of copies. In more advanced systems, he might want the capability to export the information to a spreadsheet, desktop database file, or text file format. In addition, he might want the report to be mailed to other staff or management.

Managing Report Parameters

One characteristic of a reporting-system user interface is the repetition of report parameters— the same parameters are used over and over for several reports. Many times reports display similar business data in multiple ways, but the underlying business data remains the same. Likewise, the underlying criteria to choose and display the data remain the same. You will find that if you have 10 reports, each of which has 20 controls (including labels), you do not need to use 200 controls (10×200). Many will be repeats. With careful design, you can reduce the number of controls to perhaps 40 or so. This increases display speed and decreases the drain on system resources.

In the example application (shown in Figure 4.2), the criteria controls were placed on top of, not into, each tabsheet of the tab control. The downside of not placing controls into each tabsheet is that they will not retain their values as the user moves around from report to report. For example, suppose a user decides to run a Sales Transaction report and enters the necessary parameters for that report. Then, the user selects the Sales Analysis report. A minute later, the user changes her mind again and re-clicks on the Sales Transaction report tab. Because users look for logical consistency and because this user just left the Sales Transaction report, she logically expects that the parameters will still be there when she returns to the original report. Therefore, you need to save the parameters for the UI to be logically consistent.

Managing the user interface and the report parameters can be very complex unless you plan for them well. One effective method uses parallel data structures. The three structures (including their declarations) are shown in Listing 4.1.

Listing 4.1. Front end control structures.

```
Dim fCriteriaControls() As Control
Dim fCurReport(n) As tRptData                    '"n" = Number of reports
Dim mReport As tRptData
```

`fCriteriaControls()` is an array of controls; each element in the array is a control that is associated with a specific report. `fCurReport()` is an array that holds the default or selected parameters for each report while the user is clicking tabs to move from report to report. `mReport` holds the report parameters after the user has clicked the Create Report button to start the print job. Using these three structures in combination reduces the front-end code dramatically.

When `fCriteriaControls()` is loaded, it is ReDimed to a two-dimensional array, as shown in Listing 4.2.

The first dimension of the structure is the `Reports` dimension. The second dimension is the `controls` dimension. When you are re-dimensioning `fCriterialControls`, set the upper bounds of the first dimension to the current number of reports (`iNumReports`) minus one. Set the upper bounds of the second dimension equal to the total number of unique controls (`iNumCriteriaControls`) that all of the reports could have, minus one. For example, suppose you have two reports. The first report has `CustomerName` and `InvoiceDate` criteria controls; the second has `InvoiceDate` and `CustomerCity` criteria controls. The total number of unique controls is three: `CustomerName`, `InvoiceDate`, and `CustomerCity`. Therefore, `iNumCriteriaControls` equals 3.

Listing 4.2. `ReDim fCriteriaControls.`

```
'Set the number of reports
iNumReports = 3

'Set the maximum number of controls
iNumCriteriaControls = 10

ReDim fCriteriaControls(iNumReports - 1, iNumCriteriaControls - 1) As Control
```

As you learned earlier, `fCriteriaControls` is used to control the user interface. When loading or accessing the elements of the structure, the first dimension is the index of the report (`iRptIndex`). The second dimension is a control or an empty value. The existence of a control in `fCriteriaControls()` for a specific report (as specified by `iRptIndex`) indicates that the control is used for entering criteria for that report. `fCriteriaControls()` is used to manage the enabled properties of each control and determine whether the contents of a control should be loaded and saved for a given report. Note that `iRptIndex` is always the same as the `.Tab` property of the report's tabsheet.

`FCriteriaControls` contains controls that might be the parent to other controls that are dealt with as a group. For example, `fraOrderDate` is a frame control that contains `mskOrderDateStart`, `mskOrderDateEnd`, and a label control. Because you always deal with `mskOrderDateStart` and `mskOrderDateEnd` together, you place them on a panel and enable/disable them at the panel (`fraOrderDate`) level. Likewise, in the procedure `SaveCurRptData`, if the `fraOrderDate` panel control exists in the `fCriteriaControls()` array, the values for `mskOrderDateStart` and `mskOrderDateEnd` are always saved.

Listing 4.3 demonstrates how to load each element of the array.

Listing 4.3. Using `Set` to load each element of the `fCriteriaControls` array.

```
iRptIndex = SalesTransactions       'Sales Transactions
   Set fCriteriaControls(iRptIndex, 0) = txtReportTitle
   Set fCriteriaControls(iRptIndex, 1) = txtReportSubTitle
   Set fCriteriaControls(iRptIndex, 2) = fraOrderDate
...
```

As the user clicks a tab to move to another report, you can determine which report tab the user came from and to which he is going. By looping through the control array for a specific report (iRptIndex), you know which control is valid for which report. Therefore, you can easily save the data from the report from which the user came, enable (or make visible) the appropriate controls for the report to which the user is going, and get the control values for the report to which the user is going. If the control exists in the array for the "from" report, data is saved; otherwise it is not. If the control exists in the array for the "to" report, the control is enabled and the default data for that control is loaded.

Because you know that only the valid controls for a specific report will be in the fCriteriaControls array, you can use a small number of procedures for all reports. SaveCurRptData in Listing 4.4 is a procedure used for all reports. It saves the data only for those reports where the controls are used. As you add more reports to the UI, you simply add the report's iRptIndex and controls to the fCriteriaControls array. If new criteria are added (that is, not from the current superset of all report criteria), ensure that you add Save<*ParameterType*> procedures for the parameter types. The procedure for retrieving parameter control defaults (GetCurRptData) is very similar.

Listing 4.4. The SaveCurRptData procedure.

```
Private Sub SaveCurRptData(iPreviousTab As Integer)
    iRptIndex = iPreviousTab

    For iCurControl = 0 To UBound(fCriteriaControls, 2)
        Select Case fCriteriaControls(iRptIndex, iCurControl).Name
            Case "txtReportTitle"
                Call SaveReportTitle(iRptIndex)
            Case "txtReportSubTitle"
                Call SaveReportTitle(iRptIndex)
            Case "fraStoreName"
                Call SaveStoreName(iRptIndex)
            Case "fraBookTitle"
                Call SaveBookTitle(iRptIndex)
            Case "fraBookType"
                Call SaveBookType(iRptIndex)
            Case "fraOrderDate"
                Call SaveDate(iRptIndex, OrderDate)
            Case "fraSortBy"
                Call SaveSortBy(iRptIndex)
            Case "fraGroupBy"
                Call SaveGroupBy(iRptIndex)
        End Select
    Next iCurControl
End Sub
```

Listing 4.5 shows the EnableRptControls() procedure. The EnableRptControls() procedure enables specific controls for a specific report. Using the fCriteriaControls array, the EnableRptControls() procedure for enabling report controls for a specific report is trivial. Again, maintaining fCriteriaControls is all that is necessary to maintain this procedure.

Listing 4.5. The `EnableRptControls()` **procedure.**

```
Public Sub EnableRptControls(iRptIndex As Integer)
    For iCurControl = 0 To UBound(fCriteriaControls, 2)
            fCriteriaControls(iRptIndex, iCurControl).Enabled = True
    Next iCurControl
End Sub
```

The `fCurReport(n)` and `mReport` report parameter data structures are used as central repositories for report parameters. The exact type of structure you use is not critical; use the ones with which you are most comfortable. Here, for the sake of illustration, we use structures of user-defined data types because these two data structures must be synchronized, and user-defined data types provide the advantage of making it easy to define both structures using the same data type. As you add new elements to the user-defined data type, both structures are automatically synchronized. In the example application, the user-defined data type `tRptData` is declared as shown in Listing 4.6.

Listing 4.6. Declaring `tRptData`.

```
Type tRptData
    RptIndex As Variant       'Index of report
    RptTitle As String
    RptSubTitle As String
    BookType As String
    BookTitle As String
    StoreName As String
    OrderDateStart As Variant
    OrderDateEnd As Variant
    SortBy0 As String
    SortBy1 As String
    SortBy2 As String
    SortDirection0 As String
    SortDirection1 As String
    SortDirection2 As String
    GroupBy As String
    CurDate As Date
    NumCopies As Integer
    Preview As Integer
End Type
```

> Use report parameter data structures to capture intermediate and final report parameters. They keep the user interface logically consistent and reduce database query coding.

`fCurReport(n)` is a UI form-level structure that stores the user's selections for each report (each tab) while the user is selecting the report(s). When the user selects another tab, the values from the controls on the current tab are saved to the structure and the values for the new tab are retrieved from the structure and loaded into the controls. This data structure is defined as an array of a user-defined data type. The array is dimensioned to the number (n) of reports. For example, if you had three reports, the array would be dimensioned like this.

```
Dim fCurReport(3) As tRptData
```

The index to each element of `fCurReport` matches the `.Tab` property of the tab control. Therefore, if the Sales Transactions report is tab 0 (tabs are zero-based), the parameters for the Sales Transactions will be stored in the first element of `fCurReport()`—that is, they would be in `fCurReport(0)`.

Also note that the `fCriteriaControls()` array is used to control the loading to and retrieval of data from `fCurReport()`, but these are not similar structures. As discussed before, `fCriteriaControls()` works at a higher level than `fCurReport()`; `fCurReport()` contains the specific values of each criteria control. Also note that when the data is passed to `fCurReport()`, it is formatted so that it can be used to create SQL queries.

The second structure is a module-scope variable of type `tRptData` that holds report data for the selected report. It is dimensioned like this:

```
Dim mReport As tRptData
```

It is loaded with the data from `fCurReport(iRptIndex)` where `iRptIndex` is the `.Tab` property of the currently selected tab. It is loaded after the user starts the report-creation process by clicking the Create Report button on the user interface (refer to Figure 4.2). `mReport` is dimensioned at a module level to allow more flexibility in design and reduce resource load.

Starting the Report

From the user interface, the user selects the report that he or she wants to produce and chooses selection, sorting, grouping, and formatting parameters. Then the user clicks OK to produce the report.

First, the parameters for the selected report are copied from the `fCurReport()` array to the `mReport` variable in the `RptUtil` module. For every code or form module that requires the data in `mReport`, a local `mReport` or `fReport` declaration is made. Whenever data is needed in that module, the local module's `mReport` variable is passed into `RptUtil.GetModRptStruct` as an argument to the function, loaded with report data from `RptUtil.GetModRptStruct`, and passed back to the calling form or code module.

Next, the print report dialog box (`frmPrintReport`) is loaded, which prompts the user for the number of copies to be printed and whether the output will be sent directly to the printer or to a print preview window (see Figure 4.3). `frmPrintReport` prompts the user for the number of copies to be printed and whether the output will be sent directly to the printer or to a print preview window. During the loading of frmPrintReport, fReport (a form-level duplicate of RptUtil.mReport) is loaded with the contents of RptUtil.mReport. The user makes his or her selections and clicks OK.

Figure 4.3.
*Setting print parameters
with the Print Report
dialog box.*

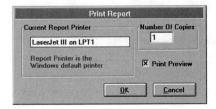

After the user clicks OK, the number of copies and the print preview parameters are loaded into the fReport variable. The fReport variable is passed as an argument into LoadRptUtilStruct() in RptUtil; this reloads RptUtil.mReport. mReport now contains the print control parameters.

At this point, RptMod1.StartReport() is called. This procedure uses a simple SELECT CASE statement that executes a report-specific procedure based on the report index stored in mReport.RptIndex. In the example application, because mReport.RptIndex = 0, we call SalesTransactionsRpt().

SalesTransactionsRpt(), in Listing 4.7, is a core, report-specific procedure. Up until this point, with the exception of the contents of fCriteriaControls, all of the front-end code discussed has been designed to work for all reports. Now it's time to start writing code that has to be report-specific.

SalesTransactionsRpt() starts the print job. Then it creates the user-specific result tables on the server (CreateSTSvrTables), sets the report header (SetRptHeader), sets report grouping and sorting (SetReportGrouping and SetRptSortFields), and sets the contents of report formulas (SetSTRptFormulas). Having manipulated the report successfully, it executes the print job (RunReport). Finally, after the report has finished dumping to the printer, or if the user closes the print preview window, the CRW Pro Print Engine is stopped (due to part of RunReport) and drops the result-set tables (DropTable).

RunReport is the key print-control utility procedure. It performs three critical functions:

■ Sets the print output—The user-selected print output, either print preview or directly to printer, is set.

■ Logs on and sets the location of the server and database—To ensure database independence, you set the database location and the logon account information for all tables used in the report. (If you've optimized, this should be just one table.) Then the procedure logs on the CRW Pro Print Engine to the server.

■ Shuts down CRW Pro—After the print job is complete, the CRW Pro print job and Print Engine are closed down.

Although the code is report-specific, you can use the first report-specific procedure (in this case, SalesTransactionsRpt()) as a template for other reports. To use it as a template, you have to modify report-specific constants and strings and use new, report-specific procedure calls. In Listing 4.7, the following conventions apply.

- Report-specific procedure calls are marked with >>.

- Report-specific strings and constants are marked with >.

Listing 4.7. Creating SalesTransactionRpt, **the master report procedure.**

```
Sub SalesTransactionsRpt()
  'Init Status
  RptStatusOpen "Print Report"
> RptStatusUpdate "Sales Transactions Report", "Processing"

  'Create a string version of @@SPID (server process ID)
  'This will allow intermediate tables and final result sets
  '(both tables and views) to be unique.
  sSPID = "_" & Trim$(GetSvrSPID)

  'Create the tables and views on the server
>> Call CreateSTSvrTables(sSPID)

  'Open Print Job for the specific report type
  'Note that "SalesTransactions" is a Global constant whose value
  'is the same as the iRptIndex used in frmRptUI
> iPrJob = OpenPrintJob(SalesTransactions)

  If iPrJob = 0 Then
     'Close the print job
     Call PEClosePrintJob(iPrJob)

     'Unload the report status form
     RptStatusClose

     Exit Sub
  End If

  'Set report header fields - SetRptHeader uses mCriteriaControls()
  Call SetRptHeader(iPrJob)

  'Set report group field
> SetReportGrouping "Sales_Transactions_T1", iPrJob

  'Set report sort fields
> If Not SetRptSortFields("Sales_Transactions_T1", iPrJob) Then
     Stop
  End If

  'Set report formulas
> If Not SetSTRptFormulas("Sales_Transactions_T1", iPrJob) Then
     Stop
  End If
```

continues

Listing 4.7. continued

```
'Run the report
Call RunReport(iPrJob, sSPID)

'Clean up - Drop the tables and views
>   If Not DropTable("Sales_Transactions_T1" & sSPID) Then
      Stop
   End If
```

At this point in the development cycle, if you are using the example application as a template, you will want to rem out several procedure calls to get the system running from front end to back end. Then, when the basic system is running, return and fill in the additional items. These procedures are discussed in the next two sections. The procedures to rem out are CreateSTSvrTables(), SetRptHeader(), SetReportGrouping(), SetRptSortFields(), SetSTRptFormulas(), and DropTable().

Choosing Between the CRW Print Engine and Custom Controls

To this point, we have made references to the CRW Print Engine. CRW Pro ships with two methods of controlling a CRW report file dynamically from a VB front end. The first is using the Crystal Reports Print Engine API. The Print Engine is a DLL that opens the CRW Pro reports, passes parameters to the reports, and executes that report. The second is using CRW Custom Controls. These are a 16-bit OCX and VBX and a 32-bit OCX. The custom controls are object-oriented wrappers around the Print Engine.

Which is the best for developing reporting systems? That depends on the needs of the project. It would be wonderful to use the CRW Custom Controls (we are using the 32-bit version of VB4)—properties, methods, all sorts of good object "stuff." Unfortunately, CRW's object orientation is not quite robust enough for our needs. The following are some major limitations:

■ The CRW Custom Controls will not work with RDO; the Print Engine will.

■ The CRW Custom Controls do not give you the control that you need. They have no "get" functions, so you cannot determine what the report's current sort or group sections are. Neither can you determine the report's current table names dynamically unless you first know in what order the reports were entered into the report file.

■ The Print Engine API has 99 functions. The OCX currently has 75. However, be aware that Print Engine functions return multiple parameters, whereas the OCX typically returns only one. For example, PEExportTo has 11 parameters that are handled by 11 separate properties or methods in the OCX. Therefore, of the 99 Print Engine functions, 57 have no OCX analog.

■ Using the Print Engine API, you can control when the Print Engine is loaded and shut down. With the OCX, the Print Engine is loaded and shut down automatically with every report. Under some conditions, OCX will be slower than the Print Engine.

For now, use the CRW Pro Print Engine API for developing reporting systems until the Custom Controls have been improved.

Maintaining Unique Result Sets

A major goal of system design is to optimize the use of the server and create a final result set on the server. But there is a problem with this. You are running the report on a multiuser system. The front end creates the same result set for the same report for all users. Therefore, if two users run the same report at the same time, they could easily overwrite their data. This is a major problem.

One alternative is to use server-created temporary tables. With systems such as SQL Server, there are two types of temporary tables: global and local. *Global temporary tables* can be viewed by all users. *Local temporary tables* can be viewed only by the user whose connection created the table. Because you need to shield other users from using the tables, global temp tables are obviously not appropriate. Unfortunately, local temp tables will not work either, because CRW Pro logs on to the server with a different connection. It cannot see the temporary table that Visual Basic created! Now you have another major problem.

It turns out that the solution is relatively simple. When you create any table or view (including the final result set) on the server, you append a unique number to the table or view name. Then, when the report is run, you reset all table names in the report at runtime to be the original name, plus this unique number.

In Listing 4.7, notice the procedure GetSvrSPID. This procedure returns the SQL Server *server process ID*, or *SPID*, a unique ID for this user connection to the database server. Alternatively, you could use the first *n* digits of a VB connection identifier to create a unique name. Another solution would be to create a random number of 10 digits or so.

Also notice the string Sales_Transactions_T1. This is the root table name of the final result set. By convention, you use the same table name whether you're creating the table manually to test the report or creating it dynamically from VB. By appending the sSPID (string variable that is set to the SPID) to the final result root table name, you create a user-specific table. For example, if the SPID for this connection is 13, the final result-set table (with an appended underscore) would be Sales_Transactions_T1_13.

One final note: At this point in the process, you are not dynamically creating the result set data. Therefore, rem out the following:

```
sSPID = "_" & Trim$(GetSvrSPID)
```

and add the following:

```
sSPID = "_"
```

At this point, you should be able to run the basic report from the front end without passing parameters.

Report Parameter Procedures

The next step in the report-creation process is to add the code necessary to modify report parameters at runtime. The primary reasons for this are to maximize flexibility and minimize the number of report files that you have to maintain. Do not think of the report file as a static piece of art that is "painted" once and then left to dry. Instead, think of it as a dynamic view of data that you control on the fly.

> Modify report parameters, such as report formulas, sorting, and grouping, at runtime. This maximizes flexibility and minimizes the number of report files.

CRW Pro has 99 Print Engine functions. Of the 99, 18 are utility functions. These include logging on and off the server, opening and closing the Print Engine and print jobs, and error handling. The other 81 functions provide a broad array of options to modify reports at runtime. These functions range from simple ones that reset the report title to complex functions that enable you to point the report to a different server and table, reset the format of the detail section or any group, set graphics output, distribute the data by mail, and translate it to different formats (for example, Excel .XLS).

Although all of this flexibility is nice, you probably will use the utility functions much more. This chapter covers functions in three areas: setting report formulas, sort fields, and group sections.

Setting Report Formulas

What is a formula? To quote from the CRW Pro help file, "A formula is a symbolic statement of the manipulations you want performed on certain data before it is printed on your report." This means that you can process the report data after it has been queried from the database server. You can sum rows and columns, extend price and quantity columns, compute months from dates, and perform a wide variety of other calculations. But it does not cover the way to look at formulas when you can modify them from a front end such as Visual Basic.

If you combine the concept of formulas with the capability to modify them from the front end at runtime, report formulas expand the flexibility of the system greatly. In this context, you need to view them in two ways. First, when used in the traditional fashion to calculate data in the report, they are referred to as *calculation formulas*. Second, when used as labels in the report, they are referred to as (you guessed it) *label formulas*.

> Formulas must exist in a report file before they can be modified from the front end. You cannot create a formula at runtime.

To CRW Pro, there is no distinction between calculation formulas and label formulas—they are both formulas. Furthermore, both types of formulas are set using the same CRW Pro Print Engine function: PESetFormula(). The distinction is how you perceive and use them. In a CRW Pro formula, if you enter a string and enclose it with single or double quotes, CRW Pro simply displays the string. If you reference a table column or put some syntactically correct calculation in the formula *without* quotes, it will display the value of the column or the result of the calculation.

> Modify report parameters such as report formulas, sorting, and grouping at runtime. This maximizes flexibility and minimizes the number of report files.

Because you can set the formulas on the fly, you now have a way of greatly modifying both the look and the contents of the report at runtime. From the front end, you pass quote-bounded strings to label formulas to modify the look of the report. You pass strings without quotes to change the way the report is calculated. The distinction is that setting label formulas is easier than setting calculation formulas. For example, if you make a spelling mistake in a label formula, it is easy to correct. If you make a spelling or syntax error in a calculation formula, you will get an Error 515, Error in Formula, when you try to run the report. Here is a way of checking for and correcting these errors:

1. Place a breakpoint at the point in your VB code where you suspect the error occurs.
2. Debug.print the suspected PESetFormula formula string to the debug window.
3. Copy the formula string.
4. Open the report file in CRW Pro and edit the target formula.
5. In the Edit Formula dialog box, paste the formula string into the formula.
6. In the Edit Formulas dialog box, click the Check button. (If no errors are found, CRW Pro will display a dialog box saying No errors found.)

In the VB front end for the Sales Transactions report, there are two procedures that set CRW Pro formulas: SetRptHeader(iPrJob) and SetSTRptFormulas("Sales_Transactions_T1", iPrJob).

SetRptHeader, shown in Listing 4.8, is a utility function that uses RptUtil.mCriteriaControls() to get parameters from the mReport structure and set the formula name. It passes these procedures to ChkSetCRWFormula. ChkSetCRWFormula checks to determine if a formula exists with sFormulaName and then passes vFormulaValue to the report formula. This function can be used for all reports.

Listing 4.8. Changing a report heading with `SetRptHeader`.

```
Public Sub SetRptHeader(iPrJob As Integer)
    For iCtrlIndex = 0 To UBound(mCriteriaControls())
        sCtrlName = mCriteriaControls(iCtrlIndex).Name

        Select Case sCtrlName
            Case "txtReportTitle"
                sFormulaName = "ReportTitle"
                vFormulaValue = mReport.RptTitle
            Case "txtReportSubTitle"
                sFormulaName = "ReportSubTitle"
                vFormulaValue = mReport.RptSubTitle
            Case "fraStoreName"
                sFormulaName = "StoreNameCriteria"
                vFormulaValue = "Store(s): " & mReport.StoreName
            ...
            Case Else
                sFormulaName = ""
        End Select

        If sFormulaName <> "" Then
            If Not ChkSetCRWFormula(iPrJob, sFormulaName, vFormulaValue) Then
                Stop
            End If
        End If

        sFormulaName = ""
    Next iCtrlIndex
```

`SetSTRptFormulas` sets report formulas in the report (see Listing 4.9). In this case, you are setting the report formulas such that they will display group section labels and subtotal formulas correctly to match the group-by criteria that the user chose in the front end.

Listing 4.9. Setting the report's formulas with `SetSTRptFormulas`.

```
Function SetSTRptFormulas(sResultTable As String, iPrJob As Integer) As Integer
    'First get the group by parameters
    sSelectedGroupBy = mReport.GroupBy
    iArrayItem = GetSrtGrpArrayIndex(mGroupArray, sSelectedGroupBy)
    sGroupByColumn = mGroupArray(iArrayItem).ColumnName

    'Now apply it to each formula (with formatting)

    'GroupTotalLabel
    sCurFormulaName = "GroupTotalLabel"
    sCurFormula = "'Total For: ' + GroupName ({" & sResultTable & "." _
            & sGroupByColumn & "})"
    If Not ChkSetCRWStringFormula(iPrJob, sCurFormulaName, sCurFormula) Then
        Stop
    End If

    'GroupTotal
    sCurFormulaName = "GroupTotal"
```

```
sCurFormula = "Sum ({" & sResultTable & "." & "qty},{" & sResultTable & "."
    & sGroupByColumn & "})"
If Not ChkSetCRWStringFormula(iPrJob, sCurFormulaName, sCurFormula) Then
    Stop
End If

SetSTRptFormulas = True

'Give CRW a chance to set the fields
DoEvents
```

The GetSrtGrpArrayIndex procedure is used in combination with the mGroupArray to retrieve the sGroupByColumn. mGroupArray is an array of user-defined data type tSortGroupArray. This array holds the display string that was displayed in the Group By combo box and the table and column name associated with that name. GetSrtGrpArrayIndex simply searches for the group by name (from mReport.GroupBy) in the array and returns the index. The table and column now can be retrieved by specifying the index.

ChkSetCRWStringFormula is similar to ChkSetCRWFormula (used previously). ChkSetCRWStringFormula does not apply CRW Pro formatting to the formula value; you supply the formatting. ChkSetCRWFormula checks the VB data type and then applies the correct CRW Pro formatting. Use ChkSetCRWFormula when you want to pass a label formula. Use ChkSetCRWStringFormula when you want to pass a calculation formula.

Use DoEvents to allow CRW Pro to process the formula.

Setting Report Grouping and Sorting

Two functions in the sample application perform set grouping and sorting parameters in the report:

```
SetReportGrouping(sResultTable As String, iPrJob As Integer)
SetRptSortFields("Sales_Transactions_T1", iPrJob)
```

The code is relatively straightforward. Both use GetSrtGrpArrayIndex in the same fashion as seen in Listing 4.9. However, here are some idiosyncrasies of which you should be aware:

- When you create the report file during design time, you must create as many group sections as you think you will need. You can hide any or all of these group sections, but they must exist if you want to reset them at runtime.

- Sorting is performed first by group sections(s) and then by sort column. For example, if you group by state and then by book title, CRW Pro will always sort by state and then by book title before it sorts by any other column that the user specifies in the sort criteria.

- If a report has a group section or a sort column, CRW Pro will always sort the data using them. Even if you group and sort the data on the server, CRW Pro will always re-sort it according the group sections and sort columns specified in the report. When you create queries, do not group and sort your data on the server; it wastes time.

- When you set the Group Conditions columns and the Sort Conditions column, the columns have to be qualified with the table name of the original table that the report was created with at design time. For example, when you created the report, you created a group section and specified that the default grouping would be on table `Sales_Transactions_T1` and the column `state`. If at runtime you wanted to reset this to group on `title` (book title) for the `sConditionField`, you would pass the string `"Sales_Transactions_T1.title"`.

- When you set the group and sort columns, you need to pass in the same result-set table name with which the report file was created. Just before the report is run, the result-set table name that the report file was originally created with is reset to the user-specific result-set name that you created at runtime. At that time, all of the table names specified in the report's formulas, group sections, and sort criteria are automatically reset to the new result-set table name.

Database Query Procedures

The final step in the process of developing your first reporting system is to create the database query procedures. These procedures generate 0 to *n* number of intermediate result sets and a final result set.

There are two goals in creating these procedures. The first is to maximize the performance of the system. The second is to create user-specific intermediate and final result sets. The first is important to the user who is running the report. The second is important for system security.

Stored Procedures Versus Embedded SQL

There are two general approaches to querying the database: embedded SQL and stored procedures. Embedded SQL is so called because it is embedded in a procedural language such as Visual Basic.

Choosing between embedded SQL and stored procedures can be somewhat difficult. The primary advantage of stored procedures is that they can execute much faster than embedded SQL. This is because they are precompiled, and the execution plan is saved with the stored procedure.

The downside is that stored procedures are less flexible than embedded SQL. Another downside of stored procedures is that they are somewhat more difficult to write. As a procedural language, Transact-SQL is much less robust than Visual Basic. Finally, stored procedures are extremely fast when execution time is short. However, if the execution time is long, the performance gain of stored procedures might be less noticeable.

One issue is specifically related to developing a server with this methodology: creating user-specific final result set tables. If you are using MS SQL Server 6.0 or later, you can have the best of both worlds. You use the EXECUTE statement to execute a string combined with a stored procedure parameter. You pass in the user-specific result-set name, and concatenate it with a string containing the correct CREATE TABLE syntax. The stored procedures will then create the result-set table and continue processing as normal. For example, to create a final result table called "Sales_Transactions_T1_13" using a stored procedure, first create the stored procedure as in the following code:

```
CREATE PROC sps_SalesTransactionRpt
    @ResultTableName varchar(30)
AS

EXEC ("CREATE TABLE " + @ ResultTableName + " (Col1 int)")
...
(The rest of the code.)
```

Then, call the stored procedure as in the following:

```
EXEC sps_SalesTransactionRpt @ResultTableName = "Sales_Transactions_T1_13"
```

To use this methodology with versions of MS SQL Server prior to 6.0, you are limited because all server objects must be hard-coded at design time. One alternative is to use stored procedures for intermediate result sets and embedded SQL to create and populate the final result set. For other servers, check your documentation to determine if you can create tables using stored procedure parameters.

> When you are creating the final result set, do not group and sort your data on the server. It wastes time, because CRW Pro will regroup and resort the data when it queries the final result set.

Optimizing Queries

Optimizing queries is the third way you can have the most impact on performance. (Recall that database design and index optimization were covered in previous sections.) Although query optimization depends on the database that you use and the specific needs of the query, the following are several methods that can improve query performance:

■ Execute queries that will limit the result set first, especially if they can use indexes. This can be implemented as a subquery or by inserting the result set into an interim result table. Included in this is breaking apart complex joins.

■ Limit the use of Aggregate and Convert functions, IN/OR queries, and NOT EQUAL TO operations.

■ One area that catches many developers of operational systems is the use of *outer joins.* Many reports require outer joins to return correct data. An outer join differs from an equijoin in that it returns rows from one table even when there are no matching rows in the other join table. For example, referring to the SQL Server pubs database, you might want to retrieve a list of all publishers including those that do not currently have books listed in the Titles table.

The performance impact of outer joins comes with more complex queries where you have three or more tables. For example, suppose you have three tables: A, B, and C. You need to join them to get your data. But you want all rows in A even if no rows match in B, and all rows in B even if no rows match in C. Unfortunately, this will not work in one query. In Transact-SQL, you will receive an error when you try to execute the following:

```
A *= B *= C
```

The impact on you as a report-query developer is that many times you will be forced to create and use intermediate tables (typically temp tables) to shield against this problem. This can have a significant effect on performance.

Characteristic Functions

Characteristic functions are both a methodology and a unique way of utilizing SQL. They solve many difficult problems that tend to crop up in writing report queries. In some conditions they can greatly speed up query execution and reduce the amount of code required.

One problem that these functions solve easily is table folding. *Table folding* is a situation in which the source data is in a column (vertically) and you want to "fold" it to multiple columns (horizontally). For example, Pubs.Sales includes three columns: stor_id, ord_date, and qty. Report requirements call for reporting the sum of qty by stor_id in 12 columns, one for each month. Using traditional SQL, you would write the code shown in Listing 4.10.

Listing 4.10. The #tmpQueryResults script in traditional SQL.

```
INSERT INTO #tmpQueryResults
SELECT
        store_id,
        FebAmt = SUM(qty)
FROM
        Sales
WHERE
        ord_date BETWEEN '1/1/95' AND '1/31/95'
GROUP BY
        store_id

UPDATE #tmpQueryResults
SET
        FebAmt = SUM(qty)
```

```
FROM
        Sales
WHERE
        ord_date BETWEEN '2/1/95' AND '2/28/95'
AND     (#tmpQueryResults.store_id = Sales.store id)
GROUP BY
        store_id
```

This last section of code, beginning with the line

```
UPDATE # tmpQueryResults
```

and to the end, will be repeated ten times to perform the script completely.

Listing 4.11 shows the same query using characteristic functions.

Listing 4.11. The #tmpQueryResults script using characteristic functions.

```
INSERT INTO #tmpQueryResults
SELECT
    JanAmt = SUM(qty*(1-ABS(SIGN(DATEPART(month,ord_date)-1)))),
    FebAmt = SUM(qty*(1-ABS(SIGN(DATEPART(month,ord_date)-2)))),
    MarAmt = SUM(qty*(1-ABS(SIGN(DATEPART(month,ord_date)-3)))),
    ...
    DecAmt = SUM(qty*(1-ABS(SIGN(DATEPART(month,ord_date)-12)))),
FROM Sales
GROUP BY store_id
```

Although it looks strange at first, this methodology is really quite simple to understand. In general, the query will take one pass through the database and return 12 columns of values, one for each month. Each column with be the sum of the qty column for orders that fall in that month.

First, let's review. All of these functions are standard, built-in Microsoft SQL Server functions. DATEPART() returns an integer indicating the specified date part (in this case, month) for the specified date (in this case the value in the ord_date column). SIGN() returns -1 for negative values, 0 for zero values, and +1 for positive values. ABS() returns the absolute value of the argument. SUM returns the sum of the values for each GROUP BY level.

Now look at the JanAmt portion of the query.

```
JanAmt = SUM(qty*(1-ABS(SIGN(DATEPART(month,ord_date)-1))))
```

Here, we wish to return a column with one value that is the sum of all quantities (qty) where the order date (ord_date) is in January. In this case, the month is specified with an integer. In the code, DATEPART(month,ord_date)-1, the 1 is the integer that specifies January as the target month. If you want to return values where the ord_date is in February, you would use the value 2 in the function.

Therefore, assume that the ord_date for the first row in the table is in January. Therefore, the inner expression DATEPART()-1 returns 0 (one minus one). Then, the next outer expression SIGN() returns 0 (SIGN(0)=0). Then, the next outer expression ABS() returns 0 (ABS(0)=0). Then, the next outer expression 1-0 returns 1. Then, the next-outer expression returns the quantity for that row (qty * 1). Finally, the SUM() expression returns the sum of all quantities for a specific month. In this case, because the ord_date is in January, the quantity is returned, and the quantity is included with other January quantities in the JanAmt column.

Now, assume that the ord_date for the first row in the table is in February (not January). Therefore, the inner expression DATEPART()-1 returns 1 (2-1). Then, the next outer expression SIGN() returns 1 (SIGN(1)=1). The next outer expression then ABS() returns 1 (ABS(1)=1). After that, the next outer expression 1-1 returns 0. Then, the next-outer expression returns a zero quantity (qty * 0). Finally, the SUM() expression returns the sum of all values for a specific month. In this case, because the ord_date is not in January, the quantity (qty) for that row is not returned (a zero quantity is returned instead) and the quantity for that row is not included with other January quantities in the JanAmt column. Instead, the quantity is included with the February quantities in the FebAmt column.

Besides the obvious fact that this code is easier to read (once you have gotten used to the concept), it can be much faster. Using a standard SQL approach, the procedure would have to scan the table 12 times. Using characteristic functions, the table is scanned once.

One potential downside of using characteristic functions is the system overhead. For large queries with long characteristic functions, you might receive error messages saying that you have exceeded a page-count limit. Consult your database system's documentation for specifics.

This is a very brief overview of characteristic functions; they have much wider breadth than has been presented here. The concept and implementation of characteristic functions was developed by David Rozenshtein, Anatoly Abramovich, and Eugene Birger. Strongly recommended is their small but concise book:

> David Rozenshtein, Anatoly Abramovich, and Eugene Birger, *Optimizing Transact-SQL: Advanced Programming Techniques*, (Fremont, CA: SQL Forum Press, 1995)

Summary

Building a reporting system that operates effectively and efficiently can be a challenge. When built with a sensitivity to the users' needs using a modular approach based on an architecture, the reporting system that you build can be fast, expandable, and supported with a minimum of effort.

The SysInfo Control

by James E. Bettone

When you are developing within the Windows environment, you have at your disposal a rich set of APIs to support the environment. All of these are exposed to Visual Basic via a type library or by "declaring" each API call. Another aspect of the Windows environment are *messages*. These Windows messages normally are hidden to the Visual Basic developer, and only a select few of these developers know how to manipulate them from within Visual Basic.

Visual Basic 4.0 mostly solves this problem by providing an OCX or custom control called the SysInfo Custom Control, which provides events and properties that enable the developer to respond to a particular type of message called a *system message*.

This chapter reviews the different properties and events of the SysInfo control and provides samples and code to demonstrate some of its capabilities.

The SysInfo Control

The SysInfo control enables you to respond to certain types of messages called system messages. *System messages* are messages that are broadcast to all the applications that are currently running. These messages are usually broadcast when something in the operating system has changed. For example, if the user goes into the Control Panel and changes the color scheme from Brick to Desert, the operating system will then broadcast a message to all open or running applications that the color scheme has changed. Your application could then reflect these changes as appropriate by responding to the system message.

This is where the SysInfo control comes in handy. Normally, the messages and message queues of the operating system are something that we developers are insulated from, because they are fairly complex and a potentially dangerous thing to mess around with. The SysInfo control eliminates this complexity (and the danger) by putting a nice friendly user-interface control between the developer and the operating system (OS). (See Figure 5.1.)

Figure 5.1.
*The SysInfo control sits
between your application
and the OS.*

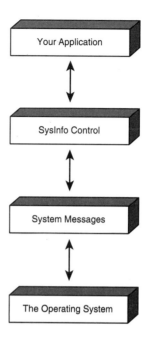

Adding the SysInfo Control to Your Project

You can find the SysInfo control on the Visual Basic 4.0 CD in the \Tools\Sysinfo directory.
To include the control in your project, follow these steps:

1. If you already have a copy and/or have registered the SysInfo control, then skip the
   next steps and go to step 4.

2. Copy the SysInfo.OCX and SysInfo.OCA files to the System directory of your
   Windows directory.

3. Copy the file SysInfo.HLP to your Visual Basic directory.

4. Start Visual Basic.

5. From the Tools menu, select Custom Controls.

6. Search in the Custom Controls list for Microsoft SysInfo Control. If you can't find
   the control in the list, then proceed to the next step; otherwise, select the control (so
   that an X is in the box) and proceed to step 8. See Figure 5.2 for an example of this
   dialog box.

Figure 5.2.
The Custom Controls dialog box.

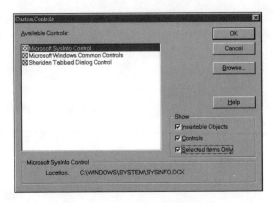

7. Select the Browse button and select SysInfo.OCX from the System directory of your Windows directory. See Figure 5.3 for an example of this screen.

Figure 5.3.
The SysInfo OCX.

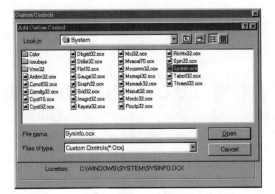

8. Click OK.

You should now have the SysInfo control in your project. The control will be in the bottom part of the toolbar and look something like that shown in Figure 5.4.

Figure 5.4.
The SysInfo control.

For a complete example of this control, see the SysInfo example included on the CD that accompanies this book. See Figure 5.5 for a screen shot of the example.

Figure 5.5.
The SysInfo example.

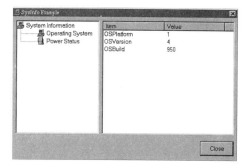

Monitoring Changes Within the OS

The main purpose of the SysInfo control is to notify your application of system events and properties. The control does this through a variety of properties and events that can be grouped logically together into a few areas, such as system changes and properties, power status, and plug-and-play changes.

System Changes and Properties

The SysInfo control has a variety of properties and events that enable the developer to respond to changes within the OS or to view properties of the OS. The following section explains what each property or event represents.

The `OSPlatform`, `OSVersion`, and `OSBuild` Properties

The `OSPlatform`, `OSVersion`, and `OSBuild` properties return a value that you can use to determine under which type of platform, version, and build your application is running.

The `OSPlatform` property returns a set of integer values as shown in Table 5.1.

Table 5.1. The values of the `OSPlatform` property.

Value	Description
0	Windows, Windows for Workgroups
1	Windows 95
2	Windows NT

The `OSVersion` and `OSBuild` properties return a value that identifies the version and build number, respectively, of the current platform.

These properties can be used to determine exactly what version, build, and platform your application is currently running under, in order, for example, to use a different set of APIs or set of routines that maybe wasn't supported on a different platform or build.

The `ScrollBarSize` Property

The `ScrollBarSize` property returns a value, in twips, indicating the width of scrollbars throughout the operating system.

The `WorkAreaHeight`, `WorkAreaLeft`, `WorkAreaTop`, and `WorkAreaWidth` Properties

These properties are used to determine the area of the desktop that is visible (minus the Windows 95 taskbar, if applicable). You can use these properties to resize your form if it is supposed to be the height of the display. For example:

```
If Screen.Height > frmSysInfo.SysInfo.WorkAreaHeight Then
    frmSysInfo.Height = frmSysInfo.SysInfo.WorkAreaHeight
Else
    frmSysInfo.Height = Screen.Height
End If
```

Configuration Changes

The SysInfo control has events that monitor when the System Registry has been edited, changed, or deleted. These events can be used to determine if a value in the registry that your application uses has been changed. For example, a user changes the registry setting that stores which type of toolbars your application is using—large or small. When the user changes this value, your application will respond to this event and change to the correct type of toolbar.

The `QueryChangeConfig` event occurs when a user is about to change the configuration or registry setting. This message is broadcast to all currently running applications. If the configuration does change (for example, by clicking OK), then another message is broadcast and the `ConfigChanged` event fires off. Likewise, the `ConfigChangeCancelled` event fires off if the configuration change was cancelled (for example, by the user clicking Cancel).

System Changes

There are a number of events available to monitor changes within the system such as when a user changes the time, system color, or a device's setting. This property is useful when your application relies on the setting of a specific device within the operating system. When the device's setting changes, the appropriate event is triggered, and your application has a chance to respond to this. Table 5.2 lists the events and their descriptions.

Table 5.2. The values of the system-change events.

Event	Description
DevModeChange Event	Occurs when the user changes a device's setting
DisplayChanged Event	Occurs when the user changes display settings.
SettingChanged Event	Occurs when the user changes system settings.
SysColorsChanged Event	Occurs when the user changes the system colors.
TimeChanged Event	Occurs when the user changes the system date/time.

Monitoring Power Status

The SysInfo control supports a number of properties and events to monitor power-source activities and properties. These properties and events are useful for applications that run on a portable power source such as those found in laptops and notebooks.

The Power-Status Properties

The power-status properties are used to determine different things about the power source for the computer that is running your application. This is useful if your application does a power-intensive operation and needs to be aware of the power source for the computer system.

The ACStatus Property

The ACStatus property returns a value specifying which type of electricity the computer system is using. This is mostly applicable on laptops and notebooks wherein it might be important to know where the power is coming from. Table 5.3 shows the possible values.

Table 5.3. Values for the ACStatus property.

Value	Description
0	The computer is not using AC power.
1	The computer is using AC power.
255	Cannot determine if AC power is being used or not.

The Battery-Status Properties

The battery-status properties are used to determine how much charge remains in the battery, how much battery life remains (how much longer it will still hold a charge), and how much time the battery will keep the computer running. Of course, these properties are not useful when the app is running on a desktop computer system, but they can be very useful when your application is running on a portable system that uses batteries.

With these properties, your application can be aware of how long the power source for the computer will continue to provide power for its needs.

The `BatteryFullTime` and `BatteryLifeTime` Properties

The `BatteryFullTime` and `BatteryLifeTime` properties can be used to determine how long the battery is supposed to last and how much time is left in the battery, respectively.

The `BatteryLifePercent` Property

The `BatteryLifePercent` property returns a value between `0` and `100` that indicates how much life is still in the battery.

The `BatteryStatus` Property

The BatteryStatus property is used to determine the status of the battery—that is, whether its charge is full, low, or critical. Table 5.4 lists the various values of this property.

Table 5.4. The values of the `BatteryStatus` property.

Value	Description
1	Battery charge is high.
2	Battery charge is low.
4	Battery charge is critical.
8	Battery is charging.
128	The system has no battery.
255	Battery charge status is unknown.

The Power-Status Events

The power-status events are used to monitor when power status has changed.

The `PowerQuerySuspend` and `PowerSuspend` Events

The `PowerQuerySuspend` and `PowerSuspend` events are the events that trigger prior and more immediately prior to the power being suspended. Most desktop as well as portable computers suspend power during periods of idle activity. You can use these events to warn the user during critical operation that the computer is about to go into suspend mode—or even cancel the power-suspend mode altogether. (You do this from within the `PowerQuerySuspend` event.)

The `PowerResume` Event

The `PowerResume` event will trigger immediately after the power has resumed. You can use this to determine when it is safe to start a critical operation.

The `PowerStatusChanged` Event

The `PowerStatusChanged` event occurs when a change in the power or the status of the power is detected. For example, this event will trigger when the power has changed from AC to DC, when the battery is low, or when the battery has finished recharging. See Table 5.5 for other possible events.

Table 5.5. The power-status events with descriptions.

Event	Description
PowerQuerySuspend	Triggers when power is about to suspend.
PowerResume	Triggers when power is about to resume.
PowerStatusChanged	Triggers when power status has changed.
PowerSuspend	Triggers immediately before the power is suspended.

Monitoring Plug-and-Play Changes

Last but not least, the SysInfo control has properties to monitor when plug-and-play devices have been changed, deleted, or added (see Table 5.6). You can use these events to monitor if a critical device has been removed or changed while your application is running.

Table 5.6. The plug-and-play events and their descriptions.

Event	Description
DeviceArrival	Occurs when a device has successfully been installed.
DeviceEventOther	Occurs when the other events aren't appropriate.
DeviceQueryRemove	Occurs before a device is removed.
DeviceQueryRemoveFailed	Occurs when the device removal failed.
DeviceRemoveComplete	Occurs when the device removal is successful.
DeviceRemovePending	Occurs immediately before a device is removed.

The `DeviceRemoveComplete`, `DeviceRemovePending`, `DeviceQueryRemove`, and `DeviceQueryRemoveFailed` Events

These events, described in the following list, can be used to monitor device removal in the system, including network drives, additional hardware, or disk drives.

- `DeviceQueryRemove` occurs immediately before an attempt by the user to remove a device from the system.

- `DeviceQueryRemoveFailed` occurs immediately after an attempt by the user to remove a device has failed or the user has cancelled the operation.

- `DeviceRemovePending` occurs after all the applications that are currently executing return an OK to the system. When a device is removed, the system sends out a message to all applications that are executing, notifying them of the pending device removal. If this is OK, the applications respond appropriately back to the system. This event will trigger immediately after this has happened.

- `DeviceRemoveComplete` occurs immediately after a device has been removed.

Both of these last two events have properties that describe the device that is affected by the removal. There are properties for the `DeviceType`, `DeviceID`, or `DeviceData`, and `DeviceName`. See the online help under `DeviceRemoveComplete` for descriptions of these values.

The `DeviceArrival` and `DeviceEventOther` Events

The `DeviceArrival` and `DeviceEventOther` events occur when devices are added to the system or when all other events are inappropriate. Both of these events support the same set of properties and property values as the above mentioned `DeviceEvents`.

Summary

In this chapter, you learned the System Information or SysInfo control—how it works, what it can do, and how it can benefit you as a developer to make more Windows-aware applications. This control is a very useful tool for doing just that, and it can be a valuable addition to any project.

Using the Win95/ Win32 API

by Michael Murphy

CHAPTER

6

The Visual Basic programming language is very powerful and flexible. It enables you to develop sophisticated Windows applications quickly and easily. There are, however, boundaries within native Visual Basic. Fortunately, you can break through these boundaries by accessing external procedures. Indeed, the capability to call external procedures, including the Windows Application Programming Interface (API), is probably the most powerful feature of Visual Basic.

The introduction of the 32-bit version of Visual Basic 4.0 opens up a whole new set of opportunities and challenges for accessing external procedures. Developers can now take advantage of the power of the Windows 32-bit API, known as the Win32. The Win32 contains hundreds of new functions.

This chapter examines the powerful capabilities of calling external procedures. It also shows you how to use the Windows API and gives some examples of how easy it is to include this functionality in your Visual Basic application.

Overview of the Windows API

The Microsoft family of Windows operating systems (Windows NT, Windows 95, and Windows 3.*x*) contains several dynamically linked libraries (DLLs) that make up what is called the Windows Application Programming Interface (API). The API is a standard set of functions that can be called from your Visual Basic application (or other Windows applications). In fact, all Windows applications use the Windows API to perform tasks such as creating windows, changing the window size, reading and writing files, and so on. This set of standard functions, collectively known as the API, is the very heart of the operating system and one of the key strengths of the Windows environment. It enables you to take advantage of pre-written functions, which you can use in your Visual Basic application.

To better understand the Windows API, it is important to understand the difference between static and dynamic linking. First, *static linking* is the process of including all functions used by your program in the program executable. The compiler scans your code for references to functions and then includes those functions in your .EXE file when you compile. Several programming languages, such as C and Pascal, give you the ability to statically link your application. On the other hand, *dynamic linking* is the process of loading functions (contained in external files) when your application is loaded. These functions reside externally to your application and are simply used when your application calls them. The Windows API is composed of dynamically linked libraries. The functions contained in these DLLs are not compiled into your application; instead, they are dynamically linked to your application and loaded into memory when an application uses the DLL, and then they are unloaded when the application is closed.

There are several advantages of DLLs:

- Functions can be reused and shared among many applications.
- You need only one copy of the DLL (not one for each of your applications).
- You can modify the DLL without modifying your application (assuming you don't change the `Declare` statement).
- DLLs are usually written in the C/C++ programming language. These DLLs tend to be faster because they are statically linked and compiled into a stand-alone executable—unlike VB code, which is first translated.

The Windows 3.*x* API is made up of three main DLLs: GDI.DLL, Kernel.DLL, and User.DLL. These DLLs were replaced in Windows 95 and Windows NT by the following 32-bit versions: GDI32.DLL, Kernel32.DLL, and User32.DLL. In addition to these DLLs there are now several other DLLs that make up the Windows 95 and Windows NT API. These 32-bit DLLs contain system-related procedures that include functions, data structures, data types, messages, and statements you can take advantage of while developing applications to run under Windows 95 and Windows NT.

These files are usually located in your System directory under Windows 95 and Windows 3.X and are in the System32 directory under Windows NT.

Overview of Win32

The Microsoft Win32 API builds on the Win16 API to take advantage of 32-bit operating systems. Like its predecessor, the Win32 is made up of functions, messages, and structures to perform general Windows functions.

The Win32 is the first major change to the Windows API since the introduction of the Win16. Sure, the Win16 added new functions over the years; however, the fundamentals remained the same. Prior to the release of Visual Basic 4.0, the developer could simply declare an API function and be confident that it would work on all Windows desktops. Now, with Win32, the developer needs to make a conscious decision about which API to use. And of course, for those who have existing Visual Basic applications that contain Win16 API calls, you need to decide if you are going to port your application.

Why Use the API?

As a Visual Basic programmer, you have probably used the Windows API at one time or another. Maybe you have used `WritePrivateProfileString` and `GetPrivateProfileString` functions to read or write .INI files to store configuration information. Or maybe you have used `GetWindowsDirectory` to get the Windows directory. In either case, you could have written lines and lines of code to accomplish the same thing. But why would you want to spend time doing that if you could accomplish the same thing in one call to API? Writing to an .INI file and getting the Windows directory can be done in VB; however, there are times when you have to make external procedure calls that you can't do in Visual Basic. For example, how do you make a network connection in Visual Basic? You need to use the API.

There are two major advantages of the Win32 API:

- To break through the 64KB memory barrier
- To maintain compatibility across Microsoft's 32-bit platforms: Windows 95, Windows NT 3.1, and Windows 3.1 with Win32s

Declare Your API Routines

In order to use the Windows API, or any other function contained in DLLs, you must first declare the function you want to use. By declaring the function, you give Visual Basic the information it needs to make the appropriate call to the external procedure. After you have declared the appropriate function, you simply call it like any other function in your project. The declaration of the function contains the following information:

- The name of the function you want to call
- The name of the DLL you are calling
- The number of arguments and their datatypes to be passed to the DLL
- The datatype of the returning value (if the procedure is a function)

There are two basic steps to making a call to an external procedure:

1. Use the Declare statement to tell VB which procedure to call and the arguments it expects.
2. Make the call to the procedure.

The Structure of API Routines

The Declare statement is used to declare a reference to an external procedure. You simply declare the external procedure in the declarations section of any form, standard, or class module. Declarations for a DLL procedure in a standard module are public by default—they can be called from anywhere in the application. However, if you declare a procedure in a form or class module, you need to use the Private keyword. Remember, when you use the Private keyword, the procedure is available only within the module in which the declaration is made.

If the external procedure returns a value, it will be declared as a function and is declared with the following syntax:

```
Declare Function publicname Lib libname [Alias alias] [([[ByVal] variable
➡[As type] [,[ByVal] variable [As type]]...])] As Type
```

For example:

```
Declare Function GetDriveType Lib "kernel32" Alias
➥"GetDriveTypeA" (ByVal nDrive As String) As Long
```

If the external procedure does not return a value, it will be declared as a Sub and is declared with the following syntax:

```
Declare Sub publicname Lib "libname" [Alias "alias"] [([[ByVal]
➥variable [As type] [,[ByVal] variable [As type]]...])]
```

For example:

```
Declare Sub FreeSid Lib "advapi32.dll" Alias "FreeSid" (pSid As Any)
```

It is very important that you declare the procedure correctly. The best way to do that is to copy and paste the declaration from a source such as the Windows API view (discussed later in this chapter). You can also refer to the Microsoft Windows Software Development Kit.

> Functions in the Win32 API are case-sensitive. Functions in the Win16 API are not.

The Lib clause in the Declare statement specifies the name of the DLL you are calling and can also specify the exact location of the file. The following example will specify the kernel32.DLL in the c:\windows\system directory:

```
Declare Function GetDriveType Lib "c:\windows\system\kernel32.dll"
➥Alias "GetDriveTypeA" (ByVal nDrive As String) As Long
```

Most external procedure calls do not contain the fully qualified path of the DLL. Instead, the name of the DLL is given without the path and the .DLL extension. If the path and extension is not included in the Lib section, VB assumes a DLL extension and will look for the DLL in the following order:

1. Directory of the application
2. Current directory
3. Windows 32-bit system directory (in Windows NT)
4. Windows system directory
5. Windows directory
6. The PATH environment

The Alias section and passing arguments to the external procedure are discussed in the following sections.

Aliasing API Calls

The optional keyword Alias is often used in the declaration of an external procedure. There are several occasions when you need to use the Alias clause when you declare a procedure:

- When the external procedure name is the same as a keyword in Visual Basic
- When the external procedure has the same name as a public variable, constant, or any other procedure within the same scope
- When the external procedure name is not allowed by the DLL naming convention in Visual Basic
- When the external procedure does not contain names of the procedure; instead, you must specify the ordinal number for the procedure

If you find that an external procedure name is the same as a keyword in Visual Basic, you must alias the procedure. For example, the API function SetFocus is also a keyword in Visual Basic, and you must alias this function. Also, if the procedure name is already a public variable, constant, or other procedure within the same scope, you must alias the procedure. You might find this useful if, for example, you write a great deal of code and you later add external procedure calls and find that the name of the procedure has already been used as a variable. Instead of going back and replacing all occurrences of the variable, you can simply alias the procedure to give Visual Basic the unique name it needs to make the appropriate procedure call. The alternative is to do a global search-and-replace of your variable. For the sake of standards, this approach is preferred.

The following paragraphs describe occasions 3 and 4 (from the preceding list) in more detail.

When the external procedure name is not allowed by the DLL naming convention in Visual Basic, you need to alias any external procedure that contains characters that are not allowed by Visual Basic. The procedure name must contain alphanumeric characters or the underscore character (_). However, the first character of the procedure must begin with a letter. The following is an example of a function call that uses the Alias clause because the function contains an underscore as the first character:

```
Declare Function lclose Lib "kernel32" Alias "_lclose"
➡(ByVal hFile As Long) As Long
```

When the external procedure does not contain names of the procedure, you must specify the *ordinal number* for the procedure: Each procedure in a DLL is assigned a number, called the *ordinal number.* You can call the procedure by its name (if it exists) or by the ordinal number. The ordinal number is another way of referencing the procedure you are calling. In fact, some DLLs do not contain the name of the procedure—only the ordinal number. Although calling the procedure by the ordinal number is slightly faster than calling it by its name, it is recommended that you call the procedure by name, because the name of the procedure is usually descriptive of the function call. In contrast, calling a procedure by the ordinal number does not give you any hint as to which procedure you are calling. Therefore, calling the procedure by name is easier to read, and it is less likely that you will call the wrong procedure.

If you call a procedure by ordinal, you must first know the number that you want to call. You need to reference the documentation for the DLL you are calling. You then alias the procedure by inserting the number sign (#) and then inputting the ordinal number you are calling. The following is an example of a fictitious external procedure call using the ordinal number instead of the name:

```
Declare Function MyRemoveSpaces Lib "MyDLL" Alias "#100"
➥(ByVal lpszMyArgument As String) As Long
```

Now the same procedure call using the name:

```
Declare Function MyRemoveSpaces Lib "MyDLL" Alias "RemoveSpaces"
➥(ByVal lpszMyArgument As String) As Long
```

Passing Parameters

When you pass parameters to a DLL, you must make sure you pass arguments that the DLL expects, both in terms of order in which they are passed as well as the data type of the argument. Additionally, you must specify how the argument is passed. Making sure you pass the right argument(s) is the most difficult part of making DLL calls. If you pass the wrong datatype to an external procedure, for example, you can cause a Windows General Protection Fault (GPF), which will most likely cause Visual Basic to crash. If you generate a GPF, it is also quite possible that Windows will become unstable.

> Make sure to save your work before you run a project that contains Windows API calls. If you make a call to an API that is formatted incorrectly, you will likely get a GPF and will lose all the work that was entered since the last time you saved.

By default, Visual Basic will pass all arguments ByRef (by reference). Passing an argument to a procedure ByRef means that you are passing a pointer to a memory address of the variable, not the actual value. When you pass ByRef, you give the calling procedure the capability to change the actual value of the variable rather than simply changing a copy of the variable. Unlike ByRef, ByVal actually sends the variable to the procedure. Most DLLs expect arguments ByVal, which means that a copy of the actual value is passed to the procedure. As you can probably deduce, passing ByRef is more efficient that passing ByVal, because you are simply passing the memory address of the variable rather than passing the entire variable to the procedure.

Of course, there is an exception to every rule. The exception to this rule is using ByVal to pass a string datatype. Visual Basic handles string datatypes a little differently. In order to compensate for the differences and be able to pass the string in a format that the external procedure can use, passing a string ByVal is slightly different from passing other datatypes. Passing a string ByVal actually means that you are passing the memory address of the first data byte in the string (kind of like what the ByRef does). The first data byte in the string gives the calling procedure the information it needs to access the variable. Passing a string ByRef actually means you are passing the memory address where another address is located.

The Registry and .INI Files

Under Windows 3.*x*, the standard way of storing configuration information such as the hardware configuration, installed software applications, user preferences, and other settings is in the form of initialization files (.INI files). These .INI files normally reside in the Windows directory, and there are often dozens of .INI files (depending on the number of applications installed in the computer). In order to organize and consolidate these settings, Microsoft released the Registry in Windows 95 and Windows NT. The Registry is a system-defined database that contains all system settings. To view entries in the Registry, simply run the regedit application in Windows 95 or the regedt32 application in Windows NT. For additional information on the Windows Registry, please refer to the documentation provided by Microsoft Windows.

The following sections give you some examples of the WritePrivateProfileString and GetPrivateProfileString API calls (for use with Windows 3.*x*) and also show you how to use the Registry to save settings under Windows 95 and Windows NT.

Interacting with Registry and .INI Files

You might want to save configuration information or store user preferences for your Visual Basic application. The Windows Registry is a good place to save those settings. The following examples of saving user preferences include saving settings to .INI files as well as saving to the Windows Registry. Although writing to .INI files is still supported, the preferred method of saving settings is to the Windows Registry. The following examples show you how to read and write to .INI files and also to read and write to the Windows Registry. They are intended to show you the differences between the two methods and also to give some examples of API calls.

Writing to .INI Files

As discussed earlier in this chapter, when you use the Windows API, you must first declare the function you are calling. Using the WritePrivateProfileString API function call will open an .INI file you specify. Write the section, key name, and setting provided in the argument list, and then close the file. If the .INI file does not exist, the API will automatically create the file in the default Windows directory. You can find the default Windows directory by calling the GetWindowsDirectory API call. The following is an example of writing a user preference for the MyApp application that saves the default location of the database.

First, declare the function in a module:

```
Declare Function WritePrivateProfileString Lib "kernel32" Alias
➡"WritePrivateProfileStringA" (ByVal lpApplicationName As String, ByVal
➡lpKeyName As Any, ByVal lpString As Any,
➡ByVal lpFileName As String) As Long
```

Next, simply call the function with the appropriate parameters:

```
Private Sub cmdWriteSetting_Click()
   Dim lngReturnValue As Long
    lngReturnValue = WritePrivateProfileString("Settings", "DataBase Path",
    ➡"c:\MyApp\Database", "MyApp.INI")
End Sub
```

Note that the preceding example requires the Win32 API and the 32-bit version of Visual Basic. The returned datatype is Long; the 16-bit counterpart returns an Integer. If you were going to use the Win16 API, you would use the following example:

```
Declare Function WritePrivateProfileString Lib "Kernel" (ByVal
➡lpApplicationName As String, ByVal lpKeyName As Any,
➡ByVal lpString As Any, ByVal lplFileName As String) As Integer


Private Sub cmdWriteSetting_Click()
    Dim intReturnValue As Integer
    intReturnValue = WritePrivateProfileString("Settings", "DataBase Path",
    ➡"c:\MyApp\Database", "MyApp.INI")
End Sub
```

The 16-bit and the 32-bit version will yield the same results, as shown in Figure 6.1.

Figure 6.1.
*Display of MyApp.INI
file.*

If you plan to develop your application for both Win32 and Win16, you should use the conditional compile option described later in the book.

Reading from .INI Files

Now that you have saved a setting to the MyApp.INI, you need to be able to retrieve that setting. You can do this by using the GetPrivateProfileString API call. The following is an example of how to read the setting that was written in the previous example. Because you are retrieving a string value, you will notice that you have to do a little more work with this API call. Remember from the earlier section called "Passing Parameters" that strings are handled a little differently from other datatypes. The ByVal lpReturnedString As String in the following Declare statement actually means that it is looking for a pointer to a memory address. Therefore, you need to allocate memory for the string that the function can access; that is why you have to specifically define the length of the string. The API call will change the string value and will return the length of the returned string.

```
Declare Function GetPrivateProfileString Lib "kernel32" Alias
➡"GetPrivateProfileStringA" (ByVal lpApplicationName As String, ByVal
➡lpKeyName As Any, ByVal lpDefault As String,
➡ByVal lpReturnedString As String, ByVal nSize As Long,
➡ByVal lpFileName As String) As Long
Private Sub cmdGetSetting_Click()
    Dim lngReturnValue As Long, strReturnString As String * 255
    lngReturnValue = GetPrivateProfileString("Settings", "Database Path",
    ➡"", strReturnString, 255, "MyApp.INI")
    strReturnString = Left$(strReturnString, lngReturnValue)
End Sub
```

The 16-bit version is nearly the same; make sure you use the 16 API declaration and use an Integer as the return value instead of a Long.

Writing to the Registry

Because the SaveSetting statement is now a part of the functionality in Visual Basic, you do not need to declare it as you would with the API call to WritePrivateProfileString. The following is the syntax for the SaveSetting statement:

```
SaveSetting(appname, section, key, setting)
```

Writing to the Registry then becomes quite easy. The following is an example that writes to the Windows Registry:

```
Call SaveSetting("MyApp", "Settings", "Database Path", "c:\MyApp\Database")
```

As you can see from Figure 6.2, using the SaveSetting statement in VB writes to the Registry database in HKEY_CURRENT_USER\Software\VB and VBA Program Settings.

Figure 6.2.
Display of saved Registry settings.

Reading from the Registry

Similar to the SaveSetting statement, the GetSetting function is also a part of Visual Basic and does not need to be declared as an API call. Notice that because SaveSetting returns a value, it is a function. The following is the syntax for the GetSetting function:

```
GetSetting(appname, section, key[, default])
```

The following example returns the setting written in the previous example into the variable vntReturnValue:

```
Dim vntReturnValue As Variant
vntReturnValue = GetSetting("MyApp", "Settings", "Database Path")
```

You can also read and write to the Registry via Win32 API calls; however, because Visual Basic has this functionality built-in, it is much easier to use this approach when accessing registry settings in HKEY_CURRENT_USER\Software\VB and VB Program Settings. If you want to read and write to other sections of the Registry, you need to use Win32 API calls.

Using the API Viewer

The API Viewer that ships with the Professional and Enterprise version of Visual Basic (see Figure 6.3) provides a great way for you to get your API declarations into your project quickly and easily. For those of you who have used the API view, you know how easy it is. Simply open the application by clicking on the API Text Viewer from the Visual Basic 4.0 application group and then click on File | Load Text File.

Figure 6.3.

Opening Win32api.TXT file in the Visual Basic API View.

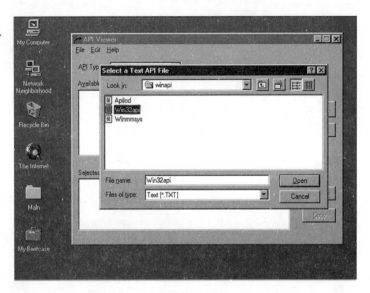

Select one of the text files from the \VB\WINAPI directory. Notice that because I only installed the 32-bit version of Visual Basic on this computer, I only have the 32-bit version of the API reference. If you plan to develop your applications for Win16, you can install the 16-bit version of Visual Basic in the same directory. You will then get the 16-bit version of the API reference. The API Viewer will prompt you to convert the text file to a database: Yes/No (see Figure 6.4). Heck, it says it'll be faster, so go for it.

Figure 6.4.

Converting Win32api.TXT file to a database.

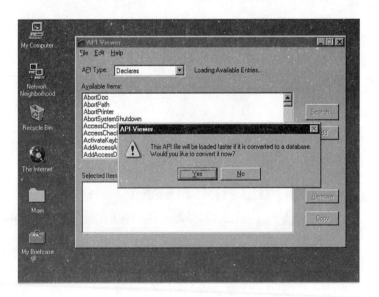

Now you are ready to start copying. Select the desired APIs and click Add. A nice feature of the API View is that it enables you to select multiple items as shown in Figure 6.5. When you have selected all the APIs you want, click Copy, and then switch over to your VB project and paste them in. That's all there is to it.

Figure 6.5.
Visual Basic API View.

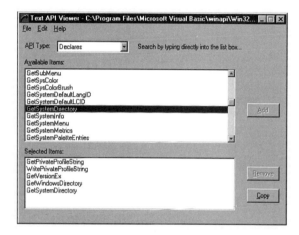

> You can also reference the Win32API.TXT or Win16API.TXT for the same APIs. For obvious reasons, you don't want to include the contents of the entire WinXXAPI.TXT in your project (unless you are trying to make your application slow).

Summary

This chapter gave you an introduction to using the Windows API in your Visual Basic application. It also gave some examples of how to make calls to both the Win16 and the Win32 API.

However, we have barely scratched the surface of the power and flexibility of the Windows API. The API is a topic that really requires a detailed discussion to be fully understood. (The information in this chapter might be just enough to make you dangerous.) There are dozens of books on this subject, and I would strongly recommend you purchase one of these books and familiarize yourself with the more detailed concepts and implementations. I think you'll find it worth your time.

Using OLE and OLE Automation

P A R T

2

Object-Oriented Concepts

by Shawn Oberst

This chapter is a short introduction to object-oriented concepts. If you are unfamiliar with objects, including some of the fundamental manifestations of objects, you should read this chapter. If you are familiar with the concepts of objects, including classes, encapsulation, inheritance, polymorphism, and persistence, you probably can skip this chapter. Chapters 8 through 11 explain how to implement object-oriented concepts using Visual Basic 4.0.

The object-oriented model is a set of design principles that can be applied to just about any development task and implemented in just about any programming language. When I say that a language like Visual Basic 4.0 is more object-oriented than Visual Basic 3.0, I am saying that there are more constructs built into Visual Basic 4.0 to enable developers to easily apply these object-oriented design principles.

What Is an Object?

Many people have been talking about objects for several years. Most of the time, however, they only tell half the story, and much of that is fiercely debated. I, too, once longed for an opportunity to release to the world my grand scheme for exactly how objects should look and behave. After stepping down from my intellectual high horse and mucking about in the muddy waters of experience, however, I have acquired a much more Taoist perspective on objects. I believe this simpler and more experimental perspective is worth more than any amount of detailed explanation I could give. An object in a computer system always should be modeled so that it looks and behaves as closely as possible as its equivalent object in the real world. Although it often is helpful to read various "expert" opinions on structure and style, you always should remember to look back at the physical or conceptual objects you are modeling and ask yourself, "What is that object?"

Creating an *object* is merely an attempt to create something in a computer system exactly as functional, reusable, and persistent as an object with which people are familiar in their everyday experience. The argument for why someone might want to do such a thing is fairly simple. If you could create something inside your computer that looked and acted in every significant way exactly like a phone, for example, then that something would be as easy and intuitive to use as your phone. Just as important, it would have to change only whenever your phone changed. You easily could identify exactly when a change should be made to your system, what changes you should make, and where you should make those changes.

This is quite significant when you consider the well-documented fact that 70 percent of the costs of a computer system involve maintaining the system, and the majority of these costs is in attempting to ensure that the computer system is in line with changes occurring in the real world. An interesting and significant side argument is that, at some point, it wouldn't even be necessary for these objects to exist in the physical world at all. In other words, at some point the phone object inside your computer could be your phone. Of course, these arguments and countless others you can read about apply equally well to any information or communications-based object or concept.

So, to answer the question of what you can expect of objects in a computer system, you must ask yourself what you know to be fundamentally true about the objects that surround you. A myriad of conclusions can be drawn and debated when it comes to such questions of fundamental existence, but I will be bold and choose three that I think are most significant to this subject: Objects have properties, behavior, and relationships.

Properties means that there are certain features of objects that indicate that object's current state of being. Currently, the Color property of the title bar on my word processor is red, the Length property of my mouse's cord is 48 inches, and, fortunately, the Count property of the collection of fingers on my left hand is five.

Behavior means that there are certain features of objects that enable them to respond to external or internal stimuli. I currently am exhibiting the behavior of typing in response to a message I received a few weeks ago from the primary author of this book. In order for me to exhibit this behavior, I first had to possess the ability of being able to type. Therefore, the capabilities or methods of an object are merely manifestations of the full set of behaviors an object can exhibit. My word processor possesses a spell checking method that is invoked when I send it a stimulus by selecting Spelling from the Tools menu or a stimulus of pressing the F7 key.

Relationships means that there are certain features of objects that indicate their association with other objects. I am related to my wife by marriage, I am related to my computer by ownership, and my laptop's monitor is related to my laptop by virtue of being a part of it. This chapter is related to my word processor by virtue of having been created by it.

What Is a Class?

Often, the terms *class* and *object* are used almost interchangeably when people discuss object-oriented technology, but there is an important distinction between these terms. An *object* is an instance of a *class*. That is, an object is a specific example of a class. I am an object of the class human. You are also an instance of the class human. We are two distinct objects but we are of the same class. When I say that I have two eyes, I am really getting this property from being an instance of the class human. When you breathe, it is because you are able to exhibit this behavior due to a capability that is inherent to humans. This is sometimes hard to grasp, but it is important to realize that human is only a concept and that there isn't anything you can point to and say, "That is human." You can point and say, "That is *a* human," but what you really are saying is, "That is an *instance* of a human."

One way to be sure you have an object rather than a class is to try to identify values of the properties of the thing you have. One of my properties is my name, the value of which is Shawn. The fact that I can give a specific value to my Name property is what proves that I am an object. It is equally true that one of the properties of a human is a name. But you cannot give a specific value to this property because each human has a different name. This proves that human is a class.

A *class* is a concept that enables you to group multiple objects based on common properties, behaviors, and relationships. Because these commonalties are more inherent to the classes of objects than the objects themselves, when you implement objects in an object-oriented programming language, you actually assign them to the classes. This means that when someone says the Volume property of my radio is currently seven, what he really is saying is that he has a class radio, which has the property of Volume and that the particular instance of that class he is dealing with has the current setting of Seven for that property.

Why Use the Object-Oriented Model?

"Necessity is the mother of invention." It often is helpful when trying to understand an invention to explore what necessity conspired to bring it about. The object-oriented (OO) model was born of simulation and the relative inability of other programming models to adequately handle the event-driven nature of simulation. Scientists of other disciplines have concluded that the world can be viewed as an event-driven process. Physical scientists call this *action/reaction*, psychologists call this *stimulus/response*, and there are countless other terms based on observations of the physical world. *Simulation* is merely an attempt to capture these event-driven object interactions in a computer system so that the entire set of possible interactions can be explored in a relatively short time.

You can think of every computer system as a simulation. The purpose of every computer system is to model a system, process, or state in the physical world so thoroughly that an agent interacting with the system can directly cause a change in the real world or reach a conclusion that will guide him in making a change. If you accept that the object-oriented model is an excellent approach to simulation and, in turn, accept that every computer system can be modeled as a simulation, then logic demands that you accept the object-oriented model as a reasonable approach to every computer system.

Therefore, you have concluded that OO is a reasonable approach, but what should persuade you that it is the most ideal approach for your development at hand? Ideally, you want your systems to have the following qualities:

> Robustness
> Reusability
> Extensibility
> Compatibility
> Efficiency
> Ease of use
> Integrity

These were the principles on which OO was designed.

Robust means that the object is free of errors and capable of defending itself from the errors of other objects or other system components. OO is robust because every object owns its own interface and therefore is capable of protecting itself and isolating its own exceptions.

Reusable means that the object is designed flexible enough that it is capable of solving many problems of the same problem domain instead of just the singular problem at hand.

Extensible means that the object can evolve as requirements placed upon it evolve. OO is reusable and extendible because every object has virtually the same functionality as its real-world equivalent and therefore can be reused or extended in the same situations.

Compatible means that the object gets along well with other objects. This means that it neither unnecessarily impedes their capability to perform their function nor makes unnecessary requirements upon them to perform its function. OO is compatible because each object makes as few assumptions about other objects as possible, subject to the necessity to relate and interact with other objects.

Efficient means that the object performs its task quickly with as few resources as possible. Although there is nothing specific to the OO model to cause it to be more efficient than other models, the related increase in code reuse promotes the adoption of the most efficient algorithms for each problem domain.

Easy to use means the object behaves in a way that requires little training to understand. The object-oriented model promotes ease of use because it enables you to view your computer system with the same clarity and intuitive base as you have with your physical system.

Integrity means that the system of objects does not appear to contradict itself or the world around it. OO promotes integrity by clearly identifying the external object interactions and by making it possible through messaging to verify and enforce required relationships.

As you learn major features of the OO paradigm in the following sections, you will learn how many of these features support the qualities of good language design referred to in this section.

The better your model reflects the real world, the higher the probability that your code will exhibit the aforementioned qualities. This makes design the paramount activity of the OO development process.

Encapsulation

Encapsulation is the idea that an object should be a relatively self-contained, identifiable entity. Most objects you encounter in the world have reasonably well-defined boundaries. You usually can tell whether something is part of an object. Your hand is part of you, but your shirt is not. Most people have even become adept at identifying the true origin of a behavior. When someone presses the button next to the door outside your house, your house appears to ring. Of course, you know that it is really the doorbell located in the entry hall that is ringing. This is because the ringing function of the doorbell and the relationship between the doorbell and that button are part of the doorbell's well-defined interface. The key to encapsulation is in properly defining the interface that forms the border between what is external to the object and what is a part of the object.

The unit of encapsulation in the OO world is the *class*. This means that if you want to know nearly everything that might be useful to know about an object, you should be able to go to wherever that object's class is defined. This also means that someone trying to use an object should be able to assume that, given the same stimulus, the object will behave consistently unless it has changed due to changes in the world or due to a change taking place in some other object on which it depends.

You should understand four major concepts in order to understand encapsulation: identity, modularity, information hiding, and coupling. These terms are described in the following sections.

Identity

Identity is the concept that it should be possible to uniquely identify a particular object from all other objects—particularly from other objects of the same class. This is why people have names and why, when that fails, we give people nicknames and, when that fails, the government goes to the trouble of giving everyone a unique Social Security number to end the problem once and for all (which, of course, it hasn't). The point is that you should try very hard to uniquely identify an object because the closer you come, the easier your life will be.

Modularity

Modularity is the concept that your mother tried to teach you when you were 10. It's simply a fancy word that means everything should have a logical place and everything should be in its place. If this is done correctly, it greatly limits how often you will need to have things redundantly defined all over the place just so that you know it will be available when you need it.

Modularity is the secret to robustness. If something is handled only in one place and in one way, it has a much lower potential to go wrong. Just think of how often human processes go awry because more than one person was responsible for something. I know that when my mother told my sister and me that one of us had to make sure the dog was fed each day when we came home from school, the poor dog starved for three days. On the other hand, when she tried to fix the situation by telling me to feed the dog when I came home and then telling my sister to check the dish when she got home, the dog quickly learned that if he ate fast enough, he could get two meals a day.

Information Hiding

Information hiding is a powerful technique practiced all too infrequently in this world. We are in the midst of an information explosion where the secret to success is no longer in trying to acquire rare pieces of information. It is now in trying to sort through mountains of information to isolate those few strategic pieces from which you can obtain maximum leverage. Wouldn't it be fantastic if, as a student, you could somehow obtain magic copies of your college text books that automatically filter out all information that isn't relevant to the final exam?

Information hiding is the principle that you should not expose something in an object's interface unless some other object is interested in that thing you are exposing. If the only object that cares about some property is that very object that possesses the property, that property should be kept private. Likewise, if some object wants to ensure that it is the only object that can perform a certain action, it should keep its method for doing that action private. Information hiding adds to the robustness of a system because it enables an object to protect those things for which it is responsible by making them private to itself. Information hiding adds to the ease of use of a system because anyone using the system only has to worry about publicly exposed interfaces.

Coupling

Coupling is the most elusive concept of encapsulation. *Coupling* refers to the degree to which one object or set of objects depends on another object or set of objects to function in a reasonable way. If there are not many dependencies, the objects are *weakly coupled*. If there are many dependencies, the objects are *strongly coupled*.

The secret here is that objects in the computer system should be coupled at roughly the same degree at which they are coupled in the real world. If in doubt, you should err toward the weakly coupled side. The button in front of your house is naturally strongly coupled with your doorbell because it serves virtually no purpose if your doorbell ceases to exist. Therefore, it would be reasonable for you to strongly couple those two objects in your computer system. Your VCR is loosely coupled with your television because your television is still a fairly useful device without your VCR, and your VCR still keeps track of time without your television (although it's a rather expensive time-keeping device).

Inheritance

Inheritance in the object-oriented world has more to do with the idea that you got your mother's quirky sense of humor and your father's big ears than the idea that you received a couple of treasury bonds and an attic full of scratched phonograph records. Inheritance in the OO sense of the word is similar to the classifications of living species. Because you are a human, you are capable of walking erect and you have opposable thumbs. This is not directly due to the fact that humans have this capability, but instead is indirectly due to the fact that primates have this capability and humans are primates. Humans inherit this capability from primates. Likewise, because I am human, I am capable of growing hair (except on certain portions of my head, for some inexplicable reason). This is not directly due to the fact that humans can grow hair but instead is due to the fact that humans inherit this capability from primates, who, in turn, inherit this capability from mammals.

A line of inheritance such as that formed by humans, primates, and mammals is referred to as an *inheritance chain*. Each class above a given class in this chain is called a *superclass*, and each class below a given class is called a *subclass*. *Mammal* is a superclass of *primate* and *human* is a subclass of *primate*. All superclasses in the chain above a given class are ancestors of that class, and all subclasses in the chain below a given class are descendants. Primates and mammals are ancestors of humans, and humans and primates are descendants of mammals.

The value of inheritance is to avoid redundancy in definition, which can lead to errors and a loss of integrity. If I had a system with a class for each and every mammal on earth, it would be a difficult task to include in the definition of each of those classes that the objects of that class are all capable of growing hair. It would be doubly hard to have to go back to each and proclaim that they are capable of bearing live offspring. By the time I got around to telling each that it is a vertebrate, I'd probably be stark-raving mad (more so). The point is that it would be much more efficient for me just to tell each that it is a mammal and then define that all mammals are capable of growing hair and bearing live offspring, and that they possess vertebrae. More important, there is no chance that someone will forget to specify that one particular species of mammal is a vertebrate and subject the poor instances of that class to being picked on by all the other mammals and labeled spineless little ninnies.

Abstract Superclasses

An *abstract superclass* is a fairly scary-sounding term that refers to any class for which you cannot find any objects that are purely instances of that class. Primate is really an abstract superclass. You will never come across something that is merely a primate rather than some specific form of a primate. You can find a specific instance of a human. Presumably, you are an instance of a human (unless this book becomes much more popular on the galactic market than I imagine). You can find a specific instance of a gorilla (Donkey Kong is my personal favorite), but you can't find something that is a primate and only a primate. As a matter of fact, all levels of the categories of living species above the lowest level are abstract superclasses.

Multiple Inheritance

Multiple inheritance is along the lines of the idea that you get some of your genes from your mother and some from your father. That is, you have two inheritance chains to consider when you are trying to determine who is to blame for those knobby knees that embarrass you when you are wearing shorts. The argument for using multiple inheritance is that it meets the golden rule of the object-oriented model. Objects behave this way in the real world and, therefore, they should behave this way in your computer system that is attempting to model the real world. The compact disc player I am listening to right now is also a radio and an audio cassette player. The company that sells this unit also sells units that are just compact disc players, just radios, just audio cassette players, and combinations of all these. It would simplify their specifications for these units a great deal if they could just create specifications for each of the three components and then inherit from these specifications for each combination unit.

Multiple inheritance also introduces some new complexities, which is why it is sometimes a controversial aspect of OO. It is obvious that my stereo system inherited its rewind button from the audio cassette player and its tuning knob from the radio.

If it is possible for the same feature to be inherited from more than one chain, however, it is not always easy to determine or to properly specify which chain a feature comes from. All three of the ancestors of my stereo had a volume knob. So, which ancestor did my stereo inherit its volume knob from? You might wonder why it matters, and it is true that sometimes it doesn't matter because the behavior is the same either way. But sometimes, while the public behavior is the same, the private behavior that is happening behind the interface may be drastically different.

Digital amplification of sound is a very different process than analog amplification of sound, for example, and yet amplifiers capable of doing both can use mostly the same interfaces. The interfaces can be the same because both the control and the net result from the user's perspective is the same. Someplace internal to the class definition of an object that multiply inherits similar features, a determination must be made where each feature should come from. When I stimulate my amplifier to simulate surround sound, it must make a determination internally as to whether to use a digit or an analog process for doing this.

Behavior Classes

Behavior classes are perhaps one of the most controversial of all OO constructs. If they are used improperly, it is possible to degrade a system back to a point where it is not object-oriented at all and gains few of the advantages of the OO model. I believe that all good ideas have a proper application, however, and I do not believe in censoring a good idea simply because it can be put to poor use.

Behavior classes are a means of grouping similar behavior in one place without immediately attaching that behavior to any real object. Of all the animals in the world, for example, only some have the ability to swim. Those that do swim have different maximum swimming speeds, depths at which they can swim, and maximum times during which they can stay below the surface of the water. If you tried to define these features associated with swimming in the fish class, you would exclude mammals, birds, and amphibians that swim, or you would have to redundantly define these behaviors in these other classes. If you went farther up the inheritance chain to include all these groups, you also would include a number of animals that are completely incapable of swimming. The solution to this dilemma is to create a behavior class that represents the behavior of swimming and all features associated with this behavior. Then, for every class of animal in the inheritance chain capable of swimming, you could multiply inherit from the swimming behavior class you defined.

Polymorphism

Polymorphism means "many shapes" and refers to the idea that two things might be considered the same at some level of abstraction and behave fairly differently at another level of abstraction. Both spiders and frogs jump, for example, and these behaviors are conceptually rough equivalents for each animal. By examining the anatomy of these two animals, however, you learn that what each does to jump is drastically different. A frog jumps like most vertebrates by pulling on muscles that pull on ligaments, which pull on bones, which push on the ground, and off it goes. Spiders jump by rapidly filling their legs with blood, which pushes the legs out in a fashion similar to a hydraulic pump. People trying to simply command the spiders and frogs to jump for their exotic pet shows probably have no interest in knowing that there is anything different about the way their frogs jump from the way their spiders jump, and simply would prefer to consider these the same action.

Polymorphism enables you to maintain the same or a similar interface and behavior across multiple classes even when the underlying implementation is different. Polymorphism promotes ease of use and the principle of information hiding.

Of course, the power of polymorphism goes beyond merely being able to tell multiple objects what to do with the same simple command without knowing how each is actually doing it. You can use polymorphism to tell an arbitrary object what to do, without even knowing what kind of object you have.

Suppose that you are inventing a coin-sorting machine. The machine takes a bag of mixed coins as input and returns separate bags of coins for each type of coin you give it. If you are trying to make a reusable machine that can operate properly in any country in the world, it would be a poor design idea for you to assume that the coins are any particular size. For simplicity, however, assume that no country has two coins of exactly the same size. The operation of the coin machine is simply to grab each coin, determine the coin's size, and then place it in the bag that it has identified for coins of that size. The point is that the coin machine functions correctly without any knowledge of what type of coin it really has. It only knows that every coin has the feature of possessing a unique size.

Persistence

Persistence is something people were pretty comfortable with in the physical world up until new physics came along. It is simply the idea that objects have a tendency to stay around unless someone goes to some trouble to get rid of them. Other than socks in dryers, most objects are still in the same place and in roughly the same form when you go to get them as they were when you left them. Somewhat oddly, you frequently don't automatically apply this principle when it comes to objects in computer systems. I am typing this document in a word processor, for example. If I simply turn off my machine and walk away, portions of this document will not be here when I come back. This is because word processing documents are not persistent by nature. You must explicitly save them to a more permanent medium if you expect to be able to recover them later.

This same nonpersistent-by-nature concept occurs throughout computer systems in practice simply because computers are much more efficient at dealing with nonpersistent objects than persistent ones. You once again must apply the golden rule of OO, however, and admit that, ideally, objects should be as persistent in your computer model as they are in the real world. In practice, this means that a well-behaved object sometimes must save portions of itself even without being explicitly asked to, because this occurs naturally in the real-world object. Because there are significant performance considerations in most computer systems, you must strike a balance when deciding where to draw the lines of control.

Summary

This chapter introduced a number of key concepts of the object-oriented model. It was not meant to be a comprehensive account of the subject, nor was any of the discussion specific to Visual Basic. The goal of this chapter simply was to lay a foundation for the next four chapters, which cover applying object-oriented principles using Visual Basic 4. As such, it concentrated on those OO concepts most important for you to understand to effectively use the tricks and techniques presented in the following chapters.

In Chapter 8, "Using the Object-Oriented Constructs of Visual Basic 4," you begin applying these concepts using the object-oriented constructs that are built into VB4.

Using the Object-Oriented Constructs of Visual Basic 4

by Shawn Oberst

CHAPTER

8

This chapter and the two chapters that follow assume that you are familiar with object-oriented (OO) concepts. Therefore, these chapters focus on how you can apply these concepts in Visual Basic 4.0 (VB4). If you are unfamiliar with the OO model or would simply appreciate a refresher, refer back to Chapter 7, "Object-Oriented Concepts." This chapter assumes that you have at least reviewed the manuals provided with VB4 to pick up basic content and are familiar with how to use the development environment. You should be familiar with how to create, name, save, and retrieve a class module, for example, so this chapter only attempts to add some insight into what to put into a class module.

Obviously, a concept can be applied in many ways, and OO concepts are no exception to this rule. This chapter, as well as the next two chapters, are filled with some of the most effective ways to apply OO concepts in VB4. I have used nearly everything covered in this chapter in my work as an information systems developer. Some of these approaches are among the most advanced available and are the culmination of many years of thought and evolution through hard-knocks experience.

However, you should keep in mind that sometimes you must make trade-offs between various design principles and real-world constraints. You need to consider development time and efficiency, as well as physical computer system constraints such as memory, storage space, and processor speed. You might want to modify these approaches to fit your needs or find ways to integrate them with other tricks and techniques of your own. Many times, I demonstrate multiple approaches to solving the same problem and discuss the advantages and disadvantages of each. You must determine for yourself which approach best fits your design criteria.

This chapter discusses how to build and create classes and libraries, how to construct and use objects, how to compile classes into OLE servers, and how to construct and use OLE server objects in VB4. Even if you are already familiar with these topics, I encourage you to read this chapter. I have not seen some of the ideas presented here in any other book on this subject.

If you are the type of person who likes to see something even if you don't quite know what you are looking at, you can jump forward to the section "The Die Example" before returning to this section to delve into the details. On the other hand, if you are the type of person who likes to understand something first, just read on.

Designing a Class

Classes are implemented using properties and methods. *Properties* implement primitive typed properties, which return values indicating the state of an object, as well as relationships between an object and other objects in the system. *Methods* implement the behavior of the object.

Implementing Properties

In VB4, properties usually are implemented in one of three ways:

- Declaring a property in the declaration section of the class.
- Using a combination of declaring the property in the declaration section and then exposing the property through property let, property set, and property get procedures.
- Enabling only the constructor of the class or other controlled methods to set properties and then using a property get procedure to expose some properties directly for read-only access.

Suppose that you are implementing a class CPoint to handle a point in two-dimensional space. If you recall from algebra, a point consists of an X coordinate and a Y coordinate. The simplest implementation of these two properties is to place the following two lines of code in the declaration section of Cpoint:

```
Public X As Double
Public Y As Double
```

The advantage of this approach is that it is very simple. The disadvantage is that it exposes the implementation of CPoint to the outside world, which makes it difficult for you to make any radical changes later. The other disadvantage is that it is difficult for CPoint to protect its own state because anyone can change the values for X or Y.

A slightly safer approach is to declare X and Y privately and then expose them by using the property let and property get procedures:

```
Private pX As Double
Private pY As Double

Public Property Let X(dX As Double)
  pX = dX
End Property

Public Property Get X() As Double
  X = pX
End Property

Public Property Let Y(dY As Double)
  pY = dY
End Property

Public Property Get Y() As Double
  Y = pY
End Property
```

The advantage of this approach is that the implementation of X and Y within CPoint is not exposed outside of CPoint. You therefore can change the implementation radically and the interface remains the same. The disadvantage is that anyone still can change the values of X or Y. This implementation does little to protect X and Y.

The final implementation is to make it so that X and Y can be changed only in the class constructor or in other well-defined methods. The class constructor simply can initialize X and Y to the origin, for example, and it can require a call to an initialization method to set the point someplace else. In this implementation, X and Y still are declared private, and you also might want to keep the property get procedures as defined earlier. The property let procedures are removed, however, and these lines of code are added:

```
Private Sub Class_Initialize()
  pX = 0
  pY = 0
End Sub

Public Sub Initialize(dX As Double, dY As Double)
' Initialize sets the initial values of the properties of the class
  pX = dX
  pY = dY
End Sub
```

The advantage to this approach is that you protect both the implementation and the state of your objects. The disadvantage is that the implementation might become quite complex when you are dealing with complex objects.

The CPoint example in this section demonstrates how you can implement primitive typed properties. *Primitive typed* refers to properties for which the declared types are among those intrinsic to the VB4 language. Both X and Y are of type double, which is one of the types intrinsic to VB4. You can use VB4's online Help feature or manuals to get a list of all the intrinsic types.

Implementing Properties to Represent Relationships

Sometimes a property is quite complex. When this happens, the property becomes an object unto itself and the implementation of that property becomes a relationship to this new object. An Employee object might have a property for the spouse's name, for example. If this is all you keep track of about employees' spouses, this is implemented as a property of type string using one of the techniques discussed in the preceding section. If you start keeping track of the spouse's name, Social Security number, date of birth, and medical and dental plan, however, then the spouse becomes complex enough to evolve into a class of objects in his or her own right. At this point, you attach all these new properties to the new Spouse class, and the Employee objects simply have relationships to these new Spouse objects.

To implement one of these relationship properties, you must declare a reference to the related object in your class. Like all other properties, you also must expose a means of accessing and changing this relationship. The simplest way of implementing your employee spouse example is to put the following line of code in your CEmployee class declaration:

```
Public Spouse as CSpouse
```

If you want to use the second technique for implementing properties where every property has two property procedures, you need to make a small but important change. You must use a property set procedure instead of a `property let` procedure. This is because the property being referenced is an object and not a primitive type. The code using this technique follows:

```
Private pSpouse as CSpouse
Public Property Set Spouse (dSpouse As CSpouse)
  Set pSpouse = dSpouse
End Property

Public Property Get Spouse () As CSpouse
  Set Spouse = pSpouse
End Property
```

Implementing Properties Representing Multivalued Relationships

Most relationships between objects are multivalued. Although in most places in the world you can have only one spouse, you usually can have more than one child. You cannot use the `property set` and `property get` procedures for these multivalued relationships because assignment is only a binary operator. As a matter of fact, these multivalued relationships are so complex that they require an entire object separate from either of the objects in the relationship just to handle the relationship. The most powerful and flexible technique is to use the `collection` class, which is built into VB4.

You can implement multivalued relationships as a collection of relationships, which is effectively a collection of references to other objects. VB4 collections enable you to add, remove, order, label, retrieve, and count relationships automatically. Usually, this is all the functionality you need in order to deal with a multivalued relationship. The simplest way to add a `Children` property to your `CEmployee` class is with the following line of code:

```
Public Children As New Collection
```

This is a very simple technique and has a great deal of merit based on that alone. It does have the disadvantage that the `Children` property does not protect itself from someone arbitrarily changing its content, however. In some cases, you might need to use the more complex technique that follows.

If your multivalued relationship has constraints it must enforce, or if you simply want to further protect the relationship, you cannot use the simple approach just discussed. But it would be a shame to re-implement all the wonderful collection functionality that VB4 gives you. The trick here is to encapsulate VB4's general collection inside another application-specific collection. Suppose that your `Children` collection has to enforce the rule that no one is allowed to have more than four children. You can create a class `CChildrenCollection` containing the following code:

```
Private Col As New Collection
Public Sub Add(dObject As CChild,Optional dKey,Optional dBefore,
Optional dAfter)
' Add inserts a new member into the collection
  If Col.Count = 4 then
```

```
       ' Raise an error using your favorite error handling technique
    Else
       Col.Add dObject, dKey, dBefore, dAfter
    End If
End Sub

Public Sub Remove(dKey As Variant)
' Remove deletes a member from the collection
    Col.Remove dKey
End Sub

Public Function Item(dKey as Variant) As CChild
' Item retrieves a member of the collection
    Set Item = Col.Item(dKey)
End Function

Public Function Count()As Long
' Count provides a count of the number of members in the collection
    Count = Col.Count
End Function
```

Your CEmployee class then contains the following line of code:

```
Public Children As New CChildrenCollection
```

Notice that this technique also gives you the flexibility to add new methods to the collection of relationships. You might want to add a method to remove all relationships at once, for example:

```
Public Sub RemoveAll()
' RemoveAll removes all members of the collection
    Dim I As Long
    For I = Col.Count to 1 Step -1
      Col.Remove 1
    Next I
End Sub
```

The astute OO student will observe that CChildrenCollection is a specialization of the collection class. Through this implementation, you have effectively inherited functionality from collection, overloaded its Add method, and then added new functionality with the RemoveAll method. This is basically how inheritance is implemented in the absence of any supporting constructs in VB4. The next chapter elaborates on this issue.

Implementing Methods

You use methods to implement the behavior of an object. Methods are implemented with nonproperty subroutines and functions. If you want your CPoint to be able to return a string equivalent of itself in standard algebraic notation, for example, you can add the following function to the CPoint class definition:

```
Public Function StrVal() As String
' StrVal provides the string equivalent of the point in standard
' algebraic notation
    StrVal = "(" & X & "," & Y & ")"
End Function
```

If you want your CPoint object to be able to be translated by another Cpoint object, you can add this subroutine to the CPoint class definition:

```
Public Sub Translate(dPoint As CPoint)
' Tranolate moves the puint relative to the point provided according to
' the rules of vector addition
  X = X + dPoint.X
  Y = Y + dPoint.Y
End Sub
```

If you want your CPoint to be able to return the distance between it and another Cpoint, you can add this function to the CPoint class definition:

```
Public Function Distance(dPoint As CPoint) As Double
' Distance provides the distance between the point and the point provided
  Distance = sqr( (X-dPoint.X) ^ 2 + (Y-dPoint.Y) ^ 2)
End Function
```

If some part of the behavior of an object is not useful to any other object, or if it is dangerous to expose that behavior to other objects, you should declare those methods private in the object's class definition. This simplifies the interface for those developers attempting to use objects of that class, and it also helps the object protect itself from accidental misuse. Because VB4 only supports private and public scoping, however, you must err on the liberal side sometimes and declare more things public than you might in another language with more scoping constructs. Specifically, VB4 does not offer the capability to enable only certain specified objects access to some methods while restricting other objects' access to those same methods. As soon as any other object needs the information, it must be made public to all other objects.

Creating and Using Objects

This section concentrates on how to create or declare objects that you have previously defined and then on how to use the properties and methods of those objects.

Creating Objects

Objects are incredibly intuitive to create and use; otherwise, they would defeat most of the intention of the OO model. You can think of a class as nothing more than a complex user-defined type. To define that an object is of a certain class, you simply dimension that object to be of that class, just as you would dimension a variable to be of a type. If you want to create a point object of the class Cpoint, for example, you can use this line of code:

```
Dim Point As CPoint
```

Notice how similar this declaration is to the following code, which declares a variable Count to be an integer:

```
Dim Count As Integer
```

There is only one difference between dimensioning an object and dimensioning a variable, but it is a very significant one. When you dimension Count to be an integer, you declare Count as an integer and automatically create a space in memory to store Count. When you dimension Point to be a Cpoint, however, you only declare Point to be a CPoint. You then create space in memory for Point by adding the following line of code:

```
Set Point = New CPoint
```

You must add this line of code somewhere after your dimension statement, although not necessarily immediately following it. You can do both these things by using a single line of code:

```
Dim Point As New CPoint
```

You might wonder why VB4 doesn't just automatically allocate the space required for Point. Because this is a common area of confusion and an important concept to understand, we will revisit this issue later, in the section "Explicitly Allocating Space for Objects."

Using Objects

If you are familiar with using custom controls, you already know how to use objects. To use an object, you simply first specify which object you want to use, then a period (referred to as a *dot*), and then the feature of that object you want to use. If you want to create two point objects, initialize each, translate one by the other, and then display the distance between the two, you can use these lines of code:

```
Dim P1 As New Point
Dim P2 As New Point
P1.X = 1
P1.Y = 2
P2.X = 5
P2.Y = 7
P1.Translate P2
Msgbox "The distance between " & P1.StrVal & " and " & P2.StrVal
& " is " & P1.Distance(P2)
```

Explicitly Allocating Space for Objects

There are three very good reasons why VB4 doesn't just automatically allocate the space for an object when it is declared:

■ All the intrinsic types of VB4 take up very little space in memory. So little that it is not worth bothering to try to find a way not to waste the space. But the objects you create could take up an extremely large amount of space. Whenever you are using a large amount of any resource in a computer, it is important that you manage that resource. In order to manage a resource, you must have a way to control your use of that resource.

■ You often will need a new reference to an object that already exists. My sister is also my mother's daughter. If I had a reference to an object that was my sister and my mother had a reference to a different object that was her daughter and we each interacted with these objects separately, then these two objects probably would become out of sync. This, of course, would not be sensible, because they are the same object in the real world.

To see how you can reference the same object, suppose that you have a class CHuman with the two Relationship properties of Sister and Daughter. For simplicity, assume that each is a single-value relationship, although this is obviously not what they would be in a real system because it is possible for someone to have more than one daughter and more than one sister. The following lines of code cause Me.Sister and Mom.Daughter to reference the same object in memory:

```
Dim Mom As New CHuman
Dim Me As New CHuman
Dim Sis As New CHuman
Set Me.Sister = Sis
Set Mom.Daughter = Sis
```

Now, any change made to Me.Sister automatically is made to Mom.Daughter because they both refer to the exact same object. That is, they are both referencing the exact same area of memory.

The Die Example

I have come across people who have read a dozen definitions of what an object is and they still don't get it. This is not because they are stupid or because objects are amazingly complex things, which can be understood only by those with computer science degrees. An object is one of those concepts that sometimes is easier to understand by looking at a few good examples instead of reading a half dozen explanations. One of the best examples I have ever come up with is a six-sided die. It can be seen as having exactly one interesting property and one method, and yet it is still a very useful object. The only interesting property of a six-sided die is its current value (the number of dimples on the top face). The only interesting thing that a six-sided die does is roll. Therefore, the CDie class definition follows:

```
Private lValue As Long
Public Property Get Value() As Long
  Value = lValue
End Property

Public Function Roll() As Long
  lValue = Int( 6 * Rnd + 1 )
  Roll = lValue
End Function
```

This really is a fully functioning class that I have used and, most important, reused in many game programs I have written. As the following code shows, to use this die you simply create it, roll it, and then see what you get.

```
Dim SixSidedDie As New CDie
SixSidedDie.Roll
MsgBox SixSidedDie.Value
```

This example is a good opportunity to talk about the evolution of an object. I reused this CDie class many times until one day my problem changed slightly and my class had to change with it. I wrote a game in which I needed dice of all numbers of sides. For this game, I needed dice with eight sides, 10 sides, and even 100 sides. I was able to evolve my object easily to accommodate this new functionality and yet still preserve the same interface for those applications already using my CDie. Here is the new implementation:

```
Public NumberOfSides As Long
Private lValue As Long

Public Property Get Value() As Long
  Value = lValue
End Property

Public Function Roll() As Long
  lValue = Int( NumberOfSides * Rnd + 1 )
  Roll = lValue
End Function
```

All I did was add a new property, NumberOfSides, and then change the roll method to use this new property. This would have worked fine if these were the only changes I made to my class, except for two anomalies. First, my class would have behaved sort of strangely if I forgot when using this die to tell it how many sides it had. The roll method always would have produced the value of one. Second, all the games I already had made using my six-sided die would have had to change. I would have had to add the statement to set the number of sides of all my new CDie objects to six. To resolve both of these issues, I added a statement to the Class_Initialize method to set the default number of sides to six:

```
Private Sub Class_Initialize()
  NumberOfSides = 6
End Sub
```

Because the Class Initialize method always is run whenever a new object of that class is created, every die is a six-sided die until it is told otherwise. Now, a six-sided die can be used the way that it always has been, and yet I also can create and use a 10-sided die:

```
Dim TenSidedDie As New CDie
TenSidedDie.NumberOfSides = 10
Msgbox TenSidedDie.Roll
```

This process of evolving an object to accommodate new needs while preserving the old interface for legacy systems is a natural part of object-oriented development. Many people make the mistake of thinking the object was not constructed correctly in the first place, and that they are fixing it with their changes. But this ignores the fact that every design reflects some system of design criteria and is the product of trade-offs between those criteria. Currently, my CDie class only accommodates generating random numbers with a normal or constant distribution, for example. I cannot simulate a weighted or skewed distribution without adding to this class and its interface. Adding to the interface of Cdie, however, makes it a little more complicated to use. So I would have to decide whether I felt the additional functionality was worth the additional complication.

Designing a Class Library

A *class library* is simply a group of classes that are somehow related. These classes usually are related through many interdependencies, which means that the classes of a library are *strongly coupled*. How classes are grouped into libraries is more of a design decision than an implementation decision, however, so it is more important to focus on determining the "natural" groupings of the classes. That is, it is more important to group classes into libraries according to how much the objects of those classes are related to each other in the real world. I have never witnessed anybody using a tennis racquet without using a tennis ball, and when people are using tennis balls, they usually also are using tennis racquets. These objects are "naturally" related to each other in the real world and therefore probably should be contained in the same library.

It is important to keep in mind that a library shouldn't do anything. If it did something, then it would be a program. It should be regarded as a collection of tools just waiting to be used. After these tools are combined with instructions on how to build something, you have a program. Extending this analogy, you might have one library dedicated to woodworking tools, another dedicated to auto mechanics, and a third dedicated to electronics. If you are creating a program to fix the electrical systems in your car, you probably will borrow some of the objects in your auto mechanics library and some of the objects in your electronics library. The library exists simply because these objects can be reused effectively in a variety of applications.

A library in VB4 is much less obvious than in some other object-oriented languages because no file exists that explicitly defines which classes belong to a library. In VB4, every class has its own class module stored in its own file. Unless you are making a library into an OLE server, you must explicitly include each class in each program that uses that class. This is somewhat monotonous, so I am confident that it will be fixed in a future version of VB4; for now, though, you are stuck with this task. Even though there isn't a construct to enforce a library, it is still a good programming practice to create a library because it helps library users understand how different classes interrelate.

You create a library simply by including all classes that belong to the library in a project all by themselves. If the classes of the library share some global resource, such as a group of global constants or variables, you can include a Basic module in the library that holds these resources. Also, if any of the classes depend on an existing class outside of this library or on a custom control, you should include that resource in the library or annotate the dependency in a comments section. If you are not going to include the resource, you should place this information in a comments section at the top of the library's Basic module.

Creating an OLE Server

Until recently, creating an OLE server was a daunting task requiring a great deal of Windows development background and an extremely technical reference guide. Fortunately, VB4 has simplified this process so that it is now possible to create an OLE server without even really knowing what an OLE server is. Because of this and the fact that there is a plethora of other literature out there on this subject, I will not bother to give a detailed explanation of OLE servers. Suffice it to say that an OLE server is a class library that is registered with the Windows operating system and therefore is capable of being referenced from any OLE client-compliant application.

To create an OLE server, you simply create a class library, set the class properties to expose your OLE server classes publicly, and then set up and compile the OLE server.

To expose your OLE server classes publicly, you must set the Public and Instancing properties of the class. If you want the clients of your OLE server to be able to get handles on an object of one of your classes, then you must set that class's Public property to True. If the objects of that class are used only internally by your OLE server, however, you should leave the Public property set to False.

If the Public property is set to False, you should leave the Instancing property set to Not Creatable. If the Public property is set to True, you must decide whether you want your clients to be able to create objects of the class on-the-fly or whether they will have to get objects of that class from another class. If the latter is the case, leave the Instancing property set to Not Creatable. If the former is the case, then you must decide whether you want your class to be SingleUse or MultiUse and set the Instancing property accordingly. SingleUse causes a separate instance of the OLE server to be created each time a new application needs a new object. That is, there is a separate independent server for each client. MultiUse causes only one instance of the OLE server to be created to service all clients.

The advantage of SingleUse is that there is a separate set of global variables for each instance of the server and there is no way that one client can monopolize the server and block out other clients. The advantage of MultiUse is that there is only one copy of the server in memory and that you can share memory across clients through global variables. If in doubt, use MultiUse until you have a reason to use SingleUse.

To set up and compile the OLE server, give your project the same name as that of the OLE server registered with the operating system. Then, if the class library does not contain any forms that can be referenced as the project start-up form, you must put a Sub Main procedure in the OLE server's Basic module. It is perfectly acceptable that this procedure hasn't any code in its body. However, if you want to initialize the server before someone uses it, then the Sub Main section would be a good place to do so because you are guaranteed that this procedure with the special name Main will be called when the server is initialized at runtime. Now you simply compile the library into an OLE server using any of the techniques discussed in the manuals and Help files that accompany VB4. You do not need to separately register the server on your development machine because VB4 does this for you automatically.

Examining In-Process Versus Out-of-Process OLE Servers

If you compile your OLE server as a DLL, it executes as an *in-process* OLE server; it runs in the same process space as the client application that is using it. The primary advantage of this is that it runs faster than an out-of-process OLE server. If you have no reason to use an out-of-process server, you probably should use an in-process server.

If you compile your OLE server as an EXE, it executes as an out-of-process OLE server. This means that it runs in its own process space separate from the client application that is using it. There are four cases in which you must use an out-of-process OLE server:

- If you must support 16-bit clients.
- If you want to share global variables, the OLE server must be out-of-process and the Instancing property must be set to MultiUse.
- If you want to prevent one client from being blocked by another client dominating the OLE server, the OLE server must be out-of-process and the Instancing property must be set to MultiUse.
- If you want to use remote procedure calls and have your OLE server actually run on a different machine than your client, it must be an out-of-process OLE server.

Registering an OLE Server

When you compile an OLE server, it is automatically registered on your development machine. Before you can use your OLE server on another machine, however, it must be registered for that machine. To register an out-of-process OLE server, you can run the EXE and it automatically registers itself before executing. Or, you can run the EXE with a /REGISTER command-line option so that it registers itself without executing. To register an in-process OLE server, you must use REGSVR32.EXE and pass it the DLL to be registered. Although it is important to know how to register OLE servers to support your development and testing, in practice you rarely have to register OLE servers on your customers' machines directly. If you use the VB4 Setup Wizard to create your Setup application, it registers the OLE servers for you.

Creating and Using an OLE Server Object

You can create an OLE server object in almost exactly the same way that you create a VB4 object. The only addition is that you must let VB4 know which server possesses the object's class definition. Assuming that you already have compiled your CPoint class into an OLE server named Shapes, you can use any of the following code to create this object:

```
Dim Point As New Shapes.CPoint
```

or

```
Dim Point As Shapes.CPoint
Set Point = New Shapes.CPoint
```

If Shapes happens to be the only OLE server on your machine with a CPoint class, then you can also drop the Shapes qualifier and use any of the following code:

```
Dim Point As New CPoint
```

or

```
Dim Point As CPoint
Set Point = New CPoint
```

Another method of creating OLE server objects is the same in concept but different in syntax. This is the older method used in VB3 applications, which is sometimes necessary when supporting older OLE servers. You first must declare the object and then create the object. You can declare the object to be of the generic class object or to be of a specific class. Then, to create the object, you can use the CreateObject function or the GetObject function. The CreateObject function creates a new object of whatever class you specify. The GetObject function tries to get a reference to an object that presumably already has been created. After you create an OLE server object, you can use it in exactly the same way as any other VB4 object. To create and use a CPoint object, you can use the following code:

```
Dim Point As Object
Set Point = CreateObject("Shapes.CPoint")
Point.X = 3
Point.Y = 4
Msgbox Point.StrVal
```

By declaring Point to be a generic object, you are forcing it to use *late binding*. This means that the interpreter will not know until runtime what type of specific object you are creating. This makes it difficult for the compiler to warn you about misuse of the object during compile time.

Raising Errors in OLE Servers

To cause an error to be propagated back to the client of your OLE server, you must use the Raise method of the Err object. This error can be trapped using any of the built-in exception-handling mechanisms of VB4, such as ON ERROR GOTO. A typical use of this method follows:

```
Err.Raise vbObjectError + 1234
```

By adding vbObjectError, you can ensure that you do not conflict with any built-in VB4 error numbers.

Deciding Whether to Use an OLE Server or a VB4 Class Library

A common point of confusion is determining when a class library should be compiled into an OLE server and used as such. There are no simple answers to this question. Currently, OLE servers are slower than class libraries because class libraries are compiled right into the application. Much of this performance disparity can be eradicated by compiling the OLE server into an in-process DLL, however. You still take a performance hit when the server is initialized and a slight hit when you create objects, but the subsequent use of the object is just as fast. This slight hit on creating objects can become a very large aggregate hit with repetitive operations, so you should consider the probable use of your objects as well. The advantages to OLE servers are simplicity and separation.

If you use OLE servers, your applications will become simpler because you will not have excessive code in your program declaring a bunch of things that you don't even use. The advantage of the separation is that if you have several programs using the same class library and that library's internal implementation needs to change, you simply can make the change and recompile the OLE server. If you do not change the interface, you will not have to reincorporate the new library into each of these applications or recompile them.

Summary

This chapter focused on creating and using classes, objects, and libraries using the constructs built into VB4. You learned how to implement objects with simple properties and methods using very few tricks and techniques beyond what is native to the language.

The next two chapters focus more heavily on taking a complete object-oriented approach, which the language makes possible but does not readily support.

Extending the Object-Oriented Constructs of VB4

by Shawn Oberst

CHAPTER 9

Chapter 8, "Using the Object-Oriented Constructs of Visual Basic 4," focused on creating and using classes, objects, and libraries with the constructs built into VB4. This chapter focuses on extending VB4 to handle the more advanced object-oriented concepts of inheritance and polymorphism. If you are unfamiliar with or a little rusty on OO concepts, refer to Chapter 7, "Object-Oriented Concepts," before you read this chapter.

Some people are quick to point out that VB4 does not support inheritance at all, nor does it completely support polymorphism. These people write off the language altogether for OO implementations based on this assumption alone. The truth is that it is possible to do an OO implementation in virtually any language. The key to reaping the benefits of the OO model is in the prudent application of its design principles. When someone states that some language is an OO language, they really are saying that the language has some built-in constructs to more easily support applying OO principles than many other languages.

Therefore, when you evaluate the effectiveness of a language for implementing OO applications, you cannot simply ask whether the language has built-in constructs for supporting each of the principles. You must look at each principle and ask how difficult it is to implement that principle using whatever constructs the language does supply. This chapter shows you that most OO principles can be applied relatively easily using the constructs available in VB4.

Inheritance

Inheritance is simply the concept that a given object should be able to inherit properties and behaviors from all those classes of which its own class is a specialization. I am a human, for example, and humans are simply a specialization of a primate. Therefore, not only should I have all the features of a human, but I also should have all the features of a primate. In some OO languages, this desired capability happens automatically for you simply by your declaring that the class Human is derived from the class Primate. This is admittedly a very useful construct and is unfortunately missing from VB4.

Even many of the advanced languages run into problems after a class inherits features from multiple classes, however. It becomes necessary to override the implementation of various shared methods to explicitly state from where the method is being inherited or to combine the functionality of the methods of each class. In other words, the automatic functionality of the language breaks down and it becomes necessary for the specialized class to explicitly call the appropriate methods of the more general classes. Even without multiple inheritance, it is extremely common for a specialized class to partially override the functionality of many of the methods of the general class from which it is derived. It does this first by calling the general class's equivalent method in its own method and then doing a few extra operations of its own to handle things that are specific to it.

You can implement inheritance in VB4 simply by using the fallback technique described in the preceding paragraph for all cases. Any time a specialized class needs to inherit a feature from a general class, it simply calls the equivalent feature of the general class. Of course, it must have a handle on an instance of the general class.

An Example Technique

In this section, you'll create a general class called CShape, which represents any arbitrary shape that can be drawn on a canvas. CShape could have the following implementation:

```
Public LineThickness As Long
Public LineColor As Long

Public Property Get ClassName() As String
' ClassName provides the name of the class
  ClassName = "Shape"
End Property

Public Property Get LibraryName() As String
' LibraryName provides the name of the class library
 LibraryName = "Shape"
End Property

Public Function StrVal() As String
' StrVal provides the string equivalent of the object's properties
StrVal = "LineThickness " & LineThickness & chr(13)
  StrVal = StrVal & "LineColor " & LineColor
End Function

Public Sub Draw(Canvas As Object)
' Draw renders the shape on the canvas.
' This method is purely abstract and is included here solely to document
' the fact that it should
' be included as a method of every derived class
' and should have this signature.
End Sub
```

Also assume that you have a class CRectangle, which is a specialization of CShape and, as such, inherits the features of CShape. The class CRectangle builds off of the class CPoint, which was discussed in Chapter 8. CRectangle could have the following implementation:

```
Private Shape As New CShape
Public UpperLeft As CPoint
Public LowerRight As CPoint

Public Property Let LineThickness(pLineThickness As Long)
  Shape.LineThickness = pLineThickness
End Property

Public Property Get LineThickness() As Long
 LineThickness = Shape.LineThickness
End Property
```

```
Public Property Let LineColor(pLineColor As Long)
   Shape.LineColor = pLineColor
End Property

Public Property Get LineColor() As Long
   LineColor = Shape.LineColor
End Property

Public Property Get LibraryName() As String
' LibraryName provides the name of the class library
   LibraryName = Shape.LibraryName
End Property

Public Property Get ClassName() As String
' ClassName provides the name of the class
   ClassName = "Rectangle"
End Property

Public Function StrVal() As String
' StrVal provides the string equivalent of the object's properties
StrVal = "UpperLeft " & UpperLeft & chr(13)
   StrVal = StrVal & "LowerRight " & LowerRight & chr(13)
   StrVal = StrVal & Shape.StrVal
End Function

Public Sub Draw(Canvas As Object)
' Draw renders the shape on the canvas.
   Canvas.DrawWidth = Shape.LineThickness
   Canvas.ForeColor = Shape.LineColor
   Canvas.Line Step(UpperLeft.X,UpperLeft.Y)
   ➡- Step(LowerRight.X,LowerRight.Y)
End Sub
```

The first peculiar thing you'll notice when you review these two class definitions is the Draw method of the class CShape. This method actually doesn't do anything at all. You might wonder why you would even bother to declare such a method. The reason is that, by declaring this method, you are making a statement to anyone who wants to inherit from this class. You are saying that all classes inheriting from this class must have a method named Draw and that method should take only one parameter, which is a reference to the canvas on which you want the shape drawn. A declaration of a method, including all the parameters it requires, is referred to as a *signature* and is very important when it comes to polymorphism (this idea is elaborated on throughout this chapter).

The next thing of importance to inheritance in this example is that CRectangle actually contains a private instance of the general class CShape. This is necessary because you cannot invoke any of the properties or methods of a class without having a reference to an instance of that class. This instance also acts as a convenient place to store the inherited properties.

Because CShape has some properties that need to be exposed in CRectangle's interface, you need to create the property let and property get procedures that you see in CRectangle's class definition. You must overcome an extra level of indirection because these properties actually are stored in the CShape class. By using these property procedures, this extra level of indirection, which otherwise would be quite confusing to the users of the CRectangle class, is completely transparent. This is an excellent example of the power of information hiding applied to protecting your underlying implementation.

The LibraryName property of CRectangle is an example of normal inheritance. The CRectangle class should be in the same library as CShape because it is very strongly coupled with CShape. The easiest way for CRectangle to implement the LibraryName property, therefore, is simply to inherit it. In the technique you are using here, you can accomplish simple inheritance by declaring a procedure with the same signature in the specialized class and then implementing that procedure with a single call to the same procedure in the general class.

CRectangle overrides CShape's ClassName property entirely. This makes sense because the names of the classes are constants and they are clearly different. It is acceptable for a class feature to be overridden by a derived class as long as two criteria are met.

- First, the meaning of the overriding feature must be the same as the feature being overridden. Otherwise, the usage of this feature will become very confusing to the user of these classes.

- Second, the signature of the feature must remain the same; there should be no more or fewer parameters required by the specialized class's feature than there was required by the general class's feature.

The only slight exception to this second rule is that optional parameters may become more restrictive. In other words, parameters that were optional in the general class now may be required in the specialized class.

The StrVal method of the CRectangle class is a classic example of a specialized class leveraging the existing functionality of the parent class for the very method it is overriding. In practice, this inheritance behavior occurs quite frequently. The purpose of the StrVal method is to expose the properties of the object in a form that can be displayed easily using a function like Msgbox. Because the properties of CRectangle are by definition a superset of the properties of CShape, all the StrVal method of CRectangle needs to do is add its own properties to the list of those already provided by the StrVal method of CShape. The advanced reader should note how complex this same functionality can be in some languages that attempt to handle inheritance for you automatically and how simple this is in comparison.

The Draw method of CRectangle fulfills the implied contract established by the existence of the Draw method of CShape. Because this method is purely abstract in CShape, it must be given an actual definition in CRectangle so that it can be invoked. Notice that Draw in CRectangle has the same signature as Draw in CShape. This makes it possible for a user of this library to invoke Draw for a shape without even knowing what kind of a shape he has. This topic is explored in greater depth later, in the section "Polymorphism."

Essentially, you are using this technique to create one private object for each level of abstraction of an exposed object, and then to ensure that each object in the inheritance chain has the handle of the next higher object in the chain. The CShape example has only one level of abstraction, so the only reference to a private object is when the CRectangle class contains an instance of CShape. If you were implementing the Human, Primate, Mammal inheritance chain, for example, you would expect Human to contain a reference to an instance of a Primate; Primate, in turn, would contain a reference to an instance of Mammal. Because only Human would be public, it appears to the user of a Human object that he has only one object that is doing everything a human should be able to do. In fact, there are three objects working together to provide the functionality.

An Alternative Technique

Now take a look at an alternative approach to implementing the CShape and CRectangle classes with the same functionality. CShape could have the following implementation:

```
' Public LineThickness As Long
' Public LineColor As Long
' These properties are purely abstract and are included here solely to document
' the fact that they should be included as properties of every derived class.

Public Property Get ClassName() As String
' ClassName provides the name of the class
   ClassName = "Shape"
End Property

Public Property Get LibraryName() As String
' LibraryName provides the name of the class library
  LibraryName = "Shape"
End Property

Public Function StrVal(Specialization As Object) As String
' StrVal provides the string equivalent of the object's properties
StrVal = "LineThickness " & Specialization.LineThickness & chr(13)
   StrVal = StrVal & "LineColor " & Specialization.LineColor
End Function

Public Sub Draw(Canvas As Object)
' Draw renders the shape on the canvas.
' This method is purely abstract and is included here solely to document the
' fact that it should
' be included as a method of every derived class and should
' have this signature.
End Sub
```

CRectangle would then have the following implementation:

```
Public LineThickness As Long
Public LineColor As Long
Public UpperLeft As CPoint
Public LowerRight As CPoint

Public Property Get LibraryName() As String
' LibraryName provides the name of the class library
   LibraryName = gShape.LibraryName
End Property
```

```
Public Property Get ClassName() As String
' ClassName provides the name of the class
  ClassName = "Rectangle"
End Property

Public Function StrVal() As String
' StrVal provides the string equivalent of the object's properties
  StrVal = "UpperLeft " & UpperLeft & chr(13)
  StrVal = StrVal & "LowerRight " & LowerRight & chr(13)
  StrVal = StrVal & gShape.StrVal(Me)
End Function

Public Sub Draw(Canvas As Object)
' Draw renders the shape on the canvas.
  Canvas.DrawWidth = LineThickness
  Canvas.ForeColor = LineColor
  Canvas.Line Step(UpperLeft.X,UpperLeft.Y)
➥- Step(LowerRight.X,LowerRight.Y)
End Sub
```

The first thing you will notice about this technique is that there is no longer one instance of the abstract superclass CShape for each CRectangle object. Instead, both the LibraryName and StrVal properties reference a mysterious gShape object that was never declared anywhere. The assumption is that gShape has been made somehow globally visible, and if it hasn't, the CRectangle object will produce an error at runtime. The standard means of ensuring that these globally accessible abstract superclasses are available at runtime is to include a Basic code module with your library to declare a public instance of each.

The next thing you might notice is that all the properties that were once part of the implementation of CShape now are implemented entirely within CRectangle. This is done for two reasons.

■ First, it simplifies much of the implementation because you no longer have the level of indirection for the CShape properties. This, in turn, enables you to implement these properties as public variables instead of property let and property get procedures.

■ Second, it is not possible to implement these properties in the CShape class if you are sharing a single global instance of this class among multiple CRectangle objects, as you are in the example here. This is because if you changed the LineThickness property of one rectangle, it would mysteriously (and probably erroneously) change the LineThickness property of all rectangles because the value for this property is stored in only one place in memory.

Another difference you will notice is that the StrVal property of CRectangle actually passes a reference to itself to the StrVal property of the global instance of CShape. This is because the StrVal property of gShape needs a reference back to the rectangle object so that it can access the LineThickness and LineColor properties of that particular instance. This is actually a foreshadowing of the major technique of polymorphism, which is discussed later in this chapter.

This technique sometimes is referred to as *rolling down* the inheritance chain. This is because you actually pushed virtually all the implementations of the abstract classes down the inheritance chain into the non-abstract classes. Because every inheritance chain terminates with a non-abstract class, you can apply this technique across an entire library. Of course, if it were applied for every feature of every class, there wouldn't be any inheritance left in the implementation at all. Some people then might argue that you no longer are using the object-oriented model according to the strictest definition.

I argue, yet again, that you are using OO as long as you are applying OO design techniques, and that your physical implementation is less relevant. If I compiled a library using either of these techniques into an OLE server, and you implemented that same OLE server in a more pure object-oriented language, there would be no way for a user to tell the difference between these two OLE servers. They both equally encapsulate the state and behavior of these objects and expose identical interfaces.

It is important to note that these techniques are not mutually exclusive. If a class inherited features from three other classes, for example, it might roll down the features from one class, contain an instance of another class, and still reference a globally available instance of the third class.

Advantages and Disadvantages of These Techniques

Some purists will argue that what I have done to implement inheritance is simply to turn all inheritance relationships into association relationships, which therefore is no longer true inheritance. Of course, they are quite correct in their assertion, but who cares? If it looks like a rose and smells like a rose, then for all intents and purposes, it is a rose. The point is that if my public interface and functionality are identical to theirs, the particular implementation I choose to accomplish this is not relevant as long as it is equally flexible, robust, reusable, and so on. In fact, this is precisely the point of the principle of encapsulation.

I must concede that this implementation is not equally flexible and, therefore, it does have one disadvantage when compared to inheritance, which is built into the language. If any feature of an abstract class changed its public interface, this change normally would have to be made only in a single place. It would be made in the definition of that abstract superclass, and it would propagate automatically to all subclasses.

Using either of the techniques discussed here, the object developer must propagate such changes down the inheritance chain manually. Of course, this argument is somewhat weak because it is extremely poor programming practice to change a public interface of a reusable component in the first place. You never know how many client applications may no longer function properly. This is particularly germane when it comes to OLE servers, because the user of the application that relies on this OLE server might not even know that such a dependency exists. Suddenly, one of his applications that has been stable for a long time no longer functions properly when he installs an unrelated application on the same machine simply because the new application also did a silent upgrade to a shared OLE server.

Therefore, in the end there are only two valid disadvantages:

- You must write more code because none of the inheritance happens automatically.
- These techniques require that you have more discipline when you develop an object, because the compiler will not complain if you fail to implement an inherited feature in a descendent class.

Somewhat oddly, this second disadvantage is also an advantage of these techniques. The inheritance as implemented in virtually all object-oriented languages uses a strictly additive model; every derived class has all the features of its immediate superclasses plus some additional features.

You cannot subtract from the functionality of a superclass, however, because all its functionality is inherited automatically. But subtractive inheritance exists in real-world objects and so you would like to be able to represent it in your implementation. A platypus is a mammal, for example, but it does not bear live offspring, as do all other mammals. It would be convenient if it were possible to state in the definition of a platypus that it inherited everything from `Mammal` except those properties and methods associated with bearing live offspring. This is not possible in most OO languages. Because you must implement all inheritance relationships manually using the technique described here, however, you can subtract from any subclass's features simply by not implementing the features you don't want to exist.

Another major advantage comes into play when you consider multiple inheritance. In many OO languages, it sometimes is difficult to define and control which features are being inherited from which subclasses when a subclass inherits from many superclasses with similar features. This becomes particularly difficult when some of these superclasses inherit from identical superclasses themselves. In other words, two inheritance chains merge at a common node. Because of the complexities involved, some pragmatists advise against using multiple inheritance at all. Of course, I find this unacceptable because multiple inheritance exists in real-world objects and therefore must be represented somehow in the implementation.

Professional library developers usually solve this problem by rolling down some of the inheritance chains and then implementing very short chains with the remaining classes. In many cases, they go to the extreme of implementing chains that are never more than one level deep. This, of course, makes it impossible for them to ever need to inherit from a common superclass because there must be at least two levels of abstraction. Of course, all they are doing is punting all the complexities that need to be addressed into their user community instead of dealing with them.

If you use these techniques, however, you really don't need to deviate from an ideal model based on language restrictions or complexities. Because you already are required to specify exactly from where each feature is being inherited, you might as well reap the rewards of this extra labor. If you must inherit similar features from two different superclasses, you need to have a reference to each.

Which reference you use in the subclass's implementation of that feature specifies from which superclass you inherit that feature. In some cases, you also might need to use both references and, because you have both of them, you can. In other cases, you might want to create an independent reference to the common multiply inherited-from superclass and only use this reference to inherit multiply inherited features. Because this technique greatly simplifies multiple inheritance, I have found that the number of superclasses I have for a given subclass has increased dramatically. With this increase, I have enjoyed a greatly enhanced code modularity.

Polymorphism

Polymorphism is the idea that it is logical to get two different objects to do similar things using similar commands. I once read in an anthropology book about a society in which the words men used for something were very frequently different than the words women used for that same thing. It was almost as if the men and women in the society spoke two different languages—as if communication between the sexes weren't already complicated enough. The point is that men and women usually experience and interact with the world in a very similar manner and, therefore, the commonality of terms and approaches is more important than the differences. You want to lower the complexity for those people using your objects by using the same terms and the same signatures for things that are logically very similar.

Polymorphism is one of the areas that sometimes gets quite a *wow* when demonstrated in practice. It is an example of one of those fantastic engineering feats that make it possible for someone to do something useful with a tool without really knowing what the tool is or how it works. I run across excellent examples of how good engineering makes this possible every day. When someone buys an electronic device at the store, the first thing you can be sure of is that he won't read any of the instructions. This is so universal that I found it amusing to learn that most manufacturers have started placing the instructions at the bottom of the box instead of at the top so that they can be sure their customers' first interaction with their product is a positive one.

The point is that somehow all these people who have never read the instructions are using these products quite successfully—in part, due to polymorphism. As a matter of fact, the very first thing they do with their new electronic device is extraordinarily polymorphic. They attempt to give the device power by plugging it in or by putting batteries in it. How did they know they had to give this device power and how did they know which part of this strange new device needed to be plugged in? The answer is that all electronic devices share the behavior of needing power and all expose similar methods for doing so.

The good news is that VB4 is incredibly polymorphic by nature. The reason is that when the compiler cannot be sure of the exact object it will use at runtime, it delays the decision as to what to do with that object as long as possible. This usually is referred to as *late binding*, which is just an interpreter's way of saying that it's going to wing it and assume that it will know what to do when it gets there.

Suppose that I tell you I'm going to hand you a few objects one at a time and I want you to consume the objects I hand you, and you quite foolishly agree. Because you're not sure what the objects are going to be, you don't really know exactly how you are going to consume them, but you assume (like the interpreter) that you'll figure it out as you go along. First, I hand you an apple and you eat it. Second, I hand you a glass of water and you drink it. Finally, I hand you a vacuum cleaner and you protest. You exhibited polymorphic behavior when I handed you the apple and water and told you to consume them because you did two different but logically similar things. When I handed you the vacuum cleaner, you did exactly what VB4 does if you hand it an object at runtime that does not contain the feature you are asking the interpreter to use. You'll be happy to know that VB4 would protest to consuming the vacuum cleaner as well.

A Practical Example

To see a more practical example of polymorphism in VB4, revisit the CShape and CRectangle examples. Suppose that you also derived two other classes from CShape named CEllipse and CTriangle. Each of these new classes has the same properties and methods as CShape. Also assume that you have a class CDrawing, whose purpose is to encapsulate an entire drawing consisting of multiple shapes—rectangles, ellipses, and triangles.

First, assume for a moment that you don't know about polymorphism and you call the Draw method of the CRectangle class DrawRectangle, the Draw method of the CEllipse class DrawEllipse, and the Draw method of the CTriangle class DrawTriangle. Part of the implementation of the CDrawing class includes the following code:

```
Public Shapes as New Collection

Public Sub Draw(Canvas as Object)
  Dim Shape as Object
  For each Shape in Shapes
    Select Case TypeName(Shape)
    Case "CRectangle"
      Shape.DrawRectangle(Canvas)
    Case "CEllipse"
      Shape.DrawEllipse(Canvas)
    Case "CTriangle"
      Shape.DrawTriangle(Canvas)
  Next
End Sub
```

In this example, Shapes is a collection of CShape objects. Some of these CShape objects actually will be declared from the class CRectangle, some from CEllipse, and some from CTriangle. But they are all added to the same collection together. Therefore, the Draw method of the CDrawing class must check what each object is before it attempts to draw the object so that it knows which Draw method to use. First, you'll notice that this is a rather ugly, redundant solution. More important, this means that every time you add a new subclass of CShape to your library, you will have to remember to come back to this routine and update it so that this Draw method will know which Draw method to call for objects of the new class.

Now, assume that you do know about polymorphism and so you wisely choose to name the Draw method of every subclass of CShape Draw. The Draw method of CDrawing can be implemented like this:

```
Public Sub Draw(Canvas as Object)
  Dim Shape as Object
  For each Shape in Shapes
    Shape.Draw (Canvas)
  Next
End Sub
```

Notice how simple, concise, and yet extraordinarily powerful this routine is. You can add as many new subclasses of CShape as you want and, as long as they also implement a method named Draw with the same single parameter of the Canvas being provided, this method will continue to function properly without change. This obviously is enormously important to the concepts of reuse and ease of use.

It is important to note before going on that this routine is still calling three different Draw methods, depending on which class of object it finds in the Shapes collection. It also is important to keep in mind that the implementation hidden in each of these methods might, in fact, be drastically different. After all, the code for drawing an ellipse is much more complex and quite different in nature than the code for drawing simple polygons like rectangles and triangles. But Draw logically means the same thing to each of these objects and therefore exposes identical interfaces.

Extending Polymorphism with Inheritance

So far, I have demonstrated only how polymorphism already works in VB4 using the constructs readily available. But this chapter focuses primarily on how to extend VB4 to implement OO design that is not readily supported by the language. The area of polymorphism that is not so straightforward is when polymorphism is mixed with inheritance.

Sometimes, in order for a superclass to accomplish one of its methods, it must know something about the subclass for which it is accomplishing the method. You saw this in the StrVal method of the CRectangle class in the section, "An Alternative Technique." The CShape class needed to display its properties but, because you rolled its properties into the CRectangle class, it no longer possessed a handle on its own properties. It therefore was necessary that the CRectangle class actually pass a reference to itself to the StrVal property of CShape through the built-in Me pointer. It was valid for the StrVal method to assume that the reference being passed to it would be to an object that would contain the LineWidth and LineColor properties because these properties actually were inherited from it. That is, it knew that the reference would be to a subclass of itself and, therefore, by definition, this subclass would have to support the same properties that it supported.

Polymorphism combined with inheritance is abstract even as OO concepts go, so I will try to clarify it a bit with another example. Suppose that you have three classes: CDie, CCoin, and CRouletteWheel. These are subclasses of CRandomDevice. Assume that CRandomDevice has an abstract method NewValue and one actual method Average. The implementation of CRandomDevice can include this code:

```
Public Function NewValue() as Long
' Generates a new value and returns that value
' This method is purely abstract and is included here solely to document
' the fact that it should
' be included as a method of every derived class
' and should have this signature.
End Function

Public Function Average(Specialization As Object, NumberOfAttempts
  as Long) as Double
' This method returns the average of a specified number of attempts
' at using the random device
Dim I as Integer, Sum as Long
  Sum = 0
  For I = 1 to NumberOfAttempts
    Sum = Sum + Specialization.NewValue
  Next I
  Average = Sum / NumberOfAttempts
End Function
```

The implementation of CDie can include the following code:

```
Public PipsOnTopFace as Long
Public RandomDevice as New CRandomDevice

Public Sub Roll()
  PipsOnTopFace = Int(Rnd * 6 + 1)
End Sub

Public Function NewValue() as Long
  Roll
  NewValue = PipsOnTopFace
End  Function

Public Function Average(NumberOfAttempts as Long) as Double
  Average = RandomDevice.Average(Me, NumberOfAttempts)
End Function
```

The implementation of CCoin can include this code:

```
Public Face as Boolean ' True = Head and False = Tales
Public RandomDevice as New CRandomDevice

Public Sub Flip()
  Face = (Int (Rnd * 2) = 1)
End Sub

Public Function NewValue() as Long
  Flip
  NewValue = 0
  If Face Then NewValue = 1
End  Function

Public Function Average(NumberOfAttempts as Long) as Double
  Average = RandomDevice.Average(Me, NumberOfAttempts)
End Function
```

The implementation of CRouletteWheel can include the following code:

```
Public SlotNumberOfBall as Long
Public RandomDevice as New CRandomDevice

Public Sub Spin()
  SlotNumberOfBall = Int(Rnd * 38)
' Note that there are two chances at zero on a Roulette wheel
  If SlotNumberOfBall = 37 Then SlotNumberOfBall = 0
End Sub

Public Function NewValue() as Long
  Spin
  NewValue = SlotNumberOfBall
End  Function

Public Function Average(NumberOfAttempts as Long) as Double
  Average = RandomDevice.Average(Me, NumberOfAttempts)
End Function
```

The Average method of CRandomDevice is implemented in each subclass, and yet all each subclass needs to do is call the same method of the superclass. This is just normal inheritance behavior using a technique discussed earlier in this chapter. The Average method of the CRandomDevice superclass cannot actually accomplish its defined task without invoking an abstract method NewValue for the specific subclass that invoked it in the first place, however. Of course, it doesn't have a handle on the specific subclass that called it unless that subclass supplies one. This is why the first parameter each subclass provides to the Average method of the CRandomDevice superclass is a reference to itself through the built-in Me pointer.

The Average method of CRandomDevice knows that it can call the NewValue method using the reference it was provided because it knows that the reference is to a subclass of itself and that this subclass must have a method with this name and signature. Notice how the NewValue method is truly polymorphic because the implementation in each derived class is different even though each accomplishes a logically equivalent task of generating a random value and returning this value to the caller.

Summary

This chapter focused on extending VB4's object-oriented capabilities with inheritance and polymorphism. You learned about two approaches to implementing inheritance by rendering inheritance relationships into associations between classes and rolling down features into non-abstract subclasses. You also learned how to use the late binding nature of VB4 to implement polymorphism and how to pass the Me pointer to a superclass so that you can use polymorphism with inheritance.

The next chapter focuses on two approaches to object persistence. The final chapter on the object-oriented model, Chapter 11, focuses on building OLE servers using and extending Microsoft's OLE server standards.

Persistent Objects

by Shawn Oberst

CHAPTER

10

When I say that an object is *persistent*, I mean that the object is capable of being saved onto a more permanent storage media (such as a disk) and then retrieved intact at a later point in time. When I say "intact," I mean that not only should all the properties be just as you left them when you last interacted with this object, but so should all of the relationships between the object and all the other objects. Of course, if one of the other objects was destroyed in the meantime or the other object dissolved the relationship, then these changes in state should be reflected as well.

The idea of persistent objects is another one of those object-oriented (OO) concepts on which there are many hotly debated schools of thought. As I stated before, I am one of those people who believes that every good idea has an application someplace, and so I don't try to decide whether one technique is better than another, as much as to decide what are the merits of each. Knowing the merits of each enables me to make a decision about which to use when I come across a specific problem.

There are two major schools of thought when it comes to implementing persistent objects. One is to implement them in an Object-Oriented Database Management System (OODBMS), and the other is to implement them in a Relational Database Management System (RDBMS). Of course, most people don't have OODBMSs, and most of the ones that do exist are not very efficient. However, that doesn't prevent you from using the OO approach any more than the fact that VB4 doesn't have constructs for inheritance prevents you from using VB4 for developing OO applications. With just a few simple tricks, you can partially implement an OO approach to persistence on an RDBMS.

You do not need to be familiar with OODBMSs to understand this chapter. However, if you are unfamiliar with RDBMSs, then this chapter will be extremely challenging to read.

Defining Persistence in an RDBMS

Before I talk about each approach, let's first analyze what parts of an object must be made persistent in order for an object to be persistent in an RDBMS. An object has simple properties, relationships, and behavior. However, the behavior of an object is already persistent because it is fully captured in the methods of that object. Therefore, you must find a way to preserve the properties and both the single-valued and multi-valued relationships.

The relational model enforced by the RDBMS also imposes one additional requirement. All records in an RDBMS must be uniquely identifiable in order to be stored and retrieved properly. This means that whatever schema you propose must have a unique way of identifying an object.

Some Example Objects to Make Persistent

To illustrate each approach to object persistence, you need some sample objects. I chose to do a bizarre experiment for you that involves people and their pets because it contains each type of relationship I need to demonstrate. In this experiment, the pets can be either cats or dogs. The hypothesis that you are attempting to prove is that women who are not married have more cats than average, and men who are not married have more dogs than average. Additionally, we hypothesize that there is an inverse correlation between the number of children people have and the number of pets they have, and that this correlation becomes stronger as the average age of the children increases.

For adults, you need to keep track of their names, gender, spouse, children, and pets. For children, keep track of their names, gender, and age. For pets, keep track of their name and age. Additionally, for each cat, you'll keep track of whether it catches mice and what its favorite toy is; for each dog you'll keep track of whether it chases cars and its favorite place to go for a walk. You keep track of this extraneous information about the specific cats and dogs so that if it is necessary to call back to get additional information in the future, our telephone survey people can sound more friendly.

To implement this experiment, you will need to have at least four classes: `Adult`, `Child`, `Dog`, and `Cat`, and possibly a fifth abstract class, `Pet`. There are also five relationships of four different types. The relationship between adults and their respective spouses is what is referred to as a *one-to-one relationship* because every husband can have only one wife and every wife can have only one husband.

The relationship between an owner and that owner's pets is what is referred to as a *one-to-many relationship* because in this system you assign each pet to exactly one owner, but an owner can have many pets.

The relationship between parents and their children is what is referred to as a *many-to-many relationship* because parents may have many children and children may have many parents.

The last type of relationship is called an *"Is A"* relationship, and it represents the inheritance relationship. You have two of those in this system: a cat is a pet, and a dog is a pet.

If you are familiar with object modeling techniques (OMT), then Figure 10.1 should be useful in visualizing the objects and relationships just described. Even if you are not familiar with this technique, you should be able to match the description to this diagram and surmise its meaning.

Figure 10.1.
A sample OMT diagram.

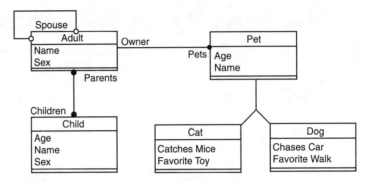

Using an OO Approach on an RDBMS

Both the OO and relational approaches you will be learning dictate that each class should have its own table and that each object should be a record in one of those tables. In the OO approach, a table for each class is the only table necessary.

Also in both approaches, the simple properties of each class are just fields of that class's table. The types of these fields should match as closely as possible to the types of the equivalent property. The values stored in these fields are the values of those properties of the given object that the record represents. For example, our Adult class would be stored in the Adult table, which would have the fields Name and Gender for its simple properties.

I am an Adult object, and therefore I would appear as a record in the Adult table. The values for my name and gender properties would be Shawn and Male, respectively. Because the type of the Name property of Adult is likely String, the Name field of the Adult table would probably have a type like VarChar(30), Text(30), or Char(30). The exact type depends on the particular RDBMS you are using.

In the OO approach, you use an object identifier to uniquely identify each object. What is particularly interesting about these object identifiers is that they uniquely identify the object within the entire system, not just within a single table, as the relational model dictates. The other important distinction between these object identifiers and a simple relational key is that they are assigned by the system itself. These identifiers have no logical equivalent in the real world but are merely necessary for the physical implementation.

If there were no relationships between the objects in this example application, then your database could be implemented as five tables named Adult, Child, Pet, Cat, and Dog. Those five tables would have the same schema as the tables in Figure 10.2 without the Relationships fields.

Figure 10.2.
Sample RDBMS tables for the OO approach.

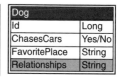

Adult	
Id	Long
Name	String
Gender	Char
Relationships	String

Child	
Id	Long
Name	String
Gender	String
Age	Long
Relationships	String

Pet	
Id	Long
Name	String
Age	Integer
Relationships	String

Cat	
Id	Long
ChasesMice	Yes/No
FavoriteToy	String
Relationships	String

Dog	
Id	Long
ChasesCars	Yes/No
FavoritePlace	String
Relationships	String

Relationships Using an OO Approach

If you are the type of person who gets lost in all the computer jargon and prefers to look at examples, then you might wish to refer to the next section, "The Flintstones Example," while reading this section. The next section guides you through a concrete example of all of the conceptual stuff that this section explains.

Whether relationships are single-valued or multi-valued, they are implemented with a single field appended to the end of every table that handles all relationships. For the sample experiment, these fields are lightly highlighted in Figure 10.2. In each case, this field is composed of a series of numbers broken into groups of three, called *tuples*. Each tuple represents exactly one relationship between the object to which this relationship field belongs and some other object. Each tuple is composed of a number that identifies the relationship type, a number that identifies the class to which it relates, and a number that identifies the object being related.

Every time a relationship between two objects A and B is created, two tuples are created to represent that relationship. The first tuple is appended to the relationship field of A, and it represents A's relationship to B. The second tuple is appended to the relationship field of B, and it represents B's relationship to A. Each of these relationships must have a unique relationship identifier because in some relationships, it is not otherwise possible to determine which direction the relationship goes.

For example, both objects involved in the spouse relationship are adults. If you did not keep track of gender and if you used only a single relationship identifier, then you could not determine which adult is the husband and which is the wife. In this experiment, this does not matter, but in other cases it might. The term *reflexive relationship* was coined to refer to the opposite relationship to the one you are creating. Wife is the reflexive relationship of husband, and husband is the reflexive relationship of wife. If the relationship between A and B is destroyed at some point, then both of the tuples must be removed from their respective relationship fields.

To effectively implement this approach, every class must be assigned a unique class identifier, and every relationship must be assigned two unique relationship identifiers. These must be decided upon at design time and remain constant for the life of the system. The object identifiers are the same as those that appear in the Id field and are assigned automatically by the system each time a new object is created.

The Flintstones Example

Because this field behaves so strangely, let's use the experiment as an example to make it more tangible. Suppose that for this experiment you assign the class and relationship identifiers shown in Figure 10.3. There is no particular reason why the relationship identifiers need to be a disjointed set from the class identifiers, but I made them as such to make the explanation more clear.

Figure 10.3.

Sample class and relationship Id tables.

Class	Id
Adult	1
Child	2
Pet	3
Cat	4
Dog	5

Relationship	Id
AdultChildren	10
AdultWife	12
AdultPets	14
PetIsACat	16
PetIsADog	18

Reflexive	Id
ChildParents	11
AdultHusband	13
PetOwner	15
CatIsAPet	17
DogIsAPet	19

To demonstrate how the relationship fields work, let's suppose that you create two adult objects, Fred and Wilma, who are married and have one child, Pebbles, and one pet, Dino, who is a dog (sort of). You will assign Fred the object identifier of 100, Wilma 101, Pebbles 102, and Dino 103. To create the spouse relationship between Fred and Wilma, you would add the tuple (12,1,101) to the relationship field of Fred's record to establish Wilma as his wife. You can see from the table in Figure 10.3 that the 12 in this tuple represents the AdultWife relationship and the 1 in this tuple represents the Adult class. The 101 in this tuple is Wilma's object identifier.

After adding Fred's relationship to Wilma you must add Wilma's relationship to Fred. To do this you would add the tuple (13,1,100) to the relationship field of Wilma's record to establish Fred as her husband. Again, you can see from the table in Figure 10.3 that the 13 in this tuple represents the AdultHusband relationship and the 1 in this tuple represents the Adult class. The 100 in this tuple is Fred's object identifier.

Figure 10.4 shows how each of the relationships described in this paragraph would be implemented. In the remaining sections of this chapter I will not describe in such detail how these tuples are created. It is always the same algorithm as described in this section.

The functioning of this field is highly unorthodox by modern programming practices, and it violates the relational model. However, it is extremely flexible and efficient for doing single-object-at-a-time interactions. Remember that the relational model was designed to perform operations on large numbers of records efficiently with a much lesser regard for single-record-at-a-time operations. These single-record-at-a-time operations occur much more frequently in OO designs. Also, note that much of the ugliness of this field can be encapsulated inside a class dedicated to relationships.

Figure 10.4.

The Flintstones OO example.

Relationship	Table	Record	Tuple	Table	Record	Tuple
Fred is Wilma's spouse	Adult	Fred	(12,1,101)	Adult	Wilma	(13,1,100)
Pebbles is Fred's child	Adult	Fred	(10,2,102)	Child	Pebbles	(11,1,100)
Pebbles is Wilma's child	Adult	Wilma	(10,2,102)	Child	Pebbles	(11,1,101)
Dino is Fred's pet	Adult	Fred	(14,3,103)	Pet	Dino	(15,1,100)
Dino is a Dog	Pet	Dino	(18,5,103)	Dog	Dino	(19,3,103)

Multi-Valued Relationships Using the OO Approach

Both single-valued and multi-valued relationships are made persistent using the same relationship field described in the preceding section. However, sometimes order matters in a multi-valued relationship. That is, sometimes it is important to know not only that A is an element of the collection B, but that it is, in fact, the third element of that collection. The Add method of VB4 collections supports this ordering concept through the Before and After parameters, and so you must have a way to make this ordering persistent. Fortunately, the solution to this is quite simple in the OO model. Instead of simply appending the tuple representing a relationship to the end of the relationship field, you can insert it some place in the middle, ensuring that you preserve the order.

For example, let's assume that Fred had another child before Pebbles that you just now learned about. Oh no, scandal in the Flintstone family! What is this world coming to? This child's name is Rocky, and we assigned him the object identifier of 104. Before adding Rocky to the collection of children that Fred fathered, Fred's relationship field looked like this:

`(12,1,101)(10,2,102)(14,3,103)`

This field value was derived by concatenating all of Fred's tuples from Figure 10.4. If you did not care about order, then you could simply append Rocky's tuple (10,2,104) to the end. However, to show that Rocky is the first element of Fred's collection of children, you must insert Rocky's tuple before Pebble's tuple. That is, it must be inserted before the tuple (10,2,102). After the insertion, Fred's relationship field would look like this:

`(12,1,101)(10,2,104)(10,2,102)(14,3,103)`

If you want to support all the functionality of VB4 collections, you still need to add one more thing before your relationship field is complete. VB4 collections enable you to attach an arbitrary string to each member of a collection through the Key parameter of the Add method. Because this key has nothing to do with either object in the relationship but is an attribute of the relationship between the two objects, it is necessary to store this key in the relationship. To do this, you must add a fourth element to each tuple. After adding a few keys, Fred's relationship field might look like this:

```
(12,1,101,Lover)(10,2,104,First Born)(10,2,102,Second Born)
➥(14,3,103,Best Friend)
```

Using a Relational Approach on an RDBMS

The relational approach to implementing persistent relationships should look far more familiar and be easier to follow if you are accustomed to working with normalized relations in an RDBMS. In fact, the approach should seem virtually identical to an approach you might take if you weren't trying to create objects at all, but simply trying to save this same information as records.

Just as with the OO approach, this approach implements each class as its own table, and each simple property is a field of the class's table. The types of these fields should match as closely as possible to the types of the equivalent property. The values stored in these fields are the values of those properties of the given object that the record represents.

I am an Adult object, and therefore I would appear as a record in the Adult table. The values for my name and gender properties would be Shawn and Male, respectively. Because the type of the Name property of Adult is likely String, the Name field of the Adult table would probably have a type like VarChar(30), Text(30), or Char(30). The exact type depends on the particular RDBMS you are using.

Unlike the OO approach, it is not actually necessary to have unique object identifiers because you may use any unique key to show a relationship. However, you should note that there are many advantages to using these unique object identifiers as keys, and therefore, they are often used in practice. First, the object identifiers tend to simplify the code used to traverse relationships because you can always be sure that you will be traversing the relationship with a single integer field. Second, there is a higher performance of join operations performed on integer values than on strings. Finally, by having relationships represented using an identifier that is automatically generated by the system and therefore has no logical equivalent in the real world, you eliminate the chance that a foreign key might have to change when its corresponding primary key changes. That is, you do not have to contend with the cascade update of a primary key. To make the distinction between these two approaches more salient, I will ignore these advantages and refrain from using unique object identifiers in this section.

If there were no relationships between the objects in the survey example application, then your database could be implemented as five tables named Adult, Child, Pet, Cat, and Dog. Those five tables would have the same schema as the tables in Figure 10.5 without the lightly highlighted fields.

Figure 10.5.
Sample RDBMS tables for the relational approach.

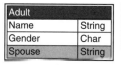

Adult	
Name	String
Gender	Char
Spouse	String

ParentChild	
Parent	String
Child	String

Child	
Name	String
Gender	String
Age	Long

Pet	
Name	String
Age	Integer
Owner	String

Cat	
Name	String
ChasesMice	Yes/No
FavoriteToy	String

Dog	
Name	String
ChasesCars	Yes/No
FavoritePlace	String

Relationships Using a Relational Approach

When using the relational approach, one-to-one and one-to-many relationships are implemented through the use of foreign keys. For the sample experiment, the one-to-one relationship between a husband and wife is implemented through the self-referential foreign key Spouse in the Adult table. Similarly, the one-to-many relationship between owners and their pets is implemented through a foreign key Owner in the Pet table. Many-to-many relationships are implemented through the use of link tables. As a result, the many-to-many relationship between parents and their children is implemented with the ParentChild link table. Of course, nothing prohibits you from also using link tables for one-to-one and one-to-many relationships, and it often simplifies things to do so if a relationship is heterogeneous.

Inheritance relationships are implemented by using identical primary keys for the superclass and all of its subclasses. For our sample experiment, the inheritance relationships that a Dog is a Pet and that a Cat is a Pet are implemented through the fact that the name fields of both Dog and Cat are the Dog and Cat tables' primary key and that the name field of Pet is also its primary key. The set of pet names is identical to the union of the set of cat names and the set of dog names. The lightly highlighted fields of Figure 10.5 need to be added to represent the relationships of our sample experiment.

The Flintstones Example Revisited

To demonstrate how this new approach works for the sample experiment, let's revisit the Flintstones. To represent the fact that Fred is the husband of Wilma, you could place the name Fred in the spouse field of Wilma's record, or you could place the name Wilma in the spouse field of Fred's record, or you could do both. It doesn't matter a great deal which you choose, as long as you ensure that you do not get duplicate relationships when you do your join operation later. Doing both makes it easy to find the spouse's name from either spouse but does so at a cost of two write operations.

To represent the fact that the parents of Pebbles are Fred and Wilma, you need to add two new records to the ParentChild link table. The first record will place Fred in the Parent field and Pebbles in the Child field. The second record will place Wilma in the Parent field and Pebbles in the Child field.

To represent the fact that Dino is Fred's dog, you simply place the name Fred in the Owner field of Dino's pet record. Note that the fact that Dino is a dog is represented by the fact that Dino has a record in both the Pet table and the Dog table and that in each case, the primary key name is Dino.

After all these relationships are made persistent, your experimental tables will contain the records shown in Figure 10.6.

Figure 10.6.
Experimental tables with object records.

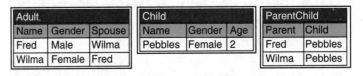

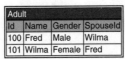

It is worth noting again at this point that you could have implemented unique object identifiers assigned by the system as the primary keys of each object; in which case, each of the foreign key relationships in this example would have referenced those primary keys. If you would have taken this approach, then the tables would have looked something like Figure 10.7.

Figure 10.7.
Experimental tables with object identifiers.

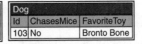

Multi-Valued Relationships Using the Relational Approach

As discussed in the section titled, "Multi-Valued Relationships Using the OO Approach," multi-valued relationships in VB might require order or keys. This capability is supported by the Add method of the collection class. Unfortunately, arbitrary ordering is a complex problem in the relational model. The relational model is based on set theory, which assumes that order does not matter. Therefore, RDBMSs assume that you wish to order only on fields of the tables you are joining in a `select` statement. Furthermore, the keys used to select records are usually keys of the tables that contain the objects themselves, not keys of the relationships between these objects.

To implement collection keys, you simply need to add an extra indexed field to whichever table you added the foreign key. That is, in a one-to-many relationship implemented with a foreign key on the many side, you simply add an extra collection key field to the many side as well. In a many-to-many relationship where the foreign keys are in the link table, you simply add an extra collection key field for whichever collection you wish to have a key value. If you wish to have one for both collections represented by the link table, then you must add two collection key fields, one for each relationship.

Implementing order in multi-valued relationships using the relational approach is very similar to how it's done with collection keys, but it's a whole lot uglier. Like collection keys, you simply add an extra indexed field to whichever table you added the foreign key. The problem is that you must calculate what value to place in these fields to cause the record to be in the correct order when a sort operation is performed in a `select` statement.

The simplest way to do this is to assign the first object added to the collection an order of zero. Each subsequent object added to the beginning or end of the collection is assigned an order that is some constant binary offset from the first or last element of the collection. If an object is inserted into the middle of the collection, then the average of the order values for the two elements that the new object is being inserted between is taken, and this becomes the order value of the new element. If there is no longer any space between the two elements that an object is to be inserted between, then either the entire collection or some localized subset of it must be reordered to make room. These periodic reorderings can be expensive, so knowing the common usage patterns of your collection can be highly useful when you are determining a proper binary offset.

Because this algorithm is a bit complicated, I will attempt to clarify it with an example. Assume that you have chosen a binary offset for your collection of 64. You begin by adding an object A to your collection, and this object is assigned an order of 0. You then add two objects B and C to the end of your collection, and they are assigned orders of 64 and 128, respectively. You then add two objects D and E to the beginning of your collection, and they are assigned orders of -64 and -128 respectively. The current order of your collection is D, E, A, B, C.

Now you decide to insert an object F between A and B. The order of A is 0 and the order of B is 64, and therefore, F is assigned an order of 32. You then decide to insert an object G between F and B. The order of F is 32 and the order of B is 64, and therefore, G is assigned an order of 48. Note that if you performed a `select` statement ordered by the order field, you would still correctly retrieve the objects in the order D, E, A, F, G, B, C, so the algorithm seems to work great. However, there are now only 15 numbers left between G and B. If you continued to insert elements between these two elements, then eventually you would run out of elements, and you would have to reorder your collection to make room.

To see how the table schema would look, let's assume that you have decided to both order and key the `Children` and `Pets` relationships of the sample experiment. The new schema and some example values are shown in the tables in Figure 10.8.

Figure 10.8.
Ordered and keyed relationships.

ParentChild			
Parent	ChildOrder	ChildKey	Child
Fred	1	First Born	Rocky
Fred	2	Second Born	Pebbles
Wilma	1	First Born	Pebbles

PET				
Name	Age	OwnerOrder	OwnerKey	Owner
Fred	8	1	BestFriend	Fred

Advantages and Disadvantages of Each Approach

The OO approach is fairly fast for single-relationship traversals. It is particularly fast if you are doing multiple single-relationship traversals from the same object, because all of the relationships are in one field and therefore are guaranteed to be read with a single disk read. Such traversals are important to consider because they tend to occur more frequently in OO implementations than in more traditional functional implementations.

The OO approach is slower than the relational approach with respect to create, update, and delete operations on relationships, because every relationship is stored in both objects involved in the relationship. However, you should keep in mind that in most systems far more read operations are performed than write operations. The OO approach is also slower than the relational approach in mass read operations because it violates first normal form and therefore cannot take advantage of the query optimization capabilities built into the RDBMS.

If you expect to do a fair amount of batch processing operations of moderate-to-large size, then the relational approach is probably superior based on this alone. If you are uncertain of your future needs for your objects, then you should keep in mind that your worst-case performance scenarios for the OO approach are likely to be worse than your worst-case performance scenarios for the relational approach. However, in practice, I find that a prudent mix of each based on design trade-offs works better than either alone. You can always wrap relational operations inside of methods to help maintain a consistent interface.

In short-term usage, the relational approach is simpler to implement because most of what you need to implement it is already built into the RDBMS. However, in the long term, the OO approach is simpler to implement. This is because, in the relational approach, different types of relationships are implemented in different ways, and therefore, you must always think about what kind of relationship you have when you try to determine what its implementation should be. In the OO approach, all relationships are implemented using the relationship field in exactly the same way. In fact, this approach is so flexible that it is even possible to add new kinds of relationships or to change the cardinality of a relationship on-the-fly at runtime. All you need to do to add a new kind of relationship is to put a new record in the table which keeps track of relationship identifiers.

The relational approach is easier to maintain. If the relational tables somehow get messed up, it is a fairly straightforward process to examine the tables and manually set the relationships back to the way that they should be. It is often quite complex for a human to attempt to sort out the cryptic tuples of the relationship fields and determine where things are pointing in the wrong direction. It is often so complex that it requires some automated utilities to help in the process. Along these same lines, the relational approach is usually easier to sell within an organization because often people are already trained to understand it and many more training resources are available.

The relational approach also enables you to leverage the query engine, referential integrity constraints, stored queries, and other capabilities already built into the RDBMS. The OO approach requires that you invent proprietary approaches to many of the types of functions.

In my opinion, the relational approach is overall the best approach, but it requires a bit more work and planning. Because the required planning is little more than one should do anyway as part of a good OO analysis, this seems like a reasonable cost to bear for all the advantages. However, you should keep an eye out for a good OODBMS that would enable you to use the OO approach without suffering from many of its present disadvantages.

Rolling Up or Rolling Down the Inheritance Hierarchy

When you are deciding on the physical database schema of a class hierarchy, one of the biggest decisions is whether to roll up the inheritance hierarchy, roll it down, or leave it as is. *Rolling down* the inheritance hierarchy means that all properties and relationships of the abstract superclasses are duplicated in the subclasses so that tables for the abstract superclasses are no longer necessary. *Rolling up* an inheritance hierarchy means to aggregate all the properties and relationships of all the subclasses and place them in the same table as the abstract superclass so that tables for the subclasses are no longer necessary. When you leave the inheritance hierarchy alone, there is a table for each superclass and each subclass.

The main reason why you might want to roll up or down the inheritance hierarchy is that doing so usually increases performance for create, read, update, and delete operations. This is because to do one of these operations for a single object requires a separate read or write operation for each class in the inheritance chain of the object. In the example, if I wanted to read in the Dino object, I would have to read from both the Dog table and the Pet table.

In this experiment, if you decided to roll down the Pet superclass, the Pet table would go away, and the Cat and Dog tables would have the schema shown in Figure 10.9.

Figure 10.9.
Rolling down the abstract class Pet.

Cat	
Name	String
ChasesMice	Yes/No
FavoriteToy	String
Age	Integer
Owner	String

Dog	
Name	String
ChasesCars	Yes/No
FavoritePlace	String
Age	Integer
Owner	String

On the other hand, if you decide to roll up the Pet superclass, then the Cat and Dog tables would go away, and the Pet table would have the schema shown in Figure 10.10.

Figure 10.10.
Rolling up the abstract class Pet.

Pet	
Name	String
Type	String
Age	Integer
ChasesMice	Yes/No
FavoriteToy	String
ChasesCars	Yes/No
FavoritePlace	String
Owner	String

A final variation would be to roll up the inheritance chain and overload similar fields between subclasses. In the example, the ChasesMice property of Cat and the ChasesCars property of Dog are very similar, and therefore, you could overload them in the rolled up Pet table. Also, the FavoriteToy property of Cat and the FavoritePlace property of Dog are very similar and could be overloaded. If you did this, then the Pet table would have the new schema shown in Figure 10.11.

Figure 10.11.
Rolling up and overloading fields of Pet.

Pet	
Name	String
Type	String
Age	Integer
Chases	Yes/No
Favorite	String
Owner	String

Advantages to Rolling Up or Down

The advantage to keeping the inheritance hierarchy's physical implementation the same as its logical form is that it minimizes duplication of properties. In the experiment, the age of every pet is in exactly one table. If I want to determine the average age of the pets in the experiment, I could write a very simple aggregating query.

The disadvantage of rolling down an inheritance hierarchy is that properties are duplicated across multiple tables. In our example, the age of dogs is stored in the Dog table, and the age of cats is stored in the Cat table. If I want to determine the average age of the pets, I would need to perform some subqueries to create a union of the ages of the cats and dogs before I could perform my aggregation query. This problem would only get worse if there were a great deal more subtypes of Pet. What makes this problem particularly difficult is that every time I add a new subtype of Pet, I would have to remember this query and all the others like it and make the appropriate modifications. This defeats some of the purpose of using an OO approach.

The disadvantages of rolling up an inheritance hierarchy are that it violates Boyce-Code normal form, and it can create a sparse matrix and therefore waste storage space. It violates Boyce-Code normal form because some of the properties are not fully functionally dependent on the primary key. All of the properties that belong solely to a single type depend on the combination of the primary key and the type field. It's fairly simple to see why rolling up an inheritance hierarchy can create a sparse matrix. Notice that the ChasesMice and FavoriteToy properties will be empty and useless to all the Dog records, and the ChasesCars and FavoritePlace properties will be empty and useless to all the Cat records. You can imagine how sparse this matrix would become if we were to add Bird, Reptile, and Fish classes and all five pet classes have ten unique properties each.

Overloading fields is an attempt to mitigate some of the sparse matrix problems of rolled-up tables. However, now you've violated first normal form because every field does not have only a single meaning. The overloaded field Chases of our rolled-up table Pet means ChasesMice for a Cat and ChasesCars for a Dog. Overloading fields is essentially the same thing as having variant records, which is a violation of first normal form. The problem is that if you someday want to add the FavoriteToy property to our Dog class, it's going to be necessary for you to write a data conversion routine first to separate the cat FavoriteToy properties from the dog FavoritePlace properties. Because it is next to impossible to predict the future requirements on a system, overloading fields should be employed rarely and with a great deal of forethought.

The disadvantage to keeping the physical implementation of the inheritance hierarchy the same as its logical form is that it requires multiple writes to create, read, update, or delete an object. In fact, it requires one extra write per superclass in the inheritance chain. If the chain is deep or bushy, then this can become prohibitively expensive. Conversely, if you have rolled up or down the inheritance chain, then each of these operations would always only require exactly one write no matter how deep or bushy the chain gets.

Why Not Both?

In general, it tends to be best to roll up the inheritance hierarchy when the abstract superclass contains a great deal of properties and relationships of its own and the quantity of subclasses is small or the subclasses have few properties and relationships of their own. In general, it tends to be best to roll down the inheritance hierarchy when the abstract superclass contains very few properties and relationships of its own. There is no particular reason why you cannot roll up some parts of your inheritance hierarchy, roll down other parts, and leave some just as they are in the object model. In fact, applying rules of thumb and mixing and matching these techniques is usually the best of all alternatives to achieve maximum performance without significant loss in flexibility. This is particularly true if you use stored queries to encapsulate your physical implementation.

Stored Queries

To shield you from making a mistake in your choice of physical implementation, which can be somewhat costly later, I suggest that you write stored queries for all create, read, update, and delete operations. I use the term "stored queries" to refer to any one of the various database technologies that enable you to save a query with a name for future execution. The stored queries effectively become the contract between the data services layer and the object services layer, and encapsulate the physical implementation of the data services so that the object services are less affected by any implementation changes that might be required later.

There are many complex approaches to writing these stored queries, which go beyond the scope of this book. However, the simplest approach I have found is to create one create query, one read query, one update query, and one delete query per class. Then create two read queries, two add queries, and two remove queries per relationship type, one for the relationship from each object's perspective.

To illustrate, look yet again at the sample experiment, and focus on the Adult and Child classes and their relationship as parents and children. Table 10.1 shows the set of queries, the input parameters for those queries, and the expected result for these two classes and this relationship. For read queries, the third column in this table shows the schema of the resultant record set and states whether one or many records are expected on a given read.

Table 10.1. Sample experiment stored queries.

Query Name	Input Parameters	Expected Result
AdultCreate	Name,Gender	Creates a new adult object
AdultRead	Name	Returns one {Name,Gender}
AdultUpdate	Name,Gender	Updates Gender for Named adult

Query Name	Input Parameters	Expected Result
AdultDelete	Name	Deletes an existing adult object
ChildCreate	Name,Gender,Age	Creates a new child object
ChildRead	Name	Returns one {Name,Gender,Age}
ChildUpdate	Name,Gender,Age	Updates Gender,Age for Named child
ChildDelete	Name	Deletes an existing child object
AdultChildrenAdd	AdultName,ChildName	Adds a new ParentChild relationship
AdultChildrenRemove	AdultName,ChildName	Removes a ParentChild relationship
AdultChildrenRead	AdultName	Returns many {Name,Gender,Age}
ChildParentAdd	AdultName,ChildName	Adds a new ParentChild relationship
ChildParentRemove	AdultName,ChildName	Removes a ParentChild relationship
ChildParentRead	ChildName	Returns many {Name,Gender}

Notice that this approach is very simple, but it makes updating primary keys a complex matter. To do this, you must delete an existing object, cascading the deletes to all relationships to that object, add the object back with its new primary key, and then add back all the relationships. Some relational theorists agree that it should be this difficult because changing a primary key is a very significant matter. However, if you use object identifiers that are assigned by the system, then there is never a reason to change the primary key, and therefore, you never have to perform this complex operation. Table 10.2 shows the queries for the Adult object when the Adult table contains a system assigned Id field as its primary key. In this example, you can change either the Name or the Gender of the Adult with ease.

Table 10.2. Sample experiment stored queries with object identifiers.

Query Name	Input Parameters	Expected Result
AdultCreate	Id,Name,Gender	Creates a new adult object
AdultRead	Id	Returns one {Id,Name,Gender}
AdultUpdate	Id,Name,Gender	Updates Name,Gender for Ided adult
AdultDelete	Id	Deletes an existing adult object

Summary

This chapter focused on various topics related to object persistence. You learned both an OO approach and a relational approach to implementing persistent objects on an RDBMS and also learned the advantages and disadvantages of each. You also learned rolling up and rolling down an inheritance hierarchy to achieve higher performance. Finally, you learned how to use stored queries to encapsulate your database implementation so that it might be able to evolve without severely affecting your business servers that depend upon it.

Visual Basic 4 Persistent Object OLE Server Standards

by Shawn Oberst

CHAPTER 11

Chapters 8, 9, and 10 focus on the language and implementation of object-oriented techniques in Visual Basic 4.0. The code snippets and database schema shown in the examples in those chapters are similar in style, form, and content to those that I regularly come across as an information systems developer for Microsoft. Recently, Microsoft has set a new focus on addressing the needs of this particular development community and because of this has begun creating standards and tools to aid in developing three-tier client/server applications.

The tools are well documented in Microsoft's documentation, in this book, and in other books like it; this chapter focuses more closely on the standards and the design they imply. Some of these standards are those published by Microsoft with the release of Visual Basic 4 (VB4) and have been included here for context and closure. However, most of them are the standards that are prescribed and practiced internally in Microsoft's Information Technology Group. This is the group responsible for developing business object OLE servers for Microsoft's internal use. However, you should understand that other than those standards which are published with the VB4 manuals, the standards in this chapter are not formally endorsed or prescribed by Microsoft.

It might strike you as a bit strange to dedicate an entire chapter of this book to a subject like standards, but you must remember that a standard is merely a formalized design approach, and design is the paramount activity of all object-oriented (OO) development. All objects evolve over time, and business objects do this even more than most.

Therefore, it can be assumed that no amount of analysis can capture all future needs of an object. The trick to a flexible implementation that can be reused across a variety of applications and yet still evolve as the needs of the business change is in solid design based on solid design principles. Once those design principles have been properly analyzed and tested, the way to solidify your design with uniform application across business services is through standards that are both as rigid and flexible as appropriate.

The other key benefit to adhering to a design standard is that your OLE server user community can begin to depend on a consistent interface. This benefit is analogous to the advantages reaped by the consistencies of the graphical user interface across most Windows applications. Almost all Windows users know by now that if they want to open, close, save, print, or create a new document in a Windows application, they can simply go to the File menu and select the appropriate option. Because of this, I haven't looked up how to save a document in over half a decade. Wouldn't it be fantastic if people could use most of the services provided by our OLE servers without having to look up anything?

The rest of this chapter is an extension of the Microsoft VB4 OLE server design standards. Most of the extensions revolve around object persistence, which currently does not have a standard. There are also enhancements to implement common object behavior found in other OO programming languages. Finally, there are a few enhancements designed to simply increase the usability of the objects. From this point forward, this chapter reads like a standard so that you can incorporate it, in part or in full, into your own business object OLE server standards if you so choose. However, you are strongly advised to review each part of this standard internally with your organization and adapt it as necessary to fit your unique requirements.

General Requirements

If you are certain any one of the classes or features discussed in this chapter is not useful to the particular server you are creating, you simply shouldn't include it. However, it would be a violation of this standard to include a feature that fulfills the same logical purpose as one of these features and yet name it something different or give it a different signature when a signature is provided. If it is necessary to add to the signatures provided, the additional parameters should be placed at the end of the parameter list and, if possible, be made optional to maintain backward compatibility. Likewise, it is acceptable to not implement every functionality of the methods described here. However, if you choose to implement the functionality, it should work as described in this chapter.

Error-Handling Approach

All errors will be returned by raising exceptions. If it is necessary to return multiple errors from a single invocation, you should form an error queue and raise an exception to alert the invoker that there are errors on the queue.

Persistence Approach

You don't want to reinvent the database wheel to implement persistent objects. With ODBC, DAO, and RDO all readily available and the upcoming OLE DB just out of reach, it is pointless to embed powerful database features such as connection management and transactions beneath the object layer and out of reach of the application developer. However, if you held the application developer responsible for all database operations, your OLE server would provide much less value in terms of simplification and encapsulation. But there is a compromise solution by which simple, everyday operations can be handled by the OLE server automatically while keeping more advanced database operations directly available to the application developer when he needs them.

The technique, which I call *plugging-in* the object layer, was developed from a recognition of a pragmatic flaw in the traditional three-tier model. The *three-tier model* places the object layer as a firm intermediary between the user-interface layer and the database layer. This implies that the application developer never needs to deal with the database directly. This assumption has two practical problems. First, it imposes an unnecessary dependency for the user interface on the object layer. If the database layer evolves to expose new functionality, the application cannot take advantage of this new functionality until the object layer evolves. Second, there is an unnecessary additional burden for the object layer when the assumption does not hold true and the application developer does need to access some of the functionality of the database layer. In this situation, the object layer is required to expose pass-through methods in its own interface.

The *plug-in model* (see Figure 11.1) recognizes the application as the owner of both the database layer and the object layer independently. The application simply creates an instance of each layer and then "plugs" the object layer into the database layer to activate its persistent features. In this way, the application still possesses a handle on the database layer and can handle advanced operations directly when it needs to. This provides the additional benefit of making it possible to plug multiple OLE servers into the same database environment or to redirect a server to another environment on-the-fly.

Figure 11.1.
The plug-in model.

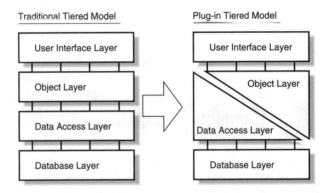

Note that in this model all of the normal access paths are still through the object layer. However, the tip of the data-access layer is exposed so that it is still possible for the application developer to get a handle on it if necessary. By default, the object layer could establish the data-access layer through some means that is hidden to the user-interface layer, but this could be overridden in exceptional cases.

Features to Consider for All Classes

The following features have been included in the standard for necessity or extreme utility; they are not all necessary, *per se*, but those that are not necessary are so useful that you probably should think long and hard before you choose to leave them out.

The `ClassName` Property

This read-only property returns the name of the class as a string. This is useful when you are trying to determine what type of object has been retrieved from a multityped collection.

The `StrVal` Property

This read-only property returns the object's entire structure in a string that can be easily passed to the `Msgbox` function. This is a useful property for debugging.

The Initialize Method

If an Initialize method exists, it needs to be called before the object is generally useful. It can be thought of as an extension to the constructor for the object. In many languages, the constructor would do all the setup and initialization that this method is supposed to do. However, in VB4, there is no way to pass parameters to a constructor, so when parameters are necessary for proper construction, this method is necessary. Likewise, sometimes an object needs information from the outside world before it is useful. The Initialize method can be used to pass information to the object so that it can set itself up properly.

The Deinitialize Method

Notice that VB4 does not require a destructor in most cases because of automatic garbage collection. Moreover, if a class must do some clean-up work before shutting down, you should first consider the class's default destructor. However, if your destructor needs parameters or needs to return a value, you must use this Deinitialize method.

The CopyFrom Method

This method's signature is as follows:

```
CopyFrom(Obj,optional Depth as long = -2)
```

CopyFrom makes another copy of an object in memory. It needs you to give it an existing object of the same type as the one you are copying. How much of the object is copied depends on the value of the Depth variable as indicated by Table 11.1. Depths of one or more indicate various class-specific depths.

Table 11.1. Depth **variable values.**

Depth	Meaning
0	Nothing
1	Key properties
2	Non-key properties
3	All primitive properties
4	Relationships
5	Key properties and relationships
6	Non-key properties and relationships
7	All properties and relationships

The `InitializeFrom` Method

This method's signature is

```
InitializeFrom(Obj)
```

If an object exposes all of its initialization properties publicly, it is possible for one object to be initialized from another object. This is particularly useful when you don't know how the other object was initialized in the first place.

The `IsEqual` Method

This method's signature is as follows:

```
IsEqual(Obj,optional Depth as long = -1) as boolean
```

It determines whether the object provided and this object are equivalent. They are considered equivalent if they possess some salient properties that have equivalent property values. If provided, the `Depth` property can be used in those cases in which there can be various definitions of equivalence for the same class. In other words, the `Depth` property provides a means of customizing which properties are considered salient and should be checked for equality. Standard depths are shown in Table 11.1. Depths of less than zero can be used for class-specific equivalencies. Note that all positive odd depths indicate that the two objects are actually the same persistent object because they share the same key.

The `IsIdentical` Method

This method's signature is as follows:

```
IsIdentical(Obj) as boolean
```

This method determines whether the object provided is the same object as the object which possesses this method. To be considered the same object, there must be a guarantee that if one of the two objects changes the other object will automatically reflect that change. Most of the time, this will indicate that they are, in fact, the exact same physical object in memory. However, in some cases, they might just cache their properties in the same place or use some means of automatic change notification.

The `Application` Class

Every OLE server should have one class called `Application`. This class represents the root of the class library; that is, it is the root of the association matrix. It should not be mistaken for the root of the inheritance hierarchy. `Application` is a class for which there is expected to be only one instance per application using the library. It should be possible to get to any object that cannot be retrieved through any other association from the `Application` object. This includes such things as independent collections of objects and other objects for which there is expected to be only one instance per application.

At a minimum, the `Application` class should contain the features described in the following sections.

The `Version` Property

This read-only property returns the version and release number using the standard dot notation for this release of the OLE server. This makes it possible for application developers to write client code that can detect whether the client has access to an OLE server in the correct release range.

The `Environment` Property

This relatively innocuous-looking property is the main key to simplifying object persistence. This property is a reference to a database environment object such as an `rdoEnvironment` or a DOA Workspace. It is assumed that this environment has been properly instantiated before this property is set to reference it. This is the plug of the "plug-in" approach described in the "Persistence Approach" section in this chapter.

The `Initialize` Method

This method's signature is

```
Initialize(optional ConnectToDBLayer = True)
```

Every `Application` class needs to provide an `Initialize` method, which is the method that establishes the connections between the object layer, the data-access layer, and the database layer. By default, this connection will be established by the `Initialize` method constructing its own data-access objects, checking the registry for a predefined constant name, and then connecting to the database associated with that name. However, if the `ConnectToDBLayer` property is set explicitly to `false`, the application developer will be responsible for creating his own data-access objects, connecting to a database, and then plugging in the object layer using the `Environment` property. Note that if other parameters need to be added to a server's `Initialize` method, they will probably be added before the `ConnectToDBLayer` parameter.

You should also consider adding the following features that have already been discussed in the "Features to Consider for All Classes" section:

- `ClassName`
- `Deinitialize`

Other optional features include those described in the following sections.

Cache

This is a reference to the cache object as described in the "The Cache Class" section of this chapter.

ObjectBroker

This is a reference to the ObjectBroker object as described in the next section, "The ObjectBroker Class."

The ObjectBroker Class

There are many times in OO programming that one needs to dynamically create an object of a class that is not known until runtime. Unfortunately, there isn't any construct for doing this in most programming languages. The ObjectBroker is a unique class that is given the strange role of being able to create an instance of any other class simply by being provided with the name of the class. As you can well imagine, the ObjectBroker is strongly coupled with the OLE server to which it belongs. The ObjectBroker object is one of those objects of which there will only be one instance in an application. Therefore, if a server has an ObjectBroker, the Application object should have a property named ObjectBroker that returns a reference to this ObjectBroker object.

The NewObject Method

The NewObject method's usage is

```
NewObject(ClassName)
```

It returns an object of the class with the class name specified. Because the Initialize methods for different objects have different signatures, it is not possible for ObjectBroker to invoke these methods. Therefore, the application developer has to initialize the returned object manually if it needs to be initialized.

Business Object Classes

In addition to the properties and behaviors inherent to the specific business object, you should consider adding all the features detailed in this section. You should also consider adding the following list of features that were discussed in the "Features to Consider for All Classes" section.

- Deinitialize
- CopyFrom
- ClassName
- IsEqual
- StrVal
- IsIdentical

The `Initialize` Method

`Initialize` is described in the "Features to Consider for All Classes" section, earlier in this chapter. At a minimum, a business object's `Initialize` method should call the `Initialize` methods of all `DependentCollections` and `DependentRelationships` if they have not already been called in the constructor.

The `Create` Method

The `Create` method creates a persistent instance of the object on disk and commits all relationships that have been established between this object and other objects.

The `Update` Method

The `Update` method updates the existing persistent instance of the object on disk and commits all new relationships that have been established or destroyed between this object and other objects.

The `Save` Method

The `Save` method determines whether it is appropriate to create or update the object and then does that. This method should be provided by your business object so that the client developer does not have to keep track of which is appropriate. Note that if it is appropriate to update the object but the server finds that the object does not exist, it will not attempt to create the object automatically.

The `Delete` Method

The `Delete` method deletes the persistent instance of the object. Note that this does not delete any of the relationships between this object and other objects.

The `CascadeDelete` Method

The `CascadeDelete` method not only deletes the persistent instance of the object, but also all relationships between that object and other objects.

The `Read` Method

This method's signature is

```
Read(optional KeyProperties...)
```

This method reads the object from disk. If the key properties are not provided directly as parameters to this method, they should be provided by instantiating the appropriate properties of the object before invoking this method.

The `IsDirty` Property

The `IsDirty` property can be used to determine if an object has changed since the last time it was saved. This can be used to do things like check to see if you should prompt the user to save his changes before closing a window. You should also know that the `Create` and `Update` methods check this property before attempting their operation so that they won't perform any unnecessary and expensive writes to disk. This gives the application developer the convenience of being able to simply tell the object to save itself without having to worry about whether the object really needs to be saved.

The `TableName` Property

The `TableName` property returns the name of the table in which the objects of this class are persistent.

Simple Collection Classes

The *simple collection classes* are an optional implementation feature designed to make independent collections even simpler for the application developer. Simple collection classes are implemented by creating a specific collection for every business object class in your server. For example, if your server had the class `CEmployee`, there would also be a class `CEmployees` that would default to a collection of all `CEmployee` objects.

Note that everything that a specific simple collection class can do can be accomplished by the far more generic `IndependentCollection` class. This is why it is optional to implement simple collection classes within a server. Because simple collections are just simplified independent collections, they should be implemented through a thin layer over the independent class.

At a minimum, simple collections should possess all the read-only capability of VB4 collections. That is, they should contain the following features with identical signatures as VB4:

- Count
- Item (Key)

Additional features of this class are detailed in the following sections.

The `ClassName` Property

The `ClassName` property is a read-only property that returns the simple collection's class name; for example, `"CEmployees"`.

The `StrVal` Property

The `StrVal` property returns the string equivalent of the collection. It iterates over the entire collection and concatenates the `StrVal` property for all members of the collection. This is useful for debugging purposes.

Reusable Objects

The following sections document classes that can be reused across multiple business object OLE servers or compiled into an independent OLE server which is itself used by multiple business object OLE servers.

The `IndependentCollection` Class

`IndependentCollections` are collections of objects that are dynamically created by querying a database of persistent objects. Because there is no simple method of guaranteeing that objects added to these collections fit the definition prescribed for the collection, these are read-only collections.

At a minimum, independent collections should possess all the read-only capability of VB4 collections. That is, they should contain the following features with identical signatures as VB4:

- ■ Count
- ■ Item(Key)

Additional features of this class are as follows.

The `ClassName` Property

The `ClassName` property is a read-only property that returns `"CIndependentCollection"`.

The `Initialize` Method

This method's signature is

```
Initialize (MembersClassName as String, SQLStatement as String,
optional ReadNow as boolean=True)
```

This method defines the `IndependentCollection` that is to be dynamically created. The `MembersClassName` parameter sets the name of the class of objects that the query is expected to return. The `SQLStatement` parameter is the query to be executed. `ReadNow` indicates whether the `Read` method should be called automatically at this time. It defaults to `True` so that the application developer need only define the collection he wants and then can begin using it immediately.

Note that the `IndependentCollection` class utilizes the `ObjectBroker` described previously to actually create the objects on-the-fly. Because the `Initialize` methods for different objects will have different signatures, it is not possible for IndependentCollection to invoke these methods. Therefore, the application developer will be required to invoke these methods if invocation is necessary.

The IsInitialized Property

This method's signature is

```
IsInitialized() as boolean
```

This read-only property returns true if the class has been initialized. Otherwise, it returns false.

The Read Method

The Read method reads the members of the collection from disk. It is not possible to use a collection until a retrieve is performed. However, it is possible to independently invoke this method because retrieving the collection might be very expensive, and therefore it is assumed that the application programmer might want to have control over it when it occurs.

The StrVal Property

The StrVal property returns the string equivalent of the collection. It iterates over the entire collection and concatenates the StrVal property for all members of the collection. This is useful for debugging purposes.

The DependentCollection Class

DependentCollections are collections of objects that must be retrieved through another object. For example, to retrieve the collection of children for a person, you must first retrieve the person. DependentCollections are used to implement all multivalued relationships.

At a minimum, DependentCollections should possess all the capability of VB4 collections. That is, they should contain the following features with identical signatures as VB4:

- Count
- Add(Object, Key, Before, After)
- Remove(Key)
- Item(Key)

Additional features of this class are detailed in the following sections.

The ClassName Property

ClassName is a read-only property that returns "CGDependentCollection".

The `Initialize` Method

This method's signature is

```
Initialize(Parent As Object, Slde As Long, LeftSuperClassName As String,
LeftRelatedClassList As String,LeftRelationshipName As String,
RightSuperClassName As String, RightRelatedClassList As String,
RightRelationshipName As String, Geneology As Long, lCardinality As Long,
Embedded As Long, LeftKeyFieldCount As Long, RightKeyFieldCount As Long,
Optional RetrieveNow as boolean=False)
```

The `Initialize` method defines the `DependentCollection` before it can be utilized by the application developer.

It is obvious that the quantity of parameters being passed to this method are ominously large. However, you should note that a user-interface developer will never have to call this method. Because these are `DependentCollections`, their `Initialize` method will be called in the constructor of the class on which they are dependent. Therefore, only object developers will have to understand the interface of this method.

The `IsInitialized` Property

This method's signature is

```
IsInitialized() as boolean
```

This read-only property returns `true` if the class has been initialized. Otherwise, it returns `false`.

The `Save` Method

The `Save` method saves all changes to disk made to the collection since the last retrieve or save. To keep track of all of the operations that have occurred, the `DependentCollection` utilizes the `ObjectTransaction` class described in the section "The `ObjectTransaction` Class."

The `Read` Method

The `Read` method reads the members of the collection from disk. It is not possible to use a collection until a read is performed. However, it is possible to independently invoke this method because reading the collection might be very expensive, and therefore it is assumed that the application programmer might want to have control over when it occurs.

The `RemoveAll` Method

The `RemoveAll` method deletes all members of the collection. It is provided so that it is possible for the collection's owner to perform a cascade delete.

The `Move` Method

This method's signature is

```
Move(Key, Before, After)
```

The `Move` method will move the member identified by `Key` to another place in the collection identified by `Before` or `After`. This method only works for ordered collections.

The `StrVal` Property

The `StrVal` property returns the string equivalent of the collection. It iterates over the entire collection and concatenates the `StrVal` property for all members of the collection. This is useful for debugging purposes.

The `DependentRelationship` Class

Whereas `DependentCollections` are used to implement multivalued relationships, `DependentRelationships` are used to implement single-valued relationships. For example, to retrieve the spouse of a woman you might use the `Husband` `DependentRelationship` of that woman.

The `ClassName` Property

The `ClassName` property is a read-only property that returns `"CGDependentRelationship"`.

The `Initialize` Method

This method's signature is

```
Initialize(Parent As Object, Side As Long, LeftSuperClassName As String,
LeftRelatedClassList As String,LeftRelationshipName As String,
RightSuperClassName As String, RightRelatedClassList As String,
RightRelationshipName As String, Geneology As Long, lCardinality As Long,
Embedded As Long, LeftKeyFieldCount As Long, RightKeyFieldCount As Long,
Optional RetrieveNow as boolean=False)
```

See "The `Initialize` Method" of "The `DependentCollection` Class" section, earlier in this chapter.

The IsInitialized Property

This method's signature is

```
IsInitialized() as booloan
```

This read-only property returns true if the class has been initialized. Otherwise, it returns false.

The Item Property

The Item property is a read-write property that can be used to set or get the related object.

The Save Method

The Save method saves all changes to disk made to the relationship since the last retrieve or save.

The StrVal Property

The StrVal property returns the string equivalent of the related object. This is useful for debugging purposes.

The Cache Class

The *cache* should be a loosely coupled, optional class that can be used to increase performance or left out to decrease complexity or size. The cache should reflect the best known current persistent state of the object. That is, the property values for the object in cache should be the same as those which are expected to be in that object's record on disk at that time. It is important to differentiate this object cache from memory or disk caching, which occurs automatically in the operating system and RDBMS. The cache object is one of those objects of which there will only be one instance in an application. Therefore, if a server has a cache, the Application object should have a property named Cache that returns a reference to this cache object.

If the CacheSize is set to a value greater than zero, all retrieved objects will be copied into cache if they are not already there. If they are already in cache, they will not be retrieved from disk. When a create is performed, the new object is added to cache. When an update operation is performed, the old object is removed from cache, and the new object is added. When a delete is performed, the deleted object is removed from cache. When a refresh is performed, the old object is removed from cache, retrieved from disk, and then added back to cache. The cache follows a first-in, first-out (FIFO) model. All objects are added to the bottom of the cache and, on overflow, items are removed from the top of cache.

Note that only the CacheSize property and the Refresh method should actually ever be called by an application developer. The rest of the interface is used internally.

The `CacheSize` Property

The `CacheSize` property sets or gets the maximum cache size. If this is set to zero (which it is by default), the `Cache` is disabled.

The `Add` Method

This method's signature is

```
Add(Obj, Key)
```

The `Add` method adds an item to cache with the specified key.

The `Remove` Method

This method's signature is

```
Remove(Key)
```

The `Remove` method removes the item in cache with the specified key.

The `Item` Method

This method's signature is

```
Item(Key)
```

The `Item` method finds the item in cache with the specified key.

The `Refresh` Method

This method's signature is

```
Refresh(Key)
```

The `Refresh` method refreshes (re-reads) the item in cache with the specified key.

The `RefreshAll` Method

The `RefreshAll` method refreshes (re-reads) the entire cache.

The `ObjectTransaction` Class

`ObjectTransaction` is a completely decoupled, optional class that can be utilized when transaction logic that is independent of the database transaction is required by an application. If an application wants to gather a number of create, modify, and delete operations before submitting them to the database, these operations can be gathered in an `ObjectTransaction` first. With `ObjectTransactions`, these operations can be submitted in batches that can be committed or rolled back as a whole. It is important to keep in mind that this is an extra transaction mechanism that is separate from, but can work in conjunction with, the transaction logic of the RDBMS. Most of the time, you will simply want to utilize the built-in, database-controlled transaction class.

The `Create` Method

This method's signature is

```
Create(object)
```

This method marks the object for creation in the transaction. The object is not actually created on disk until the commit.

The `Update` Method

This method's signature is

```
Update(object)
```

The `Update` method marks the object for update in the transaction. The object is not actually modified on disk until the commit.

The `Delete` Method

This method's signature is

```
Delete(object)
```

The `Delete` method marks the object for deletion in the transaction. The object is not actually deleted on disk until the commit.

The `Commit` Method

The `Commit` method commits to disk all object create, update, and delete operations in the transaction.

The `Rollback` Method

The `Rollback` method rolls back all object create, update, and delete operations in the transaction. The objects should reflect the same state they had before the transaction occurred. This will require refreshing (re-reading) all objects in the transaction.

The `Free` Method

This method's signature is

```
Free(object)
```

The Free method releases the specified object from the transaction. Nothing that occurred to this object in this transaction is reflected in the commit. However, the object will remain in its current state. It will not be refreshed from disk.

The FreeAll Method

The FreeAll method releases the entire transaction. This is similar to a rollback, except that all objects remain in their current state. They will not be refreshed from disk.

Summary

This chapter documents a standard of OLE server design of persistent business objects. At the time of this writing, this standard is backed by some moderately complete working implementations of real business object OLE servers.

Office Solutions and OLE Automation

by Merrill Mayer

CHAPTER 12

OLE automation is the portion of the object linking and embedding (OLE) technology that you use to automate the control of objects exposed by a separate application. It enables you to create object-oriented software by combining reusable components or objects into a single application.

This chapter introduces you to using OLE automation with Microsoft Office products and your Visual Basic applications. It covers how to incorporate Microsoft Office products as components of your applications and presents coding techniques and recommendations for implementing OLE. Information on how OLE works is also presented.

Using OLE Automation

You should use OLE automation if you want to integrate more than one application into a single tool or if you require functionality that can be found only in another application. OLE automation enables you to develop document-centric rather than application-centric software. In the *document-centric* world, the end user is not forced to navigate among a variety of applications to accomplish a task. For example, with OLE, you can write code that puts numbers in the cells of a spreadsheet without relying on any end-user activity to directly manipulate that spreadsheet. In addition, using OLE prevents the duplication of functions that already exist in other applications. You might need to use a spell checker for documents created in your application, for example. In this case, using OLE automation to access the spell checker from Microsoft Word is far easier than designing a spell-checking algorithm for your application.

Differences Between OLE Servers and Controllers

An application or tool can function as an OLE automation controller, a server, or both. An OLE automation server exposes programmable objects to other applications, enabling other applications to use the server's properties and methods. The OLE automation objects still are part of the server application. The Microsoft Office products, such as Word and Excel, are examples of applications frequently used as OLE automation servers. An OLE automation controller manipulates the objects exposed by the server application. The controller application has a reference to the objects exposed by the server. It can set and read the properties of the server application as well as execute its methods. You can use Visual Basic 4.0 to create OLE automation controller applications and OLE automation servers.

The Visual Basic development environment itself is an OLE automation server. This is very useful in developing add-ins for Visual Basic. This topic is covered in Chapter 3, "Creating a Good Interface."

Using In-Process and Out-of-Process Servers

OLE automation servers can be in-process or out-of-process servers. An *in-process* server is contained within a dynamic link library (DLL). Data is transferred directly between an in-process server and the controller application, which usually results in good performance. The server and controller must both be 32-bit or 16-bit applications. A 32-bit controller application cannot use a 16-bit DLL, for example.

An *out-of-process* server is contained in an executable file. Data is transferred indirectly between an out-of-process server and the controller application. Although performance can be much slower than when using an in-process server, out-of-process servers have their advantages. Out-of-process servers can be used in remote automation where the server is on a different computer than the controller. They can also isolate the controller application from server errors. For example, when an in-process server has a critical error, the controller application will fail. This occurs because an in-process server runs in the same address space as the controller. However, the controller application can still continue to execute even when an out-of-process server fails because the server runs in a separate address space. When used as servers in OLE automation, all Microsoft Office products are out-of-process servers.

Although there are no problems mixing 16- and 32-bit applications when you are using an out-of-process server, you should be aware that the 16-bit and 32-bit versions of Visual Basic use different character sets. The 16-bit version uses ANSI characters, and the 32-bit version uses Unicode. If you use the 16-bit version of Visual Basic on a 32-bit platform such as Windows 95 or Windows NT, the 32-bit version of the OLE server is used if both the 16- and 32-bit servers are available. In this situation, strings are converted automatically to Unicode when they are passed to the server and then converted back to ANSI when they are returned back to the controller. On the other hand, if the 32-bit version of Visual Basic is using a 16-bit OLE automation server, Unicode strings are converted automatically to ANSI when they are passed and then are converted back to Unicode when they are returned.

Using OLE Automation Controllers

An OLE automation controller is connected to an OLE automation server by a process known as binding. *Binding* is the means by which a name or variable is associated with the OLE object to which it refers. Binding puts an object into Run mode, enabling its properties and methods to be invoked.

An OLE automation controller uses one of two methods to connect to an OLE server: late binding or early binding.

Using Late Binding

Late binding is supported by all OLE automation servers. *Late binding* is runtime binding. This means that you do not receive a compile or syntax error if you invoke a property or method that is not valid for an OLE automation server. Instead, a runtime error is generated when this situation arises.

In Visual Basic, you can use late binding by declaring a variable using the generic type Object, as in the following code:

```
dim myWord as Object

set xl = CreateObject(""Word.Basic"")
```

Using the OLE Control as a Binding Method

In Visual Basic, you can use an OLE control to bind the OLE automation controller to an OLE automation server. OLE control binding is a form of late binding, so you do not get syntax checking. The OLE control's Class property is set in the same way as if the control were being used for linking or embedding. You also might want to use OLE automation to access the properties and methods of the class to which the OLE control refers. To do this, you specify the Object property of the OLE control, followed by the property or method you want to invoke for the class. You do not need to declare a variable to set the object reference because a reference is established with the Class property of the OLE control. If the Class property is set to Excel.Sheet.5, for example, you can set the value of cell A1 as shown in this code:

```
Ole1.Object.Range("A1").Value = 500
```

Using Early Binding

Early binding is compile-time binding. This means that syntax checking is provided and you are informed when an invalid property or method is invoked.

You can use early binding in Visual Basic by declaring a variable of a specific type, as shown in the following code examples:

```
dim myWord as Word.WordBasic

set myWord = CreateObject(""Word.Basic"")
```

or

```
dim myAccess as New Access.Application
```

When early binding is available, it usually is the preferred method of connecting an OLE automation controller to a server. Early binding not only allows syntax checking but also provides performance improvements over late binding.

Not all OLE automation servers support early binding. To support early binding, the server must provide an object library. Object libraries are discussed in the section, "Using Object Libraries," later in this chapter. To determine whether an object library is provided and early binding is supported, consult the documentation for the server that you are using. If early binding is supported, you must make sure that you have established a reference to the object library using the References option on the Tools menu. After you establish a reference, you can use the Object Browser to view and use the object model. For more information on using the Object Browser with OLE automation servers, see "Using the Object Browser," later in this chapter.

You also can use the References option on the Tools menu to determine whether an OLE automation server provides an object library. If the server or application that you are looking for is not listed, use the Browse button to search for type libraries (*.TLB or *.OLB), DLLs, or executable files.

Examining Object Models

OLE is based on a component object model (COM). *COM* is a standard binary interface that enables communication between objects, which allows components or objects to be integrated through OLE regardless of the programming language in which they are written. COM does not determine how objects are structured but how they function together. In this way, COM provides the interface between the components themselves and the users of those components. In other words, COM provides the basis for the communication between OLE automation servers and their controllers.

Using Object Libraries

The Component Object Manager helps components communicate by using object libraries. As discussed earlier, object libraries are essential to the use of early binding in OLE automation. Object libraries represent a hierarchy of objects exposed by the OLE automation server to the OLE automation controller. This gives the controller application access to the properties and methods of the server.

The object library hierarchy is divided into several levels. Usually, the top level contains a single object that represents the actual application being used as an OLE automation server. In Microsoft Excel, for example, the top level corresponds to the Excel application itself. You can think of the object hierarchy as a process of containment, where the higher-level objects contain the objects below them. As you progress down the object hierarchy, the levels become more specific and have a narrower scope. Again, using Excel as an example, the Application object is followed by the Workbook object at the next level, which is followed by the Worksheet object at the third level. Understanding the hierarchy of object libraries is important when you need to create references to the OLE automation servers and navigate through the various properties and methods they expose. This is covered in "Implementing OLE Automation," later in this chapter.

Using OLE and the System Registry

The system registry makes OLE automation possible. It also makes object libraries available for use by OLE automation controllers. In the system registry, every object has a ProgID. The *ProgID* is the identifier or class you use when you are creating an instance of an OLE automation server with CreateObject() or GetObject().

For example, Excel.Application is a ProgID. The ProgID maps to a class ID (CLSID), which points to the OLE automation server via the LocalServer or LocalServer32 subkey. If you look in the system registry under HKEY_LOCAL_MACHINE, the subkey SOFTWARE, and then Classes, you can find the registry entry for Excel.Application. You then can look at the CLSID key to determine the class ID for Excel.Application. Next, you can back up in the registry listings to find the CLSID subkey that is on the same level in the registry hierarchy as the Excel.Application subkey you just examined. Here, you can find the LocalServer and/or LocalServer32 entry that indicates the OLE automation server. So, if the CLSID is "00020841-0000-0000-C000-000000000046" you would find the LocalServer and/or LocalServer32 entry under "HKEY_LOCAL_MACHINE\SOFTWARE\Classes\CLSID\{00020841-0000-0000-C000-000000000046}". Figure 12.1 shows an example of how the Excel.Application registry entry might look, and Figure 12.2 shows the LocalServer32 entry.

Figure 12.1.

A registry entry for Excel.Application*.*

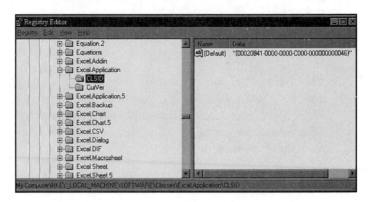

Figure 12.2.
A registry entry for
`LocalServer32.`

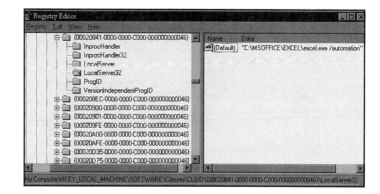

Implementing OLE Automation

After you understand the basic principles behind OLE automation, you can develop applications that use it. Several tools are available in the Visual Basic environment to assist you in your efforts. The capabilities to record macros and to use the Object Browser are included with these tools.

Recording Macros

Developing OLE automation applications means writing the code to invoke the properties and methods of the server you are using. This seems to imply that you need a thorough understanding of the object hierarchy of many different OLE automation servers. Many servers provide a shortcut, however: the macro recorder.

You can use the macro recorder to record or capture your actions as you go along, generating the code that can replicate your actions at another time. After you record a macro, you can paste the code into your controller application and modify it to run in the controller environment. This process always involves qualifying the commands generated by the macro recorder with the object variable that refers to the instance of the server. You can use the macro recorder in Microsoft Excel, for example, to create a simple procedure that places numbers in cells A1, B1, and C1; formats them to show two decimal places; and finally adds a title in a bold font. Listing 12.1 shows the recorded macro, and Listing 12.2 shows how you can modify the recorded macro to run in Visual Basic 4.0. Remember that you must also set a reference to Microsoft Excel in order for the Visual Basic code to compile.

Listing 12.1. A macro recorded in Microsoft Excel.

```
Sub MyMacro()
    ActiveCell.FormulaR1C1 = "100"
    Range("B1").Select
```

continues

Listing 12.1. continued

```
      ActiveCell.FormulaR1C1 = "200"
      Range("C1").Select
      ActiveCell.FormulaR1C1 = "300"
      Range("A1:C1").Select
      Selection.NumberFormat = "0.00"
      Selection.Font.Italic = True
      Rows("1:1").Select
      Selection.Insert Shift:=xlDown
      Range("C1").Select
      ActiveCell.FormulaR1C1 = "My Spreadsheet"
      Range("C1:D1").Select
      Selection.Font.Bold = True
      Range("E1").Select
End Sub
```

Listing 12.2. A recorded macro modified to run in Visual Basic 4.0.

```
Public Sub SetRange()

    Dim xlApp As Excel.Application

    Set xlApp = CreateObject("Excel.Application")

    With xlApp
        .Workbooks.Add
        .ActiveCell.FormulaR1C1 = "100"
        .Range("B1").Select
        .ActiveCell.FormulaR1C1 = "200"
        .Range("C1").Select
        .ActiveCell.FormulaR1C1 = "300"
        .Range("A1:C1").Select
        .Selection.NumberFormat = "0.00"
        .Selection.Font.Italic = True
        .Rows("1:1").Select
        .Selection.Insert Shift:=xlDown
        .Range("C1").Select
        .ActiveCell.FormulaR1C1 = "My Spreadsheet"
        .Range("C1:D1").Select
        .Selection.Font.Bold = True
        .Range("E1").Select
    End With

End Sub
```

In addition to modifying the recorded macro for use in Visual Basic 4.0, you can use the Run method of the application to execute code in an Excel module. For example, if you saved the macro myMacro, found in Listing 12.2 in the Excel spreadsheet, testMacro.xls, the code in Listing 12.3 could be used to run that macro from Visual Basic.

Listing 12.3. Executing an Excel macro from Visual Basic 4.0.

```
Public Sub SetRange()

Dim xl As Excel.Application

    Set xl = CreateObject("Excel.Application")
    xl.Workbooks.Open filename:="C:\WINDOWS\Personal\testMacro.xls"
    xl.Run ("myMacro")

End Sub
```

Obviously, how you record or run a macro differs, depending on the OLE automation server you use. You should consult the documentation or help files for the server you are using.

Using the Object Browser

Just as recording macros in the OLE automation server application can assist you in the development process, so can using the Object Browser. The Object Browser enables you to paste the properties and methods of the OLE automation server you are working with directly into your OLE automation controller code. Remember that you first must establish a reference to the OLE automation server using the References choice on the Tools menu. After you establish a reference, you can select the OLE automation server you are using from the Libraries/Projects drop-down list in the Object Browser. At this point, using the Object Browser to paste OLE server methods and properties has the same effect as pasting any other methods and properties into your code. Figure 12.3 shows how you can select the Range method of the Worksheet object in Microsoft Excel from the Object Browser. Listing 12.4 shows the result of pasting in the code.

Figure 12.3.
Using the Object Browser.

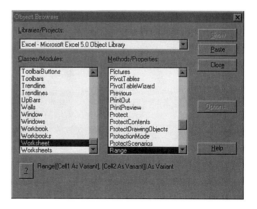

Listing 12.4. Pasting the Range **method from the Object Browser.**

```
Dim xlSheet As Excel.Worksheet

    Set xlSheet = CreateObject("Excel.sheet")


    xlSheet.Range(Cell1:=, Cell2:=)
```

> The code shown in Listing 12.4 would have to be modified to provide values for the
> cell's argument before the code could run. The following modification would run and
> select the range of cells A1 through C3, for example:
> ```
> xlSheet.Range(Cell1:="A1", Cell2:="C3").Select
> ```

The Object Browser not only provides the capability to paste the properties and methods of OLE
automation servers into your application but also enables you to use the Help system for those
objects. You can click the ? button in the Object Browser, as shown in Figure 12.3, for example,
to get help on the Range method. You also can use the Object Browser to view and paste the
constants defined in the server application. Figure 12.4 shows the Microsoft Excel application
constants in the Object Browser.

Figure 12.4.
*Using Microsoft Excel
constants with the Object
Browser.*

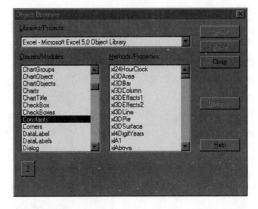

You also can use the Object Browser to navigate through the object library to see how the exposed
server objects, properties, and methods fit together. If you examine the Microsoft Excel 5.0
Object Library in the Object Browser and select Application from the Classes/Modules listbox,
for example, you can see the properties and methods of the Application object. If you examine
the Methods/Properties listbox, you will find that several of them also are listed in the Classes/
Modules listbox.

An example of this is the Workbooks method. Notice that Workbooks appears in both the Classes/ Modules and Methods/Properites. Therefore, Workbooks represents a dependent object of the Application object as well as a class. In addition, you will notice that both Workbooks and Workbook are present in the Classes/Modules listbox. You can be fairly certain that Workbooks represents a collection of Workbook objects. You can verify this by using the online Help system. Continuing with this process, you can look for the properties and methods of the Workbook object and then continue searching through the object library hierarchy. The capability to use the Object Browser to navigate through an object library's hierarchy becomes more significant as you write the code that accesses OLE automation server objects.

Using Named Versus Ordered Arguments

You use ordered arguments to pass the parameters to a procedure in a specified sequence. Using the Range method as an example, you can invoke it and pass its arguments in sequence, as shown in Listing 12.5.

Listing 12.5. Using ordered arguments.

```
Dim xlSheet As Excel.Worksheet

    Set xlSheet = CreateObject("Excel.sheet")

    xlSheet.Range("A1","C3").value = 500
```

Because the Range method does not have a large number of arguments, it is easy to keep the arguments in the correct order. If a large number of arguments is passed, however, their order easily can be confused, and the purpose of each argument can be lost. In addition, with named arguments, you do not need to include placeholders, such as commas, for the arguments you do not want to specify. It therefore often is clearer to use named arguments.

Named arguments use the following syntax:

Name of Argument := Value

Listing 12.6 shows the code from Listing 12.5 with the necessary modifications to use named arguments.

Listing 12.6. Using named arguments.

```
Dim xlSheet As Excel.Worksheet

    Set xlSheet = CreateObject("Excel.sheet")

    xlSheet.Range(Cell1:="A1", Cell2:="C3").Value = 500
```

You can use the Object Browser to become familiar with named arguments. Code pasted from the Object Browser always uses named argument syntax.

Referencing Objects

To use OLE automation objects, you need to somehow reference them. In Visual Basic, you use the Dim and Set statements to create variables that refer to OLE automation objects.

Using the New Keyword

The simplest way to declare a variable for a specific object type is by using the New keyword. Using the New keyword automatically initializes the variable so that a Set statement is not required. Because it only works with specific object types, the New keyword requires an object library and results in early binding of the controller application to the server. The syntax for using the New keyword follows:

```
Dim variable As New Application.ObjectType
```

Many OLE automation servers, such as Excel, do not support the New keyword. Therefore, despite its simplicity, you probably should avoid using it.

Using the CreateObject Function

If you do not use the New keyword or if an object does not have an object library, you must use the CreateObject() function to create a reference to a new object. The CreateObject() function is used with the Dim statement. Two examples of the syntax for CreateObject() follow:

```
Dim myObject as Object                          'late binding

Set myObject = CreateObject("Application.ObjectType")

or

Dim myObject as Application.ObjectType          'early binding

Set myObject = CreateObject("Application.ObjectType")
```

Notice that the first example results in late binding whereas the second example results in early binding. Late and early binding are discussed earlier in this chapter.

Using the `GetObject` Function

You use the `GetObject()` function to get a reference to an existing object in an OLE automation server. If more than one instance of a particular server is running, you cannot determine which instance will be the active instance when the `GetObject` function is used. The syntax for the `GetObject()` function follows:

```
Set myOjbect = GetObject([pathname][,class])
```

Both `CreateObject()` and `GetObject()` behave differently, depending on the OLE automation server specified, what arguments are passed, and whether the referenced OLE server is running. Although the `CreateObject()` function has the class as its only argument, `GetObject()` includes *pathname* as its optional first argument. You can use the *pathname* argument to specify the fully qualified path to an existing file or an empty string. Specifying a path normally causes `GetObject()` to use an existing instance of the server, whereas using an empty string normally results in creating a new instance as though `CreateObject()` were used.

> Many OLE automation servers, such as Microsoft Word or Microsoft Excel, do not enable you to open files with the `GetObject()` function. Instead, you must use a method of the OLE server to open a file. Use the `Workbooks.Open` method in Excel or the `FileOpen` method in Word, for example.

Table 12.1 shows the different results you get when you use the `CreateObject()` and `GetObject()` functions when you are referencing top-level (`Application`) objects for Microsoft Office products.

Table 12.1. Using `CreateObject()` **and** `GetObject()`**.**

Server Name	Server Running	Function	Result
Microsoft Excel	No	`CreateObject("Excel.Application")`	Creates a new instance
Microsoft Excel	Yes	`CreateObject("Excel.Application")`	Creates a new instance
Microsoft Excel	No	`GetObject(,"Excel.Application")`	OLE automation error
Microsoft Excel	Yes	`GetObject(,"Excel.Application")`	Uses an existing instance
Microsoft Excel	No	`GetObject("","Excel.Application")`	Creates a new instance

continues

Table 12.1. continued

Server Name	Server Running	Function	Result
Microsoft Excel	Yes	`GetObject("","Excel.Application")`	Creates a new instance
Microsoft Word	No	`CreateObject("Word.Basic")`	Creates a new instance
Microsoft Word	Yes	`CreateObject("Word.Basic")`	Uses an existing instance
Microsoft Word	No	`GetObject(,"Word.Basic")`	OLE automation error
Microsoft Word	Yes	`GetObject(,"Word.Basic")`	OLE automation error
Microsoft Word	No	`GetObject("","Word.Basic")`	Creates a new instance
Microsoft Word	Yes	`GetObject("","Word.Basic")`	Uses an existing instance
Microsoft Project	No	`CreateObject("MSProject.Application")`	Creates a new instance
Microsoft Project	Yes	`CreateObject("MSProject.Application")`	Uses an existing instance
Microsoft Project	No	`GetObject(, "MSProject.Application")`	OLE automation error
Microsoft Project	Yes	`GetObject(, "MSProject.Application")`	Uses an existing instance
Microsoft Project	No	`GetObject("","MSProject.Application")`	Creates a new instance
Microsoft Project	Yes	`GetObject("","MSProject.Application")`	Uses an existing instance
Microsoft Access	No	`CreateObject("Access.Application")`	Creates a new instance
Microsoft Access	Yes	`CreateObject("Access.Application")`	Creates a new instance
Microsoft Access	No	`GetObject(, "Access.Application")`	OLE automation error
Microsoft Access	Yes	`GetObject(, "Access.Application")`	Uses an existing instance

Server Name	Server Running	Function	Result
Microsoft Access	No	`GetObject("", "Access.Application")`	Creates a new instance
Microsoft Access	Yes	`GetObject("", "Access.Application")`	Creates a new instance

Qualifying References

When you refer to OLE automation objects, it is very important to fully qualify all references. This means using the library name as the first-level qualifier. You can find the library name in the Libraries/Projects drop-down list of the Object Browser. The information in this list consists of the library name followed by the reference title. The library name for the Microsoft Excel 5.0 Object Library is Excel, and the library name for Microsoft Access for Windows 95 is Access.

Fully qualifying object references is essential in order to distinguish between the various applications used in OLE automation because many OLE automation servers have the same properties and methods. If object references are not fully qualified, your Visual Basic application uses the properties and methods from the object library with the highest priority. As discussed earlier in this chapter, object libraries are made available in the Visual Basic environment through the References dialog box, which you access by choosing References from the Tools menu. The References dialog box displays object libraries by their priority in descending order. It also enables you to adjust the priority of object libraries by using the priority buttons. In Figure 12.5, you can see that the Microsoft Excel 5.0 Object Library has a higher priority than the Microsoft Project 4.1 Object Library.

Figure 12.5.
Object Library priorities.

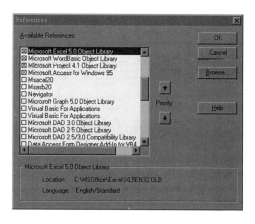

If you try to implement OLE automation using Microsoft Excel and Microsoft Project as servers, you can see the results of both the priority structure of the object libraries in Visual Basic and the results of qualifying or not qualifying references. Note that when you use the CreateObject() or GetObject() function, you are establishing the object library reference, thereby ensuring that the variable you define with Set provides the means to fully qualify object references.

In Listing 12.7, you can see what happens when you qualify the Parent property to ensure references first from Microsoft Excel and then from Microsoft Project. Finally, an unqualified reference is used. The MsgBox statements show that the qualified references give the expected results, and the unqualified reference returns Microsoft Excel as the Parent property because it has a higher priority than Microsoft Project. From this example, it's easy to see how failing to qualify references can lead to unpredictable results.

Listing 12.7. Qualifying object references.

```
Sub QualifyReferences()

    Dim xlApp As Excel.Application
    Dim projApp As MSProject.Project
    Dim sParent As String

    Set xlApp = CreateObject("Excel.Application")
    Set projApp = CreateObject("MsProject.Project")

    sParent = xlApp.Parent
    MsgBox "xlApp.Parent = " & sParent

    sParent = projApp.Parent
    MsgBox "projApp.Parent = " & sParent

    sParent = Parent
    MsgBox "Unqualified = " & sParent

    xlApp.Quit
    projApp.Application.Quit
    Set xlApp = Nothing

    Set projApp = Nothing
End Sub
```

Using Externally Creatable Versus Dependent Objects

Only some of the objects exposed through the object library can be accessed directly by setting a reference to them from outside the OLE server that created them. These objects are considered to be *externally creatable* objects. The top-level object usually falls into this category. In the Visual Basic environment, an object is externally creatable if you can set a reference to it with the New keyword or with the CreateObject() and GetObject() functions. The Excel application object is externally creatable. Table 12.2 shows the externally creatable objects for Microsoft Word, Excel, Access, and Project.

Table 12.2. Externally creatable objects.

Application	Object type	Class
Microsoft Excel	Application	`Excel.Application`
	Worksheet	`Excel.Sheet`
	Chart	`Excel.Chart`
Microsoft Project	Application	`MSProject.Application`
	Project	`MSProject.Project`
Microsoft Word	WordBasic	`Word.Basic`
Microsoft Access	Application	`Access.Application`

Objects that cannot be accessed directly by creating references to them in the OLE automation controller applications are considered to be dependent objects. *Dependent objects* can be accessed only by using a method of a higher-level object. The `Range` object in Excel, for example, can be accessed first by creating a reference to a `Sheet` object and then by accessing it through the `Sheet` object. Listing 12.8 shows an example of how the `Range` object can be used.

Listing 12.8. Accessing the `Range` object in Microsoft Excel.

```
Public Sub SetRange()

    Dim xlSheet As Excel.Worksheet

    Set xlSheet = CreateObject("Excel.Sheet")
    xlSheet.Visible = True
    xlSheet.Range("a1").Value = 500
End Sub
```

Because many OLE automation servers, such as Microsoft Excel, expose a great number of objects, determining the structure of an object library's hierarchy is often difficult. The Object Browser provides an excellent way to view the hierarchy of a server and to determine its methods and properties.

Using Properties and Methods

After you establish a reference to an OLE automation server, you can invoke its properties and methods. Many examples of using properties and methods have already been presented in this chapter. Both the `Range` method and the `Parent` property were used to explain various aspects of OLE automation. By examining these examples, you can see that the syntax follows the usual Visual Basic Object.Method or Object.Property syntax. Although it is beyond the scope of this chapter to discuss all the properties and methods of the OLE automation servers available through the Microsoft Office products, you should examine some general concepts that apply to properties and methods used with OLE automation servers.

You probably have noticed that it often is quite cumbersome to navigate through the hierarchy of objects to finally get to the property or method you want to invoke. When you combine this with the need to fully qualify object references, you might find that you are writing very long statements when you use OLE automation. You can use a few techniques, however, to help you shorten these statements and improve the readability of your code. These techniques include using the With...End With statement, declaring object variables, and using certain properties.

Using the With...End With Statement

You can use the With...End With statement to set multiple properties for an object without specifying the object's name each time a property is set. You can nest With...End With statements, which greatly reduces the length of statements used to reference OLE automation objects and their properties. Using With...End With statements not only shortens the amount of code you have to write, but also provides a performance gain in OLE automation. When you use a With...End With statement, the connection to the server is left open so that messages can be sent far more quickly between the controller and server application. Listing 12.9 shows an example of using the With...End With statement. In this example, a Worksheet object is created and then a range is selected. Notice that another With...End With statement is nested, which sets the Font.Bold and Value properties for the Range selected.

Listing 12.9. Using the With...End With statement.

```
Sub SetRange()

    Dim xl As Excel.Worksheet

    Set xl = CreateObject("Excel.sheet")

    With xl
        .Range("A1:C3").Select
        With .Application.Selection
            .Value = 100
            .Font.Bold = True
        End With
    End With

    xl.Application.Quit
    Set xl = Nothing
End Sub
```

Using Object Variables

Using object variables shortens object expressions and reduces execution time. You can create object variables by using a combination of the Dim and Set statements. You can use a specific or generic object type when you create object variables. Listing 12.10 demonstrates how to set a reference to an Excel Application object, add two workbooks, and select a specific worksheet and range. This example uses a specific object reference to a worksheet and includes the use of the With...End With statement, along with the object variable.

Listing 12.10. Using object variables.

```
Sub AddWorkbooks()

    Dim xl As Excel.Application
    Dim mySheet As Worksheet

    Set xl = CreateObject("Excel.Application")
    With xl
        .Workbooks.Add
        .Workbooks.Add
        Set mySheet = .Workbooks(2).Worksheets(3)
        .Visible = True
    End With
    mySheet.Select
    mySheet.Range("A1:C3").Value = 100

    xl.Quit
    Set xl = Nothing

End Sub
```

Using Properties as a Navigational Shortcut

Some OLE automation servers support properties that help you navigate through the object hierarchy and shorten the expressions you use when you refer to objects. Microsoft Excel, for example, has Parent and Application properties as well as a default property for many objects. The Parent property returns the owner for the specified object. You even can use the Parent property to get the owner of the Parent object by specifying Object.Parent.Parent. Listing 12.11 shows how you can use the Parent property to obtain information. The MsgBox statement displays the objects returned by using the Parent property. In this example, the Parent object of mySheet is a workbook, and its parent is the Application object. Therefore, mySheet.Parent.Parent.Name returns the same information as xl.Name.

Listing 12.11. Using the `Parent` **property.**

```
Sub FindParent()

    Dim xl As Excel.Application
    Dim mySheet As Worksheet
    Dim sName As String

    Set xl = CreateObject("Excel.Application")
    With xl
        .Workbooks.Add
        Set mySheet = .Workbooks(1).Worksheets(1)
    End With

    sName = mySheet.Parent.Name
    MsgBox "Parent = " & sName
    sName = mySheet.Parent.Parent.Name
    MsgBox "Parent.Parent = " & sName
    MsgBox "Application = " & xl.Name

    xl.Quit
    Set xl = Nothing
End Sub
```

The `Application` property provides access to the properties and methods of the `Application` object to lower-level objects. If you define a reference to an Excel worksheet, as shown in Listing 12.12, you can use the `Application` property to get the `Name` property of the application or to invoke the `Quit` method.

Listing 12.12. Using the `Application` **property.**

```
Sub SetRange()

    Dim xl As Excel.Worksheet
    Dim sName As String

    Set xl = CreateObject("Excel.sheet")
    sName = xl.Application.Name

    xl.Application.Quit
    Set xl = Nothing
End Sub
```

Finally, many objects in Excel have a default property. A *default property* is the property accessed when no property is specified. The `Name` property, for example, is the default property for the `Application` object. This means that in Listing 12.12, you could have set the value of the `sName` variable as the following:

```
sName = xl.Application
```

Although the result of using the default property in the preceding code is the same as the code in Listing 12.12 and the expression is shorter, using default properties can be confusing. Someone reading your code might not always be sure what property you are accessing. If you forget what the default property is, you also might get surprising results in your application. Therefore, you should use the default property with caution.

Using Collections

A *collection* is a group of objects of a related type. The collection itself is also an object. The standard naming convention for collection objects is to use the plural name of the individual objects that make up the collection. The collection of worksheets in Microsoft Excel or forms in Microsoft Access are examples of collections. The individual objects in the collection do not have a fixed size or position. You therefore cannot assume that what is currently the first worksheet in the Worksheets collection always will be first.

Collections typically support the capability to add new members to the group, to remove members from the group, to get a count of existing members, and to iterate through the individual collections. Listing 12.13 shows examples of adding a new worksheet to the Worksheets collection, removing a worksheet, and getting a count of Worksheets.

Listing 12.13. Using collections.

```
Sub AddSheets()

    Dim xl As Excel.Worksheet

    Set xl = CreateObject("Excel.Sheet")
    With xl
        .Parent.Worksheets.Add
        MsgBox .Parent.Worksheets.Count
        .Parent.Worksheets(1).Delete
        MsgBox .Parent.Worksheets.Count
    End With

    xl.Application.Quit
    Set xl = Nothing

End Sub
```

Iterating Through Collections

Visual Basic provides a way to iterate through each member in a collection with the For Each...Next statement. The For Each...Next statement enables you to execute the same code for every member in the collection. Listing 12.14 shows an example of this statement. Notice that the information displayed by the `MsgBox` statement reflects the property settings for each individual member in the collection.

Listing 12.14. Iterating through collections.

```
Sub MoveThroughSheets()

    Dim xl As Excel.Application
    Dim mySheet As Worksheet

    Set xl = CreateObject("Excel.Application")
    With xl
        .Workbooks.Add
        For Each mySheet In .Worksheets
            MsgBox mySheet.Name
            MsgBox mySheet.Range("a1").Font.Size
        Next mySheet
    End With

    xl.Quit
    Set xl = Nothing


End Sub
```

Handling Errors

When you use OLE automation, it often is difficult to determine where errors occur. OLE automation errors can be passed back from the server or can be Visual Basic trappable errors. If the OLE automation server does not handle a particular error, it is passed back to Visual Basic.

You can handle OLE automation errors by using the same error-trapping techniques you normally use in Visual Basic. This category of errors presents a unique set of problems for the Visual Basic developer, however.

Handling Trappable Errors

Visual Basic can handle many types of OLE automation errors. These errors indicate a specific condition that caused Visual Basic to raise an error. You might receive an error message indicating that the OLE automation server can't create the object or that a specific property or method is not supported, for example. The Visual Basic online Help system provides a list of these OLE automation errors. Listing 12.15 shows examples of code that cause specific OLE automation errors.

Listing 12.15. Specific OLE automation errors.

```
sub myErrors()
    Dim xl As Excel.Application
    On Error GoTo myError
'generate err 429 - can't create object
    Set xl = CreateObject("Excel.Apps")
'generate error 438 - object doesn't support this property or method
    xl.workbooks.add
    xl.Workbooks(1).Worksheets(1).Range("A1").Font.ZZZZ = False
    xl.Quit
    Set xl = Nothing
    Exit Sub

myError:
    MsgBox Err.Number & " " & Err.Description
End Sub
```

> Listing 12.15 contains an error trap, so you will never get the second error unless you fix the first error by changing `"Excel.Apps"` to `"Excel.Application"`.

Handling Errors Generated by a Condition Within the Server

Sometimes the OLE automation server can pass back its own error condition to the controller application. These errors usually provide important information about what conditions caused the error. You should be careful in how you interpret these errors, however, because an OLE server error might have the same value as a Visual Basic error and cause you to misinterpret the problem. Listing 12.16 results in error 1004 with the description `Cannot find C:\WINDOWS\Personal\testMacro.xll`.

Listing 12.16. Errors passed back from an OLE automation server.

```
Sub SetRange()

    Dim xl As Excel.Application
    On Error GoTo myError
    Set xl = CreateObject("Excel.Application")
'the following generates an error
    xl.Workbooks.Open filename:="C:\WINDOWS\Personal\testMacro.xll"
    xl.Workbooks(1).Worksheets(1).Range("A1").Font.Bold = False
    xl.Quit
    Set xl = Nothing
    Exit Sub

myError:

    MsgBox Err.Number & " " & Err.Description
End Sub
```

In addition to the errors returned from an OLE automation server, you have to handle situations that arise when the server cannot immediately respond to the request from your controller application. In this case, Visual Basic displays the Server Busy dialog box, as shown in Figure 12.6.

Figure 12.6.
The Server Busy
dialog box.

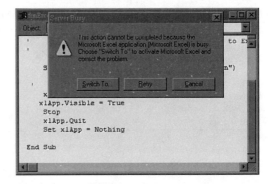

The Server Busy dialog box appears when the OLE automation server is busy and cannot respond to the controller application's request or when a long-running activity, such as a database query, is in process. In the first case, the message box represents a Server Busy condition, and in the second case, it represents a request-pending condition. The only difference in the appearance of the Server Busy dialog box is that the Cancel button is disabled (grayed out) when a request is pending. The Cancel button is disabled because you cannot cancel a request that has been accepted by the server.

Responding to the Server Busy Condition

The Server Busy condition often occurs when mouse or keyboard input is received while an OLE automation request is pending. You easily can create this situation by making your OLE server visible, entering some data directly into it, and then trying to terminate the server application in your Visual Basic code. You usually can resolve the impasse created by the Server Busy condition by switching to the server application and completing whatever activity was in progress. If you are entering data into a Microsoft Excel spreadsheet cell, for example, finishing the data-entry process enables your controller application to terminate the OLE server. In addition, to simply activate the server and correct the situation that caused the Server Busy condition, you can set several properties that increase your control over what happens when an OLE automation server cannot respond to a request.

First of all, you might want to increase the `OLEServerBusyTimeout` property to give your server more time to complete a task or perhaps decrease it to display the Server Busy dialog box more quickly. Its default value is 10000 milliseconds. In addition, you can change the Server Busy dialog box. Listing 12.17 shows an example of increasing the server time-out value and creating a custom message. The stop statement is included for demonstration purposes to enable you to actually activate Excel and enter something into a worksheet cell. Entering data into Excel causes the Save dialog box to appear if you try to terminate Excel without saving the worksheet. Figure 12.7 shows the message displayed when the Visual Basic code tries to terminate Excel. This message is displayed because Excel is waiting for a response to the Save dialog. Note that if you click the Cancel button, an OLE automation error occurs. Clicking the Retry button after completing the cell-editing procedure in Excel forces you to return once more to Excel to respond to the Save dialog box.

Listing 12.17. Customizing the Server Busy dialog box.

```
Sub SetServerBusy()

    Dim xlApp As Excel.Application

    App.OleServerBusyTimeout = 20000
    App.OleServerBusyMsgTitle = "Excel is busy"
    App.OleServerBusyMsgText =
    ➥"Please switch to Excel and complete your activity"

    Set xlApp = CreateObject("Excel.Application")

    xlApp.Workbooks.Add
    xlApp.Visible = True
    Stop
    xlApp.Quit
    Set xlApp = Nothing

End Sub
```

Figure 12.7.
Customizing the Server Busy dialog box.

Aside from the capability to customize the Server Busy dialog box, you have the additional option of forcing an error when the server is busy. You do this by setting the OLEServerBusyRaiseError property to True. When this property is set to True, Visual Basic still retries your request for the length of time set by the OLEServerBusyTimeout property. When the time-out period expires, however, the Server Busy dialog box is not displayed, even if you have set up a custom message. Instead, an error is raised, which you should handle with an appropriate error-trapping routine. Listing 12.18 demonstrates raising an error when the server is busy.

Listing 12.18. Raising an error when the server is busy.

```
Sub SetServerBusy()

    Dim xlApp As Excel.Application

    App.OleServerBusyTimeout = 20000
    App.OleServerBusyMsgTitle = "Excel is busy"
    App.OleServerBusyMsgText =
    ➥"Please switch to Excel and complete your activity"
    App.OleServerBusyRaiseError = True

    Set xlApp = CreateObject("Excel.Application")
    On Error GoTo ErrorTrap
    xlApp.Workbooks.Add
    xlApp.Visible = True
    Stop
    xlApp.Quit
    Set xlApp = Nothing
exit sub

ErrorTrap:
    MsgBox Err.Number & " " & Err.Description
End Sub
```

Handling a Request-Pending Condition

Unlike the Server Busy condition, the request-pending condition normally cannot be addressed by switching focus to the OLE server and completing the pending task. Instead, the best way to deal with a request-pending situation is to modify the server time-out intervals to accommodate any long-running tasks. In Visual Basic, you do this by increasing the OLERequestPendingTimeout property. The default value for this property is 5000 milliseconds. You also can change the message displayed by the Server Busy dialog box when an OLE automation request is pending. You use the properties OLERequestPendingMsgTitle and OLERequestPendingMsgText to accomplish this. You set these properties in the same way as the corresponding properties for handling a busy server, so refer to Listing 12.18 for more information.

Closing the OLE Server and Releasing an Object

Object reference counts are incremented every time your Visual Basic program uses a Set statement. Many OLE servers automatically close when the reference count to the object is zero. Not all OLE automation servers do this, however, so you must use a method that closes the object. Microsoft Excel is an example of an OLE automation server that requires you to explicitly close it. The code examples in this chapter demonstrate how to close Microsoft Excel with the Quit method. Because there seem to be more and more OLE automation servers available and you will not always be sure of their behavior, it is a good idea to always close all automation objects.

Aside from the need to close OLE automation objects when you are finished with them, you also should release all objects from memory by setting them to Nothing. Listing 12.19 shows how to close a WordBasic object and release the object variable from memory.

Listing 12.19. Closing OLE servers and releasing objects.

```
Sub CloseWord()

    Dim wd As Word.WordBasic

    Set wd = CreateObject("Word.Basic")
    wd.AppClose
    Set wd = Nothing

End Sub
```

> Object variables are cleared when they go out of scope, so be careful where and how you declare object variables in your controller application. The code listings in this chapter typically use procedure-level object variables in order to increase visibility between the variable declaration and the rest of the code. This technique is not meant to imply that a procedure-level variable is always the best choice.

Summary

Using OLE automation with Microsoft Office products enables you to integrate office applications with Visual Basic. You can take advantage of features already built into Microsoft Office applications and use them in your own applications.

This chapter covered how OLE automation works with Visual Basic. You learned how to navigate through an object hierarchy using the Object Browser, the differences between in-process and out-of-process servers, how to use early and late binding, and how to set object references. In addition, you learned several coding techniques such as using properties and methods, as well as error handling.

Chapter 13, "Implementing Office Automation with MSOffice Products," expands upon what you learned in this chapter. It goes into detail about how to use Microsoft Office products as OLE automation servers. It covers coding techniques for working with Work, Excel, and Access.

Implementing Office Automation with MSOffice Products

by Merrill Mayer

CHAPTER

13

In Chapter 12, "Office Solutions and OLE Automation," you were introduced to some of the technical aspects of OLE automation, as well as some basic techniques for implementing OLE. This chapter expands on those techniques to provide more complete examples of using OLE automation with Microsoft Office products. Specifically, you learn how to use Microsoft Word, Excel, and Access as OLE Automation servers from the Visual Basic environment. You also learn techniques for starting and terminating the OLE servers, sending information to and receiving information from the servers, and invoking the features and functions of the particular server.

> All the examples of Microsoft Office products as OLE servers are based on the version 7.0 (Windows 95) release of the products.

Using OLE Automation with Microsoft Excel

Your Visual Basic controller application can use the many objects exposed by Microsoft Excel via OLE automation. Microsoft Excel uses Visual Basic for Applications as its macro language, so its syntax should seem very familiar. It does, of course, have its own unique properties and methods that control things like spreadsheet and charting functions. Some of these functions are presented in this chapter.

As discussed in Chapter 12, you begin using Microsoft Excel as an OLE automation server by setting a reference to the `Application`, `Chart`, and `Sheet` objects. All other dependent objects must be accessed via a reference to the `Application`, `Chart`, or `Sheet` objects.

Starting Microsoft Excel

You can create a reference to Microsoft Excel by using the `CreateObject()` and `GetObject()` functions. Although using these functions is covered in Chapter 12, you should consider a few implementation issues here. Suppose that you want your Visual Basic application to use an existing instance of Microsoft Excel if it is available and to create a new instance if it is not. Creating a reference to Excel using `GetObject()` when there is no running instance of Microsoft Excel generates an OLE automation error. This means that your Visual Basic application must somehow handle this situation. Listing 13.1 provides a solution to this dilemma. In the code, if an instance of Excel is running, it is used. Otherwise, an error occurs and a new instance is started.

Listing 13.1. Starting Microsoft Excel.

```
Dim xl As Excel.Application

    On Error Resume Next
    Set xl = GetObject(, "Excel.Application")
    If xl Is Nothing Then
        Set xl = CreateObject("Excel.Application")
    End If

    xl.Workbooks.Add
```

Notice that the Add method is used in this sample to create a new workbook. When the code creates a new instance of Excel, this will be the only workbook. When the code uses an existing instance of Excel, the Add method creates a new workbook in addition to those already present. Typically, you use the Add method to create dependent objects, such as workbooks.

Creating New Workbooks

You use Microsoft Excel workbooks to store data. Workbooks are composed of one or more sheets, which can be worksheets, charts, or modules.

If you just created a new reference to Microsoft Excel with CreateObject() or GetObject(), the application will contain no open workbooks. By using the Add method, you can create one or more workbooks in your Excel application. When you use the Add method to create new workbooks, the workbooks you create contain the number of sheets as defined by the SheetsInNewWorkbook property. You use the General tab of the Options dialog box to set this property, but you also can set this in code. The code in Listing 13.2 adds two workbooks, each with seven sheets. It also sets the Visible property of the Application object to True, because Excel always starts in an invisible state. The code assumes that xlBook already has been declared as a module-level variable.

Listing 13.2. Creating workbooks.

```
Sub AddWorkbooks()

    Set xlBook = CreateObject("Excel.Application")
    With xlBook
        .SheetsInNewWorkbook = 7
        .Workbooks.Add
        .Workbooks.Add
        .Visible = True
    End With

End Sub
```

Opening Existing Workbooks

You can use OLE automation to open an existing workbook by using the `GetObject()` function and the `Sheet` object or the `Workbooks.Open` method. When you use OLE automation to open an existing workbook, the number of sheets in that workbook corresponds to the number of sheets present when the workbook was saved last. Listings 13.3 and 13.4 show each method, respectively. Both listings assume that the variable, `xlBook`, already has been declared. Note that in Listing 13.3, you must make the window containing the workbook visible in order for it not to be hidden when you make the application visible. You also should be aware that it is not necessary to make your server application visible if you only want to perform some behind-the-scenes functions, such as calculations in Microsoft Excel. Making a server application visible, however, does enable you to use the server application to display information as well as to receive user input.

Listing 13.3. Opening workbooks with `GetObject`.

```
Sub OpenWorkBooks()

    Set xlBook = GetObject("C:\WINDOWS\Personal\tstexprt.xls", "Excel.Sheet")

'makes workbook visible
    xlBook.Application.Windows("tstexprt.xls").Visible = True
    xlBook.Application.Visible = True

End Sub
```

Listing 13.4. Opening workbooks with the `Open` method.

```
Sub OpenWorkBooks()

Set xlBook = CreateObject("Excel.Application")
    xlBook.Workbooks.Open filename:="C:\WINDOWS\Personal\testMacro.xls"
    xlBook.Application.Visible = True

End Sub
```

Using Worksheets

As stated previously, new workbooks always contain the default number of sheets, and existing workbooks have the number of sheets that were present when the workbook was last saved. You still can add and delete sheets in a workbook, however. In addition, you can iterate through the `WorkSheets` collection just as you can with other Microsoft Excel collections.

All the collections in Microsoft Excel are one-based rather than zero-based. This means that the first worksheet is referenced as Worksheets(1).

Listing 13.5 demonstrates how to add a new workbook and three new worksheets, and then move through all the worksheets in the workbook you just added. If you do not specify the workbook, worksheets always are added to the active workbook. In Listing 13.5, there is only one workbook, so it is the active workbook. If you run the code in Listing 13.5, you are asked whether you want to save the changes you made to the Excel application. You receive this message even though you have not even made Excel visible. You cannot set the DisplayAlerts property to False in order to repress this message when you use OLE automation because Microsoft Excel immediately sets it back to True.

Listing 13.5. Using worksheets.

```
Sub AddSheets()

    Dim xl As Excel.Application
    Dim mySheet As Worksheet

    Set xl = CreateObject("Excel.Application")
With xl
        .Workbooks.Add
        .Worksheets.Add Count:=3
        MsgBox "WorkbookCount = " & .Workbooks.Count
        MsgBox "WorkSheetCount = " & .Worksheets.Count
        For Each mySheet In .Worksheets
            MsgBox "WorkSheet Name = " & mySheet.Name
        Next mySheet
        .Quit
    End With

Set xl = Nothing

End Sub
```

You can use the same technique you use to add new worksheets to add dialog sheets, modules, and charts. The following code adds a new module to the active workbook:

```
xl.Modules.Add
```

Working with Ranges

The capability to manipulate workbooks and worksheets is, in itself, not all that useful. You can use the Range method of the Worksheet object, however, to set and retrieve values. Using the Range method, you can place a single value in a specific worksheet cell, the same value in multiple cells, or even use an array to put multiple values into multiple cells. You can use the same techniques to retrieve values from a worksheet. Listing 13.6 shows how to use the Range method to set values and formulas. Note that the code starts out by creating a reference to a worksheet, thereby eliminating the need to first add a workbook in order to get access to a worksheet.

Listing 13.6. Using the Range method.

```
Sub SetRange()

    Dim xl As Excel.Worksheet
    Dim myRange As Range
    Dim myArray(1 To 3, 1 To 2) As Integer

    Set xl = CreateObject("Excel.sheet")

    'Initialize array
    myArray(1, 1) = 4
    myArray(1, 2) = 5
    myArray(2, 1) = 6
    myArray(2, 2) = 7
    myArray(3, 1) = 8
    myArray(3, 2) = 9
    With xl
        .Range("A1").Value = 100
        .Range("A1:C3").Value = 100
        .Range("D1:E3").Value = myArray
        .Range("D4").FormulaR1C1 = "=SUM(R[-3]C:R[-1]C)"
        .Application.Quit
    End With

Set xl = Nothing

End Sub
```

Not only can you put formulas into worksheet cells with OLE automation, but you can also use all built-in Excel functions. This means that your Visual Basic application can take advantage of many statistical and financial functions that are part of Microsoft Excel. You can design a form that captures the data, pass the data to Microsoft Excel via OLE automation, retrieve the results, and display them.

To illustrate how to use Excel's built-in functions with OLE Automation, you can design a small application to calculate car loan payments. To begin, design a form with three text boxes to enter loan amount, interest rate, and number of payments (in years). Name the text boxes txtLoanAmt, txtIntRate, and txtTerm. Add an additional text box to hold the results of the calculation and name it txtPayment. Set the Locked property of txtPayment to True to prevent user input. You also can use a gray back color for this text box to indicate that it is not available for user input and set its Forecolor property to Red. Finally, add a command button named cmdCalculate. When the command button is clicked, the information entered into the text boxes is processed and the results are returned. Listing 13.7 shows how to use Excel to perform the calculations. Obviously, you would have to enhance the code sample with error checking to make sure that all required fields are completed with numeric data before using it in a real-world application. Figure 13.1 shows the form as it would look after the results are obtained.

Listing 13.7. Using Excel functions.

```
Private Sub cmdCalculate_Click()

    Dim xl As Excel.Worksheet

    Set xl = CreateObject("Excel.sheet")
    With xl
        .Range("A1").Value = CSng(txtIntRate.Text) * 0.01 / 12
        .Range("A2").Value = CInt(txtTerm.Text) * 12
        .Range("A3").Value = txtLoanAmt.Text
        .Range("A4").FormulaR1C1 = "=PMT(R[-3]C,R[-2]C,R[-1]C)"
        txtPayment.Text = Format(.Range("A4").Value, "#,##0.00")
        .Application.Quit
    End With

End Sub
```

Figure 13.1.
A car payment
application.

Creating Charts

When you use a spreadsheet application like Microsoft Excel, you often want to create a graphical representation of your data. Using OLE automation, you can use the data from the active worksheet to create a chart. Listing 13.8 builds on the previous code samples from this chapter by first adding a new workbook and then using an array to fill a series of worksheet cells via the Range method. Finally, the Range is selected and a new chart is added. Excel is made visible in order to display the chart.

Listing 13.8. Creating a chart.

```
Sub CreateChart()

    Dim xl As Excel.Application
    Dim myChart As Chart
    Dim myArray(1 To 3, 1 To 2) As Integer

    Set xl = CreateObject("Excel.Application")

'Initialize array
    myArray(1, 1) = 4
    myArray(1, 2) = 5
    myArray(2, 1) = 6
    myArray(2, 2) = 7
    myArray(3, 1) = 8
    myArray(3, 2) = 9
    With xl
        .Workbooks.Add
        With .Range("D1:E3")
            .Value = myArray
            .Select
        End With
        Set myChart = .Charts.Add
        myChart.Type = xl3DBar    '3-D bar graph
        .Visible = True
    End With

End Sub
```

Closing Microsoft Excel

How and when Microsoft Excel closes depends on whether it is visible and what type of reference was used to create it. If Microsoft Excel is not visible, the active instance closes when its variable reference goes out of scope if that variable references a chart or a sheet. If the variable references the application object, you must use the Quit method to close Excel, even if the active instance is not visible. After you make the active instance visible, you cannot close it with code. Excel keeps running until it is shut down via user intervention.

Using OLE Automation with Microsoft Word

Working with Microsoft Word as an OLE automation server might, at first, seem more challenging than working with Excel. The challenge comes from the fact that Microsoft Word does not use Visual Basic for Applications. Instead, the language used to control Word is WordBasic. The challenge is reduced once you realize that many WordBasic methods are identical to the menu selections in Word itself, and the parameters match Word's dialog box items. To save a file using OLE automation with Word, for example, you use the FileSave method; to close a file, you use the FileClose method. An additional point to remember when you use WordBasic is the existence of nonstandard names. Nonstandard names use characters that have special meanings in Visual Basic, such as the dollar sign ($). You must use square brackets when you reference a method with a nonstandard name. To display the name of the current style, for example, you can use the following code.

```
MsgBox .[StyleName$]()
```

Starting Microsoft Word

You can use the `CreateObject()` and `GetObject()` functions discussed in Chapter 12 to create a reference to the `WordBasic` object. `CreateObject()` and the form of `GetObject()` that works with WordBasic behave exactly the same way, so only `CreateObject()` is used in this chapter. The one additional consideration in creating a reference to WordBasic is the use of early binding. Unlike Microsoft Excel, the WordBasic object library does not ship with Microsoft Word. It is available separately as part of the Microsoft Word Developer's Kit. Remember that it is the availability of the object library that enables you to declare a variable as a specific object type, as in the following code:

```
Dim wd As Word.WordBasic
```

Creating New Documents

Documents form the core of Microsoft Word, and you probably will find many uses for them in your OLE automation projects. Using OLE automation, you can create new documents, add text to documents, format and edit text, and save documents.

WordBasic provides two methods for creating new documents. The first, `FileNewDefault`, creates a new document using the default template (usually, Normal.Dot). The second, `FileNew`, creates a new document using a specific template. Like Microsoft Excel, Word has no open documents when a new instance is created. Therefore, creating a new document with OLE automation adds the only document to Word. If there already is a running instance of Microsoft Word, creating a new document with OLE adds a new document window to the running instance. Listing 13.9 shows how to open a new default document and how to open a document based on a specific template. Because Word starts invisibly, you need to include the `AppShow` method to make the documents visible. After placing the following line in your `Declarations` section, you can run the code in Listing 13.9:

```
Dim wd As Word.WordBasic
```

Listing 13.9. Creating a new document.

```
Sub RunWord()

    Dim wd As Word.WordBasic

    Set wd = CreateObject("Word.Basic")
    wd.FileNewDefault
    wd.FileNew "c:\msoffice\Templates\Letters & Faxes\Contemporary Letter.dot"

    wd.AppShow

End Sub
```

Opening Existing Documents

You use the FileOpen method to open an existing document. Listing 13.10 shows how to use this method. The code creates a new instance of Word and opens the document or uses a running instance. If the document already is open, it is used and a new copy of the document is not opened. If the document cannot be found, an error occurs. As in Listing 13.9, you need to declare the wd variable before you can use it in the following code.

Listing 13.10. Opening an existing document.

```
Sub OpenWord()
On Error GoTo WordError
    Set wd = CreateObject("Word.Basic")
    wd.FileOpen "myDoc2.doc"

    wd.AppShow
    Exit Sub
WordError:
    MsgBox Err.Number & " " & Err.Description
End Sub
```

Adding Information to Documents

The capability to create and open documents in Microsoft Word is only the beginning of how you can manipulate document information with OLE automation. You also can add text to your documents and modify its appearance. Listing 13.11 shows you how to add text to your document with the Insert method and then use other WordBasic methods to replace text and format that text as bold. Finally, the document is saved. The code makes Word visible with the AppShow method so that the text can be selected and replaced. If Word is not visible, the code does not select the text, so the second use of the Insert method just appends the text to the last line.

Listing 13.11. Working with text.

```
Sub WorkWithText()

    Dim sMyText As String

    Set wd = CreateObject("Word.Basic")
    With wd
        .FileNewDefault
        .AppShow
        sMyText = "Here is some text which will go into word" & vbCrLf
        sMyText = sMyText & "One more paragraph is now added to Word"
        .Insert sMyText    'add text to document
        .StartOfLine       'move to beginning of the current line
        .SelectCurSentence 'select current line
        sMyText = "This line replaces the last one"
        .Insert sMyText
        .StartOfLine
        .SelectCurSentence
        .Bold On:=1
        .FileSaveAs Name:="myNewDocument"
    End With
End Sub
```

Using Forms

Microsoft Word enables you to create forms that contain specific fields. These fields can be text fields, checkboxes, or drop-down lists. Word provides the flexibility of creating a reusable document in which information can be updated. This is similar to the capability to enter information in Visual Basic controls. Although it is beyond the scope of this chapter to describe how to design forms in Word, a brief explanation of how to use OLE automation to manage forms is presented.

WordBasic uses the SetFormResult method to place information in form fields. Listing 13.12 shows how to use this method with an existing form document. Figure 13.2 shows the form document. If you want to expand on the code presented, you can design a small Visual Basic application in which text boxes are used to gather the data passed to Word via OLE automation.

Listing 13.12. Using forms.

```
Sub SetFormFields()

    Set wd = CreateObject("Word.Basic")

    With wd
        .FileOpen "c:\windows\personal\WordForm.dot"
        .SetFormResult "Title", "Software Developer"
        .SetFormResult "Name", "Jane Doe"
    End With

End Sub
```

Figure 13.2.
Using forms.

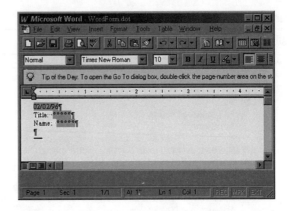

Using Mail Merge

Another one of Microsoft Word's capabilities that you can control with OLE automation is Mail Merge. To use Mail Merge, you first must set up a Mail Merge document in Microsoft Word. Using Microsoft Word to set up a Mail Merge document is beyond the scope of this chapter, but you can use Word's online Help to become familiar with the process. The Mail Merge document used in Listing 13.13 is shown in Figure 13.3. The Mail Merge fields in this document are stored in an Access database.

Figure 13.3.
A sample Mail Merge document.

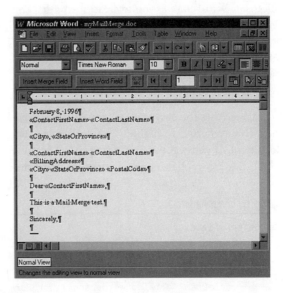

The code in Listing 13.13 opens a Mail Merge document and outputs the results to a new Word document with the `MailMergeToDoc` method. In addition to merging the document fields with the Access data, the code also uses a bookmark to provide the salesperson's name. You can use a *bookmark* to go directly to a specific place in a Word document and add text there with the Insert method. After the code in Listing 13.13 runs, Super Salesperson of the Month appears on the last line of the document before the paragraph mark, because this is where the bookmark is located. See Word's online Help for more information about bookmarks. At the end of the procedure, the code makes sure the original Mail Merge document is active by using the Activate method. This ensures that the correct document is closed by the FileClose method.

Before running the code in Listing 13.13, place the following line in your Declarations section:

```
Dim wd As Word.WordBasic
```

Listing 13.13. Using Mail Merge.

```
On Error GoTo MailMergeError

Set wd = CreateObject("Word.Basic")

With wd
'open our mailmerge template
    .FileOpen "c:\windows\personal\mymailmerge.doc"
    .AppShow
    If .AppMinimize() Then   'is Word minimized?
        .AppRestore          'Restore the Word
    End If

    .EditGoTo "SalesPersonName"
    .Insert "Super Salesperson of the Month"
'output mail merge results to a new document
    .MailMergeToDoc
'make sure mail merge document is active
    .Activate WindowTitle:="mymailmerge.doc"
'close mail merge doc without saving
    .FileClose 2
End With
Exit Sub

MailMergeError::

    MsgBox Err.Number & " " & Err.Description
    If wd Is Nothing Then    'clean up object
    Else
        Set wd = Nothing
    End If

End Sub
```

Using the Spell Checker

One of the more useful features of Microsoft Word is the Spell Checker. When you design your own applications with Visual Basic, it would be very convenient to be able to check the spelling of text input. With OLE automation, this becomes very simple.

To begin, start with a new project and add a text box and command button to a form. Name the text box txtSpelling and set its Multiline property to True. Name the command button cmdSpellCheck and set its Caption property to &Spelling. The form should look like Figure 13.4.

Figure 13.4.
A Visual Basic spell checker application.

Add the code from Listing 13.14 to the Click event of the command button. The code creates a new document and then adds the contents of your text box to the document. The spell check routine is invoked by using the ToolsSpelling method. The on error statement in the code is very important because WordBasic always returns an error when the spell check is complete. The modified text in the Word document then is selected by using the EditSelectAll method. The CharLeft method is used to move the selection one character to the left to avoid selecting the paragraph marker. The selection is pasted back into the text box, replacing what was originally there. Finally, the document is closed without saving, because this document was created solely for the purpose of using the spell checker and is not one that you need to keep.

Listing 13.14. Invoking the spell checker.

```
Private Sub cmdSpellCheck_Click()

    Dim sMyText As String

    Set wd = CreateObject("Word.Basic")
    With wd
        .FileNewDefault
        .Insert txtSpelling.Text
        On Error Resume Next
        .ToolsSpelling
        .EditSelectAll                    'select entire Word document
        .CharLeft Count:=1, Select:=1     'move selection 1 char to left
        txtSpelling.Text = .Selection()
        .FileClose Save:=2   'don't save
    End With

End Sub
```

Running Macros

Aside from invoking multiple WordBasic methods from Visual Basic to manipulate Word documents, you also can run macros. You can call Word macros by using the ToolsMacro method. You should keep a few things in mind when you invoke Word macros with OLE automation. First of all, if the macro displays a dialog box, Word must be the active application. In addition, you cannot pass parameters directly to a Word macro with OLE automation. Listing 13.15 shows how to call a Word macro from Visual Basic with OLE automation.

Listing 13.15. Using Word macros.

```
Sub RunMacro()

    Set wd = CreateObject("Word.Basic")

    With wd
'open our mailmerge template
        .FileOpen "c:\windows\personal\myDoc.doc"
.AppShow
        .AppActivate "Microsoft Word"
        .ToolsMacro Name:="myMacro", Run:=True
    End With

End Sub
```

Closing Microsoft Word

If your Visual Basic application creates the instance of Word that gets used for OLE automation, Word closes when the declared object variable goes out of scope or when it is set to Nothing. This means that if you declare an object variable in a given procedure and use it to reference a new instance of Word, Word will no longer be running when the procedure terminates. On the other hand, Word continues to run until it is closed by user intervention or by the AppClose method if your Visual Basic application referenced an instance that was already running. If you set the object variable to Nothing and your application uses an active instance of Word, you no longer will be able to use WordBasic methods, although Word will still be running. The code used to close Word and set the object variable to Nothing follows:

```
wd.AppClose
Set wd = Nothing
```

Microsoft Word Implementation Summary

The ability to use Microsoft Word as an OLE Automation server allows you to take advantage of the many features found in the product. You can create and manipulate documents, run macros, add data to forms, use mail merge, and invoke the spell checker. If you continue to work with Word as an OLE server, you will undoubtedly find many other ways to incorporate its functions into your applications.

Using OLE Automation with Microsoft Access

With the release of version 7.0, Microsoft Access can function as an OLE automation server. Before this release, Microsoft Access could function only as an OLE automation controller. Like Microsoft Excel, Microsoft Access uses Visual Basic for Applications, so its language syntax will seem very familiar to you. Access, of course, has its own unique properties and methods that are made available through OLE automation. Even though Access exposes many properties and methods, you might find that you do not often use Access directly as an OLE automation server. Because you can use data access objects (DAOs) to select and update information from Access databases, you probably will use DAOs for most of your Visual Basic and Access database interaction. To find out more about using DAOs, see Chapter 20, "Data Access Objects." Despite the availability of DAOs, there are still uses for Access as an OLE automation server.

Starting Microsoft Access

You can create a reference to Microsoft Access by using the CreateObject() and GetObject() functions. Chapter 12 explains how these functions are used. Microsoft Access always starts visible, so you do not need to set the Visible property as you do with Word and Excel. Like Microsoft Excel, you can use code to check whether Access is already running when using GetObject() and then proceed to use CreateObject() if it is not. Refer to Listing 13.1 to see how to do this.

Using Microsoft Access to Run Reports

One very useful role for Microsoft Access as an OLE automation server is its capability to run reports. You can design your reports in the Access environment, use Visual Basic and DAO to update your Access database, and then use OLE to run the reports. To illustrate this technique, assume that you have created a database called myAccess.mdb that contains Customers and Employees tables. These tables are used to create the Customers and Employees reports. You then can use Visual Basic to view or print these reports. In Visual Basic, create a new project with a form whose Caption property is set to Reports. Add a listbox named lstReports and a command button named cmdReports. Listing 13.16 shows the code to implement the report features. The code uses the start-up technique described in the section "Starting Microsoft Access," which enables you to start a new instance of Microsoft Access if there is no running instance of the server. Figure 13.5 shows what a sample form might look like.

Listing 13.16. Using Microsoft Access to run reports.

```
Option Explicit
Dim acc As Access.Application

Private Sub cmdReports_Click()
```

```
On Error Resume Next
    Set acc = GetObject(, "Access.Application")
    If acc Is Nothing Then
        Set acc = CreateObject("Access.Application")
    End If
    acc.OpenCurrentDatabase ("myAccess.mdb")
    acc.DoCmd.OpenReport lstReports.List(lstReports.ListIndex), acPreview


End Sub

Private Sub Form_Load()
    lstReports.AddItem "Customers"
    lstReports.AddItem "Employees"
    lstReports.ListIndex = 0
End Sub
```

Figure 13.5.

*A sample form to run
Microsoft Access reports.*

Closing Microsoft Access

Terminating an instance of Microsoft Access follows the same pattern as that of Microsoft
Word. If your Visual Basic application creates the instance of Access that is used for OLE
automation, Access closes when the declared object variable goes out of scope or when it is set
to Nothing. On the other hand, Access continues to run until it is closed by user intervention
or by the Quit method if your Visual Basic application referenced an instance that was already
running. Remember that once you set the object variable to Nothing, you no longer can use
Visual Basic to reference any properties or methods of Microsoft Access. The code used to close
Access and set the object variable to Nothing follows:

```
acc.DoCmd.Quit
Set acc = Nothing
```

Summary

Using OLE automation enables you to use the features and functions of Microsoft Office
products from your Visual Basic applications. Although not every Office product could be
covered in this chapter, you can build on the examples to integrate OLE into your applications.

The topics covered in this chapter should get you started using Microsoft Excel as an OLE automation server. You now have enough information to start Excel; create and use workbooks, worksheets, and charts; and place values and formulas in cells. You can use the Object Browser and online Help to pursue more information about Excel's methods and properties.

This chapter also looked at how you can use Microsoft Access as an OLE automation server to develop a Report Engine for your Visual Basic applications. You also saw how to use any of the other properties and methods that Access exposes through OLE automation. Since Access is primarily used by Visual Basic developers for its database features, you will continue to do most of your work with Access databases by using DAO to manipulate fields, tables, and queries.

Creating BackOffice Solutions with Visual Basic

by A. Nicklas Malik

The cornerstone of the Microsoft BackOffice product is SQL Server. Currently in Version 6.0, Version 6.5 will be available about the time this book hits the market. This server-based relational database management system is powerful, quick, and inexpensive, offering a way for small and medium-sized businesses to benefit from the advantages of client-server architectures.

However, there is more to running a SQL Server database than many PC-based programmers are accustomed to. Until recently, systems of this nature did not take full advantage of the Windows user interface for administering the data, including making backups, importing and exporting text files, and so on. In fact, there are still a few command-line interfaces in the SQL Server administrator's skill set.

All of this took a major leap forward, however, with the release of SQL Server 6.0. This version contains a new tool: the SQL Enterprise Manager. This tool makes it far easier for a single user to administer many different SQL Server databases from any system on the network. Everything is laid out in a nice graphics user interface (GUI), with functionality to spare.

This kind of migration to the GUI is nothing new for modern database products. However, Microsoft went one step further. In addition to providing a fully functional front-end application, Microsoft designed this tool in a powerful way: All of the functionality of the SQL Enterprise Manager is built into a set of OLE objects, called the Distributed Management Objects (SQL DMO).

Installation and Distribution of the SQL DMO

Although it is a very nice interface, the SQL Enterprise Manager is only a front end to the SQL DMO. Anyone who has installed the Enterprise Manager on their system has also, in effect, installed the SQL DMO object. In fact, you cannot distribute the SQL DMO object to any workstation that does not have SQL Enterprise Manager installed!

> Installing SQL Enterprise Manager is the *only* legal way to distribute the SQL DMO object. Although you can delete the Enterprise Manager executable after the install, leaving only the OLE object, you cannot distribute this object separately from SQL Server.

The Enterprise Manager is a part of the SQL Server Workstation product and is considered one of the SQL Server Client Tools. Therefore, your users must have one SQL Server Workstation license for every copy of the SQL DMO on their systems. This severely limits the distributable capability of any application you write that uses the SQL DMO.

Also note that the Enterprise Manager and the SQL DMO are 32-bit COM objects that are OLE-automation compatible. They can be called from 16-bit applications, but they can run only on a 32-bit system, such as Windows NT or Windows 95. Because your applications have to run on the same systems, you can go ahead and develop the app using 32-bit Visual Basic. There is no advantage to using the 16-bit version of VB4 to develop a DMO application, and I will assume for the rest of this chapter that you will be using VB4/32 to develop your DMO applications.

Using SQL DMO with SQL Server 4.2 Databases

Just as you can use the SQL Server Enterprise Manager with SQL Server 4.2 databases, you can use the SQL DMO. However, the same restrictions apply:

- SQL Server 6.x functions are not available on version 4.2 servers (obviously).

- Before the DMO can correctly access a SQL Server 4.2 database, you have to run a Transact SQL script on that server in the master database. This script sets up a number of stored procedures that are called by the SQL DMO interface to perform tasks. The script is installed with the client tools and can be found in the file `C:\SQL60\INSTALL\SQLOLE42.SQL`.

There is a corresponding script for SQL Server 6.0, but it is installed automatically with the database product, so you do not have to worry about installing it.

> Just because you can use the same object as the Enterprise Manager doesn't mean that you can get access to the list of "registered databases" that you create with the Enterprise Manager. If you are using SQL Server 6.0, you will have to keep your own list of databases or require the users to provide information each time they use your tool. This omission was fixed in SQL Server 6.5.

Doing What the Enterprise Manager Cannot Do

There is one obvious question I'd like to address: Why use the objects when you can do everything you want with the Enterprise Manager? Here is a short list of good reasons:

- Interface usability. For many users, the Enterprise Manager is too complicated. If your goal is to provide a single database-management function for users who will only perform the function intermittently, there is no need for such users to invoke the Enterprise Manager.

  This is not meant as a criticism of the Enterprise Manager. However, with any tool that packs in as much functionality as this one does, there are bound to be trade-offs. The Enterprise Manager was designed to be used on a regular basis by knowledgeable users. It is a poor tool for intermittent or occasional users.

■ Informal security. For many users, the Enterprise Manager is too powerful. Some data-administration operations require that the user have system-administrator privileges. However, this level of security bestows god-like status on the user. Someone with these privileges can do a lot more than just the functions that their organization might want them to perform.

For example, in order to add a user to a system, the administrator needs "sa" access. However, a person with sa access can also delete a database, change a dump device association, and invoke queries. It's a little like starting a campfire with a blowtorch. It can be done by anyone, but not everyone should be doing it.

Therefore, your organization might ask you to write a front-end tool using the SQL DMO. Your tool will perform individual functions on the database without offering access to more critical functions. You could then place the tool on your user's system and delete the executable for the Enterprise Manager. Although this doesn't provide perfect security, it is far better in many cases then simply telling the user "This function is bad—so don't do it."

■ Complicated processes. The SQL Enterprise Manager is a general tool. Therefore, every capability under it is exposed as a simple interaction. However, many common business processes require a long series of steps to perform. It is far better to create a small tool that will perform every step in the proper sequence than to require a person to do it, for two reasons: the increased productivity of the administrator and the decreased opportunity for mistakes. By far, this is the most common use of the SQL DMO. In fact, with SQL Server 6.5, you can create an application that performs a complicated process, and you can add it to the Enterprise Manager as an external tool.

The DMO Object Hierarchy

An object hierarchy is an interesting thing. It provides a way to view the capabilities of an OLE object, and to see how to access each part of it, without answering the most important question: How do I use it? You start with the object map. (See Figure 14.1.) Then you learn how to read it. The process of using it constitutes the remainder of this chapter.

How to Read the Object Map

The shaded boxes represent collections. Note that the name of each collection is a plural noun. The name of each object in the collection is the singular form of the same noun. Therefore, the Rules collection is made up of Rule objects.

Figure 14.1.
SQL Server 6.0 Distributed Management Object.

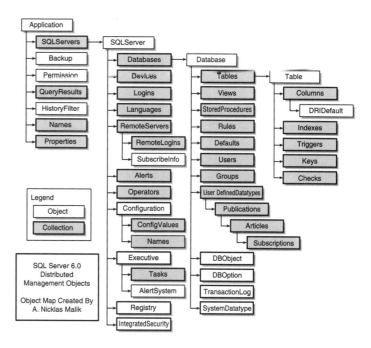

However, the map does not show the Rule objects, because there are no objects below the Rule object. This was done to reduce the complexity of the diagram. Therefore, when you see the Logins collection, you would correctly assume that it contains Login objects.

I explicitly drew the relationship between the collections and the objects within for three of the collections: SQLServers, Databases, and Tables because the objects in these collections are more complicated. They each contain other objects. For these collections, I have drawn a horizontal arrow between each collection and the object class within it.

The clear boxes represent individual objects. For example, there is only one Application object, and under it, there is only one Backup object.

The diagram does not show the properties and methods of the objects, nor does it distinguish between objects that always exist (such as the Languages collection under the SQLServer object) and objects that are returned as the result of a method call (such as the DBObject object under the Database object).

For a far more comprehensive map, check out the Microsoft Developers Network CD (on or after January 1996) for the article and accompanying map from Ken Lassesen. I have this map on my wall; it is so comprehensive that even when printed on a four-foot sheet of paper, the text is so small that you have to stand a few inches away to read it.

So what does the map show? It shows you how to access your objects from Visual Basic. For example, if you want to access a `Device` object, you would declare it as follows, but you would only be able to access it from the `Devices` collection of a `SQLServer` object:

```
Dim dvMaster as SQLOLE.Device
```

Assume that I have created a SQL Server object called `ssCurrentServer`. You could then access the master device with the following code:

```
Set dvMaster = ssCurrentServer.Devices("master")
```

As a general rule, for every object on the map, you need the object above it in order to gain access to it.

> Declare any SQL DMO object as `SQLOLE.object` where `object` is the object you want, regardless of where it appears on the object map.

The exception to this rule is the `Application` object. This object is more of a placeholder than anything else. The objects that are declared below it are not directly accessible from it. Therefore, you cannot use the `Application` object to get access to the `Permission` object. Rather, this is simply the place where this object is declared in the hierarchy.

Therefore, for all practical purposes, you should only be concerned with the objects below the `SQLServer` collection.

Referencing the Object

The first step in using the SQL DMO object is to reference the object in the References dialog. On a system where the Enterprise Manager is installed, start up Visual Basic. Then, from the Tools menu, select References. In the dialog box that appears, check the checkbox on the line that reads Microsoft SQLOLE Object Library.

If this line does not appear in your references list, you should click the Browse button and find the SQLOLE32.TLB file (which should be in `C:\SQL60\DLL`). Select the file and click OK. This will add the object library to your list of references. Check the SQLOLE reference and click OK.

Connecting to a Database

The first thing you do in the code is declare a `SQLServer` object. You then create the object and use its `Connect` method to establish a connection with a database. It looks like this:

```
Dim ssvServer as SQLOLE.SQLServer
Set ssvServer = New SQLOLE.SQLServer
ssvServer.Connect "Emissary", "NickMalik", "dmoguru"
```

In this example, the server is called Emissary, and the user name and password are NickMalik and dmoguru, respectively.

It is a good idea to declare your SQLServer object in the declarations section of a form or module. As soon as this variable leaves scope, your connection will be dropped. If you want to disconnect from the server without discarding the object (so that you can use it again to connect to a different server), then you should use the Disconnect method, like so:

```
ssvServer.Disconnect
```

When you are finished with the object, it is good form to release the connection explicitly by disconnecting from the database and then dropping the object, like this:

```
ssvServer.Disconnect
Set ssvServer = Nothing
```

Neither of these statements are actually required, however, because the object will automatically disconnect when it is dropped, and VB will automatically drop it when it leaves scope or your program terminates.

A Simple Example

Included on the CD-ROM that comes with this book is the project dmodemo1.vbp. If you load and run the application in Visual Basic, you will see a dialog box similar to Figure 14.2.

Figure 14.2.
DMODEMO1 sample application in action.

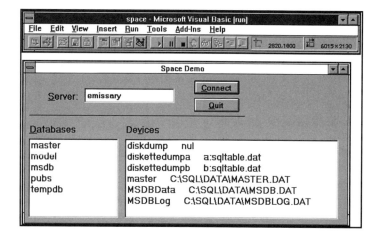

This very small application begins by prompting you for the name of a server where SQL Server is running. After you provide the name, press Enter or click the Connect button. You will be prompted for a user ID and password.

If the login is successful, a list of the databases and devices on the server will be displayed. For the devices, you will see the device name and the name of the file where the data is stored for this device (the `PhysicalLocation` property of the `Device` object).

Resources for Exploration and Information

Both the SQL Server Books Online and the Microsoft Developers Network contain a manual called *Programming the Distributed Management Objects*. This book is of some limited value, in that you can discover all of the properties and methods of every object, with one-line descriptions of most of the properties.

Unfortunately, there is nearly no documentation on how to actually use these properties and methods, and how to interpret the results, in a coherent manner. In fact, for all of the "enumerated types," there is a simple listing of the possible values that can be passed as parameters, with no documentation whatsoever for what each value means!

There is also an online help file called SQLOLE.HLP. This file provides the exact same information as the manual. It is of no further benefit.

Refreshing the Cache

The SQL DMO object layer keeps a cache of SQL Server settings in memory to optimize the calls to SQL Server. Although this is fine for efficiency, there are times when you want to see the changes that have been made in the database. That is where the `Refresh` method (of every collection object) comes in handy.

For example, if you execute a script that inserts a stored procedure in the database, and you want that new stored procedure to appear in the `Database.StoredProcedures` collection, then you will need to call the following method:

```
driDatabase.StoredProcedures.Refresh
```

Each of the collection objects has a `Refresh` method.

Changing SQL Server Configuration Settings

Viewing and changing the configuration settings of SQL Server is fairly simple. You can access any configuration setting from the `ConfigValues` collection under the `SQLServer.Configuration` property. Therefore, if you have a server object named `ssServer`, you can discover the current value for the `memory` option like so:

```
x=ssServer.Configuration.ConfigValues("memory").RunningValue
```

You can set a new value by assigning the value to the `CurrentValue` property, like so:

```
With ssServer.Configuration
    .ConfigValues("memory").CurrentValue = 8192
End With
```

Notice that I used the `With...End With` syntax to abbreviate my expression. If you are going to change more than one value at a time, using this syntax can significantly improve the performance of your application. Learn to use the `With...End With` syntax as often as possible.

So what is the difference between the `RunningValue` and `CurrentValue` properties? `RunningValue` is the value that SQL Server started with. `CurrentValue` is the value that has been set since SQL Server started.

> Changing the `CurrentValue` property is not enough to force SQL Server to accept the change. After you change all the values you want, you must issue one of two methods:
>
> ```
> ssServer.ReconfigureCurrentValues
> ```
>
> or
>
> ```
> ssServer.ReconfigureWithOverride
> ```
>
> The first method will fail if a warning message is produced by SQL Server on the attempt to change one or more of the values. Warning messages come back a trappable error in the errors collection. The second method will force all changes to be made. The only changes that cannot be made are those where the value provided by the user is outside of the minimum or maximum range provided by the configuration setting.
>
> To find out what the minimum and maximum values are for each setting, inquire on the `MinimumValue` and `MaximumValue` properties of the `ConfigValue` object.

Some SQL Server settings take effect immediately, while others will take effect only when the server is restarted. To determine when the change will take effect, you should examine the `DynamicReconfigure` property, which is a Boolean value. If this value is `True`, then changing the `CurrentValue` and issuing the `Reconfigure` method will cause SQL Server to immediately change the setting.

On your CD-ROM is a small application that mimics one of the functions of the SQL Enterprise Manager, in that it enables you to change the configuration settings on a server (assuming that you have the permissions needed to do so). The application is called config.vbp. The following code is used to load a grid with all of the configuration settings:

```
Dim cvConfig as SQLOLE.ConfigValue
' Connect to the Server
ssCurrentServer.Connect txServer.Text, sUserid, sPassword
```

```
With ssCurrentServer.Configuration
    grSettings.Rows = .ConfigValues.Count + 1
    currow = 1
    ' Fill the grid with the config values
    For Each cvConfig In .ConfigValues
        select_grid_row grSettings, currow
        sClipString = cvConfig.Name & vbTab _
                    & cvConfig.MinimumValue & vbTab _
                    & cvConfig.MaximumValue & vbTab _
                    & cvConfig.RunningValue & vbTab _
                    & cvConfig.CurrentValue
        grSettings.Clip = sClipString
        currow = currow + 1
    Next
End With
```

The preceding code begins by connecting to the SQL Server. Then, in a With block, it sets up the grid to match the number of rows in the ConfigValues collection. The call to select_grid_row simply selects a single row for the sake of the Clip call. This is a fairly fast way to load a grid control. The user interface for this sample app is shown in Figure 14.3.

Figure 14.3.
The config sample application in action.

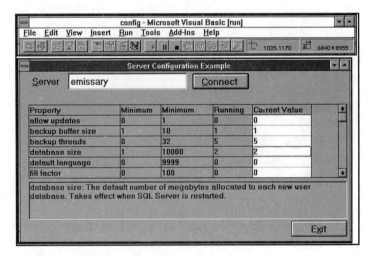

Manipulating Database Objects

At the next level in the object map, below the SQLServer object, is the Databases collection. In order to manipulate a database, you should first assign a database object to the entry in the Databases collection in which you are interested. For example:

```
Dim sdPubs as SQLOLE.Database
set sdPubs = ssCurrentServer.Databases("pubs")
```

Although you could easily reference the object with its full derivation, it would be very slow to do so, and the code would be difficult to read. Assigning a pointer into the hierarchy to work from is far more efficient.

One of the frequently used features of the Enterprise Manager is the ability to create the Transact-SQL source code needed to re-create a stored procedure, table, trigger, or any other database object. From the SQL DMO, you access this functionality from the Script() methods on each of these database objects.

When you use the Script method on an object, SQL Server will write a script for you. If you execute the script, the object will be re-created. This is a very handy feature. Most organizations will keep a script file for every object in the database, so that the database and all objects within it can easily be re-created at a later date. This method also enables the script file to be saved in a source code control system like Visual SourceSafe, where changes can be documented during the life of a project.

The Script method takes two parameters. The first parameter, ScriptType, takes a flag value specifying what settings SQL Server should use when creating the script. The list of possible flag values is provided in the online docs. You can specify as many constants as you want, as long as you join them with the OR operator.

The second parameter, ScriptFilePath, is the name of a file to which you want the script file saved. Both parameters are optional. If the ScriptType parameter is omitted, then the PrimaryObject setting is used by default. If the filename is omitted, the script will not be written to a file. Either way, the script text is returned as a string from this method (unless you specify a ScriptType value of ToFileOnly). For example, you can use any of the following four method calls to generate a script:

```
myval$ = spMyProc.Script()    ' use defaults only

flags = SQLOLEScript_Drops Or SQLOLEScript_IncludeIfNotExists
myval$ = spMyProc.Script( ScriptType := flags )

myval$ = spMyProc.Script( ScriptFilePath := "outfile.sql")

flags = SQLOLEScript_Drops Or SQLOLEScript_IncludeIfNotExists
myval$ = spMyProc.Script( ScriptType := Flags, _
                          ScriptFilePath := "outfile.sql")
```

A list of some of the values for the Flags parameter follows. Note: many of these flag values require that you combine them with the SQLOLEScript_Default flag to get them to work.

- SQLOLEScript_Default. Specifies the default settings for creating a script.

- SQLOLEScript_Drops. Specifies that statements will be added that drop the object before creating it.

- SQLOLEScript_ToFileOnly. Specifies that the script will be written to the filename provided by the ScriptFilePath parameter, but will not be returned as a string return value.

- SQLOLEScript_AppendToFile. Specifies that the script will be appended to the script file. If this option is not specified, the script file will be opened for writing, which will discard any existing contents of the file.

- ■ SQLOLEScript_NoDRI. Unless this option is specified, any CREATE TABLE scripts will use the Declarative Referential Integrity constraints that are a major feature of SQL Server 6.*x.* These constraints include the PRIMARY KEY and FOREIGN KEY declarations of the CREATE TABLE statement.

- ■ SQLOLEScript_UDDTsToBaseType. Specifies that the attributes of a table created with a CREATE TABLE script should be declared with their base types instead of any user-defined data types that are currently used in the database object.

- ■ SQLOLEScript_42Syntax. Specifies that the script should conform to SQL Server 4.2 syntax. Note that this implies SQLOLEScript_NoDRI.

- ■ SQLOLEScript_ODBCSyntax. Specifies that the script will conform to ODBC syntax.

- ■ SQLOLEScript_Indexes. Specifies that statements will be added to the script to generate the indexes on a Table object. For obvious reasons, this option is useful only for Table objects.

Your CD-ROM contains a sample application that will generate a script for any stored procedure in any database that you can connect to. The application is called StProc.vbp. The user interface is illustrated in Figure 14.4.

Figure 14.4.
StProc sample extracts a stored procedure script.

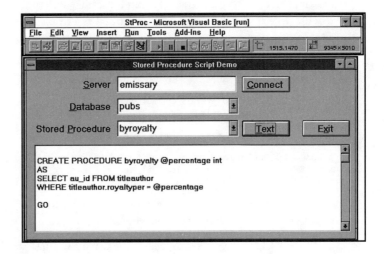

Many of the objects in the SQL DMO have a special requirement associated with them. If you want to change any of the properties or collections in these objects, you must use the .BeginAlter and .DoAlter methods. The objects are:

```
Alert
AlertSystem
Article
Executive
Operator
Publication
```

```
RemoteServer
SubscriberInfo
Subscription
Table
Task
```

For each of these objects, you would begin your changes by issuing the .BeginAlter method on the object. Then, after making your changes, you would issue the .DoAlter method to cause the changes to be made in SQL Server. For example, if I wanted to insert a new column called Gender in the Authors table of the sample pubs database, the code would look like the following listing. Note, in this example, the database object dbPubsDB has already been assigned.

```
Dim aTable as SQLOLE.Table
Dim colGender as SQLOLE.Column

Set aTable = dbPubsDB.Tables("authors")
Set colGender = New SQLOLE.Column
colGender.AllowNulls = True
colGender.Datatype = "char"
colGender.Length = 1
colGender.Name = "auGender"
aTable.BeginAlter
aTable.InsertColumn colGender, ""
aTable.DoAlter
```

Suggested Naming Conventions

There is a large number of objects in the SQLOLE hierarchy. In order to keep them straight, it is a good idea to establish a naming convention for using them. I would like to suggest the following naming convention for the most common SQL DMO objects.

Prefix	Object	Example
ss	SQLServer	ssCurrentServer
sdv	Device	sdvLogDevice
sln	Login	slnCurrentLogin
sd	Database	sdCurrentDatabase
st	Table	stServerTable
sv	View	svBusinessObject
sp	Stored Procedure	spInsertByKey
sr	Rule	srBoundLimits
su	User	suCurrentUser
sg	Group	sgSuperGroup
stc	Column	stcTableColumn
sti	Index	stiPrimary
str	Trigger	strInsertTrigger
stk	Keys	stkForeign
stc	Checks	stcBoundary

Summary

This chapter covered a very small sample of the functions and capabilities of the SQL DMO objects. In addition to the ability to manipulate the objects shown, you can use these objects to create and manipulate database objects such as tables, columns, triggers, users, groups, and logins. You can set up alerts, queue tasks, and read your integrated security configuration. You can even execute SQL statements (check out `Database.Execute`), which will return a collection of `QueryResults` objects.

It is unfortunate that Microsoft did such a poor job of documenting these objects. There is a great deal of power in them, as is evidenced by the SQL Enterprise Manager.

Every one of the examples in this chapter was developed by experimentation. Most of the settings are documented well enough in the help file, and in SQL Server Books Online, to get you past the guessing stage. If all else fails, take note of all of the values, and then see what the Enterprise Manager shows for the same function. You might be able to take your code that last step when you see how it is handled in the Enterprise Manager.

Above all, when you discover a new function or feature that is poorly documented (or not at all), send code to the Internet or CompuServe forums that support Visual Basic. Ultimately, if Microsoft won't document this rich object, we will.

Remote Automation

by James E. Bettone

CHAPTER

15

The Enterprise Edition of Visual Basic 4.0 introduces an interesting and useful capability called *remote automation*. Remote automation enables the developer to build distributed client/server applications that communicate via OLE automation. For many of us who have been waiting for OLE capabilities across an enterprise network, remote automation raises many issues and questions as well as possibilities, which are explored in this chapter.

In this chapter you learn the basics of remote automation, its capabilities and its future, the differences between OLE and remote automation, and security issues.

Remote Automation—An Overview

Building distributed component-based applications presupposes a means to deploy components across an enterprise network. Remote automation gives the developer this ability, precluding the need for the release of distributed or network OLE.

Because remote automation is based on exactly the same OLE interface concepts as local OLE automation, it is completely scaleable and supports client- or server-side execution. This means OLE servers can run on either the client or the server without recompiling the client application or OLE server. This capability also enables the servers to be run locally for debugging and testing. When debugging and testing are complete, the application can simply and seamlessly switch over to remote automation. Figure 15.1 illustrates a standard OLE implementation.

Figure 15.1.
A standard OLE application.

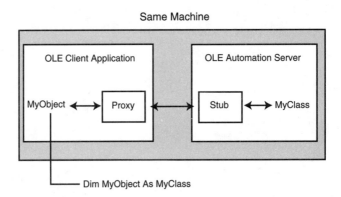

Remote automation enables developers to build distributed client/server applications that use the three-tiered client/server business model. Business rules can now be separated from the front and back ends and stored within scaleable, flexible business objects located on a remote server. These servers can then be implemented remotely throughout a network.

The remote system must be running either Windows NT or Windows 95. Remote automation is supported only on these two operating systems.

Visual Basic supports remote automation over both local and wide area networks with little or no code changes to either the client application or server objects. For the most part, remote automation OLE servers are developed in the same way as is a locally implemented OLE server. Figure 15.2 illustrates a remote automation implementation.

Figure 15.2.
Sample remote automation application.

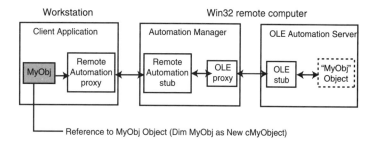

OLE Automation Terms and Definitions

You need to be familiar with the following terms in order to understand OLE and remote automation. OLE terms are addressed in a remote automation chapter because remote automation is another implementation of OLE that is used over a network. These terms apply in both contexts (local and remote OLE).

Local, or Standard, OLE

Applications in which the client and server components reside on the same machine use *standard OLE*, which can be implemented as either an in-process or an out-of-process OLE server. For example, standard OLE servers can be such applications as a locally installed version of Excel or Word.

Network OLE

Network OLE, also referred to as the Distributed Component Object Model (DCOM), is the "networked" version of standard OLE, which means it provides the ability to remotely access an application's objects. In other words, network OLE enables you to use the Excel Workbook object from another machine's installed copy of Excel.

In-Process OLE Servers

In-process OLE servers are usually implemented as a DLL and share the same process space and thread as the calling or client application. Calls to an in-process OLE server use the same stack space as the client application, and both the client application and the in-process OLE server can access each other's data directly without marshaling the data (see the following section titled "Marshaling"). Figure 15.3 illustrates an in-process server implementation.

Figure 15.3.
An in-process server implementation.

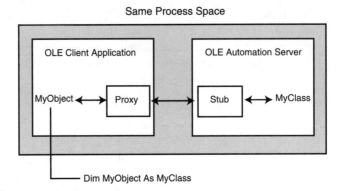

Figure 15.4.
An out-of-process server implementation.

Out-of-Process OLE Servers

Out-of-process OLE servers are implemented as an executable (.EXE) file and have their own process space. Because the client application and the out-of-process OLE server don't share the same process space, data has to be "marshaled" to move it across the process boundary between the two. Essentially, data referenced by the client application in the OLE server is copied locally into the client's process, so the client application points to a local address space within its own process. The same is true if the out-of-process OLE server references data from the client application. Figure 15.4 illustrates an out-of-process server implementation.

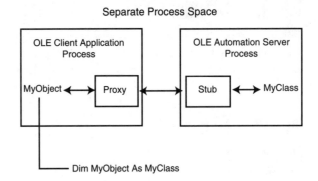

Marshaling

What is marshaling? Marshaling is simply the packaging of data to be sent either across a process boundary via local remote procedure calls (LRPCs) or across a machine boundary via remote procedure calls (RPCs). The process of packaging the data into something a network protocol can understand is *marshaling*. *Unmarshaling* is the process of unpacking the data into something the client application or the automation server can understand. Figure 15.5 is a conceptual illustration of marshaling.

Figure 15.5.
*Conceptual illustration
of marshaling.*

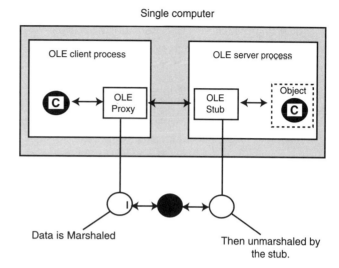

Proxies and Stubs

A *proxy* is a type of transparent object that packages data in preparation for a remote method call. A proxy usually resides in the same process as the client.

A *stub* resides in the receiver's process space and unpackages data for use by the receiver. This process is similar to how RPCs work over the network, hence the term LRPC, or the local version of RPC. A proxy marshals data to the corresponding stub, which unmarshals the data. Proxies and stubs are how OLE clients and servers communicate with each other.

What Is Remote Automation?

Remote automation enables remote access of objects on an enterprise network. With standard OLE limitations, the server application or object had to reside on the client's machine. For example, if you wanted to use the Excel Workbook object, you would need to have installed Excel on the same machine on which your application resides. This meant that applications using OLE automation had the requirement of ensuring that the automation servers resided on the same machine as the application.

To overcome the limitation of having the automation servers such as Word and Excel installed on the same client machine as the application, network OLE was born. Network OLE, also formally known as the Distributed Component Object Model (DCOM), will enable access to automation servers located remotely on an enterprise network. A lot of developers have been waiting for the release of network OLE. Thus was born remote automation, which succeeds in bringing us a step closer to true network OLE.

Remote automation works essentially the same as standard OLE except for the addition of the Automation Manager. The Automation Manager is the interface between the client application and the automation server. It handles the communication between the client and the server applications via remote procedure calls (RPCs).

Standard OLE uses a type of RPC called a local remote procedure call (I know it sounds like an oxymoron, but it's for real) to communicate between applications residing on the same machine. Each application has its own proxy and stub that will marshal the data to be sent. Figure 15.6 illustrates a local remote procedure call (LRPC).

Figure 15.6.

A sample LRPC.

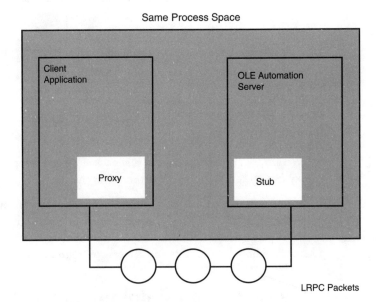

Remote automation essentially replaces the LRPC used by OLE when the client and the server are physically executing on the same machine with a full-featured remote procedure call (RPC). RPCs are like LRPCs except the boundary is between machines *and* applications. In other words, RPCs are how remote automation communicates between the client and server applications. Figure 15.7 illustrates an RPC.

Remote automation supports all seven levels of security defined for RPCs, which range from unprotected access to encrypted, authorized access. For more on security issues, see the later section in this chapter titled "Security Issues."

Figure 15.7.
A sample RPC.

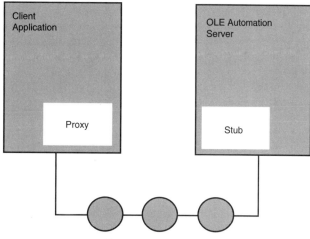

Marshaled Data sent via RPC

Remote Automation Design Issues

Remote automation servers and local servers are usually designed with mostly the same design considerations in mind. In other words, if you design your local OLE server correctly, it can easily be used for remote access (via remote automation, of course). However, for a remote automation server, there are additional design issues to keep in mind when dealing with things such as performance, error handling, and optimization methods.

A User Interface?

An OLE server that will be used remotely should never have any type of user interface when it is started using OLE. The reason for this is that an OLE server typically runs remotely on another server that is unattended. Therefore, no operator is present to respond to or interact with a user interface.

By using the StartMode property of the App object, you can determine how your OLE server started: by user interaction (when a user double-clicked the program from Explorer or File Manager, for example) or in response to an OLE request. The two values and predefined constants representing these values for StartMode are 0 (vbSModeStandalone) and 1 (vbSModeAutomation). For example:

```
If Application.StartMode = vbSModeAutomation Then
    MsgBox "Your Application has started via an OLE Automation Request!
ElseIf App.StartMode = vbSModeStandalone Then
    MsgBox "Your Application has started non OLE request(stand-alone).
End If
```

Performance Issues

You can do many things to increase the performance of your OLE server.

- Pass parameters
- Use 32-bit servers
- Limit the size of passed variables
- Handle database objects
- Monitor the number of objects that are created

Pass Parameters

Each time you access a property by either getting or setting its value, data of some sort travels back and forth across the network, and this can cause performance degradation. Instead of requiring properties to be set before a method can be called, you can design the server so that all the data is passed to the method (thus requiring fewer network calls). You can then set the appropriate properties in the method. For example, instead of setting two properties and calling a method (resulting in three network calls), you can call the same method and pass it the property values, which in turn can be set from within the method (resulting in one network call).

Use 32-Bit Servers

Whether the client application is a 16- or 32-bit application, you should always compile your OLE servers as 32-bit applications. The server will perform much more efficiently as a 32-bit application than if it was compiled as a 16-bit application.

Limit the Size of Passed Variables

You should be conscious of the size of the variables that are passed back and forth between the server and the client. The larger in size the variable is, the more time it takes to move the data back and forth between the client and server. In general, the smaller the variables (no smaller than a packet in size for your particular network), the fewer marshaled packets it will take to move the data.

Handling Database Objects

You should always avoid passing any type of DAO or RDO object back across to the client application. This will have a very bad effect on performance. If, for example, you pass back a recordset object to the client application, then each access of a property, method, field, or record will require a separate network operation.

Data from a database or recordset object should be passed back in some type of user-defined data type, variant array, or better yet, in a collection. This will limit the number of network operations significantly by passing all the data in the record in one or two operations instead of several. Recordset objects carry a lot of extra baggage or goodies that aren't necessarily used by the developer. In essence, you pass back only the data the user interface uses.

Manage the Number of Creatable Objects

Although the Automation Manager is a multithreaded, multitasking application that can handle a fairly large number of OLE objects, its performance degrades as the number of created OLE servers it has to manage increases. By carefully monitoring the number of objects that are created, you will in essence keep the remote computer running at optimal speeds.

> The number of allowable objects on the remote computer depends on the remote computer's configuration (that is, memory, processor speed, and so on). The higher-performance computer will be able to efficiently handle a larger number of OLE objects.

Trapping Errors

When you are designing a remote OLE server, you have to handle error messages differently than if the OLE server were running locally on the client machine. Usually when an OLE server is running remotely, it is running on a machine in an entirely different location from that where the client machine resides. Error messages that are displayed in a message box will then "hang up" the client until someone clicks OK on the remote OLE server's machine. As long as any error or message box is displayed from the remote OLE server, the client cannot proceed—or fail, for that matter—until someone responds to the message.

Errors should therefore always be returned to the client application. This rule is true for both local and remote OLE servers. It should be up to the client application to display the appropriate error message or take the appropriate action based on that error message.

There are two effective ways to handle error messages. The first but least advisable is to not trap any errors at all and allow them to cascade on up to the client application. The second and preferred approach is to use the Raise method to raise the error to the client application. For example:

```
Err.Raise Source:="My Neat OBJECT", Number:= 1051 + vbObjectError,
➥ Description:="Failure!"
' Returns an Error code or number of 1051
```

The `Raise` error method will properly trigger the client application's error handler. The errors that are raised back to the client are custom errors, which means they are errors that you define. OLE error values range from below 512. The rest, on up to 65,535, are user-defined error values that are defined by you. (*Error value* in this context is the error number that will be returned or raised to the client error handler.) In the preceding example, I used `1051 + vbObjectError` for the error number. This would return an error value of `1051` to the calling client application.

Dealing with Non-Trappable Errors

Some errors that can't be trapped will cause problems and potentially lock up both client and server applications. Some errors, such as the infamous "Out of Stack Space" errors, are not trappable. Therefore, when you are designing and implementing remote OLE servers, you should take extra care to ensure that errors like these never happen. The following three rules have always worked for me:

1. Stay away from recursive routines.

2. Make sure your procedure calls are not nested too deeply.

3. Be careful how data is passed between procedures (`ByVal` versus `ByRef`). Depending on how much data is passed between procedures, it is usually safe to pass most data by value (`ByVal`), which is the default. The downside is that `ByVal` uses more stack space than `ByRef`, or by reference (which only passes a pointer to the data, not the actual data itself). Please see the Visual Basic manuals or online help for further explanations of `ByVal` and `ByRef`.

Using a Pool Manager

For both local and remote automation servers, startup can be expensive because it can take several seconds for the server to initialize and start up. This time expense is an important performance factor, whether the remote automation server is already created or loaded when it is called or whether it is created on demand. Some of the larger remote automation servers can take up to several seconds to initialize; to avoid this hit in performance and help manage this issue more efficiently, the concept of Pool Managers is introduced. Pool Managers maintain pools of pre-created objects that are handed out to clients on demand, and manage load balancing and fault tolerance redundancy. Figure 15.8 is a graphical representation of how a Pool Manager is implemented.

Pool Managers can be implemented across multiple nodes in a network to provide maximum performance of remote automation servers, and they provide a simple way to handle performance issues of automation servers. Pool Managers bring the following benefits:

■ Time-consuming OLE server startups are avoided because the objects are created before the client needs them.

■ Based on the frequency of client requests, the potential number of clients (and requests), and the duration of server tasks, the Pool Manager can adjust the size of the pool (according to demand even) or the Pool Manager can, on a pre-scheduled time, create more servers.

■ The server administrator can limit the number of servers of a specific type to be created or used to a pre-determined amount. Such limits can be very useful in performance tuning.

Figure 15.8.
Sample Pool Manager implementation.

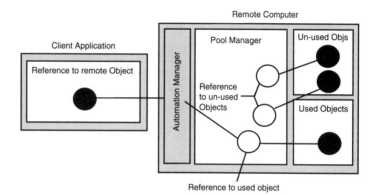

Security Issues

Remote automation supports all seven levels of security defined for RPCs, and these levels range from unprotected access to encrypted, authorized access. The Automation Connection Manager exposes four of these. See Table 15.1 for a list of these security levels.

Table 15.1. Security levels supported by RPC.

Level	Value	Description
Disallow All Remote Creates	0	No objects can be created.
Allow All Remote Creates	1	Enables any object to be created.
Allow Remote Creates by Key	2	Will enable objects to be created if the Allow Remote Activation checkbox is selected in the Automation Connection Manager.
Allow Remote Creates by ACL	3	A user can create an object only if the Access Control List for the CLSID in the Windows Registry includes the user. Windows NT only.

In addition to the Automation Component Manager, Visual Basic provides simple tools to manage remote objects, such as the Pool Manager and the Automation Connection Manager. The Component Manager enables developers to catalog, identify, locate, and distribute OLE servers in a networked environment. The Pool Manager manages OLE performance in a distributed environment by maintaining pools of objects that can be distributed to clients on demand. The Automation Manager is a multithreaded application that resides on the server (the automation server) and replaces the original OLE proxy and stub with RPCs that communicate over the network. Figure 15.9 shows an example of the Automation Manager.

Figure 15.9.
The Automation Manager.

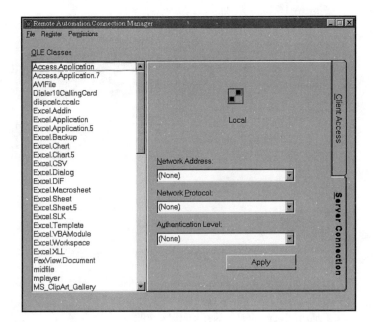

What the Future Holds

When network OLE is implemented, applications should be able to work exactly the same way they do with remote automation. Remote automation brings the developer a step closer to network OLE, which will enhance many capabilities of remote automation and OLE in general. For example, network OLE will provide a means for impersonations (the ability to log in as someone else if you have the security privileges) to chain across servers (your access privileges will be used to determine security on any server the application accesses). Your success in using remote automation will be highly dependent on your understanding of its role in the overall evolution of OLE. Remote automation enables the developer to write applications that can access remote OLE automation servers.

When network OLE does arrive, applications will be able to run with either remote automation or network OLE with no necessary code changes. The switch from remote automation to network OLE should be transparent to the users and the developer.

Summary

In this chapter you learned the implications and usefulness of remote automation and its baby step into network OLE. Remote automation can be a very powerful tool and can ease developers into creating distributed client/server applications.

Create Your Own Add-In Wizards with Visual Basic

by Merrill Mayer

CHAPTER 16

What Is an Add-In?

A Visual Basic *add-in* is an OLE server that you can add to your Visual Basic Integrated Development Environment (VBIDE). Your add-in can be either an in-process or an out-of-process server. The distinction between in-process and out-of-process servers is covered in Chapter 12, "Office Solutions and OLE Automation." Visual Basic add-ins work by manipulating the properties and methods exposed by the VBIDE through the appropriate object library (VBEXT16.OLB for 16-bit VB or VBEXT32.OLB for 32-bit VB). All add-ins are made accessible via the Add-ins menu when Visual Basic is in design mode.

Why Use Add-Ins?

You can use add-ins to extend the capabilities of Visual Basic. Add-ins enable you to do the following:

- Build Wizards to automate repetitive tasks
- Build form generators to generate forms for a new project
- Build source code controllers to enable many people to work on the same project
- Create control templates so a project will always have control with specific property defaults

Development Guidelines

Visual Basic requires that you follow certain guidelines to ensure that your add-ins operate correctly. When you develop an add-in, you should adhere to the following procedures:

- Set a reference to the Microsoft Visual Basic 4.0 Development Environment by using the References option in the Tools menu. You must set a reference to the VBIDE in order to use the properties and methods exposed by Visual Basic. Figure 16.1 shows how to set a reference to the VBIDE.

Figure 16.1.
Setting a reference to the VBIDE.

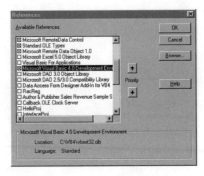

- Add a `Public` class module to the project. Every add-in must have at least one `Public` class module.

- In the `Public` class module, declare the `Public` procedures, `ConnectAddIn` and `DisConnectAddIn`. These procedures insert your add-in and delete it from the Visual Basic environment.

- Include any Visual Basic code necessary to run your add-in and manipulate the objects exposed by Visual Basic.

- Modify the VB.INI file to contain an entry that points to your add-in. This entry should include the project name and the `Public` class that contains the `ConnectAddIn` procedure. The project name corresponds to the name you enter on the Project tab of the Options dialog box. This dialog box is made available from the Tools | Options menu in Visual Basic. The VB.INI modifying entry is stored under the section named Add-Ins32 (for 32-bit Visual Basic) or Add-Ins16 (for 16-bit Visual Basic). For example, if you have a project called MyAddin and a class named `clsAddin` and you are running 32-bit Visual Basic, your VB.INI file entry would be as follows:

```
[Add-Ins32]
MyAddin.clsAddin = 0
```

> You can use code to automatically add the VB.INI entry for your add-in by calling the `GetPrivateProfileString` and `WritePrivateProfileString` APIs.

Visual Basic Objects

Like all other OLE automation servers, the Visual Basic development environment exposes a hierarchy of objects that you can manipulate with your add-in by setting properties and invoking methods. You can use the Object Browser to become familiar with the objects exposed by the VBIDE. The top-level object exposed by the VBIDE is the `Application` object and refers to Visual Basic itself. On the next level, the VBIDE exposes several more objects you can use in developing your add-in. Included among these objects are the `Menu`, `ProjectTemplate`, and `FileControl` objects.

> For more information about OLE automation and object hierarchies, please refer to Chapters 12 and 13 of this book.

The Menu Object

The Menu object is returned by the AddinMenu property of the Application object. The SubMenu object enables you to add and remove menus from the Visual Basic Add-ins menu. It is only through the Add-ins menu that you can run a Visual Basic add-in.

The ProjectTemplate Object

The ProjectTemplate object is returned by the ActiveProject property of the Application object. You can use this object to obtain information about the current project or to modify the project. For example, you can add new forms to the project or determine what components of the project are selected. Project components consist of the forms, class modules, standard modules, and resource files that are included in the active project.

The FileControl Object

The FileControl object enables your add-in to support all events concerning file control within the currently active project. By using the FileControl object, you can determine when files are added to the project or when a file is saved.

Writing the Add-In Code

After you have an understanding of how to approach add-in development and you have decided what tasks you want your add-in to accomplish, you are ready to write the code. One of the first things you will want to do is make sure to enter the correct startup form and project name in the Options dialog box. Because your add-in is an OLE server, it will typically start in the Sub Main procedure. Your project name is the name that will be stored in the VB.INI file and the name under which your add-in will be registered.

Modifying the VB.INI File

As stated earlier, you can use API calls to add an entry for your add-in in the VB.INI file. Because add-ins can run under both 16- and 32-bit Visual Basic, you should make your add-in flexible enough to support both environments. By using compiler directives, you can develop an add-in that will run in 16- and 32-bit environments. The code in Listing 16.1 shows how to declare the GetPrivateProfileString and WritePrivateProfileString APIs and how to use them to modify the VB.INI file.

Listing 16.1. Modifying the VB.INI file.

```
'In general declarations of a Module
#If Win16 Then
    Declare Function WritePrivateProfileString Lib "KERNEL"
    ➥(ByVal AppName$, ByVal KeyName$, ByVal keydefault$,
    ➥ByVal FileName$) As Integer

    Declare Function GetPrivateProfileString Lib "KERNEL"
      (ByVal AppName$, ByVal KeyName$, ByVal keydefault$,
      ➥ByVal ReturnString$, ByVal NumBytes As Integer,
      ➥ByVal FileName$) As Integer
#Else
    Declare Function WritePrivateProfileString Lib "kernel32"
    ➥Alias "WritePrivateProfileStringA"
    ➥(ByVal AppName$, ByVal KeyName$, ByVal keydefault$,
    ➥ByVal FileName$) As Long

    Declare Function GetPrivateProfileString Lib "kernel32"
    ➥Alias "GetPrivateProfileStringA"
    ➥(ByVal AppName$, ByVal KeyName$, ByVal keydefault$,
    ➥ByVal ReturnString$, ByVal NumBytes As Integer, ByVal FileName$) As Long
#End If

Sub Main()

    Dim sReturnString As String
    Dim sSection As String
    Dim liErrCode As Long

  'is add-in in the VB.INI file? If not, add it.
  #If Win16 Then
    sSection = "Add-Ins16"
  #Else
    sSection = "Add-Ins32"
  #End If

  sReturnString = String$(12, Chr$(0))
  ➥liErrCode = GetPrivateProfileString(sSection,
"ProjAddin1.clsAddin", "NotFound", sReturnString,
➥Len(sReturnString) + 1, "VB.INI")

  If Left(sReturnString, liErrCode) = "NotFound" Then
    liErrCode = WritePrivateProfileString(sSection,
    ➥"ProjAddin1.clsAddin", "0", "VB.INI")

  End If

End Sub
```

Connecting Your Add-In

When your Visual Basic add-in is installed, the ConnectAddIn procedure is executed. As a result, you must include a ConnectAddIn procedure in every add-in that you develop. The ConnectAddIn procedure is used to install menus and initialize variables. This procedure is passed one argument that indicates what instance of Visual Basic your add-in is using. Listing 16.2 shows an example of declaring the ConnectAddIn procedure.

Listing 16.2. Declaring the ConnectAddIn procedure.

```
Sub ConnectAddIn(VBINST As VBIDE.Application)

End Sub
```

You will need to make the argument passed to the ConnectAddIn procedure available to other procedures in your add-in. The recommended approach is to declare a Private object variable in your Public class (the class that contains the ConnectAddIn procedure) and pass that object reference to your other classes by means of class properties. You need to use this approach because it prevents multiple instances of your add-in from overwriting data. Although this approach is not a problem if you compile your add-in as an OLE DLL, it will definitely cause unpredictable results if you compile your add-in as an executable file. In addition, the object variable is always declared as a specific object type, VBIDE.Application. This enables early binding, which results in better performance than simply declaring the variable as a generic object type. (The concept of early binding is discussed in Chapter 12.) If you always follow this recommended approach, your add-in will have the flexibility to be compiled as either a DLL or an executable file and will achieve good performance. Listing 16.3 shows an example of this type of add-in design.

Listing 16.3. Declaring and referencing the Visual Basic instance.

```
'in the declaration section of the Public class module
Private VBIDEAppInst As VBIDE.Application
Private myClass1 As New clsMenu1

 'The ConnectAddIn Procedure of the Public class module
Sub ConnectAddIn(VBINST As VBIDE.Application)
    Set VBIDEAppInst = VBINST
    Set myClass1.VBINST = VBINST
End Sub

'in the declaration section of the clsMenu1 class module
Private mvbInst As VBIDE.Application

'the property procedure in the clsMenu1 class module
Public Property Set VBINST(pVBInst As VBIDE.Application)
    Set mvbInst = pVBInst
End Property
```

Note that the ConnectAddIn procedure sets the VBINST property of the other classes used in the add-in application. This is how the reference to the correct instance of Visual Basic is passed to the various classes used by the add-in.

Adding Menus

Your add-in can add menu items to the Visual Basic Add-Ins menu. However, your add-in cannot change any other menus in the Visual Basic development environment. Visual Basic exposes a MenuItems collection as well as SubMenu and MenuLine objects.

The MenuItems Collection

The MenuItems collection is a collection of all entries in a menu, including separator bars. The items in the MenuItems collection can be both submenus and individual menu-item objects.

The SubMenu Object

A SubMenu object is a menu in the Visual Basic environment. It contains menu lines.

The MenuLine Object

A MenuLine object represents an individual item in a menu.

Menus and Procedures

Because Visual Basic uses the Add-ins menu to run add-in procedures, your add-in must include the code that inserts new menu items in this menu. The code in Listing 16.4 uses the methods of the MenuItems collection to add a menu named Add Controls and two menu lines named TextBox and Label, respectively.

Listing 16.4. Using menus.

```
'Declarations
Private myMenu1 As VBIDE.SubMenu
Private myMenuLine1 As VBIDE.MenuLine
Private myMenuLine2 As VBIDE.MenuLine

Private myClass1 As New clsMenu1
Private myClass2 As New clsMenu2
Private VBIDEAppInst As VBIDE.Application

Sub ConnectAddIn(VBINST As VBIDE.Application)
    Set VBIDEAppInst = VBINST
    Set myClass1.VBINST = VBINST
    Set myClass2.VBINST = VBINST

    Set myMenu1 = VBINST.AddInMenu.MenuItems.AddMenu("Add &Controls")
    Set myMenuLine1 = myMenu1.MenuItems.Add("&TextBox")
    Set myMenuLine2 = myMenu1.MenuItems.Add("&Label")
```

continues

Listing 16.4. continued

```
    myMenuLine1.ConnectEvents myClass1
    myMenuLine2.ConnectEvents myClass2
End Sub
```

After you add your menu and menu items to the Visual Basic Add-Ins menu, you need to write the code that Visual Basic should execute when your menu is activated. To do this, insert a class module for each `MenuLine` you defined in your add-in. In each class module, include a procedure named `AfterClick`. The `AfterClick` procedure is executed when the menu item is activated.

If you refer back to Listing 16.4, you will notice that there are object references to two classes, `myClass1` and `myClass2`. These are the classes that represent the `MenuLine` objects, and they must contain the `AfterClick` procedures. In your add-in, you must create an instance of each class before the class can be used. Listing 16.4 also uses the `ConnectEvents` method to associate a menu item with the code that is to be executed when the menu is activated. After all these tasks have been completed in your `ConnectAddIn` procedure, you can write the code for the `AfterClick` procedures in each class. Listing 16.5 shows an example of using an `AfterClick` procedure in your add-in.

Listing 16.5. An `AfterClick` procedure.

```
Public Sub AfterClick ()
    Msgbox "This is the menu"
End Sub
```

Removing Menus

The `Remove` method removes a menu. The following code sample removes the main menu `myMenu1`. When this menu is removed, all the menu lines associated with that menu also are removed.

```
VBIDEAppInst.AddInMenu.MenuItems.Remove myMenu1
```

You also can use the `DisconnectEvents` method to disconnect a menu from an object before removing the menu. Once a disconnect event is executed, the menu item can no longer receive or respond to menu item selections. If you remove a menu completely, the `DisconnectEvents` method is not required. However, if you do use the `DisconnectEvents` method, you would need to store the identifier returned when the `ConnectEvents` method is executed. Listing 16.6 demonstrates how you could modify the `ConnectAddIn` procedure to store the identifier and then use this identifier to invoke the `DisconnectEvents` method.

Listing 16.6. Using the DisconnectEvents **method.**

```
'In the declarations section of the Public class
private liConnect1 as long
private liConnect2 as long

'in the ConnectAddIn procedure
liConnect1 = myMenuLine1.ConnectEvents(myClass1)
liConnect2 = myMenuLine2.ConnectEvents(myClass2)

'in the DisConnectAddIn procedure
myMenuLine1.DisconnectEvents liConnect1
myMenuLine2.DisconnectEvents liConnect2
```

Disconnecting Your Add-In

When your add-in is removed from the active instance of Visual Basic, the DisConnectAddIn procedure is executed. An integer value is passed from Visual Basic to your DisConnectAddIn procedure specifying why your add-in is being disconnected. If a zero is passed, it means Visual Basic is being closed. If a 1 is passed, it means the Add-In Manager is removing the add-in. Listing 16.7 shows an example of a DisConnectAddIn procedure.

Listing 16.7. The DisConnectAddIn **procedure.**

```
Sub DisConnectAddIn(ByVal mode As Integer)
    VBIDEAppInst.AddInMenu.MenuItems.Remove myMenu1
End Sub
```

Working with Forms

One major benefit of using add-ins in Visual Basic is that you gain the ability to create templates that enable you to add predefined forms and classes to any project. You can use the AddFile method to add forms, class modules, or standard modules to the active project. When you are adding forms or modules to a project, you follow the same guidelines that were previously described in this chapter. This means that you need to add the necessary classes, establish a reference to the correct instance of Visual Basic, and provide code to connect add-in menu items to the task you want your add-in to perform. Listing 16.8 shows an example of adding a form to the active project.

Listing 16.8. Adding a form to a project.

```
'declarations
Option Explicit
Private mvbInst As VBIDE.Application
```

continues

Listing 16.8. continued

```
Public Sub AfterClick()

    mvbInst.ActiveProject.AddFile App.Path & "\frmDialog.frm"

End Sub

Public Property Set VBINST(pVBInst As VBIDE.Application)
    Set mvbInst = pVBInst
End Property
```

If you want your add-in to add a new, blank form to the current project, you would use the `AddFormTemplate` method. Listing 16.9 shows how this method is used.

Listing 16.9. Adding a blank form to a project.

```
Sub AfterClick()
    Dim myNewForm As FormTemplate

    Set myNewForm = mvbInst.ActiveProject.AddFormTemplate

End Sub
```

Working with Controls

One way you work with controls in your add-in is when you use the `AddFile` method to add forms that already contain a number of controls. However, you might want your add-in to place new controls on a form in the active project. The ability to add controls to a form enables you to define controls that always conform to certain specifications. This means that the controls you add via your add-in could already have many properties set. For example, you could add a command button with its caption property set to OK and its default property set to True. You would use the `Add` method of the `ControlTemplates` collection to add a control to a form. The `Properties` collection enables you to set the various properties of a form or control. Listing 16.10 shows an example of adding a text box control to a form. The code sets the size and location of the text box, as well as its `Name` property.

Listing 16.10. Adding controls to a form.

```
Public Sub AfterClick()

    Dim myForm As FormTemplate
    Dim myControl As ControlTemplate
    Dim iTextCount As Integer
    Dim iHeight As Integer
    Dim iTop As Integer
    Dim iLeft As Integer
    Dim sTextName As String
```

```
    On Error GoTo AfterClickError
    Set myForm = mvbInst.ActiveProject.ActiveForm
    On Error GoTo 0
    iHeight = 300
    iLeft - 1100
    iTop = 120
    For Each myControl In myForm.ControlTemplates
        If myControl.ClassName = "VB.TextBox" Then
            iTextCount = iTextCount + 1
        End If
    Next myControl
    Set myControl = myForm.ControlTemplates.Add("TextBox")
    sTextName = "txtName" & Trim(Str$(iTextCount + 1))
    With myControl
        .Properties("Name") = sTextName
        .Properties("Text") = ""
        .Properties("Height") = iHeight
        .Properties("Left") = iLeft
        If iTextCount = 0 Then
            .Properties("Top") = iTop
        Else
            .Properties("Top") = iTop + ((iHeight + 60) * iTextCount)
        End If
    End With
 Exit Sub
AfterClickError:
    Exit Sub
End Sub
```

Adding Menus to Forms

Just as you can add controls to a form, you also can add menus. This enables you to develop an add-in to build forms that already have standard Windows-type menus such as File, Edit, and Window. You could even develop an add-in that enables users to pick which menus they want and then add those menus to the form.

Like controls, menus are accessed as ControlTemplate objects. You can add menus after existing menus but not between two menus. You use the AddMenuTemplate method to add menus to a form. This method enables you to set the menu name and access key. It also enables you to specify where in the menu hierarchy the menu should fit: as a top-level menu or as a menu item. You specify a top-level menu by setting the parent parameter to Nothing. For all other menu items, you must specify the ControlTemplate object that you have set as the parent menu.

Listing 16.11 shows how to add a new, blank form to the project and then add both a File and an Edit menu to that form. Notice that each top-level menu has items that appear when the menu drops down. The format of the menus is established by setting the top-level menu as the parent for the additional menu items. Figure 16.2 shows how the form looks after it has been added to the project.

Listing 16.11. Adding menus to a form.

```
Public Sub AfterClick()

    Dim myNewForm As VBIDE.FormTemplate
    Dim myMenu As VBIDE.ControlTemplate
    Dim myMenuItem As VBIDE.ControlTemplate

    On Error GoTo AfterClickError
    Set myNewForm = mvbInst.ActiveProject.AddFormTemplate

    Set myMenu = myNewForm.AddMenuTemplate("mnuFile", Nothing)
    myMenu.Properties("Caption").Value = "&File"
    Set myMenuItem = myNewForm.AddMenuTemplate("itmExit", myMenu)
    myMenuItem.Properties("Caption").Value = "E&xit"
    Set myMenu = myNewForm.AddMenuTemplate("mnuEdit", Nothing)
    myMenu.Properties("Caption").Value = "&Edit"
    Set myMenuItem = myNewForm.AddMenuTemplate("itmCut", myMenu)
    myMenuItem.Properties("Caption").Value = "Cu&t"
    Set myMenuItem = myNewForm.AddMenuTemplate("itmCopy", myMenu)
    myMenuItem.Properties("Caption").Value = "&Copy"
    Set myMenuItem = myNewForm.AddMenuTemplate("itmPast", myMenu)
    myMenuItem.Properties("Caption").Value = "&Paste"

    On Error GoTo 0
    Exit Sub
AfterClickError:
    Exit Sub
End Sub
```

Figure 16.2.
*Adding forms and menus
to a project.*

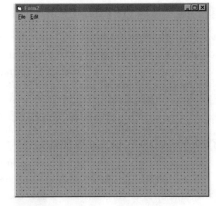

Adding Code to Forms

Not only can you add forms, controls, and menus by using add-ins, but also you can add code
to a form. You use the InsertFile method to place code from a file into a form. With the
InsertFile method, the code is inserted as though you had inserted the file using the File
command in the Insert menu. The code will appear after the last declaration and before the first

procedure in the form. If you modify the code shown in Listing 16.11, you can expand the functionality of the add-in to insert code in the new form in the project. The following line of code will insert the contents of the specified file into the new form created by the add-in·

```
myNewForm.InsertFile App.Path & "\FileAdd.txt"
```

You can enhance your add-in's capability to add code to forms by using standard file I/O to create a text file with code at runtime and then invoking the `InsertFile` method to place the file into a form.

Working with the `FileControl` Object

The `FileControl` object lets your add-in know when file events occur. You can use the `FileControl` object to determine when a file is added to a project or a file is saved. Your add-in's capability to intercept file-related events enables you to implement a complex source code controller. Although building a complete source-code control system is beyond the scope of this chapter, you learn some of the file management capabilities found in add-ins in this section.

When you design an add-in that uses the `FileControl` object, you begin by following the same steps already outlined in this chapter. This means you must still code class modules, modify the VB.INI file, and connect events. In addition, you must create code to handle any `FileControl` events. This includes invoking the `ConnectEvents` method for the `FileControl` object. Listing 16.12 shows the code for trapping the events when a new project is opened and when a file is saved under a new name. The code shows a record of the events in a text box on a form. Notice that the `AfterClick` procedure displays the form used for this add-in. A complete list of `FileControl` events can be found by using Visual Basic online help.

Listing 16.12. Using `FileControl` events.

```
'the public class
Set VBIDEAppInst = VBInst

    Set myMenuLine = VBIDEAppInst.AddInMenu.MenuItems.Add("Show File Events")

    Set myClass.myMenuLine = myMenuLine

    mClassID = myMenuLine.ConnectEvents(myClass)

    myClass.AfterClick

    'Connect our event handler to the FileControl object
    mFileEventID = VBIDEAppInst.FileControl.ConnectEvents(myClass)

 'the file events class
Public Sub AfterClick()
    frmFileEvents.Show
End Sub
```

continues

Listing 16.12. continued

```
Public Sub DoGetNewFileName (FileType As Integer,
➥NewName As String, OldName As String, CancelDefault As Boolean)
    Dim sFileType As String
    Select Case FileType
        Case vbextFileTypeForm
            sFileType = "Form"
        Case vbextFileTypeModule
            sFileType = "Module"
        Case vbextFileTypeClass
            sFileType = "Class"
        Case vbextFileTypeProject
            sFileType = "Project"
        Case vbextFileTypeExe
            sFileType = "EXE FIle"
        Case vbextFileTypeFrx
            sFileType = "FRX File"
        Case vbextFileTypeRes = "Resource"
    End Select

    frmFileEvents.txtFiles.Text = "New File Name " & NewName & " " & sFileType
End Sub

Public Sub DoGetOpenProjectName(ProjectName As String,
➥CancelDefault As Boolean)
    frmFileEvents.txtFiles.Text = "opened project " & ProjectName
End Sub
```

Installing Your Add-In

Before you install your add-in, it must be properly registered. If you compile your add-in as an .EXE file, the add-in is automatically registered the first time it is run. However, an OLEDLL file must be manually registered. In this case, you can use the Regsvr32.exe program that ships with Visual Basic to register your add-in. For example, the following code registers an OLEDLL add-in named projAddin.dll:

```
c:\vb4\clisvr\Regsvr32.exe  c:\vb4\progs\projAddin.dll
```

After your add-in has been properly registered, you can use the Add-In Manager to incorporate your add-in into the Visual Basic environment. If you try to use the Add-In Manager before your add-in has been registered, Visual Basic will display an error dialog and remove the add-in from the VB.INI file.

The Add-In Manager is available as an item in the Visual Basic Add-ins menu. Figure 16.3 shows how an add-in looks when it is selected in the Add-In Manager.

After your add-in is installed, you have completed the design and development process. You can now continue to test your add-in and enhance its features and functions.

Figure 16.3.
The Add-In Manager.

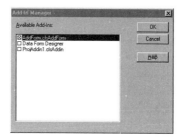

Summary

Add-ins provide a useful way to extend the Visual Basic development environment. Add-ins range in scope from defining simple control templates to developing complete source control systems, thereby enabling you to design the type of add-ins that fit your needs.

The Formula One Control

by Frank Font

17

CHAPTER

Formula One version 3.1 is a sophisticated and fast spreadsheet control that you can embed into your Visual Basic applications. It saves development time by delivering tested and high-performing Excel functionality right into your Visual Basic programs. You might say, "Why get something *like* Excel when I can have the real Excel?" From the perspective of a developer, there are at least three reasons: speed, resources, and distribution costs. Let me explain:

■ Excel is a complete end-user application that also can be used for development purposes. However, all that front-end-user interface code makes Excel much bigger and slower than Formula One. Formula One is a developer component that delivers Excel 4, 5, and 7 file compatibility into your programs.

■ It is no secret that Excel requires a lot of resources to run. If your applications will be used in a Windows 3.1 environment, this resource load is a serious consideration. It is less of an issue for Windows 95 and Windows NT users. Formula One requires fewer system resources. (On more than one occasion, I've developed an Excel application that would not run under Windows 3.1 due to system resource limitations.)

■ As an end-user application, Excel is meant to be purchased by all those who will use it. On the other hand, Formula One 3.1 is a developer tool with no runtime licensing fees. This means that, as a developer, you need to pay for Formula One, but persons running your programs do not.

This chapter explores some of the ways Formula One can help you write appealing Visual Basic programs more efficiently. Each section of the chapter focuses on one aspect of the control. Where appropriate, samples with code are presented. But before we jump into that, let's get an overview of the control and some basic spreadsheet concepts.

If you would like to compile the samples of this chapter yourself, you will need to purchase and install the Formula One control. Formula One 3.1 is a product of Visual Components, Inc. (http://www.visualcomp.com), and is not included with Visual Basic and is not on the CD-ROM that accompanies this book. The sample code from this chapter is, however, on the included CD-ROM.

Some Spreadsheet Fundamentals

Most computer professionals know that a spreadsheet is a grid of some type that can take numbers as input and process them. For those whose knowledge of spreadsheets stops there, let me mention some fundamentals about today's Excel-style spreadsheets:

■ As illustrated in Figure 17.1, sheets of workbooks are composed of cells. (In contrast to Excel 5 and 7, the Excel 4 file format did not support the "workbook" concept. It allowed only one worksheet per file. Groups of sheets saved together as one entity are workbooks.) Workbooks are just groups of these sheets "bound" together into one file. Sheets in a workbook usually have names that identify them displayed on tabs.

Figure 17.1.
A Formula One spread-sheet and its components.

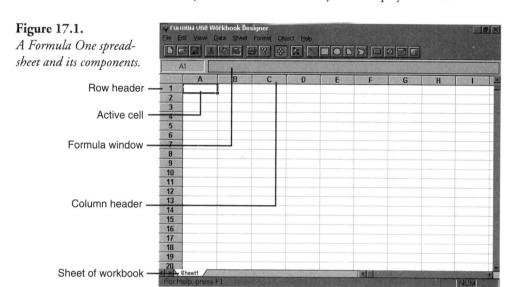

Cells can contain data or formulas. (An odd concept to get used to is that the cells with formulas also contain the result of the formula. What you see all depends on how you reference the cell. See the formula window in Figure 17.2 for an example.)

Figure 17.2.
The Formula One 3.1 16-bit spreadsheet designer interface.

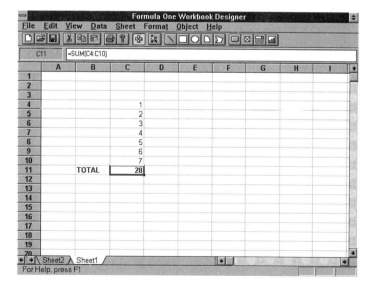

- Formulas can reference other cells in a spreadsheet or workbook of spreadsheets. Cell references are commonly of the form A1, where A is the letter of the column and 1 is the number of the row. Alternatively, cell references can be in R1C2 format, where 1 is the row number and 2 is the column number. Other referencing methods include using named ranges or offset functions.

- Each cell or group of cells can be formatted in sophisticated ways. Generally, you can add lines, edit color, and determine presentation of cell contents.

- Cells can be used for user input.

- Cells can be used for data output.

- Cell formula calculations are nonprocedural. In other words, the formula calculation sequence is determined by the spreadsheet control. The particular formulas in the cells, however, are established by the spreadsheet developer.

- Formulas are anything that begin with an equal sign. For example, the entry SUM(A1:A2) in a cell would not be interpreted by the control as a formula. However, the entry =SUM(A1:A2) would be recognized as a formula. In the latter case, the cell in which that formula is entered would display the sum of cells A1 and A2.

> A good way to comment out a formula in a workbook sheet is to precede it with the word REM. This clearly indicates that the formula has been disabled. A *very bad* way to comment out a formula is to precede it with a space. Under some viewing modes this formula will not look disabled, which can cause difficult debugging problems down the road.

As mentioned earlier, Formula One 3.1 is an Excel 7-compatible OCX. It is both file compatible and formula structure compatible with Excel 7. However, there are some limitations, as illustrated in Table 17.1. Consult the literature that accompanies Formula One for full details.

Table 17.1. Some limitations of the Formula One 3.1 component.

Feature	Limitations
Excel 4, 5, and 7 file compatible	Excel add-ins, native Excel charts, and function arrays are not supported. Also, Formula One cannot read files that have been password protected in Excel. If your Excel files contain unsupported features, you should not use them with Formula One.
Excel 7 formulas	Some Excel 7 formulas are not available in Formula One. In particular, no Excel formulas that require add-ins are supported.
Macros	Formula One does not have a macro language.

Formula One can be used to create new Excel 4, 5, or 7 compatible sheets at runtime. It supports other file formats also, as illustrated in Table 17.2.

Table 17.2. File formats supported by the Formula One 3.1 OCX control.

Format	Description
Formula One	The native file format of Formula One has a .VTS extension by default. This format supports some features not available to Excel. (The VTS format supports cell validation and its own version of password protection.)
Excel	Formula One can read and write Excel 4, 5, and 7 files. These files have .XLS extensions by default.
Tab delimited	Formula One can create tab-delimited files of its spreadsheets. These files usually have .TXT extensions.

Formula One also comes with a small user interface of its own that can be used at design time to create and format spreadsheets for use in your programs. This interface looks and behaves as you would expect a modest spreadsheet application to look and behave. The 16-bit version is shown previously in Figure 17.2. You can disable that interface so your users cannot access it at runtime. You also can elect to create your spreadsheets in your favorite application, as long as that application can save in Excel 4, 5, or 7 format.

With the Formula One component, your applications can process calculations that are defined on spreadsheets. Sometimes, sophisticated calculations are easier to implement and maintain as a spreadsheet or spreadsheet workbook. In addition, in some cases, using this component to do complex calculations can be faster and more accurate at runtime than building the same calculations in native Visual Basic code. As a bonus, Formula One can calculate some spreadsheet formulas faster than Excel.

Presentation of information has always been a use for spreadsheets. Reports that are not of the repeating-row variety are a natural to implement with this tool. Formula One has advanced and easy-to-use spreadsheet formatting features. The spreadsheets can be customized at design time to look just as you want them to and then printed at runtime. You can easily display these sheets on your screen from your program before printing them.

This section only skims the subject of what a spreadsheet is and some of the general uses. For more detail about these concepts, you should consult the documentation of a commercial spreadsheet application or the Formula One help file. However, for a practical examination of how to use the Formula One component in your Visual Basic 4 applications, read on.

Using Formula One for User Input

To illustrate how the spreadsheet cells can be manipulated at runtime from Visual Basic code, let's look at a small program. Formula One is good for collecting user input because, unlike the standard Microsoft grid and DBGrid controls that come with Visual Basic, it can store user entries directly without resorting to database tables and arrays.

The program that illustrates this use of the control is called MAKESQL and can be found on the CD-ROM that accompanies this book. Of side interest, this program constructs a legitimate SQL statement from the contents of the user entry in the displayed grid. Figure 17.3 shows what the interface looks like.

Figure 17.3.
The MAKESQL program running in the Visual Basic environment.

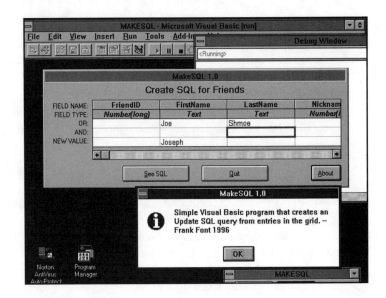

The bulk of the grid manipulations happen in the InitSQLUpdate and ParseSQLUpdate subroutines. As shown in Listing 17.1, the initialization subroutine assigns initial values to the grid and formats it.

Listing 17.1. Visual Basic 4.0 code that initializes the environment of the MAKESQL program.

```
'-----------------------------------------------------------------
'Initialize the grid control with database field names and appropriate
'formatting.
'-----------------------------------------------------------------
Sub InitSQLUpdate()
Dim tc, i%, NewRow$
Dim FieldCnt%
```

```
'Initialize the data control.
dtaWorkFile.DatabaseName = App.Path & "\SAMPLE.MDB"
dtaWorkFile.RecordSource = "Friends"
dtaWorkFile.Refresh

'Store number of FieldCnt in a local variable.
FieldCnt = dtaWorkFile.Database.TableDefs(0).Fields.Count

'Configure the grid size and cell widths.
xlsBatchChange.SetColWidth 1, FieldCnt, 18 * 256, 2560
xlsBatchChange.MaxCol = FieldCnt

'Name the columns and fill in first row of cells.
For i = 1 To FieldCnt
  xlsBatchChange.ColText(i) =
    ➥dtaWorkFile.Database.TableDefs(1).Fields(i - 1).name
  xlsBatchChange.EntryRC(1, i) =
    ➥DBFTypeName(dtaWorkFile.Database.TableDefs(0).Fields(i - 1).Type)
Next

'Select the first row of cells.
xlsBatchChange.SetSelection 1, 1, 1, FieldCnt

'Change the font.
Dim pf$, ps%, pb As Boolean, pi As Boolean, pu As Boolean
Dim pstrike As Boolean, pcr As Long, pout As Boolean, px As Boolean
xlsBatchChange.GetFont pf, ps, pb, pi, pu, pstrike, pcr, pout, px
xlsBatchChange.SetFont pf, -ps, ps, True, pu, pstrike, pcr, pout, px

'Change the background.
Dim pat%, fg&, bg&
xlsBatchChange.GetPattern pat%, fg, bg
xlsBatchChange.SetPattern 1, &HC0C0C0, bg

'Add a border.
Dim lb%, rb%, tb%, bb%, shade%, lc&, rc&, topc&, bc&, crout&
xlsBatchChange.GetBorder lb, rb, tb, bb, shade, lc, rc, topc, bc
xlsBatchChange.SetBorder -1, 1, 1, 1, 1, shade, crout, lc, rc, topc, bc

'Align the text.
Dim ph%, pw As Boolean, pv%, po%
xlsBatchChange.GetAlignment ph, pw, pv, po
xlsBatchChange.SetAlignment F1HAlignCenter, pw, pv, po

'Do not let users type in row 1.
xlsBatchChange.SetSelection 1, 1, 1, FieldCnt
xlsBatchChange.SetProtection True, False

'Let users type into row 2.
xlsBatchChange.SetSelection 2, 1, 2, FieldCnt
xlsBatchChange.SetProtection False, False

'Let users type in row 3.
xlsBatchChange.SetSelection 2, 1, 3, FieldCnt
xlsBatchChange.SetProtection False, False
```

continues

Listing 17.1. continued

```
'Let users type in row 4.
xlsBatchChange.SetSelection 2, 1, 4, FieldCnt
xlsBatchChange.SetProtection False, False

'Unselect the rows and protect the sheet.
xlsBatchChange.SetSelection 1, 1, 1, 1
xlsBatchChange.EnableProtection = True

'Activate the first cell on the sheet.
xlsBatchChange.SetActiveCell 2, 1

End Sub
```

The parsing routine reads the cells of the grid to determine what the SQL statement should contain. Listing 17.2 shows how this is done. Most of the grid-handling code is at the top of this routine.

Listing 17.2. Visual Basic 4.0 code that reads the contents of the Formula One grid to create a SQL statement.

```
'- - - - - - - - - - - - - - - - - - - - - - - - - - - - - - - - - - - - - - - - - -
'This subroutine reads the grid control for contents that describe
'the update query to construct.
'- - - - - - - - - - - - - - - - - - - - - - - - - - - - - - - - - - - - - - - - - -
Function ParseSQLUpdate() As String
  Dim i%, ValueCol%
  Dim sWHERE$, sAND$, sOR$, sSET$
  Dim FieldNames(MAXFLDS) As String, FieldName As String
  Dim OrValues(MAXFLDS), OrValue
  Dim AndValues(MAXFLDS), AndValue
  Dim SetValues(MAXFLDS), SetValue
  Dim FieldTypes(MAXFLDS) As Integer
  Dim FieldCnt%, CRLF$


  'Some initializations.
  On Error GoTo ParseSQLUpdate_Err
  ParseSQLUpdate = ""
  FieldCnt = dtaWorkFile.Database.TableDefs(0).Fields.Count
  CRLF = Chr(13) & Chr(10)

  'Parse each cell of the grid.
  ValueCol = 0
  For i = 1 To FieldCnt

    'Load the content of each column into a temporary variable.
    OrValue = Trim(xlsBatchChange.EntryRC(2, i))
    AndValue = Trim(xlsBatchChange.EntryRC(3, i))
    SetValue = Trim(xlsBatchChange.EntryRC(4, i))

    'Do we have something to process?
    If Len(OrValue) > 0 Or Len(AndValue) > 0 Or Len(SetValue) > 0 Then

      ValueCol = ValueCol + 1
```

```
      'Load the field information into the arrays.
      FieldNames(ValueCol) =
         ➥dtaWorkFile.Database.TableDefs(1).Fields(i - 1).name
      FieldTypes(ValueCol) =
         ➥dtaWorkFile.Database.TableDefs(0).Fields(i - 1).Type

      'Set the all fields to null by default.
      OrValues(ValueCol) = "/NULL"
      AndValues(ValueCol) = "/NULL"
      SetValues(ValueCol) = "/NULL"

      'Set the appropriate portions of the SQL statement.
      If Len(AndValue) > 0 Then
        'Value in the AND row.
        If UCase(Left(AndValue, 6)) = "/BLANK" Then
          AndValues(ValueCol) = ""
        Else
          AndValues(ValueCol) = AndValue
        End If
      ElseIf Len(OrValue) > 0 Then
        'Value in the OR row.
        If UCase(Left(OrValue, 6)) = "/BLANK" Then
          OrValues(ValueCol) = ""
        Else
          OrValues(ValueCol) = OrValue
        End If
      End If
      If Len(SetValue) > 0 Then
        'Value in the SET row.
        If UCase(Left(SetValue, 6)) = "/BLANK" Then
          SetValues(ValueCol) = ""
        Else
          SetValues(ValueCol) = SetValue
        End If
      End If
    End If
Next i

'Process the parsed data into a complete SQL query.
If ValueCol = 0 Then
  MsgBox "Found nothing in the grid to parse.", 48, ProgramName
Else

  'Create the AND part first.
  sAND = ""
  For i = 1 To ValueCol
    If AndValues(i) <> "/NULL" Then
      If Len(sAND) > 0 Then sAND = sAND & " AND "
      sAND = sAND & Trim(FieldNames(i)) & "="
      Select Case FieldTypes(i)
      Case dbDate, dbText, dbMemo
        sAND = sAND & "'" & Trim(AndValues(i)) & "'"
      Case Else
        sAND = sAND & Trim(AndValues(i))
      End Select
    End If
  Next
```

continues

Listing 17.2. continued

```
    'Create the OR part.
    sOR = ""
    For i = 1 To ValueCol
      If OrValues(i) <> "/NULL" Then
        If Len(sOR) > 0 Then sOR = sOR & " OR "
        sOR = sOR & Trim(FieldNames(i)) & "="
        Select Case FieldTypes(i)
        Case dbDate, dbText, dbMemo
          sOR = sOR & "'" & Trim(OrValues(i)) & "'"
        Case Else
          sOR = sOR & Trim(OrValues(i))
        End Select
      End If
    Next

    'Create the SQL SET clause.
    sSET = ""
    For i = 1 To ValueCol
      If SetValues(i) <> "/NULL" Then
        If Len(sSET) > 0 Then sSET = sSET & ", "
        sSET = sSET & Trim(FieldNames(i)) & "="
        Select Case FieldTypes(i)
        Case dbDate, dbText, dbMemo
          sSET = sSET & "'" & Trim(SetValues(i)) & "'"
        Case Else
          sSET = sSET & Trim(SetValues(i))
        End Select
      End If
    Next

    'Were any fields designated to be changed?
    If Len(sSET) = 0 Then
      MsgBox "No update fields were specified.", , ProgramName
      Exit Function
    End If

    'Write the SQL Where clause.
    If Len(sAND) > 0 And Len(sOR) > 0 Then
      sWHERE = " (" & sAND & ") AND (" & sOR & ");"
    ElseIf Len(sAND) > 0 Then
      sWHERE = sAND & ";"
    ElseIf Len(sOR) > 0 Then
      sWHERE = sOR & ";"
    Else
      MsgBox "No selection criteria was entered.", , ProgramName
      Exit Function
    End If

    'Construct the SQL command.
    ParseSQLUpdate = "UPDATE " & dtaWorkFile.RecordSource & CRLF & _
                     "SET " & sSET & CRLF & "WHERE " & sWHERE
  End If

  Exit Function

ParseSQLUpdate_Err:
```

```
      MsgBox Error(), 16, ProgramName
      ParseSQLUpdate = ""
      Exit Function

ParseSQLUpdate_ErrSQL:
      MsgBox Error(), 16, ProgramName
      ParseSQLUpdate = ""
      Exit Function

End Function
```

Formula One as a Calculation Engine

The Formula One component supports many of the formulas that Excel does. Formulas include those of the usual mathematical variety, such as `SIN()`, `TAN()`, `SUM()`, and so on; those of the logical kind, such as `OR()`, `AND()`, and `IF()`; and the text-handling types, such as `LEN()`, `LEFT()`, and so on. Consult the Formula One help file for a complete list of formulas and usage details.

> Programs based on spreadsheets open up a terrific opportunity to coordinate the efforts of technical and nontechnical people. One good strategy that maximizes the benefit to all involved parties is as follows:
>
> 1. Identify all the input values the program will need to collect for calculations.
>
> 2. Identify all the output values the program will calculate.
>
> 3. Agree on a spreadsheet layout with respect to where the input values will be placed on the spreadsheet and where the output values will appear.
>
> 4. Let the calculation expert work independently on the calculations of the spreadsheet and the software developer work independently on the interface features of the program. (The programmer is working with a "dummy" sheet in the meantime. This dummy sheet has test values placed into the output cells of the spreadsheet. The programmer works to place values into the input cells of that same sheet.)
>
> 5. When the calculations are done, the programmer replaces his or her dummy sheet with the real sheet.
>
> This can be a highly productive strategy because it decouples the work of the person who implements the calculations from that of the programmer who develops other aspects of the program. Some advantages of this technique, besides saving time, are as follows:

- The programmer is not in a position to misinterpret or misimplement a calculation because implementing the calculations is the task of the calculation expert working with the spreadsheet. This spreads responsibility around and takes some pressure off the programmer while reducing the chance of error.

- Because the calculations are not translated from what the calculation expert is familiar with, that person can continue to maintain the calculations in the future. This makes updates easier.

- Calculations can be tested and independently verified before the program is complete. This does not have to involve the programmer, and thus does not distract the programmer from his or her development effort. In addition, the calculation expert will not have to wait for the programmer to finish translating his or her calculations into code before trying them out.

- In many cases, sophisticated calculations both are easier to code in a spreadsheet and will run faster than they will if coded in standard Visual Basic.

Few techniques can compare to this one for coupling the development potential of nontechnical calculation experts and software developers.

Formulas are calculated by the Formula One control automatically if the `AutoRecalc` property is true. Otherwise, they calculate when the `Recalc` method is issued for the workbook by the program. A workbook can contain one or many sheets.

You can use the techniques shown in Listing 17.2 of the MAKESQL program to place values into input cells of a workbook sheet for calculation. You can use those same techniques to read the results back into your program for other processing. A good sequence of events for this type of operation with `AutoRecalc` set to false is as follows:

1. Place values into the input cells of a workbook sheet that is used for calculations.

2. Issue the `Recalc` method.

3. Read the results from the output cells of the workbook sheet.

If you will use sheets internally for calculation purposes, keeping `AutoRecalc` off is generally a good idea because it gives you greater control over the timing of the workbook calculations. If the workbooks contain many formulas or are very complex, this setting can be a significant source of performance benefit.

If you want to keep your formulas away from prying eyes, don't save your workbooks to disk. Instead, keep them as part of the control. This is the default state of any sheets created at design time using Formula One. Alternatively, you can hide rows and protect a workbook with a password if it is saved as a .VTS file on disk.

Sharp Reports

You can take advantage of Formula One's formidable layout and formatting features to create form-style reports. The forms to be printed are just workbook sheets that have been laid out in whatever manner is appropriate, such as to look like a standard form that otherwise would be filled out manually. The general sequence of steps to implement something like this is as follows:

1. Place a Formula One control on a form.
2. Create the report layout that you desire using the Formula One designer, Excel, or some other spreadsheet tool. This is the time to create borders, define number formats, and determine colors.
3. At runtime, place values into the appropriate cells of the sheet.
4. Print the sheet.

> When you are formatting a workbook sheet, consider compressing some rows and columns to zero height or width so they remain between visible rows and columns but are not visible themselves. Should you ever need to add another column or row between those that already exist, you will then be able to do it without affecting the addresses of existing entries. Adding a new row or column in that case is just a matter of unhiding what has always been there. (This is knowledge from the school of hard knocks.)

You can place values onto a workbook sheet through Text, Formula, FormulaRC, or Entry properties of the sheet cells. Alternatively, formulas on the report sheets can directly reference cells of other workbook sheets in the project. For example, if a project has a calculation workbook where one of the values to be printed in a report is in cell A10 of Sheet1, and that calculation workbook is called xlsMainCalcs, then a cell of the report sheet could reference that value with the following formula:

```
=[xlsMainCalcs]Sheet1!A10
```

Issuing a Recalc method to a report sheet just before printing the sheet would refresh it with the contents of the calculation sheet from which the report sheet draws numbers. This method of updating report forms can be easier to maintain than paste operations coded in Visual Basic.

Once you are satisfied that a report sheet is ready for printing, you can send it to the printer by issuing a FilePrint method on the workbook object. For example, to print the active worksheet of a workbook called xlsWorkBook, you would issue the command xlsWorkBook.FilePrint in your Visual Basic program. Table 17.3 shows some of the properties and methods available for printing workbook sheets. Many of these methods and properties work two ways: You can use them to read values and also use them to set values. Consult the Formula One help file for syntax details.

Table 17.3. Some methods and properties important for printing worksheets.

Method or Property	Brief Description
FilePageSetupDlg	Shows the Page Setup dialog box.
FilePrint	Prints the current sheet of the workbook.
FilePrintSetupDlg	Displays the Windows Print Setup dialog box.
PrintArea	Enables you to define what section of the current worksheet you want to print.
PrintBottomMargin	Sets the bottom margin.
PrintColHeading	Disables the printing of column headings.
PrintDevMode	Enables you to access the Windows API DEVMODE printer structure.
PrintFooter	Defines the current page footer.
PrintGridLines	Determines whether the gridlines will print.
PrintHCenter	Defines the horizontal centering setting.
PrintHeader	Defines the current page header.
PrintLandscape	Toggles landscape printing.
PrintLeftMargin	Defines the left margin.
PrintLeftToRight	Determines the order in which sheet content is printed. This option is relevant when more than one paper sheet will be required.
PrintNoColor	Determines whether color will be used.
PrintRightMargin	Defines the right margin.
PrintRowHeading	Disables printing of the row headings.
PrintTitles	Defines the text to print on each page.
PrintTopMargin	Defines the top margin.
PrintVCenter	Defines the vertical centering setting.
SetPrintAreaFromSelection	Sets the print area.
SetPrintScale	Sets scaling or fit to pages.
SetPrintTitlesFromSelection	Defines the current selection as the text to print on each page.

Summary

The advantages of Formula One over full spreadsheet applications such as Excel are higher speed, lower resource usage, and lower distribution costs. In addition, you can achieve greater functional control of the spreadsheets through the combination of this component and Visual Basic than you can achieve under the scripting language of full-fledged spreadsheet applications.

This chapter illustrates some of the methods and mentions some properties of the Formula One control. A sample program is included that formats the cells of an embedded workbook sheet and reads the cell contents after user input. Some cell formula syntax also is shown to demonstrate referencing cells between separate workbooks.

Some spreadsheet concepts are introduced superficially early in the chapter. For more information on spreadsheets and spreadsheet concepts, consult the help file that comes with Formula One. Additional insight can be gained by reading materials that cover Microsoft Excel, because many Excel concepts and methods overlap with those of Formula One.

Tapping Into Databases with Visual Basic

PART 3

Using the Data Control and the Bound Controls

by Christopher Rotberg

CHAPTER

18

Welcome to the wonderful world of the Data control. In this world, everything is done for you, without the need for code. Why can't everything be this easy? Because not writing code comes with a price: memory usage. Although the Data control is very easy to use, it requires more memory than does using code. This is not always a bad thing; I just wanted to make you aware of the trade-offs of using the Data control versus code. Now that I have shown you the dark side of using the Data control, it's time to jump right into the Data control and its companions, the bound controls. The Data control has been enhanced extensively in Visual Basic 4.0 and now includes new bound controls.

What's New in Visual Basic 4.0?

Before beginning the discussion of what the Data control is, I want to list some of the changes for version 4.0. If you haven't used the Data control before, then just read through the changes for now. I go into greater detail about the changes later in this chapter. The following is a list of what's new in version 4.0:

- New `Align` property positions the control automatically to the top or bottom of the form.
- `BOFAction` and `EOFAction` properties provide greater control when the record set reaches the beginning or end of a record set.
- New `RecordsetType` property enables the Data control to set a record set type. Selections include table-type, dynaset-type, and snapshot-type.
- Record sets created by the Data control or directly through code (with the Professional or Enterprise Edition) can now be assigned to any other Data control.
- New DAO and Jet features for versions 2.5 (16-bit) and 3.0 (32-bit).

What Is the Data Control?

The *Data control* is a custom control that automatically provides access to data stored in databases. It offers the user the ability to move between records and to view and manipulate data of bound controls. The Data control acts as a intermediary between data bound controls and the Jet engine. After a bound control's `Data Source` property is set to a valid Data control, the bound control does not have to know anything about the database; the Data control takes care of all the database activity for the bound control. It is this capability to provide a level of indirection that makes the Data control so useful for using bound controls. The bound control doesn't know the difference between a Microsoft Access database or a Paradox database, and it doesn't care. It just waits for the Data control to give it data.

How Does the Data Control Work?

All of the Data control's magic is performed through its use of properties and methods. It has properties that specify the database name, location, and type, the type of record set to use, and what actions to take when the database requests information. The main properties set by the user are DatabaseName, RecordSource, and RecordsetType. When your Visual Basic 4.0 application starts up, it looks for Data controls used in the project. When it encounters a control, it reads the DatabaseName, RecordSource, and RecordsetType properties, and then creates a new Database object and a new Recordset object of the type specified by the RecordsetType property. The Data control's DatabaseName and RecordSource properties now point to the newly created objects in memory. The Data control's methods will now operate on the newly created objects. When the user chooses to move to the next record, the Data control increments the record in the Recordset object. It is important to note that when a Data control creates a record set, the record set is automatically populated.

This is a brief overview of the Data control; the next section goes into more detail about the Data control's properties and methods.

Properties and Methods of the Data Control

Although there are over 30 properties and methods of the Data control, this chapter covers only several of the most important. In Visual Basic, many of the custom controls share the same properties, such as BackColor, Appearance, and Caption. This chapter highlights those that are unique to the Data control.

Properties of the Data Control

The properties you will use most often are Align, BOFAction, and EOFAction (new properties); Connect, Database, DatabaseName, EditMode, Exclusive, Options, RecordSet, RecordSetType, and RecordSource.

Align (New)

The Align property designates where the Data control should be positioned. The default for a (non-MDI) regular form is no alignment (0); for a MDI form, the default is aligned to the bottom (2).

BOFAction (New)

The BOFAction property enables you to control what happens when the Data control reaches the beginning of the record set. Its settings are vbBOFActionMoveFirst and vbBOFActionBOF.

- vbBOFActionMoveFirst (0): Instructs the Data control to use the first record as the current record.

- vbBOFActionBOF (1): Causes a validation event to occur if you try to move back beyond the first record. The validation event triggers a reposition event, which disables the Move Previous button on the Data control.

EOFAction (New)

This property performs similarly to BOFAction, but it controls records for the end of the record set. The following are the three settings for EOFAction:

- VbEOFActionMoveLast (0): Ensures that the last record is the current record.

- VbEOFActionEOF (1): Causes a Validation event to occur if you try to move forward beyond the last record in the record set. The Validation event triggers a Reposition event, which disables the Move Next button on the Data control.

- VbEOFActionAddNew (2): This property is similar to VbEOFActionEOF except that the Validation event occurs on the current record, followed by an automatic AddNew, followed by a Reposition event on the new record.

The AddNew action positions the current record to a new record in the copy buffer. If the user makes changes to this record and then moves the record pointer to another record, the changes are automatically saved. If no changes are made, the new record is discarded.

VbEOFActionAddNew is helpful in situations in which the record set is returned with no records or after the last record has been deleted. A new record is always available as the current record.

> AddNew action has no effect when you are manipulating the Data control through code. It works only when you are manipulating the Data control with the mouse.

Connect

The Connect property returns or sets a value about a database that is open or used in a pass-through query or for attached tables. Connect strings are commonly used when you are making a connection to an ODBC data source. A string consisting of DATABASE (default database), UID (user), PWD (password), and DSN (ODBC data source name) is passed to make the connection.

Database

The Database property specifies the Data control's underlying database object.

DatabaseName

The `DatabaseName` property returns or sets the name and the location of the Data control's data source. This can be a network path such as `\\SERVER\SHARE\DATABASE.MDB` or `C:\DATABASE.MDB`. For ODBC databases, this property can be empty if a valid connect string is given. A valid string includes a DSN (ODBC data source name) registered in the ODBC.INI file.

> If you change the data source after the data object is open, you must use the `Refresh` method to open the new database.

EditMode

`EditMode` is the Visual Basic equivalent of an `IsDirty` property. This read-only property will return the current state of editing for the current record. It offers three settings to help you trap for record changes: `dbEditNone`, `dbEditInProgress`, and `dbEditAdd`:

- `dbEditNone`: No editing is in progress.
- `dbEditInProgress`: Editing has taken place, and the current record is in the copy buffer. You can use this property in conjunction with the `LockEdits` property to determine if the current data page is locked.
- `dbEditAdd`: `AddNew` has been called, and a new record is now in the copy buffer.

Exclusive

The `Exclusive` property sets or returns a value indicating whether the underlying database is open for single- or multiuser access. A value of `True` indicates the database is open for single-user access, while `False` indicates multiuser. Multiuser is the default and enables others to make changes while the database is open.

This value is used when the database is being opened; if you later change the value, you must use the `Refresh` method to update those changes.

> The `Exclusive` property is ignored when you are using databases through ODBC.

Options

The `Options` property returns or sets values that affect how the underlying record set can be used. The values for this property are shown in Table 18.1. They can be used alone, or you can combine them to achieve greater control (add the values to use more than one parameter).

Table 18.1. Value combinations for the Options property.

Parameter	Value	Description
dbDenyWrite	1	Other users cannot make changes to the records in the record set. (Applies to the multiuser environment.)
dbDenyRead	2	Other users cannot read the record set. (Applies to multiuser environment for table-type record set only.)
dbReadOnly	4	Cannot make changes to the record set.
dbAppendOnly	8	New records can be added, but existing records cannot be read.
dbInconsistent	16	Updates can take place in all fields of the record set, even if they break join constraints.
dbConsistent	32	Only fields that do not break the join constraints can be updated.
dbSQLPassThrough	64	Sends SQL statements to the ODBC data source when the RecordSource property is a SQL statement.
dbForwardOnly	256	Record set is forward only; MoveNext is the only valid move statement. Note: This cannot be used with the Data control.
dbSeeChanges	512	Generates a trappable error if more than one user tries to update the same record.

The dbSQLPassThrough parameter is available for compatibility with previous versions of the Jet engine; using a previously created SQL PassThrough QueryDef object is the preferred method.

RecordSet

The RecordSet property sets or returns the Recordset object as defined by the Data control's properties or by an existing record set. When your application starts, the Data control creates a new record set as designated by the Data control's current property settings. If you choose to set the Data control's properties at runtime, you must explicitly use the Refresh method to tell the Jet engine to create the record set.

RecordsetType

The RecordsetType property returns or sets the type of record set you want to create. The default type is Dynaset. The three options are vbRSTypeTable (0), vbRSTypeDynaset (1), and vbRSTypeSnapshot (2).

> If you create a new record set without the Data control and then assign it to a Data control, the Data control RecordsetType will change to conform to that of the record set.

RecordSource

The RecordSource property sets or returns the table, SQL statement, or QueryDef that creates the underlying record set for the Data control. After the Data control creates the record set from its RecordSource, all bound controls have access to the fields in the table.

The following is an example of a valid RecordSource:

```
Data1.RecordSource= "Select * from Publishers"
```

> Make sure to use the Refresh method whenever you change the RecordSource property at runtime. In addition, a bound control's DataField property might be invalid if the RecordSource is changed to a new record set that doesn't contain the field specified in the DataField.

Data Control Methods

Now that you are familiar with the data properties of the Data control, you can start to put the control to work. You make the Data control work for you by calling its methods. The methods carry out an action by reading the control's property settings and then calling functions. It is true that the Data control has relatively few methods, but sometimes less is more.

The following sections discuss the methods available for data manipulation.

Refresh

If you use the Data control, Refresh will be your favorite method. You must use this method whenever you change a data property at runtime. Changing the RecordSource or DatabaseName properties has no effect until the control is refreshed. The Refresh method causes the current record set to close and a new record set to be created. This can be very handy when you want the Data control to be the source for multiple bound controls. Listing 18.1 shows the code for the Refresh method.

Listing 18.1. Using the Refresh method.

```
Private Sub Form_Load()

Data1.DatabaseName = "C:\BIBLIO.MDB" ' Set the database

' Set the RecordSource to a Table.
Data1.RecordSource = "Publishers"
Data1.RecordsetType = vbRSTypeSnapShot ' Create snapshot-type Recordset.
Data1.Refresh

' Set ListField to Publisher Name
DBList1. ListField = "Name"

End Sub
```

In this example, the Data control is initialized with a snapshot-type record set of the Publishers table. I am using a bound listbox to display all the publisher's names. Listing 18.2 shows how the same Data control and bound listbox can now be used to show data in the Authors table.

Listing 18.2. Using the Refresh method: Example 2.

```
Private Sub Command1_Click()

Data1.DatabaseName = "C:\BIBLIO.MDB" ' Set the database

' Set the RecordSource to a SQL statement at runtime.
Data1.RecordSource = "Select * from Authors ORDER BY author"
Data1.RecordsetType = vbRSTypeDynaset ' Create dynaset-type Recordset.
Data1.Refresh

' Set ListField to Publisher Name
DBList1. ListField = "Name"

End Sub
```

Assume that you have pressed the Command1 button. You now have a dynaset-type record set of the Authors table, and the listbox now displays a list of authors. You have only one Data control and one bound control serving dual purposes, first for Publishers and then for Authors. Your applications will run much more efficiently if you can reduce the amount of redundant controls. Try to design your applications using just what is needed to get the job done. It is more efficient to use one Data control for four functions than four Data controls soaking up valuable memory space. You will learn more optimization tips later; for now, it's time to get back to those methods.

UpdateControls

The UpdateControls method is handy for validation routines. Often when a user edits a record and then decides not to save the changes, the edited record is still displayed. The record is in limbo. This is where the UpdateControls method comes in. After you have established that the user does not want to save changes to the current record, you can invoke UpdateControls to return the record to its original state. It is essentially making the current record current again.

This method would be a great choice for an Undo button on a custom toolbar. Listing 18.3 shows how a button can be added to the toolbar to add an Undo function.

Listing 18.3. The UpdateControls method.

```
Private Sub Toolbar1_ButtonClick(ByVal Button As Button)

    Select Case Button.Key
    Case "Undo"
        Data1.UpdateControls
    Case "Copy"
        bReturn = Copy()
    End Select

End Sub
```

If the user chooses copy and then the copy function is performed, the copy can then be undone by pressing the Undo button.

UpdateRecord

The UpdateRecord method forces the record set to be saved without triggering the Validation event. This would be useful if you wanted to save the current record without causing a reposition action to occur. A Save button on a toolbar would be a good place to invoke this method. The record set is updated, and the current record still stays current.

Visual Basic not only provides properties and methods but also events. It's in these events that you often use the various methods. Following are some of the most notable events.

Data Control Events

Take a look at some of the events in which you can use the Data control's properties and methods.

The `Validate` Event

The `Validate` event is called before the current record is changed, before the `Update` method (unless the data is saved with `UpdateRecord`), and before a `Delete`, `Unload`, or `Close` operation. This event is most often used to prompt the user to save changes and to enforce that certain parameters are adhered to. This event has three parameters that are passed in at runtime: `Index`, `Action`, and `Save`.

`Index` is used to identify the instance of the control if it is used in a control array.

The `Action` value indicates what action caused the validation event to occur. The 12 values are shown in Table 18.2.

Table 18.2. `Action` values.

Parameter	Value	Description
`vbDataActionCancel`	0	Indicates the action was canceled.
`vbDataActionMoveFirst`	1	A `MoveFirst` method was invoked.
`vbDataActionMovePrevious`	2	User selected the `MovePrevious` action.
`vbDataActionMoveNext`	3	A `MoveNext` method was invoked.
`vbDataActionMoveLast`	4	A user selected the `MoveLast` operation to move to the last record.
`vbDataActionAddNew`	5	A new record has just been created.
`vbDataActionUpdate`	6	The Data control was instructed to update the record set.
`vbDataActionDelete`	7	A user has deleted one of the records.
`vbDataActionFind`	8	The `Find` method has been invoked.
`vbDataActionBookmark`	9	A bookmark has been set by the user.
`vbDataActionClose`	10	The `Close` method has been called.
`vbDataActionUnload`	11	The current form is being unloaded.

The `Save` argument indicates if data in the bound controls has changed. Once data has been changed, `Save` will be set to `True`. If when the `Validation` event exists, the `Save` property is still `True`, the changes are saved. If `Save` is `False`, the changes are lost.

The example in Listing 18.4 shows how to use the `Validation` event and the `Save` parameter to prompt the user to save changes.

Listing 18.4. Validating records with the Data control.

```
Private Sub Data1_Validate(Action As Integer, Save As Integer)

    Dim Msg As String, Style As String, Title As String
    Dim Response As Boolean

    Msg = "Do you want to save this record ?"   ' Define message
    Style = vbYesNo + vbCritical + vbDefaultButton2 ' Define buttons
    Title = "Confirm Save"  ' Define title

    If Save Then
    response = MsgBox(Msg, Style, Title)
        If response Then    ' User chose Yes.
            Save = True     ' Perform some action.
        Else
            Save = False ' Perform some action
        End If
    End If
End Sub
```

In the code in Listing 18.4, the `Validation` event is used to prompt the user to save changes. The `Save` property will initially be `True` if the record is dirty (that is, if the record has been modified). If the user wants to save changes, `Save` has to be true when the function ends; this will invoke both the `Edit` and `UpdateRecord` methods. To nullify the changes, simply set `Save` to `False`.

The `Reposition` Event

In contrast to the `Validate` event, the `Reposition` event occurs after a record becomes the current record. This event is useful if you want to run a process based on a record becoming current. For example, if you have a combo box that displays states and a listbox displays cities in that state, you could use the `Reposition` event to trap the current state and fill the listbox with the corresponding cities.

Your code might look like that in Listing 18.5.

Listing 18.5. Utilizing the `Reposition` event.

```
Private Sub Data1_Reposition()

    Data2.RecordSource = "Select cities from City where state ="
    ➡& Data1.Recordset("State")
    Data2.Refresh

End Sub
```

Using ODBC with the Data Control

If you use Visual Basic, at some point you are going to use ODBC. ODBC is important because it can provide access to data located on a SQL server, spreadsheets, text files, and so on, and it provides you with a level of indirection. It is much easier to change a data source if your application is using a static DSN (data source name) rather than a hard-coded path to the data. The application looks for the DSN and reads the path to the data. This path can be changed manually or automatically at runtime by the application; it is very flexible. Because ODBC is useful, it would make sense that the Data control be able to take advantage of it—and it does. The easiest way to attach to ODBC via the Data control is to set the Data control's Connect property to ODBC.

Figure 18.1 illustrates how this is done.

Figure 18.1.

Setting the Connect *property.*

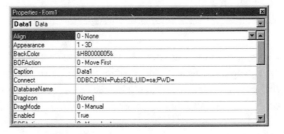

Notice that the connection string contains the data source type, ODBC, the DSN, a UID (user identification name), and a PWD (user's password). You can also add the keyword DATABASE to define the database name, but this can be done through the ODBC manager when you set up the DSN. These entries comprise the string needed to access a SQL server database through ODBC; it gives the Data control enough information to retrieve the data.

> If you just put ODBC in the Connect property, the ODBC dialog box will appear at runtime and prompt for a DSN source, the user name, and password. Additionally, most Microsoft Access databases that do not have security implemented have a UID = "Admin" and a PWD= "".

After the connection has been made, the Data control will return the records from the table specified in the RecordSource property. An ODBC record set is treated like any other native record set in Access. The RecordSource can even accept SQL, as Figure 18.2 indicates.

This has been a brief summary on using ODBC. The Data control is capable of retrieving data from many more types of data sources. Take a look and explore a few on your own.

Figure 18.2.
Setting the RecordSource property.

Optimizing Applications with the Data Control

The Data control is a controversial control. Some programmers do not touch it, while others use it liberally. Seasoned programmers who do everything in code shun the Data control, while beginners lavish in its simplicity. So should you use it? The answer is yes. For some tasks, the Data control provides too much built-in functionality to ignore—especially when the development cycle is short. A good example of this is the DBGrid control. It is very easy to give the DBGrid a Data control source and let it work its magic. As you add, modify, and delete rows, the grid updates the Data control's record set for you automatically. Of course, there are times when code is essential, but for many tasks the Data control is the wise choice to use with the DBGrid.

How To Optimize the Data Control

You can follow several strategies to increase not only the performance of the Data control but of your application, as well. You can do the following:

- Implement control re-use.
- Set the Exclusive property to True.
- Use the appropriate RecordsetType.
- Use indexes on your key database fields.

Control Re-Use

No other control can bring an application to its knees as can the misuse of Data controls. Each time you use a Data control in your application, you are creating a new Database and Recordset object. Each of these objects robs valuable memory from your program; therefore, the goal is to re-use one Data control over and over. In the Refresh method example in Listing 18.1, I first initialized the Data control to the Publishers table; then later if the user selected the command button, I changed the Data control's source to the Authors table. I opened two different views with only one Database object and one Recordset object. This technique reduced the overhead of having redundant objects sitting in memory. This technique also works well with controls such as bound listboxes, comboboxes, and text boxes, because you can use only one control to represent different views. Because every control on your form takes memory, try to design your application with re-usability in mind.

The `Exclusive` Property

If you are not operating in a multiuser environment, set the `Exclusive` property to `True`. This will speed up your application. The Data control does not have to handle concurrency issues when the database is exclusive. It can save changes without having to check if someone else is already changing the same record.

Use the Appropriate `RecordsetType`

If you have a relatively small database and none of the records are going to change, use `vbRSTypeSnapshot` when you create your record set. This type of record set is generally faster because it's all in memory or in a temp file. A snapshot-type record set does not worry about page locking or multiuser issues. This type is perfect for supplying data to fill combo or listboxes; the data is static and is used only for selection purposes. For larger databases, external databases, or if the records are going to change, use `vbRSTypeDynaset`.

Use Indexes

In general, it is a good idea to use indexes when you design your databases. The Data control in Visual Basic 4.0 now utilizes the index of the database much better than before. You can improve the performance of your searches when the data is already in order. Try to make the Bound column match the Index column of your table.

Bound Controls

Users of Visual Basic would have no use for a Data control if bound controls did not exist. The main purpose of the Data control is to provide advanced data functionality with no coding required; but if you had to code to get at the data, what would be the savings? The Data control is useful because it hides the data-gathering process and works with bound controls that hide the data-manipulation process. You do not have to know a thing about displaying records or searching the record set. Just set a few properties, and the controls handle it automatically. Bound controls can literally update, search, sort, and navigate the record set without requiring you to write a single line of code. This kind of functionality can dramatically increase the speed in which an application can be developed. Less code is required because the nice people at Microsoft have done the coding for you. This is not to say that you can't enhance a control's functionality through your own code. I just want to point out that you don't have to code to get an application running.

Now that I have justified the existence of bound controls, take a look at what Visual Basic has to offer. The bound controls that ship with Visual Basic are illustrated in Table 18.3.

Table 18.3. The bound controls.

Icon	Name	Description
A	Label	Use for static text that the user cannot change, like a caption for a graphic.
abl	TextBox	Use to provide a read/write text field that is bound to a data field.
☑	CheckBox	Use to provide a read/write (True or False) field; control can bound to a Boolean field.
	ComboBox	Use to provide a combo box; the list is manually loaded, and the user's selection from the list is bound to the field.
	ListBox	Use to display a list of items; the list is manually loaded, and the user's selection from the list is bound to the field.
	PictureBox	Use to display a graphical image; can be bound to an image/binary data field.
	Image	Use is the same as PictureBox, but it uses less resources. The image is purely decorative.
	DBCombo	Use to provide combo box; the list is manually loaded, and the user's selection from the list is bound to the field.
	DBList	Use to display a list of items; the list is manually loaded, and the user's selection from the list is bound to the field.
	DBGrid	(Data Bound Grid) Use to provide a grid of multiple records in columns and rows. The data is bound to fields.

Table 18.3 shows the icons for each control so it will be easy for you to identify them on the toolbar. The following sections cover each control; but instead of approaching each control one by one, the controls are grouped into sections. The first section covers the *Simple controls* (Label, TextBox, CheckBox, ComboBox, ListBox), and then the *Graphic controls* (Image, PictureBox) are covered. The third section covers *Advanced controls* (DBCombo, DBList), and the final section covers the *Bound Grid* (DBGrid).

Simple Controls

I refer to the controls in this group as *simple* because they all have just one direct link to a data field and do not offer complex data manipulation. It is true that the ComboBox and ListBox controls provide more functionality than that of the Label control, but this functionality is achieved by using code. For example, to fill a listbox, the user has to load each item with the AddItem method; items cannot be automatically loaded. The ListBox control simply passes the selected item to the Data control via its DataField property. The Data control then validates the data and saves it to the database.

All of the controls in this section connect to the Data control via a DataField and DataSource property. The DataSource property is the name of a valid Data control on the form, whereas the DataField is a valid field within the Data control. The field specified by the DataField is considered to be the bound field; thus the changes made in the control are reflected in the field used for the DataField.

The following looks at each of these controls in more detail:

■ Label: The Label control is primarily used to display static data from the record set. Typical uses would include a caption under a picture control or to display support information. Examples of support information could include social security number, telephone number, or birth date. This type of support information is displayed on the screen but cannot be updated.

■ TextBox: The TextBox control is used in much the same way as that of the Label control, except that it can also be used as an input device. The control is perfect for collecting data from the end user and then storing the data into a database. Text boxes would be used to collect information on a field-by-field basis.

■ CheckBox: The CheckBox control is used to display or collect Boolean information. A field that holds True/False or Yes/No data is typically displayed with a CheckBox control.

■ ComboBox: The ComboBox control enables a user to make a selection from a predefined list or enter new information to be stored in the bound field. This type of control is handy because it lets the user add information that is not contained in the list. In situations in which the control is set to read-only, the text-editing portion of the ComboBox acts as a search criteria window. As the user types, the control searches for a match in the list portion. The items displayed in the list must be added with the AddItem method. The selected item in the list or the newly entered item is saved to the bound field as specified by the DataField.

■ ListBox: The ListBox control is essentially a ComboBox that cannot be edited. The list is read-only, and is used purely for selecting an entry from the list. Items are loaded into the list using the AddItem method, and the selected item in the list is bound to the field as specified in the DataField.

Graphic Controls

The graphic controls in Visual Basic 4.0 include the Picture control and the Image control. These controls have a DataSource and a DataField property that work with various files such as bitmaps (BMP) and picture files (PCX). Picture information is usually stored in a database as a binary field; thus the DataField property reads binary data. Use the Image control if you just want to display a picture, and use a Picture control if editing is required.

Advanced Controls

I refer to the controls in this section as advanced because they provide additional features not found in the regular ComboBox or ListBox controls. These advanced controls continue to provide the bound data features found in other bound controls and add new features such as automatically populating the list portion, the capability to add a level of indirection to data selection, and advanced search features. Take a look at how these new features can enhance your programming.

Populating the Listbox

One of the new features introduced in the DBCombo and DBList controls is the capability to automatically fill the list portion with data. Remember, ComboBox and ListBox needed to use the AddItem method to fill the list portion. All items added or removed from the list were the programmer's responsibility; the new DBCombo and DBList fill the list automatically.

This functionality is provided through two new properties:

- RowSource: The RowSource property stores the name of the Data control that is the source for the records in the listbox. Generally, this is going to be a different Data control than the one used as the DataSource property. The table used by the Data control is what will be available to the bound control. *This property is not available at runtime.*

- ListField: This property is used to specify which field to use when you are populating the listbox. Once a RowSource has been set, the ListField property will display a listing of all fields in that record set. The field you choose will be the one that is displayed in the list portion.

There are several limitations to these properties that you should be aware of when trying to use this functionality:

- The RowSource can be set only at design time. I know what you're thinking: How can I take advantage of control re-use if I can't access more than one table? The list portion will always display data from the same table. The answer is in the Data control. When you want to switch tables, reset the Data control's RecordSource property and then refresh. Now just change the ListField property (this property can be modified at runtime) to the appropriate data field, and you can use the same listbox for several purposes. There is a work-around for everything!

■ The ListField can display only one field at a time. This means you have to pick one field and one field only; but you want two fields. How can you get two fields if it displays only one? The answer is once again in the Data control and, yes, the RecordSource property. This RecordSource property comes in handy, doesn't it? The answer is to simply alias the fields you want into one field. Take a look at some code that does just that.

In Listing 18.6, I wanted both the publisher ID and the name in the listbox, and I wasn't going to take no for an answer.

Listing 18.6. Populating the listbox with multiple columns.

```
Private Sub Command1_Click()

    'Use SQL string to alias PUBID and Name into one field
    'called IDName. Work around for list box one field limitation.

    Data1.RecordSource = "Select [PUBID]& String(5,32) & [Name]"
    ➥& "AS IDName,PUBID,Name,Address From Publishers "

    'Create new recordset
    Data1.Refresh

    DBList1.BoundColumn = "Name"

    'Set Listfield to display new alias field
    DBList1.ListField = "IDName"

End Sub
```

Notice that I inserted a bit of code in between the field names in the SQL statement. This statement String(5,32) tells Visual Basic that I want five spaces padded between the two fields. In case you haven't looked at ASCII in a while, Chr(32) is the space character. It's cleaner to use the String function to repeat the space five times rather than typing Chr(32) five times. I wanted to add some spaces to make the string more readable to the user. Now that I can present the user with a formatted string of my choice, how do I pull that string apart to record my selection? What else, more properties!

■ BoundColumn: This property enables the programmer to specify what field of the list portion's record set is to be passed to the bound DataField. Once a selection is made from the list, the selected item is then passed to the DataField property to be saved in the database. The BoundColumn can be any of the fields in the RowSource record set. A trappable error occurs if the field designated as the BoundColumn cannot be located in the record set.

If the ListField property is left empty, the BoundColumn is used to fill the list.

■ `BoundText`: Returns or sets the selected item in the control's listbox. This property corresponds to the actual selected text in the field defined by the `BoundColumn`. The `BoundText` does not have to be associated with the column displayed in the listbox.

You might have noticed from Listing 18.6 that I used the `BoundColumn` to reference the `"Name"` field in the record set. I was actually displaying the alias field `"IDName"` in the list, but once a selection was made, I wanted the `"Name"` to be passed to the `DataField`. This enabled me to offer the user a friendly, readable choice but allowed me to reference only the information I needed.

Listing 18.7 illustrates how `BoundText` is used.

Listing 18.7. Using `BoundText` control versus `Text` control.

```
Private Sub Command2_Click()
    'For this example I used DBList1.BoundColumn = "PUBID"

    'List box is using the IDName field derived from the previous
    'example. List box displays

    '5    Brady Pub.

    'for the fifth entry.

    MsgBox DBList1.BoundText

    'Message displays 5 which is the PUBID

    MsgBox DBList1.Text

    'Message displays 5    Brady Pub.

End Sub
```

Searching Functions

Before discussing the `DBGrid` control, I want to talk about the new built-in searching functions for VB4. `DBCombo` and `DBList` now have a property called `MatchEntry`, which enables the listbox to be searched. In previous versions of Visual Basic, searching listboxes was a chore that the programmer had to implement. This was usually accomplished by trapping the keys on the `KeyDown` event and using the `SendMessage` API. Fortunately for you, all of this is now done automatically.

The `MatchEntry` property can have the following options:

`vbMatchEntrySimple`	*Basic Matching*: (0) Default—This value instructs the control to search for a match for the character typed by the user. The match is attempted by using the first character of the entry in the listbox. Typing the same letter over and over moves through all of the entries in the list beginning with that letter.

VbMatchEntryExtended	*Extended Matching*: (1)—This value instructs the control to search for an entry matching all characters entered. The search is performed as the characters are being typed by the user.

Data Bound Grid

The DBGrid is the last bound control discussed in this chapter, and by far the most powerful. The DBGrid offers so many properties and methods that I cannot cover them all in the remaining pages of this chapter. Instead, I'll cover the most important features and some tips that are not apparent from reading the Help file. Look at some of the properties, methods, and events that you will use most often.

The DBGrid's properties include the following:

AllowAddNew	Returns or sets a value enabling the user to add new records to the record set. If this property is True, the last row is left blank for the new record. The underlying database might not allow the changes to occur even if this property is True.
AllowDelete	Returns or sets a value enabling the user to delete records to the record set. The underlying database might not allow the changes to occur even if this property is True.
AllowRowSizing	Returns or sets a value enabling the user to resize the rows in the DBGrid. Any changes in row size cause a RowResize event to occur.
AllowUpdate	Returns or sets a value enabling the user to make changes to the records in the record set. Any changes made while this property is False are ignored.
Columns	This property returns a collection of column objects. The following returns the value in column 1:
	`MsgBox DBGrid1.Columns(1).Value`
DataMode	DataMode indicates if the grid is to be bound or unbound. A value of 0 binds the control to a data source, and a value of 1 instructs the grid to retrieve its data through the unbound events.
DataSource	Specifies the Data control or record set that is the source of data for the DBGrid.
DefColWidth	Returns or sets a value indicating the default column width for all columns in the bound grid. If DefColWidth is set to 0, the control automatically sizes all columns based on the width of the column heading or the Size property setting of the underlying source field, whichever is larger.

RecordSelectors   Returns or sets a value indicating whether the record selectors are displayed in the grid. Record selectors appear on the left side of the record.

SelBookmarks   Returns a collection of bookmarks for all selected items in the bound grid.

The following code shows how the SelBookmarks property is used:

```
Do While DBGrid1.SelBookmarks.Count <> 0
  Data1.Recordset.Bookmark = DBGrid1.SelBookmarks(0)
  Data1.Recordset.Delete
Loop
```

VisibleCols   Returns a value indicating the amount of visible columns.

The following discusses some useful methods that can be used with the DBGrid. Use these controls to manipulate Grid data.

Rebind   The Rebind method causes the DBGrid control to reset the columns, headings, and other properties based on the current Data control properties. This method is equivalent to the operations performed when the control is set to a valid DataSource.

Refresh   This method is used to refresh the underlying record set for the DBGrid. If you programmatically change any of the cell values, use the Refresh method to update the underlying record set to reflect your changes.

You can't set the value of a column directly. You can only set the data in the underlying record set and then do a grid refresh. The following code changes the value in the second field of the first record:

```
Data2.RecordSet.MoveFirst
Data2.RecordSet.Edit
Data2.RecordSet.Fields(1) = "New Value"
Data2.RecordSet.Update
DBGrid1.Refresh
```

GetBookmark   Returns a value containing a bookmark for a row specified to the current row in the DBGrid control. The specified row can be before, after, or the current row plus *n* rows. This method can be useful if you want to programmatically check the position of the current row relative to other rows in the grid.

Listing 18.8 shows an example of how to use the GetBookmark method.

Listing 18.8. Using the GetBookmark **method.**

```
Private Sub Command4_Click()

    'Display text in the first column, for the current row.
    MsgBox DBGrid1.Columns(1).CellValue(DBGrid1.GetBookmark(0))

    'Display text in the first column, for the row previous to the
    'current row.
    MsgBox DBGrid1.Columns(1).CellValue(DBGrid1.GetBookmark(-1))

    'Display text in the first column, for the row following the
    'current row.
    MsgBox DBGrid1.Columns(1).CellValue(DBGrid1.GetBookmark(1))

    'Display text in the first column, for the current row
    '+ 5.
    MsgBox DBGrid1.Columns(1).CellValue(DBGrid1.GetBookmark(0 + 5))

End Sub
```

Scroll   The Scroll method allows for quick movements within the DBGrid. The focus can be moved to a specific column and row. Positive values move down and to the right, whereas negative values move up and to the left. The following code will move the focus 1 row to the right and 18 rows down:

```
DBGrid1.Scroll 1, 18
```

There are also many useful events that help you as the programmer to guide the end user while they are using the application:

BeforeUpdate   This event is called when the user tries to move to another row or if the Data control's UpdateRecord method is called. This event is a good place to ensure that the user has entered all the required data for a record, before that record is committed. The user cannot move focus off the current record until the requirement is met.

Listing 18.9 shows an example of how to use the BeforeUpdate event to capture and validate the end user's data entry.

Listing 18.9. Validating data in the BeforeUpdate **event.**

```
Private Sub DBGrid1_BeforeUpdate(Cancel As Integer)

    'This procedure checks if the user has left the
    'Company column blank, if so it displays a message.

    If DBGrid1.Columns(2).Value = "" Then
        MsgBox "You must enter a value in the Company column!"
        Cancel = True
```

```
    End If
End Sub
```

BeforeColUpdate   This event is similar to that of BeforeUpdate, except that it works on individual columns. If the user tries to change focus from the column, the event is triggered. This is a good place to put your validation code for values in that column. In Listing 18.10, BeforeColUpdate is used to verify that the user has typed "Redmond" or "Issaquah"; if not, an error occurs.

Listing 18.10. Trapping user input with BeforeColUpdate.

```
Private Sub DBGrid1_BeforeColUpdate(ByVal ColIndex As Integer,&
➥OLDValue As Variant, Cancel As Integer)

    Dim sVal

    'Check to see if user entered Redmond or Issaquah for Column 1
    If ColIndex = 1 Then
        sVal = DBGrid1.Columns(1).Text

        If sVal = "Redmond" Or sVal = " Issaquah" Then
            Cancel = False
        Else
            Cancel = True
            MsgBox "You must enter Redmond or Issaquah."
        End If
End Sub
```

DBGrid Tips

This section shows you some shortcuts that are not easily found in the Help file. You learn how to automatically populate the DBGrid with table information from the Data control and how to insert and delete columns at design time. Both of these shortcuts use the right mouse button.

Setting Up the DBGrid

You have a Data control and a DBGrid on your form, so how do you tell the grid what fields you want to use? You could do it all manually by setting the properties of individual columns in the property sheet (see Figure 18.3), or you could just use the Retrieve Fields command as described after Figure 18.3.

Figure 18.3.
Using the DBGrid
property sheet to
modify columns.

Do the following to activate the Retrieve Fields command:

1. Place a DBGrid control on a form, and then click on the DBGrid.
2. Press the right mouse button to activate a shortcut menu similar to that in Figure 18.4.

Figure 18.4.
The shortcut to retrieve
fields.

3. Choose Retrieve Fields.

The DBGrid will now read the record set of the Data control and build the columns for you. This is assuming that you have set the DBGrid's DataSource to a valid Data control. The DBGrid now knows what columns are in the record set and even builds the column headers. What could be easier? There is one problem: How do you add or delete columns?

Adding and Deleting Columns

Setting up the DBGrid seemed straightforward enough, but what about modifying columns? How do you add or delete a column? Don't look for the property sheet here because you won't find anything to help you.

You can always add a column at runtime with the following code:

```
DBGrid2.Columns.Add (2)
DBGrid2.Columns(2).Caption = "hello"
DBGrid2.Columns(2).Vioiblc = True
DBGrid2.Refresh
```

This works OK if the application is running, but what about the design environment? There is a simple method to add and delete a field, and it's done with the click of a mouse.

To add or delete a field, use the Add or Delete command from the Edit menu.

1. Place a DBGrid control on a form, and then click on the DBGrid.

2. Press the right mouse button and choose Edit (see Figure 18.5).

Figure 18.5.
The shortcut to the Edit mode.

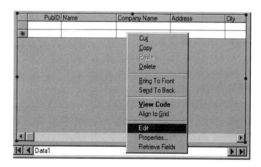

3. The DBGrid is now in Edit mode. Choose the appropriate command from Figure 18.6.

Figure 18.6.
Using the shortcut menu to insert new columns.

This is the easiest way to modify column settings in the DBGrid control.

I want to show you one last screen before I conclude the section on the Data Bound Grid. The Properties screen makes it very easy to set most of the properties discussed earlier. To open the screen, you simply click on the DBGrid, click the right mouse button, and choose Properties. You will notice in Figure 18.7 that all the relevant properties are covered among the four tabs.

Figure 18.7.
*The DBGrid Properties
sheet.*

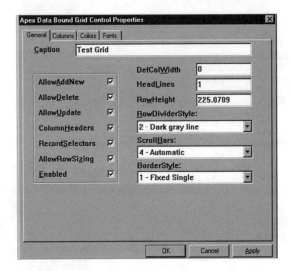

Summary

This chapter introduces you to the Data control and its bound cousins. It shows you how they can be used to aid in the development of Visual Basic applications and gives some insight on why you might want to use them. These controls definitely have their purpose in Visual Basic and they can, and should, be used. I hope that this chapter has given you an indication of why and when to use these controls. Ultimately, it is up to you to select the right control for the job, but your decision should be based on your personal needs and programmability level, not on other people's personal bias. Good luck!

The Jet Database Engine

by Dwayne R. Gifford

In the development of a database management system, the database engine is often one of those behind-the-scenes players that no one pays much attention to. Users are focusing on the business rules, and analysts are working on the data to support them. Database administrators are looking at the structure of the database, and programmers are writing the code to access the data.

Surprisingly, a database engine affects all of these areas. The Microsoft Jet 3.0 engine contains validation rules, self-enforced referential integrity, rich data typing, configurable performance settings, and more. Being aware of the existence and use of these features is a key factor to your success in the development of a database management system.

Version Soup: Jet History

Since VB3 was first introduced, the Jet engine has changed substantially. VB3 included the Jet 1.1 engine, which was formerly introduced with Access 1.1. The next revision, Jet 2.0, came with Access 2. Unfortunately, the databases created by Jet 2.0 were not file-compatible with Jet 1.1. In order to allow users of VB3 to address Jet 2.0 databases, the Visual Basic Compatibility Layer (VBCL) was released.

After Jet 2.0 came Jet 2.5, which appeared in an Access service pack. Jet 2.5 is the current 16-bit version of the Jet database engine and supports the same .MDB file structure as does Jet 3.0, the current 32-bit version of the engine. VB4 enables full access to both the Jet 2.5 and 3.0 engines.

Functional Components of the Jet Engine

Although the Jet engine is powerful, it does rely on other components to deliver its functionality. The following lists identify the differences.

Components of the Jet Engine

Specifically, the Jet database engine includes

- Data access objects (DAO)
- Security
- File services for accessing native Jet databases (such file services are referred to as Indexed Sequential Access Method (ISAM))
- The query engine, including the query optimizer
- Internal tracking logic to support replication

Services Related to the Jet Engine

Services that work with the Jet engine, but are outside the core functionality include

- VBA expression evaluation
- ODBC Driver Manager and driver files
- Replication management and shuttle services
- Non-Jet ISAM drivers

Figure 19.1 depicts the relationship between the functional components just discussed. Components integral to the Jet engine are displayed inside the gray box. Outside the box, the services and accessories used by the Jet engine are connected with lines, indicating paths of communication.

Figure 19.1.
Functional Components of the Jet Engine.

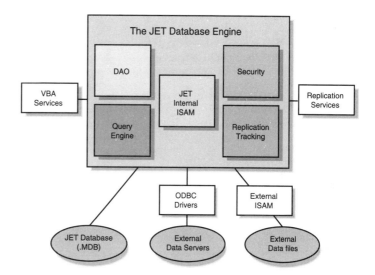

Physical Components of the Jet Engine

While database engines are often evaluated by comparing the logical functions performed, a lesser amount of attention is given to how these functions are actually implemented. Every function performed by the Jet engine is contained in a library or executable file. Knowing which files are used for each function is useful in many situations, such as resolving a support question after a failed setup. By understanding which functions are not working, you can usually determine which files are missing.

Components of the Jet engine are implemented primarily in Dynamic Link Library files (files with an extension of .DLL) and can be found in the Windows SYSTEM directory on your computer. The files noted as 32-bit always refer to Jet 3.0, whereas the 16-bit files reference Jet 2.5.

Primary Jet Engine Components

- MSJT3032.DLL (32-bit) and MSAJT200.DLL (16-bit) implement the majority of the Jet database engine, including data storage and retrieval, the query engine, and security functions.
- MSJINT32.DLL (32-bit) and MSJetINT.DLL (16-bit) provide localized language support. These files contain language-specific strings for Jet.
- MSJTER32.DLL (32-bit) and MSJetERR.DLL (16-bit) provide error-handling services and localized error messages.

DAO Interface Components

- DAO3032.DLL (32-bit) contains the type library and object layer interface to the engine.
- DAO2532.DLL (32-bit) provides a compatibility layer to obsolete DAO objects, such as Snapshots and Dynasets.

Jet-Specific VBA Files

VGAJet32.DLL (32-bit) initializes VBA expression evaluation services for the Jet engine.

Replication Service

- MSWNG300.DLL is the main replication engine, which provides creation and reconciliation.
- MSJTCLR.DLL supports replication services for the Microsoft Windows 95 Briefcase component.
- MSJTTR.EXE and MSAJetFS.DLL are the shuttle services that interface with and move data between replicas and masters.
- MSJRMI30.DLL and MSJRCI30.DLL provide localized language support. This file contains language-specific strings for the replication components.

External ISAM Files

Each ISAM database driver uses a different file to access that type of database. The following list indicates the ISAM drivers that ship with VB4, and the corresponding .DLL file used.

Driver	Filename
Access 1.x and 2.0	MSRD2X32.DLL
Paradox 3.5 – 5.0	MSPX3032.DLL

Driver	Filename
Xbase: Dbase III – V, FoxPro 2.0 – 3.0	MSXB3032.DLL
Excel 3.0 – 7.0	MSXL3032.DLL
Lotus 1-2-3 1.x – 4.x	MSLT3032.DLL
Text files	MSTX3032.DLL

The Jet Database

The other major physical component of the Jet engine is, of course, the Jet database. The data types that are native to the Jet database are shown in Table 19.1.

Table 19.1. Jet database native data types.

Data Type	Storage Size	Stores
Boolean	1 bit	Boolean data; also known as Yes/No
Byte	1 byte	Numbers 0 through 255
Integer	2 bytes	Numbers –32,768 through 32,767
Long	4 bytes	Numbers –2,147,483,648 through 2,147,483,647
Currency	8 bytes	A scaled integer, this field stores numbers with up to 19 digits—15 digits left of the decimal point, and 4 to the right
Single	4 bytes	$+- 3.4 \times 10^{38}$
Double	8 bytes	$+- 1.8 \times 10^{308}$
Date/Time	8 bytes	Dates from 1 January 100 to 31 December 9999 and times from 0:00:00 to 23:59:59
Text	Up to 255 bytes	Variable length text
OLE Object	N/A	OLE objects and other large variable-length binary data (often referred to as long binary data)
Memo	N/A	Large variable length text
GUID	16 bytes	Used for replication; this is a system-generated number that is guaranteed to be unique

Structure of the .MDB File

The Microsoft Jet database (.MDB) stores all tables, indexes, query definitions, security information, relationship information, and validation rules in a single .MDB file. In addition, if Microsoft Access uses the database, any forms, reports, macros, or modules created there are also stored in the .MDB file.

All of these items are written onto *pages*, or equally sized file spaces. Pages can be thought of as 2048-byte-wide rows in a file. It is possible (and likely) that more than one record will be located on a single page.

Figure 19.2 shows an example of how a typical database with both customer records and order records can be allocated onto database pages. Note that the records are not necessarily contiguous, among pages, nor is the same type of record necessarily located near other records of the same type.

Figure 19.2.
The relationship between database pages and data records.

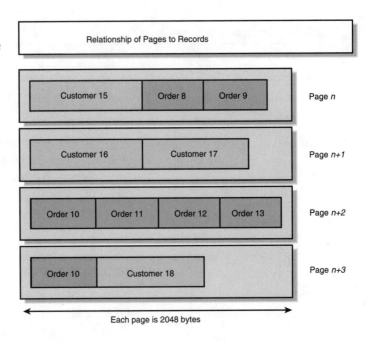

Several different types of pages exist in a Jet database. The first page in the database is referred to as the *database header page*. This page is used to track multiuser operations in the database. Other page types include pages to store normal data, long-value data (MEMO and OLE types), system tables, and indexes.

In order to track the inventory of tables, queries, rules, security settings, and relationships, the Jet database uses system tables. Four system tables are used to store this information. MSysObjects stores information about tables and queries in the database. MSysQueries stores additional information about the queries in the database, including the query type, the fields and tables referenced in the query, sort columns and sort order, query criteria, and any parameters used in the query. MSysACES feeds the security routines in the engine by storing permission information. MSysRelationships stores relationships between objects in the database.

It's important to note that if the database is used with Microsoft Access, you can create other system tables to keep track of Access forms, reports, and modules.

Structure of the .LDB File

The .LDB file helps control multiuser access to the database by tracking the current database *sessions*. One session is created for every user that references Jet's OpenDatabase method. A user can have multiple sessions in the database if, for example, they open the database with a VB program as well as having it open with MS Access.

No action is necessary to create the .LDB file—it is automatically created when the database is first opened in non-exclusive (shared) mode. The file always resides in the same directory as the database, and it has the same name up to the dot-three extension. For example, the sample database accompanying VB4 is called BIBLIO.MDB; it would have a locking file called BIBLIO.LDB. With Jet 3.0, the .LDB file is deleted when the last user closes a shared database with a few exceptions: the .LDB file is not deleted if the database is corrupt, or if the user doesn't have delete rights to the directory.

The file is structured quite simply: Each session's user information is stored within a 64-byte block. The first 32 characters hold the workstation name of the computer, and the last 32 bytes hold the security name (for example, Admin). Note that the file is not a completely accurate picture of who is currently logged on to the database—the entry for users who log off the database will not be erased. The entry can be overwritten by a user who later logs on. In other words, Jet doesn't reshuffle or optimize the .LDB. Internally, Jet is associating session numbers corresponding to these entries in the .LDB file. Jet will use this information when it needs to display an error message, referencing the session information, for example: Couldn't update; currently locked by user 'EmilioB' on machine 'Finance04'. Figure 19.3 illustrates the layout of the .LDB file.

Figure 19.3.
Structure of the .LDB file.

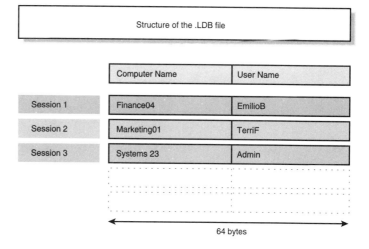

Multiuser Data Access

Like most databases, Jet controls access to shared data using locks. Jet uses a page-locking model. When Jet needs to lock an individual record, it locks the 2048-byte page containing that record. This type of locking scheme has less overhead and provides much greater efficiency than locking individual records. However, it can create headaches for programmers because by locking a page, Jet might actually be locking more than one record at a time. Referring back to Figure 19.2, when a user changes data for customer 16, customer 17 will be locked as well.

In order to give the programmer flexibility in dealing with this type of situation, Jet provides two multiuser locking schemes: *optimistic* and *pessimistic* locking. The default method is optimistic locking. In this scenario, Jet doesn't request a page lock until the user directs Jet to update the record. The advantage of this scheme is that the page is locked for a very short amount of time, minimizing the number of potential locking conflicts. On the other hand, the disadvantage is that two users could be editing the same record at the same time. The application must then deal with the situation in which more than one user attempts to save different versions of a record.

One way that applications resolve contention conflicts under optimistic locking involves using a Last Updated field in the record. The application checks this field to ensure that the value has not changed since the user started editing the record.

The situation is handled differently under pessimistic locking. Using the pessimistic scheme, Jet will immediately lock the page containing the record when the user begins to edit the record (that is, the user invokes the edit method on a record set). From the time between the invoking of the edit method and the calling of the update method, no other user will be able to edit any record on that page. Although the page is locked from edits, the records are still viewable.

Many applications using pessimistic locking employ some sort of visual cue (for example, an international NO symbol in the status bar) to signal to the user that the record is currently unavailable for editing. When the record becomes available, the program must know to refresh the displayed information, because another user might have changed data in the record.

Security

Another multiuser consideration is that of security. Security for Jet databases is based upon a workgroup model. A central workgroup security file named SYSTEM.MDW defines account names and passwords for each user. This file contains a unique ID, called the system user ID (SUID), for each user in the workgroup.

This ID is referenced in each .MDB database where the user has permissions. In addition, users can be assigned to groups with common security settings. An SUID will be assigned to the group, and permissions can then be given to all users in a group in one operation. For example, users in the Human_Rooources gioup would have read-write permissions on the Employee table. On the other hand, users in the Phone_Operators group would have select permissions on all columns of the Employee table, but perhaps they would have read-write access on the PhoneExtension column.

Prior to VB4, dealing with Jet security meant doing most of the work in Access. The improved DAO now provides full programmatic control over security with Jet databases. In other words, you can create and modify users and groups, assign passwords, and set permission levels on databases directly from Visual Basic. The one caveat here is that VB4 does not have a mechanism to initially create the secure SYSTEM.MDW database containing workgroup account names. This file is created when Access is installed. After the SYSTEM.MDW file is created, Visual Basic can add and delete accounts at will. Note that the SYSTEM.MDW file is not needed by Visual Basic unless security features are enabled.

Query Engine

The query engine is a complex subset of the database engine. In summary, its role is to accept a query that the user has submitted, analyze the query (noting which tables will be needed to perform the query), choose the most efficient plan of execution, and finally, execute the query and return the results to the user.

Functions

Although the query engine is complex, it can be broken down into three major steps: compilation, optimization, and execution.

Compilation

The compilation pass of the query first checks the syntax of the query. It compares the names of columns and tables in the query to the set of columns and tables currently available in the database. It also compares any references to functions in the query to those available in the environment. After the query passes the syntax check, the query is converted from SQL into an internal structure, with pointers to the referenced columns and tables. If the source of the query is one or more querydefs, the source querydef(s) are evaluated and also placed into the internal structure. For example, suppose you wrote a query entitled "May Renewals," which referenced a querydef entitled ActiveSubscriptions. The SQL of your query might be:

```
SELECT DISTINCTROW * FROM [ActiveSubscriptions]
➥where ExpiryDate between 5/1/96 and 5/31/96;
```

And the querydef `ActiveSubscriptions` can be based upon a query:

```
SELECT DISTINCTROW * FROM Subscriptions
➥where StatusFlag = "A"
```

In this stage of query compilation, the querydef `ActiveSubscriptions` is evaluated based upon the original table that it references, in this case `Subscriptions`.

Optimization

The Jet query optimizer uses statistics to determine the most efficient way to execute a query. Statistics (such as record counts) are used to determine the cost (in terms of time) of accessing data from each table. Because the use of indexes and different methods of table access will affect the cost, the optimizer considers all of the possible methods, and then chooses the one of least cost for each particular task (for example, reading data from the `Authors` table). When the query involves several tasks (as it nearly always does), the optimizer will build lists of possible tasks, and then choose the least expensive list.

In considering the statistics, Jet takes into account the following:

- The record count. The number of records in a table affects the join strategy that will be used.

- The data page count. The more pages the engine has to read, the longer the query will take to execute.

- The selectivity of available indexes. Selectivity refers to the uniqueness of the value in an index.

  Suppose you are considering indexing a table of 100,000 employees. Choosing to index a column containing `birth_month` would give a very low selectivity. Because there are only 12 months, each index value would probably point to over 8000 employees. `Birth_date` is somewhat better, but still has a low selectivity, because over 250 employees would share the same birth date (assuming fairly equal distribution of birth dates!). The greatest selectivity can be achieved by a unique index, because every value is distinct.

- Index pages count. As with data pages, the query cost will increase with the number of index pages read.

- Index rules for the particular database format. For example, certain ISAM or ODBC data formats allow nulls in indexes.

Because much of the optimization is based upon the use of statistics, the accuracy of such statistics will certainly affect the query performance.

Statistics can become out of date on any database platform. The Jet .MDB database is no exception. This can happen if many transactions are rolled back, or if a user turns off his or her machine with the database still open, thus not allowing the engine to refresh the statistics before closing.

In order to refresh the statistics, it is necessary to compact the database. In addition to updating the statistics, Jet 3.0 will physically realign the data based upon primary key order. This realignment is known as *clustering* and is a new feature of Jet 3.0. Note that the clustering is performed only upon compacting, and it is not maintained as new data is added to the table. Finally, compacting may speed up queries simply because it is faster to scan the compacted, contiguous pages rather than scanning fragmented pages.

The statistics are used by the optimizer to choose a join strategy. A join strategy dictates how columns and indexes will be used to form a join between tables.

With each potential join, strategy is a consideration of the "base-table access plan." The term "base-table" means the table underlying the query. For example, in the SQL statement SELECT * FROM Authors; the base table is Authors. In the statement SELECT * FROM 1996AuthPub, where 1996AuthPub is a querydef referencing a join between authors and publishers, then the base tables are Authors and Publishers. Thus the "base-table access plan" is the method the engine will use to retrieve the data from the base tables.

Figure 19.4 illustrates the relationship between access plans and join combinations.

Figure 19.4.
The relationship between join strategy and base-table access plan.

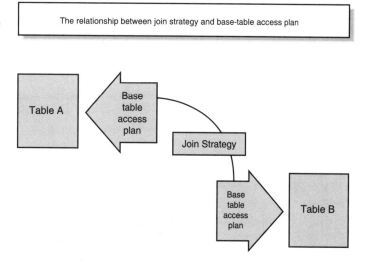

Jet will consider three different base-table access plans and five different join strategies in determining the most optimal query plan.

The three methods of base-table access are:

1. Rushmore restriction. This method is considered when more than one indexed column is involved in the query criteria or in the join criteria. Rushmore is able to restrict the number of data pages that need to be read by considering multiple indexes.

2. Index range. This method is used if part of the query involves limiting the number of records in a table based upon a single index. When the query is executed using Index Range, the query will use the index to access data in the base table.

3. Table scan. This method is usually not desirable because it is a one-time pass through every record in the table. As a result, every data page in the table must be read.

The five join strategies Jet considers are:

1. Nested iteration join. This is the least optimal join, which pairs each record in one table to another. For each record in table A, every record in table B might need to be examined to find a match.

2. Index join. This method tends to be favored when the data is being retrieved from just one table, and a second table is linked simply for the purpose of limiting results.

3. Lookup join. Similar to an index join, the lookup join first creates a temporary sorted table based upon one of the tables, for the purpose of reducing the size of the join. The join is then performed on the smaller temporary table.

4. Merge join. In order to perform a merge join, the join columns from each table must be sorted. The records are then paired by moving down through each table and locating matches in the sorted join columns.

5. Index-merge join. When both tables are in the native Jet database format, an index-merge will be considered if both tables have non-null indexes over the join columns.

Execution

Once the query optimizer has chosen the best plan, the joins are processed and the query is executed.

Analyzing Query Performance with ShowPlan

Once the optimizer has chosen the plan of lowest cost, the query is executed. Typically, information about the chosen plan is not exposed to the user or developer. However, Jet 3.0 has an undocumented feature called ShowPlan, which reveals the chosen execution plan.

ShowPlan is a method in which the Jet engine will, for purposes of development, create a text file containing the chosen query execution plan.

> The ShowPlan feature is unsupported, and there is no guarantee that it will exist in future releases or that it will have similar functionality. ShowPlan is available only in the 32-bit version of the engine, Jet 3.0. Jet 2.5 does not have this feature.

Enabling ShowPlan

In order to enable the ShowPlan feature, it is necessary to add a key to the registry.

1. For Win95 users, choose Run from the Start menu, type REGEDIT in the box, and click OK. For Window NT 3.5x users, choose Run from Program Manager, type REGEDT32, and press Enter.
2. From the registry tree, expand the following by clicking on the + sign next to each:

   HKEY_LOCAL_MACHINE

   SOFTWARE

   Microsoft

   Jet

   3.0

   Engines
3. Create a new key (Edit | New Key) called Debug.
4. Click the Debug key.
5. Create a new String Value, JetSHOWPLAN (this must be in all caps). For Windows NT 3.5x, the data type is called REG_SZ. For the value, type ON.

After ShowPlan is activated, Jet will append text containing the execution plan to a file SHOWPLAN.OUT located in the default directory on your computer. For Windows NT users, the default directory is usually \USERS\DEFAULT. For Win95 users, it is often \WINDOWS. If you're uncertain of the default directory, you might end up having to perform a search out of File Manager or the Start Menu in order to locate the file for the first time.

While ShowPlan is activated, any client accessing the Jet 3.0 engine will write query execution plans to this file. If you have much database activity on your computer (such as Access 95), this file can quickly grow large.

Disabling ShowPlan

To turn off the ShowPlan feature, go back into the registry editor and locate the Debug Key. Select JetSHOWPLAN, and change the value to OFF. ShowPlan will now be disabled.

Analyzing ShowPlan Results

The queries used for the sample ShowPlan results come from the sample database Northwind.MDB, which ships with Access 95.

The Order Details Extended Query

The SQL for the Order Details Extended query is

```
SELECT DISTINCTROW [Order Details].OrderID, [Order Details].ProductID,
➡Products.ProductName, [Order Details].UnitPrice,
➡[Order Details].Quantity, [Order Details].Discount,
➡ CCur([Order Details].[UnitPrice]*[Quantity]*(1-[Discount])/100)*100
➡ AS ExtendedPrice
FROM Products
➡INNER JOIN [Order Details]
➡ON Products.ProductID = [Order Details].ProductID
ORDER BY [Order Details].OrderID;
```

The ShowPlan output is

```
— Order Details Extended —

01) Inner Join table 'Products' to table 'Order Details'
    using index 'Order Details!ProductsOrder Details'
       join expression "Products.ProductID=[Order Details].ProductID"
02) Sort result of '01)'
```

The Invoices Query

The SQL for the Invoices query is

```
SELECT DISTINCTROW Orders.ShipName, Orders.ShipAddress,
➡Orders.ShipCity, Orders.ShipRegion, Orders.ShipPostalCode,
➡Orders.ShipCountry, Orders.CustomerID, Customers.CompanyName,
➡Customers.Address, Customers.City, Customers.Region,
➡Customers.PostalCode, Customers.Country,
➡[FirstName] & " " & [LastName] AS Salesperson, Orders.OrderID,
➡Orders.OrderDate, Orders.RequiredDate, Orders.ShippedDate,
➡Shippers.CompanyName, [Order Details].ProductID,
➡Products.ProductName, [Order Details].UnitPrice,
➡[Order Details].Quantity, [Order Details].Discount,
➡CCur([Order Details].[UnitPrice]*[Quantity]*(1-[Discount])/100)*100
➡AS ExtendedPrice, Orders.Freight
FROM Shippers
➡INNER JOIN (Products
➡ INNER JOIN ((Employees
```

```
➥    INNER JOIN (Customers
➥     INNER JOIN Orders
➥      ON Customers.CustomerID = Orders.CustomerID)
➥        ON Employees.EmployeeID = Orders.EmployeeID)
➥    INNER JOIN [Order Details]
➥     ON Orders.OrderID = [Order Details].OrderID)
➥   ON Products.ProductID = [Order Details].ProductID)
➥ ON Shippers.ShipperID = Orders.ShipVia;
```

The ShowPlan output for this query is:

```
— Invoices —

01) Sort table 'Orders'
02) Inner Join table 'Shippers' to result of '01)'
      using temporary index
      join expression "Shippers.ShipperID=Orders.ShipVia"
03) Sort table 'Employees'
04) Inner Join result of '02)' to result of '03)'
      using temporary index
      join expression "Orders.EmployeeID=Employees.EmployeeID"
05) Inner Join result of '04)' to table 'Customers'
      using index 'Customers!PrimaryKey'
      join expression "Orders.CustomerID=Customers.CustomerID"
06) Inner Join result of '05)' to table 'Order Details'
      using index 'Order Details!OrdersOrder Details'
      join expression "Orders.OrderID=[Order Details].OrderID"
07) Sort table 'Products'
08) Inner Join result of '06)' to result of '07)'
      using temporary index
      join expression "[Order Details].ProductID=Products.ProductID"
```

Summary of the Jet Improvements

As mentioned earlier, the Jet engine has changed substantially since VB3 was introduced. The following summary explains the major changes between the versions.

Improvements from Jet 1.1 to 2.0

Many new features were added to Jet 2.0. In addition, existing features were improved, and the SQL language was greatly expanded. The major additions are listed in the following sections.

Engine-Level Rules

Providing engine-level rules enables the user to specify conditions for data validation. For example, the user can specify that the column Priority must be a number between 1 and 3, or that the InvoiceAmount must be entered before the record can be saved.

SQL Pass Through (SPT) Flag

One of the complaints about Jet 1.*x* was that the engine seemed to be quite slow when accessing normally fast remote databases such as SQL Server. One of the reasons was that ODBC had to translate the query provided by Jet into something native to that server. The SPT flag enables the query to be sent directly to the remote database server, thereby bypassing the query interpreter engine.

Remote Index Join

Another reason the queries against remote databases could be slow was the Jet 1.*x*'s design of requesting all records in the remote table, and then performing the join locally. Jet 2.0 performed a remote index join, requesting only those records in the remote table matching a local key value. This resulted in a reduction of network traffic as well as an improved performance.

Rushmore

The Rushmore query engine was originally available only in FoxPro, a product praised for very high performance. The Rushmore technology dramatically improved query performance.

Data Definition Queries

Jet 2.0 included a richer SQL, which enabled the users to define data structures, such as CREATE TABLE, ALTER TABLE, and CREATE INDEX.

Cascading Updates and Deletes

Beginning with Jet 2.0, it became possible to define relationships between tables, and optionally enforce relational integrity. If relational integrity was enforced, the user could also specify to cascade updates and deletes.

Union Queries and Subqueries

Jet 2.0 supported the UNION syntax in queries. In addition, Jet 2.0 introduced the capability to perform subqueries. These powerful features are used mainly in decision support systems.

TOP N Queries

Support of Top N queries is probably the most popular addition in Jet 2.0. Users can easily perform queries to answer questions such as, "Who are my top 10 customers in terms of sales?"

Improvements from Jet 2.0 to 2.5

Jet 2.5 is very similar to Jet 2.0. Both engines use 16-bit architecture. Primarily, Jet 2.5 corrected a bug that would cause the database to behave as if it were corrupted if a user exited Windows improperly.

Improvements in Jet 3.0 Over 2.0 and 2.5

A great deal of effort was put into developing the 32-bit version of the Jet database engine. Improvements were made in the areas of performance and usability.

32-Bit Engine

The 32-bit engine virtually eliminates the "query too complex" messages, because the query is no longer restricted to compiling within a 64KB page.

Multithreading

The engine takes advantage of the multithreading capabilities of Windows NT and Windows 95. By default, the engine uses three threads.

Implicit Transactions

In Jet 2.x, users could improve the performance of iterative processes by first calling a BEGIN TRANSACTION, performing the processes, and then calling COMMIT. Jet 3.0 performs this function by default.

Dynamic Buffering

Jet 2.x supports a maximum cache size of 4MB. Jet 3.0's cache is dynamically allocated at startup and has no limit. The cache begins with approximately half the available memory, allowing effective memory usage on computers with larger amounts of memory.

Replication

Jet 3.0 was designed to support a master-replica replication scheme.

New Sort Engine

Many of the sort algorithms from Microsoft FoxPro are now used in Jet 3.0.

Long Types in Separate Tables

Long values, such as OLE types or memos, are now stored in separate tables. Prior versions of Jet stored all such values in a single table, which ended up causing a lot of contention for this data when there were many columns of long data in the database. In addition, the location of each long data value is indexed, resulting in faster seek times for random positioning.

Page Handling

Improvements in page handling in the areas of page reuse, page allocation, and delete logic bring faster, more efficient operations to Jet 3.0.

Clustering Indexes on Primary Key

As mentioned earlier in the chapter, compacting the databases results in a clustering of the indexes based upon the primary key.

Summary

The Jet database engine is the behind-the-scenes player that enables powerful database management systems. Jet has been extensively revised since its introduction several years ago; the current 32-bit version contains many powerful functions found nowhere else in the market. Learning how to harness all of this power requires some effort, but the payoff lies in the powerful applications that can be quickly developed.

More than ever before, the Jet engine is revealing its inner workings. With the `ShowPlan` function, the developer can quickly identify problems with slow queries. Once the problem is identified, you can take action to make the query run more quickly.

Data Access Objects

by James E. Bettone and Mitchell Guzman

In previous chapters you learned how to access data through the Access user interface. *Data Access Objects*, or *DAO*, provides a set of objects and collections that enable the developer to programmatically create and manipulate database components. Each object or collection has properties and methods that describe and manipulate these database components, respectively. These objects and collections form a hierarchical model of the database and its components that you, the developer, totally control.

In this chapter you learn Data Access Objects, its hierarchical model, and the different types of objects and collections that comprise the hierarchy. You learn about the power of DAO and much more.

What Is DAO?

DAO, or *Data Access Objects*, is the mechanism that enables other applications to communicate with database systems such as Microsoft Access and Microsoft FoxPro. This mechanism is responsible for retrieving and storing user data in a database system. DAO is installed fully supported by Visual Basic. The following are the versions of DAO that are available with Visual Basic 4.0:

- 16-bit version of DAO version 2.5. This version (for 16-bit applications) includes all of the new features available and provides backward compatibility with applications created using DAO 1.1 or DAO 2.0. DAO 2.5 is compatible with databases created using Access 2.0.

- 32-bit version of DAO version 2.5/3.0 compatibility layer. This version includes all of the new features available in DAO and also provides backward compatibility with applications created using either DAO 1.1 or DAO 2.0. DAO 2.5 is compatible with databases created using all versions up to and including Access 2.0. This 32-bit version is provided to allow easy transition to DAO 3.0.

- 32-bit DAO version 3.0. This version is not 100% backward compatible with the previous version of the DAO engine. Modifications are required to some areas of your application to take full advantage of DAO 3.0 and its features. DAO 3.0 is fully compatible with databases created using Access 7.0.

New Features in Microsoft DAO Version 3.0

There have been some major changes in DAO 3.0. If you're converting your application to Access 95, you'll probably want to take full advantage of this new functionality. Following are some of the changes made to DAO (for more information, see the section titled "DAO Compatibility" in this chapter or the online help for DAO).

- New index structure. This results in the substantial reduction in storage size and a substantial time savings because time isn't wasted creating duplicate indexes.

■ No more read locks on index pages. This will remove many locking conflicts and eliminate the need for the developer to call FreeLocks in Visual Basic 4.0 32-bit.

■ New way for page reuse. In Microsoft DAO 2.x, if a user deletes a lot of data, the last user out pays a substantial time penalty while the recycled page identifiers are being processed into available page identifiers. In Microsoft DAO 3.0, the process is significantly faster.

■ New compacting method. Compacting the database now stores the indexes in a clustered-index format. The clustered index isn't maintained until the next compact; performance is still improved. This differs from Microsoft DAO 2.x, where rows of data are stored the way they were entered.

■ New way for page allocation. In DAO 2.x each page contains data from a different table. In DAO 3.0, each table maintains clusters of grouped-together pages (eight pages), eliminating every other page having data from different tables.

■ Multithreading. By default, Microsoft DAO uses three threads to perform read-ahead, write-behind, and cache maintenance.

■ Implicit transactions. Users are no longer forced to explicitly use BEGINTRANS and COMMITTRANS to gain performance improvements.

■ Dynamic buffering. DAO 2.x supports a maximum cache size of 4MB. DAO 3.0 cache is dynamically allocated at startup and has no limit.

■ DBEngine.INIPath property: Windows 95 and Windows NT no longer support the use of INI files, but instead store INI type information in the system registry. INIPath now returns the path in the system registry. For example:

```
DBEngine.IniPath = "HKEY_CURRENT_USER\Software\VB and VBA Program
➥Settings\MYDBApp"
```

■ Recordset object. Rows from a Recordset object can now be retrieved into an array using the GetRows method. Previously, in order to populate an array with records from a recordset, you would usually have to iterate through the recordset. With the GetRows method, shown in Listing 20.1, you can now retrieve whole blocks of records or smaller blocks.

Listing 20.1. An example of the GetRows method.

```
Public Sub GetRowsSample()
    Dim dbsDatabase As Database, rstSampleRecordSet As Recordset
    Dim varMyRecords As Variant, iCount As Integer

    Set dbsDatabase = CurrentDb()
    ' Place this all on one line
    Set rstSampleRecordSet = dbsDatabase.OpenRecordset("SELECT FirstName, " &
    ➥"LastName, Title FROM Employees", dbOpenSnapshot)

    varMyRecords = rstSampleRecordSet.GetRows(3)
```

continues

Listing 20.1. continued

```
Debug.Print "First Name", "Last Name", "Title"

' The first subscript of the array identifies the Fields
' collection (moves horizontally across the record)
' Print the first field in the first record
Debug.Print varMyRecords(0, 0),

' Print the second field in the first record
Debug.Print varMyRecords(1, 0),

' Print the third field in the first record
Debug.Print varMyRecords(2, 0)

' The second subscript of the array identifies the record number
' (moves vertically through records)
' Print the first field in the second record
Debug.Print varMyRecords(0, 1),

' Print the second field in the second record
Debug.Print varMyRecords(1, 1),

' Print the third field in the second record
Debug.Print varMyRecords(2, 1)

End Sub
```

■ The `AllPermissions` property of the Containers/Document Object returns the permissions pertaining to each of the objects (either a `Document` or `Container` object) to which a user or his or her group has access. `AllPermissions` differs from `Permissions` in that it includes the permissions for the group as well as the permissions for the user. If the `UserName` property is set to a group, then `AllPermissions` and `Permissions` will function the same.

■ Replication: This is a new feature to Access 95 and DAO that allows for replication of databases. For more on this feature, please see the section titled "Replication" in Chapter 23, "Design of a Three-Tier Client/Server System."

■ Backward compatibility: You can use either the DAO 2.5/3.0 Compatibility Library for compatibility with older versions of DAO or, by deselecting this reference from Tools | References and selecting the DAO 3.0 library, use the DAO 3.0 library only (which has no backward compatibility). The latter removes support for the older objects, properties, and methods.

It is important to note that older functionality is partitioned off into separate versions or libraries. This is because this functionality will not be supported after Visual Basic 4.0. It is probably wise to suffer the pain (albeit minor) of converting over to the newer version of DAO now rather than wait until the older functionality is no longer supported.

The DAO Hierarchy

DAO in Visual Basic 4.0 is a set of OLE objects that represents the functionality of the DAO engine. This layer of objects sits between your application and the database you're trying to manipulate. This insulates you, the developer, from the complexities of database programming while providing a high level of flexibility and control.

> Each object in the DAO is actually a class. A class is not unlike a data type. You dimension an object as type `class` just like you dimension a variable as some data type. For example:
>
> ```
> Dim MyWorkSpace As Workspace
> Dim iCount As Integer
> ```
>
> Because most of the discussion in this chapter is about objects that you create and manipulate, we use the term "object" instead of "class" to keep things clear.

Each data access object has its own properties that help define it and methods that manipulate it. Almost every object has its own collections as well. *Collections* are simply a means for an object to contain other, usually like, objects. In other words, an object can have a collection that contains other objects with collections that contain other objects, and so on. This is how the hierarchy is implemented—through collections. For more on objects, properties, methods, and collections, see Chapter 7, "Object-Oriented Concepts."

The DAO hierarchy can be confusing at times, but once you can see the whole forest, you will begin to see the ease of use and power of DAO. Figure 20.1 shows the DAO hierarchy (each object/collection is represented by one object).

DBEngine

The DBEngine object is the topmost object in the DAO hierarchy and is predefined (you don't have to create an instance of a DBEngine objcct). (See Figure 20.2.) It represents and directly manipulates the DAO database engine. Therefore, the DBEngine object isn't an element of a collection; it is the object that contains everything else.

> Prior to version 3.0 you could have only up to 10 instances of the DBEngine object. Version 3.0 has this limitation removed; you can run as many instances as you want.

Figure 20.1.
The DAO hierarchy.

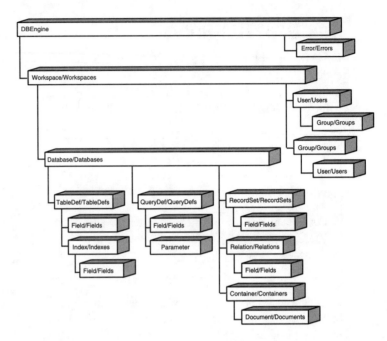

Figure 20.2.
The DBEngine *object.*

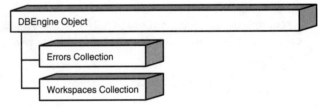

The DBEngine object can be used to compact or repair databases, register ODBC databases, get the DAO version number, and set the login timeout. Errors that occur from DAO actions are placed into the DBEngine object's Errors collection. Table 20.1 outlines the properties, methods, and collections of the DBEngine object.

Table 20.1. Methods, properties, and collections of the DBEngine object.

Methods	Properties	Collections
CompactDatabase	DefaultPassword	Errors
CreateWorkSpace	DefaultUser	Workspaces (default)
Idle	IniPath	Properties
RepairDatabase	Version	
RegisterDatabase	LoginTimeOut	
	SystemDB	

Errors

The Error object is the object that receives all errors when an action or activity performed by DAO fails. (See Figure 20.3.) The error collection is cleared and all errors that occurred are placed into the (same) error collection. This is because multiple errors might occur during a given activity or action by DAO. Errors in the Errors collection are ordered by error number—that is, the error with the lowest number is the first element, the next higher error number the next element, and so on. Error handling for this collection is discussed in more detail later in this chapter in the section titled "Handling Errors."

Figure 20.3.

The Errors collection and the Error object.

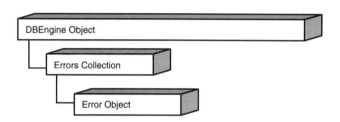

The following is an example of using the Error object:

```
Err.Clear

'Need to suppress any errors
On Error Resume Next

'Causes an overflow error
Err.Raise 6

'See the properties of the error object
Msgbox "Error " & Err.Description & " " & Err.HelpFile  & " " & Err.HelpContext
```

Table 20.2 lists the properties and collection of the Error object.

Table 20.2. Properties and collection of the Error object.

Properties	Collection
Description	Properties
HelpContext	
HelpFile	
Number	
Source	

Workspaces

To define a session for a user, use the `Workspace` object. (See Figure 20.4.) This object contains all open databases for a user and a transaction scope for that user. Transactions within a `Workspace` object are global across all databases for that `Workspace` object. Access, by default, creates a `Workspaces(0)` object that, if there is no security set up for the current database, sets the `Name` and `UserName` properties to `#Default Workspace#` and `Admin`, respectively. The `Workspaces(0)` object is commonly referred to as the *default workspace*.

Figure 20.4.

The Workspaces *collection and the* Workspace *object.*

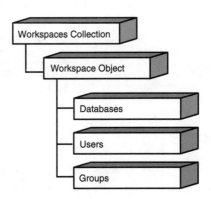

The `Workspaces` collection is a collection of all `Workspace` objects.

The following example depicts the update (secure database, omit workspace name, user name, and password on a nonsecure database) of the field `Unit Price` multiplied by 0.1, and then prompts the user to commit his changes or roll back any changes.

```
Dim sSQL as String
Dim wMyWorkspace as Workspace

wMyWorkspace  = DBEngine.Workspace("guzz",
➥"UserGuzz", "GuzzPassword").beginTrans
sSQL = "UPDATE Products SET [Unit Price] = [Unit Price] * 0.1"
  db.Execute Ssql, dbFailOnError

'Prompt the user if they want to save the changes
iReturn = MsgBox ("Are you sure you want to make these changes? ",
➥vbYesNo, "MYAPP")

'If yes commit the changes
If iReturn = gsYES then
 wMyWorkspace  = DBEngine.Workspace("guzz", "UserGuzz",
➥"GuzzPassword").CommitTrans

'Else rollback the changes
```

```
Else
   wMyWorkspace = DBEngine.Workspace("guzz", "UserGuzz",
   ➡"GuzzPassword").Rollback
End IF
```

The OpenDatabase method of the Workspace object is used to open a connection to a database. The following are some examples of the OpenDatabase method:

```
Dim db as Database
Dim wk as Workspace

Set wk = DBEngine .CreateWorkspace (0)
```

This example opens a database with full read and write conditions:

```
Set db = wk.OpenDatabase("c:\guzz\guzz.mdb", False, False)
```

This example opens guzz.mdb database as a read-only database:

```
Set db = wk.OpenDatabase("c:\guzz\guzz.mdb", False, True)
```

This example prompts the user to select a valid ODBC data source:

```
Set db = wk.OpenDatabase("", False, True, "ODBC;")
```

Table 20.3 lists the methods, properties, and collections of the Workspace object.

Table 20.3. Methods, properties, and collections of the Workspace **object.**

Methods	Properties	Collections
BeginTrans	IsolateODBCTrans	Databases (default)
Close	Name	Groups
CommitTrans	UserName	Properties
CreateDatabase		Users
CreateGroup		
CreateUser		
OpenDatabase		
Rollback		

Databases

The Database object represents a database that has been opened by or created with DAO. (See Figure 20.5.) If you use the CreateDatabase method of the Workspace object, the database is automatically appended to the Databases collection. Closing the Database object (using the Close method) will remove it from the Databases collection.

Figure 20.5.

The Databases *collection and the* Database *object.*

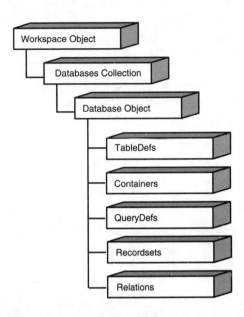

If you use the Close method to close a Workspace or Database object, this will close all open Recordset objects and roll back any pending updates or changes you have made. Also, it is important to note that if your Workspace or Database object falls out of scope, any pending updates or changes will also be rolled back.

The Databases collection is a collection of all the Database objects opened by DAO, including the current database that was opened by Access. It is important to note that the "internal" or hidden databases (wizards, system.mdw, and so on) used by Access aren't in this collection. The database collection contains database objects that have properties such as Connect (which shows the connect string used to connect or open the database), Name, and RecordsAffected (which shows the number of records affected by the Execute method of the database object).

The following example depicts the use of the Connect, Name, and RecordAffected properties:

```
Const dbSortGeneral  = 0
  Dim GuzzDatabase as Database
  Dim GuzzTable as TableDef
  Dim tTableName as String
  Dim iTotalRecsProcs as integer

  set GuzzDatabase = Workspaces(0).OpenDatabase("Guzz.mdb")
  set GuzzTable = GuzzDatabase.CreateTableDef("DBFTable")

 'Attach a paradox table
```

```
GuzzTable.Connect = "PDX;DATABSE=C:\DBF\DBF1.DB"
GuzzTable.SourceTableName = "Employee"
 tTableName = GuzzTable.Name

 ' Update the first record and column
 GuzzTable.MoveFirst
 GuzzTable.Edit
 GuzzTable.Fields(0) = 4
 GuzzTable.Update

 'Return the number of records affected
 iTotalRecsProcs = GuzzTable.RecordsAffected
 GuzzTable.Close

 ' Check to see if the action worked correctly
 if iTotalRecsProcs = 1 then
     Msgbox "The record is updated", vbOKOnly,"Guzz Program"
Else
     Msgbox "The record is not updated", vbOKOnly + vbCritical,"Guzz Program"
End If
```

Table 20.4 list the methods, properties, and collections of the Database object.

Table 20.4. Methods, properties, and collections of the Database object.

Methods	Properties	Collections
Close	CollatingOrder	Containers
CreateProperty	Connect	Properties
CreateQueryDef	Name	QueryDefs
CreateRelation	QueryTimeout	Recordsets
CreateTableDef	RecordsAffected	Relations
Execute	Transactions	TableDefs (default)
MakeReplica	Updatable	
OpenRecordset	V1xNullBehavior	
Synchronize	Version	

Users

Each User object represents users that exist in the workgroup database or the system.mdw. (See Figure 20.6.) User objects represent a user's account as defined in the workgroup database. For more information on workgroup databases, see the online help under system.mdw or workgroup database.

Figure 20.6.
The Users *collection and the* User *object.*

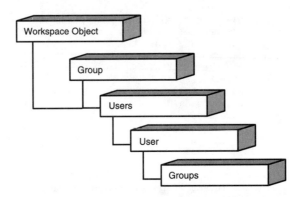

Table 20.5 lists all the methods, properties, and collections of the User object.

Table 20.5. Methods, properties, and collections of the User object.

Methods	Properties	Collections
CreateGroup	Name	Groups (default)
NewPassword	Password	Properties
	PID	

Groups

The Group object is similar to the User object; it represents groups that have been defined in the workgroup database or system.mdw. (See Figure 20.7.) A Group object usually represents groups of users and their appropriate security. Each user in a group is represented by a User object in the Users collection of the Group object.

Figure 20.7.
The Groups *collection and the* Group *object.*

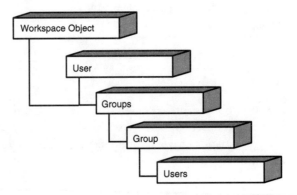

Table 20.6 lists the method, properties, and collections of the `Group` object.

Table 20.6. Method, properties, and collections of the `Group` object.

Method	Properties	Collections
CreateUser	Name	Users (default)
	PID	Properties

QueryDefs

Each query that has been defined in Access or created using `CreateQueryDef` is represented by a `QueryDef` object in the `QueryDefs` collection. (See Figure 20.8.) With the `QueryDef` object, you can create `Recordset` objects, add your own properties (more on this later in the "Properties" section), and pull out the SQL to see if it returns records or if you can just execute it. Because `QueryDefs` are precompiled SQL statements, they generally run faster than dynamic SQL (DAO doesn't have to compile it on-the-fly). You can create queries with the `CreateQueryDef` method.

Figure 20.8.
The `QueryDefs` collection and `QueryDef` object.

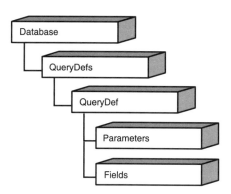

The following is an example of `CreateQueryDef`:

```
Dim MyDatabase as Database
Dim MyNewQueryDef as QueryDef
Dim MyRecordset as Recordset

Set MyDatabase = Workspaces(0).OpenDatabase("Guzz.mdb")

'Create our New QueryDef
Set MyNewQueryDef = MyDatabase.CreateQueryDef("Managers",
➥"Select Name from Employees where Title = 'Managers';")

    'Open our recordset
  Set MyRecordset = MyDatabase.OpenRecordset ("Managers")
```

```
'Populate our list box
MyRecordset.MoveFirst

Do Until MyRecordset.EOF
   MyListBox.Additem MyRecordset.Fields(0)
   MyRecordset.MoveNext
Loop
```

Table 20.7 lists the methods, properties, and collections of the `QueryDef` object.

Table 20.7. Methods, properties, and collections of the `QueryDef` object.

Methods	Properties	Collections
CreateProperty	Connect	Fields
Execute	DateCreated	Parameters (default)
OpenRecordset	LastUpdated	Properties
	LogMessages	
	Name	
	ODBCTimeout	
	RecordsAffected	
	ReturnsRecords	
	SQL	
	Type	
	Updatable	

TableDefs

`TableDef` objects represent tables or stored table definitions in a given database. (See Figure 20.9.) This could be a table in the current database or an attached table from an external database. With the `TableDef` object, you can tell whether the table is attached, what its validation rules are, whether it can be updated, or the number of records in the table. Also, tables can be created in code using the `CreateTableDef` method as described next.

When a table is attached, the properties that define its definition are read-only. You must go back to the source database (where the table resides) and make changes there.

Figure 20.9.
The TableDefs *collection
and the* TableDef *object.*

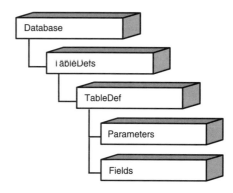

The following is an example of CreateTableDef:

```
Dim MyNewField as Field
Dim MyNewTableDef as TableDef
Dim MyDatabase as Database
Dim MyRecordset as Recordset
Dim ix as Integer

Set MyDatabase = Workspaces(0).OpenDatabase("Guzz.mdb")

'Create our tabledef object
Set MyNewTableDef  = MyDatabase.CreateTableDef("Managers")

'Need to add our Field to our created Tabledef
Set MyNewField = MyNewTableDef.CreateField("Name", dbText)
MyNewTableDef.Fields.Append MyNewField

'Append the new tabledef to our collection
MyDatabase.TableDefs.Append MyNewTableDef

'Lets populate our new table with the managers from our list box
MyRecordset = MyDatabase.Recordset("Managers")

For ix = 0 to MyListBox.ListCount - 1
  MyRecordset.Addnew
  MyRecordset.Fields(0) = MyListBox.List(MyListBox.ListIndex(ix))
  MyRecordset.Update
Next ix
```

Table 20.8 lists the methods, properties, and collections of the TableDef object.

Table 20.8. Methods, properties, and collections of the TableDef object.

Methods	Properties	Collections
CreateField	Attributes	Fields (default)
CreateIndex	ConflictTable	Indexes
CreateProperty	Connect	Properties

continues

Table 20.8. continued

Methods	Properties	Collections
OpenRecordset	DateCreated	
RefreshLink	LastUpdated	
	Name	
	RecordCount	
	SourceTableName	
	Updatable	
	ValidationRule	
	ValidationText	

Indexes

Indexes of a `Recordset` or `TableDef` object are represented by the `Index` object. (See Figure 20.10.) This enables the developer to set the index for a table, for example, just by referring to an index in the `Indexes` collection.

Figure 20.10.
The `Indexes` collection and the `Index` object.

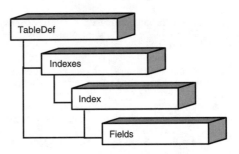

The following is an example of how to use the `Index` object's properties and methods:

```
Dim MyDatabase as Database
Dim MyTable as Table
Dim MyIndex as Index
Dim MyField as Field
Dim iTotalIndex as Integer
Dim sInexName as String

Set MyDatabase = Workspaces(0).OpenDatabase ("Guzz.mdb")
Set MyTable = MyDatabase.OpenTable("GuzzTable")

    'Store the number of current indexes in our collection
    iTotalIndex = MyTable.Indexes.Count
```

```
'Create our Index object
Set MyIndex = MyTable.CreateIndex("Index1")

'Create our unique index key
Set MyField = MyIndex.CreateField("Index1")

'Need to add some Index properties
MyIndex.Unique = True
MyIndex.Primary = True
MyIndex.Required = True
MyIndex.IgnoreNulls = False

'Need to append the index to the index collection
MyIndex.Fields.Append MyField
MyTable.Indexes.Append MyIndex

'Prompt the user on that the index was/was not created.
If iTotalIndex <> MyTable.Indexes.Count  then
   Msgbox "The index " & MyIndex.Name & " has been added", vbOKOnly, "MyApp"
Else
   Msgbox "The index " & MyIndex.Name & "has not been added.",
   ➥vbOKOnly + vbCritical, "MyApp"
End If
```

Table 20.9 lists the methods, properties, and collections of the Index object.

Table 20.9. Methods, properties, and collections of the Index object.

Methods	Properties	Collections
CreateField	Clustered	Properties
CreateProperty	DistinctCount	Fields (default)
	Foreign	
	IgnoreNulls	
	Name	
	Primary	
	Required	
	Unique	

Fields

Field objects represent common columns of data sharing similar properties and a common data type. (See Figure 20.11.) Relation, Recordset, TableDef, QueryDef, and Index objects all have a Fields collection. For example, if you're looking at a table using Access, each column of information is a field and is represented by a Field object. The Attributes property of a Field object represents the different characteristics of the Field object.

Figure 20.11.
The Fields *collection and the* Field *object.*

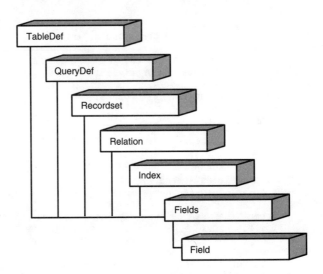

The following is an example of how to use the Field object and the Fields collection:

```
Dim MyDatabase as Database
Dim MyRecordSet as Recordset
Dim MyField as Field
Dim MyQuery as String

Set MyDatabase = Workspaces(0).OpenDatabase("Guzz.mdb")

'Build our SQL Statment
MyQuery = "Select [Home Address] as Home From GuzzTable;"

'Create our Recordset
Set MyRecordSet = MyDatabase.OpenRecordset(MyQuery)
MyField = MyRecordSet.Fields(0)
Msgbox "The original Source Table is " & MyField.SourceTable
➡& " and the original Field Name is" & MyField.SourceField, vbOKOnly, "MyApp"
```

Table 20.10 lists the methods, properties, and collection of the Field object.

Table 20.10. Methods, properties, and collection of the Field **object.**

Methods	Properties	Collection
AppendChunk	AllowZeroLength	Properties
CreateProperty	Attributes	
FieldSize	CollatingOrder	
GetChunk	DataUpdatable	
	DefaultValue	
	ForeignName	

Methods	Properties	Collection
	Name	
	OrdinalPosition	
	Required	
	Size	
	SourceField	
	SourceTable	
	Type	
	ValidateOnSet	
	ValidationRule	
	ValidationText	
	Value	

Recordsets

The Recordset object is probably the most used and also the most powerful object DAO provides. (See Figure 20.12.) With this object, a developer can programmatically access DAO tables as well as attached tables from SQL Server, ORACLE, or an ISAM database. This type of object is somewhat different from the other objects in that you create Recordset objects each time your application runs. These objects are never stored on disk—or anywhere, for that matter (except in memory)—they are just temporary.

Figure 20.12.
The Recordsets
collection and the
Recordset object.

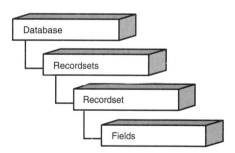

The properties, methods, and collections of a Recordset object vary depending on the type of the record set. See the DAO online help for a complete listing of properties, methods, and collections for this object.

The following is an example of the different types of `Recordset` objects in DAO:

```
Dim MyWorkspace as WorkSpace
Dim MyDatabase as Database
Dim MyRecordset as RecordSet

Set MyWorkspace = DBEngine.CreateWorkspace(0)
Set MyDatabase = MyWorkspace.OpenDatabase("Guzz.mdb")

'Create a Dynaset object
Set MyRecordset = MyDatabase.OpenRecordset("Select * from Employees",
➥dbOpenDynaset)

'Open a  snapshot
Set MyRecordset = MyDatabase.OpenRecordset("Select * from Employees",
➥dbOpenSnapShot)

'Open a table object
Set MyRecordset = MyDatabase.OpenRecordset("Select * from Employees", dbOpenTable)
```

Relations

All relations of an Access database are represented by a `Relation` object. (See Figure 20.13.) A *relation* is defined as a relationship between fields in two or more tables. The `Relations` collection contains all of the defined relationships for that `Database` object.

Figure 20.13.
The `Relations` *collection
and the* `Relation` *object.*

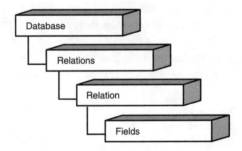

The following is an example of how to create a relationship:

```
Dim MyRelation as Relation
        Dim MyDatabase as Database
        Dim MyRelField as Field

        Set MyDatabase = Workspaces(0).OpenDatabase("Guzz.mdb")

        ' Create the new relation object
        Set MyRelation  = MyDatabase.CreateRelation("MyRelation-1")
        MyRelation.Table = "Employee"
        MyRelation.ForeignTable = "States"
        MyRelation.Attributes = dbRelationUpdateCascade
        Set MyRelField = MyRelation.CreateField("EmpState")
```

```
MyRelField .ForeignName = "StCode"
MyRelation.Fields.Append MyRelField

'Need to update our new relation to our collection
MyDatabase.Relations.Append MyRelation
```

Table 20.11 lists the methods, properties, and collection of the Relation object.

Table 20.11. Methods, properties, and collection of the Relation object.

Methods	Properties	Collection
CreateField	Attributes	Fields (default)
ForeignTable	Properties	
	Name	
	Table	

Parameters

In Access, you can define queries that require formal parameters and supply these parameters at runtime. Formal or *explicit* parameters are parameters that have been defined in a querydef's SQL using the PARAMETERS keyword. These formal parameters are represented in the Parameters collection by the Parameter object, shown in Figure 20.14. It is important to note that only *explicit*, not *implicit*, parameters are represented. The Parameter object provides information only on existing parameters. You cannot append objects to (or delete objects from) the Parameters collection.

Figure 20.14.
The Parameters collection and the Parameter object.

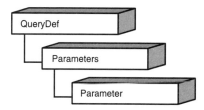

The following is an example of the use of the Parameter properties and methods:

```
Dim MyDatabase as Database
Dim MyQuery as QueryDef
Dim MyParameter as Parameter
Dim MyRecordset as Recordset
Dim MyParamName as String
Dim MyParamType as String
Dim MyParamValue as String

Set MyDatabase = Workspaces(0).OpenDatabase("Guzz.mdb")
Set MyQuery = MyDatabase.CreateQueryDef("GuzzQuery")
```

```
'Create two Parameter objects
MyQuery.Parameters("Title") = "Manager"

'Run our query
MyRecordset = MyQuery.OpenRecordset()

'Lets expose some of the properties
MyParamName = MyParameter.Name
MyParamType = MyParameter.Type
MyParamValue = MyParameter.Value

'Display some of the values of the created Parameter object.
Msgbox "The created Parameter " & MyParamName &
➥"contains the following values:" & " Type = " & MyParamType
➥& " Value = " & MyParamValue, vbOKOnly, MyApp
```

Table 20.12 lists the properties and collection of the `Parameter` object.

Table 20.12. Properties and collection of the `Parameter` object.

Properties	Collection
Name	Properties
Type	
Value	

Containers

The `Containers` object, shown in Figure 20.15, is one of the ways DAO achieves its application independence. It is an object that stores things like Access forms, databases, and modules. This object is generic enough to store these types of objects, yet flexible enough to maintain independence from any one application. The `Container` object contains document objects which are described next.

Figure 20.15.
The `Containers`
collection and the
`Container` object.

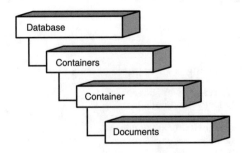

Table 20.13 lists the properties and collections of the `Container` object.

Table 20.13. Properties and collections of the `Container` object.

Properties	Collections
AllPermissions	Documents (default)
Inherit	Properties
Name	
Owner	
Permissions	
UserName	

Documents

The Document object, shown in Figure 20.16, represents each individual application's object. For example, when you create your database, DAO creates a Forms Container that contains a Document object for each form in the database. This is the object that actually represents each *individual* application object (such as forms, modules, or tables).

Figure 20.16.

The Documents collection and the Document object.

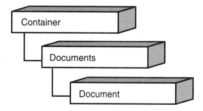

Table 20.14 lists the properties and collection of the Document object.

Table 20.14. Properties and collection of the `Document` object.

Properties	Collection
AllPermissions	Properties
Container	
DateCreated	
KeepLocal	
LastUpdated	
Name	
Owner	
Permissions	
Replicable	
UserName	

Properties

A `Property` object represents the characteristics of an object. (See Figure 20.17.) Every object in DAO has a `Properties` collection, and each `Property` object can be a built-in or a user-defined characteristic. The developer can manipulate these properties at runtime, and can even add new properties using the `CreateProperty` method if necessary.

Figure 20.17.
The `Properties`
collection and the
`Property` *object.*

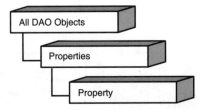

User-defined properties are properties added at runtime to a specific instance of an object.

> It is important to note that properties added to an object type are only for that instance of that object type. The developer is responsible for setting and changing values in user-defined properties.

These are the only types of properties that can be deleted from the `Properties` collection; built-in properties cannot be deleted.

The following is an example of how to create properties:

```
Dim MyProperty as Property
        Dim MyDatabase as Database
        Set MyDatabase = Workspaces(0).OpenDatabase("Guzz.mdb")

        'Example of the creation of a new property object
        Set MyProperty = MyDatabase.CreateProperty("NewProp")

        'Set some new properties for our new property
        MyProperty.Type = dbBoolean
        MyProperty.Value = False
        MyDatabase.Properties.Append MyProperty

        'Return the successful created property
        'value or else return the error
        If Err = 0 then
Msgbox "The Property has been created with the following value "
➥ & MyProperty.Value, vbOKOnly, "MyApp"
        Else
 Msgbox "The new Property has not been created. " & vbCRLF & Error,
 ➥ vbOKOnly + vbCritical, "MyApp"
        End If
```

Table 20.15 lists the properties and collection of the `Property` object.

Table 20.15. Properties and collection of the `Property` **object.**

Properties	Collection
Inherited	Properties
Name	
Type	
Value	

DAO Basics

Now that you understand the hierarchy, we can get down to the basics of using DAO. By now you're probably comfortable accessing data through the user interface of the Data control. Much of the hierarchy is hidden beneath the Data control that calls DAO directly. This section covers the basics of using DAO, such as the Application Model, declaring DAO, and objects and collections.

The `Application` Object Model

DAO can now be accessed from any OLE-compatible client (Microsoft Visual Basic 4.0 32-bit, Microsoft Excel 95, or Microsoft Access 95), and all of the objects, properties, and methods are exposed to the developer as an OLE in-process server. For an example of the Application Model, see Figure 20.18.

Figure 20.18.
The `Application` *object model.*

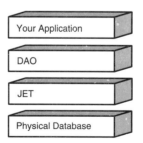

In-process servers are OLE Automation servers that are compiled as DLLs and share the same process space as the calling (your) application. What is the difference between a DLL and an OLE server, you ask? An OLE server exposes all of its objects, properties, and methods to the developer (just like a DLL), but an OLE server also exposes descriptions and explanations of each object, property, and method in an associated *type library*.

During design time you can browse the type libraries of all the OLE servers in your application by using the Object Browser. You can get to the Object Browser from the Visual Basic toolbar by pressing F2, or by choosing Object Browser from the View menu. For an example of the Object Browser, see Figure 20.19.

Figure 20.19.
The Object Browser.

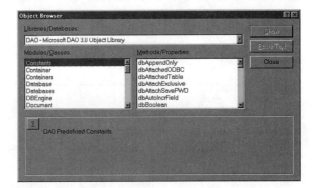

Objects and Collections

The concepts of objects and collections are very important in DAO. In the hierarchy (refer to the section titled "The DAO Hierarchy" earlier in this chapter), most objects have collections that contain that object type's members. For example, the DBEngine object has a Workspaces collection that contains individual Workspace objects. Most objects are part of a collection that has objects which in turn can also have collections.

Usually in the object-oriented (OO) world, a collection's name is the plural of the name of the object type that the collection contains. For example, the Workspaces collection contains Workspace objects. This convention is useful to know when you don't know the name of the object's collection; for example, the DBEngine has a collection of Workspace objects, and you want to use that collection but don't know the name. Just pluralize Workspace and you've got it!

Declaring DAO

In order to use DAO, you first must declare an object variable of whatever object type you would like to use. Earlier in this chapter, we discussed that the DAO is actually a hierarchy of classes but opted to refer to the classes as objects to avoid confusion. Classes are usually a type of object that you declare something as and can't use directly. For example, I don't have an object called Workspace, but instead have a variable wksMyWorkspace of the Workspace type or class as in the following example:

```
Dim wksMyWorkspace as Workspace
```

Object Variables

Due to the nature of DAO's hierarchical structure, it could become rather cumbersome to keep referring to objects through the DAO hierarchy without declaring anything. In comes a thing called *object variables*. Object variables are simply pointers or references to other objects. Using an object variable instead of using the hierarchy directly will make your code more readable and easier to type (no typing those long references!). The downside of using object variables is that dereferencing occurs at runtime, which could cause some rather tricky debugging situations. Overall, the advantages outweigh the negatives, and you should always use object variables if you reference a property more than once. For example:

```
Dim rstMyRecordset As Recordset, strName As String, strConnect As String
Dim iCount As Integer, strUpdatable As String, dbsMyDatabase As Database

Set dbsMyDatabase = CurrentDb

' This is the SLOW method (DON'T DO THIS)
' References get resolved through each iteration
For iCount = 1 To 10
    Debug.Print dbsMyDatabase.Name

Next

' This is the FAST method
' References get resolved just once
strName = dbsMyDatabase.Name
For iCount = 1 To 10
    Debug.Print strName

Next

' Use a With/End With Structure when referring to
➥' the same object a bunch of times
With dbsMyDatabase
    strUpdatable = .Updatable
    strName = .Name
    strConnect = .Connect

End With
```

Using the Current Database

Usually when you develop Access applications, you are using the database that was opened from the design environment. DAO has a function named CurrentDB that is a pointer to the currently open database. This is a very handy little function to have around—whenever you need to reference the current database, there is already a reference established.

CurrentDB references the database the same way DBEngine.Workspaces(0).Databases(0) does. In Access, you can't close Databases(0) as well as CurrentDB (CurrentDB.Close has no effect and is ignored). Although the second method is supported in Access 95 and probably will be there in future versions, it is recommended that you use the `CurrentDB` function instead. Why? The `CurrentDB` function is a lot more friendly in multiuser environments than the older method. `CurrentDB` creates another instance of the open database (similar to using `Opendatabase` on the current database) instead of referring back to the open instance.

A Special Note on the `Close` Method

The `Close` method is one of the methods that can really cause a lot of strange problems in an application. Strange problems normally don't pop up until the final release of your application. In older versions of DAO, the `Close` method would cause an error if it was used at the wrong time (when you had `Recordset` objects open), or would cause problems if it wasn't used at all (especially the next time your application started).

The reason we have devoted a small section to the `close` method is because of its new behavior. For the most part, the biggest change in this method is what happens when you use it. If you close an open database using the `close` method, all objects referencing that database will be de-referenced and any pending transactions or edits will be rolled back. All recordsets against that database will be closed, too. Any object that falls out of scope will have similar results (if you don't explicitly close the object).

The gist of the story is always explicitly close your `Database`, `Recordset`, `TableDef`, or `Workspace` objects.

Handling Errors

Error handling is done with the `DBEngine`'s `Errors` collection of `Error` objects. Whenever an error occurs, you can examine the `Errors` collection for all errors that occurred. Basically, the `Errors` collection holds all errors that occur during an action or transaction and each error is represented by an `Error` object. If you're writing a generic error handler, you can examine the `Errors` collection and report errors (based on an `Error` table or a basic `Select Case` statement). For example:

```
On Error Goto ErrorBlock_Err:

Dim dbsMyDatabase as Database, errErrorObject as Error

Set dbsMyDatabase = OpenDatabase("BogusDB.MDB")
dbsMyDatabase.Close
Exit Sub
ErrorBlock_Err:
    For Each errErrorObject in dbsMyDatabase.Errors
        Debug.Print errErrorObject.Description
        Debug.Print errErrorObject.Source
        Debug.Print errErrorObject.Number
    Next
Resume Next
```

DAO Compatibility

With the new and improved object model, some of the following objects, methods, and properties are no longer supported in DAO 3.0. Table 20.16 shows the object, method, or property with its accompanying replacement.

Table 20.16. DAO compatibility.

Functionality not present in DAO 3.0	Recommended DAO 3.0 replacements
FreeLocks	Not needed in Access 95 (use the Idle property instead)
SetDefaultWorkSpace	DBEngine.DefaultUser/ DBEngine.DefaultPassword
SetDataAccessOption	DBEngine.IniPath
BeginTrans (Database object)	BeginTrans method of Workspace object
CommitTrans (Database object)	CommitTrans method of Workspace object
RollBack (Database object)	RollBack method of Workspace object
CreateDynaset (Database object)	(Database) OpenRecordSet of the type Dynaset
CreateSnapshot (Database object)	(Database) OpenRecordSet of the type Snapshot
DeleteQueryDef (Database object)	QueryDefs collection's Delete method
ExecuteSQL (Database object)	Execute method and RecordsAffected property of the Database object
ListTables (Database object)	TableDefs collection of the Database object
OpenQueryDef (Database object)	QueryDefs collection of the Database object
OpenTable (Database object)	(Database) OpenRecordSet of the type Table
Table ListIndexes	Indexes collection of the TableDef object
CreateDynaset (QueryDef object)	OpenRecordset method of QueryDef object
CreateSnapshot (QueryDef object)	OpenRecordset method of QueryDef object
ListParameters (QueryDef object)	Parameters collection of the QueryDef object
Dynaset object	Recordset object of type Dynaset

continues

Table 20.16. continued

Functionality not present in DAO 3.0	Recommended DAO 3.0 replacements
Snapshot object	Recordset object of type Snapshot
Table object	Recordset object of type Table
ListFields method (Table, Dynaset, and Snapshot)	Fields collection of Recordset object
CreateDynaset (QueryDef and Dynaset object)	OpenRecordset method of object with type Dynaset
CreateSnapshot (QueryDef and Dynaset object)	OpenRecordset method of object with type Snapshot

If your project contains some of the older objects, properties, or methods, you just might want to convert to DAO 3.0 or use the Microsoft DAO 2.5/3.0 Compatibility Library. This library provides backward compatibility with older versions of DAO. To check if you're using this type library, choose References from the Tools menu to bring up the References dialog box (see Figure 20.20); look for the Microsoft DAO 2.5/3.0 Compatibility Library option. Future versions of Visual Basic will not support the older methods and properties of previous versions of DAO.

Figure 20.20.
The References dialog box.

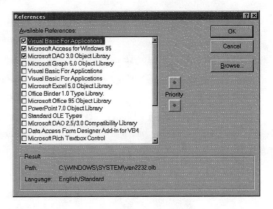

It is important to note that applications created in Visual Basic 3.0 will automatically reference the Compatibility type library. Likewise, applications created using Visual Basic 4.0 will not have this reference and will only reference the DAO 3.0 type library. If you have an older application and are not sure if you're using any of the older objects, deselect the Microsoft DAO 2.5/3.0 Compatibility Library option and select Start with Full Compile from the Run menu. If your application recompiles without errors, you don't have to use the Compatibility Library.

To ensure proper compatibility with future versions of DAO, it is recommended that you convert to DAO 3.0. Your application won't have the additional overhead of another layer and you won't have to distribute the Compatibility Library with your application. Again, future versions of Visual Basic will not support the older versions of DAO. For an example of the References dialog box and the Compatibility Library option, see Figure 20.21.

Figure 20.21.
The Compatibility Library.

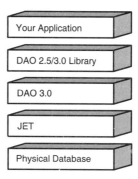

If you have installed the 16-bit version of Visual Basic, it will install DAO 2.5. The 32-bit version installs DAO 3.0 (which is fully 32-bit).

Optimizing DAO

As always, optimization and speed issues are important in database applications. The following sections discuss a few of the things to do to optimize your application when you use DAO.

Bang (!) Versus Dot (.) Usage

In previous versions of DAO, you could use either the bang or the dot separator when you referred to members of a collection. In DAO 3.0, most objects don't support the use of the dot separator. Eventually, support for the use of the dot separator will go away (and rolling over to new versions of DAO won't be as easy). Therefore, any future applications you develop should use the bang separator only. For example:

```
MyRS!Employee_ID  ' This is OK
MyRS.Employee_Name ' This is OK, but not recomended
DBEngine.Workspaces(0) ' No longer supported
DBEngine!Workspaces(0) ' Correct usage
```

Use Object Variables

As stated previously, whenever your application needs to reference a DAO property, store its value in a variable. This is probably one of the most common mistakes made by Access developers. Here's a simple rule of thumb: If the same object or property is used more than once, use an object variable.

Default Collections

All objects have a default property or collection. This can make your code difficult to read (some developers might get confused as to which property you're using if you're referring to the default property or collection), but it will run faster because the compiler doesn't have to resolve an extra reference. For example, the default collection of the DBEngine object is the Workspaces collection:

```
DBEngine.WorkSpaces(0).Databases(0)
```

You could use this instead:

```
DBEngine(0).Databases or DBEngine(0)(0)
```

The latter refers to the default collection of the default collection of the DBEngine object. Confusing? Not really, once you learn what the default collections are for each object. After you have done one application using DAO, you get pretty familiar with them.

Refreshing

Avoid refreshing unless it's absolutely necessary. *Refreshing* a collection will give an up-to-date view of that collection's objects and properties, but in a multiuser environment or a speed-critical application, this is a very expensive method to use. This method should be used only when it can't be avoided.

Using Queries

Queries are precompiled SQL stored in Access. When your application uses *dynamic SQL* (SQL created on the fly), DAO still needs to optimize and compile the SQL statement during runtime. If you use queries whenever possible, the optimization and compilation are done beforehand (when the query is created in Access) and you don't suffer the hit at runtime.

Accessing Remote Databases

Some applications made with Access will be used against a remote database such as SQL Server or ORACLE. It is important to note that DAO is optimized for use with DAO and ISAM databases, not with remote databases such as SQL Server. If you're ever going against a remote database, use RDO instead of DAO (see Chapter 24, "Remote Data Control/Remote Data Objects").

Take Advantage of Rushmore

Rushmore is a technology that enables you to query sets of records very efficiently. With Rushmore, you can use certain types of expressions in a query criteria (like the WHERE clause) that will make your query run much faster.

Cloning

Instead of opening new Recordset objects, use the Clone method of the Recordset object and clone existing record sets. This can result in substantial time savings when you are dealing with a similar, large, or duplicate record set.

Use Snapshot Record Sets When Possible

Record set objects of type dbOpenSnapshot are generally faster than dbOpendynaset-type record set objects. How much and what type of data you are retrieving should be the deciding factors in which type of object to use.

Use the Forward-Only Snapshots When Possible

Normally, snapshots can be bidirectionally scrolled by default. But if all that you need is to make a single pass through the records in the snapshot, use the dbForwardOnly option when you create the record set. For example, use this when you are populating a list box or combo box with values from the database.

Summary

DAO is a fairly extensible object library that enables the developer to manipulate many types of databases. This chapter informs you about DAO's extensive hierarchy, how to use DAO, and how to optimize and increase the efficiency of your application when you use DAO.

Make sure you understand DAO completely before leaping into a project. This way you can take full advantage of the new features in DAO 3.0 and have a solid application to boot.

Client/Server Programming with Visual Basic

P A R T 4

Using an Access Database from Visual Basic

by Dwayne R. Gifford

One of the most difficult parts of developing any application is deciding how you will save the data the application needs in order to operate. Currently, one of the best ways available is to use an Access database file and then use Microsoft Jet to access the data from Visual Basic.

This chapter gives you some very important information on how to create an Access database, how to modify data in the database, and how to secure the data so that not just anyone can get to it.

Creating Databases

The first step in using an Access database from Visual Basic is to create the database. You can do this in two ways: You can use Visual Basic, or you can use Access. The first method is discussed in the following sections. The second method is outlined in the "Implementing Security for Your Database" section, later in this chapter.

Using 16-Bit or 32-Bit Databases

To create the database from Visual Basic, you can use the Set command, as shown in the following code:

```
Set database = workspace.CreateDatabase (databasename, locale [, options])
```

Explanations of this code follow:

database	Must be set to a variable set to database.
workspace	A variable representing the Workspace object.
databasename	A string expression that will be the new database file. This must include the full path, which can be just D:\temp\temp.mdb, for example, or \\computer\sharename\temp.mdb.
locale	A string expression specifying the collating order for creating the database. For a list of available options, use the Visual Basic online Help and search on CreateDataBase.
options	Defines whether the database is a 16-bit or a 32-bit database. This parameter is optional. Use dbVersion25 to create a 16-bit database or dbVersion30 to create a 32-bit database. If you leave this parameter blank, Visual Basic creates a database based on your current working environment.

Creating a Table

To create a table in the database, you first need to set a `tabledef` variable equal to the new table name. Use the following `Set` code:

```
Set variable = database.CreateTableDef
➡([name[, attributes[, source[, connect]]]])
```

`variable`	Set this to a `TableDef` variable type.
`database`	Must be a variable that has been set to a database variable type.
`name`	A string expression equal to the new table name.
`attributes`	A `Long` variable type and the variable needs to be set to the sum of all the characteristics that you wish the new table to be made of. Table 21.1 lists the possible options.
`source`	A `String` variable set to the name of the original source of the data, this being the name of the table in an external database.
`connect`	A string expression containing information about the open database, this being made up of the database identifier and the database path.

Table 21.1. Available attributes for `CreateTableDef`.

Constant	Description
`dbAttachExclusive`	Tells Jet to attach the table in Exclusive mode.
`dbAttachedODBC`	Specifies an attached ODBC table.
`dbAttachSavePWD`	Tells Jet to save the connection information.
`dbAttachedTable`	Specifies that this is a non-ODBC table and that it is attached.
`dbHiddenObject`	Specifies that the hidden table is for temporary use and is read-only.
`dbSystemObject`	Specifies that `Systemtable` will be read-only.

After you set up the table, you should add fields to it. To do this, use the following code:

```
Set variable = object.CreateField([name[, type [, size]]])
```

`variable`	Declared as a field.
`object`	A variable set to `TableDef`.
`name`	Uniquely identifies your field from the other fields in the table.
`type`	Should be set to one of the available integer constants. Table 21.2 lists these available options, as well as possible `size` options.
`size`	If the `size` option is required with any of the `type` options, then the possible values will be in the final column of Table 21.2.

Table 21.2. Available attributes for `CreateField`.

Value	Setting	Description	Size
1	dbBoolean	Boolean	Not Required (NR)
2	dbByte	Byte	NR
3	dbInteger	Integer	NR
4	dbLong	Long	NR
5	dbCurrency	Currency	NR
6	dbSingle	Single	NR
7	dbDouble	Double	NR
8	dbDate	Date/Time	NR
10	dbText	Text	1-255
11	dbLongBinary	Long Binary (OLE object)	NR
12	dbMemo	Memo	NR

After you set the field object, you can add any of the properties that are listed in Table 21.3.

Table 21.3. List of available properties for `CreateField`.

Property	Brief Description
AllowZeroLength	Enables the field to be set to NULL when a new record is inserted.
Attributes*	Covered in more detail after this table.
CollatingOrder	Refer to Table 21.4 for valid values for this property.
Count	Returns the number of fields in the current tabledef.
DataUpdatable	Once a record has been added, it makes this field read-only.
DefaultValue	Covered in more detail after this table.
ForeignName	Works with a relationship property of Foreigntable. Is set to the name of the column that the foreign relationship will be based on.
Name	The name that will be used to represent the field.
OrdinalPosition	This will allow you to specify a field order for the table that you are working on.
Required*	Covered in more detail after this table.
Size	For data types and is size-applicable; refer to Table 21.2.
SourceField	Indicates the name of the field that the data is to be retrieved from.
SourceTable	Indicates the name of the table that the Sourcefield is from.

Property	Brief Description
Type	Refer to Table 21.2 for valid field data types.
ValidateOnSet	Specifies if the value is to be immediately validated when the value is set.
ValidationRule	Identifies what is valid data for the current field.
ValidationText	Indicates what text to display if the data does not meet the ValidationRule.
Value	Is used to display what the current records value is set to.

The properties with an asterisk (*) are covered in more detail later in this section. If you want to see all the properties in the list, open Visual Basic Help, do a search on the Fields collection, and then click on Properties.

Table 21.4 lists the values you can set for the Attributes property.

Table 21.4. Available values for the Attributes property.

Constant	Description
dbAutoIncrField	Automatically incremented, creating a unique index value.
dbDescending	Specifies that the field is sorted in descending order if the field is the indexed object. If this field is the constant, leave it blank, and ascending order is assumed.
dbFixedField	Fixed in Size field.
dbUpdatableField	Field value can be updated.
dbVariableField	Variable Text field.

You can set the Required property to True or False. If it is set to True, no NULL values are accepted. If you set the DefaultValue property, the record becomes equal to the default value. You can overwrite this value by setting the Value property. After you set all the fields, you should append the fields to the table using this code:

```
collection.Append object
```

The collection variable, in this case, is required to be set to the tabledef.fields, and the object should be set to the Fields variable. The following code is an example:

```
tdProducts.Fields.Append fldProducts(0)
```

After you add the fields to the table, the last step is to add any indexes that might be required. First, create an index variable by using this code:

```
Set variable = tabledef.CreateIndex([name])
```

Explanations for the syntax follow:

> variable   Should be an index variable.
>
> tabledef   Must be set to a tabledef variable.
>
> name   Specifies a unique string expression to identify the new index.

The following list contains all the properties you can set before creating the index on the field of the table:

```
Clustered
Foreign
IgnoreNulls
Primary
Required
Unique
```

You can set all these properties to True or False.

To set one of these properties, for example, you can use this code:

```
indProduct.Primary = True
```

The indProduct is a variable set to index. After you set these parameters, it is time to call CreateField again. This time, the object is set to the index object instead of the tabledef object. An example follows:

```
Set fldIndex(0) = indProduct.CreateField("ProductID")
```

After you set the field variable, you should append the index to the index object. After the index is appended to the index object, you must append the index object to the indexes collection. The final step in the process to build a table is to append the tabledef object to the tabledefs collection.

You need to repeat this process for each table you want to create. After all the tables have been built, the only step left is to close the database.

For an example of the whole process of building a new database and adding tables plus indexes, refer to build.vbp, which is located on the CD-ROM included with this book.

Attaching Tables

You also can attach tables from other supported Jet databases. The connection information is stored in the database that is making the attachment call. This also enables the database to automatically reconnect the attached table when the database is opened. Attaching a table is just like making a new table, with one exception: You cannot add new fields or indexes to the table.

The first step in attaching an external table is to set a tabledef variable. The following code shows you how to do this:

```
Set tdProducts = dbPExample.CreateTableDef("Products")
```

After you set the TableDef variable, you need to set two properties that tell Jet there is an external table. These two properties are SourceTableName and Connect. SourceTableName is the actual name by which the table is known in its own database. In the following example, the table name is Software Products:

```
TdProducts.SourceTableName = "Software Products"
```

The connect string needs to tell Jet what type of database it is connecting to and the path to the database. Before the database path and name, you need to place the string Database= and append a semicolon (;).

Table 21.5 gives you a complete list of possible database types and the keyword required for the connect string.

Table 21.5. Database string values.

Database Type	Required Specifier
Btrieve	Btrieve;
dBASE III	dBASE III;
dBASE IV	dBASE IV;
Excel 3.0	Excel 3.0;
Excel 4.0	Excel 4.0;
Excel 5.0	Excel 5.0;
FoxPro 2.0	FoxPro 2.0;
FoxPro 2.5	FoxPro 2.5;
FoxPro 2.6	FoxPro 2.6;
Jet database engine	;
Paradox 3.x	Paradox 3.x;
Paradox 4.x	Paradox 4.x;
ODBC	ODBC;
Text	Text;

> The ODBC string in Table 21.5 is an example, and it might not be complete for all servers. It is the minimum required string for a connection to Microsoft SQL Server, however.

In all cases except for the ODBC string, you are required to add the `Database=` string before the path and filename. You can use the following example to connect to an Access database called Temp.mdb and in `C:\Temp`:

```
TdProducts.Connect = ";Database=C:\Temp\Temp.mdb;"
```

Modifying Your Database

After you create the initial database, you need to make changes to it at some point. You can add or delete tables, fields, indexes, and queries. Because this chapter already has discussed adding tables, fields, and indexes, this section focuses on deleting these types of objects. When dealing with an Access database, you need to be aware of two other important features that could help you avoid some major problems: `CompactDatabase` and `RepairDatabase`.

Deleting Tables

To delete a table from the `TableDef` collection, you use the following code:

```
collection.Delete objectname
```

Descriptions of this syntax follow:

> *collection*   A variable set to `TableDef`.
> *objectname*   The table you want to delete.

The following example deletes the table Customers from the currently open database:

```
dbExample.TableDef.Delete "Customers"
```

> If the table does not exist in the database, an error is raised.
>
> Remember that when you delete a table, you also are deleting the data that is in the table. Therefore, after the `Table` object is deleted, it is impossible to undelete the table.

Deleting Fields

To delete a field, you use this code:

```
collection.Delete objectname
```

The syntax follows:

collection	Set to the `Fields` collection.
objectname	Set to the field you want to delete.

> You cannot delete a field if it is part of an index or relationship. You first must remove the index or relationship before you can delete the field.

The following example deletes the `ProductDescription` field from the Products table:

```
products.Delete productdescription
```

To make a change to a field, such as renaming the field or setting it to a new size, you need to build the new table with the changes. After you create the table, move the data to the new table, and then delete the old table. To learn how to move the data from one table to the other, see "Making Bulk Changes," later in this chapter.

Deleting Indexes

As changes occur to the database, you might need to remove an index so that you can delete an unwanted field or add a new index to replace the old index. The following example removes an index named `ProductId` from the Products table:

```
dbExample.TableDefs("Products").Indexes.Delete "ProductID"
```

> If the index is part of a relationship or does not exist, an error occurs.

Using Queries

One of the most effective ways to increase the speed of a SQL statement being used in the `OpenRecordset` is to use an already created query. To learn more about the `OpenRecordset`, see "Creating Record Sets." This section covers how to create a temporary `querydef` or a permanent `querydef`. Then you'll learn how to remove a `querydef` after it has been created.

Adding Queries

To add a new `QueryDef`, use the following command:

```
Set querydef = database.CreateQueryDef([name][, sqltext])
```

Explanations of the syntax follow:

querydef	A variable set to querydef.
database	A database variable.
name	The name used to uniquely identify the query.
sqltext	Made up of a valid SQL statement.

The following SQL statement returns all the records from the Products table:

```
Select ProductID, ProductName, ProductDescription from Products
```

To learn more about writing and using SQL, you might want to read *Teach Yourself SQL in 14 Days* or *Developing SQL Windows Applications,* both by Sams Publishing. To create a temporary `QueryDdef`, you need to leave the `name` parameter as an empty string.

After you set the `querydef` variable, it is appended automatically to the `querydef` collection. There is no need to append the `querydef` to the `querydefs` collection yourself. The following code shows you how to create a `querydef` called Product Search:

```
Set qdExample = dbExample.CreateQueryDef("Product Search",
➥"Select * from Products")
```

You can create two types of queries: an action query and a parameter query. An *action query* consists of a SQL statement that will use `Update`, `Insert`, or `Delete` instead of `Select` statements. These keywords are used in action queries because they return no data, but instead manipulate the data.

The parameter query has the following syntax:

```
PARAMETERS name datatype, ...;
```

The syntax for `PARAMETERS` follows:

name	Uniquely identifies the parameter.
datatype	Specifies the parameter's data type.

The following example shows how to create a parameter query:

```
Set qdExample = dbExample.CreateQueryDef("Example Parameter", "
➥Parameters [ProductID]; Select * from Products
➥where ProductID = [ProductsID];")
qdExample.Parameters("ProductsID") = 1
qdExample.Parameters("ProductsName") = "New"
```

To get a parameter query to work correctly, you need to add the *n* number of parameters to the `querydef` variable before setting the `recordset` variable equal to the `querydef`.

Deleting Queries

To remove a query from the database, you need to remove it from the querydefs collection. If you have added a querydef called New Query, you need to use the following code to have it removed from the database:

```
dbExample.QueryDefs.Delete "New Query"
```

In this case, dbExample must be set to a database variable.

Compacting and Repairing a Database

As you remove data from the database, you will find that the database grows at an unbelievable rate and to an incredible size. The database grows because Access does not remove the data until it is told to actually remove this deleted data. To tell Access to remove the data from the database, you must compact the database. Also, at times, you will find that your database has become corrupted. This section will help you fix both these problems.

Compacting a Database

To compact the database, you can use the following code:

```
DBEngine.CompactDatabase olddatabase, newdatabase [, locale [, options]]
```

Explanations for the CompactDatabase syntax follow:

olddatabase	Specifies a string equal to the database you want to compact.
newdatabase	A string expression equal to the name of the new database.
locale	A string expression used to specify collating order. If left blank, the new database will be created with the same option as the original database used. For a list of available options, refer to the Visual Basic online help and search on CreateDatabase.
options	This is optional, and can be left blank if you want to use the same options that the original database used. This can be made of two parts. The first is dbEncrypt or dbDecrypt. The second part consists of one of the following: dbVersion10, dbVersion11, dbVersion25, and dbVersion30.

> If you compact a dbVersion25 database and you leave the options part empty, the database is upgraded to a dbVersion30.

When you are compacting the database, using a different value than the original value used to create the database does not totally convert the database; it just converts the data format.

Repairing a Corrupted Database

To repair a corrupted database, use the following code:

```
DBEngine.RepairDatabase dbname
```

Here, *dbname* is a string expression equal to the database you want to repair. If the database cannot be repaired, a trappable error occurs. It is important to remember when you are working with Access databases to always make backups because it is possible to have a database that is impossible to repair.

> In order for you to be able to repair a database, you must be the only user on the database.

Working with Databases

After you add the objects to the database, you need to know how to actually work with the data. The first step in working with the data is to open the database. Then you can work with the data in one of two ways: by using record sets or by using query definitions. The query definitions were covered earlier in the chapter, in the section "Using Queries," so this section focuses on record sets.

Opening Databases

To open the database, use this code:

```
Set database = WorkSpace.OpenDatabase(dbname[, exclusive[,
➥read-only[, source]]])
```

Definitions of the syntax for OpenDatabase follow:

database	Must be set to a database variable.
WorkSpace	Can be a variable set to the workspace that will contain the database, or it can just be set to the default workspace, which is specified by Workspace(0). To define a new workspace, you can use the CreateWorkSpace command. This command takes three parameters: Name, User, and Password. Each needs to be set to a string expression. The Name option must begin with a letter and be no longer than 40 characters.

	User must be set to a name or group that is in the `users` or `groups` collection. `Password` is for the current user or group.
dbName	Must be set to a string expression that evaluates to an existing database.
exclusive	This is optional. If it is left blank, shared is assumed.
read-only	This option is `True` (to specify read-only) or `False` (to specify that it is not read-only).
source	Can be added if you need to evaluate to an ODBC connect string.

The following example opens the database access7.mdb as read-only:

```
Set db = Workspaces(0).OpenDatabase("d:\data\examples\access7.mdb", ,True)
```

Leaving the empty parameter between the `"d:\data\examples\access7.mdb"` and the `True` makes the function call use the default value. If you did not put in the extra comma (,), the call would assume that you want the database opened in Exclusive mode. Finally, after the database is open, it is time to actually start working with the data.

Creating Record Sets

To actually get at the data to work with it, you need to work with the record set collection. You can get to the data in Access by using one of five methods: `CreateDynaset`, `CreateSnapShot`, `OpenTable`, `OpenQueryDef`, or `OpenRecordSet`. The method most used in Visual Basic is `OpenRecordset`, because it gives you as the developer the most flexibility and options.

To use `OpenRecordSet`, you need to call one of the following codes:

```
Set variable = database.OpenRecordSet(source[, type[, options]])
```

or

```
Set variable = object.OpenRecordSet([type[, options]])
```

Definitions for the `OpenRecordSet` syntax follow:

variable	Must be set to a `RecordSet` data type.
database	Must be set to an existing database object.
object	Must be set to an existing `TableDef`, `RecordSet`, or `QueryDef` object. If you are dealing with a `RecordSet` object that refers to a table type original, it now will be set to a `Dynaset` type. Otherwise, the type will not change from the original type.
source	A string expression that will evaluate to a valid table name in the `TableDefs` collection, a query name that is in the `QueryDefs` collection, or a valid SQL statement that will return data.

type   Can be set to any of the following reserved constants:

dbOpenTable: Opens the record set as a table type. Cannot be used if an attached table is being referenced.

dbOpenDynaset: Opens the record set as a Dynaset type.

dbOpenSnapShot: Opens the record set as a SnapShot type.

options   Can be set to any combination of the items listed in Table 21.6.

Table 21.6. Options **variables.**

Variable	Function
dbDenyWrite	Locks the record set so that no other users can modify or add records.
dbDenyRead	Locks the records so that no other users can even view the records.
DbReadOnly	Sets you in View mode only.
DbAppendOnly	Enables you to add records only. This option is available only with the type Dynaset.
DbInConsistent	Enables you to add new records without enforcing referential integrity on the new record. Can be used only with the Dynaset type. Cannot be used with dbConsistent.
DbConsistent	Forces referential integrity when a new record is added. Can be used only with a type of Dynaset. Cannot be used with dbInConsistent.
DbForwardOnly	Enables you to scroll forward only through the record set.
DbSQLPassThrough	The Jet Engine is bypassed, and the source argument is passed to an ODBC server to be processed.
DbSSeeChange	Generates a runtime error if another user is editing the same data that you are editing. This option helps enforce referential integrity on the database.

Because this chapter deals with an Access database, you should not use the dbSQLPassThrough option in an OpenRecordSet call. Also, unless you are in a multiuser environment, you should not call DBSSeeChange.

As you can see, because OpenRecordSet gives you the capability to act like OpenTable, SQL statements, QueryDefs, SnapShots, and Dynasets, OpenRecordSet is the best choice of the five statements mentioned. In addition to these options, you will find that the OpenRecordSet is the most flexible.

The following examples show how you can use the OpenRecordSet call:

```
set rcdProducts = dbExamples.OpenRecordSet("Products",dbOpenTable)

set rcdProducts = dbExamples.OpenRecordSet("Select * from Products",
➥dbOpenDynaset)
```

If you do a SQL statement and put the dbOpenTable as the type, a Can't find object error is generated. The major difference between a Dynaset type and a SnapShot type is that Dynaset can be modified and added to, but SnapShot cannot. If you need to get a list that will never be updated while you have it, you should use the SnapShot type. The major difference between Dynaset and Table types is that you can perform finds on a Dynaset but not on a table. You can perform a seek on a table, but not on a Dynaset. Therefore, if you look at the advantages and disadvantages, you will see that the Dynaset type gives you the most flexibility. To learn about more properties and methods for a record set, do a search on Recordset in Visual Basic Help.

Sorting and Filtering

You can use two properties to sort or filter a SnapShot or Dynaset type of a record set. For performance, however, I recommend that you don't even go near them. These are very slow methods and there are better ways to sort or filter data. If you wish to know how to use them, do a search on Sort or Filter in Visual Basic Help.

The best way to apply a sort is to use a SQL statement and append an order by clause. The order by clause has the following syntax:

```
ORDER BY fieldname [desc]
```

The desc is optional. If you don't use it, ascending order is assumed. The following is an example of how to use the order by clause:

```
'This example does a SQL statement to retrieve the data but now with an orderby
set rcdProducts = dbExamples.OpenRecordSet("Select
➥* from Products order by ProductName",dbOpenDynaset)
```

This sample retrieves all the records from the products sorted by the product name. To use the filter, you need to add a where clause to the SQL statement. The syntax of the where clause is where fieldname.

In the following example, you add a where criterion, which is an expression that the records must equal in order to be included in the record set. The following example shows you how to retrieve all product records that have a product name containing the word ROM. Also, it still orders the retrieved words by product name.

```
'This example does a SQL statement to retrieve the data but now with an orderby
'Also filter out Product Names that do not have ROM in them
set rcdProducts = dbExamples.OpenRecordSet("Select * from Products
➥where ProductName like '*ROM*' order by ProductName",dbOpenDynaset)
```

> When you are using data from a database to fill a listbox, it is faster to actually change the listbox to a combo box and get the users to type the first *n* characters of what they want to see. The last thing you want to do to a user is make him wait for the listbox to be filled at startup. Then he must search through the list of items he does not want to see. For an example of how to do this, refer to listbox.vbp on the CD that comes with this book.

Navigating the Record Set

The next step in using the data is being able to navigate between records. The less movement between records, the better. To change a record and repopulate the form takes time and usually annoys the user. To avoid this type of problem, it is best to get the data required to the smallest possible set to start with. To do this, you must use the where clause more and more in the SQL statement when opening your record sets. After you have your data to the smallest set, you have three ways of navigating through your data set: Move, Find, and Seek. But first, you need to know your record set limits, or you could be in trouble.

Locating the Limits of the Record Sets

Before you actually start to navigate through the data, the most important thing to know is the limit of the record set. To do this, you first can check to see whether you actually got data back. One way to do this is to check the Recordcount property. If it is not equal to zero, then data has been returned.

After you know that you have data, you can do a MoveLast, which moves you to the last record of the record set. By doing this, you also set the Recordcount property to be equal to the value of the last record. So at this point, you know that the first record is 1 and the last record is what every record count is equal to at this present time.

Another way to move through the data is to watch for the End of File (EOF) and the Beginning of File (BOF) properties. It is really up to you to decide how you move through the data and how you watch for the limits of the data, but this method ensures that you do not run past the limits of your record set.

Using the Move Method

All types of OpenRecordset can use the Move command. The available methods for Move are MoveFirst, MoveNext, MovePrevious, MoveLast, and Move. The syntax for each of these records follows:

```
Object.MoveFirst
Object.MoveNext
```

```
Object.MovePrevious
Object.MoveLast
Recordset.Move rows[,start]
```

The `Object` in this case must be a variable set to a record set. The `MoveFirst`, `MoveLast`, and `MovePrevious` methods are not supported if the record set is opened with `dbForwardOnly`. If you use `MoveNext` twice after you are on the last record, an error occurs; before the second call, the `EOF` property is set to `True`. Likewise, if `MovePrevious` is called twice after the last record, an error occurs; after the first call, the `BOF` property is set to `True`.

When you are navigating through records, it is important that you always know where you are in reference to the last record and to the first record. One way to do this is to use bookmarks. The `Rows` property for the `Move` method must be set to a `Long` value, specifying the number of rows to move. A positive number means forward and a negative means backward. If you add `Start` as a valid bookmark string, the rows move from the bookmark. If you try to move past the EOF of the data set, you are placed on the last record of the set. Likewise, when moving backward, if you go past the BOF, you are placed on the first record. Also, if you have a record set with no records and you try to use the `Move` method, an error occurs.

Using the `Find` Method

Another way to navigate through records is to use the `Find` methods. These methods are not available for table types of record sets. Four methods are available: `FindFirst`, `FindNext`, `FindLast`, and `FindPrevious`. The syntax for each of the methods follows:

```
recordset.FindFirst criteria
recordset.FindLast criteria
recordset.FindNext criteria
recordset.FindPrevious criteria
```

The elements that make up the `Find` method are `recordset`, which must be a variable set to a record set, and `criteria`, which is a string expression that is equivalent to a SQL `where` statement without the word `where`.

If you have narrowed down your data to the smallest possible size, you should never use the `Find` methods. Instead of using the `Find` method, you should have `criteria` as part of the SQL statement when you retrieve the data from the database. A sample of a `Find` follows:

```
rcdProducts.FindFirst "ProductName like '*ROM*'"
```

Notice that this is the same type of statement I used in the data example in the "Sorting and Filtering" section. I suggest that you use the `Find` methods sparingly because they will slow down your application if your data set is too large to begin with.

Using the Seek Method

The Seek method is available only for the table type of a record set. If the table on which you want to run the seek does not have an index, the method will not work. The first step in calling the Seek method is to set recordset.index. To do that, you need to call the following code:

```
Object.index = indexname
```

In this case, the Object is a record set variable and the indexname is a string expression equal to the index name for this table. The Seek method has the following syntax:

```
table.seek comparison, key1, key2, key3...
```

An example of using Seek follows:

```
rcdProducts.index = "ProductID"
rcdProducts.Seek ">", 2
```

The Seek method only moves you to the first occurrence of the record in the data set. After you find this record, it is up to you to get to other data from here, because if Seek is called again, it moves you back to the same record.

I strongly recommend that you use SQL statements that will bring you to this point before your data is retrieved from the database. Always try to keep to a minimum the amount of data being pulled from the database.

Working with Records

Now that you can get your data, the next step is to actually do something with it. You don't always want to bring back data just to view it. At times, you will need to make changes to the data, delete some data entirely from the database, or add some new data. This section gives you some ideas on how to do this.

> You cannot update data if you are working with a SnapShot object because a SnapShot is read-only.

Modifying Your Data

To modify data, you first need to create an OpenRecordset equal to the data you want to edit. Remember that the best way to edit the data is to use a Dynaset type. If you are not on the exact record you want to edit, first move to that record. Then you need to tell the record set that you are going to make a change. To do this, you call recordset.edit, where recordset is set to the variable recordset. Then you can go ahead and make the changes. The last step is to save the record set to keep the changes. To do this, you need to call recordset.Update, where, again, recordset is equal to a recordset variable. An example of editing the product name follows:

```
Set rcdProducts = dbExample.OpenRecordSet("Soloot * from Products
➥where ProductID = 4")
If rcdProducts.RecordCount <> 0 Then
    rcdProducts,MoveFirst
    rcdProducts.Edit
    rcdProducts("ProductName") = "New Product"
    rcdProducts.Update
End If
```

Notice how I set the record set to bring back only the records I wanted to edit. To do this I added the where statement to my SQL statement. After I made the change, I updated the record set.

Adding a Record

Adding a record is similar to modifying records, except that you need to first call recordset.AddNew. Then you need to set each mandatory field to a value. Next, you should update your record. An example of adding a product record follows:

```
Set rcdProducts = dbExample.OpenRecordset("Select * from Products
➥where ProductID = 4")
If rcdProducts.RecordCount <> 0 Then
    rcdProducts.AddNew
    rcdProducts("ProductName") = "New Product"
    rcdProducts("ProductDescription") = "New Product for example"
    rcdProducts.Update
End If
```

Sometimes, when you add records to a table, it is best to use an OpenTable type when you create a record set.

Deleting a Record

To remove a record from your table, you need to move to the record you want to delete and then call recordset.Delete. A sample of how to delete a record follows:

```
Set rcdProducts = dbExample.OpenRecordset("Select * from Products
➥where ProductID = 4")
If rcdProducts.RecordCount <> 0 Then
    rcdProducts.MoveFirst
    rcdProducts.Delete
End If
```

Unless you are using transactions, it is impossible to retrieve a deleted record.

Making Bulk Changes

To perform mass updates, you need to use QueryDefs unless you wish to move through each item as you update them. Performing a mass update takes a little bit of practice and learning how to work with SQL statements. The first step is to use the following code:

```
Set querydef = database.CreateQueryDef([name][, sqltext])
```

Refer to the "Using Queries" section for explanations of the syntax of this statement. An example of bulk updating follows:

```
Set qryProducts = dbEX.CreateQueryDef("", "Update Products
➥Set ProductName = 'Visual Basic Guru' where ProductID > 2")
qryProducts.Execute
```

Leaving the name blank makes the querydef a one-time thing, and the querydef is not appended to the querydefs collection.

Using Transactions

A way to guarantee that all changes occur is to implement transactions. To implement transactions, you need to use an object.begintrans, where the object in this case is the workspace variable. Then, if there are no problems and you want to commit the changes, you should use object.committrans. This tells Jet to commit the changes to the database. If something goes wrong, you will need to use an object.rollback statement. This tells Jet to get rid of the changes you just made. An example of how to use transactions follows:

```
Set wrkExample = Workspaces(0)
Set dbExample = wrkExample.OpenDatabase("C:\Temp.MDB")
Set rcdExample = dbExample.OpenRecordset("Select * from Products",
➥dbOpenDynaset)
wrkExample.BeginTrans
rcdExample.MoveFirst
On Error Resume Next
Do While Not(rcdExample.EOF)
    rcdExample.Edit
    rcdExample("ExampleTitle") = rcdExample("ExampleTitle") & " 50"
    rcdExample.Update
    If Err <> 0 Then
intError = 1
    End If
    rcdExample.MoveNext
Loop
If intError = 0 Then
    intReply = MsgBox("All Changes have been made, save changes",
    ➥ vbYesNO + VBQuestion)
If intReply = vbYes Then
        wrkExample.CommitTrans
Else
        wrkExample.Rollback
End If
```

```
Else
    MsgBox "Errors were encountered removing transactions!"
    wrkExample.Rollback
End If
```

When you are doing a lot of bulk changes, it is always wise to use transactions around them. If you do not, you will never be able to determine the state of the database.

Refreshing Record Sets

The last task you need to know about when you are working with data is how to make a change, such as adding new records and then updating the data without closing the record set and then opening it again. To do this, you need to call *recordset*.requery, were *recordset* is equal to a variable set or to a recordset variable. An example follows:

```
rcdExample.Requery
```

If you added any new data or any other user has added any new data since the rcdExample was created, this new data now is part of the rcdExample record set.

Implementing Security for Your Database

Now that you have seen how to build and use an Access database from Visual Basic, it is time to learn how to make sure that the data in the database is secure. This task will ensure that unwanted visitors cannot get access to the data. To secure an Access database, you need to have a Workgroup file (System.mdw). You are required to have this file and cannot build it from scratch, because Visual Basic does not have the capability to build this file. After you have this file, you can implement the security from Visual Basic or from Access. In this section, you will learn how to secure your database from Access. Then you will learn how to maintain your security using Visual Basic code.

Securing an Access Database

To secure an Access database using Microsoft Access, you need to follow four steps:

1. Create a new workgroup file.
2. Add a password to the Admin user.
3. Add the new Admin user.
4. Create a secure database.

The following sections explain these steps in more detail.

Creating a New Workgroup File

You should create a new workgroup file to make sure that there are no other users or groups other than the default users and groups. Also make sure that the security you are adding is hard to break. To create your own workgroup, you need to follow these steps:

1. Open the Workgroup Administrator; to do this you will need to run workgadm.exe. When you are in the Workgroup Administrator, click the Create button. The Workgroup Owner Information dialog box appears, as shown in Figure 21.1.

Figure 21.1.
The Workgroup Owner Information dialog box.

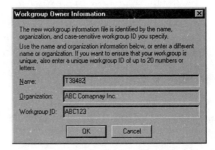

2. Type your name in the Name field. You can type in a maximum of 39 alphanumeric characters.

3. Type the company name in the Organization field. You can type a maximum of 39 alphanumeric characters.

4. The last piece of information you need to supply is the Workgroup ID. The maximum number of characters you can enter is 20 alphanumeric characters. The workgroup ID is case-sensitive.

5. Click OK. The Workgroup Information File Location dialog box appears.

6. Enter the name under which you want to save the workgroup. If you are not sure of the location, you can click Browse and use the Select Workgroup Information File Locator to determine where to place your new workgroup.

> You should save the information used here to create the new workgroup file in a safe place, just in case you need to create a new workgroup file.

7. Click OK. The Confirm Workgroup Information dialog box appears as in Figure 21.2, prompting you to confirm the information you just entered.

Figure 21.2.
The Confirm Workgroup Information dialog box.

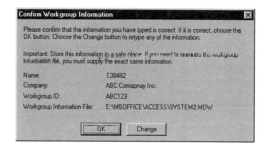

8. Click Change if you want to change any information.

9. Click OK to create the workgroup file. If the file already exists, you are prompted to confirm the overwrite of the existing workgroup file. When the file has been created, a confirmation dialog box appears, informing you that the workgroup was created.

Adding a Password to the Admin User

You need to add a password to the admin user so that you can sign on as the new admin user. To change your password, choose Tools | Security | User and Group Accounts. The dialog box shown in Figure 21.3 appears.

Figure 21.3.
The Change Logon Password tab of the User and Group Accounts dialog box.

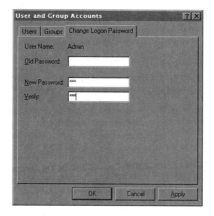

Select the Change Logon Password tab. Here, you are required to enter three pieces of information:

■ The old password

■ The new password

■ A verification of the new password

In this case, the old password is blank. If the old password does not match the current password, you will not be able to change the password. If the new password and the verification password do not match, you will not be able to change your password. After you enter the old, new, and verification passwords, you can click Apply or OK to accept your password changes. Clicking Apply leaves you in the User and Group Accounts dialog box, and clicking OK returns you to the Database window. Once you have accepted the password change, there is only one way to cancel the change and that is to change it.

Adding the New Admin User

You need to add the new admin user at this point because you are required to close Access and then open it using the new admin user. To add the new admin user, you need to reopen the User and Group Accounts dialog box by choosing Tools | Security | User and Group Accounts. This will open the Users tab of the User and Group Accounts dialog box.

To add the new admin, follow these steps:

1. Make sure that the active tab is Users. Then click the New button. A dialog box appears, prompting you to enter the user name and personal ID.

2. If you are on a network, I strongly suggest that you use the user's login name from the network. Otherwise, make sure that the user's login name is unique for each user of the workgroup. Also ensure that you use a unique personal ID.

3. After all the information has been added for the new user, Click OK. Or if you do not wish to add this user, then click Cancel. By either clicking OK or Cancel you are returned to the Users tab in the User and Group Accounts dialog box.

4. Select the Admins group in the Available Groups box.

5. Click the Add button, this will make the new user a member of the Admins group.

6. At this point you can click Cancel to cancel all of your actions up to this point. Or click Apply or OK. Both will accept the changes. Clicking Apply leaves you on the Users tab in the User and Group Accounts dialog box and clicking OK will return you to the database window.

For more information on how to add new groups or add users to existing groups, see "Adding and Deleting Users" and "Adding and Deleting Groups," later in this chapter.

Creating a Secure Database

To create a secure database, you first must sign into Access as the new admin user. Then create the new database by using the new admin to make the owner of the database the current user. To make sure that the database is secure from a user opening it into the Access environment, follow these steps:

1. Add a new group for all users to be members of. For more information on adding a group, see the following section called "Adding and Deleting Groups."

2. Give the user group no access to the database. Choose Tools | User and Group Permissions and then select Database from the Object Type listbox. Then click the Groups radio button and select the Users group from the listbox. Then make sure that no checkboxes are selected and click Apply.

3. Close Access, this will make the new permissions take effect.

4. Now reopen Access and the database that you are trying to secure.

5. After the database has been opened, you need to remove the admins group from the Admin user, leaving Admin with only users as a group. To do this, click on Tools | Security | User and Group Accounts. First make sure that the active tab is User and then select the user Admin from the Name listbox. Now select the Admins Group from the Member of listbox and click the Remove button.

By removing the Admins group from the Admin user and removing all permissions to the Users group, you make sure that no user can open the database unless you have given him or her permission. To understand more on the fundamentals of users, groups, and assigning users to groups, read the following sections.

Adding and Deleting Users

To add or delete a user, you must be a member of the Admins group. To add a user, follow these steps:

1. Click on Tools | Security | User and Group Accounts. This will open the User and Group Accounts dialog box.

2. Click the New button. An Add User/Group dialog box opens, prompting you for a user name and a personal ID.

3. If you are on a network, I suggest that you use the user's login name from the network. Otherwise, make sure that user's login name is unique for each user of the workgroup. Also ensure that you use a unique personal ID.

4. To accept the new user, click OK; otherwise, click the Cancel button.

This returns you to the User and Group Accounts dialog box, and the active user will be the user that you just entered.

To delete a user, follow these steps:

1. Click on Tools | Security | User and Group Accounts. This will open the User and Group Accounts dialog box.

2. Select the user from the User Name listbox. Click the drop-down arrow and click on the user you want to delete.

3. Click the Delete button. A confirmation dialog box appears, asking whether you are sure that you want to delete the currently selected user.

4. If you are sure, click Yes; otherwise, click No.

You are returned to the User and Group Accounts dialog box. To return to the database window, click either the OK or Cancel button.

Adding and Deleting Groups

To add or delete a group, you first must Click on Tools | Security | User and Group Accounts. This will open the User and Group Accounts dialog box. To add or delete groups you will need to activate the Groups tab. To add a group, follow these steps:

1. Click the New button. The Add User/Group dialog box is opened prompting you to enter a new group name and a personal ID for the group.

2. Enter the name and personal ID.

3. Click OK to accept the new group or click Cancel to not accept the new group.

You are returned to the User and Group Accounts dialog box, and the active group will be the group that you just entered.

To delete a group, follow these steps:

1. Select the group from the Name listbox.

2. Click the Delete button. A confirmation dialog box appears, asking whether you are sure that you want to delete the currently selected group.

3. If you are sure, click Yes; otherwise, click No.

You then are returned to the User and Group Accounts dialog box.

> When you add a new user or group, the name must be unique to both users and groups. You cannot have a group and a user with the same name. If you attempt to assign the same name, a Microsoft Access Account Name Already Exists dialog box appears.

Adding or Removing a User From a Group

It is important to remember that not all users will belong to the same groups. After you add the groups, you must tell the users to which groups they belong. The first step is to click on Tools | Security | User and Group Accounts. This will open the User and Group Accounts dialog box.

To add a user to a group, follow these steps:

1. After opening the User and Group Accounts dialog box, select the Users tab.
2. Select the user from the Name listbox.
3. In the Group Membership area, click on a group in the Available Groups listbox, and then click the Add button to add the currently selected group to the user.
4. When you are finished adding and removing users from Groups, click OK or Cancel to return back to the database window.

To remove a user from a group, follow these steps:

1. In the User and Group Accounts dialog box, select the user from the Name listbox.
2. In the Group Membership area, click on a group in the Member Of box, and then click the Remove button to remove the currently selected user from the group.
3. When you are finished adding and removing users from Groups, click OK or Cancel to return to the database window.

All users must be at least a member of the users group.

Setting User and Group Permissions

After you add the users and their groups, it is time to define the permissions that these groups or users will have on the objects in the database. To do this, you must be signed in as a member of the Admins group. After you access your database, choose Tools | Security | User and Group Permissions to access the dialog box shown in Figure 21.4. This dialog box has two tabs available: Permissions and Change Owner.

Figure 21.4.
The User and Group Permissions dialog box.

The Permissions Tab

The Permissions tab is the active tab in Figure 21.4. It consists of three components:

- The first component is a list of users or groups, depending on which List radio button is selected.

- The second component is the Object Name drop-down listbox, which consists of all objects that match the object type selected in the Object Type drop-down listbox. Because you are designing a database for use from Visual Basic, this section covers only the permissions for tables, queries, and the database itself. The Object Name drop-down listbox is a multiselect listbox. This means that you can select more than one object in the list at a time; simply hold down the Shift key while you select contiguous objects with the mouse cursor. To select noncontiguous objects, just press the Ctrl key while you select each object with the mouse cursor.

- The last area is the Permissions settings for the currently selected user or group and the selected object.

To change the permissions on an object in the database, follow these steps:

1. Select the user or group in the User/Group Name listbox. If you want to change from a user list to a group list, click the List radio button named Groups.

2. Select the object from the Object Name drop-down listbox. To change the list to a different type of object, click the Object Type drop-down listbox and select the object for which you want to change permissions.

3. Based on the type of object you have selected and the user/group selected, the Permissions checkboxes will be filled in appropriately. To remove a permission or add a permission, click on the corresponding Permission checkbox.

4. After you change the permissions for the active object, you can click Apply to apply the permissions without confirming them, or you can select a new object and see a prompt asking you whether you want to apply your changes. If you have made a change and you try to close the dialog box or try to select a new object, a Change dialog box appears asking whether you want to save the permission changes.

You can select from different permissions available for each object type in the database. The available permissions are dependent on the active object type. Some things to remember when trying to turn on or off permissions on a table object follow:

- If you mark any of the Data options (Read, Update, Insert, or Delete), Read Design automatically is selected for you.

- If you select any data option other then Read, Read Data is selected automatically.

- If you unselect Read, all other data options and design options are turned off, except Read Design.

■ If you select Modify Design, then Read, Update, and Delete Data automatically are selected.

■ If you select Administrator, all Design and Data options automatically are selected.

Some things you should remember when trying to turn on or off permissions on a query object follow:

■ If you mark any of the Data options (Read, Update, Insert, or Delete), Read Design automatically is selected for you.

■ If you select any data option other than Read, Read Data automatically is selected.

■ If you unselect Read, all other Data options and Design options are turned off, except Read Design.

■ You can select Read Design with all the data options or none of the data options.

■ If you select Administrator, all Design and Data options automatically are selected.

The last database object you can set permissions on is the database itself. To do this, select the database for the Object Type listbox. Notice that in the list of object names, there is only one available: Current Database. Also, you have only three permissions options available to you:

■ Open/Run: Enables the user or member of the group to open and run the database.

■ Open Exclusive: Enables the user or member of the group to open the database exclusively. If you want to make sure that no user opens the database exclusively, this is the best way to do it.

■ Administrator: All other permissions are selected automatically.

If a group needs to be able to only open the database, open the forms, and run reports, the minimum permissions you need to give this group follow:

■ Tables: The group needs to have Read/Design permissions and Read Data or Forms permissions; it will not be able to open reports.

■ Queries: To have the queries operate, you need to grant the group Read/Design and Read Data permissions.

■ Forms: In order for the forms to be opened by the group, you need to select Open/ Run.

■ Reports: In order for the reports to be run/printed, you need to select Open/Run.

■ Macros: If any macros will be run or open by the forms/reports, you should select Open/Run.

■ Modules: You do not need to select anything in order for the modules to function correctly.

■ Database: The group must have Open/Run selected or the group's users will not be able to open the database.

The Change Owner Tab

If you are working with a database that already exists, you will need to change the ownership of the objects in the database. To open the User and Group Permissions dialog box click on Tools | Security | User and Group Permissions and set the active tab to Change Owner (see Figure 21.5).

Figure 21.5.

The Change Owner tab of the User and Group Permissions dialog box.

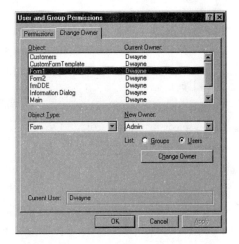

The Change Owner tab consists of three components:

- Object and Current Owner listbox: This derives its list from the Object Type combo box, and the default is Form.
- New Owner combo box: This is derived from the List item selected—Users or Groups.
- Change Owner button: Takes the currently selected object and changes the owner to the selected new owner. If you have permissions to change the owner, it is updated to the new owner; otherwise, an error dialog box appears, telling you that you are unable to change the owner of this object. There are three buttons to select here. Clicking the OK and Cancel buttons returns you back to the User and Group Permissions dialog box. Clicking the Help button opens Help and gives you some information on how to fix the problem. You can change all objects in the database this way, except the actual owner of the database.

To change the owner of a database, follow these steps:

1. Start Access, sign in using the New Owner, and then create a new database. By doing this you make the current user the administrator for this new database.
2. Choose File | Get External Data | Import. The Import dialog box appears.

3. Make sure that the type of file is set to Microsoft Access. Then navigate through the folders until you locate the database for which you want to change the owner. Select the database and then click Import.

4. The Import Objects dialog box will open, giving you the ability to import all objects from the other database. Make sure that you select all objects under each of the six tabs.

5. Click OK. The dialog box changes from the list of objects to a status report for the import.

When you finish importing all the objects, you will have successfully created a new database under the new owner. To complete the database owner change you will need to make a backup of the old database. After you have a backup, delete the old database and rename the new one the old name.

> When you assign ownership of objects, it is possible to assign the owner to groups. The database object must be assigned to a user, however.

Opening Secure Databases

After you secure the database, you need to tell Visual Basic where to find the workgroup file, whom to use as the user, and the user's password. Without supplying these three options, you will not be able to open the database.

The first step is to tell Visual Basic where the workgroup file is located. To do this, you need to set systemdb to equal the path plus workgroup filename:

```
DBEngine.SystemDB = "c:\Access\system.mdw".
```

> For 16-bit Visual Basic, set the IniPath variable to equal the private INI of the application. Then, in the INI file, you would use this code:
>
> ```
> set SystemDB= C:\ACCESS\SYSTEM.MDW
> ```
>
> The entry also must be located in the Options section of the INI file.

After you set the SystemDB, you need to set the user and password that will be used for this workgroup file. To do this, you set the default user and the default password. After you set the user name and password, you need to open the database. The syntax for opening the database follows:

```
Set database = workspace.OpenDatabase(dbname[,
➥exclusive[, read-only[, source]]])
```

The following code is an example of how to open a secured database:

```
'Load the system file that will be used by Jet
    strValue = GetSetting("Example7", "Engines\Jet", "SystemDB")
'Let DBEngine know where the system file is
    DBEngine.SystemDB = strValue
'Set the user name that Jet will use to sign into the database with
    DBEngine.DefaultUser = "New User"
'Set the user password that Jet will use to sign into the database with
    DBEngine.DefaultPassword = ""
'Open the database
    Set db = Workspaces(0).OpenDatabase("d:\data\examples\access7.mdb")
```

> After you have set the SystemDB and a database has been opened using this workgroup file, it is impossible to change the workgroup file without closing the application first.

Adding and Removing Users

After a database is secured, it is important to be able to add or remove users. To add or delete a user, you do not need to actually open the database; just use the systemdb, defaultuser, and defaultpassword set. Also, the default user must be part of the admins group or an error will occur. The reason for this is that the users are stored in the workgroup file rather than the actual database.

Adding a User

To add a new user to the database, you need to actually add the new user to the user collection. To do this, you need to call CreateUser. The syntax for this call follows:

```
Set variable = object.CreateUser([name [,pid [,password]])
```

Explanations of the CreateUser syntax follows:

variable	Set to the user type.
object	Set to group or workspace variable.
name	A string expression equal to the new name of the user.
pid	A string expression that is the personal identifier for this new user.
password	The password the user will use to sign into the database.

The following example shows you how to add user New Product User to a workgroup file that has been set to SystemDB:

```
Dim wrkExample As workspace
Dim usrProduct As user
Set wrkExample = DBEngine.Workspaces(0)
```

```
Set usrProduct = wrkExample.CreateUser("New Product User")
usrProduct.PID = "New Product User"
usrProduct.Password = ""
wrkExample.Users.Append usrProduct
```

To add the new user to a group, you need to call `CreateGroup`:

```
userobject.groups.append object.CreateGroup([name])
```

Explanations of this syntax follow:

userobject	Must be set to a user variable.
object	Must be set to the same user object as `userobject`.
name	A string expression equal to a group name that is already part of the database.

The following is a sample of how to add the New Product User to the Users group:

```
usrProduct.Groups.Append usrProduct.CreateGroup("Users")
```

> If the group does not already exist, an error occurs when you try to add the user to the group.

Removing a User

To remove a user, you need to remove the user from the users collection rather than the user object. Use the following code:

```
Object.delete objectname
```

In this case, *Object* must be set to users, and *objectname* is set to the name of the user you want to remove.

The following example removes the user New Product User:

```
Dim wrkExample As workspace
Sim usrProducts As users
Set usrProducts = wrkExample.Users
usrProducts.Delete "New Product User"
```

> If the user does not exist in the users collection, an error occurs.

Adding and Removing Groups

When you are working with secure databases, it is important and easier to add permissions to a group instead of users; it just makes it so much easier to add or remove permissions to one source instead of *n* number of sources. So the next step in using a secure database is adding and removing groups from the workgroup.

Adding Groups

To add a new group, you need to append the group to the group object. To add the new group, use the following code:

```
Set variable = object.CreateGroup([name[, pid]])
```

Explanations of this syntax follow:

variable	Must be set to the group variable.
object	Must be set to a workspace's variable.
name	The new group name.
pid	An option value that identifies this new group.

The following code shows you how to add a new group called New Product Users:

```
Dim grpProduct As Group
Sim wrkExample As workspace
Set grpProduct = wrkExample.CreateGroup("New Product Users",
➥"New Product User")
wrkExample.Groups.Append grpProduct
```

> If the group is already part of the groups collection, an error occurs.

Removing Groups

To remove a group, you need to remove the group from the groups collection. To remove a group, use the following code:

```
Object.delete objectname
```

In this case, *Object* must be set to a group's variable, and *objectname* is a string expression equal to the name of the group you want to remove.

The following example removes the group New Product Users:

```
Dim grpProduct As Groups
Dim wrkExample As Workspace
Set grpProducts = wrkExample.Groups
grpProducts.Delete "New Product Users"
```

If the group is not part of the groups collection, an error occurs.

Setting Passwords

After you add a user to the database, it is important to allow him or her to set his or her own passwords. To do this, call the following code:

```
object.NewPassword oldpassword, newpassword
```

Explanations of this syntax follow:

object	Set to a user variable.
oldpassword	A string expression equal to the old password.
newpassword	Equal to the new password the user wants to use now. Only the user or a member of the admins group can actually change a password. The password property is write-only, meaning that you are unable to view the current value of the password.

The following code sets the old password to equal a space for the user New Product User:

```
Dim wrkExample As Workspace
Dim usrProduct As User
Set usrProduct = wrkExample.Users![New Product User]
usrProduct.NewPassword "", " "
```

If the old password is not equal to the actual current password, or the user does not exist, an error occurs. Remember that all passwords are case-sensitive.

Setting Permissions

After you set up the users and their groups, it is time to set the permissions to the object for each user or group. Remember that it is better to set the permissions at a group level instead of the user level because after you set the permissions on a group, all users that are part of that group inherit the permissions from the group.

To set the permissions on an object, you need to use the following code:

```
object.Permissions [= value]
```

object is set to a valid container or document. Table 21.7 shows data permissions that can be set on the table object.

Table 21.7. Valid permissions on tables.

Constant	Description	Access Equivalent
dbSecRetrieveData	Can retrieve data from the document	Read Data
dbSecInsertData	Can add records	Insert Data
dbSecReplaceData	Can modify records	Modify Data
dbSecDeleteData	Can delete records	Delete Data

To see other possible permissions, do a search in Visual Basic Help on the Permissions property.

Encrypting and Decrypting Databases

After you secure the database, there is one more step you can take to make sure that no user is able to view the data. You can encrypt the database, making sure that it cannot be read by a utility program or by a word processor application. To encrypt a database, you can add the encrypt option to the CreateDatabase command or use Access. To decrypt the database, you can use Access or Compact. For more information on this, see "Compacting a Database," earlier in this chapter. For more information on the CreateDatabase command, see the section "Creating Databases," earlier in this chapter.

To encrypt the database using Access, follow these steps:

1. Open Access when no database is open.
2. Open the Encrypt tool after choosing Tools | Security | Encrypt/Decrypt Database. The Encrypt/Decrypt Database dialog box opens.
3. Navigate through folders on your local machine or on your network share until you locate the database you want to encrypt/decrypt.
4. Select the database and click OK. The Encrypt Database dialog box appears, prompting you for the new database name and location in which to save it.
5. Enter the location and name, and then click Save.

> To encrypt or decrypt the database, you must be able to open the database in Exclusive mode, which means that no users can be using the database. Also, you must have at least Modify Design permissions on the table objects.

To decrypt a database, follow the same steps, except that you are prompted for the decrypt database name instead of the encrypt database name. To decrypt the database using Visual Basic, refer to the section "Compacting a Database," earlier in this chapter.

Summary

The goal of this chapter is to give you some ideas on how to use an Access database as the place to hold the data for your application. You learned how to create a database, open the database, move within the database, manipulate the data in the database, and secure the database.

The Three-Tier Client/Server Model

by A. Nicklas Malik

CHAPTER

22

There is much talk these days about the three-tier client/server model and the concepts of client/server programming. This is a fairly new technology, but its concepts are not difficult to learn. Every new solution comes with trade-offs. This chapter describes the three-tier model and discusses many of the decisions and considerations that come with it.

This is a new technology. Although its roots are in distributed mainframe computing, the definitions have been shifting every year. The alphabet soup is full of terms such as OLTP, RDBMS, ODBC, DAO, RDO, OLE, and RA. I might use a definition that conflicts with that of another author or expert—no problem. As this technology takes hold, a *de facto* standard definition will emerge. The definitions presented here are a reflection of the emerging standard.

Why are there a dozen different definitions of client/server? Part of the reason is that moving to a three-tier environment is not an obvious transition to make. Once you get used to it, a three-tier environment makes sense. On the surface, though, it is crazy. When was the last time you heard a good programmer promise to speed up your application by *adding* a code layer? Before you answer, consider this: How quickly could you drive through a busy city if there were no traffic lights? Don't red lights just slow you down?

The Market Is Exploding, and VB Is in the Middle

Three-tier client/server systems are largely an enterprise solution, but they are no longer the exclusive domain of large companies. When you use a UNIX server and a database system that costs over $50,000, you can see why a local hardware chain with only five stores cannot afford it. Today, with Microsoft aggressively leading the way, however, you can set up a solid two-tier client/server system for under $10,000 for software and licenses.

Suddenly, the world of client/server is open to the small and medium-sized businesses that conduct the overwhelming majority of the commerce in North America, Japan, and Europe. This market is exploding, and Visual Basic is strategically placed to take advantage of this new wave.

However, VB programmers are traditionally not mainframe experts. Mostly, they work in the same small and medium-sized businesses that can benefit the most from this wave. This chapter explains many things that are probably well-known in the big-iron environment but that might be new to the designers and developers leading the charge for the rest of the world.

An Analogy for the Three-Tier Client/Server System

The core concepts of three-tier systems are easy to comprehend. In fact, our society is organized around the same concepts. The best way to remember them is with an analogy. It goes like this:

The customer, a program, walks into a bar. He sits down at one of the tables and waits for a waitress to come over.

The waitress says, "What will you have?"

The customer responds, "Give me a drink, and make it strong."

The waitress walks over to the bartender and says, "My customer wants a Long Island iced tea."

The bartender mixes the drink and hands the glass to the waitress, who delivers it to the customer's table. The customer finishes the drink and hollers for the waitress to return. "I want 55 more!"

Without hesitation, the waitress says, "Are you nuts? They will arrest me for program slaughter. One drink at a time; that's the rule."

The customer concedes and reduces his request. "OK. Give me one more."

The waitress returns to the bar and asks the bartender for another Long Island iced tea. This time, the bartender refuses. "We are out of Triple Sec," he replies.

The waitress returns empty-handed and explains that the drink cannot be served. The customer leaves the bar.

Some points to note are:

- Who is a server? The waitress is a server, because she serves the customer. The bartender also is a server, because he serves the waitress.

- Who is a client? The customer is a client, because he asks for a drink. The waitress also is a client of the bartender. Thus, the waitress is both a server and a client, which is perfectly normal.

- How do you know who is a client and who is a server? The client initiates the request, whereas the server fills the request.

- How many people are involved? There is a customer, a waitress, and a bartender—three people, three tiers. Note that I do not mention other customers. To qualify as a tier, a person must be part of the sequence of events from the request ("I want a drink") to its fulfillment (the waitress returns with a glass).

- The customer does not explain how to make the drink or even what is in it. The waitress creates the specific request for the bartender to follow.

- The waitress does not have to ask the bartender if she should serve 55 drinks to one customer. She already knows the rules, and she prevents the request from going any further. Likewise, if the waitress asks the bartender for 10 drinks, he can safely assume that she has 10 customers.

- Nothing prevents the waitress from physically carrying 55 drinks to the customer's table. Nothing prevents the bartender from physically making 55 drinks. The limit is imposed by the business itself. This is an example of a business rule.

Note as well that

- The server is not a slave. The waitress can say, "No, you cannot have 55 drinks." Likewise, the bartender can say, "No, we are out of an ingredient." In this respect, the server is a peer of the client.

- When the client orders the drink, the waitress does not bring the entire bar, nor does she bring each of the five bottles of liquor required to make the particular drink. She brings a glass with one drink in it. Her tray might have other glasses on it, but that does not affect this request.

- If the bartender were serving another customer when the waitress approached, that would not be a problem. This particular transaction is isolated in the sense that the possible presence of other transactions does not impact the system's capability to perform this one.

Consider these issues:

- If the customer sat at the bar instead of at a table, only two people would be involved—a client and a server. In this case, the bartender must know that he should not serve 55 drinks to one customer. This is a two-tier client/server system.

- Suppose that 75 people were in the establishment, and they all had to crowd at the bar to get drinks. Is there a limit to the number of people who can effectively be served directly from the bar?

- If the customer jumped over the bar and mixed his own drink, it would be a one-tier system. What prevents the customer from making a bad-tasting drink? Spilling all the rum by accident? Paying the wrong amount into the register? Serving himself 55 drinks?

I refer to this analogy throughout the rest of this chapter. It is powerful because it is fairly close to how we actually work in the real world—except that we normally tell the waitress specifically what drink we want.

Comparing One-Tier, Two-Tier, and Three-Tier Systems

The following sections discuss the one-tier, two-tier, and three-tier models. Pay careful attention to what each program is responsible for doing. You should be familiar with most of the terms here, but don't be too concerned if some of them are a little unusual. If they are important to three-tier systems, they are covered later in this chapter.

One Tier: One Program Does All the Work

A one-tier system uses one program to do all the work. Figure 22.1 shows a single application program running on a mainframe system. It is responsible for every facet of the system: user interface, input validation, business rule enforcement, query processing, and data file input and output.

Figure 22.1.
A one-tier mainframe system.

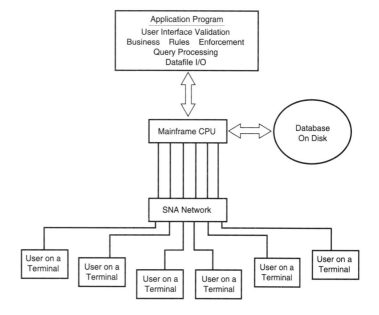

Another example of a one-tier system is a file server-based PC system, as in Figure 22.2. This type of system is common in small companies that have fewer than 10 workstations on a local area network sharing an Access or FoxPro database. Although the topography is different, the functions being performed by the application program itself are exactly the same as in the mainframe example.

The terms *one-tier* and *client/server* are mutually exclusive. By definition, a client/server system must have at least two tiers—one to represent the client and the other to represent the server.

In Figure 22.2, in addition to "Database On Disk," which hangs off the file server, there is "Database In RAM" on the client system. This is because one-tier systems rely on the capability of the operating system to get to the data. The application truly believes that the files are on the local machine. This means that the application must take total control of the database file itself.

All inserts, updates, deletes, index changes, and garbage collection must be done by the application program. To accomplish this, a large portion of the file itself must be moved back and forth across the network. "Database In RAM" represents this fact.

Figure 22.2.

A one-tier PC system.

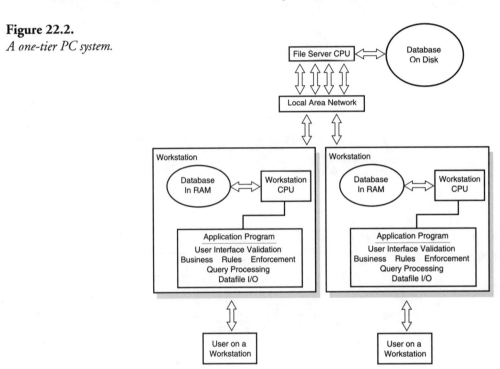

In terms of the bar analogy, either the customer is behind the bar making the drinks, or the waitress—the network—must carry the entire shelf of drinks to the customer. Either method works if there are no other customers, but both methods break down quickly when there are 25 other thirsty people in the establishment.

Two Tiers: Working Smarter, not Harder

A two-tier system, shown in Figure 22.3, is the first real step toward multiprocessing. This is the most common form of a client/server system today. In theory, there is no requirement that the system on the server be a relational database. Most of the concepts of partitioning and business rules enforcement that are discussed in this chapter still apply. In practice, however, the vast majority of applications that use this architecture provide access to a relational database management system on the server.

Figure 22.3.

A two-tier client/server system.

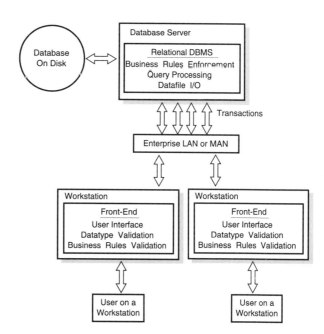

In this type of system, the tasks of the application program have been divided into two parts. The client—the front-end application—collects the user's input, validates the data types (such as dates and telephone numbers), and does simple business rule validation (such as making sure that an order cannot be placed for a product that the company does not carry). The server side is responsible for actually enforcing the business rules. This means that it must act as a gatekeeper, turning down any request that causes invalid data to be saved in the database.

This model is considerably easier on the network than a one-tier system. The client does not need the server to pass large portions of a database file over the network. In this example, the client application provides a string of ASCII text that describes either a subset of data that it wants to see (a query) or a change that must be made to the data (a transaction). In almost every real-life example, these requests are written in Structured Query Language (SQL). The text strings are interpreted on the server side by a relational database system such as Oracle, Sybase, Informix, or Microsoft SQL Server.

The business rules appear in two places in Figure 22.3. Simple validation occurs on the client side, and enforcement occurs on the server side. The drawback is that any change in the business rules of the enterprise causes a change in both the client and server sides of the equation.

There are many reasons why the business rules are broken up like this. First, the server can be some distance away on the local area network. Forcing the server to validate all the data integrity would slow down the application. Second, the application's user interface can be designed to take advantage of the business rules. For example, the user could be presented with a drop-down list of choices rather than be required to type in text for a field that must contain one of a predefined set of values. Third, for the client to create statements in SQL, it must be aware of the details of the database implementation. Because the database schema is derived from the needs of the business, it is inherently representative of the rules of the business. It is, therefore, subject to change as the business rules change.

Business rules do change—that is their nature. To prevent the changes in business rules from causing massive rewrites of a two-tier system, it is best to limit the amount of business-specific work that is done at the front end. This enables the majority of changes to be trapped in the back-end code.

> A common term for a client application that is overly laden with business rules is a *fat client*. On the other hand, a server that is doing so much work on each transaction that it bogs down is called a *fat server*. In a two-tier system, your goal lies somewhere in the middle.

There is an even better method of isolating business rules to prevent pain and suffering: Use a three-tier system.

Three Tiers: The Doorway to Distributed Processing

A three-tier system, sometimes called an *n-tier system,* is a paradigm shift from earlier models. As Figure 22.4 shows, the front-end client is much smaller. It contains only enough code to collect the data cleanly and efficiently. Business rules are moved as much as possible to a middle layer, called the *services* (or *middleware*) *layer.* This layer is responsible for creating the transactions that are sent to the database servers.

Three-tier systems are sometimes called *n-tier systems,* because the middle layer can actually be quite complicated, with many interacting components. If we were to count each component as a tier, we could end up with quite a large number. (I have seen a system that could legitimately be called a six-tier system.) For this reason, some authors refer to it as *n-tier*, while others use a completely new term, *the services model* (where the middleware components are described as services). I may switch back and forth between the terms *three-tier* and *n-tier* in discussions of complicated systems (where they mean the same thing). I describe the services model soon.

Two-tier systems rely on SQL for most communication between layers. Unfortunately, SQL is an interpreted language, which means that every statement must be checked for syntax and validity before it can be executed. Although this is great for sending requests from one platform to another—such as from a PC to a UNIX system—it is not efficient for fast program-to-program communication.

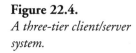

Figure 22.4.
A three-tier client/server system.

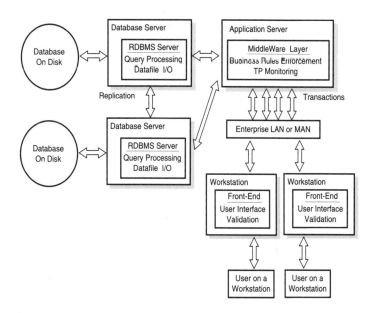

Three-tier systems of the recent past still sent text strings to handle communication. This means that middleware layers were either slow (because they had to interpret the strings) or dumb (because they treated the strings as an enclosed quantity going from one place to another—much as the post office treats a letter).

With the emergence of Microsoft as the platform of choice for the PC world and the upcoming release of Network OLE, there is a well-defined interface for applications to communicate that does not have to be translated into text on the sending side and interpreted on the receiving side. This opens the door for cleaner, more effective communication. Currently, Remote OLE Automation is not very fast, but you can expect the speed to improve dramatically in the near future.

A further advantage is that in a three-tier model, you can move away from using SQL for encoding the business rules. In two-tier systems, the business rules are located on the server, and the servers speak only in SQL. Because SQL is based on set theory, it is ideal for framing data queries against large sets of data. SQL, however, is lousy at describing business rules. The rules of the business tend to be easier to describe in a procedural language such as VB or C++.

The Services Model: Everything Has a Job to Do

Going from two to three tiers does not sound like a large move, so why is it a paradigm shift? Isn't just another box added in the middle? Actually, in a three-tier environment, the concept of a tier being represented by a single program running on a single box loses all meaning. Suddenly, distributed computing becomes a reality.

In two-tier systems, the client and the server are nearly always developed together; each one is designed specifically to communicate only with the other. In many two-tier systems, in fact, any access of the back end by anything other than its designated counterpart is considered a breach of security.

In three-tier systems, the middle layer is a set of programs that provide services to the front end. If these services are written generically in a way that can be encapsulated down to a single business function, there is no reason why you cannot create an entire array of middle-layer service programs. These programs can provide all the necessary services for a host of front-end programs, as shown in Figure 22.5.

Figure 22.5.

The services model.

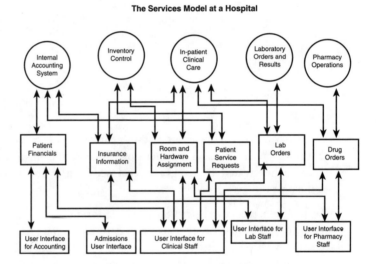

Note that Figure 22.5 is a simplified diagram of the services model. In addition to leaving out about two-thirds of the detail of a real organization, it does not make clear that the middleware components can call one another. In fact, the components themselves can be layered to create increasingly abstract, and increasingly functional, super components that act as agents between the front-end client applications and the data servers.

Why would anyone do something this complicated? The answer is because they already do. Most organizations have more than one database system in place. Code sometimes has been written to automate the replication of information from one database to another or to combine data from different databases for the creation of a report. In the real world, these connections are often achieved by using business processes instead of direct computing solutions. In many organizations, critical information can be gathered only by using two or three different applications or by perusing various reports. In these cases, users are required to make the connections manually. In many organizations, the information needed to make strategic business decisions might not be available at all.

The promise of three-tier systems is the promise of true distributed processing. This is not distributed processing for its own sake; it is distributed processing for the sake of making enterprise data readily available to the enterprise that created it and that can best use it.

In this fantasy world, a sales order begins its journey at the user interface. From there, it propagates through the business rule objects and lands in one or more server-based databases. When it does, you can be fully confident that the data is valid, has met all the business requirements, and maintains enterprise-wide referential integrity and domain integrity constraints. More importantly, the front-end application does not know the majority of the business rules. They are encapsulated in well-designed components within the middleware cloud. Other front-end applications can immediately access the changes that were instigated in the database by the processing of this sales order. Clever users can create combinations of information not foreseen by the database designers by using powerful tools to do serious business analysis.

As business rules change, an individual component can be replaced to reflect the change without affecting any other components. Ideally, you would not need to recode or recompile any of the other components. In fact, you do not need to distribute anything at all to the client workstations. You swap only one component—on the server—and the change takes effect.

This scenario is a fantasy, of course. Many factors can come into play that prevent this from occurring in most organizations, given the present technologies. You can get closer to this goal than ever before, though. As time goes on, these factors will come under control.

Common Design Goals of a Three-Tier Client/Server

Client/server systems can effectively address many difficult technical issues. Three-tier systems are not a perfect solution, though. By adding components that can be changed at runtime, you add considerable complexity to the configuration. As the number of objects increases, you must worry about compatibility, security, and network issues at a whole new level. This increases the need for good management of the system long after the programming is done—a significant and often overlooked expense.

Three-tier systems are not cheaper than two-tier systems. They can reduce the costs of creating the front-end programs because they are less complicated and reuse existing components, but the increased costs incurred during the support phase can consume those early savings. The middle layer is difficult to design, requiring a significant up-front investment in expertise and analysis. Likewise, three-tier systems can drive changes in the network hardware and topology, for greater reliance is placed on moving data from one system to another, quickly and reliably. Therefore, if you do not need—or cannot afford—the power, flexibility, or potential for future savings that a three-tier system can provide, don't spend the money to buy one.

All too often, an organization decides to use the technology of a two-tier or three-tier client/server system, but the final product does not live up to the expectations of the users or even the designers. Remember, a client/server system is just a tool, and no tool is useful unless you know how and when to use it. Keeping your eyes on the overall design goals of three-tier client/server systems can help you make strategic decisions when you are in the trenches, writing code.

User Scalability

There are two ways to look at scalability: adding more users to an existing database versus moving all or part of a database to where more users can see it. They mean the same thing: More people can access the data. The solutions are different, however.

> For the sake of this discussion, I call the desire to add an infinite number of users to a data system *user scalability*. I call the desire to move all or some of the data into a wider domain *data scalability*.

Adding users to an existing data source is an issue because the technology of most database designs limits the number of users who can use it. Notice that I do not say, "the number who can use it concurrently." I include the access method in my statement, and the number of people who actually use a database at any one time is directly tied to how it is implemented.

For example, if you create a front-end application that connects to a server directly, gets one record, updates one value, and disconnects, in 30 seconds or less, you can support a huge number of users because the access method was written efficiently. Therefore, to calculate the actual limit on the number of users, you must consider both the physical limits on concurrent connections and the amount of time during which the connection is held open by the middleware or front-end application.

Let's say you can calculate the "magic" number of users that your system can support at one time. What happens when that number is exceeded? Part of the answer is structural, and part is technical. Either way, you want to plan for that day from both a structural and a technical standpoint.

The structural standpoint refers to the possibility of limiting the number of users of a system not because of any technical or security issues, but solely on the basis of the limits of the system itself. You can do this by limiting the number of users with the software physically installed or by limiting the number of logins to a database. From a technical standpoint, you must create systems that have as few limits as possible, understand the process needed to overcome the limits, and prepare your clients and customers for the costs involved with this process. The use of *n*-tier systems addresses only a small part of this puzzle. Specifically, you have relieved many of the limits on the number of users by understanding the bottlenecks in your system and by relieving the stresses on those bottlenecks.

To see how an *n*-tier system addresses user scalability, consider the customer in a bar analogy. Suppose that the customer—the program—walks into a liquor store and buys the necessary components to make a Long Island iced tea—it requires five different kinds of liquor. While there, 50 other people come rushing in, all looking for the same components. Imagine how crowded it would be. How long would it take to pay and get out? Most stores would run out of stock. The system has reached a limit in user scalability.

The customer gets frustrated and walks down the street to a small pub. He goes up to the bar to order a drink. Suddenly, 50 other customers come rushing in. Although the bartender is overwhelmed for a few minutes, the customer still gets his drink. The system has achieved a fair level of scalability.

What if 100 more customers come in? Now there is no way to get close to the bar, and the bartender can barely hear an order over the constant roar of voices. The system has broken down under the weight of additional users.

Now suppose that customer goes down the street to a large restaurant. He sits at a table and asks the waitress for his drink. There is no crowding at the bar, even though the restaurant has 200 customers, because the waitresses are busy taking orders and carrying the drinks to the tables.

The first example, in which the customer buys from a liquor store, is a one-tier system. Although the customer enjoys more flexibility—he can make his drink very strong—the system does not support many users simultaneously. The second example is a two-tier system. It supports a greater number of users, but it still has a fairly small maximum number—unless you can get the customers to leave the bar and watch a sporting event on television. The third example is the three-tier example from the beginning of this chapter. Here, a large number of customers can be handled easily with the least amount of difficulty and confusion. This is what is meant by user scalability. It is one of the strengths of a three-tier system—and one of the goals that you need to keep in mind when you design one.

Data Scalability

Data scalability is the discovery that a stream of data that has been the sole domain of a small part of the organization is valuable to a considerably larger audience than previously expected.

Suppose, for example, that your organization has been installing or creating client/server systems to automate sales, marketing, human resources, inventory, and so on. The supplier database, however, has been running on an IBM AS400, sitting quietly in the corner of the data center, untouched by anyone except the group in charge of supplier relationships. One day, a new manager in the accounting department breaks one of the unwritten rules; she asks to compare the data from the accounts payable system directly with information from the supplier database and make updates directly to the supplier system. The IS department howls loudly, as does the supplier relations group—they could lose their jobs. This seems like a perfectly logical request, yet there is no way to do it. No one has ever tried to do more than the simple data feed that runs every night, downloading a file to a PC and uploading it to another system for processing. It would require writing a program that knows the business rules of the supplier database.

This is a data scalability issue. So how does a three-tier system help?

Imagine that you have just been appointed to head the team to replace the archaic front end on the supplier system. You choose to go with a three-tier architecture. In this case, you have no choice—just try to get data from an AS400 in two tiers. The middleware is a gateway to the AS400 and a few OLE objects that you write in Visual Basic that run on the gateway machine. The middleware talks to the gateway with ODBC. The front end talks to the middleware with Network OLE.

Gateway software is available from a number of different vendors, depending on the platform and the network. You don't write it; you buy it. The result is that your AS400 DB2 database can be accessed like any other ODBC data source on your local area network.

So far so good. Now you are in the middle of the design process. Remember the manager from the accounting department; she needed to make updates to the database in complete accordance with the business rules by using some other tool. You should write your middleware objects so that they incorporate enough functionality to make the data available throughout the enterprise—even if your front end does not require it.

This means that your middleware must know the business rules for reading, updating, and interpreting the data. There must be no gaps. Don't leave things out for later—later never comes. This requires work, but it is work that you have to do only once. It is infrastructure. In doing so, you have planned for data scalability. You have exposed data objects, not just databases, to the enterprise. Now when someone asks for direct information from the supplier system, you can not only provide the data, but also support the updates without having to go back Into the process of defining the business rules again.

This is different from user scalability. You did not use three-tier because you wanted to add 500 more users. You used three-tier because you wanted to add one more user with different data requirements. Note that you do not have to provide an interface to every detail of the underlying system if doing so violates a wise security policy. What you are trying to do is to enable your organization to create another pathway to the data or a part of the data.

Distributed Processing

Isn't distributed processing part of the point of a three-tier environment? Not really. In many cases, the middleware layer might be running on the client machine or the server machine, not on an independent system. There is no requirement that the middleware should get its own Pentium chip to play on.

What goes into your middleware depends on your design. If you have created a middleware layer with serious processing capabilities, providing calculation or manipulation services that go beyond simple "get the record" operations, however, you might seriously want to consider taking advantage of the distributed nature of a network by giving your heavy objects a dedicated processor. Of course, these should be considerations during the design stage. Once you move an object to another box, it runs up a much higher expense in communicating over the network than if it sits on the same machine as its client or server. Passing a byte from an application to a DLL that it is calling is cheap. Passing a byte from one application to another application on the same box is fairly expensive. Passing that byte over the network to another machine is downright extravagant.

> Take special care that relegating a processor-intensive function to a distant server does not cost you more time than simply waiting for it to occur on your local box because of the amount of data that must be passed over the network to get the job done.

Distributed Data Sources

Some questions cannot be answered by searching a single data source. For them, you might need to create middleware objects that inspect or update information in multiple databases. You might also use a combination of other middleware objects that provide business object access to the databases.

In an ideal world, these things would be easy, because everyone would use data values that are consistent across an organization. In the real world, this is nearly never the case. IS departments are routinely called on to write specialized programs to translate data from one format or domain set to another.

Suppose, for example, that a hospital uses a standard patient number assigned by the admissions system when a patient is first entered. Everyone gets a patient number, whether he or she shows up at the clinic or comes in through the emergency room. So far, so good.

Now suppose that you want to ask, "What is the average dollar amount of the pharmacy orders per patient, compared with the total billed cost of the patient's stay, broken down by length of stay?" This sounds reasonable enough. You get room assignment dates from the admissions system, cost of stay information from the billing system, and pharmacy orders from the pharmacy system; you link on patient numbers. The problem is that the billing system can support multiple currencies, whereas the pharmacy system supports only your local currency. It is difficult to get a meaningful value, for example, if 10 percent of your patients pay their bills in Canadian dollars while the rest pay in U.S. dollars.

One way to address this problem with middleware is to start with a common, enterprise-wide effort to define the standard meanings and formats of every data item that the organization uses. For example, you might let the billing system allow multiple currencies while still defining the bill amount data items only in U.S. dollars. When you write your middleware objects, every value that is put out should meet these standards, and every value that comes in must be in one of the standard formats. That way, the different systems of your organization can continue to use whatever formats they need to use, while all the applications that sit on top of your middleware layers see only uniform meanings and data formats.

By having the middleware objects themselves handle the data conversions into and out of their local formats, you gain many benefits:

■ If the underlying system changes, you do not have to fix a dozen different translation or extraction programs, which move data into or out of the system. You change one middleware object, and everything else continues to function.

■ Cross-database joins become much easier to perform if the data can be interpreted uniformly.

■ By requiring that a common set of definitions be created for every data item, you build the infrastructure so that future systems can be coded to require as little translation as possible. You get the added bonus of discovering places where different departments of the organization used different definitions for the same data item and simply assumed that the other departments used the same definition.

Localization of Changes to Business Rules

Business rules change—or at least they should change. In many organizations, there is an implicit agreement not to change business strategy or structure in any way that significantly affects business rules because of the difficulty of changing the software that runs the business. This is a prime example of the tail wagging the dog. About the only way to begin to address this problem is to recognize that a flexible and responsive IS organization can keep up with changing business rules to meet the needs of global competition.

To achieve this goal, you must localize the code that changes. When a rule changes, you should not have to make that change in 1,000 different places in the system. In an ideal world, you make the change in one routine that is used by all of those 1,000 different objects. In the past, this still meant recompiling the applications to the new library and running unit and functional tests on each program that changed, before any change could occur across the system.

The goal of creating middleware objects is to be able not only to localize a change, but also to easily test an object when a change has been made. If the object meets its unit and functional testing, you should be able to roll it into the system without a massive retest effort on every component that uses the updated business rule.

Therefore, when you design middleware objects, do your best to design them as flexibly as possible to accommodate changes, yet still keep them small enough to be tested comprehensively. You must be able to convince yourself and your organization that a change will not destroy a functioning system before it rolls in, without incurring a huge bill for retesting thousands of component programs.

Design the component to be tested, and create the testing script or testing application that will perform your comprehensive test. Not only can you use this testing script during the development cycle, but it can stay around to help test the component when the rules that govern it are changed.

A Stricter Definition of Client/Server Computing

Now that you have learned about the concepts of a client/server system, it is time for a more rigorous definition of the term. This definition incorporates the design goals already covered.

A Client/Server Information System

A client/server information system is composed of two or more programs running independently that communicate with one another using a well-defined language or protocol. In any individual interaction, the one that initiates an information or calculation request is called the client, whereas the program that fulfills that request is called the server. In general, a client program is one that acts as a consumer of information, and a server program is one that acts as a provider or manager of information.

To meet the full definition of a client/server system, the information system must meet three requirements: multiuser access, isolation, and flexible communication.

Note that nothing is said about a network. There is nothing inherent in the client/server programming model to suggest that a network is a requirement for implementing a client/server system. As such, it is possible to create a client/server system on a single workstation. Nevertheless, the real power of client/server technology lies in the scalability inherent in networking operations.

Although many observations have been made about client/server systems—and about what separates good systems from bad ones—these rules of thumb do not define what a client/server system is. Therefore, you cannot disqualify a system from this definition on the grounds that it is poorly designed. For example, a system can still be called client/server, even though it requires 5MB of data to flow from the server to the client on startup. The definition requires that a system *has* inherent power and flexibility, not that it uses it.

Multiuser Access

The server component must be able to support multiple clients running concurrently without requiring multiple copies of the server to run. Likewise, the server component must always be aware of how many concurrent users are connected.

Database applications described as *one-tier*, *single-tier*, or *file server* systems do not meet this criterion.

Many server systems launch a new thread to handle servicing a new connection. This multithreaded approach is not a violation of the prohibition of multiple copies. On the other hand, statically linked code libraries that provide data access services violate this prohibition, because each instance of a client application loads its own copy of the server code into memory.

Isolation

The server must not allow an error in one client to prevent it from servicing other clients in a timely manner. This includes the capability of the server to recover from errors or exceptions that occur on the client side. Likewise, an exception in the server must be recoverable by the client.

To meet this criterion adequately, the server component must be isolated from errors in the client components. To prevent a bug in a communication pipeline from shutting down a server, the operating system must support preemptive multitasking; Windows NT, OS/2, and UNIX do. As a result, this criterion is not well met when multiuser server components run on Microsoft Windows 3.*x* systems.

This criterion rules out the use of the term *client/server* when the server code resides entirely in one or more dynamic link libraries, because a bug in a server DLL can wipe out a client without any warning or opportunity to recover.

Flexible Communication

The communication protocol must be able to handle, at a minimum, a simple command-and-response interaction structure. This enables a client to ask for a portion of the total available information. The server responds with the information requested, and no more. At present, the most common form of client/server application-level protocol is SQL.

Summary

This chapter provided an informal definition by example of a client/server system and a simple analogy to three-tier systems. We discussed each of the different models, focusing on the overall services provided in each tier.

Beyond the informal discussion, we covered design goals that can be achieved when you use a three-tier model. These goals include user scalability, data scalability, distributed processing, distributed datasources, and localizing changes to business rules. We rounded out the discussion by examining a rigorous definition of the term *client/server information system*.

The next step is to design and build a three-tier system. Once you create a useful system, you can learn about some of the issues of testing, deployment, management, and support.

Design of a Three-Tier Client/Server System

by A. Nicklas Malik

CHAPTER 23

Peeling the Onion: A Detailed View of Each Tier

This chapter deals with many of the details you'll need to know when you are trying to design a new client/server system. It discusses the five layers of a three-tier system:

- Front-end client
- Back-end server functionality
- Middleware functionality
- Conversation between the client and the middleware
- Conversation between the middleware and the server

You need to take into account each of these layers in order to completely get a handle on designing a three-tier system.

The Functions of the Front-End Client

The front-end client component uses the concepts you should already be familiar with because Visual Basic was, for the first few years of its existence, relegated exclusively to this portion of the enterprise solution.

Now, much of that has changed with the newer releases of Visual Basic. Considerably more emphasis has been placed on positioning Visual Basic as a middleware tool, in addition to honing the capabilities of the front end.

So what does the front end do? As little as possible.

If you create your front end to do a vast amount of data manipulation, cross-checking, and other kinds of work, you will quickly discover that the capabilities you built into one application are something that you need in another. If this is the case, you need to see how many of these capabilities can be accomplished in the middleware. Increasing the capabilities of the middleware will allow the following two things to happen:

- Creating another front end with similar functions will be significantly easier to do.
- If a change comes along for this functionality, you will have to make the change in only one place.

Therefore, after pulling out all the "real work" that a front end can accomplish, you are left with the following tasks:

- Providing a visual interface to the functions provided by the middleware objects.
- Validating that the data that is being entered into the middleware objects meets the following objectives: domain integrity (the value falls in a predefined range); datatype and format correctness (the value is expressed in an agreed manner); and referential integrity (foreign key columns can only be given data that corresponds with data in a linked table).

It is not possible to create a front-end application that is free of business rules. It simply cannot be done while maintaining any kind of usability on the interface. Both domain integrity and referential integrity are aspects of database design, and the database schema is a direct reflection of the business rules that were known when it was being designed.

Attempting to create a front end that is so generic that it contains no business rules will give you Microsoft Excel. Although our goal should be "use no business rules," the reality is something closer to "use as few rules as possible."

The Functions of the Back-End Server

Originally, the concept of a server-based relational database was fairly simple. Structured Query Language (SQL) would be used to pull information from a server. The real-world need for manageability was the reason for the addition of stored procedures, and the need for referential integrity spawned the concept of triggers and declarative constraints.

In modern RDBMS systems, however, there are extensions to handle everything from security to iterative control. Some extensions even provide capabilities to SQL that were once reserved for traditional procedural languages: case statements, loops, and one-record-at-a-time control (cursors). This is especially true of SQL Server 6.0.

While I am not minimizing the utility of these constructs, the need that is driving their addition to RDBMSs is simple: Database designers frequently want to pull as much functionality as possible into the database layer. This may come from experience with poor front-end designs or a lack of database security from the prying eyes of ODBC-enabled applications such as Excel and VB.

However, I'd like to propose a radical concept: Let databases do what databases are good at. This means that you should not incorporate the entire security strategy entirely within the back end. This means that you should consider allowing a tightly-coupled "agent" application to bypass the stored procedure layer and perform SQL operations directly against the tables if doing so can improve performance.

All too often, the database has been handed tasks that can be justified from a data architecture point of view but do not make sense for performing at the back end. This is usually because business rules have been hard-coded into the triggers and stored procedures in the database layer.

If you view the business rules as a component of the database, then it simply becomes an integrity issue when a change in one table should cause changes in other tables. However, *business rules are not data.* They should not be treated as part of the data integrity in a three-tier system.

Why? For the same reason for moving to three tiers in the first place. Inserting the business rules into the database architecture implies a change in the database when a business rule changes. This is a high price to pay for a fairly frequent event.

There is another good reason for pulling business rules out of the database layer: SQL is an extraordinarily poor language in which to implement declarative or procedural business rules. Unfortunately, the majority of business rules fall into this category.

This is why SQL languages such as SQL Server's Transact-SQL are getting procedural language constructs. They are still slow. Use a procedural language for procedures.

Comparing Various Approaches to System Architecture: An Example

Imagine a system to be used by a large collection agency. In this agency, each phone collector has a PC on his or her desk. When they complete a call, the system will go to a database and get information on the next account that needs to be handled.

If a customer has made a promise to pay, the agency will hold off calling them for a few days to give time for the check to arrive in the mail. Additionally, if a payment is received, then an account in the call list should be postponed until the next payment is due. Therefore, there are two business objects: a list of accounts, and a subset that represents the accounts that should be called (the call list). Add the following requirement: Due to some other business need, you *must* maintain a separate table for the call list, rather than just flagging accounts in the accounts table.

In the mainframe days, the "call list" would be generated the night before, and any changes to the account, although they would be available to the collector from the front-end application, would not be able to affect membership in the call list. In other words, it would be perfectly normal for a collector to get the name of a customer to call in the afternoon whose payment was received in the morning.

In the client-server world, it is expected that this information is available "on-the-fly." This means that a change to the status of an account will immediately affect the membership in the call lists.

This means that an update operation can be a complicated thing. Changing information in an account can directly affect the status of the account, which might mean that the account needs to be added from, removed from, or reprioritized in one of the "to be called" lists.

There are no fewer than five ways to do this. Each way has advantages and disadvantages. My preference is to use either of the last two methods, as explained in the following list:

- Method One: Create a stored procedure (SP) to update the account table. This SP would detect that an account change requires an update to the calling lists. A transaction would begin. The updates would be made to all tables. The transaction would be committed, and the procedure would end.

- Method Two: Add code to the update trigger for the account table. In this trigger, determine if the changes to the record warrant a change to the call list tables and force that change to happen.

Figure 23.1 illustrates these two methods. Note that I encased each table in stored procedures (for update, insert, and delete) and triggers. This is a common architecture for ensuring integrity and data security. As you can see, both of these methods require that the business rules are encoded in the database layer.

Figure 23.1.

Two approaches to a business rules update.

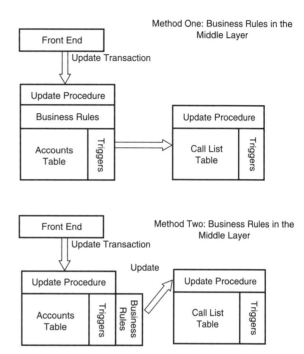

■ Method Three: Have the front-end application make multiple calls to the database to directly affect both the update to the account table and the update to the call list. The capability to determine if a change in an account would imply a change in the call list is encoded into the front-end application. This is similar to a two-tier system, so I won't go into further detail on this method.

■ Method Four: Have the front-end application invoke an update method in a middle-layer object. The middle-layer object would update the database tables. This object would invoke other objects to determine if a change in the call lists is required, and the other objects would call separate stored procedures to update the call lists. This method is illustrated in Figure 23.2.

■ Method Five: Have the front-end application invoke an update method in a middle-layer object. The middle-layer object would affect the update, as well as insert the key into a small "to be reviewed" table. A separately running "agent" application is polling this table on occasion to see if any account records come up that should be reviewed.

If so, the account record is evaluated to see if a call-list change should be made, and the agent application will make the change. (See Figure 23.3.)

Figure 23.2.
Three-tier transactional approach to business rules update.

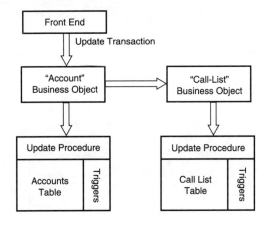

Method Four: Business Rules in the Middle Layer

Figure 23.3.
Three-tier agent-based approach to business rules update.

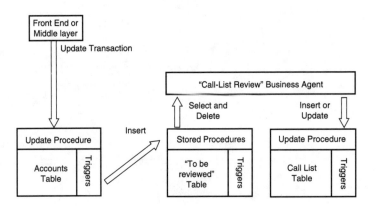

Method Five: Business Rules in a Business Agent

The only advantage of this architecture over the previous one might be performance. Because the agent is acting asynchronously, the update transaction occurs very quickly. Because you are using a separate table for "to be reviewed," you don't need to create an unbalanced index on a flag field in the accounts table. This speeds the update and prevents the need for repeated SELECT calls on the accounts table (which could cause a bottleneck on that table).

The data layer should be used to organize the data for the insert, update, and delete operations in a consistent, secure, transaction-based manner. The data layer should *not* be allowed to grow "fat" with excessive operations and business rules.

The Functions of the Middleware Layer

There are two primary uses of middleware objects in a three-tier system. The first use is the one I've been discussing: *business rules encapsulation*. Another use of this layer is *transaction management*. I describe both uses here, but they are discussed further later in the chapter.

Business Rules Encapsulation

The list of business rules under a system is the conceptual foundation on which a system runs. Whether explicitly stated or implied by the developer, these rules always exist. Managing change in this list is one of the largest issues in the long-term maintenance of any system.

Using the middle layer in a three-tier system as a place to encapsulate business rules is not a new idea. However, with the changing face of technology, particularly on the Windows platform with the evolution of Object Linking and Embedding (OLE) under Visual Basic, this idea is gaining momentum.

It is not possible to isolate the other layers from the data-oriented business rules (like the list of information items that the system tracks). However, the middleware layer provides a way of isolating the most volatile business rules from the rest of the system, but only if you have identified which rules are the most volatile.

Deciding which layer to put a process or function in is called *partitioning*.

Transaction Management

There is not a lot of discussion on using middleware for the purpose of transaction management, and for two fairly good reasons: This is the original reason for the existence of middleware, and a number of mature (and somewhat expensive) products are already on the market; and some of the justification for doing transaction management has been the high price of maintaining multiple connections to a database (either due to hardware requirements or because of the high price of software licenses). These prices are coming down at an intense rate.

Transaction management is the handling of queries and responses as "sealed packages" of data with definable characteristics. The following are the characteristics that are always present:

- One query can generate many result sets and, possibly, a return code.
- Each result set can be expressed as a two-dimensional array of variant values (as a table).
- The average query will take a fairly short period of time to execute, followed by longer periods of idleness on the connection.
- One of the largest expenses of client/server access is the time required to initially connect to the server.

With transaction management, you can create objects that connect to the database before an application needs them; you can also create objects that can stay connected for a short period of time after they are released so they can be quickly assigned to another application. Additionally, you can manage the number of open connections to the database at any one time. This means that you can determine, with certainty, how many licenses are being used and how fully they are used.

The Conversation Between Client and Middleware

A great deal of effort is often spent discussing the components of the layers themselves, without any reference to the conversation that goes on between the layers. However, if you have layers running on distant machines across a WAN and their conversation is exceptionally busy, your users will quickly grow tired of the poor performance that results.

There are a number of common methods used to communicate between the front-end application and the middleware layer. In Visual Basic, this is usually the OLE interface (local or remote out-of-process servers). However, you could also be communicating with Named Pipes or with the Open Data Services API. These are details for the networking types out there and are beyond the scope of this discussion. What is more important is not "how data is flowing" but rather "what data is flowing."

Exactly what is being said depends on how you are using the middleware layer. If you are creating a business object interface to your data, then the information passing out of the front end is transactional business information. For example, you might be passing the data for an updated invoice item.

When you are using the OLE interface, it is important that you know where the object is. Every call to an out-of-process object is seriously more time consuming than a call to a local object. Therefore, beware of using a remote object repeatedly to retrieve information. If all of the information can be retrieved in a single call, you should support that method.

Imagine a simple three-tier system. The front-end application simply displays results from a few canned queries. The middleware is responsible for invoking the queries and returning the results. The architecture of this example is illustrated in Figure 23.4.

Now it's time to dig a little deeper. What would happen if the middleware layer would return an rdoResultSet object to the front end? This result set represents the data returned from the query, and this is exactly the same format that the Remote Data Objects (RDO) will provide. Why not just pass the object straight through to the front end?

Because the front end would then have to use the RDO object's properties and methods to get the data out of the object and onto the screen. Every time the front end executes one of these methods and properties, a call is made to the RDO object (which is running in the middleware server, *not* in the client).

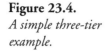

Figure 23.4.
A simple three-tier example.

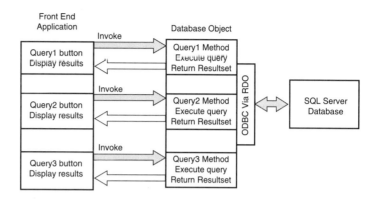

A simple loop that gets the value for each of 10 fields from a 25-record result set would cause 250 cross-process OLE calls to take place. This very small result set would result in a *huge* delay to retrieve it from the middleware layer.

On the other hand, the middleware layer can collect all the data from the RDO object. Then, the middleware can place the result set data in a two-dimensional variant array and pass the entire array back as a single variant. Then, when the front end begins the display routine, no further OLE calls have to be made to gather all of the information.

When you are using OLE to communicate across processes, you need to be aware of a few performance tips.

- If you pass an object that is native to your process to another process, any uses of that object by the other process will incur the cross-process OLE call penalty, even if the object you are passing is native to Visual Basic. In other words, if your server returns an object of type RecordSet (a DAO type), every use of the object will cause OLE to call the server, even if the application is using the DAO library locally, as well.

- You can move fairly large amounts of information across process lines in a single call. This is nowhere near as expensive as making multiple calls to get small subsets of the information. Remember that you can pass an entire array in a variant.

- Many VB programmers are tempted to set up their objects similar to the VB3 common dialog controls, where the user would set a number of properties and then call an .Action method of some kind. This is slow. It is faster for the user to make a single method call and to pass parameters to the method.

The Conversation Between Middleware and Server

The most common form of communication between any application and a database server is Structured Query Language (SQL). However, even this apparent uniformity can take many twists.

For example, consider the simple goal of executing a simple SELECT statement and returning the result set to the middleware. There are a few ways to accomplish this task:

■ Hard code the SQL statement in the native dialect. There is no reason why you couldn't perform a query simply by executing the SQL statement directly from the code. For example, the following RDO statement would execute the SQL statement:

```
Dim sSQL as String
Dim rdoConn as rdoConnection
dim rdoResult as rdoResultSet
sSQL = "SELECT au_id, au_lname FROM Authors where au_state = 'CA'"
Set rdoConn = rdoEnvironments(0).OpenConnection( _
"MyDataset", rdDriverPrompt)
Set rdoResult = rdoConn.OpenResultset(sSQL)
```

This is not an ideal solution. You are creating a fairly strong coupling between the internals of your database schema and the middleware code that will access it. For example, what if you change the Authors table by pulling out multiple addresses for each author into its own table? In that case, the preceding query would have to be rewritten.

You are also creating a dependency, in your code, on the dialect of SQL used by the server itself. If the preceding connection was being made to SQL Server, then it would work. However, some dialects of SQL require that you terminate your SELECT statement with a semicolon (;). The preceding code would not work with those databases.

■ Hard code the SQL statement in ODBC format. If you are using an ODBC driver, you can overcome one of the preceding drawbacks: the dependency on the server. Even though your code still has hard-coded database schema information, you can rely on the ODBC syntax for your SQL statements.

The full ODBC syntax is described in the *ODBC Programmer's Reference Guide*, which is shipped as part of the Open Database Connectivity SDK. (The current version of the SDK is 2.10.)

■ Hard code calls to stored procedures. This is a popular solution to the problem. Instead of placing actual native SQL statements into your code, you use Execute statements or the ODBC Call syntax to place calls to stored procedures. This allows you to isolate your code somewhat from changes in the database schema.

You are still tied to the database, and somewhat to the brand of server software (because not all servers, and not all ODBC drivers, support stored procedures). However, you've abstracted your code from changes in the database.

This third method has the advantage of providing security to the user. To do this by using SQL Server, you would revoke all SELECT, INSERT, UPDATE, and DELETE privileges for all users except the system administrator (sa) or database owner (dbo). Then you would create the stored procedures while logged in as dbo. When the procedure is running, it will take on the privileges of its creator, in this case, dbo.

What this means is that the user cannot access or modify the data in the database except by using your stored procedures. No worries about ad-hoc queries slowing down a production system. No worries about a user issuing an update statement that destroys data integrity.

The downside of this method is that ad-hoc tools such as Excel and Access will not be able to get any information from the server database. If you want these tools to be able to perform ad-hoc queries but not updates, then simply grant SELECT privileges and leave UPDATE, INSERT, and DELETE privileges revoked.

You should also be aware of some other tips in the SQL communication process:

- There is no reason to pull large amounts of data to your application, only to use one column or a few rows. Narrow down your SELECT statements as much as possible.

- If you have an application that is loading large amounts of data from the server into controls on the form, consider finding a way to avoid this altogether. You cannot call your application "user friendly" if you are forcing your users to scroll through a list box with more than 200 rows in it. One idea that works well is to have the user provide a couple of characters to "prime" the search. Then, the result set is smaller, so the query is faster, and the user isn't overwhelmed with too much data.

- Tailor your stored-procedure interface to suit the needs of the application. If your database design calls for stored procedures that perform canned SELECT statements for you, that is fine. However, if you find that you need to perform one procedure to get a chunk of data that you use to perform another procedure, consider writing a customized stored procedure that will accomplish all the work in one call. This will speed up your access dramatically.

- If you have to bring a large amount of fairly static data to your application on startup, consider setting up a local JET database to contain your static data. Then, when you start up, issue a Querydef that will update the database with only those records from the server that have changed. This "delta-update" method has the price of having to load JET at startup, but will begin to pay for itself if your static tables are large or are on a slow link (like a transatlantic WAN connection).

Basically, the key to optimizing this connection is this: Bring as little data as you can, as rarely as you can, and remember what you've recently brought over so you don't have to do it again anytime soon.

Focus on the Middle: Creating the Middleware

There are three tiers to choose from, so why did I start with the middle? Because the most important decision you can make when you are designing the overall architecture of your three-tier application is the answer to this question: What functions will be in the middle layer?

Partitioning is the process of determining what functions should sit in the front end, what functions should sit in the middle, and what functions will exist at the back end.

This is extraordinarily important in the final product, because the information that has to flow across process boundaries is expensive in terms of execution time and effort. Therefore, if you do not carefully select the functions that will operate in each tier, then you could end up forcing one tier to make hundreds of cross-process calls to get the results it needs from another tier, which can dramatically slow down the application.

Remember, what looks good on paper can be horribly slow in real life if you underestimate the number of calls that will have to be made across process boundaries.

The first step in creating your middleware is to take your overall architecture and break it down into class objects. Because VB will enable you to run a class as in an in-process server (DLL) at the front end, as well as an out-of-process server (EXE) in the middle layer, you have some flexibility in deciding where the object will end up.

Look for interactions that are similar in nature to the "simple command and response" model that SQL uses. These are the interactions that work well across process boundaries. Therefore, if you have an object that requires extensive massaging to set up and then returns information across many methods and properties, it is a bad idea to place that object in a different tier from the code that calls it.

Creating these objects is all about creating generic interfaces. This is the stuff of object-oriented programming (OOP). I will not go into detail about creating good encapsulated interfaces here, because there are other chapters in this book that deal with the correct ways to use objects.

My only concern is that the interface must be generic, testable, and flexible. *Generic* means that you should be able to replace the underlying class with one of a different design without breaking the calling interface. *Testable* means that the interface must produce predictable, reliable results that can be compared against known "good values" for the sake of a unit test. *Flexible* means that additional functionality can be added to the class without breaking the code used to call it today.

With these three conditions met, you can break open your design and make your objects available to be used by anonymous applications over which you have no direct control.

One design tip that you might want to use when building a partitioned system is the following: If you provide an in-process DLL that acts as an interface to the out-of-process middleware that the user can call, you can do all of your parameter checking in the client. This means that you can reduce the amount of parameter checking you have to do on the server because you control both the calling and the called code.

As I mentioned earlier, there are two good uses of middleware: encapsulation of business rules and transaction management. The following section discusses the encapsulation of business rules in greater detail.

Discovering Business Rules

This section describes some of the methods used today for discovering what business rules exist in a system or potential system. Understanding how to encapsulate these rules is the most important step to understanding, and using, three-tier architecture.

What Are Business Rules?

According to Barbara Von Halle, a regular columnist in the magazine *Database Programming and Design* and an expert on data architecture, a *business rule* is "a statement [that] constrains the business, [that is,] is intended to control or influence the behavior of the business." In other words, a business rule is a well-defined statement that defines a business term or describes how business concepts relate.

There are five types of business rules: definitions, facts, constraints, derivations, and actions.

■ A *definition* introduces a business concept into the rules repository and can be expressed by using the phrase "is defined as."

■ A *fact* is a business rule that relates business concepts. Facts connect the defined concepts in meaningful ways and can be expressed with verb phrases such as "can do" or "can be composed of."

■ A *constraint* is a rule that describes mandatory conditions that must be applied to the data before it can be saved. Therefore, a constraint has the effect of prohibiting actions that would lead a constraint to be "broken." Phrases such as "must do," "must have," and "must not have" are common in these type of rules.

■ A *derivation* is a rule that describes how one fact can be inferred from, or calculated from, another. An inference rule would usually be phrased as "if Fact A is true, then Fact B must also be true." A calculated rule would use the phrase "is calculated from."

■ An *action* is a rule that describes an occurrence that should take place when data reaches a defined state. Actions can be phrased as "When Fact A is true, then I must do Thing B."

The following table provides examples of each from a fictitious collection agency business:

Rule Type	Business Rule
Fact	An Account is defined as a record of a debt.
Constraint	An Account must be assigned by a single creditor with whom the agency does business.
Constraint	An Account must have at least one debtor associated with it but can have more.

continues

Rule Type	Business Rule
Fact	A creditor is defined as a client company or individual on whose behalf a debt is collected.
Fact	A commission is defined as a percentage of the total amount collected that is retained by the agency as payment for collection services.
Fact	Every account has a commission associated with it.
Fact	A commission is associated with an account at the time it is assigned by the creditor to the agency.
Derivation	The value of the commission is derived from the number of months past due when the account is assigned and the credit score of the debtor.
Action	If a creditor recalls an account, then it must be marked as inactive, and all collections on the account must cease.
Action	If all of the debtors on an account enter into bankruptcy proceedings, then all collection activity on the account must cease, and the account must be handled by the legal department.

The first stage of your analysis is the process of collecting these business rules. You need to make a solid effort to ensure that your list is complete before you begin to design the system.

One way to ensure completeness is to start with every business rule, and to determine the data that you need to store and manipulate in order to facilitate that rule. Then, consider every operation on that data: insert, update, and delete. Are there any hidden or unstated business rules related to these operations? Are there any other data needs that are revealed by this process?

Unfortunately, your users do not normally start with well-defined statements about how their business works. Users usually start with loose statements. Von Halle calls these statements "business ramblings." Refining these business ramblings can distill the business rules that you can then use.

After you have created a set of business rules, you can further formalize them into a "rule formalism." Von Halle offers the following definition of "rule formalism": a disciplined syntax for a formal, precise implementable expression of a business rule. There are some emerging tools that can use rule formalisms to assist in the analysis process. This can be quite important on large or complicated systems. I won't go into rule formalisms any further because they are beyond the scope of this discussion.

What Can Make Your Business Rules Change?

It is part of the nature of a business to adapt itself to changes in legal regulations, new technologies, and demanding customers. As a programmer, you need to have an appreciation for the things that can cause business rules to change. Armed with the following list, you can better justify the need for isolating business rules, to your clients and to yourself:

- Technology changes: Some things that were not possible before are now commonplace (for example, pagers in the e-mail system). Resource allocations that made sense in the past might no longer be efficient given new technology (for example, PCs as a dumb terminal or an office-automation island).

- Regulatory changes and deregulation: Government regulations are common in industries such as banking, utilities, transportation, medical care, and insurance. However, as difficult as changing regulations were to cope with, the current push toward deregulation has been worse, forcing organizations that were designed around accommodating government regulations to pay more attention to the market.

- Market and competitive constraints: When a competitor introduces a new innovation that is causing a shift in market share, your company might have no choice but to change, and that change might cause a shift in business rules.

  Automated teller machines is an often-quoted example, but I would also include economies of scale when a larger company moves into a neighborhood (for example, the ability to return a video to a different store than it was rented from benefits big companies at the expense of small video outlets).

- External economic changes: Changes in interest rates, monetary exchange rates, or fluctuations in the stock or bonds market can have a profound influence on some organizations. Because the rules that govern these forces changes periodically, business rules must change, as well.

  Examples: High interest rates that narrowed the profit margins for banks in the late 70s pushed them into adding "fees" as an income stream. Also, the growth of the mutual fund market forced changes in the retail side of the business for most brokerage houses.

- Business strategy changes: As a way of gaining market share, or to prop up a part of a business that is losing money, organizations routinely change their strategy for working within the marketplace. Flexibility in business rules can be the difference between a surgical strike and just barely keeping up.

- Business process reengineering: As organizations downsize, right-size, and reorganize, they are developing completely new sets of business rules. Often, these rules have existed outside of the existing information systems.

  An example would be a business process where a paper form is routed by four different departments. The cover page of the form has to be signed and dated by responsible parties in each of the departments. Reengineering may capture the existence of this rule, allowing the IS organization to provide ways to make the process smoother and more efficient.

The Process of Discovering Business Rules

Business rules don't come out of the woodwork easily. They have to be coaxed out into the light. Often, the most restrictive and difficult of dependencies doesn't surface until very late in design, which can cause quite a bit of consternation and late-night mumbling.

One well-worn method of gathering business rules is the "use case scenario." This method requires the analyst to define "actor" roles for all external forces in a system. This includes the people who add data, the people who extract information, and any other systems that feed data or require data feeds.

Then, the complete interaction of the user with the system is described from a functional standpoint. In effect, the analyst "walks in the shoes" of the actor, to work out the roles that each actor plays.

One result of the use-case is an implied order in which the resulting business ramblings are supposed to take place. As much as possible, remove any unnecessary sequencing from the rules. Unnecessary sequencing of the business rules can hamper the flexibility of a system.

After you have a set of rules, you can refine them in much the same way that a data architect would refine a database design in the process of normalization. To refine business ramblings, massage them until they meet the requirements that follow (from an article by Barbara Von Halle in *Database Programming and Design* magazine).

A high-quality business rule is

- Atomic. This rule defines or constrains the data environment in a single way.
- Business-oriented. This rule uses business terms, not computing or database constructs.
- Unique. This rule is not already in the repository.
- Consistent. Uses the same units and measures as other rules.
- Precise. Accurately specifies the complete limits of the data.
- Complete. If a constraint, represents the constraint's full intent, not a limited set of database update events.
- Declarative. This rule is worded as a declaration, without unnecessary sequencing implied in the definition.

Tools for Capturing Business Rules

Business rules can get complicated. Making sure that all of the rules that you have discovered are reflected in the tool is difficult. A number of new tools are hitting the market that make the collection of business rules easier and more consistent.

Products such as Vision Storyboard are tailored specifically for Visual Basic. Other environments might have an easier time using products such as Forte, Sapiens USA's Ideo, Trinzic's ObjectPro, Axiant from Cognos, and the Dynasty Development Environment from Dynasty Technology.

Many of these systems create SQL scripts to encapsulate a complete transaction model in an effort to reduce delivery time and minimize errors in the output. Others are more adept at assisting with the task of application partitioning. All assist with the creation and manipulation of the rules repository.

The repository is a place where all of the business rules are stored. However, it is more than a data dictionary because both data and procedures are stored in the repository. In this way, it is an object-oriented concept.

A Focus on the Three-Tier Front End

A few issues in front-end development are fairly specific to the three-tier design. With the emphasis on moving large portions of the effort of the front end out into the middle layer and making "thin clients" for the sake of data entry, you have to pay special attention to issues such as record updatability and error handling.

This section focuses on the issues that arise when developing front-end clients for three-tier client-server systems.

All Three Tiers on the Desktop

I have been asked the following question many times by Visual Basic developers eager to get into client/server programming: Can I do this at home without a network?

The answer is yes, with a caveat. There is absolutely no reason why a network has to be involved in the initial development stages and during the learning stages. In fact, you don't really have to use SQL Server or any other server-based database. Access will do just fine.

Now comes the caveat: When you are first learning to create client/server applications, the most common mistakes are often ones of partitioning. You are most likely to place a function in the wrong tier, causing unusually large amounts of traffic between the tiers. If you place all three tiers on the same workstation, you are not as likely to catch this error until very late in the process, because the expense of cross-tier communication is primarily network delay.

So if the answer is yes, what do you need to buy? Windows NT Workstation, SQL Server Workstation, and, of course, the Enterprise Edition of Visual Basic. Put them all on the same machine. You will be able to run SQL Server in Windows NT (you cannot run the server under Windows 95). You can also run Visual Basic on the same platform.

SQL Server Workstation comes with the complete SQL Server engine. It is simply not licensed for more than a few remote connections. However, don't assume that SQL Server, Server Edition is therefore a better choice for developers. Only the workstation comes with all the nifty tools that you will grow to love, like ISQL/W and SQL Enterprise Manager. Use the Workstation Edition for development, but use the Server Edition for deployment.

Of course, this all-on-one-box configuration requires a machine with a fast processor and a hefty chunk of RAM. I would recommend a minimum of a Pentium-90 with 32MB of RAM. Given that fact, it might be less expensive to create a small LAN and move SQL Server and NT off to a dedicated server on the LAN, thus freeing your development environment from the burden of running SQL Server itself. Your dedicated server can be a 486/33 with 16MB to 24MB of RAM. If you do this, I recommend that you keep NT on the client station anyway because of the increased reliability of the system. Windows 95 is a nice OS, but it is not a developer's workstation.

Working Within the Interfaces

Coding in the front end is not that different from coding in the middle layer in one important way: You have to create the object interfaces first, and then code within them. For front-end development, this is a little tougher because the GUI is the forte of traditional Visual Basic programmers, and object-oriented concepts are fairly new to this crowd.

However, consider this: Why is it easier to create your system "as you go" than to plan the entire thing out, when it is not easier to build a house by taking some wood and nails and drywall and getting started, without a floor plan of any kind?

The engineering concept is the same, and you have to change your thinking from one of artisan to that of engineer and builder. This means that you have to plan out the project and draw the blueprints, before you show up with a hammer and nails. That is the difference between a child's clubhouse nailed to a group of trees and a house that you can live in.

This is true of all programming, but it is especially true of client/server programming. If you don't plan the entire object infrastructure, how will you know if you are partitioning your application in the right place? You could guess, and you might even get lucky. But if you want to be a little more certain that your application won't end up running so slowly that you will have to start over, you will have to start with a comprehensive object design.

Error Handling at the Front End

One of the biggest issues when dealing with three-tier systems is how to handle errors. With the possibility that an error can occur somewhere in the "services" cloud, how should the front end expect to get an error message back, and in what format?

The first thing you need to do is to become familiar with the `.Raise` method of the error object. This allows you to provide large amounts of error information in your services layer that can be used in the front end to decipher what the error is and how to handle it.

> If you decide to use `Err.Raise` in your class modules, make sure to carefully examine the settings in the Advanced Tab of the Options dialog box. In the Error Trapping group, set the option for Break on Unhandled Errors. The default is Break in Class Module, which will prevent your errors from propagating out of the class where you generate them.

Be aware of one thing: the `Err.Raise` method does not create an `Errors` collection like you would get from the DAO or RDO objects. It causes the current error record to be discarded and replaced with the one you specify. If you are in a class object and you are trapping an error from another class object, you might not want to overwrite that object's `Error` method.

In this case, you might want to investigate the following idea: Create your own error collection object. When you trap an error in your class, add an error to your collection and then raise a generic error that can be caught by the front end. The front end would then be coded to use this collection to get all of the error information.

Data Security

Data security is a bit of a sticky issue. Windows NT currently allows the creation of "integrated security" tokens, which enable an NT workstation to log onto a SQL Server database without providing any access information. NT hands this token to SQL Server under the hood. (The mechanism that NT uses is not important to this discussion.)

Unfortunately, if you are using remote automation and the software that is performing the connection is running from an application server, then the token that gets passed to SQL Server is the token for the application server, not the user's workstation. This means that all users of that application server get the same privileges. In effect, security can be compromised.

The goal is for this security flaw to be addressed with Network OLE, where the application server will be allowed to impersonate the user when it makes the connection to the server on the user's behalf. At the time of this writing, the details are not yet available to determine if this future product will live up to this expectation.

In the short term, you might need to simply pass the ODBC connect information from the client station to the middleware layer for the sake of an ODBC login. In these cases, it is good to provide enough ODBC information so that an ODBC DSN does not have to exist on the application server. This is called a *DSN-less connection.*

Updating Database Information

Forget the data control. When you are using three-tier systems, you will invariably have most of your data access routines hidden in the middleware layer. In fact, there is no reason that the front end should even be aware, in anything more than the most simple sense, of more than one record at a time even being in existence.

Ultimately, you will be invoking update methods in class objects that will handle the modification of the database for you. In a well-designed three-tier system, there is no reason to expect that the front end will even be aware of what kind of server is being run, or even how the data is organized in the database.

Transaction Processing

You need to make sure that the design of your data movements still meets the criteria of transaction processing. In other words, just because you are sending data to a middle layer instead of a database server, that doesn't mean that you shouldn't know what would happen if the update was not successful.

In transaction processing, you can group a number of changes to the database with a `BeginTrans` statement and end the block with a `Commit` (or `Rollback` if you encounter an error).

When you are designing the application, make sure of two things:

- The code that is directly interfacing with the database server must be calling stored procedures that perform transaction processing, or the code is calling the `BeginTrans` and `Commit` itself.

- No operation consisting of a call to the middleware from any other operation can fail and leave information in the database in an inconsistent state.

Replication as a Design Consideration

Client/server systems can be very quick, or they can be very slow, depending on the methods that you use to move data from the database to the front end.

One of the common practices that is used in validating user input is to provide a list of known possible values for the user to select from. Therefore, instead of having the user specify that an invoice is paid with "CASH," you would provide a drop-down list with the choices CASH, VISA, MC, Amex, Other, and the user would select the correct one.

The problem comes when you extend this metaphor to the point where relatively large amounts of data have to be moved to the front end, either for data entry or for reporting lookup. By large amounts, I mean anything over about 90KB of data at startup.

At design time, this is simple. You issue a few queries at startup to get commonly accessed information and store it at the workstation so that lookups or data entry can be speeded up. Unfortunately, this can become cumbersome in the final product. I have seen systems where startup times ranged into minutes due to large amounts of data traveling over slow WAN lines.

There are a number of different techniques that can be used to speed up the movement of nearly static information around a client/server system. I consider all of them to fall under the category of replication, even though, at the fastest end, the term "cache" is often used, as well. Either way, the issues are the same: timeliness of data delivery versus certainty of data validity.

Replication is the act of making copies of portions of the database and placing those copies in a location where your application can access them more quickly than it can from the database itself.

For example, if your timesheet application downloads a list of company departments from the database every time it starts up, you could create a table on the local hard drive that would be used instead. Your application could update the table on occasion in the background, rather than doing the work every time the app is started. Depending on the amount of data involved, it is usually quicker to read data from a local table than it is to read it from a distant database.

The problems come from the fact that the data you are using at the front end is not data pulled from the central database. It is data pulled from your replicated store. This means that changes made in the central database might not be reflected in the data that you have.

Another problem in replication applies only to tables that are writeable as well as readable. If your application has the capability to write information to a table that is replicated, it needs to save the changes in two places: in the central database and in the replicated store. Alternatively, your application could make the change only to the replicated store and rely on another process to make the corresponding change to the central database.

Remote Server Replication

If you have a situation in which large amounts of data have to flow across a slow WAN connection, it might make sense to completely replicate your database from one server to another. For example, if your company has a main office in New York but the Tokyo branch is too busy to wait for the slow trans-Pacific connection, you could place a SQL Server box in the Tokyo data center and replicate the database from New York to Tokyo and back.

This type if replication is the kind most likely to rely on a separate process for keeping the servers in sync. The Tokyo users would go ahead and update the Tokyo server, and you would have a process that runs every hour that copies changes from Japan to the U.S. and vice versa. During this update process, only the records that changed locally would get copied across to the other side.

The biggest problem with replicated changes of this nature is how to handle deletes. If a record is inserted in Tokyo, it is easy to see that it needs to be moved to New York. If a record is updated in New York, the timestamp information can tell you that it should be copied to Tokyo. However, if a record is deleted in New York, there is nothing left to tell you that a change needs to be made in the Tokyo database.

For this reason, databases that rely on server replication often do not allow deletion per se. A record gets deleted by flagging it as "deleted." Because the change is really an update, the update can be propagated to the other server without problem. Optionally, you could implement a process that would actually delete records from both servers if they have been marked for deletion in both databases for more than a fixed length of time.

Local Drive Replication

Local drive replication is a process in which you copy tables from a remote server to files or a local database that is fully under your control. These files are usually on a local hard drive, but there is no reason why local drive replication couldn't be creating a file on a shared LAN drive.

This kind of replication rarely relies on any kind of separate process to keep the files in sync. Usually, the application that makes a change to the central database will also make the same change to the replicated store. It is the application's responsibility to occasionally run an update process to get central changes into the file.

Memory Caching

Memory caching is the shortest-lived form of data replication. Many client/server applications have been able to speed up their throughput by copying the contents of common queries into arrays in memory. Then, if the application needs to get the information, it looks to the memory array first.

If the replicated data changes occasionally (at the source), then you need to implement a method of knowing how long it has been since the data has been replicated from its source. My personal favorite is to take the average length of time between updates on a particular table, subtract two standard deviations, and you get the amount of time that a cache should be allowed to exist before refreshing it.

Deployment Issues in Three-Tier Systems

For the novice or unprepared, shipping a client/server application is a unique exercise in frustration. Unlike a stand-alone application, client/server applications require a considerable amount of forethought in order to prevent the rollout from coming to a complete halt a few weeks after it begins.

The tips in this section are simply notes from experience and do not reflect a comprehensive list of things that can go wrong.

Network Timeout

Client/server systems rely far more heavily on network bandwidth issues than stand-alone applications do. If you have a problem with a router or an overloaded subnet, your app can appear slow and buggy.

Make sure to design your error-handling routines to elegantly handle situations of network timeout. Usually, informing the user that the network is slow and then reissuing the SQL call is sufficient. However, you might want to allow the user to cancel the query and abort the operation, instead of reattempting the query.

Scheduled Maintenance

As with all enterprise-wide systems, there has to be a plan of how often to take the database system down for table repairs and database consistency checks. Various database servers require different amounts of time to clean them up. At a minimum, the database indices should be checked every week, and the data itself should be backed up every day.

Managing a Distributed Database

One of the greatest features of three-tier systems is that it enables portions of the data layer to exist in different databases. This means that the front-end applications can operate on data that is actually stored in multiple databases across the enterprise.

Originally, this meant that you could create a few tables in SQL Server that would be used to augment a legacy database that was being accessed through a DB2 Gateway. In this way, you could add schema to operational systems without impacting the performance or reliability of those systems.

Now this concept has become more generalized. Conceptually, the walls between data tables in different databases are beginning to break down. Users want to be able to combine data from various sources across the enterprise and create a viable and useful result.

However, there are a couple of things to consider when you explore the applicability of this concept in your environment. Once again, this is a list from experience and is not intended to be comprehensive in any way.

Referential Integrity Across an Enterprise

Referential integrity is a property of relational databases. It means that you will not allow a record X to be added to Table B if one of the fields in B has a foreign key relationship to Table A, and the key field in X does not refer to an existing record in A. In other words, you can't add an invoice item to the items table unless an invoice header already exists for the inserted item to refer to.

This process can often be handled by the server database system itself. Simply by declaring the relationship, you can force the server to look up the relationship before adding record X to Table B. However, when Table A is in one database and Table B is in another, it becomes considerably more difficult to maintain referential integrity.

There are a couple of different approaches to this problem. First approach: Cross your fingers. This approach allows integrity to be discarded completely, which forces the routines and processes that will later join these tables to cope with possible variations in the data model.

Second approach: Remote procedure calls. Many database systems, including SQL Server, enable you to issue stored procedure calls across database servers. This allows you to check the integrity of a value at the time it is being inserted. This approach is the most reliable of these listed.

Third approach: Replicated reference tables. In some cases, remote procedure calls are not feasible (like across database platforms), or the performance is not acceptable for the application. In these cases, it is common to replicate just enough information from the source database into the target database to be able to validate the integrity of a proposed addition.

Fourth approach: Disciplined updates. The calling application will check the values of the field to be added against the master database before submitting the record to be inserted into the target database.

All but the first approach have a basic assumption under them: that the data types and formats of the key fields will match between the source and target databases. This does not happen by magic. In fact, in many organizations where replicated reference tables are used, the reason for replicating the data is that it has to be converted from a different format.

This issue speaks to the need for an organization to create a common data repository. This is a knowledge base in which information is kept on what the data elements of the enterprise are, how they are derived, and what they can be used for. The sheer act of creating the repository can cause changes to occur in large systems, but the real value of the data repository is in the creation of new systems, which can benefit from the existence of standardized definitions.

Domain Integrity

Domain integrity is another property of relational databases. This time it refers to the constraints placed on a particular column in a table. If all of the values in the column are within a range of "allowable" values, then domain integrity is intact.

This is another issue for the data repository to address. A data value must be stored in a consistent manner in each of the different databases that store it, with all of the databases agreeing whether NULL values are allowed for the column, as well as all databases agreeing on what the valid range is.

Distributed Queries

Visual Basic has direct support for queries in which the data is combined from two different databases. This is done, primarily, by creating an Access database that uses linked tables from each of the two sources. The distributed query and update is done directly by the Access (Jet) engine as though the linked tables were local.

Two-Phased Commit

When you issue an update statement and it has to cause changes to occur in two separate databases, you have a situation that requires *two-phased commit*.

Here is how it works. Suppose that you are adding an author Bob Jones to your list of authors in a publishing house. You also want to send Mr. Jones an advance check for the book he presented for publication. Suppose that this means that you have to add records to your authors database, from which the advance check will be printed. You also need to add Mr. Jones' book to your publications list. You are currently enforcing referential integrity by using a replicated table of authors in the publications database.

Therefore, your transaction breaks down into three parts:

1. Update the authors table.
2. Update the replicated table of authors in the publication database.
3. Update the publications table.

However, a single `BeginTrans` will not work to force all of these operations into a single transaction. That is where two-phased commit comes in handy.

On both databases, you issue a `BeginTrans`. Then on the first database, you insert the records. Then on the second database, you insert the records. Then you go back to the first database and issue `Commit`. Then you return to the second database and issue the `Commit`. A failure anywhere along the way would cause a `Rollback` in both databases.

At this time, there are no ODBC drivers that directly support two-phased commit. However, there is no reason why this cannot be done in a middleware module.

Front-Line System Support

Support for a client/server system is also somewhat different than for a stand-alone application. Because users will share common modules across the network, issues of compatibility and availability will come into play. Therefore, a large part of the value added by the help desk will be in problem diagnosis, in determining what objects are available, and from where.

The Needs of the Help Desk

After you have created the initial design for your two- or three-tier client/server application, consider the needs of the people who will have to support it. The information that the front end makes available to the user is the same information that will later be available to the help desk when they are trying to diagnose a problem.

The following tips have proven effective at increasing the productivity of the support team for a client/server application:

- *Automated logging.* Every time your tool starts, have it delete and re-create a log file. Record every significant transaction and every error message in this log file. In my systems, the log file also contains timing information for significant functions. That way, if a user complains that a function is slow, I can find out exactly what they mean.

- *ODBC setup.* If your tool requires an ODBC data source in order to correctly function, provide a callout directly to ODBC to run the ODBCINST utility. Place the call under a button labeled "ODBC Settings."

- *System and connection information.* In the About box, provide information to the user about the system they are on and the connection they have made to their middleware and server. This information can come in quite handy when you are attempting to re-create the problem.

- *Provide simple tools to the help desk.* These tools can be run from help-desk machines or from "help" servers on the network. These apps will establish communications with the various components of the system (the server via TCP/IP, open the database and execute a proc that everyone is allowed to execute, open various business objects). This will vastly simplify the problem of finding out where the problem lies.

- *Provide training to the help desk operators.* This may be as little as a Frequently Asked Questions sheet or as much as a classroom-style session. Any documents and training that you give to the help desk you should also make available to the users.

References and Further Reading

A great deal of the information in this chapter on business rules comes from the following sources:

Baum, David, "The Right Tools for Coding Business Rules," *Datamation*, March 1, 1995, v41 n4 p36(3).

Moriarity, Terry, "The Origin of Business Rules," *Database Programming and Design*, June 1995, v8 n6 p65(3), Miller Freeman Publications.

Ross, Ronald, *The Business Rule Book: Classifying, Defining, and Modeling Rules.* Boston: Database Research Group Inc., 1994.

Von Halle, Barbara, "Uncovering Business Rules," *Database Programming and Design*, Dec 1995, v8 n12 p13(3), Miller Freeman Publications.

Von Halle, Barbara, "Life Beyond Data," *Database Programming and Design*, Sept 1995, v8 n9 p13(3), Miller Freeman Publications.

Von Halle, Barbara, "Back to Kindergarten Tee-ball: Uncovering the Mysteries of Business Rules at the Playground," *Database Programming and Design*, July 1995, v8 n7 p11(4), Miller Freeman Publications.

Summary

As you can see, the process of creating a three-tier system is a fairly complicated one. Even the decision to use more than one tier can have lasting consequences on how the application is designed, deployed, and maintained.

After all is said and done, the process of designing and implementing a system of this nature is fairly clear. Using the knowledge you gained in this chapter, you break up your application into layers. You should take extra caution to understand and isolate your business rules so that they can be changed.

You must work out the details of communication between the layers of your system. This can be the difference between a clean application that is easy to implement and maintain, and a nightmare waiting to happen.

Remote Data Control/Remote Data Objects

by Brad Midstokke and Bryce Ferguson

24

CHAPTER

Visual Basic developers have sought solutions to client/server problems for as long as the term "client/server" has been around. Our first obstacle as developers was getting access to any sort of database. We saw any number of DLLs or VBXs that helped us talk to databases, mostly Xbase-type databases. These worked fairly well for the most part, but we still had to write procedural code to get at all the features of these tools, especially the DLLs.

Then, with version 3.0, Visual Basic gave us a native database using the Jet 1.1 engine. It enabled us to use databases built with Access as well as Xbase tools, Paradox, and others using an object-oriented approach with Data Access Objects (DAO). We could also use ODBC (Open Database Connectivity) data sources such as SQL Server through Jet and get the easy development that DAO offered. The problem with this use of ODBC is that Jet imposed a performance penalty on us that was often not acceptable. We had to turn to VBSQL.VBX and DBLIB or to the ODBC API (Application Programming Interface) to get the performance we craved.

All this changed with Visual Basic 4.0 Enterprise Edition. Besides DAO, which was improved to talk to Jet 3.0 databases, VB includes the *Remote Data Objects (RDO)* and the *Remote Data Control (RDC)*. We now have a set of tools that gives us an object-oriented approach to SQL Server application development similar to DAO without the performance penalties of DAO.

The only significant problem that remains is documentation. There is a lot of material on the objects, their methods, and properties in reference form but precious little on how to actually solve problems with them.

The goal of this chapter is to provide real-life examples demonstrating techniques that most developers will need to know in order to effectively use RDO. Most of the examples have been constructed by using Microsoft's SQL Server version 6.0 and the sample "Pubs" database that comes with it.

As with any platform or tool, there are many ways to solve the same problem. The solutions here show just some of the possibilities. Hopefully, they'll get you started in the right direction and get you to think about other and even better ways.

RDO Architecture

RDO is a thin object-oriented layer of functionality around ODBC that uses *OLE (Object Linking and Embedding)* as its interface to VB. It is specifically optimized to work with the Microsoft SQL Server 6.0 database driver, although it has been known to work well with other database drivers. It improves on DAO as an ODBC access layer by giving the developer access to the connection and result set handles, not to mention removing the ponderously large Jet engine layer from the mix. If you've been using the ODBC drivers directly, this will be very familiar turf. RDO provides a considerable amount of ODBC housekeeping and enables the developer to devote more attention to the construction of the application.

It should be noted early on that RDO is currently available for 32-bit Visual Basic only. For applications that are required to use a SQL Server 6.0 database and still run on 16- or 32-bit Windows, it might be desirable to build a 32-bit data access component as an out of-process server running on a 32-bit platform using remote automation. The 16-bit version of your application can then get some of the lift of using 32-bit database access without forcing an operating system upgrade on the workstation until it's more feasible to do so.

VBSQL.VBX is the most common 16-bit tool that has been used in the past to accomplish efficient throughput for client/server applications. You paid for that speed with a considerable amount of code. To perform asynchronous calls to the back end, the code size would grow even larger. As far as overhead is concerned, RDO layering is very similar to VBSQL.VBX. The following table lists the comparable layers between RDO and VBSQL.VBX:

VB 16-bit application	VB 32-bit application
VBSQL.VBX	MSRDO32.DLL
DB3LIB.DLL	SQL Server ODBC Drivers

The ODBC API is the other way to get good client/server performance. Everything you do with this mechanism requires code. There is nothing object-oriented about it unless you make your code look that way. Given the classes, DLLs, and OLE servers you can now build with VB4, this is not out of the question; however, with RDO already sitting in front of you, why go through the pain?

RDO Hierarchy

RDO is built with a clean hierarchy of objects. The top-level object is rdoEngine, which represents the remote data source. It contains all other objects in the hierarchy.

Object	Definition
rdoEngine	This is the top-level object in the hierarchy. It represents the remote data source and contains all other objects in the hierarchy.
rdoEnvironments	This collection contains all active rdoEnvironment objects of the rdoEngine object.
rdoEnvironment	This object contains a logical set of connections for a particular user ID.
rdoConnections	This collection contains all open rdoConnection objects opened or created in an rdoEnvironment object of the remote database engine.
rdoConnection	This object represents a single connection to a remote data source and a specific database on that data source.

continues

Object	Definition
rdoPreparedStatements	This collection contains all rdoPreparedStatement objects in an rdoConnection.
rdoPreparedStatement	This object is a stored definition of a query. It corresponds to a prepared query definition. It can be thought of as a compiled SQL statement.
rdoColumns	This collection contains all stored rdoColumn objects of an rdoResultset, rdoPreparedStatement, or rdoTable object.
rdoColumn	This object represents a column of data with a common data type and a common set of properties.
rdoParameters	This collection contains all the rdoParameter objects of an rdoPreparedStatement object.
rdoParameter	This object is a parameter associated with an rdoPreparedStatement object.
rdoResultsets	This collection contains all open rdoResultset objects in an rdoConnection.
rdoResultset	This object is the set of rows that results from running a query.
rdoTables	This collection contains all stored rdoTable objects in the database.
rdoTable	This object is the stored definition of a base table or a SQL view.
rdoErrors	This collection contains all rdoError objects in the rdoEngine object.
rdoError	This object contains details about a single operation involving remote data objects that resulted in an error.

With either VBSQL.VBX or the ODBC API, it's up to you to manage all the connections, result sets, and so on. RDO manages all this for you using a clean object hierarchy. For example, if you close an rdoConnection, all open result sets, prepared statements, and so on will be closed along with it.

At the very top of this hierarchy is the rdoEngine. Default properties for rdoEnvironments can be set at this level. The properties are straightforward, and there aren't any hidden "gotchas." There are two methods available for the engine: rdoCreateEnvironment and rdoRegisterDataSource. The rdoRegisterDataSource method will enable you to bypass the ODBC dialog box and programmatically register an entry to the Windows 95/NT registry. Use rdoCreateEnvironment to create a new environment to avoid potential settings collisions with something like the RDC.

The rdoEnvironment is where things start to get interesting. Again, the properties are easy enough to understand except for the hEnv property. This is where RDO opens up the ODBC handles down inside the driver. RDO enables access to the handles for the ODBC environments, connections, and statements. Be forewarned, however: Use these handles only if you're a seasoned ODBC programmer. You can shoot yourself and your database in the foot with these things.

The rdoEnvironment has methods that will enable you to control transaction processing. You can begin commit and rollback transactions through the methods in this object. This is also the level in the hierarchy where you can start to code. There is already an environment object at your disposal, rdoEnvironment(0), and this is where I prefer to code. You do have to be a little careful when using this environment object, especially when you use RDO alongside the RDC. We'll discuss using both RDO and the RDC a little later in the chapter in "What About RDC?"

RDO Versus DAO

To the unaided eye, RDO bears at least some resemblance to DAO. In fact, there are a lot of similarities, but the names have been changed to protect the innocent. The original designers of RDO wanted to follow the DAO object hierarchy but use names that were perhaps more meaningful to RDBMS developers.

If you're already a DAO expert, the following table should help you down the road of understanding RDO's object mapping by showing the RDO objects equivalent to familiar DAO objects.

DAO	Equivalent RDO
DBEngine	rdoEngine
Workspace	rdoEnvironment
Database	rdoConnection
TableDef	rdoTable
QueryDef	rdoPreparedStatement
Recordset	rdoResultset

Some terminology differences exist between RDO and DAO. In a relational database such as SQL Server, records are referred to as *rows,* and fields are referred to as *columns.* Where DAO talks about RecordSets, RDO uses the more RDBMS style ResultSet.

You can still use popular DAO methods such as MoveFirst and MoveNext to navigate through an RDO result set. In addition, RDO gives you "settable" properties like AbsolutePosition and PercentPosition to reposition the current row pointer.

There are some DAO components missing from RDO because DAO supports the ISAM structure of Jet and other installable ISAM databases. RDO is specifically intended to communicate with relational databases, especially SQL Server 6.0. As such, objects such as Index and methods such as Seek are not supported in RDO.

RDO Versus DAO 3.1

DAO 3.1 is a new creature that Microsoft introduced just prior to the release of this book. It is an extension to DAO 3.0 that has added new methods and properties to support RDO. By toggling one property, you can tell DAO to use Jet or bypass Jet and go straight to RDO. Although it's still a little early, some informal benchmarks seem to show that this extra layer is about as thin as RDO itself and therefore doesn't impose a noticeable performance penalty.

There is something of a price to pay, however. DAO 3.1 does not expose the ODBC handles that RDO does. If you don't have a need for this, perhaps this is not a problem.

RDO Versus VBSQL

There are a lot of differences between RDO and VBSQL. Although the end results of using either one can be the same, the code path you go down is significantly different. As such, it is beyond the scope of this chapter to attempt to compare them directly.

With SQL 6.5, there is now a VBSQL.OCX available. It has the distinct benefit of being at least somewhat plug-and-play compatible with the old 16-bit VBX. The trouble is that it seems to be less of a performer than developers would like. Basically, whereas RDO is a very thin OLE object layer around the ODBC API, VBSQL is a much thicker OLE object layer around DBLIB with the accompanying performance penalties that implies.

Why Should I Use RDO?

The decision to implement RDO in an application depends on many factors. An obvious key factor is the back end you need to communicate with. If it's SQL Server 6.0, your best bet is easily RDO. If it's an Access database, go straight to Jet through DAO rather than adding the ODBC layer to the mix. Other gifts you get with RDO are the following:

- Fast access to ODBC data sources, especially SQL Server
- Capability to run SQL Server stored procedures with parameters, return status, and output values
- Management of multiple result sets
- Transact-SQL support
- Establishment of query row limits
- Choice of ODBC or server-side cursors based on back-end availability

■ Asynchronous query execution
■ Availability of ODBC handles
■ Small memory footprint

What About RDC?

The *Remote Data Control (RDC)* is a wrapper object for RDO that enables you, the programmer, to automatically bind controls on a form to columns in the RDC result set. It has the advantage of insulating you from the intricacies of when to save data, how to populate the display with data, and so on. On the other hand, it has the disadvantage of insulating you from the intricacies of when to save data, how to populate the display with data, and so on. As you can see, it's a bit of a two-edged sword.

This seeming paradox is also true for DAO and the data control. I've had the experience of working with someone else's VB3 application that used an Access database back end and used the data control for navigation. Data validation code was placed in the `Validate` event, and display preparation code was placed in the `Reposition` event. The problem was that the `Validate` event was triggered several times for each record navigation operation, causing no end of grief in trying to figure out why my display was trashed when I moved to another record using the data control. While I'm not as far along in male pattern baldness as my compatriot, this problem was accelerating the process too much for my taste!

The solution here was to yank the data control, retain the essence of the `Validate` and `Reposition` event code, and simulate the data control visuals by adding discrete buttons and a label control for record navigation. I had complete control when everything happened.

This lesson learned: It is the humble opinion of this particular developer that the data control and, as an extension, the RDC are best left to small applications that will never require the benefits of a three-tier client/server architecture. This includes fairly simple administrative-type applications or small data entry applications where you can afford to let the data controls do the work for you. However, if you have business rules that need to be shared among different applications, the RDC simply doesn't fit.

You also have to be careful if you plan to mix RDO and RDC in the same application. That's because RDC always uses `rdoEnvironments(0)` to do its work. This can be a problem if RDC decides that a cursor is not updatable and you want to do some updates with RDO.

It's easy enough to fix, just not abundantly obvious. Just create your RDO connections through a new environment such as `rdoEnvironments(1)` and let the RDC have `rdoEnvironments(0)` all to itself. You'll learn more about these objects a little later in the section titled "RDO Environments."

In a nutshell, here are some reasons to avoid the RDC:

- It places an inordinate amount of traffic on the network.
- You are forced to apply business rules entirely on the back end through stored procedures or on the front end through hard coding your application.
- It eats resources on the server or the client by using cursors to manage the row edits.
- After you edit a cell and move to another row, the changes are committed to the back end; you can't back out of an edit.
- You run the risk of settings conflicts when using RDC alongside RDO connected through rdoEnvironments(0).

Controlling RDO

When you first make an access to RDO, an instance of the rdoEngine is automatically created. It provides parameters and options that apply across RDO. New instances of rdoEnvironment, rdoConnection, and rdoResultset objects will use the defaults provided by rdoEngine unless you override them.

A number of interesting properties are associated with the rdoEngine object. These properties provide overall control over the default RDO environment.

Property	Definition	Default Value
rdoDefaultCursorDriver	Cursor driver type; this can be ODBC or server-side	rdUseIfNeeded
rdoDefaultUser	SQL Server logon ID	" " (empty string)
rdoDefaultPassword	Password associated with the logon ID	" " (empty string)
rdoDefaultErrorThreshold	Level of severity above which errors are fatal	-1 (disabled)
rdoDefaultLoginTimeout	Time to wait before abandonment of connection attempt	15 seconds

Registering a New Data Source

It's possible to install a new ODBC data source through code. This obscure and not well-documented capability can be useful if your application needs to work in concert with an Access database, an Excel workbook, or something else that can only talk to SQL databases through ODBC.

The code to do this is fairly straightforward. Simply build up a DSN attributes string and call the rdoRegisterDatasource method of the rdoEngine object. The following example uses the server name as both the data source name and description to simplify any user interface you provide. You can, of course, build a user interface to collect more of the parameters, but because your app is probably going to call this transparently, it's probably not necessary. It is probably also a good idea to try a quick DSN-less connection before you actually register the data source. This will let you make sure the data source is valid before you commit it.

```
Dim sAttribs As String
sAttribs = "Description=" & sServerName & Chr$(13)
sAttribs = sAttribs & "OemToAnsi=No" & Chr$(13)
sAttribs = sAttribs & "Network=(Default)" & Chr$(13)
sAttribs = sAttribs & "Address=(Default)" & Chr$(13)
sAttribs = sAttribs & "Database=" & sDatabase
'/// validate datasource before committing
'/// assuming it's valid, register the datasource
rdoEngine.rdoRegisterDataSource DSN:=sServerName, _
               Driver:="SQL Server", _
               Silent:=True, _
               Attributes:=sAttribs
```

RDO Environments

Connections to databases in RDO are made through rdoEnvironment objects. When you first fire up RDO, you get the first one, rdoEnvironment(0), for free.

There are a number of reasons why you might want to create a new environment in which to work. First, the kind of cursor your result set will use is determined by the environment. If you want to use server-side cursors for some operations and ODBC driver cursors for others, you'll want to create an environment for each. The new environment is automatically added to the rdoEnvironments collection.

Another reason is demonstrated by the RDC scenario you saw earlier. It's probably possible to mix the remote data control with calls to RDO in the same environment, but in my case, it didn't seem to work. To play it safe, create a new environment for use by the RDO calls and leave the RDC to its own devices in the default environment.

An interesting thing to note is the capability to create a named environment. This makes sense when you think about it. rdoEnvironments is a collection of rdoEnvironment objects. When you make your own collections in VB, you can set up a named key for the members of the collection, theoretically making it easier to get at them. In the case of the rdoEnvironments collection, you could create different named environments such as "log," "entry," or "reports" to help you easily go after the correctly configured environment for a particular kind of operation.

Now, like always, there are penalties to be paid with multiple environments, so use them with care. You'll need to decide if the price is too high for your application. Specifically, you can't have a single transaction block span multiple environments, and there's additional connection overhead.

The following is an example of creating a new environment. Notice that I use the name "Log" for the new environment because I'm always going to use it for status logging operations.

```
Dim rEnv As rdoEnvironment
Dim rConnect As rdoConnection

sConnect = GetDashboardConnect()
If rdoEnvironments.Count = 1 Then
    Set rEnviron = rdoCreateEnvironment("Log", gsUID, gsPWD)
End If

Set rConnect = rdoEnvironments("Log").OpenConnection("", _
    rdDriverNoPrompt, False, sConnect)
```

Data Source Connections

To connect to a data source, you need to use the OpenConnection method on an environment object. As stated in the preceding section, the default RDO environment, rdoEnvironments(0), is yours free of charge, right out of the box.

There are many ways to call the OpenConnection method, from letting ODBC dialog boxes collect all the needed information to letting you control the whole thing through your own dialog boxes.

The following example takes full advantage of the ODBC prompt. It takes the least code and lets ODBC do all the work.

```
Dim SqlCn As rdoConnection
On Error Resume Next
Set SqlCn = rdoEnvironments(0).OpenConnection(dsName:="", _
            Prompt:=rdDriverPrompt, _
            Readonly:=True, _
            Connect:="")
If SqlCn = Nothing Then MsgBox "ODBC connection not successful."
```

There are a number of options for the Prompt argument to give you varying degrees of control over the connection dialog boxes that ODBC will give you.

Prompt Option	Definition
rdDriverPrompt	ODBC will always show the prompt dialog box.
rdDriverComplete	ODBC will show its own prompt dialog box only if the supplied data is incomplete.
rdDriverNoPrompt	ODBC will assume that you know what you're doing and never show you its prompt dialog box.

You can use many combinations to accomplish automatic prompting for user login properties. But sometimes you just want to get things done without any dialog box at all. In those cases, you can open a DSN-less connection.

DSN-Less Connections

Creating an ODBC data source is the conventional way of telling RDO about the database to which you want to connect. This is nice, but it does take some time to actually make a connection with a named data source. There's an even faster way called a *DSN-less connection* that also has the advantage of letting you control the user interface and avoid the ODBC dialog boxes.

To build a connect string, you must include all of the following:

Element	Description	Example
DSN	This MUST be empty, which means there can be no space between = and the semicolon (;).	DSN=;
DRIVER	ODBC driver name enclosed in curly braces. (This must be a C programmer's revenge on Visual Basic developers.)	DRIVER={SQL Server};
SERVER	Server name where the database lives.	SERVER=MyServer;
DATABASE	The name of the database.	DATABASE=MyDb;
UID	User login ID.	UID=MyID;
PWD	User password.	PWD=MyPwd;

The following example accomplishes a DSN-less connection:

```
Dim SqlCn As rdoConnection
On Error Resume Next
sConnectStr = "DSN=;DRIVER={SQL Server};SERVER=MyServer;"
sConnectStr = sConnectStr & "DATABASE=MyDb;UID=MyId;PWD=MyPwd;"
Set gSqlCn = rdoEnvironments(0).OpenConnection("", _
                        rdDriverNoPrompt, _
                        True, _
                        sConnectStr)
If gSqlCn = Nothing Then MsgBox "ODBC connection not successful."
```

You can also do the same thing with the RDC:

```
sConnectStr = "DSN=;DRIVER={SQL Server};SERVER=MyServer;"
sConnectStr = sConnectStr & "DATABASE=MyDb;UID=MyId;PWD=MyPwd;"
With MSRDC1
    .Prompt = rdDriverNoPrompt
    .Connect = sConnectStr
    .SQL = sQuery
End With
MSRDC1.Refresh
```

A Simple Inline Query

It's time to get down to basics. After you have a connection, the next step is to construct a simple query to fetch data. After opening a result set, you need to retrieve the data from the server. The `rdoColumn` object is the key to extracting data from the result set. The following code fragment retrieves the column value, places a tab delimiter between each column, and places a carriage return to delimit each row. Note the use of the `rdoColumns` collection to iterate through all columns in the row.

```
Dim oResult As rdoResultset
Dim oCol As rdoColumn
Dim sText As String
Dim sDataStr As String
Set oResult = SqlCn.OpenResultset(Name:="Select * from authors", _
                                  Type:=rdOpenForwardOnly, _
                                  LockType:=rdConcurReadOnly)
Do While Not oResults.EOF
    sText = ""
    For Each oCol In oResults.rdoColumns
        sText = sText & oCol & Chr$(9)
    Next iCol
    sDataStr = sDataStr & sText & Chr$(13)
    oResults.MoveNext
Loop
```

Cursors

You use *cursors* to keep track of where you are in a result set. With RDO, it is possible to use either client-side or server-side cursors. There are advantages and disadvantages with each, and their use should be thought out with some care. As a rule, however, using ODBC driver cursors, the client-side kind, will give you more benefits. You can set this as the default by setting the `RdoDefaultCursorDriver` property of the `rdoEngine` object to `rdUseOdbc`.

You need to bear some things in mind when deciding on the appropriate cursor library for your application.

Use server-side cursors for large SELECT operations where one of the columns returned is a known unique key on the result set. This works well when you include the primary key in your query. If your result set does not contain a known unique key, your server will have to try to create an index to support the cursor. This can have a serious performance impact on your application.

Use ODBC cursors when your result sets are smaller or you wish to return multiple result sets in a single query.

It is possible to mix server-side cursors and ODBC cursors. This requires a different environment for each. The disadvantages are not being able to have a single transaction across the environments and having to establish an additional connection to your data source.

The following table describes the options you have and the strengths of each:

Cursor	Definition
rdUseIfNeeded	ODBC will choose the cursor driver for you. It tries to use server-side cursors if they are available, which is a problem if you wish to run a multiple result-set query.
rdUseOdbc	The ODBC cursor driver will be used. Cursors are built on the workstation. It has the advantage of supporting multiple result-set queries but has the disadvantage of consuming workstation resources to store the keysets.
rdrdUseServer	This forces the use of server-side cursors, assuming they're available. The keysets are stored on TempDb on SQL Server. If you try to set this against SQL Server 4.2.1a, the ODBC driver says nothing and automatically switches to the ODBC cursor driver.

Error Processing

Error processing in RDO is very different from in VBSQL.VBX. The VBX triggered events, and message and error processing was accomplished in two separate blocks of code. Error conditions in SQL Server are passed back to RDO to the rdoErrors collection in a FILO order (First In, Last Out). The most recent error, and usually the most interesting one, can be found in the first element of the collection, rdoErrors(0). Both warnings and errors are processed in the same manner. However, only the errors will make their way into the Visual Basic error collection.

In order to determine that you have an RDO error, you must inspect the rdoErrors(0).Number. If it's greater than zero, then it will be picked up by the VB error collection. Otherwise, you get a warning, and further inspection is required. The key to this part of the operation is the rdoErrors(0).SQLState. This is a string property that is made up of a two-character class value followed by a three-character subclass value.

The class value component of the SQLState property can be "01," which indicates a warning and is accompanied by a return code of SQL_SUCCESS_WITH_INFO. Other class values, except for "IM," indicate an error and are accompanied by a return code of SQL_ERROR. The class "IM" is dependent on the implementation of ODBC and applies to both warnings and errors. For all classes, the subclass value "000" identifies implementation-defined conditions for the given class.

I would recommend writing code to parse out the SQLState and to trap for the information that can be buried in here. There are conditions such as a back-end SQL syntax error or a bad handle that you need to trap.

You can use the rdoErrors collection to examine the failure in detail. Each member of the collection is an object called rdoError. Use a loop to iterate through all available members of the collection. The following example demonstrates how to do this:

```
Dim rError As rdoError
For Each rError In rdoErrors
    With rError
        Debug.Print .Number,
        Debug.Print .Description,
        Debug.Print .Source,
        Debug.Print .SQLState
    End With
Next
```

In a real error handler, you could choose to show only the number and description of the entire collection, or you could show all components of the first member of the collection. During early stages of application development, it might be useful to put all members of the entire collection into a grid for easier display. Check out the RVisData sample that comes with Visual Basic 4 Enterprise Edition for an example of this.

RDO Prepared Statements

An rdoPreparedStatement enables a VB4 application to construct a single point of interface to a SQL stored procedure that can pass input parameters and capture return values and output parameters. The syntax to establish this little gem might be a little confusing at first, but it works. The benefit is that you can build it once, perhaps as part of the application initialization, and it becomes an object in the rdoPreparedStatements collection that RDO manages. Once added to the collection, you can iterate through the collection searching for the right prepared statement by name.

The rdoPreparedStatement is also the only way to handle multiple result sets that may be returned from a SQL stored procedure. More about that later in the "Multiple Result Sets" section.

In essence, the prepared statement can appear very much like a Visual Basic function. Like a VB function, there are a million and one ways to construct an rdoPreparedStatement. The example provided here will have a little of everything: a return value, two input parameters, and one output parameter. The first order of business is to create the object in the rdoConnection collection. You need to place a question mark (?) in the statement wherever a parameter or a return value is required.

The following example assumes a global rdoConnection variable called gSqlCn:

```
Dim oResult    As rdoResultset
Dim ps         As rdoPreparedStatement
sQuery = "{ call ?=bspAddAuthor(?,?,?) }"
Set ps = gSqlCn.CreatePreparedStatement("MyStatement", sQuery)
Set oResult = ps.OpenResultset(Type:=rdOpenForwardOnly, _
                               LockType:=rdConcurReadOnly)
```

Note the curly braces around the call. They are required to call a stored procedure in the prepared statement. It is also possible to build the SQL code at this level and call it as a prepared statement. To do so, you will need to eliminate the curly braces. Here's a very simple example:

```
Dim oResult     As rdoResultset
Dim ps          As rdoPreparedStatement
sQuery = "select * from authors where au_id = ?"
Set ps = gSqlCn.CreatePreparedStatement("MyStatement", sQuery)
Set oResult = ps.OpenResultset(Type:=rdOpenForwardOnly, _
                                    LockType:=rdConcurReadOnly)
```

The next step is to identify how each parameter is to be used. That is, is it an input parameter, an output parameter, both, or is it a return value?

```
Ps.rdoParameters(0).Direction = rdParamReturnValue
Ps.rdoParameters(1).Direction = rdParamInput
Ps.rdoParameters(2).Direction = rdParamInputOutput
Ps.rdoParameters(3).Direction = rdParamOutput
```

The syntax to use this prepared statement might look something like this:

```
Ps.rdoParameters(1) = 40
Ps.rdoParameters(2) = "Foobar"
Ps.Execute
Print Ps.rdoParameters(0)
Print Ps.rdoParameters(2)
Print Ps.rdoParameters(3)
```

Depending on the goal of the stored procedure you're calling, you can also use the OpenResultset method:

```
Set oResults = Ps.OpenResultset(Type:=rdOpenForwardOnly, _
                                    LockType:=rdConcurReadOnly, _
                                    Options:=rdAsyncEnable)
```

If you're a firm believer in placing all record updates, additions, and deletions on the back end, use the prepared statement. There is a little more work in constructing the functions to retrieve the result sets, but it's worth the effort. The fact that it's the only way to catch multiple result sets is a good enough reason.

To further illustrate, suppose that you have an unbound grid that you're using for data display and you're allowing the user to edit row-based data. The user completes the edits on a particular set of rows, and then presses the Update button. A prepared statement can be constructed that can be executed for each row that has been touched by the user. The same statement can also return an integer or character value indicating whether the update was successful. If you want to get more detailed, it could also return a SQL output value to be processed or displayed by the front end. This has the advantage of lower network traffic than a bound control.

```
Dim ps As rdoPreparedStatement
SPname= "spUpDateData"
sQuery = "{ call ?= " & sSPnam & "(?,?,?)"

Set ps = gcnSql.CreatePreparedStatement(Name:=sSPname, SqlString:=sQuery)
```

```
ps.rdoParameters(0).Direction = rdParamReturnValue
ps.rdoParameters(1).Direction = rdParamInput

'for each row in the grid to update
    ps.rdoParameters(1).Value = sNewValue
    ps.Execute()
    'assuming that the stored procedure returns 0 for success
    If ps.rdoParameters(1).Value <> 0 Then
        'display an error message
    End If
'next row
```

Asynchronous Queries

Asynchronous queries are a nice feature that returns control to your application as soon as the rdoPreparedStatement or rdoOpenResultset has been called. Your app can now go off and do other things, such as submitting other queries, allowing data entry, and so on. If you do a synchronous query, there's no way to control when you quit. You have to wait for the query to return, successful or not.

Here's a code fragment that shows a simple example of what you can do with async queries:

```
'/// launch async query
    Set rResults = rConnection.OpenResultset(sQuery, _
        rdOpenStatic, _
        rdConcurReadOnly, _
        rdAsyncEnable)

    '/// wait for resultset
    Dim iCount As Long
    Do Until rResults.StillExecuting = False
        '/// test exec time to see if we're out of bounds
        '/// also test giAbort to see if the Abort
        '/// button was hit on the status form
        If Abs(DateDiff("n", vStart, Now)) > gDatapoint.iExectime _
                Or giAbort = True Then
            rResults.Cancel
            rResults.Close
            rConnection.Close
            iRows = 0
            If giAbort = True Then
                Call WriteDetailLog("User abort", 1, _
                        "ExecCommand: stored procedure")
                ExecCommand = ddm_UserAbort
            Else
                Call WriteDetailLog("Time exceeded", 1, _
                        "ExecCommand: stored procedure")
                ExecCommand = ddm_TimeExceeded
            End If
            Exit Function
        End If
        frmStatus.lblStatus(2).Caption = "Status: running " & _
                Format(Now() - vStart, "hh:mm:ss")
        frmStatus.Refresh
```

```
        Call Wait(WAIT_TIME)
    Loop
```

You have a structure member, gDatapoint.iExectime, that tells you how many minutes to expect the routine to take plus a fudge factor. There is also a Boolean global variable, giAbort, that tells you when the operator presses an Abort button on a status display. Notice the setup of a Do..Loop to continue waiting until rResults.StillExecuting = False. Inside the loop, check for elapsed time against gDatapoint.iExectime and check for the value of giAbort. If you've exceeded execution time or giAbort = True, call the rResults.Cancel method to tell the server to cancel the query.

You can also display an elapsed timer on a status form if you wish. This is a good idea just to let the user know something is going on and to give the user an opportunity to cancel the query if he or she thinks it has gone on too long.

A little later in the chapter, in the RdoServer section, there are a few examples that show real implementations of async queries and that demonstrate what you can do with them.

Multiple Result Sets

RDO is able to handle stored procedures that return multiple result sets. With DAO, you could only get the first set of results, which was usually not the most interesting set. A couple of things are needed to get ready for this kind of stored procedure. First, set RowsetSize on the rdoPreparedStatement object to 1. Here's a section of code to illustrate:

```
Dim oResult    As rdoResultset
Dim ps         As rdoPreparedStatement
sQuery = "{ call bspGetReport() }"
Ps.RowsetSize = 1
Set Ps = gSqlCn.CreatePreparedStatement("MyReport", sQuery)
Set oResults = Ps.OpenResultset(Type:=rdOpenForwardOnly, _
                                LockType:=rdConcurReadOnly)
```

To retrieve the data from a multiple result set query you need to use the RDO method MoreResults to move to the next result set. The following is a code example. Notice the nested Do..Loop construct with the MoreResults method called outside the inner loop.

```
Do
    Do While Not oResults.EOF
        sText = ""
        For iCol = 0 To iColCount - 1
            sText = sText & oResults.rdoColumns(iCol) & Chr$(9)
        Next iCol
        sDataStr = sDataStr & sText & Chr$(13)
        oResults.MoveNext
        lRow = lRow + 1
    Loop
Loop Until oResults.MoreResults = False
```

You can find the complete source code for getting result sets in the source file RDOSERVER.CLS on the CD-ROM that comes with this book.

Using ODBC Handles

Handles are something hard-core ODBC programmers enjoy using. RDO exposes four handles to the ODBC driver:

Handle	Description
rdoEnvironment.hEnv	ODBC environment handle
rdoConnection.hDbc	ODBC connection handle
rdoPreparedStatement.hStmt	ODBC statement handle
rdoResultset.hStmt	ODBC statement handle; refers to the statement underlying the result set

These ODBC handles can be used to link client forms to running result sets. This is helpful if you need to cancel all running jobs or close all open connections before letting the user bail out of your application. It's also useful when you want to tell an OLE server doing RDO for you that you have the results you want to clean up. The function shown here is used in the RDO Pubs example found on the CD-ROM that comes with this book:

```
Public Function CloseConnectionFb(oCaller As Object) As Boolean
'
' Purpose: Spin through all connections and their result sets and look for
'   a resultset that matches one in the oCaller object
'   when found, close pending result sets and close the
'   associated connection

    Dim oConn    As rdoConnection
    Dim oRS      As rdoResultset
    Dim bFound   As Boolean
    Dim nErrType       As Integer
    Dim bValidCaller   As Boolean

    On Error GoTo CloseConnectionErr
    bFound = False
    CloseConnectionFb = bFound

    ' if we don't have a valid object, bail out
    If oCaller Is Nothing Then
        Exit Function
    Else
        bValidCaller = True
    End If

    For Each oConn In rdoEnvironments(0).rdoConnections
        If oCaller.hDbc = oConn.hDbc Then
            If oConn.StillExecuting Then
                oConn.Cancel
            Else
                oConn.Close
            End If
```

```
                oCaller.bActive = False
                oCaller.hStmt = 0
                oCaller.hDbc = 0
                bFound = True
                Exit For
        End If
    Next oConn

    CloseConnectionFb = bFound
    Exit Function

CloseConnectionErr:
    Call ErrProcessS("CloseConnection Error ")
    Exit Function

End Function
```

Getting Started with RDO

Before you go running off and coding to RDO, you need to be sure that the project in which you want to use it knows it exists because, by default, RDO is not included in a project's references list. To use it, you must add it to your project in the Object Reference dialog box. To add a reference in your project to RDO, use the following steps:

1. Choose Tools | References.
2. Find Microsoft Remote Data Objects in the References list.
3. Click Microsoft Remote Data Objects from the list.
4. Choose OK.

Data Collection Utility—Simple RDO

A recent project provided an excellent opportunity to use RDO. The code was fairly project-specific, so only the fragments shown as examples are in a code module on the CD-ROM that comes with this book for you to use, reuse, and abuse to your heart's content.

The back-end requirement called for collecting small amounts of data from a moderately large number of data sources at various times of the day, every day of the week. All servers were running SQL 6.0. The data was to be summarized using stored procedures and the results for each stored procedure placed in a separate table in the target reporting database. Each stored procedure was likely to return a different set of columns, so the utility needed to be fairly generic. It also needed to run asynchronously so you could periodically check status and entertain the user with an elapsed timer display.

Another key was the short time frame given to complete the project. The clear winner? VB4 and RDO. The following sections describe the key functions and subroutines written for this utility.

ExecCommand

This function does the real work of running the query and interpreting the results. Note the DSN-less connection. This is built from information in a control table in the main database.

Note the use of rdAsyncEnabled when you make the call to get the result set. This enables you to set up a User Entertainment dialog box with a label showing the elapsed time of the job. It also enables you to abort the stored procedure by setting the giAbort flag to True or testing if it has been running longer than it ought to. If this were a more substantial interactive application, you could declare a module-level result-set object and look for the StillExecuting property to go to False using a timer control.

Because this utility uses a single, fairly static target database location, a function called GetConnect was used that reads the needed values from the Windows 95/NT registry and builds the connect string.

```
Function ExecCommand(dtDate As Date, iRows As Integer) As Integer

        '/// fire up the stored procedure
        Dim iLoginFailCount As Integer
        Dim vStart          As Variant
        Dim bUpdate         As Boolean
        Dim sConnect        As String
        Dim sQuery          As String
        Dim rConnection     As rdoConnection
        Dim rResults        As rdoResultset
        Dim rTargetDB       As rdoConnection
        Dim rTarget         As rdoResultset

        Const WAIT_TIME = 1

        '/// build dsn-less target connection for the
        '/// datapoint we're working on
        sConnect = "DRIVER={SQL Server};"
        sConnect = sConnect & "DATABASE=" & Trim(gDatapoint.sDatabase) & ";"
        sConnect = sConnect & "SERVER=" & Trim(gDatapoint.sServer) & ";"
        sConnect = sConnect & "UID=" & Trim(gDatapoint.sUser) & ";"
        sConnect = sConnect & "PWD=" & Trim(gDatapoint.sPassword) & ";"
        sConnect = sConnect & "DSN=;"

        On Error GoTo Err_ExecCommand

RetryConnection:
        Set rConnection = rdoEnvironments(0).OpenConnection("", _
                        rdDriverNoPrompt, False, sConnect)
        If rConnection Is Nothing Then
            iLoginFailCount = iLoginFailCount + 1
            If iLoginFailCount = 3 Then
                '/// three strikes and you're outta here!!
                ExecCommand = ddm_NoConnect
                Exit Function
            Else
                Call Wait(20)
```

```
            Call WriteDetailLog("Retrying", 1, _
                "ExecCommand: remote database connection")
            GoTo RetryConnection
        End If
End If

Call WriteDetailLog("Starting", 1, "ExecCommand: stored procedure")

'/// build query string
sQuery = "exec " & Trim(gDatapoint.sProcedure) & " 0, '" & dtDate & "'"
frmStatus.lblStatus(6) = "Exec: " & sQuery
frmStatus.Refresh

'/// set exec start time
'sStart = Time
vStart = Now()

'/// launch async query
Set rResults = rConnection.OpenResultset(sQuery, _
    rdOpenStatic, _
    rdConcurReadOnly, _
    rdAsyncEnable)

'/// wait for resultset
Dim iCount As Long
Do Until rResults.StillExecuting = False
    '/// test exec time to see if we're out of bounds
    '/// also test giAbort to see if the Abort button
    '/// was hit on the status form
    If Abs(DateDiff("n", vStart, Now)) > gDatapoint.iExectime _
            Or giAbort = True Then
        rResults.Cancel
        rResults.Close
        rConnection.Close
        iRows = 0
        If giAbort = True Then
            Call WriteDetailLog("User abort", 1, _
                "ExecCommand: stored procedure")
            ExecCommand = ddm_UserAbort
        Else
            Call WriteDetailLog("Time exceeded", 1, _
                "ExecCommand: stored procedure")
            ExecCommand = ddm_TimeExceeded
        End If
        Exit Function
    End If
    frmStatus.lblStatus(2).Caption = "Status: running " & _
            Format(Now() - vStart, "hh:mm:ss")
    frmStatus.Refresh

    Call Wait(WAIT_TIME)
Loop
Call WriteDetailLog("exec complete", 1, _
                    "ExecCommand: stored procedure")

'/// wait for results
```

```
        rResults.MoveLast
        iRows = rResults.RowCount
        If iRows = 0 Or rResults.rdoColumns.Count = 0 Then
            rResults.Close
            rConnection.Close
            ExecCommand = ddm_NoData
            Call WriteDetailLog("no data", 1, "ExecCommand: resultset")
            Exit Function
        End If
        rResults.MoveFirst

        '/// append results to target table, verify columns
        Call WriteDetailLog("Connecting", 1, "ExecCommand: reporting database")

        sConnect = GetConnect()
        Set rTargetDB = rdoEnvironments(0).OpenConnection("", _
                        rdDriverNoPrompt, False, sConnect)
        sConnect = "select * from " & gDatapoint.sTargetTable
        Set rTarget = rTargetDB.OpenResultset(sConnect, _
                        rdOpenDynamic, rdConcurRowver)

        Call WriteDetailLog("appending rows to " & _
                gDatapoint.sTargetTable, 1, _
                "ExecCommand: reporting database")
        Dim col As rdoColumn
        Dim iColumn As Integer
        iColumn = 0
        Do Until rResults.EOF
            rTarget.AddNew
            rTarget(0) = giLogID
            iColumn = 0
            For Each col In rResults.rdoColumns
                rTarget(iColumn + 1) = col.Value
                iColumn = iColumn + 1
            Next
            rTarget.Update
            rResults.MoveNext
        Loop

        Call WriteDetailLog("closing", 1, "ExecCommand: cleanup")
        rTarget.Close
        rTargetDB.Close
        rResults.Close
        rConnection.Close
        Call WriteDetailLog("done", 1, "ExecCommand: cleanup")
        Exit Function

Err_ExecCommand:
    Call WriteDetailLog(Err & ": " & Error$, 1, "ExecCommand: error trap")
    Resume Next

End Function
```

Now, the preceding code shows a very procedural, non-event driven way of getting the job done. It works and is probably adequate for the task for which it was developed. It's also a bit long and possibly difficult to maintain. A better way to implement the code might be to make the connection, execution, waiting, and retrieval parts of this function separate, something like the following:

```
Option Explicit
'/// scope the connection and resultset
'/// objects to the module level
Private mrConnect As rdoConnection
Private mrResults As rdoResultset
'/// we'll use this in a variation of the sp exec
Private mrStmt As rdoPreparedStatement

Sub ExecCommand(dtDate As Date)
    If OpenConnection = 0 Then
        Call ExecuteSP(dtDate)
        timWait.Enabled = True
    End If
End Sub
```

You've set the source database connection and result set objects to be module-level, addressable by all the necessary routines. Notice that you're enabling a timer after firing up the stored procedure. This timer gives you the least resource-intensive way of waiting for something to complete.

Use the following function to make the source database connection:

```
Function OpenConnection() As Integer
    Dim sConnect        As String
    Dim iLoginFailCount As Integer

    '/// build dsn-less target connection for the
    '/// datapoint we're working on
    sConnect = "DRIVER={SQL Server};"
    sConnect = sConnect & "DATABASE=" & Trim(gDatapoint.sDatabase) & ";"
    sConnect = sConnect & "SERVER=" & Trim(gDatapoint.sServer) & ";"
    sConnect = sConnect & "UID=" & Trim(gDatapoint.sUser) & ";"
    sConnect = sConnect & "PWD=" & Trim(gDatapoint.sPassword) & ";"
    sConnect = sConnect & "DSN=;"

    On Error GoTo Err_OpenConnection

RetryConnection:
    Set mrConnect = rdoEnvironments(0).OpenConnection("", _
                    rdDriverNoPrompt, False, sConnect)
    If mrConnect Is Nothing Then
        iLoginFailCount = iLoginFailCount + 1
        If iLoginFailCount = 6 Then
            '/// retry 6 times before failing
            OpenConnection = ddm_NoConnect
            Exit Function
        Else
            Call Wait(10)
            Call WriteDetailLog("Retrying", 1, _
                "ExecCommand: remote database connection")
            GoTo RetryConnection
        End If
    End If
End If
```

```
        Call WriteDetailLog("Starting", 1, "ExecCommand: stored procedure")
End Function
```

The next function, ExecuteSP, will build and execute the stored procedure call. The variation in the following is simply an extract of what was in the large ExecCommand function:

```
Function ExecuteSP(dtDate As Date) As Integer
    Dim sQuery As String
    '/// build query string
    sQuery = "exec " & Trim(gDatapoint.sProcedure) & " 0, '" & dtDate & "'"
    frmStatus.lblStatus(6) = "Exec: " & sQuery
    frmStatus.Refresh

    '/// launch async query
    Set mrResults = rConnection.OpenResultset(sQuery, _
        rdOpenStatic, _
        rdConcurReadOnly, _
        rdAsyncEnable)
End Function
```

The following variation shows the same thing set up as a prepared statement:

```
Function ExecuteSP(dtDate As Date) As Integer
    Dim sQuery As String
    '/// build query string
    sQuery = " {call ?=" & Trim(gDatapoint.sProcedure) & " (?,?) }"
    frmStatus.lblStatus(6) = "Exec: " & sQuery
    frmStatus.Refresh

    '/// launch async query
    Set mrStmt = mrConnect.CreatePreparedStatement( _
                gDatapoint.sTargetTable, sQuery)
    mrStmt.Parameters(0).Direction = rdParamReturnValue
    mrStmt.Parameters(1).Direction = rdParamInputOutput
    mrStmt.Parameters(2).Direction = rdParamInput

    mrStmt.Parameters(1) = 0
    mrStmt.Parameters(2) = dtDate

    Set mrResults = mrStmt.OpenResultset(Type=:rdOpenStatic, _
        LockType:=rdConcurReadOnly, _
        Options:=rdAsyncEnable)

End Function
```

The Timer event subroutine gets fired at any interval that makes sense for the given application. Because mrResults is a module-level object representing the async query, you can examine the StillExecuting property to see if there are any results to go get. If there aren't, check to see if the elapsed time is out of bounds or if the giAbort flag was set. If you have results, call the routine to retrieve the results into your target database.

```
Sub timWait_Timer()
    Static vStart As Variant
    If IsNull(vStart) Then vStart = Now()
```

```
    If mrResults.StillExecuting Then
        If Abs(DateDiff("n", vStart, Now)) > gDatapoint.iExectime _
            Or giAbort = True Then
              mrResults.Cancel
              mrResults.Close
              mrConnect.Close
              iRows = 0
              If giAbort = True Then
                  Call WriteDetailLog("User abort", 1, _
                      "ExecCommand: stored procedure")
              Else
                  Call WriteDetailLog("Time exceeded", 1, _
                      "ExecCommand: stored procedure")
              End If
              Exit Sub
        End If
        frmStatus.lblStatus(2).Caption = "Status: running " & _
            Format(Now() - vStart, "hh:mm:ss")
        frmStatus.Refresh
    Else
        Call RetrieveResults
    End If
End Sub
```

This is just about the end of the line for this process. The Timer event in the preceding has determined that you now have results to process. The next function validates the results and appends them to the specified target table in the target database.

The .BOF and .EOF properties of the rdoResultset object can be used in tandem to determine if the result set has anything in it.

The way the stored procedures for this project are written, it's possible for them to return no columns, so you need to test for this condition. The rdoColumns.Count property lets you do that nicely.

```
Sub RetrieveResults()
    Dim rTargetDB As rdoConnection
    Dim rTarget As rdoResultset
    Dim col As rdoColumn
    Dim iRows As Integer
    Dim iColumn As Integer
    Dim iReturn As Integer
    Dim sConnect As String
    iReturn = mrResults.Parameters(0)
    If (mrResults.BOF And mrResults.EOF) Or _
            rResults.rdoColumns.Count = 0 Or _
            iReturn <> 0 Then
        rResults.Close
        rConnection.Close
        Call WriteDetailLog("no data", 1, " RetrieveResults: resultset")
        Exit Sub
    End If

    '/// append results to target table, verify columns
```

```
        Call WriteDetailLog("Connecting", 1, _
            "RetrieveResults: reporting database")

    sConnect = GetConnect()
    Set rTargetDB = rdoEnvironments(0).OpenConnection("", _
                    rdDriverNoPrompt, False, sConnect)
    sConnect = "select * from " & gDatapoint.sTargetTable
    Set rTarget = rTargetDB.OpenResultset(sConnect, _
                    rdOpenDynamic, rdConcurRowver)

        Call WriteDetailLog("appending rows to " & _
            gDatapoint.sTargetTable, 1, _
            "RetrieveResults: reporting database")
    iColumn = 0
    Do Until mrResults.EOF
        rTarget.AddNew
        rTarget(0) = giLogID
        iColumn = 0
        '/// loop through the rdoColumns collection
        '/// the output is offset by one to make room
        '/// for the batch ID at column index 0
        For Each col In mrResults.rdoColumns
            rTarget(iColumn + 1) = col.Value
            iColumn = iColumn + 1
        Next
        rTarget.Update
        rResults.MoveNext
    Loop

    Call WriteDetailLog("closing", 1, " RetrieveResults: cleanup")
    rTarget.Close
    rTargetDB.Close
    mrResults.Close
    mrConnect.Close
    Call WriteDetailLog("done", 1, "RetrieveResults: cleanup")
    Exit Function

Err_RetrieveResults:
    Call WriteDetailLog(Err & ": " & Error$, 1, _
        "RetrieveResults: error trap")
    Resume Next

End Sub
```

WriteDetailLog

It's important to log activity throughout a process, especially when a product is under development. WriteDetailLog logs the status at various points along the way. It too uses RDO and a DSN-less connection. It also uses the Open-Write-Close method to minimize the number of simultaneous connections to the server.

```
Sub WriteDetailLog(sStatus As String, _
                iSeverity As Integer, _
                sStage As String)
```

```
    Dim iLoginFailCount As Integer
    Dim bUpdate        As Boolean
    Dim sConnect       As String
    Dim sQuery         As String
    Dim rConnection    As rdoConnection
    Dim rResults       As rdoResultset

    sConnect = GetConnect()

RetryConnection:
    Set rConnection = rdoEnvironments(0).OpenConnection("", _
                    rdDriverNoPrompt, False, sConnect)
    If rConnection Is Nothing Then
        iLoginFailCount = iLoginFailCount + 1
        If iLoginFailCount = 3 Then
            '/// three strikes and you're outta here!!
            Exit Sub
        Else
            Call Wait(20)
            GoTo RetryConnection
        End If
    End If

    sQuery = "select * from ddm_detail_log"
    Set rResults = rConnection.OpenResultset(sQuery, _
                rdOpenDynamic, rdConcurRowver)

    rResults.AddNew
    rResults!i_datapoint_id = gDatapoint.iDatapointID
    rResults!dt_time = Format(Now(), "mm/dd/yy hh:mm:ss")
    If Len(sStatus) > 60 Then sStatus = Left(sStatus, 60)
    rResults!c_status = sStatus
    rResults!i_severity = iSeverity
    If Len(sStage) > 30 Then sStage = Left(sStage, 30)
    rResults!c_stage = sStage
    rResults.Update

    On Error Resume Next

    'frmStatus.Show
    frmStatus.lblStatus(0).Caption = "Last log entry: " & _
                        Format(Now(), "mm/dd/yy hh:mm:ss")
    frmStatus.lblStatus(1).Caption = "Stage: " & sStage
    frmStatus.lblStatus(2).Caption = "Status: " & sStatus
    frmStatus.Refresh

    rResults.Close
    rConnection.Close
    Exit Sub

Err_WriteDetailLog:
    Call ProcessError()
    Resume Next

End Sub
```

WriteSummaryLog

Although you might not need or want to do summary logging like the collection utility did, I thought it useful to include my function for that here. Its purpose is to show me in one line the current status of all jobs. Also, it helps me retrieve data for specific dates when it's time to do reporting. I chose to create the log entry before the job actually started and to update the entry at various stages.

```
Sub WriteSummaryLog(iLogID As Integer, _
                    dtDate As Date, _
                    sStatus As String, _
                    iSeverity As Integer, _
                    iRows As Integer)

    Dim iLoginFailCount As Integer
    Dim bUpdate         As Boolean
    Dim sConnect        As String
    Dim sQuery          As String
    Dim rConnection     As rdoConnection
    Dim rResults        As rdoResultset

    sConnect = GetDashboardConnect()

RetryConnection:
    Set rConnection = rdoEnvironments(0).OpenConnection("", _
                    rdDriverNoPrompt, False, sConnect)
    If rConnection Is Nothing Then
        iLoginFailCount = iLoginFailCount + 1
        If iLoginFailCount = 3 Then
            '/// three strikes and you're outta here!!
            Exit Sub
        Else
            Call Wait(20)
            GoTo RetryConnection
        End If
    End If

    If iLogID <> 0 Then
        bUpdate = True
        sQuery = "select * from ddm_summary_log "
        sQuery = sQuery & "where i_summary_log_id = " & iLogID
    Else
        bUpdate = False
        sQuery = "select * from ddm_summary_log"
    End If
    Set rResults = rConnection.OpenResultset(sQuery, _
                    rdOpenDynamic, rdConcurRowver)

    If bUpdate Then
        rResults.MoveLast
        rResults.Edit
        rResults!dt_complete = Format(Now(), "mm/dd/yy hh:mm:ss")
    Else
        iLogID = GetID("ddm_summary_log", "i_summary_log_id") + 1
        rResults.AddNew
        rResults!i_summary_log_id = iLogID
```

```
                rResults!i_datapoint_id = gDatapoint.iDatapointID
                rResults!dt_start = Format(Now(), "mm/dd/yy hh:mm:ss")
                rResults!dt_GMT = dtDate
            End If

            rResults!i_rows = iRows
            If Len(sStatus) > 60 Then sStatus = Left(sStatus, 60)
            rResults!c_status = sStatus
            rResults!i_severity = iSeverity
            rResults.Update

            rResults.Close
            rConnection.Close
            Exit Sub

Err_WriteSummaryLog:
        Call ProcessError()
        Resume Next

End Sub
```

ProcessError

ProcessError is a short routine to display the most relevant pieces of each member of the rdoErrors collection:

```
Sub ProcessError()
    Dim rError As rdoError
    Dim sError As String
    For Each rError In rdoErrors
        With rError
            sError = sError & .Number & " - "
            sError = sError & .Description & " - "
            sError = sError & .Source & " - "
            sError = sError & .SQLState & vbCrLf
        End With
    Next
    MsgBox sError, vbExclamation, "RDO Error"
End Sub
```

Async Example

The Data Collector utility demonstrates some basic RDO techniques. It also shows how you can begin to take advantage of some of the more interesting capabilities that RDO provides.

To demonstrate the real power of asynchronous queries, you're going to walk through the construction of an MDI client/server application. The RDO Pubs project is on the CD-ROM that comes with this book. It uses the Pubs database that comes with SQL Server.

The RdoServer was constructed with the intent of encapsulating and simplifying RDO and SQL Server asynchronous communications. The VB4 DLL was designed to be called from a 32-bit VB4 MDI application. One of the problems involved in an application where many queries can be executing at once is associating the query result set to the correct MDI child form. This is accomplished through the use of two classes found in the DLL: the RdoServer class and the AsyncClient class. The Client class contains a form property that is assigned immediately after a new instance of the class has been initialized. The client also has a result object that completes the association between form and result set when the async query is finished. A polling mechanism must be established, usually a VB timer control, that calls an RdoServer method to poll through all pending connections and queries for a result set that is ready for retrieval. RdoServer will also accomplish synchronous queries.

One of the requirements for this application is that it enables the user to bring up two or more child windows to perform edits on different parts of the database. Each window has a distinct query to fill a grid. When the user has performed all edits desired, updates are accomplished by means of a menu pick or button. Because some of the queries can be time consuming, you need a method of performing those queries while enabling the user to perform other tasks in the application.

I have built an in-process DLL to perform all RDO asynchronous queries. The server class executes all queries, fetches all results, and manages error processing. All code pertaining to RDO is contained in the DLL. The MDI main form instantiates an RdoServer object.

One of the problems I have faced in previous client/server systems is how to link a VB form with a result set from a query. I used the VB sample code for callbacks to construct an AsyncClient class to accomplish this task. This class contains an rdoResultset object and a copy of the form handle. It also adds itself to an object collection in the DLL upon initialization.

The MDI form is the container and controller for this application. There are several MDI child forms, and each one corresponds to a query or group of queries you want to call and is used to contain the result set of that query. The problem you now need to solve is to match the child form with the appropriate result set from the associated asynchronous query.

AsyncClient **Class**

The AsyncClient class is the "glue" between the RDO result set and the VB form in the application that will use the data in the result set. The class should be instantiated in the Form_Load event of the MDI child form. One critical item of importance in initializing the class is to assign the form property of the class with the hwnd property of the VB form. An example is provided in the following code:

```
Dim foCallBack          As Object
Set foCallBack = New AsyncClientClass
    foCallBack.Form = Me
    foCallBack.Name = gsFormID
```

The last item in the Form_Load event is to make a call to AsyncIO(). This is a subroutine that should be placed in each form that uses the AsyncClient class. The AsyncIO routine is where all RDO calls come and go. When the form needs to make a data request, it is done through this routine by using a call to ExecAsyncFb:

```
Select Case iAction
    Case ACT_OPENRESULT
        bSuccess = goRdoSvr.ExecAsyncFb(oCaller:=foCallBack, _
                                        sBatchSP:=gsSPname, _
                                        sParams:=gsParameters, _
                                        iAction:=ACT_FILLGRID, _
                                        lTimeoutSeconds:=glQryTimeout)

    Case ACT_FILLGRID
    'do something with the data
…
End Select
```

One of the hidden properties of the AsyncClient class is an rdoResultset. The call to ExecAsyncFb initializes this property with a call to the RDO method OpenResultset(…). The result will have a property StillExecuting that will equal TRUE until SQL Server has returned data. Here is where a VB timer comes into play. You need some way to tell when the StillExecuting property turns FALSE. A timer is an easy way to check. Place the timer on the MDI parent with an interval of 500. This will trigger an event to occur every half second. Place a call to the RDO DLL routine, CheckDataReadyS, in the event code for the timer.

The code in CheckDataReadyS polls through all of the rdoConnections, rdoResultsets, and the collection of AsyncClients to check for any result set that is not StillExecuting. If it finds one, it calls the RDOHook method in the AsyncClient class, which in turn calls AsyncIO. The iAction parameter that was placed in the original call to ExecAsyncFb is used in the callback to AsyncIO and is used as an index into the select statement to perform the action desired to process the data returned by the result set.

In this example, Update, Add, and Delete are performed by SQL stored procedures. This places the business rules of the application in the back end. You might call this a "fat server" application because all the logic is kept on the database.

Set up for the result set by creating a prepared statement. If the procedure you want to call has parameters, you add code to handle that here. After you create the prepared statement, open the result set. Notice the use of Options:=rdAsyncEnabled. This tells RDO to give you control immediately.

```
Set Ps = SqlCn.CreatePreparedStatement(sBatchSP, sQuery)

Ps.RowsetSize = 1
Set oResults = Ps.OpenResultset(Type:=rdOpenForwardOnly, _
                                LockType:=rdConcurReadOnly, _
                                Options:=rdAsyncEnable)
```

Timers

Use a timer control to detect the completion of any queries that are running. You can set the interval to whatever seems to make the most sense. In the following example, the `Interval` property is set to `500` to check the completion status every half second. The `Timer` event will call the `AsyncIO()` function to handle the notification retrieval tasks.

```
Private Sub RdoTimer_Timer()
    On Error GoTo RdoTimerErr
    Call goRdoSvr.CheckDataReadyS
    Exit Sub
RdoTimerErr:
    MsgBox Error, vbInformation, "Rdo Timer error"
    Exit Sub
End Sub
```

The following code snippet is from the RDO DLL; it detects query execution status for all async result sets in all connections. If one of the result sets in a given connection is finished executing, the inner `For Each…Next` construct matches the client with the result set through the ODBC statement handle. It then calls the `RDOHook` method of the `AsyncClient` class to send the results back to the client.

```
Dim oConn    As rdoConnection
Dim oRS      As rdoResultset
Dim oClient As Object
On Error GoTo RdoTimerErr
For Each oConn In rdoEnvironments(0).rdoConnections
    For Each oRS In oConn.rdoResultsets
        If Not oRS.StillExecuting Then
            For Each oClient In gcoClients
                If oClient.bActive Then
                    If oRS.hStmt = oClient.hStmt Then
                        'make the callback and exit the routine
                        Call oClient.RDOHook(oClient.iAction)
                        Exit Sub
                    | End If
                End If
            Next oClient
        End If
    Next oRS
Next oConn
```

Adding a Reference in Visual Basic

In order to use the `RdoServer` class, you must add the RdoServer as a reference in the Object Reference dialog box. This is the same dialog box you use to add the RDO reference. To add the DLL as a reference, follow these steps:

1. Choose Tools | References.
2. Scroll down to the bottom of the list.

3. Click on RdoServer.

4. Choose OK.

The `Server` Class

The RdoServer has been unit tested with one server object. Multiple server objects have not been implemented. To begin using the RdoServer, you must declare a variable as an object and set that object by using the following syntax:

```
Test.bas
...
Global goRdoSvr As Object
...

Main.frm
....
'create a link to the Async server
    Set goRdoSvr = CreateObject("RdoServer.RdoSqlClass")
```

The `Client` Class

A subroutine must be placed in each form `Public Sub AsyncIO(iAction as Integer) as Integer` to serve as a callback for the client. When an async query is ready for retrieval, the RdoServer will call a method in the client class `RdoHook` that in turn calls `AsyncIO` on the form. The RdoServer will not function properly without this subroutine.

You can instantiate one or more instances of an `AsyncClientClass`. For code clarity and maintenance, a `Client` class should be created for the initial load from the server and another for updates. For example:

```
Const ACT_REFRESHDATA = 0

Private Sub Form_Load()
Dim oCallBack      As Object
Dim oBatchCallBack As Object

Set oCallBack = New RdoServer.AsyncClientClass
    oCallBack.Form = Me
    oCallBack.Name = "MyFirstCallBack"

Set oBatchCallBack = New RdoServer.AsyncClientClass
    oBatchCallBack.Form = Me
    oBatchCallBack.Name = "MyUpdateCallBack"

    '....get things started
    Call AsyncIO(ACT_REFRESHDATA)
...
End Sub
```

RdoServer **Class**

This section serves as programmer documentation for the RdoServer class. It enumerates all the available methods and properties exposed in the object. Feel free to use it, adapt it, and learn from it.

Methods

Upon initialization, the RdoServer class opens a log file RdoServer.Log. If the file already exists, it is truncated.

ConnectToDBFb **Method (RdoServer)**

The ConnectToDBFb function is offered as a method for testing a login.

Syntax

success= *rdoserver*.ConnectToDBFb()

The ConnectToDBFb method syntax has these parts:

Part	Description
success	A Boolean variable
rdoserver	An object that evaluates to an RdoServer object

Example

```
Dim oRdoSvr     As Object

    'create a link to the Async server
    Set oRdoSvr = CreateObject("RdoServer.RdoSqlClass")

If oRdoSvr.ConnectToDBFb() <> True Then
    MsgBox "Login failure, must exit"
    End
End If
```

Returns

Returns True if successful, and False if an error occurs.

CheckDataReadyS **Method (RdoServer)**

The CheckDataReadyS method iterates through all connections and their result sets searching for an asynchronous result set that is not StillExecuting. Upon finding such a creature, the Client method, RDOHook, is called with the given action (sent in the ExecAsyncFb call).

Syntax

rdoserver. CheckDataReadyS()

The CheckDataReadyS method syntax has these parts:

Part	Description
rdoserver	An object that evaluates to an RdoServer object
Variables Affected:	AsyncClientClass object method RDOHook()

Example

```
'In this example, a timer control named "RdoTimer "
'has been placed on the MDIParent form.

Private Sub RdoTimer_Timer()

    On Error GoTo RdoTimerErr
    Call goRdoSvr.CheckDataReadyS

    Exit Sub

RdoTimerErr:
    MsgBox Error, vbInformation, "Rdo Timer error"
    Exit Sub

End Sub
```

GetSyncTabStringFs **Method (RdoServer)**

The GetSyncTabStringFs method opens a synchronous PreparedStatement from the given sBatchSp and sParameters.

Syntax

rdoserver.GetSyncTabStringFs(*client, name, parameters*)

The `GetSyncTabStringFs` method syntax has these parts:

Part	Description
rdoserver	An object that evaluates to an `RdoServer` object
client	An object that evaluates to an `AsyncClientClass`
name	A string containing the name of a SQL stored procedure
parameters	A string containing the parameters for the stored procedure

Returns

A single tab-delimited string from the result set is returned from this method.

Example

```
Dim sSPname    As String
Dim sParameters As String

sSPname = "bspGetDepartmentAccess"
sParameters = "'C77' , 'A01'

sRet = goRdoSvr.GetSyncTabStringFs(oCaller:=foCallBack, _
                          sBatchSP:=sSPname, _
                          sParams:=sParameters)
```

GetResultSetFi Method (RdoServer)

The `GetResultSetFi` method enables the caller to obtain the result set from an async query.

Syntax

```
rows = rdoserver.GetResultSetFi(caller, _
       results, datastr, [hdrstr], [fielddelimiter], [rowdelimiter])
```

The `GetResultSetFi` method syntax has these parts:

Part	Description
rows	The name of an integer that will hold the number of rows returned
rdoserver	An object that evaluates to an `RdoServer` object
caller	An object that evaluates to an `AsyncClientClass`
datastr	The name of a string that will contain a string with the delimited rows and columns
hdrstr	(Optional) The name of a string that will contain the delimited column header

    fielddelimiter   (Optional) The characters to be used for field delimiters; default is a tab

    rowdelimiter   (Optional) The characters to be used for row delimiters; default is carriage return line feed

Variables Affected

sDataStr is the output container for the result set.

[sHdrStr] can contain the first result set column names.

Returns

The function returns an integer value indicating the number of rows retrieved in the result set.

Example

```
Public Sub AsyncIO(iAction As Integer)
'
' Purpose   : This routine is part of the callback functionality for the
'             RDO Async client.
'
    Dim sResultData As String
    Dim sHeader     As String
    Dim bSuccess    As Boolean

    On Error GoTo AsyncErr

    Select Case iAction
    Case ACT_OPENRESULT
        Screen.MousePointer = vbHourglass
        lblStatus.Visible = True
        lblStatus = "running report..."

        Debug.Print "glQryTimeout", glQryTimeout

        bSuccess = goRdoSvr.ExecAsyncFb(oCaller:=foCallBack, _
                                sBatchSP:=gsSPname, _
                                sParams:=gsParameters, _
                                iAction:=ACT_FILLGRID, _
                                lTimeoutSeconds:=glQryTimeout)
        Screen.MousePointer = vbDefault

    Case ACT_FILLGRID
        Screen.MousePointer = vbHourglass
        lblStatus = "Getting result set..."
        lblStatus.Refresh
        fiTotalRows = goRdoSvr.GetResultSetFi(oCaller:=foCallBack, _
                    oResults:=foCallBack.Result, _
                    sDataStr:=sResultData, _
                    sHdrStr:=sHeader)
```

```
            bSuccess = goRdoSvr.CloseConnectionFb(oCaller:=foCallBack)
            Debug.Print "CloseConnection= ", bSuccess

            'clip the data into the grid
            lblStatus = "Filling grid..."
            lblStatus.Refresh

            ssSheet.MaxRows = fiTotalRows
            ssSheet.MaxCols = goRdoSvr.RSCols
            Call FillSpreadS(sResultData, sHeader, ssSheet, 1, 1, fiTotalRows)

            If fiTotalRows < 0 Then
                MsgBox "Error in filling grid"
            End If
            lblStatus = ""
            lblStatus.Visible = False
            Screen.MousePointer = vbDefault

    End Select

    Exit Sub
AsyncErr:
    Screen.MousePointer = vbDefault
    MsgBox Error, vbInformation, "Database Error"
    Exit Sub

End Sub
```

ExecAsyncFb Method (RdoServer)

The ExecAsyncFb method opens an asynchronous SQL query.

Syntax

success = *rdoserver*.ExecAsyncFb(*oCaller*, *name*, *params*,*iAction*, [*seconds*])

The ExecAsyncFb method syntax has these parts:

Part	Description
rdoserver	An object that evaluates to an RdoServer object
oCaller	An object that evaluates to an AsyncClientClass
name	A string containing the name of a SQL stored procedure
parameters	A string containing the parameters for the stored procedure
iAction	An integer containing a value in the Select Case statement in the AsyncIO subroutine of the caller form
seconds	(Optional) Number of seconds to apply to the query time-out

Variables Affected

The following is a list of `AsyncClient` properties that are affected by `ExecAsyncFb`. `oCaller` is the name of the `AsyncClient` class in this example:

```
oCaller
'    .iAction
'    .hStmt
'    .hDbc
'    .bActive
'    .Result
```

Returns

This function returns `True` if successful; otherwise, it returns `False`.

Example

```
Public Sub AsyncIO(iAction As Integer)
'
' Purpose   : This routine is part of the callback functionality for the
'             RDO Async client.
'
    Dim sResultData As String
    Dim sHeader     As String
    Dim bSuccess    As Boolean

    On Error GoTo AsyncErr

    Select Case iAction
    Case ACT_OPENRESULT
        Screen.MousePointer = vbHourglass
        lblStatus.Visible = True
        lblStatus = "running report..."

        Debug.Print "glQryTimeout", glQryTimeout

        bSuccess = goRdoSvr.ExecAsyncFb(oCaller:=foCallBack, _
                                   sBatchSP:=gsSPname, _
                                   sParams:=gsParameters, _
                                   iAction:=ACT_FILLGRID, _
                                   lTimeoutSeconds:=glQryTimeout)
        Screen.MousePointer = vbDefault

    Case ACT_FILLGRID
        Screen.MousePointer = vbHourglass
        lblStatus = "Getting result set..."
        lblStatus.Refresh
        fiTotalRows = goRdoSvr.GetResultSetFi(oCaller:=foCallBack, _
                      oResults:=foCallBack.Result, _
                      sDataStr:=sResultData, _
                      sHdrStr:=sHeader)
```

```
        bSuccess = goRdoSvr.CloseConnectionFb(oCaller:=foCallBack)
        Debug.Print "CloseConnection= ", bSuccess

        'clip the data into the grid
        lblStatus = "Filling grid..."
        lblStatus.Refresh

        ssSheet.MaxRows = fiTotalRows
        ssSheet.MaxCols = goRdoSvr.RSCols
        Call FillSpreadS(sResultData, sHeader, ssSheet, 1, 1, fiTotalRows)

        If fiTotalRows < 0 Then
            MsgBox "Error in filling grid"
        End If
        lblStatus = ""
        lblStatus.Visible = False
        Screen.MousePointer = vbDefault

    End Select

    Exit Sub
AsyncErr:
    Screen.MousePointer = vbDefault
    MsgBox Error, vbInformation, "Database Error"
    Exit Sub

End Sub
```

ExecBatchUpdateFs Method (RdoServer)

The ExecBatchUpdateFs method opens a synchronous SQL query using an existing connection.

Syntax

data = *rdoserver*. ExecBatchUpdateFs(*caller*, *name*, *parameters*)

The ExecBatchUpdateFs method syntax has these parts:

Part	Description
data	The name of a string that will hold the tab-delimited string for the result set
rdoserver	An object that evaluates to an RdoServer object
name	A string containing the name of the stored procedure
parameters	A string containing the parameters for the stored procedure

Variables Affected

The rdoResultset property of oCaller is initialized by this function.

oCaller.Result

Returns

This function returns a single tab-delimited string containing the result set.

Example

```
Dim sSPname      As String
Dim sParameters  As String
Dim sTemp        As String

sSPname = "bspUpdMarketSeasonFromWork"
sParameters = "12 ,'C77', 'ACT'"
oClient.Name = "MktSeasonCommitWork"

sTemp = goRdoSvr.ExecBatchUpdateFs(oCaller:=oClient, _
                                   sBatchSP:=sSPname, _
                                   sParams:=sParameters)
```

AbortAllRequestsS Method (RdoServer)

The AbortAllRequestsS method cancels all connections associated with the given Form handle. All pending results are canceled, as well.

Syntax

rdoserver. AbortAllRequestsS(hwnd)

The AbortAllRequestsS method syntax has these parts:

Part	Description
rdoserver	An object that evaluates to an RdoServer object
hwnd	An integer containing the handle of the calling form

Example

```
Private Sub cmdCancel_Click()
    Call goRdoSvr.AbortAllRequestsS(Me.hwnd)
    Unload Me
End Sub
```

Read-Only Properties

The following sections describe the read-only properties of the RdoServer class.

ColHeaders() As Integer

ColHeaders() As Integer contains the number of columns in the last result set header. You can use this to initialize a grid that will hold the data from the result set.

ConnectStr() As String

ConnectStr() As String contains the complete connection string used by RDO to connect to the server. The server, database, login, password, and driver name are found in this string.

ResultSets() As Integer

ResultSets() As Integer is the number of result sets in the last query. There are several times when you want a SQL stored procedure to return multiple result sets. One specific use is for reporting. You can execute a stored procedure that returns data for a profit-and-loss report, place the call through the RDO DLL, open an Excel workbook via OLE, and build a spreadsheet to hold the report.

RSCols() As Integer

RSCols() As Integer is a variable indicating the count of the number of columns in the last result set.

RSRows() As Long

RSRows() As Long is a variable indicating the count of the number of rows in the last result set.

Read/Write Properties

The following sections describe the read/write properties of the RdoServer class.

Password(sText As String)

Password(sText As String) is the RDO password used to log in to the server.

Server(sText As String)

Server(sText As String) is the RDO server name for the current login. It is used to build the connection string.

Database(sText As String)

Database(sText As String) is the RDO database name for the current login.

Login(sText As String)

`Login(sText As String)` contains the current RDO login name. The login must be a valid SQL Server login for the server specified in the server property.

DebugMode(bFlag As Boolean)

When the `DebugMode` is set to `True`, the `RdoServer.DLL` places log entries into `RdoServer.log`, which is located in the path of the DLL. Log entries are made at the entry and exit points of all methods in the DLL. There are also several log entries placed during execution of a given method.

AsyncClientClass

This section serves as programmer documentation for the `AsyncClientClass`. It enumerates all the available methods and properties exposed in the object. Feel free to use it, adapt it, and learn from it.

Read-Only Properties

The following sections describe the read-only properties of the `AsyncClientClass`.

bActive() As Boolean

`bActive() As Boolean` is used internally by `RdoServer` to indicate whether the `Client` object is busy with another query; if not, the `Client` object is reused.

hStmt() As Long

`hStmt() As Long` is used internally by `RdoServer` to poll completed result sets.

iAction() As Integer

`iAction() As Integer` is used internally by `RdoServer` when a result set is ready to be retrieved. The integer is passed in the call to `Form.AsyncIO`.

hDbc(lhDbc As Long)

`hDbc(lhDbc As Long)` is used internally by `RdoServer` to poll for connections containing result sets ready for retrieval.

Result() As Object

`Result() As Object` is modified and used by `RdoServer` as the primary conduit for SQL Server IO.

Read/Write Properties

The following sections describe the read/write properties of the `AsyncClientClass`.

Form(oForm As Object)

`Form(oForm As Object)` is initialized by the form containing an instance of an `AsyncClientClass`. This is the handle to the MDI child form in the application.

Example

```
Private Sub Form_Load()
Dim oCallBack as Object

Set oCallBack = New RdoServer.AsyncClientClass
    oCallBack.Form = Me
    oCallBack.Name = "MyCallBack"
...
End Sub
```

Name() As String

`Name() As String` is used by the calling application as a way to distinguish `AsyncClientClass` instances in the RdoServer log file. Each `RdoServer` method will publish entries into the log file containing the Client name as part of the entry.

Example

```
oCallBack.Name = "MyCallBack"
```

Summary

With the advent of RDO, the VB programmer now has the ability to build robust high-performance client/server applications more quickly and easily than ever before. Hopefully, we've shown you some tricks to help you get even more out of RDO and to steer you clear of some potholes we've found in the road.

The best way to get a handle on anything new like this is to get your hands dirty and try some things out. Go ahead and open up the code on the CD-ROM that comes with this book. Experiment with the objects and functions provided. Rework some of them to fit your needs. And, most importantly, have fun!

Becoming Familiar with the 32-Bit ODBC

by Dwayne R. Gifford

In almost every developer's mind are the ideas that using ODBC (open database connectivity) is difficult and that ODBC is of questionable value because it is slow. These two ideas, however, are not true. Using ODBC is almost the fastest way there is to access data on a server. Also, as you will see in this chapter, ODBC is not difficult to use.

This chapter presents the basics of using ODBC. One chapter can't possibly cover all aspects of ODBC, but this chapter does give you the footing you'll need to carry on further with ODBC development.

Installing and Configuring Data Sources

One way to make use of ODBC is to use a predefined data source. To set up a data source, you have three different possible methods: first, through the ODBC Administrator; second, programmatically; and third, through a setup program.

Using ODBC Administrator

The first step in using the ODBC Administrator is to open the Control Panel, as shown in Figure 25.1.

Figure 25.1.
The Control Panel.

In the Control Panel, double-click on the ODBC icon. Doing so should bring up the Data Sources dialog box shown in Figure 25.2, which is a view of all available 32-bit data sources.

Here you can add a new data source, edit a data source, delete a data source, or set ODBC default options; you can also add, edit, or delete system data sources.

Figure 25.2.
The Data Sources
dialog box.

Adding Data Sources

Whether you are adding a system data source or just a data source, you will need to follow the same four steps.

1. Click the Add button. This brings you to the Add Data Source dialog box shown in Figure 25.3.

Figure 25.3.
The Add Data Source
dialog box.

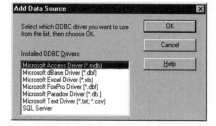

2. Select the ODBC driver on which you want the data source to be based.
3. Fill in the required information for the type of ODBC driver you selected in step 2. The example shown in Figure 25.4 is for ODBC SQL Server. With the SQL Server setup, you are required to fill in the Data Source Name box. This is how you reference the driver from a program. The Description field is simply the description for this data source you are adding.

    Next, fill in the Server box, which is a combo box. You can either type in the name of the SQL Server or drop down the list and select the server from the list. If you are using a local copy of SQL Server, select (local). Normally the network address points to the Data Management system from which the driver will retrieve the data. The Network Library field is the name of the network library DLL that the SQL Server driver will use to communicate with the network software. The Network Address and Network Library boxes for Microsoft SQL Server can be left as (Default). You can set four other options; to do so, click the Options button. The four options are these: Server Name, Language Name, Generate Stored Procedures for Prepared Statements, and Convert OEM to ANSI Characters.

4. Finally, accept the information you have entered. To do so, click the OK button.

Each driver's data source Setup dialog box is different. In this example, I covered the ODBC SQL Server Setup because this is the driver shipped with Visual Basic 4.0.

Figure 25.4.
The ODBC SQL Server Setup dialog box.

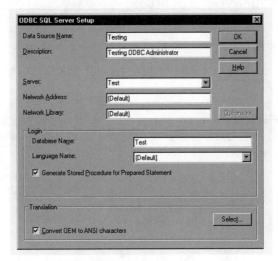

Notice that now, if you check the Data Sources dialog box again, you see the newly added data source. Also notice that it shows the data source name, not the description.

Editing Data Sources

To edit a data source, you need to select the data source and then click the Setup button. This brings you back to the ODBC SQL Server Setup dialog box. You can also use the Setup button to rename a data source. To rename the data source, change information in the Data Source Name box.

Deleting Data Sources

To delete a data source, select the one that you wish to delete and click the Delete button. The Delete Data Source Confirmation dialog box appears to confirm that you want to delete the data source. To accept the deletion of the currently selected data source, click the Yes button. Otherwise, click the No button.

Setting Up a Data Source Programmatically

To set up a data source programmatically, you first must know whether the data source exists or not. To find out, you can use the SQLDataSources API. The following is the declaration for the API:

```
Declare Function SQLDataSources Lib "odbc32.dll" (ByVal hEnv&,
➥ByVal fDirection%, ByVal szDSN$, ByVal cbDSNMax%, pcbDSN%,
➥ByVal szDescription$, ByVal cbDescriptionMax%,
➥pcbDescription%) As Integer
```

Eight parameters are expected when the SQLDataSources API is used. One is hEnv&, which is set when you call SQLAllocEnv. Another is fDirection, which can be set to one of the constants shown in Table 25.1.

Table 25.1. List of available constants for fDirection.

Value	Constants
1	SQL_FETCH_NEXT
2	SQL_FETCH_FIRST
3	SQL_FETCH_LAST
4	SQL_FETCH_PRIOR
5	SQL_FETCH_ABSOLUTE
6	SQL_FETCH_RELATIVE
8	SQL_FETCH_BOOKMARK

Another parameter is szDSN; this is set to nothing on the first call and to the DSN value from the previous call. You check the szDSN value to locate the data source that you are checking for.

The cbDSNMax parameter is set to the maximum size that can be returned into the variable szDSN. The pcbDSN parameter is the current size of szDSN. The szDescription variable will be set to the description for the currently found szDSN. The cbDescriptionMax parameter is the maximum size that can be returned to szDescription. The pcbDescription parameter is the current length of szDescription.

If you find that the data source does not exist, the next step is to call SQLConfigureDataSource. This API is different from all the other APIs I will discuss because it is a member of odbcinst.dll, not part of ODBC32.DLL.

> The ODBCINST.DLL does not always get installed when you set up Visual Basic 4.0. If it does not, look in ?:\VB\SYSTEM for it, where ? is equal to the location from which you installed VB.

The following line of code is the required declaration for SQLConfigDataSource:

```
Declare Function SQLConfigDataSource Lib "odbcinst.dll" (ByVal hwnd As Long,
➥ByVal fRequest%, ByVal szDriver$, ByVal szAttrib$) As Integer
```

The following code sample shows you how to use the SQLDataSources and the SQLConfigureDataSource APIs:

```
'Allocate environment handle
    intReturn = SQLAllocEnv(mlngHenv)

    If intReturn <> SQL_SUCCESS Then
        MsgBox "Unable to allocate environment"
        End
    End If

    intReturn = SQLDataSources(mlngHenv, SQL_FETCH_FIRST, strDSN, 32,
    ➥intDSNLength, strDesc, 255, intDescLength)

    Do While intReturn = SQL_SUCCESS
        If strDSN = "Chapter26" Then
            cmdMain(0).Caption = "Modify Data Source"
            cmdMain(0).Enabled = True
            cmdMain(1).Enabled = True
            Exit Sub
        End If
        intReturn = SQLDataSources(mlngHenv, SQL_FETCH_NEXT, strDSN, 32,
        ➥intDSNLength, strDesc, 255, intDescLength)
    Loop
    cmdMain(0).Caption = "Add Data Source"
    cmdMain(0).Enabled = True
```

The first part of the sample code is to allocate the SQL environment. Then the code goes through each DSN trying to locate a DSN named Chapter26. If it locates Chapter26, it then sets up the form to modify the data source; otherwise, it sets up the form for adding a new data source. To see all the code, refer to the sample called dsSample.vbp on the book's companion CD-ROM.

One parameter for SQLConfigDataSource is hwnd. The fRequest variable can be set to any of the values shown in Table 25.2.

Table 25.2. List of available constants for fRequest.

Constants	Description
ODBC_ADD_DSN	Used to add a new DSN
ODBC_CONFIG_DSN	Used to modify an already existing DSN
ODBC_REMOVE_DSN	Used to remove an already existing DSN

The next parameter is szDriver, which must be set to the name of the driver minus its extension. For example, szDriver would be set to sqlsrv32. The last parameter is szAttrib, which must be set to the values that you wish to have set for the new DSN.

When Installing the Application

If you are using Acme Setup that comes with the Access 95 SDK kit, you need to make three line changes to the setup.stf. The first change is to add the following:

```
ODBCSQL_Config          ConfigureODBCDriver    "SQL Server", ";",
➥"DSN=Testing;Description=Testing ODBC Config;Server=Test;OemToAnsi=No;
➥FastConnectOption=Yes;UseProcForPrepare=No;Database=Testing;
➥Filetype =SQL;;"
```

This code is made up of three parts. The first goes into column C and has the value ODBCSQL_Config. Next, you need to add ConfigureODBCDriver in column E. The last part is made up of three pieces. The first is to identify what driver you are configuring. The second is the separator value used to separate the key values in the data string. The third is the actual Data Source information. Each value has an identification name, followed by an equal sign and separated by the value that is in the separator field. Also, in the A column, you need to give the line a unique ID number.

You need to look for the following value: Maximum Object ID. This will be in column A and roughly in row 16. The Column present value will be set to the current maximum ID number. So, if you add five items and you increase them by the value 5, and if the old number was 100, then the new value will be set to the ID of the last item you just added, or in this case 125.

Next, you need to look for the following section: ==== Install ODBC SQL Server ====. Under this you will see the ODBCSQL_File that identifies all the lines that are to be run for this group. Here you must append the new IDs that you used for your ODBCSQL_Config line.

After you have made these changes, the data source will be added for you when the user installs the program.

Which APIs You Will Need

Because I am covering the basics of the 32-bit ODBC, I will go over only the basic APIs that will be required to make a connection to an ODBC data source, retrieve data, and then disconnect from the data source. To do this, you must be familiar with the following SQL APIs:

- SQLAllocEnv
- SQLAllocConnect
- SQLDriverConnect
- SQLAllocStmt
- SQLExecDirect
- SQLFetch
- SQLGetData

■ SQLFreeStmt

■ SQLDisconnect

■ SQLFreeConnect

■ SQLFreeEnv

In addition, I will cover two other APIs: SQLNumResultCols and SQLError.

SQLAllocEnv

The first call that must come before all other calls is SQLAllocEnv. This API takes a single parameter of a long variable. If it is successful in setting the Env variable, SQL_Success is returned. The following code is the required declaration for SQLAllocEnv:

```
Declare Function SQLAllocEnv Lib "odbc32.dll" (Env As Long) As Integer
```

This API call also initializes the ODBC interface.

SQLAllocConnect

After the environment variable has been set, you must call SQLAllocConnect. The declaration for SQLAllocConnect is as follows:

```
Declare Function SQLAllocConnect Lib "odbc32.dll"
➥(ByVal Env As Long, hdbc As Long) As Integer
```

The API takes the Env variable set by SQLAllocEnv as its first parameter. If the call to SQLAllocEnv is successful, it will allocate memory for the connection information and will be pointed to by the hdbc variable. If SQL_Success is not returned from the call, you must call SQLError to find out what error occurred.

SQLDriverConnect

After the handle variable has been set, it is time to actually make the connection. To do this, you can use either SQLConnect or SQLDriverConnect. In this case, I am using SQLDriverConnect because it accepts information other than DSN (Data Source Name), user ID, and password. The following is the connection string used to declare SQLDriverConnect:

```
Declare Function SQLDriverConnect Lib "odbc32.dll" (ByVal hdbc&, ByVal hwnd%,
➥ByVal szCSIn$, ByVal cbCSIn%, ByVal szCSOut$, ByVal cbCSMax%,
➥cbCSOut%, ByVal fDrvrComp%) As Integer
```

A sample call to SQLDriverConnect is as follows:

```
Connect$ = "DSN=" & strServer$ & ";UID=" & strUser$ & ";
➥PWD=" & strPassword$ & ";WSID=" & gstrUser$ & ";
➥APP=" & strApplication & ";DATABASE=" & APP_DATABASENAME
```

```
ConnectOut$ = Space(255)

intReturn = SQLDriverConnect(pHdbc, 0, Connect$, Len(Connect$), ConnectOut$,
➡Len(ConnectOut$), cbOut%, SQL_DRIVER_NOPROMPT)
```

Notice that the Connect$ variable is set to a full DSN string, including, in this case, a few extra options. Table 25.3 shows you what options are available for this string.

Table 25.3. List of available options for connection string.

Constants	Description
DSN	The data source that you want your application to reference for its connection.
DRIVER	The actual name of the driver without its extension. This is not required if you are using DSN.
SERVER	The actual name of the SQL Server.
UID	The user's login ID.
PWD	The password for the current user login ID.
*APP	The application name.
*WSID	Workstation ID—this is equivalent to the HostName used in SQL Server. If you do not include this option in the connect string, WSID will be set to the machine name.
*DATABASE	The database name (optional if the database is set in the DSN or your user is a member of only one database on the server).
*LANGUAGE	The national language.

The * is not part of the constants listed in the table; it is used to identify optional constants. Many times, it is difficult for the DBA (Database Administrator) for an application to know who is actually using the database. The way around this difficulty is to set the WSID equal to the user's name instead of letting it default to the machine's name.

If the connection was made successfully, the Connect string is copied over to the Connection Out string. The cbOut% variable is set to the length of the Connection Out string if the call was successful. The last parameter for SQLDriverConnect is fDrvrComp, which can be set to any of the values shown in Table 25.4.

Table 25.4. List of available values for fDrvrComp.

Constants	Value	Description
SQL_DRIVER_NOPROMPT	0	If the connection string is complete enough to make the connection, then the connection is made; otherwise, SQL_Error is returned.
SQL_DRIVER_COMPLETE	1	If any information is incorrect or inaccurate, the user is prompted.
SQL_DRIVER_PROMPT	2	The user is first prompted for the DSN the user wishes to use; then the user is prompted for the login ID and password. Figure 25.5 shows the DSN dialog box. Figure 25.6 shows the Login ID prompt.
SQL_DRIVER_COMPLETE_REQUIRED	3	This is the same as SQL_DRIVER_COMPLETE except that the unnecessary information is disabled from the user.

Figure 25.5.
The SQL Data Sources dialog box.

Figure 25.6.
The SQL Server Login dialog box.

If everything goes smoothly with this API call, SQL_Success will be returned.

You can also use SQLConnect instead of SQLDriverConnect to make your connection. The difference is that SQLConnect only takes DSN, user ID, and password. For more information on SQLConnect, refer to *Teach Yourself ODBC Programming in 21 Days*, from Sams Publishing, ISBN 0-672-30609-3.

SQLAllocStmt

This API sets the statement variable to a memory location for the statement information to be held, and SQLAllocStmt associates this information to the hdbc connection information. The hdbc memory location was set when the call to SQLAllocConnect was called. The following is the required declaration for SQLAllocStmt:

```
Declare Function SQLAllocStmt Lib "odbc32.dll" (ByVal hdbc As Long,
➥hStmt As Long) As Integer
```

After the memory location for the statement variable has been set, you are free to go up against the database at your pleasure. You can retrieve, insert, delete, and add at will.

SQLExecDirect

After you have allocated the SQL statement, you can execute the SQL statement. You can do this in the form of either a stored procedure or a SQL statement. The call will return either a SQL_Error or SQL_Success_with_Info upon completion. The statement is the declaration for SQLExecDirect.

```
Declare Function SQLExecDirect Lib "odbc32.dll" (ByVal hStmt As Long,
➥ByVal sqlString As String, ByVal sqlstrlen As Long) As Integer
```

For more information on using SQL statements or stored procedures, see the corresponding sections later in this chapter. The hStmt value is the value that was set when SQLAllocStmt was called. SqlString is the SQL statement or stored procedure name. The sqlstrlen is the actual length of the sqlString variable.

SQLFetch

After the SQL statement has been called, you retrieve the data. To do this, you need to call SQLFetch. This statement has one parameter, hStmt, the same value again set by SQLAllocStmt. The SQLFetch statement is declared as follows:

```
Declare Function SQLFetch Lib "odbc32.dll" (ByVal hStmt As Long) As Integer
```

The SQLFetch statement returns one row of data at a time. To retrieve each column of data after you have received the row of data, you need to call SQLGetData, stepping through the number of columns. When you are at the end of the columns, another call needs to be made to SQLFetch. When there are no more rows of data to be returned, SQL_NO_DATA_FOUND is returned.

SQLGetData

After calling SQLFetch, it is time to retrieve each column of data that must be returned. To do this, you need to call SQLGetData. The declaration for SQLGetData is as follows:

```
Declare Function SQLGetData Lib "odbc32.dll" (ByVal hStmt As Long,
➥ByVal Col As Integer, ByVal wConvType As Integer,
➥ByVal lpbBuf As String, ByVal BufLen As Long, lpcBOut As Long) As Integer
```

The parameter is hStmt, again set by the call to SQLAllocStmt. The Col value is the column data that you wish to retrieve. If there is only one column of data to be returned, this value must be set to 1. The wConvType can be set to any of the values shown in Table 25.5.

Table 25.5. List of available values for wConvType.

Value	Constants
1	SQL_C_CHAR
4	SQL_C_LONG
5	SQL_C_SHORT
7	SQL_C_FLOAT
8	SQL_C_DOUBLE

In my experience, I have always used SQL_C_CHAR and done my own conversion of the data. The lpbBuf parameter is the spot that will be used to save the data brought back. The next parameter is BufLen, which is set to the maximum size of data that this column can return to you. The lpcBOut parameter is set by the API to be equal to the size of the data being returned. If your SQL statement is returning more than one column of data, you will need to make a call to SQLNumResultCols before your call to SQLFetch. The SQLNumResultCols is covered later in this chapter. If there was a problem in making this call, a SQL_Error is returned; otherwise, SQL_SUCCESS or SQL_SUCCESS_WITH_INFO will be returned.

SQLFreeStmt

After you have retrieved all the data and received a SQL_NO_DATA_FOUND when you called SQLFetch, it is time to begin freeing up all the variables required to get the data back from ODBC. The first call is to SQLFreeStmt. The declaration is as follows:

```
Declare Function SQLFreeStmt Lib "odbc32.dll" (ByVal hStmt As Long,
➥ByVal EndOption As Integer) As Integer
```

SQLFetch only takes one parameter, the hStmt that was set by SQLAllocStmt. If there was a problem in making this call, a SQL_Error is returned; otherwise, SQL_SUCCESS or SQL_SUCCESS_WITH_INFO is returned.

SQLDisconnect

After you have called SQLFreeStmt, the next call is to Disconnect; to disconnect, you need to call OQLDisconnect. This call disconnects the connection to the database. The declaration is as follows:

```
Declare Function SQLDisconnect Lib "odbc32.dll" (ByVal hdbc As Long) As Integer
```

SQLDisconnect takes only one parameter, hdbc, which was set by SQLAllocConnect. If there was a problem in making this call, a SQL_Error is returned; otherwise, SQL_SUCCESS or SQL_SUCCESS_WITH_INFO is returned.

SQLFreeConnect

The next call is to SQLFreeConnect. Again, it takes hdbc, which was set by SQLAllocConnect. This time the call frees the memory space that the variable was using. The declaration for the call is as follows:

```
Declare Function SQLFreeConnect Lib "odbc32.dll"
➡(ByVal hdbc As Long) As Integer
```

If there was a problem in making this call, a SQL_Error is returned. Otherwise, SQL_SUCCESS or SQL_SUCCESS_WITH_INFO is returned.

SQLFreeEnv

The last call required to finish off the retrieval of data from an ODBC source is to call SQLFreeEnv. This takes only one parameter, Env, which was set by the call to SQLAllocEnv. The declaration is as follows:

```
Declare Function SQLFreeEnv Lib "odbc32.dll" (ByVal Env As Long) As Integer
```

If there was a problem in making this call, a SQL_Error is returned; otherwise, SQL_SUCCESS or SQL_SUCCESS_WITH_INFO is returned.

SQLNumResultCols

Because you probably will be returning more than one column of data per SQL statement, it is wise for you to know SQLNumResultCols. This call lets you know how many columns you can expect to retrieve. The declaration for SQLNumResultCols is as follows:

```
Declare Function SQLNumResultCols Lib "odbc32.dll" (ByVal hStmt As Long,
➡NumCols As Integer) As Integer
```

If there was a problem in making this call, a SQL_Error is returned. Otherwise, SQL_SUCCESS or SQL_SUCCESS_WITH_INFO is returned.

SQLError

SQLError can be a useful call if you are receiving errors other than the ones you might expect your SQL statements or stored procedures to return. The declaration for SQLError is as follows:

```
Declare Function SQLError Lib "odbc32.dll" (ByVal Env As Long,
➥ByVal hdbc As Long, ByVal hStmt As Long, ByVal SQLSTATE As String,
➥NativeError As Long, ByVal Buffer As String, ByVal BufLen As Integer,
➥OutLen As Integer) As Integer
```

It takes the several parameters, including Env, which was set by SQLAllocEnv, and hdbc, which was set by SQLAllocConnect. The hStmt is the variable set when you called SQLAllocStmt. SQLState is a null terminated, five-character string that will be returned by the call. NativeError is specific to the data source. The buffer parameter is what the API will return to you. The BufLen is a value set to the maximum possible size that can be returned in Buffer. The OutLen is the length of the message that came back in the buffer.

Remember that each one of these calls returns a status of its call back to you. If this status is not SQL_SUCCESS, you know that you ran into an error. You must decide how to react to the situation. Remember that if you are using raise errors in your SQL code, the Status value will be equal to this value. One of the most important parts of programming ODBC is setting up the error handling routine.

Using SQL Statements or Stored Procedures

When you are using Microsoft SQL Server drivers, you can use either dynamic SQL or stored procedures. What I mean by *dynamic SQL* is hard code SQL in the Visual Basic executable. This is a support person's nightmare; to fix anything wrong with the SQL, the support person must release a new executable. But what if the executable just called a stored procedure? Then the support person could make the change in the stored procedure, and all users are fixed at once.

If you want to use transactions with your SQL statements, you need to learn and implement SQLTransact. What if you were using stored procedures? You would implement the transaction in the stored procedure. I will not cover SQLTransact in this chapter. For details on how to use it, refer to *Teach Yourself ODBC Programming in 21 Days* from Sams Publishing or *ODBC 2.0 Programmer's Reference and SDK Guide* by Microsoft Press.

To learn SQL, I suggest that you review the Microsoft SQL Server Manuals.

To make a call to a stored procedure, you need to do the following: Build a string that has the stored procedure name, followed by its parameters. Let's say we are calling a stored procedure that retrieves all the customers whom a salesperson looks after. Here is the stored procedure:

```
create proc sCustomers
    @pSalesPerson    varchar(40)
as
    Set NoCount ON
    select   CustomerName
    from     Customer
    where    SalesPersons = @pSalesPerson
go
```

Notice that the stored procedure takes one parameter, SalesPerson. To call this stored procedure, you need to make sqlString equal to sCustomers 'Some SalesGuy'. Then use this as the sqlString when you call SQLExecDirect. If all goes well, you can carry on with the rest of the SQL API calls and retrieve the data as requested.

Summary

This chapter showed you how to set up a DSN using ODBC Administrator, through a setup program, and programmatically. This chapter went through the basic APIs required to connect, return data, and disconnect from an ODBC data source. This chapter used Microsoft SQL Server as the example because it is the driver that comes with Visual Basic 4.0.

Comparing Data-Access Methods

by Christopher Rotberg

Welcome to the chapter on data-access methods. In this chapter, I introduce the various methods of data access and give you enough information to make the appropriate choice for your needs. Choosing a data-access method is never an easy task, so don't worry if you are having a difficult time figuring out what to use. Professional developers often consult with data specialists before they start to design their applications. You must do a lot of analysis before you can make an intelligent decision. You have to answer many questions. Is the data going to be available locally on your machine or on a server? Does the data need to be updated, or is a snapshot sufficient? How much processing is required to convert the raw data into its final form? How many records are you processing and how many people need to use the data? The list goes on and on.

Only after you answer these questions can you make an intelligent choice. This chapter can help you with those decisions by providing some insight into the functionality of the data methods available to you in Visual Basic.

Looking at the Available Methods

There are many data-access methods and many ways of using them individually or combined. Some methods, such as Data Access Object (DAO), are geared toward local databases; others, such as SQL Server, are designed for server-based data. Each database you use will have its own means of access; most are proprietary to that database. DAO works on Microsoft Access databases, whereas Paradox and dBASE have their own methods. Because this book is about Visual Basic, you only need to focus here on the data-access methods available to Visual Basic.

Looking at the Methods that Ship with Visual Basic 4.0

Visual Basic 4.0 ships with two distinct data-access objects. I refer to these as *objects* because that is what they are: the *Data Access Object* (DAO) and *Remote Data Object* (RDO). These objects are not the databases or record sets, but the means of accessing the data. They provide the interface to the Microsoft Jet Engine and the SQL Server Engine. The first method, which works only on Microsoft Access databases, is DAO.

DAO has been around since version 2.0 of Visual Basic, but it has been enhanced for Visual Basic 4.0. RDO is brand-new and currently available only for Visual Basic 4.0. It is designed to manage data on remote servers. Both of these methods are OLE Automation servers that use properties and methods to access the data. Each has an accompanying data control that binds the data object layer: for DAO, it's the Data control, and for RDO, it's the Remote Data control (RDC).

Visual Basic 4.0 also can use *open database connectivity* (ODBC) to access data. ODBC is a dynamic link library (DLL) that uses Windows API calls to handle data access. You can use it to access multiple types of information (such as Microsoft Access or SQL Server), and it provides fast data-transfer rates. It is also much more difficult to use than DAO or RDO, because DAO and RDO provide a layer on top of ODBC to shield the user from the intricacies of ODBC. Because DAO and RDO both use the ODBC layer to access their data, the user does not have to know any of the API calls that ODBC is using. Unfortunately, this layer of shielding reduces the rate at which the data is transferred, because the translation is being performed for you in the background.

A fourth option available to you is *DB-Library*. This is a library of SQL API calls that operate specifically for SQL Server. The Visual Basic application communicates with these APIs through a VBX control called VBSQL (Visual Basic Library for SQL Server). You place this VBX control on a form and use its commands to send messages to the SQL API. Although this method is fast, it requires much more coding. This method does not use the ODBC layer.

Examining the Differences Between the Data-Access Methods

A major difference between the different data-access methods is the speed at which they operate and the amount of programming required to achieve that speed. The DAO and RDO objects require significantly less time to program than those of ODBC or DB-Library. This is because DAO and RDO operate on a much simpler level, shielding the user from the low-level API calls. Unfortunately, the less you have to deal with usually means the more the computer has to do automatically, and that takes time. Depending on the volume of data you have to process, the reduced transfer rates still can outweigh the amount of time it takes to program the application using ODBC or DB-Library. The following table shows each method and the amount of programming effort that goes into it. The table assumes that the user is accessing remote data on server.

Access Method	Speed 1=slower 3=faster	Programming Effort 1=least 3=most
DAO	1	1
RDO	2 (using indexes)	1
DB-Library	2	2
ODBC	3	3

Another important factor involves where the data resides. DAO is great for local databases because it goes directly to the Microsoft Jet Engine and does not have to deal with the ODBC layer. RDO also can talk to an Access database, but it first must go through DAO to accomplish its tasks. RDO therefore would not be a very good choice for accessing local data. There is a level of indirection involved because RDO does not know the Jet Engine as well as DAO does. On the other hand, if you are accessing SQL Server, DAO has to go through its layers and ODBC's layers to get to the data—too much redundancy. RDO would be a better choice because it has a direct route. For best performance, choose the right method for the right database!

RDO is a thin layer around the ODBC, while DAO has to go through the Jet Engine to get to ODBC.

Looking at the Similarities Between the Data-Access Methods

The similarities between the data-access methods can be summarized in one easy phrase: API-level calls versus non-API-level calls. Both ODBC and DB-Library involve using API-level calls. They require much more coding than RDO or DAO and, therefore, a bigger investment in time. Unless you have specific needs or you already have a significant investment in code, DAO and RDO are the way to go. Because DAO is a big part of Visual Basic and RDO undoubtedly will become more important, this chapter focuses on the similarities between DAO and RDO.

I want to concentrate on this subject because I think many people will try RDO because it feels very much like DAO. A programmer will be more comfortable moving to remote data access from DAO than messing with the ODBC interface. One of the greatest benefits of DAO and RDO is their similar programming interfaces; RDO is really quite similar to DAO except for a few variations in commands. Because DAO and RDO already are covered in depth in other chapters of this book, I will only highlight some of the terminology as it applies to the two objects. Table 26.1 lists the RDO equivalents to DAO.

Table 26.1. RDO and DAO object equivalents.

DAO Object	RDO Object
DBEngine	rdoEngine
Workspace	rdoEnvironment
Database	rdoConnection
Recordset	rdoResultset
Dynaset-type Recordset	Keyset-type rdoResultset
Snapshot-type Recordset	Static-type rdoResultset
Not implemented (No DAO equivalent)	Dynamic-type rdoResultset
Table-type Recordset	Not implemented (No RDO equivalent)

DAO Object	RDO Object
Not implemented	Forward-only type rdoResultset
	(No Jet equivalent)
SnapShot-type Recordset	(No RDO equivalent)
Error	rdoError
Field	rdoColumn
QueryDef	rdoPreparedStatement
TableDef	rdoTable
Parameter	rdoParameter
Record	row
Field	column

Aside from the differences in context, these two objects can be manipulated in a similar manner. Each method returns a record set that can be searched and updated. You can think of an rdoResultSet as a DAO Recordset. The only real difference between using DAO and RDO is the name of the objects. You still use MoveNext and MoveLast in both objects. You do not have to learn a new interface in order to take advantage of RDO.

Listing 26.1 shows some code examples.

Listing 26.1. Accessing data from the Authors table via DAO.

```
Private Sub Command1_Click()
    'DAO recordset example

    Dim MyDB As Database, Mydata As Recordset
    Dim I As Integer, MyDataCount As Integer

    Set MyDB = Workspaces(0).OpenDatabase("biblio.MDB")
    Set MyData = MyDB.OpenRecordset("Authors",dbOpenSnapshot)
    MyData.MoveLast
    MyDataCount = MyData.RecordCount

    MyData.MoveFirst
    For I = 0 To MyDataCount - 1
        lstAuthors.AddItem MyData.Fields!Author.Value
        MyData.MoveNext
    Next I

    MyData.Close
    MyDB.Close

End Sub
```

In this example, I open the Authors table and move through the record set. Each pass through the record set yields an author, and this author is then added to a list box. Listing 26.2 shows the code if I used RDO to retrieve the authors' last names from the Authors table on SQL Server.

Listing 26.2. Accessing data from the Authors table via RDO.

```
Private Sub Command5_Click()
'RDO Example

  Dim lRecCount As Long, sConnect As String
  Dim rdoParameterSet As rdoResultset, I As Long
  Dim rdoConnectSQL As rdoConnection

  rdoEnvironments(0).CursorDriver = rdUseOdbc
  sConnect = "DSN=PubSQL;UID=sa;PWD="
  rdoEnvironments(0).LoginTimeout = 0
  Set rdoConnectSQL = rdoEnvironments(0).OpenConnection
  ➥("", False, False, sConnect)

  Set rdoParameterSet = rdoConnectSQL.OpenResultset
  ➥("Select * from authors", rdOpenStatic)
**************************************************
rdoParameterSet.MoveLast
lRecCount=rdoParameterSet.RowCount


**************************************************

  rdoParameterSet.MoveFirst
  For I = 0 To lRecCount - 1
      lstAuthors.AddItem rdoParameterSet.rdoColumns!au_lname.Value
      rdoParameterSet.MoveNext
  Next I

  'Close things down
  rdoParameterSet.Close
  rdoConnectSQL.Close

End Sub
```

Notice that the logic of the code is identical to Listing 26.2; except for a few variances, the code is almost identical. The database is opened differently, a `Recordset` is called a `Resultset`, `RecordCount` becomes `RowCount`, and instead of using `Fields` to access the author, I used `rdoColumns` to get the author's last name. If you know DAO, you should not have a problem moving to RDO.

Deciding Which Method Is Better for Accessing Data on Your Local Hard Drive

Unless you happen to have a SQL Server database running on your local machine, DAO is the right choice for local data access. Most people who have data on a user's machine store that data in a Microsoft Access database or a flat file. An application that is only reading and writing data to a local database does not need to use ODBC; only communication with the Microsoft Jet Engine is needed. Using RDO in this case is not wise, because it has to go through all the DAO layers and its own layers to read the data. You can use ODBC but, again, there is a significant coding increase and only a marginal (if any) increase in data-access time. One of the only real benefits you gain is the level of indirection that ODBC provides.

Indirection refers to the capability to change the data source without having to update the application. The application is set up to read a certain ODBC data source name (DSN), it looks for that name and reads the data source associated with it. It is very easy to change the data source when the application is running because the application is still pointing to the correct ODBC DSN connection and using the database it specifies.

> If you choose to use ODBC, you will have to make sure that the user has ODBC installed on his or her system. If ODBC is not present, it is your application's responsibility to warn the user or install it automatically.
>
> You could perform a pre-installation check of the user's hard drive for some of the files that should be present for the ODBC to work. Look for the specific drivers that are required such as Access or SQL Server, and look for the ODBC-specific DLLs.

Deciding Which Method Is Better for Accessing Data on the Server

Deciding which method is better for accessing server data is not as clear-cut as accessing data on a local machine. If you where to ask five people which method is better, you probably would get five different answers. Most would agree that using ODBC and DB-Library provide the fastest data access. Unfortunately, both these methods also require the most time to code. The decision to use ODBC or DB-Library involves personal preference and the number of SQL-specific functions that need to be performed. DB-Library provides extensive control over SQL Server and Oracle databases. Some developers swear by ODBC and DB-Library for everything. There is a new breed of developers, however, singing the praises of RDO. Although RDO seems simplistic in its approach, it does provide surprising results. RDO is the newest data-access approach of the four (ODBC, DB-Library, RDO, and DAO).

Remote data object (RDO) is brand-new and available only for Visual Basic 4.0. RDO was introduced as a way to avoid the complex and time-consuming process of accessing data via ODBC or DB-Library. It consists of a thin layer around the ODBC layer and the driver manager that handles connections to the server. RDO is beneficial because it does not use the Jet Engine and it provides a small memory footprint. It has been fine-tuned for SQL Server 6.0 and can use server-side cursors to help it process data. Server-side cursors instruct SQL Server to perform processing on the server rather than on the local machine. This can increase the performance in a situation in which sophisticated processing is needed. The reduction in development time and the speed gains are helping RDO to become the solution of choice for accessing remote data.

Summary

I hope I have given you some clear insight on when to use the different data-access methods. Much of the decision involves the data requirements and the time required to complete the application. In today's world, the length of the application development cycle is becoming more and more critical. Users are willing to lose a second or two in transfer time if they can receive the application six months earlier. The introduction of RDO supports this idea. The best suggestion I have is to try the shorter solutions first; if they do not meet your needs, you then can use the more difficult approaches.

SQL Server 6.x and Visual Basic 4.0

by A. Nicklas Malik

CHAPTER

27

At the time of this writing, Microsoft has seen a huge upsurge in the popularity of its BackOffice suite of products. The flagship product in BackOffice is Microsoft SQL Server. Therefore, it is safe to assume that many of the readers of this book will want to use Visual Basic with SQL Server to create client/server solutions.

This chapter discusses some of the reasons for using SQL Server 6.*x* with Visual Basic 4.0, and some of the problems you might encounter while doing so.

Why SQL Server: The MS Advantage

If you already have SQL Server in your enterprise, you probably have discovered its power and performance. SQL Server is a well-designed server-based RDBMS product, derived from its close cousin, Sybase. To understand the real reasons for using SQL Server, however, you need to look at the competition.

A wide variety of competing server-based database products are on the market. Oracle, Informix, and Sybase account for the vast majority of the current installations of server systems, with SQL Server bringing up the rear with a small market share. There are many other products struggling below.

All of the top systems have their roots in the world of minicomputers, predominantly running some flavor of the UNIX operating system. For years, this was the only good, nonproprietary, multiuser platform available, and the market thrived. PC-based systems lacked the capability to multitask, and a single poorly designed PC application could bring down the system—something a server can never do.

These systems are expensive, however. It is not at all unusual to find that an organization has invested more than $100,000 to set up a server system with software and licenses. That is not including the network cost.

All of this is beginning to change. First, Microsoft and IBM gave us OS/2 (now exclusively an IBM product), and then came Windows NT. Both have their roots in the PC world, yet both offer a reliable, protected, multitasking environment in which to run a server-based system.

Suddenly, the low-cost hardware platforms common in the PC world are in a position to compete with the expensive platforms needed to run large-scale UNIX systems. In a price-performance comparison, PC platforms win hands down over servers when handling data on a departmental level. Small businesses can benefit from the scalability of the PC hardware platform, starting with a small, single-processor Intel 486 box in the corner of the office, and growing to a quad-Pentium without changing software.

Consider the fact that the majority of Americans work in companies with fewer than 100 employees—companies that would balk at a $100,000 price tag for a database server—and you have a marketplace that is just beginning to discover its potential. You can set up an NT-based SQL Server system, including hardware, software, and licenses, for substantially less cost with greater scalability than most of its UNIX-based competitors.

Now, add the real costs of actually maintaining a server-based system, and you begin to see the advantages of using Microsoft's SQL Server:

- **Cost of expertise.** Database expertise is expensive to begin with. Add the cost of finding a guru who knows UNIX, as well as how databases work, and your support costs go up substantially. PC expertise is plentiful, and therefore, it is easier to find the high quality of skill needed to keep your server in tip-top shape.

- **Vendor stability.** Will your vendor survive the market forces? If your vendor calls it quits, your server software will begin to age. As new hardware and software platforms become available, you might find yourself in a position where your users have upgraded to a platform with which your database cannot communicate.

- **Vendor responsiveness.** Along with the question of "Will a vendor survive to upgrade the product?" there is another question you should ask: "How long will it take for them to respond to my needs?" When Windows 95 came out, Oracle users discovered, to their dismay, that Oracle still was working on the upgrade to SQL*Net needed to work reliably on that platform. At the time of this writing, nearly nine months later, they are still waiting.

- **Interoperability with your applications.** Microsoft's applications dominate the desktop marketplace. This means that your server has to provide a reliable way to get data into and out of Microsoft-based applications.

    For the most part, you easily can do this using ODBC drivers, now available for every significant database product. Many companies still are resisting the use of ODBC, however; instead, they are relying on third-party suppliers to develop and sell ODBC drivers to their database servers.

    This is foolish. A slow or buggy ODBC driver makes the server appear slow or buggy. Microsoft has fine-tuned its SQL Server drivers, providing access that is very fast. In fact, the SQL Server ODBC driver is measurably faster, in many cases, than the original Sybase/SQL Server data-access library known as DB/Lib.

- **Finger-pointing.** When a bug is discovered in a client/server environment, one of the biggest problems is finding out which component caused the bug. When you mix and match components, you run the risk of having two companies pointing fingers at each other, leaving you stuck in the middle with the expensive job of fixing it yourself.

- **Database scalability.** Many departments move to client/server systems gradually. They start with a small database on a single workstation. That database becomes important, and it moves to the network where it can be shared. Soon, 10 people are using the database continuously, and it becomes unstable.

    How expensive is it, at this point, to convert the database into a server-based product? Microsoft provides a toolkit for converting Access applications to SQL Server. Some other companies provide versions of their servers that run as PC-based database engines (a better alternative).

This departmental database, while it was still small, needed to be fast, efficient, and have low support costs. This is the strength of the Access database system. Access is inexpensive to get started with, easy to learn and support, and fairly fast.

In addition, an upgrade to SQL Server is fairly easy. You can set up SQL Server on any system in your network—even a 386—and, with flexible licensing, your upgrade costs are within reason.

What about the competition, like Borland or Watcom? Don't they also have systems that boast scalability from file-based to server-based products? Consider what happens when your database guru leaves for another company. You can find 10 good Access programmers for every Object-PAL programmer (the language that runs under Borland's Paradox database product). This means you will spend more money supporting the product, because you will have to spend more to find and retain your new guru.

Given all these factors, it is easy to see why many organizations are choosing to use PC-based server platforms with Microsoft as their sole supplier of software.

Of course, none of these factors would mean a thing if SQL Server were a flawed product. Fortunately, SQL Server is a strong, well-designed system, and the newest version, SQL Server 6.5, has improved on itself tremendously. You learn some of the newer features of SQL Server later in this chapter.

Can I Still Use VB4 with Oracle and Sybase?

Of course, VB4 will work with any ODBC driver that meets Level 2 compliance requirements. There are plenty of drivers available, both from the RDBMS companies themselves and from third parties like Visigenics that supply high quality ODBC drivers to a wide variety of database products.

The rest of this chapter, however, focuses exclusively on SQL Server, with the greatest detail given to the version 6.5 of that product.

 # What's New in SQL Server 6.x?

Many organizations are in the process of upgrading their existing SQL Server 4.*x* systems to the new release. Of course, Microsoft says that this move is relatively painless. Take that with a grain of salt.

In many cases, depending on how well the client/server application was developed, upgrading to the newest version of SQL Server means making changes in your database code (Transact SQL) and, in a few cases, in your front-end software.

Some of the new features provided by SQL Server 6.x follow:

■ The Enterprise Manager: This new GUI for SQL Server enables you to manage multiple databases on multiple servers. You can do everything from this user interface that you previously could do only from stored procedure calls, and more. Nearly every feature of SQL Server 6.x is available from this application, including alerts, tasks, replication, and queries. (Alas, the bulk copy utility, bcp, is still available only from the command line.)

■ SQL distributed management objects (SQL-DMO): In keeping with Microsoft's push toward OLE as a means of making software reusable, the entire functional "guts" of the Enterprise Manager are available as an OLE object hierarchy. This is extremely good news for Visual Basic 4.0 programmers, who now can write their own front ends to SQL Server (see Chapter 14, "Creating BackOffice Solutions with Visual Basic").

■ Integrated data replication: Replication of data from one database to another was a major hassle in previous versions of SQL Server, often involving elaborate stored-procedure mechanisms and separate "publish and forward" databases to store transactional updates. All this was complicated and error prone. SQL Server 6.x provides built-in data replication, which you easily can set up and manage.

■ Server-side cursors: Although the capability to move one record at a time has been extended to SQL programmers with this feature, its true power may be the performance improvement potential with client applications. When used correctly, this feature can enable a client application to select a large record set and manipulate it without having to download all of it across a network.

■ Declarative referential integrity (also known as constraints): Available in PC-based products for quite some time, this new feature in SQL Server enables a database designer to specify that the database engine itself should ensure referential integrity across tables and domain integrity in columns. This greatly eases the difficulty of converting a database from Access to SQL Server as well.

■ Session setting of transaction isolation levels: This feature gives the ODBC driver more control over what the default locking mechanism should be in a client/server session. This, in turn, gives the programmer a little more control over when a record is locked for reading or updating.

■ Scheduled tasks: By using the built-in scheduling mechanisms of SQL Server 6.0, a database administrator can cause an operation to occur (such as replication) or can even run a process (such as your VB program) at a particular time or with a particular interval.

■ E-mail capability (send and receive): Using the scheduling capability and some new extended stored procedures, a database administrator can set up SQL Server to watch for incoming mail messages that are expected to contain a single query. SQL Server then responds with a mail message containing the result set.

From the front end, this capability can be very helpful. If you have a need for long-distance queued queries or queries across the Internet, this option might be your best way of requesting and retrieving data.

■ Removable media support: This feature enables SQL Server databases to be published on CD-ROM. A good example of using this is an international company using an Executive MIS database, published monthly on CD, and mailed to sites around the world.

■ Global temporary objects: When ODBC creates a prepared statement under SQL Server, it does so by creating a stored procedure. With SQL Server 6.0, this can be a true "temporary procedure" that can be flagged for deletion by the server when the connection is terminated. No more orphaned ODBC procedures (a common occurrence with SQL Server 4.2).

■ Dynamic SQL: Enables a stored procedure to piece together a string containing a Transact SQL statement, and then to execute that statement within the current transaction. This provides powerful new capabilities to SQL Server.

Upgrading from SQL Server 4.2: Expected Issues

As I previously mentioned, moving a database from SQL Server 4.2 to 6.0 can be very simple, or it can be quite complicated. The two biggest issues are the introduction of new keywords into the Transact SQL language, and the transition to stricter ANSI compliance for the ODBC drivers.

Introducing New Keywords

When you upgrade from version 4.x of SQL Server, you should have a Transact SQL programmer available to fix any stored procedures or triggers that no longer compile under SQL Server 6.x due to a keyword conflict. The likelihood of hitting this issue depends on the number of stored procedures in your databases, their sizes, and the inclination of the programmers to have used words such as add, fetch, current, pipe, and user (just a few of the new keywords in Transact SQL).

To Microsoft's credit, SQL Server does come with a utility called CHKUPG that you can run on a database to inform you of any keyword conflicts before you begin the process of upgrading the database.

Meeting ANSI Standards

Most Transact SQL development takes place using the ISQL/W utility to submit queries and create and test stored procedures. This is fine, unless your applications use ODBC to communicate with the server, as do most applications.

There are a few problems that are caused by the new ODBC drivers, and they will rear their heads in the environment I describe. This is because the new drivers use a couple of options that support ANSI compatibility—options that usually are not in effect in ISQL/W when the stored procedures and queries are being written.

The first problem with the new drivers is the quoted identifier. The ODBC driver issues the SET QUOTED_IDENTIFIER ON statement when connecting to a session. With this option turned on, a string enclosed in quotation marks is not a character string—it is the name of a database object. If you have used quotation marks in any of your stored procedures, or worse, if your application hard codes SQL statements that use quotation marks, you will have to change them. This applies to all statements executed from ODBC, including stored procedures originally saved in ISQL/W.

> If you are not sure whether an application is sending quoted strings in SQL statements, turn on ODBC tracing and put your application through its paces *before* upgrading to SQL Server 6.0 or 6.5. Then closely scrutinize the log file for SQL statements that contain quotation marks.
>
> Otherwise, you might upgrade your server, only to find that the application has to be rewritten in order to work correctly. This is not something you want to discover *after* you've killed an operational system.

The second common problem with the new ODBC drivers is *default nullability*. The ODBC driver uses the Set ANSI_NULL_DFLT_ON statement when your application first connects to the server. This seemingly benign option has the following effect: When a table is created, and the CREATE TABLE statement does not specify whether a column should be allowed to accept NULL values, this option says "Assume that the user wants NULL values." ISQL/W, on the other hand, does not set this option to ON by default, so the system assumes that the user does not want NULL values in the column.

Listing 27.1, for example, shows a table created with three columns. In the second column, I forgot to specify whether the column should be allowed to accept NULL values.

Listing 27.1. A CREATE TABLE statement with default nullability.

```
Create Table SaleItems
    (InvoiceID      smallint  Not Null,
    InventoryID     smallint,
    Quantity        smallint  Null)
```

Assume that I used the CREATE TABLE statement above to create a table in ISQL/W, where the nullability option normally is turned off. I turn around and test a number of queries and stored procedures, all of which work correctly in ISQL/W, as shown in Listing 27.2.

Listing 27.2. A SQL statement with the correct response in ISQL/W.

```
Select * from SaleItems Where InvoiceID = 2114
InvoiceID      InventoryID    Quantity
2114              181            1
2114              206            2
2114              106            8
```

Then, I try calling those statements or stored procedures from a Visual Basic front-end application through ODBC. Remember that ODBC has set the nullability option to ON. All the values for the second column, InventoryID, may be wildly incorrect, as shown in Listing 27.3.

Listing 27.3. A SQL statement with an incorrect response in ODBC.

```
Select * from SaleItems Where InvoiceID = 2114
InvoiceID      InventoryID    Quantity
2114           -12234181         1
2114           -14882206         2
2114           -59938106         8
```

Needless to say, this disparity between the values in the database and the values returned by ODBC causes problems. Stored procedures return incorrect results. Joins in SELECT statements fail to find matching columns, and so on. Note that this happens for temporary tables as well as permanent tables.

You can fix this problem by finding every instance in which you used a CREATE TABLE statement, both as a command and in stored procedures. You then can rewrite the statement to include NULL or NOT NULL for every column. If you already have populated your table with data, use the ALTER TABLE statement and specifically denote the nullability of the column.

The problems caused by default nullability are insidious, and can cause very nasty results. Just to make life interesting, these problems are not that easy to demonstrate. There are a couple of conditions that must be met before they can be reliably reproduced. Also, automated checking tools cannot find these problems in advance.

The best workaround suggestion I have is to re-create your database from a script, where it is easy to ensure that every CREATE TABLE statement has explicit nullability on every column. You can generate a script of your database schema easily from SQL Enterprise Manager.

Installing an ODBC Driver that Causes an Application to Fail

Because the new keywords and ANSI compliance problems are introduced by the ODBC driver, the following situation has been known to occur: A SQL 6.0 database is up and running. The front-end developers had used Visual Basic 3.0 to create the front-end application, and it is working just fine using the old ODBC drivers.

Then, one day, one of the users installs VB4 or Office95 on her system, which comes with the new SQL Server drivers. Suddenly, the application stops working on that machine only. Blame falls on the new software, which promptly is uninstalled by the help desk technician. Unfortunately, the ODBC drivers do not get uninstalled, so the system remains broken.

In the short term, the solution is to put the old ODBC drivers back on the user's system and immediately begin investigating the process of fixing the database (and possibly the front-end code).

Under the Hood with VB4 and SQL Server 6.x

This section tells you how VB4 features are implemented under SQL Server 6.x. Special focus is placed on showing you how to get to server-specific features from the VB front end.

There Must Be 50 Ways To Get Your Data

Well, not really 50 ways, but there are quite a few choices available to the VB programmer. In addition to the data access objects (DAO) and the remote data objects (RDO), you get the SQL Server distributed management objects (SQLDMO), which, in addition to giving you complete control over your server, provide a query interface as well. Last, but not least, you have DB/Lib, or VBSQL.OCX, which enables you to communicate through the older DB/Lib proprietary API, completely circumventing ODBC.

Each of the methods I've just named has one or more chapters devoted to it in this book, so I won't go into detail here on how to use them. I will mention, briefly, the features of SQL Server 6.x that you can access through these methods.

Accessing SQL 6.x Features from DAO and RDO

SQL Server has added many new features, as mentioned earlier in the chapter. Some of them can be used from VB4. The following is a list of the new features that you can use, along with notes on how to use them.

- Using server-side cursors: This feature actually is fairly easy to use, because server-side cursors are the default when using the ODBC drivers. Under DAO, server-side cursors are used unless you specify a passthrough query. (Passthrough queries are executed with client-side cursors, because the query could have multiple result sets.)

  With RDO, server-side cursors also are the default. You can change this by setting the CursorDriver property of the RDO Environment object, as in this code:

  ```
  rdoEnvironments(0).CursorDriver = rdUseOdbc
  ```

  In order for this statement to take effect, you need to execute it before you open a connection on the Environment object.

> If you are using RDO to execute batches or stored procedures against SQL Server 6.*x*, server-side cursors are not your friend. You should turn them off as described here. This is because stored procedures can return multiple result sets, and SQL Server 6.*x* cannot correctly handle multiple result sets with server-side cursors.

■ Using identity columns: If you use the standard DAO syntax for creating a table, and you set the attributes of a new field to AutoIncrement, Jet issues the necessary DQL DDL statements to create an identity column in SQL Server 6.*x*.

That's about it, really. Most of the remaining features are either transparent to VB, or out of reach unless you decide to use the SQL Distributed Management Objects.

Using the New ODBC Drivers

VB4 comes with the new ODBC drivers for SQL Server 6.*x*, both in 16-bit and 32-bit form. This section discusses how to use these drivers correctly.

The first issues you are likely to encounter when you use these drivers already have been discussed: the NULL columns problem and the quoted identifier problem (refer to the section titled "Upgrading from SQL Server 4.2: Expected Issues"). Beyond that, a few additional details are worth covering.

16-Bit Versus 32-Bit Drivers

Although VB4 ships with both sets of drivers, it is important to note that you should use the 32-bit drivers for 32-bit VB applications and the 16-bit drivers for 16-bit applications. This might seem obvious, but it is easy to get this wrong, because a 32-bit application can use either driver, whereas a 16-bit application can use only a data source set up with the 16-bit drivers.

Registry Issues

In the world of 32-bit Windows NT and Windows 95, the ODBC information no longer is stored in the ODBC.INI file, where it was easy for VB programs to edit. Now, the information is in the Registry (isn't everything?) at the following key:

```
HKEY_CURRENT_USER/Software/Microsoft/ODBC/ODBC.INI/datasource
```

Under this key, the following tags are located. All are string values:

■ Database: The database on the server to use with this data source.

■ Description: A text description of the data source.

■ Driver: The full path name to the driver.

- Language: The language that the client application will present information in. Blank defaults to the system language (specified in the Control Panel). This is used primarily for country-specific translations of date and time formats.
- LastUser: The login ID of the last user to use this data source.
- OEMTOANSI: Specifies whether character set translation should be performed on the queries and result sets.
- Server: The name of the server on which the database is located.
- UseProcForPrepare: Specifies whether ODBC should create a stored procedure to support prepared statements. Under SQL Server 6.*x*, true temporary stored procedures are used, eliminating the problem of orphaned stored procedures common with SQL Server 4.2 and ODBC.

Summary

With the rapid growth of SQL Server in the marketplace, more and more Visual Basic programmers will be called up to write applications that access the features of this database system. As with every area of programming, there are a few details that can be helpful to know.

Most of the minor details that come back to bite you are embedded in the ODBC drivers that ship with VB4 and many other Microsoft Office products. These include the default nullability problem, as well as the quoted identifier problem.

Additionally, the new capabilities of SQL Server can interfere with the workings of an existing application. From the default use of server-side cursors causing ODBC to choke on any multiple-result-set query, to the addition of new keywords in Transact SQL, make the step to SQL Server 6.*x* with caution.

Miscellaneous Other Visual Basic Stuff

PART 5

Opportunities for the Internet

by Delane R. Hewett

28

CHAPTER

Over the past year, the very foundations of computing and information systems have been rocked by the Internet phenomenon. No-name companies have grown and vied to topple the software giants. UNIX is back, the Mac is back, and Windows will get washed aside in the wake of this mighty wave. Well, probably not. But make no mistake, the rules have changed.

Like most Visual Basic developers, you have probably been thinking: "What happened! I was just programming along with VB, watching the development community, keeping up with the latest technology and wham! this new thing hits, the Web, the Information Superhighway, cyberspace." You probably imagined that this over-inflated hot-air-propelled Web thing would just pop, or at least the air would leak out slowly, and we could all get back to work. Well, guess what? I'm writing this and you're reading it because we both know that it's not going to happen. The good news is that the playing field is level. Everyone is starting from scratch, and Visual Basic developers are going to be a major driving influence in bringing the Internet to life.

This chapter talks about what is happening with the Internet and what you as a Visual Basic developer can prepare for. I won't focus on the typical topic of writing Internet e-mail systems using VB and an Internet API. I'll show you where the opportunities exist and how to prepare for them.

The following material is intended to give a brief summary of several important technologies that are (or should soon become) industry standards. In a general sense, the Internet has returned us to a simplicity not seen in computing in many years. Elementary school children and grandparents have created Internet sites before a majority of computing professionals learned that surfing could happen without getting wet. The complexities become apparent when we attempt to leverage all the recent investments in computing technology and apply them to the Internet.

With the Internet we have finally come to a client/server model where information processing is truly dispersed across many servers and local processing is leveraged to minimize network traffic. In order to understand what industry is calling "Active Internet Applications," it is important to understand several important technologies, all of which will contribute to the future of the Internet.

The chapter wraps up with an example that will help to tie all these technologies together and perhaps lend insight into bringing the Internet to life.

Internet "Basics"

There are many books containing details about how the Internet works. I'll just include enough basics so that you get a general idea where things fit together and how they work. The Internet is about communication. Any two computers armed with software, a modem, and a phone line can communicate with each other. This communication spans time zones, languages, and cultures. The main enabling technologies driving this phenomenon are TCP/IP and the World Wide Web (WWW). This chapter contains a lot of acronyms that I've attempted to spell out if not define. I have included a good reference for up-to-the-minute Internet definitions at the end of this chapter.

TCP/IP

What is TCP/IP and why should you be interested? TCP/IP (Transmission Control Protocol/ Internet Protocol) is "THE" network protocol that enables all the world's computers to communicate with each other and makes the World Wide Web the phenomenon that it is today. The "TCP" in TCP/IP is the part that enables two machines to set up reliable network connections with each other and communicate by passing packets of data back and forth, and the "IP" deals with the part about routing the information over the Internet.

A TCP/IP address is a hierarchical numbering scheme that uniquely defines every machine on the Internet. Your company or Internet service provider will assign you one. This address is a 32-bit string of four octets. Each octet is a number, and the four are separated by periods as depicted in Figure 28.1.

Figure 28.1.
Internet protocol addressing scheme.

Each machine also supports *numbered ports*, each port being dedicated to a particular service. Each standard service has been assigned a particular port that it works with. For example, if you want to use TCP to send mail using Simple Mail Transfer Protocol (SMTP), you use port 21; to retrieve your mail using Post Office Protocol (POP), you use port 110.

Sockets are another important element. Sockets enable two computers to communicate through one of these services. The Internet would not be very interesting if, when two computers were talking, a third had to wait if it wanted to communicate with one of the first two. To alleviate this problem, many sockets can be used at the same time to enable one computer to communicate with several machines concurrently.

Communicating over TCP/IP

Any application that wants to communicate over the Internet must use TCP/IP because the Internet is built on TCP/IP connections. This also holds true for applications that you build. A socket represents the connection between two computers on the network that use a particular service. Programming sockets requires a standard Application Programming Interface (API) in order to write to the TCP/IP stacks. Although sockets were originally designed for UNIX, sockets were also implemented for Microsoft Windows. Windows sockets are commonly abbreviated to Winsock.

Windows Sockets

Winsock is a standard API implemented in either 16- or 32-bit DLLs. Visual Basic enables developers to call functions in external DLLs, and WINSOCK.DLL is no exception. Winsock has been in existence for several years, so there are a great many references for working with the Winsock API including providing all your VB API declaration counterparts to each function, such as:

> *Building Internet Applications with Visual Basic,* Michael Marchuk, Que Publishing, 1995, ISBN 0-7897-0214-2

I describe only briefly what can be done with Winsock and devote the rest of this chapter to new stuff that has evolved literally over the last few months.

Basically, the Winsock API provides a series of functions for setting up connections, resolving names and addresses over the Internet, sending and receiving information, and managing errors. Although this doesn't seem like a lot of functionality, virtually every Internet application from browsers to e-mail servers is based on this set of primitive functions. If you want to build a Web browser, Internet news reader client, a gopher or FTP client, then this API might be for you. Later, you learn about a newer API for doing much of the same thing called WinINet.

Internet Protocols: FTP, Gopher, HTTP

File Transfer Protocol (FTP) was established some 20 years ago to enable dissimilar machines to copy text and binary files back and forth. Each operating system has a low-level set of performance-tuned functions for working with the file system. FTP enables any file system to look the same to a host connected to it. There are only a few FTP commands. Here are the most popular:

Open	Initiates the session between the two machines for file transfer.
Close	Terminates the file transfer session.
Get	Requests that a file be transferred from the remote machine to the local.
Dir	Requests a directory listing from the remote machine.
Send	Requests that a file be transferred from the local machine to the remote.

Whenever information is transferred from one machine to another, security becomes an issue. We don't, however, want to have to grant everyone permission to access each of the millions of servers and maintain this security. The concept of an anonymous user was established to deal with this situation. By logging in anonymously to a remote server, users can have some interactions within certain directories without special accounts having to be set up.

Gopher was established by the University of Minnesota as an easy method of browsing for information. The method of navigation is through directory trees that present the information in a hierarchical manner (similar to the DOS and NT file systems). The gopher protocol sends simple requests to the server and receives information in several parts:

- A textual description of the information
- Description about the type of information (directory/file)
- A pointer to where the actual information exists

Basically, interacting starts at one gopher site and branches to links to other sites, if necessary, as interaction continues. This method of interacting constitutes a precursor to the World Wide Web.

E-Mail Protocols: SMTP, MIME, POP

SMTP, MIME, and POP work together to enable powerful e-mail solutions. Simple mail transfer protocol (SMTP) is the most popular aspect of the Internet. SMTP enables anyone on the Internet to send and receive electronic mail. Although initially SMTP was text-only, it now supports binary file attachments for sending information other than text in e-mail messages. SMTP was designed to be simple to use and to program.

Multipurpose Internet mail extensions (MIME) is a standard designed to extend SMTP to enable different media (pictures, sound, proprietary format, and so on) to be transferred across the Internet in mail messages.

Post office protocol (POP) enables computers that are not continuously connected to the network to receive e-mail from others. This is a method of storage and forwarding whereby a server that is always connected to the Internet stores e-mail messages on your behalf until your computer requests that they be forwarded to your machine.

List Servers and UseNet

List servers are SMTP-based systems that enable people to subscribe to specific topics of interest. If someone sends a message pertinent to a topic on the list server, then each person subscribing to that topic will have that message forwarded to them. Typical uses involve group meetings, technical support, and any other distribution where many want to "listen in" on information about the specific topic. List servers are sponsored by organizations. UseNet News is similar to list servers except that they are typically not sponsored by an organization. They are intended for the free exchange of information between many. List servers are mainly distribution facilities, whereas UseNet is typically information collection as well as distribution.

World Wide Web Basics

The World Wide Web (WWW) is built on top of a stateless protocol that enables information to travel from a server to a client. The primary difference between gopher and the WWW is that gopher is intended to send textual information in a directory structure, whereas the WWW can send multimedia information that can display vast amounts of visual and audio content. Gopher has a concept of directory structure, whereas the WWW has a concept of a web of interconnected documents. These documents contain *links* that point to other documents so that clicking on one of these links with the mouse has the effect of moving to the new document referenced in the link. These documents are commonly referred to as *pages* and the links as *hypertext*.

When a page on the Internet is referenced with a Web browser, a file is copied from the server to the client and the Web browser renders the page from information in the file that describes how the page should look and possibly sound. The Web pages themselves can be files that are sitting out on some server, or the content can be generated on the fly by an application running on the server. Web servers themselves can be PCs, Macs, UNIX workstations, or other higher-end machines. Anyone with access to a Web server can have his or her own page on the Web. Most Internet service providers provide clients with the ability to both connect to the Internet via their service and also to host their Web pages.

The two main technologies that define the Web are hypertext transfer protocol (HTTP) and hypertext markup language (HTML). Before you can work with these, you need to understand uniform resource locators.

Uniform Resource Locators

The World Wide Web, as its name implies, is actually a web. It is comprised of millions of strands of information tied together by nodes called hyperlinks. Hyperlinks themselves look like any other text or picture in Web documents but usually appear in a different color or highlighting than the other text or images in the document. What these hyperlinks do when you click on them is determined by a uniform resource locator (URL). Information on the Web can be accessed via hyperlinks or directly via URLs. These are really the same thing as far as the Web is concerned, but hyperlinks hide the URL from you in the HTML formatting, as you will see later. URLs are the standard method of accessing information on the Web. They are strings of formatted text similar to file system paths but with additional information. There are two main parts of a URL: the access method and the path to the information. URLs display the access method first, followed by a colon and then the path. The following represent some valid URLs:

```
http://www.microsoft.com/default.htm
http://www.microsoft.com/intdev
ftp://info.uow.edu
gopher://informx.cat.com:70/00/catalog/guests/db.mdb
//sample.cool.com
```

Notice that some of the URLs present an access technology first and then a path. If the access method is not provided, then the URL is really a universal resource identifier (URI) and merely enables the information to be located.

Web Sites

Information on Web servers can be stored in what's called a *home page* or relative to the home page. A home page is a general starting point for many Web sites. Generally, they are intended to provide a person's first impression of the site and a place to navigate to the rest of the site through hyperlinks. Unlike a book or movie, navigating through a site is not a linear process but a logical process based on the interests of the person viewing the site. The concept of a home page is important because most sites contain many pages, and generally these pages are organized into a hierarchy when they are physically stored on a server.

To keep a set of pages together and portable from one physical machine to another, *relative URLs* can be used. Relative URLs do not contain all the information that the URL that it relates to has. *Virtual URLs* are URLs in which only the address of the physical computer on which they reside has been left off. This method is useful for mirrored servers where the entire site is replicated in the same directory structure but on a physically different computer with a different name.

Figure 28.2 illustrates a series of pages representing a site. The home page is typically referenced through its full URL, but individual pages in the site might use relative URLs to navigate within the site. The arrows represent links. The text displayed next to each arrow represents the URL hidden within each of the underlined hyperlinks. The links are shown: relative (such as ford.htm), absolute (such as http://monster.com/monsters/trucks/chevy.htm), and virtual (such as /monsters/trucks/dodge.htm). How the physical htm files would appear using these URLs in the directory structure of the file system on the server is shown as well.

Figure 28.2.
HTML basic links.

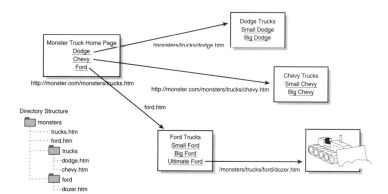

HTML Tags

The hypertext markup language (HTML) is a standard set of structured formatting that is based on the International Standards Organization's (ISO) Standard General Markup Language (SGML). In order for Web browsers to properly interpret the HTML and render the page, sections must be laid out and specific *tags* used throughout the document. The tags tell the browser where to start displaying in a particular format and where to stop that format and proceed with another. Tags are usually presented in pairs and referred to as tag and end tag with the content benefiting from the tag in the middle. The tag is enclosed in angle brackets (for example, `<TagName>`). The end tag is the same as the tag but with a slash (/) before indicating termination (for example, `</TagName>`). The major sections of an HTML document include the header and the body with other tags nested within each of these. The following is a list of the most popular tags. This is not intended to be a complete list of all tags from the W3C HTML Specification. Some options are not supported by all Web browsers.

- `A`: Stands for *anchor* and specifies a hypertext link. Everything between the `<A HREF...>` and the `</A>` (both text and pictures) becomes a clickable hyperlink to that address within an HTML document. If the anchor is `<A NAME="map1">`, then links that point to that anchor are `<A HREF="#map1">...</A>`, `<A HREF="http://www.sample.com/ home.htm#map1">...</A>` HTML 2.

  Example: `<A HREF="http://www.microsoft.com"> Llink to Microsoft.</A>`

- `Area`: Specifies the shape of a "hot spot" in a client-side image map. Client-side image maps are pictures that cause the browser to jump to different URLs depending on where you click. `COORDS="x1, y1, x2, y2, ..."` identifies the coordinates that define the hot spot's shape.

  Example: `<AREA SHAPE="RECT" COORDS="50, 25, 150, 125" HREF="http://www.microsoft.com">`

- `B`: Renders text in boldface.

  Example: `<B>This text will appear Bold</B>`

- `BASEFONT`: Sets base font value.

  `SIZE=n` (*n* is between 1 and 7 inclusive; the default is 3 and 7 is the largest). Sets the base font size. Throughout the document, relative font size settings—for example, `<FONT SIZE=+3>`—are set according to this.

  Example: `<BASEFONT SIZE=3>`

- `BGSOUND`: This tag enables you to create pages with background sounds or "soundtracks." Sounds can either be samples (.WAV or .AU format) or MIDI (.MID format). The optional `LOOP` parameter indicates how many times the sound is replayed.

  Examples: `<BGSOUND SRC="boing.wav">` or `<BGSOUND SRC="boing.wav" LOOP=INFINITE>`

- `BODY`: Indicates where the body of an HTML document begins and ends.

  Example: `<HTML> <BODY>Here's a Web page!</BODY></HTML>`

- BR: Inserts a line break. Used with optional CLEAR=LEFT, RIGHT, or ALL it inserts a vertical space so that the next text displayed will be past left- or right-aligned "floating" images. LEFT inserts space so that the next text appears aligned with the left margin directly below a left-aligned floating image. RIGHT is the same, but for the right side; and ALL puts the next text past all floating images.

  Examples: `<IMG SRC="image.gif" ALIGN=LEFT> Here's some text to the right of a picture. <BR CLEAR=LEFT> Here's some text beneath the picture.`

- CAPTION: Specifies a caption for a table and must be used within the TABLE tag. If used with optional ALIGN=LEFT, RIGHT, or CENTER, draws the caption left-aligned, right-aligned, or centered with the table borders.

  Example: `<TABLE><CAPTION ALIGN=CENTER>This caption will be centered between the left and right borders of the table.</CAPTION><TR><TD>This is a cell in the table.</TD></TR></TABLE>`

- CENTER: Causes subsequent text and images to be centered.

  Example: `<CENTER>This Text is Centered</CENTER>`

- FONT: Changes the font. COLOR=#rrggbb or COLOR=color name sets the font color. rrggbb is a hexadecimal number denoting a red-green-blue color value (the number sign is optional). It can also be set to a color name. Color names are from a standard list and include such colors as red, blue, and black.

  FACE="name [,name2] [,name3]" sets the font. You can specify a list of font names. If the first font is available on the system, it will be used, otherwise the second will be tried, and so on. If none are available, a default font will be used.

  SIZE=n SIZE=+n or -n specifies a font size between 1 and 7 (7 is largest). A plus or minus before the number indicates a size relative to the current BASEFONT setting.

  Example: `<FONT COLOR=#ff0000>This text is red.</FONT>` or `<FONT FACE="Arial,Lucida Sans,Times Roman">`

- FORM: Denotes a form.

  ACTION="URL" specifies the address to be used to carry out the action of the form. If none is specified, the base URL of the document is used.

  METHOD=GET or POST indicates how the form data should be sent to the server. GET means append the arguments to the action URL and open it as if it were an anchor; POST means send the data via an HTTP post transaction.

  Example: `<FORM ACTION="http:// www.site.com/scripts/search?" METHOD=POST> </FORM>`

- Hn: Renders text in heading style. Use H1 through H7 to specify different sizes and styles of heading (H1 is the largest). Optional ALIGN=CENTER centers the heading.

  Examples: `<H2 ALIGN=CENTER>How to Use Internet Explorer</H2>` HTML 3

  `<H1>this is heading one</H1>`

■ HR: Draws a horizontal rule the width of the window. ALIGN=LEFT, RIGHT, or CENTER draws the rule left-aligned, right-aligned, or centered. COLOR adds color to the rule. NOSHADE draws the rule without 3-D shading. SIZE sets the height of the rule in pixels. WIDTH=*n*% sets the width of the rule as a percentage of window width. WIDTH=*n* sets the width of the rule in pixels.

Example: `<HR ALIGN=CENTER>` or `<HR COLOR=#rrggbb or colorname>`

■ HTML: Denotes that the file is an HTML document.

Example: `<HTML><P>here's the whole document.</P></HTML>`

■ I: Renders text in italics.

Example: `<I> This text displays in italics.</I>`

■ IMG: Imbeds an inline image in the document.

ALIGN=TOP, MIDDLE, or BOTTOM: The surrounding text is aligned with the top, middle, or bottom of the picture.

ALIGN=LEFT or RIGHT. The picture is drawn as a left-aligned or right-aligned "floating image," and text will flow around it. (See BR CLEAR.)

ALT="text". Specifies text that will be displayed in place of the picture if Show Pictures is turned off.

BORDER=*n*. Specifies the size of a border to be drawn around the image. If the image is a hyperlink, the border is drawn in the appropriate hyperlink color. If the image is not a hyperlink, the border is invisible.

CONTROLS. If a video clip is present, a set of controls is displayed under the clip.

DYNSRC=URL. Specifies the address of a video clip or VRML world to be displayed in the window. Stands for Dynamic Support.

HEIGHT=*n*. Along with WIDTH, specifies the size at which the picture is drawn. (If the picture's actual dimensions differ from those specified with WIDTH and HEIGHT, the picture is stretched to match what's specified.)

HSPACE=*n*. Along with VSPACE, specifies margins for the image. Similar to BORDER, except that the margins are not painted with color when the image is a hyperlink.

ISMAP. Identifies the picture as a server-side image map. Clicking the picture transmits the coordinates of the click back to the server, triggering a jump to another page.

LOOP=*n* LOOP=INFINITE. Specifies how many times a video clip will loop when activated. If *n*=-1, or if LOOP=INFINITE is specified, it will loop indefinitely.

SRC. Specifies the address of the picture to insert.

START= FILEOPEN and/or MOUSEOVER. For video clips: specifies when the file should start playing. FILEOPEN means start playing as soon as the file is done opening. This is the default. MOUSEOVER means start playing when the user moves the mouse cursor over the animation.

USEMAP "map name". Identifies the picture as a client-side image map and specifies a MAP to use for acting on the user's clicks.

Examples: <IMG SRC="sample.gif" ALIGN=MIDDLE>

<IMG SRC="sample.gif" DYNSRC="test.avi">

<IMG SRC="sample.gif" WIDTH=320 HEIGHT=200>

■ INPUT: Specifies a form control.

ALIGN=TOP, MIDDLE, or BOTTOM. Used when TYPE=IMAGE. Specifies how the next line of text will be aligned with the image.

CHECKED=TRUE or FALSE. For check boxes and radio buttons, indicates that they are selected.

MAXLENGTH= "length". Indicates the maximum number of characters that can be entered into a text control.

NAME="name". Specifies the name of the control.

SIZE="size" SIZE="width, height". Specifies the size of the control (in characters). For TEXTAREA-type controls, both height and width can be specified.

SRC="address". Used when TYPE=IMAGE. Specifies the address of the image to be used.

TYPE. Specifies what type of control to use.

VALUE. For textual/numerical controls, specifies the default value of the control. For Boolean controls, specifies the value to be returned when the control is turned on.

Examples: <INPUT NAME="Control4" TYPE=IMAGE SRC="image.gif" ALIGN=LEFT>

<INPUT NAME="Control9" TYPE=TEXTBOX MAXLENGTH=20>

<INPUT NAME="Control3" TYPE=CHECKBOX VALUE=FALSE>

■ MAP: Specifies a collection of hot spots for a client-side image map. NAME gives the MAP a name so it can be referred to.

Example: <MAP NAME="mymap"> <AREA ...> <AREA...> </MAP>

■ MARQUEE: The MARQUEE tag enables you to create a scrolling text marquee.

ALIGN=TOP, MIDDLE, or BOTTOM. Specifies that the text around the marquee should align with the top, middle, or bottom of the marquee.

BEHAVIOR= SCROLL, SLIDE, or ALTERNATE. Specifies how the text should behave. SCROLL (the default) means start completely off one side, scroll all the way across and completely off, and then start again. SLIDE means start completely off one side, scroll in, and stop as soon as the text touches the other margin. ALTERNATE means bounce back and forth within the marquee.

BGCOLOR= #rrggbb or colorname. Specifies a background color for the marquee, either as an RGB triple or using a color name.

DIRECTION=LEFT or RIGHT. Specifies which direction the text should scroll. The default is LEFT, which means scrolling to the left from the right.

HEIGHT=*n* or HEIGHT=*n*%. Specifies the height of the marquee, either in pixels or as a percentage of the screen height.

HSPACE=*n*. Specifies left and right margins for the outside of the marquee, in pixels.

LOOP=*n* LOOP=INFINITE. Specifies how many times a marquee will loop when activated. If n=-1, or if LOOP=INFINITE is specified, it will loop indefinitely.

SCROLLAMOUNT=*n*. Specifies the number of pixels between each successive draw of the marquee text.

SCROLLDELAY=*n*. Specifies the number of milliseconds between each successive draw of the marquee text.

VSPACE=*n*. Specifies top and bottom margins for the outside of the marquee, in pixels.

WIDTH=*n* or WIDTH=*n*%. Sets the width of the marquee, either in pixels or as a percentage of the screen width.

Example: `<MARQUEE BGCOLOR=#EFD6C6 DIRECTION=RIGHT BEHAVIOR=SCROLL SCROLLAMOUNT=10 SCROLLDELAY=200><FONT COLOR="WHITE">This is a scrolling marquee.</FONT></MARQUEE>`

■ MENU: Specifies that the following block consists of individual items, each beginning with an `<LI>` tag.

Example: `<MENU><LI>Item1<LI>Item2<LI>Item3</MENU>`

■ META: Microsoft IIS client pull using the META tag. The META tag must be inside the HEAD tag of the HTML document.

HTTP-EQUIV= "REFRESH". Causes a document to be automatically reloaded on a regular basis, specified in seconds.

CONTENT="*n*; URL=URL". Tells the browser to reload in *n* seconds. If a URL is specified, the browser will load the URL after the time specified has elapsed. If no URL is specified, it will reload the current document. This is good for using a site for an automated presentation.

Example: `<HEAD><META HTTP-EQUIV="REFRESH" CONTENT=5><TITLE>Reload Document</TITLE></HEAD> <P>This document will be reloaded every five seconds.</BODY>`

■ NOBR: Renders text without line breaks.

Example: `<NOBR>Here's a continuous line of text that won't be broken </NOBR>`

■ OL: Specifies that the following block consists of individual items, each beginning with an `<LI>` tag. The items are numbered.

START=*n*. Specifies a starting number for the list.

TYPE=A, a, I, i, or 1. Changes the style of the list. Codes: A = use large letters; a = use small letters; I = use large Roman numerals; i = use small Roman numerals; 1 = use numbers.

Example: `<OL> <LI>Item1<LI>Item2<LI>Item3</OL>`

■ OPTION: Denotes one choice in a list box.

none. In a `<SELECT>` block, denotes one of the choices that will appear in the list.

SELECTED. Indicates that this item is the default. If not present, item number one becomes the default.

VALUE. Indicates the value that will be returned if this item is chosen.

Examples: `<SELECT NAME="choice" MULTIPLE SIZE="1">`

`<OPTION VALUE="1">choice1`

`<OPTION VALUE="2">choice2`

`SELECTED>Choice3</SELECT>`

■ P: Inserts a paragraph break and denotes a paragraph. The ending tag, `</P>`, is optional.

ALIGN=CENTER centers the paragraph.

Example: `<P>Here is a paragraph.</P>`

■ SELECT: Identifies a list box or drop-down list.

none. Specifies a list box or drop-down list.

MULTIPLE. Indicates that multiple items can be selected.

NAME. Specifies a name for the list.

SIZE. Specifies the height of the list control.

Examples: `<SELECT NAME="choice" MULTIPLE SIZE="1">`

`<OPTION VALUE="1">choice1`

`<OPTION VALUE="2">choice2`

`SELECTED>Choice3</SELECT>`

■ STRONG: Renders text as strong. Similar to boldface.

Example: `<STRONG>This is bold</STRONG>`

■ TABLE: Identifies a table.

ALIGN=LEFT or RIGHT. Specifies that the table or the text can be left- or right-aligned. The default is left-aligned for TABLE, TR, and TD. The default is center-aligned for TH.

BACKGROUND=" URL". Specifies a background picture. The picture is tiled behind the text and graphics in the table, table head, or table cell.

BGCOLOR= #rrggbb or colorname. Sets background color. rrggbb is a hexadecimal number denoting a red-green-blue color value or color name.

BORDERCOLOR= #rrggbb or colorname. Sets border color and must be used with the BORDER attribute. rrggbb is a hexadecimal number denoting a red-green-blue color or color name.

BORDERCOLORLIGHT= #rrggbb or colorname. Sets independent border color control over one of the two colors used to draw a 3-D border, opposite of BORDERCOLORDARK, and must be used with the BORDER attribute. rrggbb is a hexadecimal number denoting a red-green-blue color or color name.

BORDERCOLORDARK= #rrggbb or colorname. Sets independent border color control over one of the two colors used to draw a 3-D border, opposite of BORDERCOLORLIGHT, and must be used with the BORDER attribute. rrggbb is a hexadecimal number denoting a red-green-blue color or color name

VALIGN=TOP or BOTTOM. Specifies that the text can be top- or bottom-aligned. The default is center-aligned.

Examples: `<TABLE ALIGN=RIGHT BORDER=2 WIDTH=80%>`

`<CAPTION ALIGN=CENTER VALIGN=BOTTOM><FONT FACE="COURIER NEW" SIZE=2>Sample Table</FONT></CAPTION>`

`<TR><TD BGCOLOR=#EFD6C6>First</TD></TR>`

`<TR><TD BGCOLOR=#FFCC99>Second</TD></TR>`

`</TABLE>`

- TITLE: Specifies a title for the document. IIS uses this for the window caption.

  Example: `<TITLE>Here's the caption</TITLE>`

- U: Renders text underlined.

  Example: `<U>Underlined text</U>`

- UL: Draws lines of text as a bulleted list.

  Example: `<UL> <LI>Bullet1<LI>Bullet2<LI>Bullet3.</UL>`

I won't go any deeper into HTML because there are several good references on the subject. In addition to numerous Internet sources, here are some of the better publications.

Teach Yourself Web Publishing with HTML in a Week, Laura Lemay, Sams Publishing, 1995, ISBN 1-672-30667-0

Teach Yourself More Web Publishing with HTML in a Week, Laura Lemay, Sams Publishing, 1995, ISBN 1-57521-005-3

For a complete reference on the latest HTML standard, see http://www.w3.org/pub/www/.

For a good on-line reference to HTML see http://info.cern.ch/hypertext/WWW/MarkUp/MarkUp.html.

Security Technologies

One predominant area of security revolves around electronic commerce. Many of the software giants and the major credit card companies have engaged in serious competitive lobbying for their particular technology, hoping that theirs will come out on top. I won't go into details about the proposed technologies or what the issues were because as of February 1, 1996, the two major credit card companies announced mutual endorsement for one technology. All major players on the software side have signed up. This technology is called Secure Electronic Transactions (SET).

SET is the converged protocol (superseding Secured Transaction Technology [STT] and Secure Electronic Payment Protocol [SEPP]) that is designed to handle secure payment with bank cards over insecure data transports like the Internet. The SET specification is available on the Visa Web site at

```
http://www.visa.com/cgi-bin/vee/sf/set/settech.html
```

SET permits a user to send a credit card account number to a merchant in a scrambled form. The scrambled number will be unintelligible to anyone listening in on the Internet and even to the merchants receiving the payment. But a special code will enable the merchant to automatically check with the bank that issued the credit card to make sure that it is a valid card number and that the customer is the authorized user of the card. Scrambling of the credit card number is based on a well-known and widely used national software standard known as the Data Encryption Standard. SET is slated to be incorporated into major Internet servers and browsers by the end of 1996.

Besides electronic commerce, other information that is passed over the Internet can be private. Private Communication Technology (PCT) is a security protocol that provides privacy over the Internet. The Private Communication Technology specification is designed to secure general-purpose business and personal communications on the Internet, and it includes features such as privacy, authentication, and mutual identification. PCT enhances the Secure Socket Layer (SSL), particularly in authentication and protocol efficiency. The protocol is intended to prevent eavesdropping on connection-based communications in client/server applications, with at least one of the two always being authenticated, and each having the option of requiring authentication of the other connection. For the latest information on PCT, see `http://pct.microsoft.com`.

Active Controls

You might have seen Web pages with edit boxes, drop-down lists, checkboxes, option buttons, and standard buttons. Are these controls? Maybe, but most likely they are only static elements. These are referred to as *intrinsic controls*. Basically, the World Wide Web Consortium (W3C for short) has agreed to some standard Web elements that behave like controls but are not defined as extensible. These controls are referenced by a standard tag, and each time a new type of control comes along, it has to be proposed and accepted as a standard before it can be used widely. The following is an example of an intrinsic button:

```
<INPUT TYPE=BUTTON VALUE="Cancel" NAME="btnCancel">
```

This button is a default size and has a caption of `"Cancel"` and a name of `"btnCancel"`. It is the responsibility of each browser to render the intrinsic controls and provide their behavior. It becomes readily apparent that a better method is needed to develop new controls and have the browser "know" what to do with them.

What is an active control? To understand what a control was and what it now is, we need to look at its evolution and then break the control apart and look at its basic features. Because this is not a history lesson and we're now on Internet time, I'll only go back to the release of Visual Basic 1.0.

With release 1.0, VB introduced Visual Basic Extensions or VBX files, as they are popularly called. These files were dynamic link libraries that either shipped with VB, could be built in C++, or purchased from third-party control providers. Soon after VB's release, it became apparent that not only VB could benefit from custom controls, but other development environments could as well, and a more generalized architecture was needed. Microsoft Access 1.0 shipped with the next generation of custom controls, based on OLE, called OLE Control Extensions or OCXs for short. It wasn't until the release of Visual Basic version 4.0 in 1985 that VB used this new type of OCX control.

Moving forward requires us to look at several contributing factors to the next evolution. First, the availability of the Internet is bound by the thin wire that ties our computer into the Internet. For most people, receiving information is limited to 28.8 kilobits/second (kbps) or less. Compared with accessing information from a hard disk or even a corporate LAN, this is painfully slow. Therefore, controls will have to become as small as possible so they load fast over the Net. Second, there is the concept of content providers versus content consumers. When a control is used during design time, the control must provide features not required at runtime that enable its properties to be set via property pages, handling clipboard operations, and so on. During runtime, controls need to be small and high-performance. Control providers would like to sell their controls to content providers but give away the runtime counterpart. OLE has since relaxed the requirement of design-time features for controls. A control simply needs to support the IUnknown interface. In this sense, there is no distinction between a control and a COM object. What this means is that controls are a lot easier to build. They can even be built in Visual Basic!

Now that you have these new lightweight runtime controls, what can you do with them? You can stick them in your Web pages. Before you place a control into a Web page, look at how other things are placed. The following represents a standard bit of HTML 2.0 code used to insert an image into a page, otherwise referred to as an inline image:

```
...
<IMG SRC="mygraphic.gif" ALIGN=MIDDLE ALT="Image Loading">
...
```

The tag `IMG SRC=` says this is an image, and the file `"mygraphic.gif"` is the image displayed in the page. The tag `ALIGN=MIDDLE` indicates the relative alignment within the page and the tag `ALT="Image Loading"` tells the browser what message to display if images are not displayable in the browser.

Recently, Microsoft and several other leading companies proposed changes to the World Wide Web Consortium (W3C). The proposal was that a more powerful insert tag be standardized that enables other items besides static images to be Inserted into HTML documents. You can view this spec yourself on W3C's home page at

```
http://www.w3.org/pub/WWW/TR/WD-object.html
```

Basically, not only active controls can be inserted but also Java applets, video and sound clips, and more. The following shows how an active control could be inserted into a page using HTML:

```
<Object
   id=mycontrol1
   type="application/x-oleobject"
   code="http://www.myserver.com/activex/mycontrol.ocx
   data="http://www.myserver.com/data/mydata.dat"
>
</Object>
```

Walking through this simple example: The Object tag is the W3C proposed name for the new inserted objects, and id gives this instance of the control an identity so that scripts can set properties and invoke methods on this object. Setting properties on this object is the same as in VB (for example, mycontrol1.text = "here is the text"). Code refers to the name and location of the control in this case. Data refers to the name and location of the data stream used to instantiate the control. Later, you will see a Web application written with active controls.

Common Gateway Interface (CGI) and the Internet Server API (ISAPI)

If you are into power programming in Visual Basic, check this out.

Interactive applications or scripts can be written in almost any 32-bit programming language, such as C, Perl, Visual Basic, or as Windows NT batch files (.BAT or .CMD). Applications and script can use either of the supported interfaces, the Microsoft Internet Server Application Programming Interface (ISAPI), or the Common Gateway Interface (CGI).

The Common Gateway Interface (CGI) is a standard interface used to write applications that remote users can start by filling out an HTML form or clicking a link in an HTML page on your Web server. The remote application grabs the user-supplied information, processes it, and then returns the results in an HTML page or sticks the information into a database. Traditionally, CGI applications are written using scripting languages such as Perl and executables created in C. Because the results coming back to you from the CGI application are specific to the interaction between you and the CGI app, these types of applications are referred to as *active applications*.

By using CGI, servers can access information not readily available to the Web client (such as SQL databases). CGI then acts as a gateway between the client and the data to produce information that the client application can use. The basic mechanisms for how CGI works are important to understand as we build these new generations of client/server applications. There are some limitations to CGI today, however. The server responds to the CGI execution request from the client by creating a new process on the server. Information is optionally passed to the server through environmental variables and Standard In (stdin). The CGI application will then process the request for information or post the data passed and return information or acknowledgment through the Standard Out (stdout) of the created process.

Because each request creates another process, this solution does not scale well to large transaction databases. Problems arise when precious memory and resources are being devoured by the many concurrent processes. To avoid this problem, you should refrain from using executables in favor of DLLs that the server can load when needed and unload when necessary. DLLs provide a way for a process to call a function that is not part of its executable code. Also, this process is OK for languages that support `stdin` and `stdout`, such as C and Perl, but not very good for VB.

Internet Server Applications (ISAs) are DLLs that are loaded at runtime by the HTTP server. They are loaded in the same memory address space as the HTTP server such that all resources available via the HTTP server process are also available to the ISA. Architected in this way, there is minimum overhead executing them because there is no additional overhead associated with each request. Subsequently, performance is dramatically improved and the server scales well under heavy load.

Unlike the Environmental variable and stdin/stdout approach, interactions between the HTTP server and the ISA are managed through Extension Control Blocks (ECBs). For more details of ISAPI, see:

```
http://www/microsoft.com/intdev
```

Installing and Running ISAPI Applications on Internet Information Server

Once you have written your OLE automation server, place it in the `/Scripts` directory. This directory is a virtual directory for applications. By default, this virtual directory has Execute access to everyone.

If your application does not require data from the user, you can create a link to your application in any HTML file. If your application does require data from the user, you can use an HTML form.

For testing or specialized cases, a uniform resource locator (URL), optionally containing data parameters, can be launched from a browser. Here's an example that passes parameters:

```
http://scripts/foo.dll?Param1+Param2
```

The following is an example of a link to an application that does not require input from the user. Notice there are no parameters being passed:

```
http://www.cool.com/scripts/display.exe?
```

In both cases, /scripts refers to the virtual directory for the interactive applications.

If you are creating an application that requires input from the user, the best method to date is to create an HTML form. The following lines of HTML are used to construct a very basic form with one text box into which the user is prompted to enter text and two buttons. One button clears the value in the form and the other "submits" the form data to the ImportData.EXE program stored in the /scripts virtual root on the server. The executable program can then use the value for whatever purposes it wants, such as updating a database or writing it into a file.

```
<HTML><HEAD><TITLE>Here is a simple HTML form</TITLE></HEAD>
    <BODY BGCOLOR=#FFFFFF>
    <FONT FACE "ARIAL" SIZE=2>
    <HR>
    <!------ Let the Form begin. The next line does the real work----- >
    <FORM ACTION="/SCRIPTS/ImportData.exe" METHOD="POST">
        <B>What is your name?</B>
        <INPUT TYPE="TEXT" NAME="UserName" SIZE="10" MAXLENGTH="15">
        <INPUT TYPE="RESET" VALUE="Clear Field"><INPUT TYPE="SUBMIT">
    </FORM>
</HTML>
```

The following lines contain examples of other input types besides the text box and buttons used in the previous example. Like the text box and buttons, each of these are intrinsic controls.

Here is an example of a checkbox that is initially checked:

```
<INPUT TYPE="CHECKBOX" NAME="CHECK1" CHECKED>Check Me <P>
```

The following is an example of a couple of radio buttons. Because the NAME property is the same for both, they are part of the same group and only one can be selected at a time.

```
    <INPUT TYPE="RADIO" NAME="OPTGROUP" VALUE="1">Choose Me <P>
    <INPUT TYPE="RADIO" NAME="OPTGROUP" VALUE="2">No, Choose Me <P>
```

Here is an example of a password type text input. The typed text will not be displayed:

```
Enter 9 Digit Password: <INPUT TYPE="PASSWORD"
➡NAME="USR_PASSWORD" MAXLENGTH="9">Me <P>
```

Here is an example of a multiline text field:

```
Enter Comment Below: <BR>
<TEXTAREA NAME="Comment" ROWS="5" COLS = "60">
```

Here is some default text to stick in the box:

```
</TEXTAREA>
```

Here is a single choice drop-down listbox defaulting to Green:

```
What Color?
<SELECT NAME="Color">
   <OPTION> Blue
   <OPTION> Red
   <OPTION SELECTED> Green
</SELECT>
```

The following is a multi-select listbox with Cat and Dog preselected:

```
Select all that apply?
<SELECT NAME="Pets" MULTIPLE SIZE="6">
   <OPTION SELECTED > Dog
   <OPTION SELECTED > Cat
   <OPTION> Bird
</SELECT>
```

Any combination of these intrinsic controls can be combined into a single form and submitted using the Submit button discussed earlier. After I have introduced a few more concepts, you will see an example of using an HTML form to directly update a Microsoft Access database. At this point we are talking implementation and will rely on the Microsoft Information Server for the example.

Publishing Information Using a Database and Internet Information Server (IIS)

In the real world, information is not sitting around in static pages. In addition, it's not sitting in some huge database with no way to access it except scanning through the rows one at a time. What is needed is a way to send queries to a database and have it return the results to you across the Internet. Microsoft's Internet Information Server (IIS) ships with all the tools needed to

- Insert, update, and delete information in databases with information collected over the Internet using Structured Query Language (SQL)
- Publish information to a client browser based on a query passed over the Internet to the server

Here is how it works: Web browsers submit requests to the Internet server by using HTTP. The Internet server responds by passing back a document formatted in HTML. Access to databases is accomplished through a component of Internet Information Server called the Internet Database Connector. The Internet Database Connector, contained in Httpodbc.DLL, is an ISAPI DLL that uses ODBC to gain access to databases.

Httpodbc.DLL uses two types of files to control how the database is accessed and how the output Web page is constructed. These files are Internet Database Connector (.IDC) files and HTML extension (.HTX) files.

The Internet Database Connector files contain the necessary information to connect to the appropriate ODBC data source and execute the SQL statement. An Internet Database Connector file also contains the name and location of the HTML extension file.

The HTML extension file is the template for the actual HTML document that will be returned to the Web browser after the database information has been merged into it by Httpodbc.DLL. This HTML extension file can contain all the popular tags and multimedia effects of any other Web page.

You can get the beta of Internet Information Server with all the required DLLs from `http://www.microsoft.com/infoserv/`.

Using an HTML Form To Update an ODBC Data Source Using IIS

You will need several components to get this working correctly. First, you need a Microsoft Internet Information Server (IIS) with Windows NT 3.51, and then you need to ensure that ODBC is installed on this server. Next, you must have an ODBC data source. This example uses a Microsoft Access database.

You also need an HTML page with a form to collect the input. Then you will need to construct the IDC file to pass this information into the database. After this, you'll construct an HTX file to get the information back out of the database. Assume you have an existing Access database called Sample.MDB. This database has at least one table called `GuestList` with the fields described in the following table.

Field name	Data type	Size	Required?
`InternalID`	AutoNumber	Long Integer	Yes
`LastName`	Text	20	Yes
`FirstName`	Text	10	Yes
`Title`	Text	30	No
`TitleOfCourtesy`	Text	25	No
`HomePhone`	Text	24	No

Use an HTML form to append a record to the `GuestList` table. You can get a copy of ODBC 2.5 via anonymous FTP at the following:

FTP Address: `ftp.microsoft.com`

Path: `\byssys\sql_odbc\odbc-public\odbc25.exe`

Copy the Sample.MDB file to a destination on your IIS server. Set up an ODBC Data Source Name (DSN) for this database. You must add your DSN in the ODBC Administrator using the System DSN button. Choose the Access Driver and create a new DSN called Sample. This DSN should point to the GuestList table in the Server Sample.MDB database.

After setting up the database and the ODBC DSN, continue by building your HTML input form. Call it SampleInsert.HTM.

```
<HTML>
    <HEAD><Title>Enter a New Employee into Sample Database</Title></HEAD>
    <BODY BGCOLOR="#FFFFFF">
    <H1 Align = "Center"><FONT FACE="Arial" FONT COLOR="#000000">
    ➡Insert New Guests into the Sample Database</H1></Font><BR>
    <FONT FACE="Arial" FONT COLOR="#000000">Type in the following information
    ➡to enter a new Guest and press the Submit button
    ➡when complete</Font><BR>
    <FORM ACTION="/scripts/sampleInsert.idc" METHOD = "POST" >
    <TABLE BORDER BGCOLOR="#FFFFFF">
    <TR><TD>InternalID</TD>
    <TD><INPUT NAME="InternalID"</TD></TR><P>
    <TR><TD>LastName</TD>
    <TD><INPUT NAME="LastName"</TD></TR><P>
    <TR><TD>FirstName</TD>
    <TD><INPUT NAME="FirstName"</TD></TR><P>
    <TR><TD>Title</TD>
    <TD><INPUT NAME="Title"</TD></TR><P>
    <TR><TD>TitleOfCourtesy</TD>
    <TD><INPUT NAME="TitleOfCourtesy"</TD></TR><P>
        <TR><TD>HomePhone</TD>
    <TD><INPUT NAME="HomePhone"</TD></TR><P>
</TABLE>
    <P><INPUT TYPE="SUBMIT" VALUE="Submit" ALIGN="MIDDLE">
    ➡<INPUT TYPE="RESET" NAME="reset" VALUE="Clear all fields"
    ➡ALIGN="MIDDLE"></P></FORM>
    </BODY>
</HTML>
```

The next file is the IDC file. Call it SampleInsert.IDC. Notice that the first line contains the data source name you created in ODBC that in turn points to the sample database.

```
Datasource: Sample
Template: sampleInsert.htx
DefaultParameters: InternalID=NULL, Title=NULL, TitleOfCourtesy=NULL,
➡HomePhone=NULL
SQLStatement:
+INSERT INTO "GuestList" ("InternalID", "LastName", "FirstName", "Title",
➡"TitleOfCourtesy","HomePhone")
+VALUES (%InternalID%, '%LastName%', '%FirstName%', '%Title%',
➡'%TitleOfCourtesy%', '%HomePhone%');
#IDC-Insert FrontHTM-sampleInsert.htm ReportHTX-sampleInsert.htx
```

Now that the information has been updated, create an HTML extension template for getting the information back out. This method creates dynamic HTML and streams it to your browser with all the appropriate data from the database incorporated inside. Call this file SampleInsert.HTX.

```
<HTML>
   <HEAD><Title>Here's the results of our insert</Title></HEAD>
   <BODY BGCOLOR="#FFFFFF">
   <P><B>The following information was received.</B><BR>
   <TABLE BORDER BGCOLOR="#FFFFFF">
   <TR><TD ALIGN="RIGHT"><B>InternalID</B></TD>

   <TD><%idc.InternalID%></TD></TR>
   <TR><TD ALIGN="RIGHT"><B>LastName</B></TD>
   <TD><%idc.LastName%></TD></TR>
   <TR><TD ALIGN="RIGHT"><B>FirstName</B></TD>
   <TD><%idc.FirstName%></TD></TR>
   <TR><TD ALIGN="RIGHT"><B>Title</B></TD>
   <TD><%idc.Title%></TD></TR>
   <TR><TD ALIGN="RIGHT"><B>TitleOfCourtesy</B></TD>
   <TD><%idc.TitleOfCourtesy%></TD></TR>
<TR><TD ALIGN="RIGHT"><B>HomePhone</B></TD>
   <TD><%idc.HomePhone%></TD></TR>
   </TABLE><P>
   <A HREF="/sampleInsert.htm">Return To Data Entry Page</A>
   </BODY>
</HTML>
```

By placing the SampleInsert.HTM HTML document in your IIS Home directory (the default is c:\inetsrv\wwwroot) and placing the SampleInsert.IDC file and the SampleInsert.HTX file into the /scripts directory (the default is c:\inetsrv\scripts) you are ready to insert information into the database via the Web. All you need to do is load your Microsoft Internet Explorer browser and type in the URL http://www.myserver.com/SampleInsert.htm (assuming your server is www.myserver.com) and the form will display, ready for input. Fill in the fields and click the Submit button and the information is posted up to your IIS server where it is dumped into your database.

This is a very simple implementation. A more professional approach would be to specify Microsoft SQL Server as your ODBC data source and write stored procedures to insert and get data from SQL Server. Using this approach, instead of a series of SQL commands under the SQLStatement, in the IDC file you would substitute the stored procedure name and the values of any parameters the stored procedure expects. Nonetheless, you have just constructed an active Internet application.

WinINet API

Until recently, the only way to work with the Internet programmatically was through in-depth knowledge of TCP/IP and the Winsock API. With security and proxies thrown in, this can be quite a challenge. Bringing programming of the Internet up a level is what WinINet is about, instead of worrying about what version of the protocol to use or differentiating between the different securities of accessing the Internet resources via secure gateway servers while also accessing information on corporate intranets. WININET.DLL is the dynamic link library where all the WinINet functions reside. This DLL, a help file, and the specification for the API are available on

```
http://www.microsoft.com/intdev/sdk/docs/wininet
```

This DLL exports functions for the three most popular protocols, HTTP, gopher, and FTP. You do not need to bother with TCP/IP or sockets. WinINet, like most of the Win32 API, is handle-based. What this means to VB developers is that you don't need to write a DLL in C to wrap the functions before VB can use them. Basically, you call a function that returns a 32-bit number, and you use this 32-bit number in further calls to identify the connection.

In the WinInet API, there are several generic functions that let you connect to the Internet and even use full URLs. The URLs are parsed internally! The next set of interesting functions let you read and write streams of bytes to the server. There are `FindFirstFile` and `FindNextFile` flavors for both FTP and gopher, and you can even specify query options that let you specify options for the connection like connection timeout, connection retries, and so on. Like Win32, most functions return a BOOL (use an Integer in VB) for success or failure. Calling `GetLastError` returns the last error encountered. FTP and gopher return textual errors that provide additional information (use the `GetLastResponseInfo` function to see it). Like many APIs, WinINet provides callback functions that are really great for asynchronous operations with feedback on progress and completion.

VB does not use callbacks directly but can if the calls to the API are made through an OLE Automation Server. See Chapter 7, "Implementing OLE Servers," of *Building Client/Server Applications with Visual Basic* (included with VB4 Professional) for a great discussion of using asyncronous callbacks with Visual Basic.

So what does using WinInet buy you? First, caching of all the client-side Internet communications. Anyone who has used an Internet browser knows how nice it is when an image is in cache and isn't reloaded across the Net when the "back" button is pressed. This cache works not only on the client machine but also on the gateway server as well. Another advantage is that WinInet supports connections across proxy servers such as CERN. Programming sockets directly to do this would be a real pain. WinInet also supports a technology called "Session Keep-Alives." Normally, Web servers and browsers create a socket for every image on a page. If your Web server supports it, Keep-Alives might be able to reuse an existing socket which improves performance.

WinInet is your best bet over Winsock if all the functions you require are available in the WinINet API.

VBScript

Visual Basic Script (VBScript for short) is currently only supported on the latest high-end browsers such as Microsoft's Internet Explorer version 3.0. VBScript is a lightweight subset of Microsoft's Visual Basic language. The intent of VBScript is to provide a small, portable scripting language that can be platform-independent and operating-system-independent. VBScript is designed to be upward-compatible with the Visual Basic language. VBScript itself does not have a design environment, unlike VB. It is a component that is used by a host, such as an Internet browser or other application. The following are the differences between VB and VBScript:

- All VBScript data types are variants.

- VBScript has no platform-specific features such as Clipboard, external DLL declarations, and DDE.

- VBScript has no classes, collections, support for early binding, or calls to external OLE Automation Servers.

For the latest working draft standard for scripting, see the W3C spec

```
http://www.w3.org/pub/WWW/TR/WD-Script.htm
```

For a complete definition of the VBScript language, see

```
http://www.microsoft.com/inetsrv/
```

The following example shows VBScript used to validate the date entered in a text box by preventing it from being set before today:

```
<HTML>
   <TITLE>Check Date</TITLE>
   <BODY LANGUAGE=VBS onload="PageInit" >
      <FONT FACE = "Times New Roman" SIZE=4>Enter Date</FONT>
      <PRE> DATE: <INPUT NAME=txtDate  SIZE=60></PRE>
      <PRE> <INPUT TYPE=BUTTON VALUE="Check Date" NAME="btnCheckDate"></PRE>
   </BODY>
<SCRIPT LANGUAGE=VBS>
   Option Explicit
   '--Initialize the page when the page loads, set to today's date
   Sub PageInit
       txtDate.Value=Date
   End Sub

   '---Check the submitted date to make sure it's after today
   Sub ValidateDate
       Dim RequestedDate
       RequestedDate = Cdate(txtDate.Value)
       if RequestedDate <= Date then
          MsgBox "Sorry Date must be greater than today's date",0,"Warning"
       End If
   End Sub
   ' Call the validate subroutine when the check date button is clicked
   Sub btnCheckDate_OnClick
       Call ValidateDate
   End Sub
```

Internet Glossary

You have learned many terms here, but there are still many more. For a concise glossary of Internet terms, see

```
http://www.ucc.ie/info/net/acronyms/acro.html
```

Summary

The information presented here is intended to give a very brief description of the current state of the art for the Internet technologies. Many of the technologies mentioned are still in beta at the time of this printing. The Internet is moving at a tremendous pace, so in order for you to receive information that is both current and valuable to you as a developer, I felt it necessary to take some risk with presenting announced but unreleased products in some of this material. The good news is that most if not all of the beta software presented here can be downloaded from Microsoft's Internet Developer page. To get the latest information regarding information presented in this chapter, please look at Microsoft's Internet Developer page at

```
http://www.microsoft.com/intdev
```

Using Visual SourceSafe

by Ken Felder

This chapter discusses Visual SourceSafe, the project-oriented version control system. Visual SourceSafe offers two principal benefits to your Visual Basic development process.

- Visual SourceSafe coordinates your team's efforts, ensuring that different developers do not overwrite each other's changes.
- Visual SourceSafe tracks old versions of your project, so that you can go back in time—if, for example, a bug appears in your code.

There are other advantages, such as tracking code modules that are shared between different projects; providing a centralized place where people can browse for code; branching projects, and merging them back together; providing project-level security; and so on. But it's very unlikely that you will start using version control for those reasons. Most people start using version control for the two simple benefits just listed, and then they begin appreciating the power user features over time.

The disadvantage is that Visual SourceSafe adds an extra step to your development process: checking files in and out of a centralized database. This process is not particularly painful, but it does take getting used to, and many developers resist adopting version control for that reason. It sometimes takes a disaster—a corrupted file, or a lost version—before a team actually decides to make the switch. Once they do, they usually find that the product more than makes up for the time it costs.

The Plan

Before you dive in, I want to give you a glimpse of what's ahead.

- The chapter starts by talking about buying Visual SourceSafe, just so you can figure out whether you already have it, or how to get it.
- Then you learn how to install Visual SourceSafe. There are two sections here: one for the Visual SourceSafe administrator, and one for each individual user. When you get through the installation, you're finished with the boring part.
- The fun starts with a tutorial that runs you through a basic SourceSafe session. If you actually follow along and do the steps, you will pick up most of the key ideas by actually seeing the product work.
- After that comes a conceptual overview of Visual SourceSafe, which is the real meat of the chapter: ideas to understand and tips for usage. For convenience, this is divided into two sections. The first contains basic material that you will really need to know, and the other contains more advanced material that you can skip if you are new to version control.
- Finally, the chapter finishes with some advice specifically targeted at the Visual SourceSafe administrator.

Buying Visual SourceSafe

Visual SourceSafe comes bundled with the Enterprise Edition of Visual Basic. If you bought the Enterprise Edition for each of five developers, then you have licenses for five users of Visual SourceSafe. You don't have to buy anything more.

If you have the Professional version of Visual Basic, you do not have Visual SourceSafe. You will need to buy the separate stand-alone Visual SourceSafe box, one license for each developer who will be using the product. These licenses will cost you just under $500 per user. The actual Visual SourceSafe product you are getting is identical, feature for feature, with the product included in the Visual Basic Enterprise box. Essentially, the Enterprise box is the Pro box, with Visual SourceSafe bundled in, and other cool stuff thrown in besides. So the price is pretty good!

If you have the Standard version of Visual Basic, you can still buy and use the stand-alone Visual SourceSafe box. However, some of the tight integration into the Visual Basic IDE is not supported by the Standard edition. Therefore, you will have the same functionality as the Professional user, but noticeably less convenience.

Installing Visual SourceSafe

There are two parts of installing Visual SourceSafe: a part that the SourceSafe administrator does, and a part that each user does.

Setup By the SourceSafe Administrator

The administrator takes the first step. He or she must run SETUP.EXE, found on the SourceSafe CD (or the Visual Basic Enterprise CD, SrcSafe subdirectory). He or she is prompted with three alternatives and must choose Server Setup. Then the administrator must specify a path on a shared server to which all users have access. The Setup creates the SourceSafe database on that server. In general, there is only one SourceSafe database per group, so this process is run only once. Note that in addition to creating the database, the Server Setup copies all the SourceSafe executables to the server, and creates icons for them in the Start Menu (Win 95) or Program Manager (NT or Win 3.1).

Next, the administrator runs the SourceSafe Admin program. This program is used to define the SourceSafe user list, which is the list of all the users who are allowed to log in to this SourceSafe database. Users are added via the Add User menu, and you can probably figure out the rest. However, there are a few subtleties worth pointing out.

■ Each user's SourceSafe name should, in general, be the same as the name with which he logs into Windows and/or the network. This will make life much easier for the users!

■ There are two kinds of user: *full privilege* and *read-only*. A read-only user can see what is in SourceSafe but can never change it. A full privilege user can actually make changes, such as checking out a file.

■ Your license—that is, the number of copies of Visual SourceSafe and Visual Basic Enterprise you have—determines the number of full privilege names you are allowed to add to the user list. So if you have five licenses, you can have at most five full privilege names on this list. (Read-only users are free.) This is a legal limit—the program does not enforce it at all—so the tracking obligation is on you. The Admin user does not count against your license. The Guest account does count, and you will probably want to delete it, or make it read-only.

■ Finally, note that anyone who can run this Admin program is god as far as SourceSafe is concerned. So you will probably want to protect the Admin program. You do this by giving a password to the Admin user. *Don't forget that password.* Write it down and put it in a safe deposit box. Without it, you cannot run the Admin program, and there is no easy workaround.

That's a lot of explanation, but in general, adding all your users will take only a few minutes. You can then tell your users that it's time to do their part.

Setup By the Individual User

After the administrator has created the server installation, each user will want to create a network or client installation on his or her hard drive. The key trick is to install Visual Basic first, and then Visual SourceSafe. Part of SourceSafe's network setup process is adding itself to VB.INI, which is not there if you haven't installed VB yet. So if you install SourceSafe and then VB, SourceSafe will not be integrated into VB.

So—after installing Visual Basic, but not while you are running it—go to the directory where the SourceSafe server was installed (ask your SourceSafe administrator). In the SourceSafe directory, you will find a program called NETSETUP.EXE. Run this program. It will copy the SourceSafe executables down to your hard drive, pointing back up at the SourceSafe database on the server. It will also create icons in your Start Menu (Windows 95) or Program Manager (NT or Win 3.1), and register SourceSafe for VB integration.

Getting Started with Visual SourceSafe: A Guided Tour

The easiest way to get started with Visual SourceSafe is to take a sample project that you have been working on and start using version control on it. The following is essentially a tutorial that walks you through your first SourceSafe session. You learn some of the more general concepts after the tutorial.

1. Open a project in VB. This could be a project that you are working on or just one of the VB samples.

2. As soon as the project opens, you are confronted with your first SourceSafe dialog box. Depending on the state of your project, it might offer to add the project to Visual SourceSafe: in that case, you can just answer Yes. Or, it might instruct you to Save your project and choose Add Project.... In that case, click OK, and then click the Save icon. Then, pull down Add-Ins | SourceSafe, and choose Add Project to SourceSafe. Either way, the dialog box in Figure 29.1 comes up.

Figure 29.1.
*The Add SourceSafe
Project dialog box.*

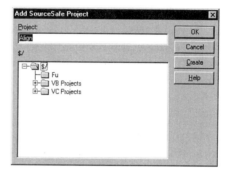

The line edit box labeled Project is the name of the new project you will be creating in SourceSafe—by default, the SourceSafe project has the same name as your VB project, and you will rarely have reason to change that default. In the list box below, you choose where in the SourceSafe project tree this VB project will be stored. (You learn more about the SourceSafe project tree later in this chapter in "The 'Project' Word.") Your administrator may have guidelines for where you should put things in SourceSafe.

3. Click OK. You are prompted with a message along the lines of Project $/Align does not exist. Create it? This is not offering to create a new VB project; it is offering to create a new SourceSafe project to house your VB project. Answering Yes brings you to the Add to SourceSafe dialog box (see Figure 29.2).

This dialog box features another odd control that you'll be seeing a lot of, the checklist box. You can click on the checkboxes to turn different items on or off; you can also use Select All to turn them all on. When you are adding a project, you will almost certainly want all the checkboxes on.

Below the list is a Comment field. Because one of SourceSafe's main purposes is to track the histories of files and projects, it's important to leave good comment trails that describe what you did. In this case, the comment should describe this project overall: something like "This is the application that displays a spinning top."

Figure 29.2.

The Add to SourceSafe dialog box.

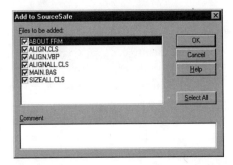

4. Click OK. The VB project is now added into SourceSafe. When the operation is complete, you return to a normal-looking Visual Basic window, with one subtle difference: next to each icon in the project window is a little red dot. If you look closer, you will see that the dot is actually meant to represent a tiny padlock. Now that the file is in SourceSafe, it is locked, and cannot be edited.

5. Pull up a form or .BAS file, and try to edit some code. Try to drag a control around the form. Try to insert a new form. You will find that these operations all fail. The reason is that your files are under Visual SourceSafe's control: you have to check them out before you can modify them.

6. Choose Check Out from the Tools menu. This brings up the (now-familiar) check-list box, giving you a selection of files to check out. Choose one or more .FRM or .BAS files, and click OK. This checks the file(s) out: the padlock in the project window turns to a checkmark, indicating a file that you have checked out.

> Earlier, I said you should get into the habit of entering good comments. You just hit the one exception: I almost never actually use a comment on Check Out. Most comments in SourceSafe last forever, but a Check Out comment lasts only until you check the file in, and then it is gone. Also, even if you do leave a Check Out comment, it's really hard to find out what you said!

7. Bring up a file that you checked out, and make a small edit to the code. Add a few lines, delete a few lines, and/or change a few lines. You will notice that the changes succeed now because the file is checked out. Save your changes.

8. Under Add-Ins | SourceSafe, click "Show Differences." A dialog box like the one in Figure 29.3 comes up.

   SourceSafe shows you the changes you made to the text. On the left is the file in SourceSafe—that is, the file before you checked it out. On the right is your local file, including the changes you made. The blue, red, and green coloring indicates lines that you deleted, changed, or added. You can use the Next Diff and Prev Diff buttons to quickly move through your changes.

Click Close to close the Differences dialog box.

Figure 29.3.
The Differences dialog box.

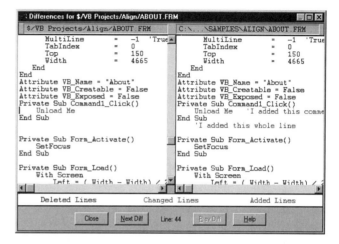

9. Choose Check In from the Tools menu. Once again, you see the check-list box, this time full of the files that you have checked out. Check all the files that you want to check in. Enter a comment, this time describing the change you made. When you click OK, the file is checked in, and the checkmark becomes a padlock once again.

> What will happen if you choose the Show Differences command now? Answer: it will tell you that the files are identical. Remember, this command compares the file in SourceSafe to your local file. So immediately after a Check In, SourceSafe always reports that there are no differences at all!

10. Under Add-Ins | SourceSafe, click Show History. A dialog box like the one in Figure 29.4 comes up.

The "history" of the file is all its old versions. You can use the Details button to see all the details of a particular version, including the all-important comment that tells you what actually happened. A subtle trick that you can play here is to use multiple selection (Ctrl+Click) to choose any two versions, and then click the Diff button to compare those two versions.

With the history, the guided tour ends. You have just used almost all of the commands that you will use on a day-to-day basis in SourceSafe: Add Project, Check Out, Check In, Show Differences, and Show History. There are a few other key commands that will be mentioned along the way, but it is time to move away from the catalog now and explain a little more of the underlying concepts behind what you've been doing.

Figure 29.4.
The History dialog box.

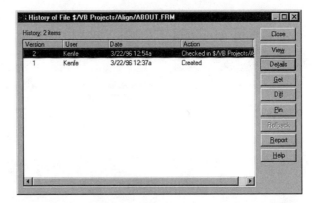

Basic Visual SourceSafe Concepts

The first thing to understand about Visual SourceSafe is that your code is actually stored in two places: on your hard drive and in the Visual SourceSafe database. Actually, to be more general, suppose you have five developers working together on a project. That project will be stored in six places: once on each hard drive, and once in the central SourceSafe database.

The database is the meeting place where the whole group comes together, so it always has the "master copy" of every file. But VB does not know about the database at all: it still works entirely in your local directory. I like to distinguish by saying that the database is where you store and track your code; your hard drive is where you edit and run your code.

The Four Key Visual SourceSafe Commands

The four key Visual SourceSafe commands—the ones on the Tools menu—are all concerned with moving files between your hard drive and the SourceSafe database. These commands are explained in Table 29.1 in order.

Table 29.1. The four key Visual SourceSafe commands.

Command	Description
Get	Copies a file from SourceSafe to your local hard drive. The file is read-only (for viewing or running, not for editing).
Check Out	Copies a file from SourceSafe to your local hard drive. The file is writable (for editing).
Check In	Ends a Check Out. Copies your changed file back into SourceSafe, "publishing" your changes for the rest of the group.
Undo Check Out	Ends a Check Out. Copies the SourceSafe file back on top of your local file, destroying all your changes.

Get and Check Out do very similar things: both copy a file, or files, from SourceSafe to your local drive. However, Get is a very simple operation that says, "I just want to look at this file." When you Get a file, you promise not to change it. Check Out, on the other hand, tells SourceSafe that you will be editing this file. In many cases, this means that no one else can check out the file until you check it back in.

Check In and Undo Check Out are similar to each other in that they both end a Check Out. But Check In says "Yes" to your changes: it copies them back up to the server and creates a new version in SourceSafe. Undo Check Out says "No" to your changes—I didn't mean them, it was all a big mistake—go back to the world before I checked this file out. No new version is created, and all your changes are lost.

Earlier in the chapter you learned about Check Out and Check In, but not Get. In fact, Get is pretty useless if you are the only person working on the project, because you already have the files. On the other hand, if you are in a multiuser project, Get might be the command you use most often, because Get is the way you get up-to-date with everyone else's changes. Even after someone checks a file into SourceSafe or adds a new file, you don't see it until you Get it.

When I'm doing development in a group, I tend to start every morning with a fresh Get of the whole project (that's what the Select All button in the Get dialog box is great for). This gives me all the changes that other people checked in the previous day. It's a pretty smart command: if you already have the latest and greatest copy of a file, Get doesn't copy it down (this is just a performance optimization). More importantly, if you have a file checked out, Get does not overwrite it. So Getting the whole project is a pretty safe thing to do.

The "Project" Word

The next key concept in Visual SourceSafe is the *project*. This is also one of the most confusing, purely because the word is overloaded: a Visual SourceSafe "project" is not the same thing as a Visual Basic "project." A Visual Basic project is a .VBP file and all the files that it references. A Visual SourceSafe project is more like a directory or folder—it is a logical organization of files that happens to live inside the SourceSafe database.

SourceSafe projects are organized into a tree hierarchy, just as directories on your hard drive are. There is a root, which is arbitrarily called $/ (just as your root directory is arbitrarily called c:\ on your hard drive). Under that root go projects, and subprojects, and so on, into as simple or as complex a tree as you want to create.

The universal rule of Visual SourceSafe project organization is that it mirrors your directory organization. So if you have a directory with three subdirectories, and you want to put it into SourceSafe, you create a project with three subprojects. In VB, this tends to mean that the .VBP and many associated files live together in a Visual SourceSafe project, but there can be subprojects that house some of the files.

In general, you don't worry about or see the Visual SourceSafe projects. However, you've already seen one exception to that rule, which is when you add a new project to Visual SourceSafe. There will be a couple of others at key points, so it is important to understand that you are creating and manipulating a new logical hierarchy of your files on the server.

Getting a Project Started

Let me jump back to a group scenario now. You have five people on your team, and they all want to work together on a project. How do they get started?

The first step is to pick someone's copy of the project as the original. If only one person has been working on the project, that's a no-brainer. If all five have been working on the project individually, you will want to sync them all up, by hook or crook—because you haven't had SourceSafe around to solve your problems—until someone has, on his hard drive, the "real" project. For simplicity's sake, let's assume that all the other people delete their local copies.

We've already seen, in the tutorial, what the first person does. He chooses Add project to SourceSafe, selects a SourceSafe project, and his files are copied from his directory to the project.

Each other person now needs to get that project down to his local hard drive so he can start working. You do this by choosing, from the SourceSafe menu under Add-Ins, Open New SourceSafe Project. The name is a bit deceptive because the project isn't new in SourceSafe, but it is new on your hard drive.

This brings up the dialog box shown in Figure 29.5.

Figure 29.5.
The Open SourceSafe Project dialog box.

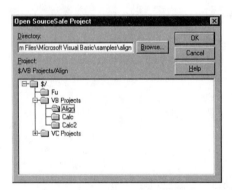

There are two key things you need to specify in the Open SourceSafe Project dialog box. First, in the project tree below, you click on the project that you want to download—the project in SourceSafe that was just created. Next, in the line edit box above, you type the name of (or Browse to) an empty directory on your hard drive. When you click OK, Visual SourceSafe actually gets that project into that directory, and Visual Basic then opens it. So you can start working.

I want to emphasize that this is something you have to do only once per project. One person did an Add, and everyone else did an Open New. But from now on, all the people will just open the project in VB, using the File menu as they always have, and SourceSafe will be ready and waiting.

> Add Project copies your directory into a SourceSafe project; Open New SourceSafe Project does the opposite. But what both of them do is establish a link between this directory and that project. This link is actually stored in a file called MSSCCPRJ.SCC, and without that file, SourceSafe would not know where to find these files. If that file is ever lost or corrupted, you can wind up in a situation in which the file exists in your directory and in SourceSafe, but they just don't know about each other. In that case, you can use either command; either Add to the SourceSafe project where it already lives, or Open New to the directory where you already work on it, and the connection will be re-established.

Check In Guidelines

The biggest guideline for checking in is, don't break the app. In all the groups I have worked for, the cardinal sin was checking in a file that broke everyone else. You can hack at the files on your hard drive to your heart's content, but before you check in, test. Test some more. Repeat if necessary.

The second guideline (always subordinate to the first!) is, don't leave files checked out for too long. When you leave a file checked out for more than a couple of days, you might be preventing someone else from being able to edit that file. And if that someone else is a savvy Visual SourceSafe user, he can figure out that you are the culprit. (He would do this under SourceSafe Properties, Check Out Status tab.)

The Project File

Every VB project is built around a project (.VBP) file. You almost never see this file inside VB, and yet it is the heart of the system. And that has certain ramifications for Visual SourceSafe.

First of all, the most important information in the .VBP file is the list of files that make up your project. Consequently, when the .VBP file is not checked out—which means you cannot edit it—you cannot add or delete files in your project. When you need to start adding and deleting, check the .VBP out.

In a one-man project, you can keep the .VBP file checked out all the time. But in a multiuser project, when only one person can have the .VBP file checked out, it's important to be considerate: check it out, do what you have to do, and then check it back in.

The problem is, the .VBP stores a lot more than just that file list. For example, the location of your project window is stored in the .VBP file. If you don't have the .VBP file checked out, what you will find is that you can move the project window wherever you want to; but next time you come into VB, it has moved right back! VB was not able to save your change. If you check out the .VBP, then VB will be able to remember where you put the project window—but after you check it in, everyone else will have to live with your new setting!

Because the .VBP file is not displayed in the project window, it isn't easy to see if it is checked out or not. To check out the file, choose Check Out—it will appear in the check-list box—and you can check it and press OK. To see if the file is checked out, the easiest way is to choose Check In and see if the file appears in the check-list box! Remember, the Check In dialog box shows only files that you have checked out. So if the .VBP appears in this dialog box, you know that you have the file checked out.

Adding and Deleting Files

As mentioned earlier, before you can add and delete files in your Visual Basic project, you must have the .VBP file checked out.

From there, things are very automatic. When you add a new file to the Visual Basic project, you are prompted to add that file immediately to SourceSafe. When you delete a file, the delete is echoed to SourceSafe immediately. Rename and Save As are similarly tracked. So it is no trouble to keep Visual SourceSafe in sync with what you are doing.

However, there is a downside to all this automation, which is that the .VBP file is still checked out. Consider the following scenario. You check out the .VBP file. Then you delete CUSTOMER.FRM, which is immediately deleted from your local .VBP file, and from the SourceSafe project. Now, someone else chooses Open New SourceSafe Project and downloads this project from SourceSafe. He gets a .VBP file that refers to CUSTOMER.FRM, but he does not get CUSTOMER.FRM. So you have violated the "don't-break-the-app" guideline, even though your local copy works fine, and you never checked anything in!

There is no perfect solution to this problem. However, you can generally avoid the problem by following this rule: after you delete or rename a file, test your changes and check in the .VBP file as soon as possible.

.FRX Files

In VB, your .FRM file is frequently (but not always) accompanied by a "silent partner," the .FRX file. For example, MYFORM.FRM will store its bitmaps in MYFORM.FRX. This file never appears in the Visual Basic interface, but it sits in the directory next to the .FRM file, and the .FRM simply will not work without it.

The Visual SourceSafe integration does a fair job of upholding VB's philosophy: use the .FRX, but hide it. For example, you never see an .FRX in the Check Out dialog box. But when you Check Out an .FRM file, the .FRX is also checked out. In a perfect world, you would never have to know that the .FRX file exists.

But alas, there are certain key SourceSafe operations where the .FRX does not follow the .FRM. You need to be very careful when you do any of the following on an .FRM file that has an associated .FRX, to make sure you don't split the pair:

- Whenever you jump into Visual SourceSafe's native interface, the Visual SourceSafe Explorer (Run SourceSafe command), you are operating on individual files. If you Check Out an .FRM from that interface, instead of going through VB, the .FRX will not automatically accompany it. This is one of the best reasons for going through VB whenever possible.

- Anything you do from the History dialog box that actually does something (as opposed to Details or Diff, which just show you information), is a source of danger. For example, if you Get an old version of an .FRM, you will still have the latest version of the .FRX, and they might not work together. In fact, the only way to safely get an old version of an .FRM is to use the Visual SourceSafe Explorer, and get old versions of both the .FRM and .FRX files.

- When you Share an .FRM file (described in the "Sharing" section, later in this chapter), you need to explicitly choose the .FRX file and Share it in the same operation. The .FRX file, if one exists, will appear in the Share list.

Advanced Visual SourceSafe Concepts

If you understand everything you've learned so far, you know everything you need to lead a happy, productive Visual SourceSafe life. But once you are comfortable with the system, there are ways to expand Visual SourceSafe into much more sophisticated project management.

The Visual SourceSafe Explorer

When you choose Run SourceSafe from the SourceSafe menu under Add-Ins, you see a whole new look at Visual SourceSafe. The Visual SourceSafe Explorer is pictured in Figure 29.6.

This Visual SourceSafe Explorer is Visual SourceSafe's native interface, outside of Visual Basic. I can't possibly itemize all the options here without rewriting the entire SourceSafe User's Manual, but now you know it's there. It offers a lot of powerful options. But for the basic options, you're always better staying in VB. This is not just for convenience: it's because VB is smart about VB, and Visual SourceSafe isn't. The .FRM/.FRX issue I mentioned earlier is just one example of how SourceSafe in VB can be a lot smarter than SourceSafe alone.

Figure 29.6.
The Visual SourceSafe Explorer.

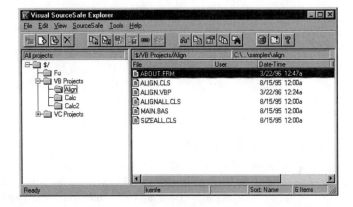

Sharing

In my personal opinion, Sharing is the most powerful and useful feature in Visual SourceSafe. The basic concept is very simple: one file can exist in multiple SourceSafe projects at once.

I said earlier that Visual SourceSafe projects are a lot like directories or folders in Windows. This is the exception: in Windows, every file lives uniquely in one directory. In Visual SourceSafe, one file can live in many different projects. When you update the file in any one project, the change automatically propagates to all the projects that are sharing that file.

As an example, suppose that someone else has written a file called SPELLING.BAS, which contains the exact spell-checking code you need in your project. So you take the following steps: first, check out your .VBP file. Then, choose Share from the Add-Ins SourceSafe menu. Navigate to the other person's project, click SPELLING.BAS, and click the Share button. (As noted earlier, if you are sharing an .FRM, make sure to explicitly share the .FRX as well.) Then close the Share dialog box.

This command actually does two separate things. First, in SourceSafe, it sets up a link between your project and that file. The file is now shared—that is, it exists in more than one SourceSafe project at once. Updates to this file in either project will immediately propagate to the other project.

In addition, the same command adds this file to your .VBP (which is why you had to check it out first). Hence, the file is being added to both "projects"—the Visual SourceSafe project and the VB project—at once.

The great power of sharing is that you do not have to worry about it after it's done. You just work on your project, fixing bugs and adding features, and some of your changes are silently echoed to other projects; you don't have to do anything special for those files. However, there are times when you want to know which projects are sharing a file. In that case, you choose SourceSafe Properties and look at the Links tab. This tab gives a list of all the projects that are sharing the selected file, so you can see who will be affected by your changes.

Multiple Checkouts

In a default Visual SourceSafe installation, all checkouts are *exclusive*. That means if you have a file checked out, other users can Get the file, but they cannot Check Out the file.

Your Visual SourceSafe administrator can elect to enable multiple checkouts. When multiple checkouts are enabled, more than one person can check out the same .BAS file at a time. When the second person checks in the file, his changes are merged with the changes of the other user, automatically. If there is a conflict (that is, both users modified the same line of code in different ways) the .BAS file is dumped back into your directory, with >>>>> and <<<<< markers around the conflict, and you have to edit the file before checking it back in. (The Visual SourceSafe user's manual goes into more detail on how to resolve merge conflicts.)

If you enable multiple checkouts, VB will still make all checkouts on .FRM and .VBP files exclusive. The Visual SourceSafe Explorer, on the other hand, will let you have multiple checkouts on an .FRM or .VBP file. I wouldn't recommend it. First of all, the .FRX file cannot be merged. Second, what are the odds that you and someone else are going to bang on the same .FRM file without any conflicts? And the .VBP is worse because minor changes can cause it to shuffle its text around a great deal. So my recommendation is to stick to code-only files for multiple checkouts.

Non-VB Files

Associated with any VB project, there are usually files that are not part of that VB project (such as specs). There is no way, from inside VB, to add those files to Visual SourceSafe. However, a good trick is to use the Visual SourceSafe Explorer to add them to Visual SourceSafe, in the same SourceSafe project as the .VBP file, or a subproject underneath. Thereafter, you will not need to use the Visual SourceSafe Explorer again: you will be able to check those files in and out from inside Visual Basic, because you have associated them with this VB project by putting them in the same place.

This brings up the obvious question: what kind of files can go into Visual SourceSafe? In principle, the answer is: any kind of files. Visual SourceSafe just tracks files, without knowing anything about their contents; so any file, text or binary, can be stored and tracked there. In practice, I use Visual SourceSafe for all the files for which I want to coordinate a team, or track versions of. Specs, images, HTML files for the Web, .RTF files for help, and so on, all go in. On the other hand, derived files—such as the .HLP file that is generated from the .RTF—don't go in SourceSafe because I can easily rebuild them from the source if I need to.

Options on History and Diff/Project Commands

As you might recall from the tutorial, when you choose Show History or Show Differences, the information comes up immediately. There is no chance to filter or change the information in advance.

However, there are times when you want to set options on how these commands are displayed. To gain access to the options, you have to bring up a pre-dialog box before the command executes. First, you go into SourceSafe | Options, click Advanced, and go to the Integration tab. Figure 29.7 shows the part of that tab which is used to control pre-dialogs.

Figure 29.7.
Checkboxes that control pre-dialogs.

If you click History, then every time you execute the History command, a dialog box will come up before the actual History, giving you options (see Figure 29.8). Similarly, Diff brings up a dialog box before each difference command.

Figure 29.8.
The File History Options dialog box.

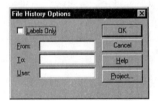

Once you have enabled the History pre-dialog, the dialog box in Figure 29.8 comes up before the History command. As you can see, it offers a variety of ways of filtering the history: you can give a date range, and you can see only changes made by a certain user.

There is also a Project button. If you click this button, Visual SourceSafe brings up a *project history*: a chronologically sorted list of all the changes to this entire project. This can be much more useful than ordinary file histories because it shows you the actual order in which changes occurred: "File MYFORM.FRM was just changed by Joyce, and before that SPELLING.BAS was changed by Mary, and before that CUSTOMER.FRM was deleted from the project..."

Similarly, the Difference pre-dialog box has a Project button. A *project difference* is a file-by-file (not line-by-line) display of what differs between your local hard drive and the Visual SourceSafe project. For example, if someone else deleted a file from the Visual SourceSafe project, but you still have it on your hard drive, Project Difference will point out the discrepancy.

For the common commands such as Get and Check Out, of course, you operate on the entire project simply by choosing the command and pressing Select All. Only History and Difference require the Project button, and an extra step to bring up a dialog box.

Personally, I like having History and Diff come up without an intervening dialog box: it saves me a mouse click. But once in a while, I want that extra filtering capability, and the Integration dialog box is a long way to go to get it. Fortunately, there's a secret trick. If you do not have the pre-dialog set to come up, but you want it to come up this time only, hold down the Shift key when you click the command. Holding down the Shift key says, "Bring up a pre-dialog before executing this command." It's not intuitive; it's not something you would ever figure out unless you stumbled onto it, but it's a great trick once you know it.

Options

If you're like me, one of the first ways you experiment with any new application is by looking for the Options tab dialog box. Visual SourceSafe has its own options, under its Add-Ins SourceSafe menu, shown in Figure 29.9.

Figure 29.9.
The Source Code Control Options dialog box.

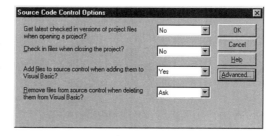

This dialog is a list of four combo boxes, each of which has three possible values: Yes, No, and Ask.

If you set them all to Yes or Ask, you are optimizing for a user who is really not used to version control at all, and doesn't want to think about it. You will be prompted to Get files when you open a project, and check files in when you close a project, so that version control will happen even if you never particularly think about it.

By the way, on the middle two—"Check in files when closing the project?" and "Add files to source control when adding them to Visual Basic?"—there's really no need to use the Ask setting. If you want the offer, just set them to Yes. What comes up is a dialog box (for Check In or Add) anyway, and you can just press Cancel if you don't want to go through with it.

Directory Mapping

Here comes an incredibly subtle point, which you can ignore completely, until one day it's suddenly in your face.

Suppose you have a VB project that consists of one directory (where the .VBP lives) and two subdirectories with other files. Let's say it's C:\ALIGN, C:\ALIGN\SUB1, and C:\ALIGN\SUB2. You put this project into SourceSafe (Add to SourceSafe), and then I get the project (Open New SourceSafe Project) to a different directory on my own hard drive: D:\DEV\ALIGN. I will get two subdirectories, called SUB1 and SUB2, because the structure of the whole thing was represented in the structure of my SourceSafe project. The question is, will my .VBP still work, given that it wants to point to "your" files?

The answer is, yes, it will still work. In general, the .VBP always stores relative paths, and even though the directory names are different, their relative positions are the same.

But now let's say you add E:\NEW.FRM to the project. This is not underneath C:\ALIGN, so there's no relative path. VB handles that fine, by putting the absolute path, C:\NEW.FRM, into the .VBP file. But what happens when you give that file to me? Do I have to create an E:\? For that matter, where is the file stored in Visual SourceSafe?

You will discover that what happens in this case, if you have Visual SourceSafe loaded, is that it will jump in when you add the file, and offer to copy it to the directory where the .VBP is. If you say yes—which I generally recommend—Visual SourceSafe will move the file and then add it. If you say no, this file will not end up in Visual SourceSafe. That means if you give anyone the .VBP, it won't work.

Refresh File Status

As you check files in and out of Visual SourceSafe from inside Visual Basic, the glyphs—the padlock and checkmarks in the project window—are updated. But what happens when other people check out files?

The answer is that the glyphs are not automatically updated. However, you can update them manually at any time by choosing Refresh File Status from the SourceSafe menu. This does not really do anything, such as Get files. But it does check on the status of the files and makes sure that the information VB displays is up to date.

In practice, I almost never do this unless I have some reason to expect that things have changed.

A Few Tips for Visual SourceSafe Administrators

The previous sections are aimed at Visual SourceSafe users (both beginner and expert). But there are a few key tips for the one person whose job it is to maintain the entire Visual SourceSafe installation: the administrator.

The Admin Program/Security

As you have seen from the installation section, the Admin program is pretty simple. You can add users, delete users, change their passwords, and make them full privilege or read-only with a few simple commands on the Users menu. You will want to give the Admin user a password—and not lose it!—to protect the Admin program.

The one advanced feature in the Admin program is the *project security system.* Go to the Options dialog box, Project Security tab, and Enable Project Security. This turns on a system in which you can give each user one of five levels of rights, on a project-by-project basis.

The project security system is documented fully in the Visual SourceSafe User's Manual, so I won't go into all the details here. But it's important to know that it's out there if you're interested in security—and it's easy to miss.

ANALYZE

In the Win32 or DOS directory in the SourceSafe server installation, you will find a file called ANALYZE.EXE. This is a command-line app: you run ANALYZE ..\DATA from a command prompt. The program looks through your Visual SourceSafe database for corruption and reports on any problems it finds.

Corruption in a Visual SourceSafe database is very rare, in my experience, but it happens. I recommend running this utility about once a month, just to see how things look.

> The ANALYZE process may take a long time, depending on the size of your database!

Back Up Your SourceSafe Database

My last tip is probably the most important, and the most obvious, but it can't hurt to say it. Back up your SourceSafe database.

In fact, it can't even hurt to say it again. *Back up your SourceSafe database!*

Your SourceSafe database (the DATA directory on the server) contains all the projects, files, and histories that make up the lifeblood of your company. If you have a good backup of that one directory, you can sleep at night; nothing can really harm you. On the other hand, if you don't have a backup, you are continually at risk of losing everything.

Summary

In this chapter, you learned to use Visual SourceSafe to follow who is working on your files and to track their histories. Visual SourceSafe is important for any professional development effort but is almost impossible to live without in a large-scale team development project.

For more tools and tips on Visual SourceSafe, check out `http://www.microsoft.com/ssafe`. It is full of white papers and tools you can download; my personal favorite is the white paper on using Visual SourceSafe to manage Web sites.

The Setup Wizard/ Setup Kit

by Christopher Rotberg

CHAPTER 30

Congratulations! Your application is finished—the hard work is over! Well, not exactly. Few people realize that a setup program can be as complicated as (or sometimes more complicated than) the actual application they are distributing. You might have spent months writing an application that has thousands of great features that maybe 40 percent of your customers are ever going to use; the setup program, however, will be used by 100 percent of your customers, so it had better work! After all, this is the first thing the customer is going to see and judge the software by, so a bad installation program easily can cast a shadow over what might be an excellent application.

The installation of a new program is a process that most customers are not very comfortable with; any bugs that surface can panic the installer. Customers will return applications they have not even run because they had trouble with the installation and they fear that the program is going to somehow "break" their computer. On the other hand, a well-written setup program might help the customer overlook a few bugs here and there in your application. The setup application is more than just an installation program—it is a chance for you to make a good first impression on the customer.

Now that I have lectured you on the importance of a good setup program, look at how Visual Basic 4.0 can help you achieve that goal. Two options are included in Visual Basic 4.0 for building setup applications: Setup Wizard and Setup Toolkit. This chapter discusses each option, as well as some tips not included in the Visual Basic 4.0 documentation.

Deciding Whether to Use Setup Wizard or Setup Toolkit

Although the documentation on these features might make it seem as though they are two separate functions, the Setup Wizard is just an automated way of using the Setup Toolkit. Even if you use the Setup Wizard, you still are using the Setup Toolkit. The difference between the two features is in the approach you take and your personal needs.

You should use the Setup Wizard for simple applications that do not require a lot of configuration settings or customization to the target system. If you want your setup program to install your application, copy some extra files, register some OLE servers (written in Visual Basic 4.0), and set up a shortcut, the Setup Wizard is for you. If you need to locate other files on the target machine, write custom entries in the Registry or to INI files, set up ODBC, or spawn other EXE files during the install process, you should look at the Setup Toolkit.

Before you choose a method, sit down and decide exactly what you need Setup to do, which files to copy, which configuration items need to be set, and what other applications need to be set up or copied in addition to your application. After you assess your needs, you can make an intelligent decision.

Examining the Setup Structure

Before you look at each setup approach, look at how the overall setup application is structured and what components go into producing a setup program. The following components comprise the setup:

- Your setup application first must know the name of the application you are distributing and its corresponding supporting files. These include your EXE, DLLs, TXT, and data files your application needs.

- The Setup.LST file contains the name, location, size, and version number of all files you are distributing, as well as the temporary supporting files you will need during the installation process. (These files are in the "Formatting The Setup.LST" section later in this chapter.)

- Setup1.EXE and Setup132.EXE are the actual EXE programs that perform the installation. They open the setup screen, check for disk space, prompt you for a destination drive, copy files, and configure settings. (These EXE programs are the result of compiling the Setup Toolkit.)

- Setup.EXE is the Microsoft Setup program that calls Setup1.EXE and Setup132.EXE to run after the Setup.EXE icon is double-clicked. It is the program that starts all the action. (This is the preinstallation program.)

Regardless of which setup approach you take, your setup application always needs these components. Before you learn the different approaches to setup applications, you should look at the Setup.LST file. This file is the road map that the completed setup application uses to copy the individual files to the correct destinations on the target machine.

Using the Setup.LST File

Setup.LST is a text file that lists all the files to be installed on the target machine. This text file follows the same basic format as that of most INI files, it is broken into sections, and contains various line items in that section. Setup.LST contains three sections: [BOOTSTRAP], [FILES], and [SETUP]. The Setup132.EXE or Setup1.EXE program reads this file to determine what files it needs during the installation. Explanations of the three sections follow:

- [BOOTSTRAP]: This section lists the files that are needed to perform the installation. These files are temporarily copied to the target machine, and then erased after the setup is complete. Typically the files in this section are runtime files that are required to make a Visual Basic application run. The file VB40032.DLL is a perfect example of a runtime file that is needed to execute a Visual Basic application. Other dependency files include: Setup1.EXE (for 16 bit) or Setup132.EXE (for 32 bit). The following code illustrates a sample of a [BOOTSTRAP] section:

```
[BootStrap]
File1=1,,setup132.ex_,setup132.exe,$(WinPath),$(EXESelfRegister),,
➥12/07/1995,174592,1.00.0029
File2=1,,stkit432.dl_,stkit432.dll,$(WinSysPath),,$(Shared),
➥8/15/1995,24576,4.0.2422.0
File3=1,,VB40032.DL_,VB40032.DLL,$(WinSysPath),,$(Shared),
➥8/15/1995,721168,4.0.24.22
File4=1,,ven2232.ol_,ven2232.olb,$(WinSysPathSysFile),,,
➥9/28/1995,37376,2.0.0.5524
```

> It is recommended that you not compress Setup.EXE, Setup.LST, or Ver.DLL. This should not be a problem because these files typically are under 100KB. Ver.DLL is not needed with 32-bit Visual Basic applications.

■ [FILES]: This section contains all the files that are needed by your application; these include executables, data, text, initialization, and dependency files. You can compress these files if you are restricted to a specific media type. Once Setup.EXE is launched and the Bootstrap files are copied, Setup1.EXE or Setup132.EXE continues the installation process by copying the files listed in this section to the target machine and performing any custom tasks that you include when you rebuild the EXE. (You learn more about customizing Setup1.EXE and Setup132.EXE later in this chapter.) The following code illustrates a sample of a [FILES] section:

```
.ex_,VIEW.exe,$(AppPath),$(EXESelfRegister),,
➥12/20/1995,385536,1.05.0003
File2=1,,dc.dl_,dc.dll,$(WinSysPath),,,12/8/1995,787968,1.1001
File3=1,,bench.ini,bench.ini,$(WinPath),,,10/25/1995,89,
File4=1,,Regsvr32.exe,Regsvr32.exe,$(WinSysPath),,,
➥8/31/1995,24064,4.00.0.0
File5=1,,Odbcji32.dll,Odbcji32.dll,$(WinSysPath),,,
➥5/12/1995,37888,03.00.20.01
File6=1,,rev05.bmp,rev05.bmp,$(AppPath),,,9/22/95,267574,0
File7=1,,access.ico,access.ico,$(AppPath),,,8/14/95,1078,0
```

■ [SETUP]: This section contains information specific to your application. It holds your application's title and default directory as well as the name of your application's executable file. Table 30.1 lists the information contained in the [SETUP] section.

```
Title=The App
DefaultDir=C:\App30
Setup=setup132.exe
AppExe=VIEW.exe
AppPath=
```

Table 30.1. Information contained in the `[SETUP]` section.

Element	Description
Title	This is the name that you want to appear in the splash screen during the setup process.
DefaultDir	This is the directory where your application is going to be installed, unless the user enters a different destination directory during the setup program.
Setup	The name of the Setup program file—normally, Setup1.Exe or Setup132.EXE. If you change the name of this file, be sure to update it here.
Btrieve	If you include Btrieve drivers, set this to a nonzero value.
AppEXE	This should be set to the name of your application, such as MYAPP.EXE.

Your application can be called anything except SETUP.EXE. This is a reserved name for the pre-installation setup application.

Formatting the Setup.LST `[BOOTSTRAP]` and `[FILES]` Sections

Each file listed in the `[BOOTSTRAP]` and `[FILES]` sections of Setup.LST must follow a predetermined format as shown here:

```
File x = y,[SPLIT],file,install,path,register,shared,date,size[,version]
```

Descriptions of this syntax follow:

x	This is the incrementor or sequence number for each file in the list. Each file must have a unique number and they must all be in sequential order.
y	This is the number of the disk on which the file resides. For network server installations or CD-ROM installations, this number is always 1.
SPLIT	An optional flag. Some of the files that you want to distribute will simply be too large to fit on one disk. This means that you will have to split the file across multiple disks. The keyword SPLIT indicates that the current line item is a member of a split file. The SPLIT keyword is not needed to conclude the split. An example of a segmented file follows:

```
File1=2,SPLIT,Oc3d.Dll, Oc3d.Dll,$(WinSysPath),,,4/28/95, 1151756
File2=3,SPLIT, Oc3d.Dl2, Oc3d.Dll
```

```
File3=4,SPLIT, Oc3d.Dl3, Oc3d.Dll
File4=5,, Oc3d.Dl4, Oc3d.Dll
```

file   This is the actual name of the file to be copied to the target system. For compressed files the last letter will be an underscore (_).

install The same name as that of the file to be distributed. Usually, this is the same name as *file*, except that *file* has an underscore for its last character. In that situation, *install* is the name the file should be after it is decompressed. (That is, the name when the last character is not an underscore.)

path   This is either an actual path or one of the built-in macro defined paths. Table 30.2 lists the macros you can use.

Table 30.2. Path macros.

Macro	Description
$(WinSysPath)	Copies files to the \WINDOWS\SYSTEM subdirectory.
$(WinPath)	Copies files to the \WINDOWS directory.
$(AppPath)	Copies files to the application directory specified by the user, or the DefaultDir value specified in the [SETUP] section.
$(AppPath)\SAMPLES	Copies files to the \SAMPLES sub directory below the application directory.
$(CommonFiles)	Copies files to the directory used for shared files: C:\PROGRAM FILES\COMMON FILES (Windows 95). C:\WINDOWS\OLESVR (Window NT, Windows for Workgroups)
$(ProgramFiles)	Copies files to the Program Files section, after you press the Start button: C:\PROGRAM FILES (Windows 95) C:\ (Windows NT, Windows for Workgroups)
$(CommonFilesSys)	Copies files to the directory used for shared file system directory: $(CommonFiles)\System (Windows 95) \WINDOWS\SYSTEM (Windows NT, Windows for Workgroups)

Do not use $(AppPath) for any entries in the [BOOTSTRAP] section because it is not determined at the time when temporary files are copied.

■ `register`: A key that indicates how the file is to be included in the user's system Registry. The possible keys follow:

`(no key)`	No registration is required.
`$(DLLSelfRegister)`	Insert this key if the file you are copying is able to self register. Usually DLL and OCX custom controls come with self-registering information.
`$(EXESelfRegister)`	Insert this key if the executable is self-registering, such as an OLE server created in Visual Basic.
`$(Remote)`	Insert this key if the file is a Remote Support file. Automation Remote OLE servers have a registration file (VBR).
`appname.REG`	Do not use this key. To update the 32-bit system registry, use the `RegCreateKey`, `RegSetNumericValue`, `RegSetStringValue`, `RegOpenKey`, and `RegCloseKey` functions in Setup1.VBP (Setup Toolkit project) and recompile Setup132.EXE. You can also use Regsvr32.EXE, explained later in this chapter.

■ `Remote#`: This line is written to the Setup.LST using information gathered in step 4 of the Setup Wizard. The Client Registration utility uses this information to register the Remote OLE Automation server. Step 4 collects information about the server address, network protocol, and authentication information. Notice the information is separated by commas, and the number matches that of the corresponding `File` entry line.

The following is an example of the line written to the Setup.LST if your application is using remote OLE Automation servers:

```
File2=1,,RSvr1.VB_,RSvr1.VBR,$(CommonFiles)\OLESVR,$(Remote),$(Shared)_
,4/10/1995,1147
Remote2="Schweiz","ncacn_ip_tcp",1

File3=1,,RSvr2.VB_,RSvr2.VBR,$(CommonFiles)\OLESVR,$(Remote),$(Shared)_
,4/10/1995,1147
Remote3=,,1
```

■ `$(Shared)`: This keyword is automatically added if the file is copied to any of the following directories:

`\WINDOWS`	Windows NT and Windows for Workgroups
`\WINDOWS\SYSTEM`	Windows NT and Windows for Workgroups
`$(CommonFiles)`	Windows 95

The presence of this entry indicates that the file is a shared resource, a blank entry indicates private scope.

■ `date`: The last date modified.

■ `size`: This is the size of the file. Setup1.EXE and Setup132.EXE use the `size` to calculate how much disk space is needed.

■ `version`: This is an optional flag. It is the internal version number of the file. If present, setup will use this version number to determine if it should overwrite an older file version. This isn't always the same version number displayed in the File Manager.

Using the Setup Wizard

The *Setup Wizard* is a tool that collects data about your application and its dependent files and then generates the Setup.LST file. As you learned earlier in this chapter, the Setup.LST file is a checklist of all the files that Setup is going to copy and configure during the installation process.

The Setup Wizard performs these actions:

■ Builds an executable (EXE) or in-process server dynamic link library (DLL) file from your project

■ Compresses all files and handles splits among disks

■ Notifies you of all dependency files that your application is going to need

■ Notifies you of the number of blank, formatted disks you'll need (if you are distributing your application on removable media)

■ Enables you to distribute from a network or a CD-ROM source

■ Determines to which directories your files should be copied

■ Creates the Setup.LST file

■ Creates a program group and icon or shortcut (Windows 95) for your program

The Setup Wizard performs a series of step-by-step procedures that walk the user through the information-gathering process.

1. The Wizard prompts you to enter the path of your Visual Basic 4.0 project (VBP) file and enables you to force a build of the EXE or DLL files. If the project has never been compiled, it automatically compiles it for you. A preexisting template also is available for you to use.

2. If your application uses the Data Control or DAO (Data Access Object), you are prompted for the database engines you want to distribute.

3. The Wizard asks you for the distribution media type.

4. The Setup Wizard searches your project for any reference to OLE automation components and includes them in a listbox on the current screen. You can add or remove files from the list. If you are using the VB 4.0 Enterprise Edition, you can select a remote OLE Automation server registration file (VBR) and specify the files that should accompany the server.

5. The Wizard also lists all dependency files needed to run your program.

6. It determines the deployment model that will be used. You can set up your program as a stand-alone file or as a shared OLE component. If you choose the latter, your application is installed as a shared OLE component in the \OLESVR directory.

> If you are using the Enterprise Edition, the OLE Automation Provider checkbox appears. If it is enabled, Setup copies AUTMGR32.EXE, AUTPRX32.DLL, RACMGR32.EXE, and dependency files.

7. This is your last chance to add and remove files. Be sure that you do not remove files that will interrupt your program. You can click the Summary Info button to see the total number of files and their uncompressed total file size. You can click the File Details button to get information on version numbers, file sizes, and dates. You can change the target location for files, but be careful about moving files that are shared files or OLE Automation servers.

You can save your template for this program from this screen prompt:

```
Press the Finish button to start the process.
```

Using the SWDEPEND.INI File

Every time you use an OCX, VBX, DLL, or reference in your Visual Basic 4.0 application, you are creating a dependency that must be taken into account. You are creating a dependency because these objects need various elements to be correct in order for them to work. They need extra files that they depend on and certain configuration requirements to be met. This is where the SWDEPEND.INI file comes in. It contains sections for all the custom controls, DLLs, and references you use and it lists each object's dependencies. As you purchase new custom controls, the installation programs for those controls are supposed to take care of updating the SWDEPEND.INI file automatically. In some cases, this does not happen and you have to do it manually. The SWDEPEND.INI file is located in the \WINDOWS directory and is a standard Windows INI file.

Step 5 of the Setup Wizard reads the SWDEPEND.INI file for dependency information to help it create the Setup.LST. If, for some reason, the SWDEPEND.INI file cannot be located, it is re-created. The 32-bit setup section [SetupWiz-32] of the SWDEPEND.INI file is re-created from the Sw32tmpl.INI file located in the \KITFIL32 directory. For the 16-bit setup section [SetupWiz] of the SWDEPEND.INI file, the Sw16tmpl.INI file located in the \KITFILES directory is used. Both these sections contain a BootStrap= entry that points to which Setup.EXE to use, as well as a key called SetupProj that indicates the path to the Setup1.VBP (Setup Toolkit) project.

Formatting the SWDEPEND.INI File

The SWDEPEND.INI file has a section for each custom control or DLL used in your Visual Basic application. Each section has three distinct lines that make up the section:

- [DEPENDENCYNAME]: This line contains the name of the custom control (OCX or VBX) or DLL for each dependency file listed in the Setup.LST. This means that every file indicated in this section is needed for you to use the file to be copied. Each control needs a separate section for 16-bit and 32-bit versions. If a section does not have an actual name for the [DEPENDENCYNAME], Visual Basic will append a "-32" to the [DEPENDENCYNAME] if it has been called by the 32-bit version of Visual Basic. An example of a [DEPENDENCYNAME] follows:

  [Section1.Dll]

- Dest=DESTINATIONDIRECTORY: This optional entry can be specified by the user or left to the Setup Wizard to handle. If you decide to use this parameter, there are several built-in entries:

$(AppPath)	Copies to the application's default directory specified in the Setup.
$(AppPath\Samples)	Copies to a specified directory under the application directory.
$(WinPath)	Copies to \Windows directory.
$(WinSysPath)	Copies to \Windows\System directory.

> It is recommended that you not use a hard-coded path such as c:\path because paths can change.

If the [DEPENDENCYNAME] line is not present, Visual Basic copies all files with extensions of DLL, OCX, and VBX to the \Windows\System directory and all other files to the application's root directory. In addition, if this line is left out of one section but another section contains a DESTINATIONDIRECTORY and a line that references the first section, the files from the first section are copied to directories according to the second section, which contains the DESTINATIONDIRECTORY. Whew! That's a mouthful, but maybe this example will simplify things:

```
[Section1.Dll]
Uses1=My.Dll
Register=$(DLLSelfRegister)

[Section2.Dll]
Uses1=Your.Dll
Uses2= Section1.Dll
Dest=$(WinSysPath)
Register=$(DLLSelfRegister)
```

The files from [Section1.Dll] are copied to the destination specified by Dest=$(WinSysPath) of [Section2.Dll] because it uses [Section1.Dll] as a dependency. I hope this clarifies things. In addition, any file that ends in :1 is copied in the \Windows\System directory in order to be compatible with Visual Basic 3.0.

■ Uses*N*=FILENAME.EXT: This key represents the name of a file or the name of a [DEPENDENCYNAME] section in the INI file. The *N* starts at 1 and increments for each additional file or section referenced. Filenames ending with :0 are copied to disks but not compressed. You should recognize the following lines:

```
Uses1=Your.Dll
Uses2= Section1.Dll
```

■ Register=REGISTERKEY: Register indicates how the object should be registered. The options follow:

$(DLLSelfRegister)	The file is self-registering.
$(EXESelfRegister)	The file is an executable that is self-registering. Applies to OLE servers created in Visual Basic.
FILENAME.REG	This file uses a REG file to be registered. It can be registered using REGEDIT.EXE and FILENAME.REG.

■ Register=$(DLLSelfRegister): If you are writing your own custom controls, you need to make sure that you update the SWDEPEND.INI file during your installation. If you are using a third-party custom control that has not modified the SWDEPEND.INI, you might need to register it manually.

Using Remote OLE Automation Servers

The previous sections discussed how step 4 of the Setup Wizard enables you to distribute OLE Servers. In order for your remote OLE automation servers to appear in this step, you must have built the EXE correctly. To make a correct EXE, follow these general steps:

1. After you select (Make EXE File) from the File menu you will be presented with a dialog box; click the Options button and check the Remote Server Support Files option. Visual Basic 4.0 creates a Visual Basic Registration file (VBR) and a Type Library (TLB) file for your EXE.

2. Step 4 of the Wizard detects that your client requires a server (assuming that the server is referenced in Tools | References on the client). Just choose Add OLE Servers to locate your server's VBR file (select type VBR from the combo box).

3. Enter the network address, protocol, and so on.

Using the Setup Wizard on 16- and 32-Bit Platforms

The Setup Wizard for 16-bit and 32-bit platforms is almost identical except for a few functional differences:

- Long filenames are supported only on 32-bit platforms; 16-bit platforms must use short filenames.

- Application-removal features are supported only with the 32-bit setup program.

- The 32-bit Enterprise Edition Setup supports both client- and server-side installation of remote OLE Automation servers. The 16-bit Enterprise Edition Setup supports only client-side OLE Automation server installation for 16-bit applications. Although remote procedure call (RPC) services are inherent to 32-bit platforms, you need 16-bit RPC support to run 16-bit servers. The Setup Wizard includes the 16-bit RPC files for you when you select the VBR file in step 4 of the Setup Wizard.

Using Setup Toolkit

Earlier in this chapter you learned the Setup Wizard and how it is used. I stated that the Setup Wizard provides an automated process of collecting information about your program's requirements. I covered the Wizard first because I wanted to show you how you can use the Wizard to help you create custom setup applications. In the Setup.LST file, there is an entry in the [BOOTSTRAP] section that refers to Setup132.EXE for 32-bit applications or Setup1.EXE for 16-bit applications. By the way, these filenames are not cast in stone; you can call this program file Myinstaller.EXE if you so desire.

The name is not important; it is what this file actually does that is important. This program file is the EXE file from the Setup1.VBP project. The Setup Wizard accesses the generic Setup1.VBP project and compiles it. This program file does most of the setup program's work. You use this project VBP file to make any modifications to customize the installation. Fortunately for you, the Setup1.VBP (Setup Toolkit) project also uses the Setup.LST created by the Setup Wizard. You can have your cake and eat it too! Run the Setup Wizard to create a list of files and their dependencies, and then just reference your version of the Setup1.VBP executable file in the [BOOTSTRAP] section of the Setup.LST.

Modifying Setup1.VBP

The Setup1 project usually is located in the vb4\setupkit\setup1 directory. This is a Visual Basic 4.0 application that has a lot of generic functions you can use and modify to meet your needs. Although you can directly modify the project in this directory, it is not a good idea. Instead, make a copy of the project and modify the copy. If anything happens, you always can get back to the original, and you still can use the Setup Wizard with a clean copy of the Setup1 project. Notice that most of the action takes place in the Setup1.FRM Load event, and it uses conditional compile for 16-bit and 32-bit applications. Load is the main processing code that calls all the functions to do hard-drive checking, directory selection, file copying, and configuring the target machine.

Adding Custom Messages

A good setup program should have the same consistent look from beginning to end. You do not want to modify the setup program so that it looks like one program with several programs inside it. Although there is nothing wrong with shelling out to other executables during the setup process, you do not want your setup program to look like you are shelling out to other processes. Installation programs that flash or periodically blank out the screen for several seconds can panic the customer who is installing. Your modifications can look just as professional as the rest of the setup program if you leverage what you already have. There is already a function that displays message boxes—why not make it display yours too? To display a custom message box, use the ShowStaticMessageDialog function.

There is one catch to using this function: You first have to add your own string to the resource file included in the project. The resource file is called Setup132.RES for 32-bit applications and Setup1.RES for 16-bit applications. If you have a C editor, you can add your own value and corresponding string to the resource file, and then include a Const for the string value in the SETUPRES.BAS file.

The following is some sample code to display a custom message that has the value of 2210 in the resource file:

```
<< SETUPRES.Bas file >>
Global Const resDSODBC% = 2210

<< form load event for Setup1.frm >>
ShowStaticMessageDialog ResolveResString(resDSODBC%)
```

The message now says Installing ODBC....

You then can use the built-in shell function to shell out to an executable that will install and configure ODBC. (Setting up ODBC is discussed later in this chapter in "Installing ODBC".)

```
sRegfile = gstrSrcPath & "ODBCInstall.exe"
fShell = FSyncShell(sRegfile, 4)
```

Manually Registering OLE Servers

There might be times when you need to register a control or OLE server and you simply cannot do it from the built-in installation routines. For these occasions, you can use Regsvr32.EXE. The following is an example of how to register an OLE server created in Visual C++ that is not self-registering:

```
ShowStaticMessageDialog ResolveResString(resDSREG%)

'Register the CCD.DLL now
sRegfile = gstrWinSysDir & "Regsvr32.exe /s " & gstrWinSysDir & "CCD.dll"
```

```
fShell = FSyncShell(sRegfile, 4)
If Not fShell Then MsgBox "We cannot register at this time."
```

Updating the Registry

In many instances, you will want to save information specific to your application after your application has closed. This might include the last window position, default database, toolbar size, or startup directory. A good place to include this information is in the Registry. Your application can read and write to the Registry at runtime, thus enabling it to know what toolbar size you preferred last time and to have it ready for you on the next startup. The functions Visual Basic 4.0 includes for writing to the Registry follow:

SaveSetting, GetSetting, GetAllSettings , DeleteSetting

These functions work only in a specific area of the Registry designated for Visual Basic. The Registry section is HKEY_CURRENT_USER\software\VB and VBA Program Settings. You can add any section names and key names you want in this directory to use in your application. The following is a brief function used to save preferences to the Registry:

```
Public Function gWriteRegistry() As Boolean

    Dim sApplication As String, sSection As String, msg As String

    On Error GoTo Errtrap

    sApplication = "View"
    sSection = "Options"

'***********************************************************
    ' Fix for Err 5 (Invalid Proc Call) for DeleteSetting
    SaveSetting sApplication, sSection, "ToolBar", "True"

    'This section is optional, but if used remember to use
    a bogus Save Setting first. DeleteSetting will not run
    if the section settings are empty.

    ' Clear out Previous Settings
    DeleteSetting sApplication, sSection
'***********************************************************

    ' ListView's View Property
    SaveSetting sApplication, sSection, "View", "3"

    ' ToolBar
    SaveSetting sApplication, sSection, "ToolBar", "False"

    gWriteRegistry = True
    Exit Function

Errtrap:
    msg = "Error # " & str(Err.Number) & " was generated by " _
    & Err.Source & Chr(13) & Err.Description
    MsgBox msg, , "Error", Err.HelpFile, Err.HelpContext
```

```
gWriteRegistry = False
Exit Function

End Function
```

> There is some exception code here that indicates DeleteSetting causes an error #5 if you try to use DeleteSetting in a section that has no entries. If you want to delete a setting, save a bogus entry using SaveSetting and then issue DeleteSetting.

Using the Setup Toolkit DLLs (Stkit432.DLL and Stkit416.DLL)

The Setup Toolkit ships with two very useful DLLs you can use to accomplish certain tasks such as creating an application group or folder and an application icon or shortcut.

If you examine Setup1.FRM in the Setup Toolkit, you will notice a function called CreateOSProgramGroup. This function creates the program group for your application. It does this by calling another function that is specific to your operating system.

For Windows 95, the function is called CreateShellGroup; for NT, it is CreateProgManGroup. These are functions in the Stkit DLLs that you can call.

To create a shortcut or icon, the code in Setup1.FRM calls the function CreateOSLink, which in turn calls CreateShellLink for shortcuts on Windows 95 and CreateProgManItem for icons in Windows NT.

Examining ODBC Installation and Configuration

OK, I know what you're thinking—I do not want to get involved with ODBC. It has to be set up and configured… it is a job better left to the end user… I will just tell him how to set up his own data sources…. Well, relax—installing ODBC and configuring it is not that difficult if you use the Installer. Yes, there is an Installer and it does work, provided that you have the supporting files set up correctly. There is far too much information on this topic to cover everything, so this section will just give you a little push to help you get started with the Installer. I show you how to use Installer to install ODBC and configure data sources for Microsoft Access and SQL 6.0. Because 32-bit drivers can be used by some 16-bit applications, and Windows 95 and NT are 32-bit, I will concentrate on 32-bit ODBC.

The Installer that you want to use for Windows 95 and Windows NT is called ODBCCP32.DLL. When provided with the correct supporting information (the ODBC.INF file), this file installs ODBC and configures your DSNs (Data Source Names).

Using the ODBC.INF File

The ODBC.INF file is the ODBC equivalent of Setup.LST. The file contains all the files needed by ODBC to run properly and configure your data sources. It contains several sections, each with a distinct purpose. The following list explains each section and its usefulness:

- [Source Media Descriptions]: This section describes the contents of the disks used for the installation. Each entry is placed in quotation marks (") and separated by commas. The period (.) at the end of the line indicates the current directory. You can specify subdirectories of the current directory by placing the directory after the period, like this: ".\win95". The files used in the other sections have a reference to one of the appropriate source media description line numbers. Consider this example:

```
[Source Media Descriptions]
"1", "ODBC Driver Libraries", "sample32.dll", "."
"2", "ODBC Driver Help Files", "odbcinst.hlp", "."
```

  The numbers "1" and "2" are referenced in the following section by using the equal sign (=):

```
[Microsoft Access Driver (*.mdb)]
"Setup"=1, odbcjt32.dll,,,, 1995-03-03,  ,,,  ,,,,,,
249856,,,, 2.0.23.17,
"Changes"=2, odbcjtnw.hlp,,,, 1995-03-03,  ,,,  ,,,,,,
83833,,,,,
"Engine"=1, msjt2032.dll,,,, 1995-03-03,  ,,,  ,,,,,,
878352,,,, 2.50.0.1117,
"Tools"=1, odbct132.dll,,,, 1995-03-03,  ,,,  ,,,,,,
78336,,,, 1.0.23.9,
```

  This tells the Installer that "Setup", "Engine", and "Tools" files are located in source media location "1", and "Changes" is located in "2". You do not have to use disks if you are performing a network installation.

- [ODBC Driver Manager]: This section indicates the files needed for the Driver Manager.

- [Generic Thunk ODBC Driver Manager]: Files in this section are used for the thunking layer with the Driver Manager on Windows 95 and Windows NT. These files enable a 16-bit application to use a 32-bit ODBC driver.

- [Win32s Driver Manager]: Files in this section are used for Win32 machines with the Driver Manager. These files enable a 32-bit application to use a 16-bit ODBC driver.

- [ODBC]: This section describes the files used by the Installer application.

- [Generic Thunk ODBC]: Files in this section are used for the thunking layer with the Installer on Windows 95 and Windows NT. These files enable a 16-bit application to use a 32-bit ODBC driver.

- [Win32s ODBC]: Files in this section are used for Win32 machines with the Installer application. These files enable a 32-bit application to use a 16-bit ODBC driver.

- [ODBC Administrator]: These are files used for the ODBC Administrator.

■ [ODBC Drivers]: This section specifies the ODBC drivers that are to be installed. The section looks like this:

```
[ODBC Drivers]
"Microsoft Access Driver (*.mdb)"=
"SQL Server"=
```

Each of the drivers then has a corresponding section for it that lists the supporting files for that driver. The Microsoft Access driver section follows:

```
[Microsoft Access Driver (*.mdb)]
"Setup"=1, odbcjt32.dll,,,, 1995-03-03,  ,,,  ,,,,,,,
249856,,,, 2.0.23.17,
"Changes"=2, odbcjtnw.hlp,,,, 1995-03-03,  ,,,  ,,,,,,
83833,,,,,
```

For each driver, there is also an optional section that lists driver attribute keywords. All ODBC 2.0 and later drivers must have driver attribute keywords associated with them. If they don't, they should not be included in the ODBC.INF. This section enables the user to set driver attributes and specify what DSN (Data Source Name) sources should be set up. You can have multiple DSN entries on one line if they are separated by a comma.

The following example sets up two data sources with the following names (in bold): OFSMDB and CCDApplication:

```
 [Microsoft Access Driver (*.mdb)-Keys]
SQLLevel=0
APILevel=1
FileUsage=2
FileExtns=*.mdb
DriverODBCVer=02.01
ConnectFunctions=YYN
CreateDSN=OFSMDB,CCDApplication
```

If you have decided to create a DSN, you will need a section that describes each DSN's attributes. This example continues with the necessary sections (in bold):

```
[OFSMDB]
Description=OFS departmental database
DBQ=C:\Program Files\source\OFSdata.mdb
DefaultDir=
DriverId=25
FIL=MS Access;
UID=admin

[CCDApplication]
Description=Data use in the CCDApplication program
DBQ=C:\CCDApplication\ccd.mdb
DefaultDir=
DriverId=25
FIL=MS Access;
UID=admin
```

The driver now sets up two Microsoft Access data source entries, complete with paths to the data stores. Each driver has different setup requirements, so you will have to check the ODBC manual for the exact format. Because many people use SQL, here is an example of a SQL driver section:

```
[Myserver]
Description=The SQL server my accounting application uses.
SERVER=Server1
DATABASE=accdata
```

In this case, SERVER is my actual server name, and DATABASE is the name of my database on Server1.

■ [ODBC Translators]: This section describes the translators shipped for each driver. It has a section that describes the files shipped for that translator. You do not need a translator section if you are not using translators.

For more detailed information on ODBC functions and settings, see the *ODBC SDK Kit Programmer's Reference.*

Installing ODBC

Earlier, I described in detail the ODBC.INF file. Now I will show you how to implement the Installer in code. The first step is to declare the Installer DLL, and then a one-line function call starts the process:

```
<< Module1.Bas file declaration >>
Declare Function SQLInstallODBC Lib "ODBCCP32.DLL" (ByVal hWnd As Long,
➡ByVal lpszINF As String, ByVal lpszSrc As String,
➡ByVal lpszDrivers As String) As Long
```

Now call the Installer:

```
Private Sub Command1_Click()
Dim bVal as Boolean
bVal=gWriteODBC(0&)
End sub
```

The actual function looks like this:

```
Public Function gWriteODBC(myhWnd As Integer) As Boolean
    Dim setupdir As String
    Dim rc As Integer
    Dim msg As String
    Dim sNull As String
    On Error GoTo Errtrap

    gWriteODBC = False

    'Setup the path to ODBC.INF
    setupdir = App.Path & "\ODBC.INF"
```

The following is the Installer line, in which I set up two drivers. You need to end the last parameter with two Chr(0) characters because ODBC is looking for a Chr(0) and a Chr(0) terminator to instruct it that you have reached the end, as I have:

```
rc = SQLInstallODBC(myhWnd, setupdir, App.Path,
"Microsoft Access Driver (*.mdb)" +
Chr(0) + "SQL Server" + Chr(0) + Chr(0) + Chr(0))
```

You also can use a universal network connection (UNC) path to a network drive:

```
rc = SQLInstallODBC(myhWnd, setupdir, "\\bcr\odbcsetup",
"Microsoft Access Driver (*.mdb)" + Chr(0) +
"Microsoft Access Driver (*.mdb)"Chr(0) + Chr(0))

    If rc <> 0 Then gWriteODBC = True
    Exit function

Errtrap:
    msg = "Error # " & Str(Err.Number) & " was generated by " _
    & Err.Source & Chr(13) & Err.Description
    MsgBox msg, , "Error", Err.HelpFile, Err.HelpContext
    gWriteODBC = False
    Unload frmMain
    End

End Function
```

The Installer will read your ODBC.INF file, install ODBC, and configure the data sources.

Configuring ODBC Data Sources

I know what you are thinking: "You just showed me how to configure OBDC; why another section on the same topic?" The reason is because you might want to configure a source without having to install ODBC again. If you are distributing your application and the target system already has ODBC installed, why install it again? You can use a function call that the nice people at Microsoft already have written for you just for configuration. It is called SQLConfigDataSource. This section presents some code examples to show you how to implement SQLConfigDataSource.

I have found that it is easier to add a DSN and then configure the DSN instead of just configuring it first. Let's take a look at an example:

```
<< Module1.Bas file declaration >>
Declare Function SQLConfigDataSource Lib "ODBCCP32.DLL" (ByVal hWnd As Long,
➡ByVal fRequest As Long, ByVal lpszDriver As String,
➡ByVal lpszAttributes As String) As Long

Your function()
```

Microsoft Access Driver Add and Configure:

```
rc = SQLConfigDataSource(myhWnd, ODBC_ADD_DSN,
➡"Microsoft Access Driver (*.mdb)" + Chr(0) + Chr(0) + Chr(0),
➡ "DSN=OFSMDB" + Chr(0) + "UID=Admin" + Chr(0) + "PDW=" +
➡Chr(0) + "DBQ=c:\ofsmdb.mdb" + Chr(0) + Chr(0))

rc = SQLConfigDataSource(myhWnd, ODBC_CONFIG_DSN,
➡"Microsoft Access Driver (*.mdb)" + Chr(0) + Chr(0) + Chr(0),
➡ "DSN=OFSMDB" + Chr(0) + "UID=Admin" + Chr(0) + "PDW=" +
➡Chr(0) + "DBQ=c:\ofsmdb.mdb" + Chr(0) + Chr(0))
```

SQL Server Driver Add and Configure:

```
rc = SQLConfigDataSource(myhWnd, ODBC_ADD_DSN,
➡ "SQL Server" + Chr(0) + Chr(0) + Chr(0),"DSN=CCDApplication"
```

```
➥ + Chr(0) + "SERVER=Server1" & Chr(0) + "DATABASE=accdata"
➥ & Chr(0) + Chr(0) + Chr(0))

rc = SQLConfigDataSource(myhWnd, ODBC_CONFIG_DSN,
➥ "SQL Server" + Chr(0) + Chr(0) + Chr(0), "DSN=CCDApplication"
➥ + Chr(0) + "SERVER=Server1 & Chr(0) + "DATABASE=accdata"
➥ & Chr(0) + Chr(0) + Chr(0))
```

Similarly, you can remove a DSN with ODBC_REMOVE_DSN. You also can use 0& instead of passing a handle to the hwnd through myhWnd.

To remove the DSNs you just added, use this code:

```
rc = SQLConfigDataSource(0&, ODBC_REMOVE_DSN,
➥"" + Chr(0) + Chr(0) + Chr(0), "DSN=OFSMDB" +
➥ Chr(0) + Chr(0) + Chr(0))

rc = SQLConfigDataSource(0&, ODBC_REMOVE_DSN,
➥"" + Chr(0) + Chr(0) + Chr(0), "DSN=CCDApplication" +
➥Chr(0) + Chr(0) + Chr(0))
```

I have covered only a few of the functions used for installing and configuring ODBC. There are many more, but I hope this gets you started.

Summary

This chapter reviews the various means available for installing your application. You now know how to leverage some of the existing functions available and have learned some tips on how to customize these functions. The ODBC topics covered here are far from simple, but I hope you have an understanding of how to use the Installer to simplify your ODBC installation and configuration. Now that you are a guru in installation applications, go ahead and write one for your application. Good luck!

Developing
International
Applications

by James E. Bettone

This chapter discusses how to develop your Visual Basic applications so that they will run the way you, the developer, expect them to run when they are used in different countries or locales. If you are targeting your application for an international market, you should try to make your application as functional in the foreign market as it is in the domestic market. Your application should run the same and act basically the same, regardless of the user's locale. This chapter covers the things you need to be aware of when you develop applications for international use and the enhanced tools available to you in Visual Basic 4.0.

This chapter introduces key concepts to help you develop Visual Basic applications for international use, such as the standard localization model, the advantages to designing software for the international market, and most important, writing and developing Visual Basic code that is easily portable to other international markets.

What Is Internationalization?

As more and more versions of Windows are introduced that are capable of working in different countries and languages, the demand for applications to support this user base is constantly increasing and is no longer a market to be ignored in today's global economy. Although the development time has significantly decreased, the need for international applications hasn't. You should consider some important concepts when you are developing your Visual Basic application. You should consider some of these before you design your application and also while the application is in its development cycle.

Looking at the Advantages

In today's global economy, there is more and more demand for international software. *International software* is defined as software that is marketable in the global economy. International software should be just as functional in the domestic markets as it is in the foreign markets.

There are two primary advantages to developing applications that are sensitive and appropriate to international-specific conventions, foreign data, and format processing:

■ After the initial development of your Visual Basic application is complete, you can launch your applications with little or no changes into foreign markets more quickly and at less cost.

■ You can develop international versions of your application without rewriting any code. You can develop an English version of your product (using the standards for developing international applications) that runs on the Japanese version of Windows without any code changes, for example.

Defining Locale

A *locale* is a unique combination of a language and a country. A locale represents the user's local conventions, language, and even the culture of the user's region. An example of a locale is French(Canada) and English(Canada).

In Canada, for example, there are two main languages: French and English. This means that there are possibly two sets of locales for Canada: English(Canada) and French(Canada). I say *possibly* because language isn't the only consideration; other local conventions such as currency or date/time formats are used to determine a locale.

An example of this is English(British) and English(United States). First, the countries are different but, aside from that, there are differences in currency between the two countries, as well as other things such as date formats. That is why these are two distinct locales; even though they both speak somewhat the same language (again, aside from being another country) the British have a different culture than the United States.

Exploring Localization Issues

Each different locale has different standards for things, such as currencies, date formats, and language. Some of the things you should consider when localizing an application follow:

- Your code should be able to handle locale-specific things, such as currencies, date format, and language. Visual Basic provides several tools to help you meet the requirements for writing international applications. Developing applications for use in other locales implies much more than just translating text messages and strings. Your application must support locale-specific dates, numeric values and separators, currencies, and language such as strings, error dialog boxes, or menus in the user interface.

- Each locale has its own conventions for displaying information, such as dates, time, currency, or numbers—Visual Basic uses English(United States) as its locale. Visual Basic gives you tools so that you do not need to know all the different conventions for your users' locales. Most of the tools provided by Visual Basic use the locale of the user's system as defined in the Control Panel settings provided by the operating system. These tools or functions that are sensitive to Control Panel settings and the Windows version are called *locale-aware*. Table 31.1 lists some locale-aware functions of Visual Basic.

Table 31.1. Locale-aware functions.

Function	Description
Ccur	Converts strings or numbers to the Currency data type using the Control Panel settings for currency.
Cdate	Converts strings to dates using the Control Panel settings for dates.
CStr, CDbl, CInt, CSng, CLng	Converts variables using the appropriate Control Panel settings.
Print	Prints out an object (forms or variables) in the current or specified context. Uses Control Panel settings.

Handling Dates

As when dealing with any locale-specific variables, such as dates, you never should hard code these within your application. There are a number of ways you can avoid this, as in the following example:

```
Private Sub cmdAction_Click()
Dim MyBirthDay as Date, OtherDate As Date

' Hardcoded date variable containing a date
MyBirthDay = "04/05/67"
OtherDate = CDate(MyBirthDay)
MsgBox "My Birthday is " & OtherDate

End Sub
```

In this example, OtherDate contains varying results, depending on the locale in which the application was executed. In most countries, the position of month, day, and year varies. In some countries where the month and day are reversed, this hard-coded date would be different. In the United States, the date derived from this format would be April 5, 1967, whereas in other countries, it would be May 4, 1967.

You can get around this issue by using date literals (remember this from database programming?) around any hard-coded dates. This forces Visual Basic to recognize the date you intended to use and to convert it properly to the locale's date format:

```
Private Sub cmdAction_Click()
Dim MyBirthDay as Date, OtherDate As Date

' If Hardcoded use literals
MyBirthDay = "#04/05/67#"
OtherDate = CDate(MyBirthDay)
MsgBox "My Birthday is " & OtherDate

End Sub
```

In this example, `OtherDate` contains identical dates in both the United States and foreign locales. So the rule of thumb here follows:

- Always place date literals around hard-coded dates.
- Always wrap dates within the `CDate` function so that dates are converted to a user's locale.

Handling Currency

As with dates, when you are dealing with currency, you have to be careful how you use them. Whenever you hard code currency within your application, avoid using the dollar sign ($) because your code won't run in locales where the dollar sign is not the currency symbol. Consider this example:

```
' Hard coded currency
MyMoney = "$196.98"
```

This example fails in locales where the dollar sign isn't the currency symbol and causes a type mismatch error. The British currency symbol is the pound symbol (£), for example, so this example fails in a British locale because of the hard-coded dollar sign ($), which isn't the valid currency symbol.

To solve this problem, don't use any currency symbols; just use numbers and a decimal as the separator (remember that Visual Basic internally uses U.S. locales). Type mismatch errors are hard to track down (depending on how well your error-trapping routines handle errors). The following code executes correctly, regardless of the user's locale:

```
' Hard coded currency
MyMoney = Ccur("196.98")
```

Also remember to wrap currency values within the `Ccur` function. This function converts numbers into currency using the user's locale information. You should remember the following when you are handling dates:

- Always wrap currency values within the `Ccur` function.
- Never use currency symbols.
- Always use decimals as the separator when hard coding values.

Handling Numbers and Separators

As with currency and dates, decimal separators must be handled in a special way. You can do this easily by using the `Cxxx` functions provided by Visual Basic.

When you are dealing with numbers, two things cause problems when you are localizing your application: the decimal separator and the thousands separator. The United States uses a decimal as the decimal separator and a comma as the thousands separator. Some countries, however, use a comma as a decimal separator and a period as a thousands separator. Confusing? Look at the following code snippet:

```
US Number  1,000,0000.10
Italy Number  1.000.000,10
```

Visual Basic makes it a little easier to handle situations such as these. As long as you wrap your numbers within CDbl, CSng, CInt, CCur, CDate, CStr, and CLng as appropriate, the numbers are locale-aware and determine the decimal separator for that user's locale.

Using Resource Files

Visual Basic 4.0 makes creating international applications much easier with the support of resource files. A *resource file* contains all string resources or text that appears in the application's user interface, such as menus, dialog boxes, and message boxes. If you use an application within a different locale from which it actually was developed, these resources must be translated to that locale. The process of adapting an application developed in another locale to that of a different locale is called *localization*. Localization is simply the translation of an application to a locale. Although this sounds fairly straightforward, localization involves more than translating each resource word for word; it also involves the meaning behind that resource.

Although this might seem time consuming, as stated earlier, all elements of the user interface should not be present within the Visual Basic application, but instead should be stored within a resource file where the resources can be loaded dynamically at runtime. The resource file usually uses the extension .RES.

> Nothing—*absolutely nothing*—is ever hard coded in an international application. If you have anything that needs to be hard coded, store it in the resource file.

The resource file can contain things like bitmaps, icons, strings, or even video clips such as AVIs, which then can be localized.

There is such a need for application localization in today's global economy that it is entirely feasible to have teams of people or even companies specializing in the localization of applications. This type of approach has several advantages:

- Cost effectiveness: After the initial development of your Visual Basic application is complete, you can launch your application with little or no changes into foreign markets more quickly and at less cost.

- Easier localization: Using a resource file and placing all string resources into that one file ensures a quick, efficient, and thorough localization process. This also reduces the chances of leaving strings unlocalized.

■ Shared code base: All international and domestic versions of the application share the same code base. This means less testing efforts, no code changes, and fewer bugs throughout the application.

Looking at a Standard Localization Model

In the standard localization model, your application is broken down conceptually into two blocks: the data block and the code block, as shown in Figure 31.1.

Figure 31.1.
The localization model.

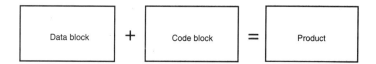

The *data block* includes all the string resources or all the resources that would be included in a resource file, but no code. The *code block* contains the code that actually runs the application, handles the locale-specific settings, and manages the resources in the resource file. Refer to the "Handling Dates" section at the beginning of this chapter for information on how to deal with locale-specific dates, currencies, and numbers.

Using this model, it is possible to change only the data block when you are localizing an application while keeping the source code for all the locales the same. The key to successfully creating international applications is separating the code and the localized data, and giving your Visual Basic application the capability to handle the different data and locales accurately.

Looking at the Advantages

There are several benefits already listed for using resource files and localization in general. Visual Basic has built-in functions for retrieving resources from a resource file: LoadResString, LoadResData, and LoadResPicture. These functions are discussed later in this chapter in the section "Using the Resource Functions." Storing resources in a resource file offers the following advantages:

■ The resources that need to be localized are contained within one resource file. This eliminates the need to change the source code or to recompile the application.

■ The application's strings, images, and user data are stored within a resource file instead of in each form in which they are used. This results in forms loading quicker because the form requests less memory resources to use and initialize.

Examining the Limitations

There are some limitations as well as advantages to using resource files; the advantages outweigh the limitations, however. A list of limitations when using resource files in Visual Basic follows:

■ In Visual Basic, you can have only one resource file in your project. Any attempt to add more than one resource file generates an error.

■ All the functions that retrieve resources have a parameter called Index. This parameter is the numerical reference to a resource inside a resource file and the parameter is limited to values up to 32,767. This might be a problem within a large project with resources of more than 32,767. (Any attempt to pass in higher values results in an Overflow error.)

Creating a Resource File

The CD-ROM version of Visual Basic (Enterprise and Professional) includes the means to compile resource files. The Resource Compiler compiles a resource *source* file (*.RC) into a resource file (*.RES), similar to the way in which Visual Basic compiles source code into an executable. Use the following steps to create a resource file (*.RES) using Visual Basic's Resource Compiler:

■ Create a source file (*.RC) with the extension of RC that contains all information about the string resources belonging to your application. (See Visual Basic's online help for the formatting for this file.) Basically, you have to associate the resource with a unique numerical identifier called a *resource identifier*. Visual Basic reserves resource identifier 1 for itself; it stores its application icon there.

■ Use the Resource Compiler to create the resource file. You then can add the resource file to your application from the design environment. See "Adding Resource Files to Your Project," later in this chapter.

Localizing Resource Files

Visual Basic does not have the capability (yet) to localize resource files. In order to do this, you must use a Resource Editor, such as Microsoft AppStudio (which ships with Visual C++).

If you are creating versions of your application for both the 16- and 32-bit platforms, make sure that you use separate resource files for each platform (16 and 32 bit).

Adding Resource Files to Your Project

To add a resource file to your project, use the File menu and choose Add. Or, use the hot key Ctrl+D. Select the resource file you want to use and click OK.

Visual Basic recognizes resource files by their .RES extension. Visual Basic won't load or recognize any resource files that don't have that extension. This also means that if a file that isn't a resource file has that extension, Visual Basic will load the file and try to use it as a resource file. An error won't be generated until the first time the resource file is accessed using Visual Basic's resource functions (LoadResString, LoadResData, and LoadResPicture), or when you try to compile the application into an EXE. Visual Basic also checks to see whether the correct resource file is used for 16- and 32-bit projects (it checks to see whether a 32-bit resource file is being used in a 16-bit project, and vice versa).

After the file is added to the project, you cannot view it in any manner (as a form or code module). In order to change anything in the resource file, you must use the External Editor (RC.EXE) or something comparable. Visual Basic now treats the file as a standard resource file.

> "There can be only one." This is true for resource files. Visual Basic allows only one resource file per project/EXE.

Visual Basic now uses and associates the resource file with your project. It is not a good idea to edit resource files while you are in the design environment. (It would be like editing the forms in your project using Notepad while Visual Basic is running with your project loaded—it's not a good idea!)

Locking Issues and Resource Files

Visual Basic does lock the resource file in certain instances in which multiple access would be treacherous (for Visual Basic). Visual Basic locks the file to prevent different applications, such as a Resource Editor, from trying to use the file at the same time. Visual Basic locks the resource file in the following situations:

- When Visual Basic is in Run or Break mode in the design environment.
- When Visual Basic is in the process of making an executable (EXE).

Using the Resource Functions

Visual Basic provides three functions to manipulate resources: LoadResString, LoadResData, and LoadResPicture. Each of these functions handles strings (LoadResString), pictures such as bitmaps or icons (LoadResData), and a miscellaneous function (LoadResPicture) to handle many types of resources. These functions are one-way functions: they only *retrieve* resources from the resource file. Visual Basic cannot update or append resources to the resource file from code.

LoadResString

LoadResString loads strings from the resource file. This is a fairly simple function because all it needs is a resource identifier or resource ID in order to retrieve that resource. (Resource IDs were assigned when you were creating the resource file.) For an example, see the following code snippet:

```
Dim MyString As String
' Loads a String
MyString = LoadResString(12)
```

LoadResPicture

LoadResPicture is used to retrieve bitmaps, icons, or cursors from a resource file. The parameters for this function are the resource ID and its format (see VB online help for a list of format options). For an example, see the following code snippet:

```
Dim MyPicture as Picture
' Loads a bitmap into picture object
MyPicture = LoadResPicture(100,0)
```

LoadResData

LoadResData is the all-around function used to load a wide variety of resources from the resource file. LoadResData can access any type of resource in the resource file (it is the variant data-type of the resource functions), including bitmaps, icons, cursors, strings, dialog boxes, user-defined resources, and font resources. For a complete list of format options, see the Visual Basic online help. For an example, see the following code snippet:

```
Dim MyPicture as Picture
' Loads a bitmap into picture object
MyPicture = LoadResData(100,2)
```

Summary

In this chapter, you learned some issues and key concepts for creating international applications. You also learned the steps from the design phase to development to implementation to easily create an international application with little code changes and reduced overall cost.

This chapter also introduced something new to the Visual Basic 4.0 developer, resource files, and the resource functions. You should now be able to use the resource functions and manipulate the resource file of your Visual Basic application.

Where To Go
For Help

by James E. Bettone

32

CHAPTER

Many resources are available to you if you are seeking solutions to tough programming problems or the mundane tasks that you know someone else already has solved. Since Visual Basic started taking off (with the release of Visual Basic 3.0), the number of publications; articles; Web sites; and News, UseNet, and user groups and forums has increased greatly. This chapter focuses on some of the major help resources available to most developers.

Internet Resources

The Internet offers a rich source of information via the World Wide Web (WWW) and UseNet groups or the NewsWire. The WWW offers instantaneous information, online publications, and even a link into Microsoft product support services. Also, UseNet groups give you the chance to network, ask questions, and bounce ideas off other developers via e-mail.

With the recent media and government interest in the Internet, the content of the Internet on the World Wide Web has drastically improved and is more available to more developers everywhere. The World Wide Web (or WWW) supplies things such as Web sites, home pages, chat groups, and online publications. By using a Web browser, such as Microsoft Internet Explorer or Netscape's Navigator, you can find a great deal of information, tips, tricks, and many other resources.

The NewsWire

Several discussion aliases or user groups are available on the Internet that cover a variety of topics, including Visual Basic. Table 32.1 lists some Visual Basic NewsWire groups.

Table 32.1. Visual Basic NewsWire groups.

Group	Discussion
comp.lang.basic.visual.misc	Miscellaneous issues not related to the other groups. For example, "How do I use the GetAllSettings function?"
comp.lang.basic.visual.3rdparty	Issues relating to add-ons, VBX or OCX controls, DLL libraries, or development utilities that enhance Visual Basic's Integrated Development Environment (IDE).
comp.lang.basic.visual.database	Database or client/server issues.
comp.lang.basic.visual.announce	Bug fixes, new product notifications, and vendor support announcements.

A very good search utility called Carl and Gary's Newsgroup Search Utility also is available. You can use this utility to search through all the newsgroup postings. It is available on the World Wide Web at `http://www.apexsc.com/vb/vb-bin/ngsearch`.

Mailing Lists

Mailing lists provide information directly to the developer via e-mail. Mailing lists are similar to UseNet groups. As with any mail group, you can use mailing lists to send and receive messages, get replies, or send replies right from your e-mail system on your desktop.

Subscribing to Mailing Lists

You can start receiving mail from a mailing list by subscribing to that list. Subscribing is fairly easy and is usually an automatic process that you have to initiate. Usually, in the body of a message you type the subscription command for that mailing list. I have included several mailing lists with the subscription information on the CD-ROM included with this book. You should replace bracketed information (for example, `[your name]`) with the appropriate information.

Using Digests

Most mailing lists support a Digest mode that you can use to receive all the messages (contained in a single file) for the mailing list at one time (usually at night). For large mailing lists, using Digest mode might be preferable to receiving the individual mail messages (this might be annoying). You can get a single mail message with all the day's mail conveniently contained in a single file and a single mail message.

Here are some of the mailing lists you can find:

Microsoft Visual Basic Forum

Send mail to: `listserv@peach.ease.lsoft.com`

Message text: `sub VISBAS-L FirstName LastName`

MS-VB Database Issues

Send mail to: `listserv@peach.ease.lsoft.com`

Message text: `sub VBDATA-L FirstName LastName`

VB App Classes

Send mail to: `listproc@ucdavis.edu`

Message text: `information vba-class`

FTP Sites

Are you looking for some cool code examples or programming solutions for easy, mundane problems (like populating a listbox with the result of a stored procedure)? You can find these through FTP sites around the world. *File Transfer Protocol* (FTP) is a means of transferring files from one computer system to another. Some Visual Basic FTP sites and their mirror sites follow. (*Mirror sites* are sites that duplicate another FTP site to spread the load between the multiple sites so that no one site is overburdened.)

CSUSM Library Technical Services: Visual Basic Archive:

```
http://coyote.csusm.edu/cwis/winworld/vbasic.html
```

Mabry Software's FTP Site:

```
ftp.halcyon.com/local/mabry/files/
```

Microsoft's FTP Site (visit the Visual Basic area in the `/developer/vb` directory):

```
ftp.microsoft.com
```

SimTel Visual Basic Archive:

```
ftp.cdrom.com/pub/simtel/win3/visbasic/
```

The Springsoft FTP Archive:

```
ftp.springsoft.com/pub/springsoft/win16/programming/
```

VB Tech Journal's FTP Site:

```
ftp.efn.org/pub/VBTech/
```

One of the most popular FTP sites is the CICA Visual Basic FTP archive. I have listed these sites separately because of the numerous mirrors around the world:

```
ftp.cica.indiana.edu/pub/pc/win3/programr/vbasic/  (this is the actual site)
ftp.cdrom.com/pub/winsite/win3/programr/vbasic/
wuarchive.wustl.edu/pub/win3/programr/vbasic/
mirrors.aol.com/pub/winsite/pc/win3/programr/vbasic/
ftp.pht.com/pub/mirrors/cica/win3/programr/vbasic/
ftp.agt.net/pub/cica-win3/programr/vbasic/
ftp.hawaii.edu/pub/ibmpc/win3/programr/vbasic/
uiarchive.cso.uiuc.edu/pub/systems/pc/cica/win3/programr/vbasic/
ftp.funet.fi/pub/msdos/Mirrors/CICA/programr/vbasic/
ftp.oleane.net/pub/mirrors/msdos/win3/cica/programr/vbasic/
ftp.esnet.com/pub/mirrors/windows95/programr/vbasic
gatekeeper.dec.com/pub/micro/msdos/win3/programr/vbasic
mjablecki.extern.ucsd.edu/pub/archive/cica/win95/programr/vbasic
ftp.rge.com/pub/systems/xxx/winsite/programr/vbasic
ftp.orst.edu/pub/mirrors/ftp.winsite.com/xxx/programr/vbasic
ftp.drcdrom.com/public/winsite-CICA/win3/programr/vbasic
```

```
ftp.drcdrom.com/public/winsite-CICA/win95/programr/vbasic
ftp.sunet.se/pub/pc/mirror/mirror-cica/win3/programr/vbasic/
```

Web Sites

There has been an explosion of Web sites dealing with Visual Basic. The World Wide Web offers instant access to a variety of information just by pointing and clicking, and it's all graphically based. Hundreds of sites are available, containing information about anything you possibly can imagine on Visual Basic. You can use a Web browser to browse or "surf" through the Web sites and view their contents.

I have included a list of Web sites on the CD-ROM included with this book. It is important to remember that these sites can go down (no longer work or become inaccessible) without any notice.

To browse through the many Web sites on the WWW, you need to have a Web browser. If you have Windows 95, you already have access to Microsoft Internet Explorer, which you can use to browse the Web. You also can use Netscape Navigator. Both applications have nice features and are easy to use. These applications are called "Web browsers" because you use them to browse through a Web site just like you browse through a magazine (but in this case it's all electronic!).

Online Publications

Most of the major publications dealing with Visual Basic now have Web sites that you can bookmark (a *bookmark* enables you to instantly return to that Web site). Many publications are located only online. I have included a comprehensive list of online publications on the CD-ROM that accompanies this book.

Really Cool Publications

Some really valuable, useful online publications are worth mentioning. These publications are rich in content, contain useful pointers, and are easily accessible.

The first publication is *Visual Basic Online*. This is a comprehensive online publication where the developer can learn of the latest developments in the VB industry. It includes a forum where Visual Basic programmers can interact with each other and with other software developers. It offers many useful articles and a *ToolBox* (a huge reference library full of information). You can see *Visual Basic Online* at http://www.vbonline.com.

Another popular publication is, of course, *Carl and Gary's Visual Basic Homepage*. There is a lot of useful information there such as mailing groups, Tips and Tricks, and Questions and Answers. Also, there are a variety of articles, white papers, and other materials available to help you in your search for Visual Basic knowledge.

CompuServe

Another resource to consider is CompuServe. CompuServe offers a forum for developers to get answers to different types of questions. Microsoft offers the MSBasic forum on CompuServe. This forum includes different sections for various types of questions. Simply post a message in one of the appropriate forums, and you'll receive an answer from someone at Microsoft Product Support or from some other user of Visual Basic. Some of the forums on CompuServe include information on the Data controls, Database issues, and OLE Automation.

The CD-ROM included with this book includes a list of the CompuServe forums relating to Visual Basic and Windows in general.

MSN

The Microsoft Network, commonly called MSN, contains rich content and a vast wealth of information on a variety of Microsoft products from Visual Basic to Windows 95 and NT. There are sample applications, articles, and white papers available to download for your perusal. Microsoft has devoted a lot of time and talent in developing MSN and, in particular, the Developer area of MSN.

To get to the Microsoft Network, use any browser and go to `http:\\www.msn.com` or `http:\\www.microsoft.com`. These are two places you definitely need to bookmark!

User Groups

Another resource to choose from is user groups. *User groups* are simply groups of people who share common interests and goals. Usually, a user group meets once or twice a month to discuss different topics and problems they have run into; sometimes they even give classes. If there aren't any Visual Basic user groups in your area, start one. It's not very hard: just supply a meeting place and invite anyone who might be interested. Usually, when you get a group of people interested in the same topic in the same room, conversation flows easily throughout the room.

This is a good way to network among other developers (the Visual Basic developer community is usually a fairly small group). Go to one or two meetings. Meet some people and get some phone numbers (or, better yet, an Internet address). That way, if you run into a problem (and it's two weeks until the next meeting), you can call someone right away. You might want to build a list of problems and bring these to the group for discussion. Make sure to express your questions so that everyone understands the problem. Saying, "I have a screen that GP faults," for example, isn't enough detail for anyone to give suggestions.

You can find a list of major user groups listed by city and state on the CD-ROM that accompanies this book.

MSDN

The *Microsoft Developer's Network* (MSDN) offers a wide range of resources, such as the Knowledge Base, white papers, and technical articles and information. MSDN is available in three subscription levels and is available from the Microsoft Corporation.

The Microsoft Knowledge base, which is available through MSN and MSDN, is a treasure chest of known bugs, how-to tips and tricks, and general programming techniques. The Knowledge Base covers many things other than Visual Basic, such as Windows 95, Windows NT, Microsoft Word, and Excel. If you want a quick tip or sample code, check here first.

Another resource available from MSDN and MSN are white papers. These are articles written by Microsoft employees, solution providers, and certified professionals from around the globe. The usually groundbreaking articles cover the hot topics of the day. This is a good resource to search if your topic is cutting edge.

Summary

This chapter introduces you to the different resources for Visual Basic developers. You learned about all the more widely used resources, including the Internet via the World Wide Web, online publications, and MSDN.

With all the popularity of Visual Basic, the Information Superhighway (the WWW), and other resources, there should be something available for you to use to help you solve programming problems or difficulties. Use all of these things to your benefit and learn from others—or better yet, show others the knowledge you've learned!

Implementing Help in Your Applications

by Christopher Rotberg

CHAPTER

33

I'm assuming at this point that your application is complete and that all that is left is to create a help application (help file). Unfortunately, creating a help application is not a trivial task to be looked upon lightly. It can be as big a project as your application itself. Because this is a book about Visual Basic and not help files, creating a help file is beyond the scope of this chapter. Instead, I will concentrate on how to integrate a finished help application into a Visual Basic application.

When discussing *integration*, I am referring to context-sensitive help and search capabilities that link to your help file topics. The help application should be seamless to the user; it should seem like the help file is part of the application, not something that is just tagged on at the end of the project. It would then seem apparent that in order to accomplish this task, you must have some knowledge of how the help file is constructed. That is the goal for this chapter; I will show enough about help file construction to allow you to properly integrate it into your application. Before I discuss the various pieces of a help file, you should know why you need one.

Why Do You Need a Help Application?

I don't know. I wrote my application so perfectly that the user should instantaneously be able to understand it as soon as he tried to use it. This dream would be nice, but it is seldom true. An obvious task to you (the designer of the application) might seem impossible to the end user. Everyone is different, and the blatantly obvious to one person is not to another. It is for this reason, and the desire to keep technical support calls to a minimum, that you should include a help application in your application.

Help applications have become such a widespread industry practice that end users actually check if an application has adequate help before they make a purchase decision. The fact that Microsoft is trying to incorporate a natural language query engine in its applications should be indication enough of the value of help files. Okay, so I have convinced you that you need a help file. Now how do you get one, and what is involved? Read on.

What Is a Help File and How Is It Created?

This is the stuff that they didn't teach you in programming school and that you have to learn on your own. You have to read books and search the online documentation. It is a topic that you need to dig deep to understand. Fortunately for you, I have already done that, and I'm prepared to share just enough with you to get you started.

A *help file* starts its life as a Rich Text Format (.RTF) document. It becomes a help file only after a valid .HPJ (precompile support file) file is created, and the Rich Text Format document is run through the HCW compiler (help compiler). The .RTF document and the .HPJ file must follow the compilers format, or the help compiler returns an error. Because a help application is nothing more than a series of topics, the .RTF document is nothing more than a series of paragraphs that are separated by page breaks. Each paragraph is considered to be a topic, and it must be formatted with special characters.

These characters are inserted into the .RTF document by the writer as footnote entries. Each topic has a corresponding footnote entry that the compiler reads to decide where the topic starts and stops. There are four basic characters that are inserted as a footnote to make up a topic, as shown in Table 33.1.

Table 33.1. RTF file footnote codes.

Code	Purpose	Description
#	Context Strings (Topic ID)	The *context string* is the unique name given to each topic in the file. This string is then used to reference the topic throughout the help file. The context string is established by the writer by placing the cursor on the first line of the paragraph and choosing the insert footnote command. The # sign is then inserted, followed by the name of the string. An example of a string that would reference a topic called Help File might be # HelpFile.
$	Topic Title	The *topic title* is the user-friendly name that appears in the search window of the help application. The user determines the title by inserting a $ character and then typing the name of title. An example of a title would be $ Using the Help File.
K	Keywords	The *keywords* entry determines the words that can be used in the search window to reference a topic. The character K is inserted as a footnote, and then the keywords are entered (each keyword is separated by a comma). For example, the previous HelpFile topic can be accessed by searching on the keywords Help, File, Using Help, Getting Help.

continues

Table 33.1. continued

Code	Purpose	Description
+	Browse Sequence	A *browse sequence* is simply the context string followed by a colon (:) and a number. The browse sequence is used when the user presses the Browse Forward and Browse Backward buttons in the help application. The help moves through the numbers for that particular topic in sequential order. For example, if the context HelpFile had two topics, +HelpFile:005, +HelpFile:006, topic 005 would come first and then 006.

After you have a sequence of paragraphs separated by page breaks and with corresponding footnotes containing the preceding characters, then you have a help file source document (.RTF document). When the .RTF document is completed, it is time for the writer to construct an .HPJ file. The .HPJ file includes items such as the title of the help application, the type of compression to use when creating the help file, the location of the bitmaps used in the help file, and the context IDs that will be used to jump to help topics in Visual Basic. Once the file is completed, it is passed as a parameter to the HCW compiler, which uses the file to create and compile the help application.

What Do I Need to Know About Help Files to Use Them in My Application?

I'm glad you asked that question. I hope you were paying attention to the previous section, because this is where the characters that were discussed become important. I mentioned that after the .RTF file is complete, you need to generate an .HPJ file. This file is simply a text file that contains information about your help file. It contains information such as the title of the help, bitmap locations, and compression information. It also contains the context string mappings. It is this mapping section that is used by your Visual Basic application.

The [Map] section lists all of your context strings and a context number for that string. Just as the context strings must be unique, so must the context numbers. By compiling these numbers along with the strings, you are creating a link to the strings from Visual Basic. All Visual Basic needs to know is the context number, and it can instruct the help file to bring up the correct help topic.

How Are Help Files Integrated into Visual Basic?

The user must inform Visual Basic that a help file will be included in the project. Help files are associated to a project by specifying the path to the help file and setting the Context ID properties of controls and forms to the appropriate context numbers. The help is then invoked at runtime by pressing F1 or the ShowWhatsThis button, and by clicking on the desired control. In this section, you learn both approaches and learn some more details on help Context IDs; but first, it's time to focus on how to set the path to the help file.

Help Path

You can enter the path to the help file directly by following these steps:

1. Choose Tools | Options.
2. Click the Project tab.
3. Enter the full path to the help file in the text box titled Help File.

   This path can also be entered at runtime by using the following code:

   ```
   App.HelpFile = "MyHelp.HLP"
   ```

As you might guess, because this property is configurable at runtime, it is easy to change between different help files after the application is running. Just remember that if you specify a new help file, make sure that the Context IDs are compatible between help files. If not, then make sure to change the IDs when you change files. You can do this with the following code:

```
DBGrid1.HelpContextID = 210
```

F1 Invoked Help (Windows 3.x)

When I refer to the F1 invoked help, I am referring to Windows 3.1-style applications. Windows 3.1 applications require the user to press F1 to activate the help. This also applies to context-sensitive help. The user has to move focus to a particular control and press F1. This style of help uses the Help Context IDs.

Help Context ID

In the previous section, you learned how to set the Context ID in code; this can also be accomplished in design mode by setting the HelpContextId property of a control to a valid number. The number entered for each control should correspond to a topic that explains its function. For example, to display custom help for a grid control on your form, you should enter the Context ID that corresponds to the grid topic in your help file. Remember, earlier in the chapter I stated that the [Map] section of the .HPJ lists all of your context strings and a context number for that string. Before you attempt to create a help file, I recommend that you have a good understanding of the help file's .HPJ. Unfortunately this topic is beyond the scope of this chapter, especially since the new Windows 95 help files use a different method to create help applications than does Windows 3.1. The new help compiler for Windows 95 shields the user from the .HPJ by wrapping it in a new help tool.

What's WhatsThisHelp (Windows 95)?

WhatsThisHelp—well, it's the new model for help in Windows 95, that's what! Windows 95 applications use a new help model that doesn't require the user to press the F1 button to invoke help. There are now actually three different methods available to invoke help, and I will explain each one in detail. Before discussing these new methods, there is one little housekeeping activity that must be taken care of. The WhatsThisHelp property of the form must be set to True before any of the commands will work. If the WhatsThisHelp property is set to False (default), the F1 button is used and the other commands are ignored. Pretend it is True, and move on.

WhatsThisHelpID

Just as the help Context ID is set for the F1 invoked help, the WhatsThisHelpID property is set for the Windows 95 style of help. If this property is set to a valid ID, the following WhatsThisHelp methods will activate the topic associated with the ID.

WhatsThisHelp Methods

Windows 95 has the following three methods for accessing help topics: the WhatsThisHelp button, the WhatsThisMode method of a form, and the ShowWhatsThis method for a particular control.

■ WhatsThisHelp button. The WhatsThisHelp button is exactly that—a button on the form that can be pressed to invoke context-sensitive help. The user can simply press the WhatsThisHelp button and then click on the desired control to receive help. The WhatsThisHelp button is the question mark button at the upper-right corner of the application's window. Figure 33.1 shows an example of the button.

Figure 33.1.
Example of
WhatsThisHelp button.

After you press the button, the mouse icon becomes a question mark. Simply move the question mark to the appropriate control and press the left mouse button to receive help.

How do you get that button on your form? There are certain requirements that must be met before the button will appear.

You must set the following properties to these values:

```
ControlBox property = True
BorderStyle property = Fixed Single or Sizable
MinButton and MaxButton = False
```

Or just set

```
BorderStyle property = Fixed Dialog
```

> It is worth noting that whenever you change BorderStyles, the Min and Max buttons' values default back to True. This will make it appear that WhatsThisHelp is not working. Make sure to check these values and check that WhatsThisButton and WhatsThisHelp are True.

■ WhatsThisMode method. This method causes the mouse pointer to change into the WhatsThis mouse pointer. After the command is invoked, it works the same as pressing the WhatsThisHelp button. Just click on a control and receive help for that control. The following code will activate this feature:

```
Private Sub mnuhelp_Click()
Form1.WhatsThisMode
End sub
```

In this example, I am calling the method from a Help menu item.

■ ShowWhatsThis method. This is the third method available to display context-sensitive help. After it's invoked, it automatically displays the topic specified in the WhatsThisHelpID property. This method has no effect on the mouse pointer. An example of using this method is the following:

```
Private Sub Command1_Click()
 Command1.ShowWhatsThis
End Sub
```

How Do I Enable a Contents and Search Menu in My Application?

If you want your application to have the standard Windows look and feel, you will need a Contents and Search item in the Help menu. The Contents section is usually the home page for the help application. This screen outlines all the sections contained in the help file. This section is not as important for help files in Windows 95 because the newer help uses a .CNT (Help Contents File) file. This new Contents screen is a series of books that are arranged in a tree structure. The books can be opened, and the topics are then expanded. The topics are depicted as a series of pages. You can double-click and browse them, just like a standard windows topic. The Search screen remains the same for Windows 3.*x* and Windows 95. It's time to see how both of these functions are invoked.

Contents Menu

An easy way to invoke a Contents menu is to use the SendKeys method. Insert the following code in the Click event of your Contents menu:

```
SendKeys "{F1}"
```

Search Menu

The Search menu is a little more difficult than the Contents menu. You have to call the WinHelp API to open the help's Search window. The Search window is invoked by passing the constant, HELP_PARTIALKEY, to WinHelp. If you are using an API, a declare is needed.

You should include the following code in the declarations section of your project's module:

```
Private Sub mnuSearch_Click()
    Dim lDummVal As Long, Temp As Long

    App.HelpFile = APp.Path & "data.hlp"
    lDummVal = 0

    'Call API to invoke search window
    Temp = WinHelp(Form1.hwnd, App.HelpFile, HELP_PARTIALKEY, lDummVal)
End Sub
```

Then place this code in your Search menu Click event:

```
Public Const HELP_PARTIALKEY = &H105     ' Call the search engine in WinHelp

#If Win16 Then
    Declare Function WinHelp Lib "User" (ByVal hwnd As Integer, _
    ByVal lpHelpFile As String, ByVal wCommand As Integer, _
    ByVal dwData As Any) As Long
#ElseIf Win32 Then
    Declare Function WinHelp Lib "user32" Alias "WinHelpA" _
    (ByVal hwnd As Long, ByVal lpHelpFile As String, _
    ByVal wCommand As Long, ByVal dwData As Long) As Long
#End If
```

When the Search Click event is fired, the API will locate your help file and open the Search window.

How Can My Error Handling Routines Reference My Help File?

Associating your help file topics is easy with Visual Basic 4.0. All it requires is the path to your help file and the correct Context ID mappings. When I talk about the correct mappings, I am indicating that your help file must have a Context ID topic that matches the error in Visual Basic. This means that if you were to receive an error 91 in Visual Basic, your help file should have a topic 91 for the error. There are ways around the need for this exact mapping, but this is the most straightforward method. First I'll show you an example that uses the mapping technique, and then I'll discuss an alternative approach.

> The help file is not automatically invoked. The user has to press the F1 key when the message box is presented on the screen.

The following example raises an error number 290. It just so happens that the help file also has an error 290:

```
Private Sub Command2_Click()

    Dim msg As String

    On Error GoTo ErrTrap:
    Err.Clear
    Err.Raise 290      ' Generate a user defined error, that is associated
                       ' with a help Context ID.
    Exit Sub
ErrTrap:
    If Err.Number <> 0 Then
        msg = "Error # " & Str(Err.Number) & " was generated by " _
        & Err.Source & Chr(13) & Err.Description

        MsgBox msg, , "Error", "d:\help\data.HLP", Err.Number
    End If
End Sub
```

The last two parameters in the message box are help file path and Context ID. Notice that I specify the path to the help file and use the Err.Number value for the Context ID. This approach works fine if I have a topic for each error I will encounter, but what if I only want certain error messages to go to the help file? A simple solution would be to trap for a certain error number and then pass the Context ID parameter a predefined value.

Here's how this would work in code:

```
Private Sub Command3_Click()

    Dim msg As String, y As Integer
```

```
    On Error GoTo ErrTrap:
    Err.Clear
    y = 1 / 0          ' Generate an error
    Exit Sub

ErrTrap:
    Select Case Err.Number
    Case 6, 7, 9, 11, 28
        msg = "Error # " & Str(Err.Number) & " was generated by " _
        & Err.Source & Chr(13) & Err.Description
        MsgBox msg, , "Error", "d:\help\data.HLP", 290
    Cas Else
        msg = "Error # " & Str(Err.Number) & " was generated by " _
        & Err.Source & Chr(13) & Err.Description
        MsgBox msg, , "Error", "d:\help\data.HLP", Err.Number
    End Select
End Sub
```

Notice that in this code, I am trapping for errors 6, 7, 9, 11, and 28. I have constructed an appropriate help topic (#290) that covers the five different error possibilities. All other messages will be mapped according to the Err.Number. Obviously, in the real world this would be very difficult to accomplish. You would probably construct a catch-all topic in your help and use that Context ID as the value. This is by no means the only way to map to your help file; I have only presented these examples as ideas. It is ultimately your job to implement the right solution for your needs.

Summary

In this chapter, I have introduced you to help files and have given you some examples of how help files can be incorporated into your applications. I think this information is important because it is rarely mentioned in the manuals and programming journals, and there is no technical support. It is unfortunate that something as useful and as widespread as help files does not receive more attention. I have tried to cover the topic as it relates to integration with Visual Basic, but there is much more to cover on creating the actual help file. I could write a complete book on help authoring alone.

For more information on creating help files, get a copy of the Microsoft Windows 95 Help Authoring Kit or read the help authoring information that ships with the Visual Basic 4.0 CD-ROM in the Tools\Hcw folder. I hope that you go out and construct your own help applications and that these tips help you create world-class applications. Good luck!

Polishing Your Applications

by Christopher Rotberg

34

CHAPTER

When I talk about *polishing*, I am referring to the intangible, little things that are easily overlooked but that add that professional touch—things that make your applications a cut above the rest. Just look at the excitement in people's faces at some of the larger product launches. I remember attending the launch for Windows 95. As new features were demonstrated, audience members looked astonished and excited. Nonprogrammers looked at these applications and wondered how the magic was accomplished. It is this response from the end user that I consider to be the icing on the cake. As programmers, we should strive not only to make the code work, but also to code in the most elegant and efficient manner possible. A well-designed application should do more than just barely run. The following sections take a look at some of the ingredients of a polished application.

What Exactly Is Polishing?

To some people, just getting the application to run is enough. However, I think that an application should not only run well but should also look and feel like a well-designed, well-planned tool. It should be *polished*. A great application should start with a good design; lay out your needs and try to get a conceptual idea of your project before you start to code. After you have the project designs in hand, start to construct the user interface. The user interface should guide the user effortlessly between its various functions, and it should have a consistent look and feel throughout the application. *Microsoft Windows User Interface Design Guide* is a good reference.

Assuming that you have accomplished the previous tasks successfully and your application runs, it is time to give your application some polishing. I devote the remainder of this chapter to several topics that I feel will make your applications more professional in appearance, performance, and quality.

Splash Screens

Almost all professional applications today include some type of *splash screen*. It is usually the first screen presented to the user.

There are two main functions for a splash screen:

- ■ To display the product's name, company name, and copyright protection warnings
- ■ To distract the user's attention from the amount of time the program is taking to load

The first function of the splash screen serves more as a mini-billboard for your company and gives you the opportunity to display your copyright warning message. A more important reason to use a splash screen is the second function.

Often one of the slowest operations your program will perform is to load itself into memory. This is a critical time for the end user because their attention is focused on starting the application. Imagine yourself clicking on an icon to start an application and not seeing anything for several minutes. At some point, usually 30 seconds after you first click the icon, you click it again, and again, and again. Does this sound familiar? It is very frustrating to click on an icon and have nothing respond. This is why the splash screen is so important. When the user clicks on the icon and you present him or her with an immediate response, the user feels like the program is running. This gives you some time to load your application into memory and satisfy the end user's demand to have something happen.

On the other hand, you can't leave the splash screen up forever; if your application is taking more than a minute to load, it is time to look at alternative methods of loading. A splash screen that stays up for several minutes can be just as annoying as an application that is just doing nothing.

A splash screen should consist of a *modal type dialog*, a window with no control box or minimize or maximize buttons. It should be centered in the screen and have no command buttons. The best place to call this screen is usually in the sub main event of the project. Display the splash screen and then process all your opening events. These typically include reading from text files or the registry and setting environmental variables. The last item in the sub main should open the main form and close the splash screen.

Crossing Your t's and Dotting Your i's

Crossing your t's and dotting your i's can be summarized by one word: *spelling*. Check the spelling of the command buttons, the label captions, help files, and so on. It doesn't matter how well you construct your screens or code your application; if the application is full of incorrect spellings, it will not present itself in a professional manner. Spelling mistakes are often tough to catch because the Visual Basic UI does not include a spell checker, and not everyone is an English teacher. (This might be a good feature for future releases.) There are some third-party tools available, but they mostly cover spelling of data that is entered into the text boxes rather than proofing the screen layout. So it is up to you, the programmer, to make sure that your work is correct. This subject might seem trivial to some, but give your badly misspelled application to a dozen software reviewers and see what happens. Think of your application as a piece of electronic literature; it deserves to be correct as much as this book does.

Include Help

A well-polished application should include a help file. It not only cuts down on support calls, but it adds that professional look to your application. Help files have become so important that customers will actually compare applications and look for such things as help files to help them make a purchase decision. For more information on how to create and integrate help, see Chapter 33, "Implementing Help in Your Applications."

Optimization Methods

The real trick to optimization is the realization that there is no one method that can be used to speed up your applications. There is no special switch that can be set to dramatically increase the performance of the program. *Optimization* is instead a collection of shortcuts—and some smoke and mirrors. There are techniques that help increase the speed of code, and there are the methods that trick you into thinking the speed has increased. The following sections discuss the methods of user-interface (front end) optimization and back-end techniques.

User-Interface Optimization

User-interface optimization can be broken into two broad categories: *actual display speed* and *user-interpreted speed*. Actual speed is related to the speed in which the windows are loaded and painted on the screen, and user-interpreted speed can be affected by changing your program's order of events. This order of events includes loading forms and data at times when the user is not aware of what is going on. First, it's time to look at what affects actual speed and then take a look at the smoke and mirror methods of interpreted speed.

Actual Speed

Because Visual Basic is a windows-based application: it has to load, unload, paint, and repaint windows on a regular basis. Depending on the controls on your form, this can be very quick or very slow. Obviously, the goal is to decrease the amount of time it takes to repaint the forms and controls.

The following guidelines can help to achieve this goal:

- Use the Image control instead of the PictureBox control. The Image control will paint faster and requires less memory. Avoid using the PictureBox control unless you need features like DDE.

> In some cases, the use of the PictureBox control can decrease repainting by enabling multiple controls to be repainted at once. If you put multiple controls into one PictureBox and then issue repaint, all controls will be repainted together.

- Set the ClipControls property to False. Unless you are using Pset, Circle, Line, or Print, setting the value to False is the preferred method. Setting ClipControls to False allows Visual Basic to ignore the work required to keep from painting over controls before they are repainted.

- Set `AutoRedraw` to `False`. The only time this property should be `True` is for a complex graphic that does not need to be repainted often. When this property is `True`, Visual Basic stores a copy of the bitmap that it uses to redraw the graphic; this bitmap can occupy a large amount of memory.

- Use the `Line` method instead of `Pset`.

- Try not to use too many controls on one form. Use one `ComboBox` control for multiple purposes.

- Use control arrays. Instead of having six combo boxes, use one control array and create the combo boxes at runtime.

- Avoid using large bitmaps or wallpaper. Although these items can add to the attractiveness of your application, they take up precious resources.

Interpreted Speed

Earlier in this chapter, I mentioned the technique of using smoke and mirrors to give the illusion of a faster application. Just as a magician uses magic to deceive the audience, you too can use illusion to deceive the end user. This illusion of speed is a very powerful tool. An application that contains several small operations and continually returns control to the user will appear much quicker than an application that is in limbo land while it is loading its forms or modules.

Like actual speed, *interpreted speed* is not a simple set of instructions that can be performed to accomplish all of your needs; it is a style of programming that includes various tricks that, when used in accordance with each other, can yield startling results. Some of these tricks are as old as Visual Basic 1.0 but are still useful today in Visual Basic 4.0.

The following is a list of helpful techniques for you to use in your programming:

- One of the oldest tricks in the book is to load the most often used forms and keep them hidden until they are needed. This is beneficial because it reduces the amount of time needed to load the form and its related module. All that is required to set the form visible is to issue the `Show` command. To the user, it appears that the form is loading very quickly, but actually it was loaded all along.

- Although including functions in modules (.BAS files) is a good practice, it can be detrimental to your application. Every time you load a form, it loads all the files that are necessary to complete its operations. This means that if the form's functions are included in several modules, all of the modules will be loaded. To optimize performance, you should include all the functions that are used for a particular form in one module. Now when the form is loaded, it will have to load only one module.

- Preload data ahead of time. If your form has a combo box that requires 10,000 names to be displayed, it could take a very long time to load the combo each time the form is displayed. A better solution would be to load the combo box during the `Load` event, when the splash screen is first opening. You could also have another form that is hidden that contains the record set for the 10,000 names, which you loaded from the database during load. Now when the application is running, all you have to do is reference the record set from the hidden form.

■ Use the timer control to perform operations in the background. The previous example of the 10,000 names can be used in this example, as well. If you do not want to build the record set during load, you could have a Timer event that processes the building of the record set while your form is being displayed.

■ Utilize a splash screen to give the user some immediate feedback.

■ Use a small application that loads the standard DLLs needed for Visual Basic applications. It might be helpful to write a small formless application that can be run from the startup group in Windows. This application can load the Vbrun DLL needed for Visual Basic. Then when it is time to run your application, the runtime libraries will already be in memory, thus dramatically reducing your application's load time.

■ The new Windows 95 common controls include a Progress Indicator control; this control can be useful for displaying the progress of your application during runtime. The goal here is to provide a distraction to the user during the slower portions of your program. Although the progress indicator is not needed for functionality, it does serve as a good way to entertain the user.

■ Show your forms instead of just loading them; this will give the user something to look at while other routines are processing.

■ Use the various Windows APIs to enhance your program. One API that I find useful is the LockWindowUpdate API. This API enables you to lock updates on a particular window until all processing is completed. I frequently use this control when I am loading the TreeView or ListView controls. You might have noticed that these controls tend to blink during the load event; not only is this annoying, but it also takes more time because the control is trying to repaint after each node is added. The LockWindowUpdate API locks the control so that no repainting occurs until after the nodes are added. After the loading is complete, you release the window back to the system.

This method is good to use when you are loading data, but be careful if your application does drag and drop. If you lock the window at the wrong time, you will get a trail of drag bitmap images across your screen as you drag your mouse. If you decide to use LockWindowUpdate, just make sure that you turn it off when your operation is complete.

The following is an example of how to use the LockWindowUpdate API.

The API declaration looks like this:

```
' Lock WindowUpdate API (Stops screen Updates)
Declare Function LockWindowUpdate Lib "User32"
(ByVal hwndLock As Long) As Long
```

My function looks like this:

```
Public Sub gLockWindowUpdating(bState As Boolean,
➥Optional OptionalhWnd As Variant)
    Dim lRetVal As Long, lHandle As Long
    If bState Then      ' Lock Window
        lHandle = OptionalhWnd
        lRetVal = LockWindowUpdate(lHandle)
    Else
        lRetVal = LockWindowUpdate(0&)
    End If
End Sub
```

To start the locking, call your procedure and pass it the hwnd of the control that you want to lock updating on—in this case, it is a listbox.

```
'Turn on window locking
gLockWindowUpdating True, List1.hWnd
```

To release the lock, simply pass a False to the function. That's all it takes.

```
' Turn on Screen updating
gLockWindowUpdating False
```

Improving the Back-End Speed

Now that you know about the user interface, it's time to go beneath the hood and tune up your code. Unfortunately, there is no magic speed switch for the back end, either; you will have to go through your code line by line and identify areas that can be improved. This is not an easy process, but I can assure you the results are well worth the effort.

I know what you are thinking: You've written hundreds of lines of code, and you do not want to start rewriting now. This is a normal reaction. It's not necessary for you to go through every function you have ever written and try to shave a fraction of a second. I am going to present some tips to use as guidelines that will help you write better code. Speed is not something that just comes from coding one For loop faster than another; it comes as a result of minimizing unneeded code throughout the application. Obviously, shaving a fraction of a second for one For loop is not going to affect overall performance; but shave that fraction for each of the 100 loops in your application, and you can see the savings start to add up.

Variables

The following are some guidelines to help you optimize your code:

- Avoid the use of `Variants`. `Variants` require 16 bytes of memory, as opposed to an `Integer`, which is 2 bytes, and `Double`, which is 8 bytes. Additionally, variable length strings take another 6 bytes, a 4-byte pointer, and 2 bytes for the null terminator. Additional memory is required if you pass the variable by reference. As you can see, a `Variant` can quickly take up valuable memory.

- Avoid dimensioning variables as global. Visual Basic 4.0 now includes form properties; it is more efficient to use these properties and reference them between forms than to set a variable global. Form properties can be referenced easily by prefacing the property name with that of the form.

  For example, to access the value of property `UserName` from the form `Users`, I could simply use the following:

  ```
  MyUser=Users.UserName
  ```

  Or I could set an object pointer to the form and use it to reference the property, like this:

  ```
  Dim frm as form
  Set frm=Users
          MyUser=frm.UserNAme
  ```

  This method enables me to access the property from anywhere in my project.

- Set string variables to a zero length string to save memory. Simply setting the variable `LogonName=""` reallocates memory that was being used by that variable.

- Set object pointers to `Nothing` at the end of your procedures. If you do not need the object pointer outside the scope of a procedure, set it to `Nothing` to release that memory back to the system. Leaving pointers that do not point to anything can cause memory leaks. The following code will delete your `frm` pointer from memory:

  ```
  Set frm=Nothing
  ```

Structure

Often, the performance of an application depends on how the code is structured. Structure is more than just knowing what certain functions do, it's how the functions are used to achieve the best performance.

- Avoid using a loop in a variant condition. This situation is slow because the loop must be re-evaluated each time through the loop. For example:

  ```
  For I = 0 to ListBox.Count
     inumber=ListBox.ListItem.index
  next I
  ```

The loop has to re-evaluate the value of Count each time it comes around. A faster approach would be to assign the value of Count to a variable and use the variable in the loop.

```
ILstCount= ListBox.Count
For I = 0 to ILstCount
    inumber=ListBox.ListItem.index
next I
```

■ Try to combine several statements in the same line. For example, the following code can be cut down to just one line:

```
x=GetValue("Toolbar")
If x= True then
    Toolbar.Visible=True
end if
```

The preceding can be shortened to this:

```
If GetValue("Toolbar") then Toolbar.Visible=True
```

It is not necessary to specifically check the value for True because this is the default value of the If statement.

■ Avoid directly referencing a control in a loop. You will notice in the following code that I am checking the value of a Textbox control from within the For loop.

```
Dim i As Integer
    For i = 0 To 2
                If List1.List(i) = Text1.Text Then MsgBox "Match"
        Next I
```

This method is slow because each time through the loop, the control's value has to be verified. This adds more overhead within the loop. A better solution would be to get the value of the text box once and then use it to compare. The code would look like this:

```
Dim i As Integer, sText as string
sText = Text1.Text
    For i = 0 To 2
                If List1.List(i) = sText Then MsgBox "Match"
        Next I
```

The revised code will now run more efficiently because I have eliminated the need to reference the control in each iteration of the loop.

Objects

Now that Visual Basic 4.0 relies so heavily on objects, it's increasingly important to know how to best utilize these objects to your advantage. The following are a few tips that will help you construct more efficient applications using objects.

■ Avoid referencing objects through each of their levels of indirection. (Reduce the number of dots when referring to objects.) For example:

```
Set db = DBEngine.Workspaces(0).OpenDatabase("Pubs.mdb")
```

can become

```
Set db= OpenDatabase("Pubs.mdb")
```

This will reduce the number of calls Visual Basic has to make to the OLE interface. Because DBEngine.Workspaces(0) is the default engine and workspace, there is no need to include them.

■ Use the Set statement to minimize the use of the dot operator. Some OLE servers can have many levels of operators. Excel is a good example of too many dots.

```
Range= Application.WorkBooks.Item(1).WorkSheets.Item("Sheet2").Range("A8")
```

It would be more efficient to set a pointer to the parent object and then go directly to the property like this:

```
Dim objwks as WorkSheet
Set objwks = Application.WorkBooks(1).WorkSheets("Sheet2")
Range=  objwks.Range("A8")
```

■ Use the With statement to set multiple properties. With statements enable you to reference the same control multiple times in an efficient manner. After you have established a handle to the control, you simply set the desired properties. In this example, I am setting the properties for a Label control:

```
With Label1
        .Caption="Label Caption"
        .BackColor=BLUE
        .Top=1289
End With
```

■ Use the For Each Next loop when dealing with objects or collections. This method will always be at least as fast as a normal For Next loop, and most often faster. It is also better suited to handle objects. The loop provides you with the current object in the collection, and it is incremented automatically. Notice how easy it is to reference the name of each control:

```
Dim objCtrl as Control, sCtrlName as String

For Each objCtrl in Form1.Controls
    sCtrlName = objCtrl.name
Next
```

The next example demonstrates how to add all the ListView controls on a form to a collection:

```
Dim objCtrl as Control
Dim lstViews As New Collection

For Each objCtrl in Form1.Controls
    if TypeOf objCtrl is ListView then
            lstViews.Add objCtr
    End If
Next
```

■ Avoid using the Before and After keys when you are adding objects to a collection. There is more overhead involved in adding objects when the collection has to move references around to reposition objects in a collection.

■ Use *early binding* instead of *late binding*. In situations in which you have a type library, it is faster to use early binding. Early binding enables Visual Basic to gain access to the properties and methods of an OLE Server at design time. This will result in faster execution at runtime because Visual Basic will not have to query the server for its capabilities. Late binding is used when a type library is not available; in this case, objects are declared as just object.

Here are some examples:

Late Binding

```
Dim xl As Object
Set xl = CreateObject("Excel.Application")
xl.Visible = True
```

Early Binding

```
Dim xl As Excel.Application
Set xl = CreateObject("Excel.Application")
xl.Visible = True
```

Be careful about how you dimension your objects. Different methods can cause problems that are not easy to detect. In the following example, I use the new keyword in my declaration.

```
Dim pp as new PowerPoint.Application
pp.Visible = True
Set pp = Nothing
pp.Visible = False
```

You would think that the last line would cause an error; however, because of the keyword new, it will actually create another instance of PowerPoint for you so it can set Visible = False. This can be a problem, especially when this last piece of code is not conveniently located after the Set pp = Nothing statement. You might end your program with objects still in memory because you are unaware that they were ever created.

Out-of-Process Servers

Here are a few tips when using out-of-process servers.

■ Be careful when you are calling functions from an out-of-process server. Unless you specify ByVal in the function, Visual Basic will perform two data copies instead of one for the variable. It will first make a copy from the calling application to the out-of-process server, and then make another copy to send back to the calling application. By using the keyword ByVal in the function header, you save yourself the second data copy.

Here is an example of using ByVal in a function header:

```
Public Function GetUser ( ByVal Name as string)
```

■ Avoid returning object pointers from functions in an out-of-process server that contains large amounts of data. This will significantly cut down on the amount of calls that have to take place between the out-of-process server and the calling application.

Remember that passing a reference to an object does not mean that all of the data associated with the object gets copied across the process boundaries. Any attempt to retrieve the data from the out-of-process server to the calling application will require another hop across the process walls, which is slow and expensive.

What Is Code Profiler?

Now that I have given you some tips on how to improve your code, where can you get information on what code needs to be changed? This is a good question. You could certainly go through every piece of code, line by line, and optimize, but this will take time. What if you are almost finished with an application and you just want to know the areas that need to be improved? Well, there is a tool that ships with Visual Basic 4.0 called *Code Profiler.* This application monitors your program while it is running; when you have closed down the application, Code Profiler will give you a complete report indicating how long each line of code took to execute and what percentage of time the line was used.

The program can be found on the Visual Basic 4.0 CD-ROM in the Tools directory in a folder called VBCP. After the program is installed, it functions as an add-in to the Visual Basic UI. You simply start your application and choose the Code Profiler from the Add-Ins menu. A screen will open that enables you to choose all or part of the components in your project. After the components are selected, click the Add Profiler Code button. This will add special code to your routines to help track the speed of execution and the pass times. The program enables the user to track line timing, function timing, line hit count, and function hit count. When your code is finished executing, you can generate a report that shows the statistics.

Figure 34.1 shows what the final statistics screen looks like.

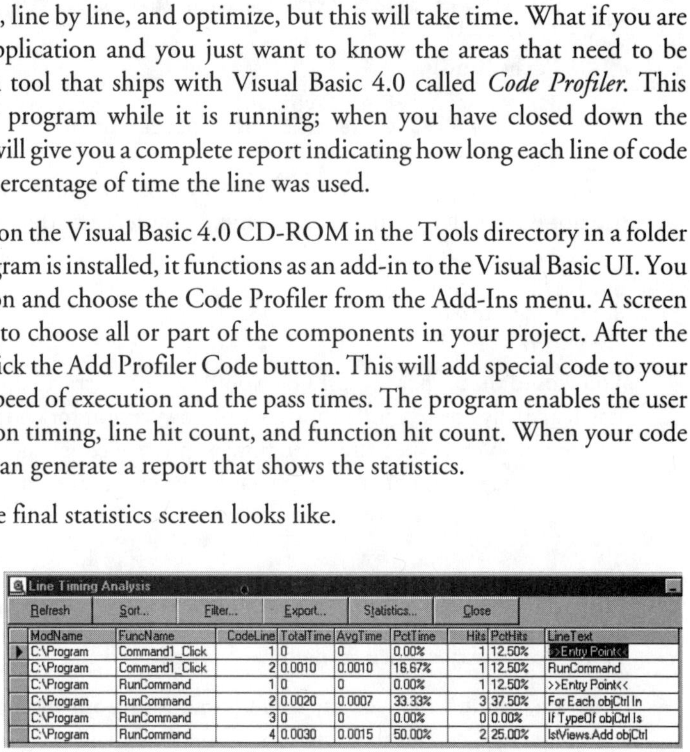

ModName	FuncName	CodeLine	TotalTime	AvgTime	PctTime	Hits	PctHits	LineText
C:\Program	Command1_Click	1	0	0	0.00%	1	12.50%	>>Entry Point<<
C:\Program	Command1_Click	2	0.0010	0.0010	16.67%	1	12.50%	RunCommand
C:\Program	RunCommand	1	0	0	0.00%	1	12.50%	>>Entry Point<<
C:\Program	RunCommand	2	0.0020	0.0007	33.33%	3	37.50%	For Each objCtrl In
C:\Program	RunCommand	3	0	0	0.00%	0	0.00%	If TypeOf objCtrl Is
C:\Program	RunCommand	4	0.0030	0.0015	50.00%	2	25.00%	lstViews.Add objCtrl

Figure 34.1.
Using the Code Profiler.

The report can be filtered, printed, and exported. There is a 16-bit and 32-bit version available. It is a good idea to remove the profiler code after you are finished running the reports. Give this tool a try and see how it works for you.

Summary

In this chapter, I have introduced you to several concepts that I feel are important to the quality of your applications. The job of the programmer is not unlike the job of an artist; of course, programmers build applications to solve a specific business problem but are also constructing something from nothing. The interface does not exist: you create it as go, you arrange the shapes, and provide the colors just as an artist paints a canvas.

Even in the back end of an application, the programmer is constantly looking for the fastest, most efficient means of executing code, in the fewest lines possible. The point is that programmers should not approach programming as a slam dunk, get-it-done-fast activity. The applications you write are being used by millions of people to perform important tasks. It is worth the extra effort to make sure your applications are polished and professional. In a world where applications come and go every six months, all you have to stand behind is your reputation. Remember that application that crashed on you every five minutes, which you ultimately returned? Would you buy its next upgrade?

Using 16-Bit Visual Basic

PART

6

Working with the 16-Bit Environment

by Dwayne R. Gifford

CHAPTER 35

Most of the books about Visual Basic 4.0 only reference the 32-bit environment, and not the 16-bit environment. The goal of this chapter is to give you a running start on building 16-bit programs. The 16-bit environment is shipped only with the Professional and Enterprise editions of Visual Basic 4.0.

This chapter covers the 16-bit environment, the standard tools that are shipped with the 16-bit environment, and some things you need to be aware of when you work in this environment.

Requirements for 16-Bit Visual Basic

When you are developing a 16-bit Visual Basic application, you must be running a 386 computer system or higher, with a minimum of 4MB of RAM. This varies, depending on the libraries and DLLs your application will be loading. You should base your memory requirement on the Windows environment recommendation, but I suggest a minimum of 8MB of RAM. You also should be running Microsoft Windows 3.1 or later, in enhanced or standard mode. If you are running Windows 95 or Windows NT 3.51 or later, you also can run applications built in 16-bit Visual Basic 4.0. To develop applications in Visual Basic 4.0 16-bit or 32-bit environments, you must have a minimum of 8MB of RAM; my recommendation is 16MB of RAM. The preferred development environment is 32MB of RAM, however.

The Environment

Working with the 16-bit environment is very similar to working with the 32-bit environment, and is similar to Visual Basic 3.0. The main differences between the old and the new are how to add and remove components, controls, and references.

Figure 35.1 shows you the 16-bit environment with the Project, Properties, Toolbox, Form, and Debug windows open.

Figure 35.1.
The 16-bit environment.

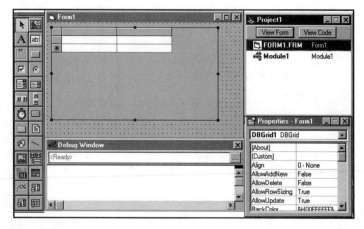

This section gives you an idea of what is new in the 16-bit Visual Basic 4.0 environment.

Starting a New Project

To start anew project, choose File | New Project. This creates a new project based on AUTO16LD.VBP. This file contains all the information required to create a new project, including the objects to be loaded and is created when you install Visual Basic the first time. The references that will be set up for the new project and the default project name also are loaded. If you make any changes to a component of the new project, a dialog box appears, asking whether you want to save your changes (see Figure 35.2).

Figure 35.2.
The save changes dialog box.

If you do not want to save the currently listed component, click the No button. To not save any more of the components from this point on, click the No to All button. To cancel the process and return to the development environment, click Cancel. To save the currently listed component, click Yes. The Save File As dialog box appears, prompting you for the name of the component and the location in which you want to save the component (see Figure 35.3).

Figure 35.3.
The Save File As dialog box.

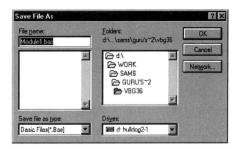

After you set the location name for the component, click OK. As each component is saved, you are returned to the Save Changes dialog box. After you specify the location in the Save File dialog box, it remains set to that location until you change it. This does not mean that you have to save each component to the same directory, but it is recommended.

Opening an Existing Project

To open a previously saved project, you can open the File menu and select it from the names of the four most recently opened projects at the bottom of the menu. Just click the project name from this list. If it is not in this list, choose File | Open Project to display the Open Project dialog box shown in Figure 35.4.

Figure 35.4.
The Open Project dialog box.

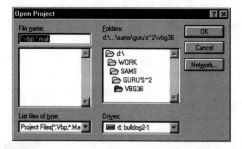

Here, you can navigate through the directories on the right side of the box trying to locate your project that will appear on the left side of the dialog. After you have located your project on the left, you will need to select the project name and then click OK.

Adding Components

You can add new components or previously saved components to your projects. To add a new component to your project, open the Insert menu. Here, you have four choices: Form, MDI Form, Module, and Class Module. To add a previously saved component to your project, choose File | Add File. This opens the Add File dialog box, which enables you to navigate to the component, select it, and then click OK to add the component to the current project (see Figure 35.5).

Figure 35.5.
The Add File dialog box.

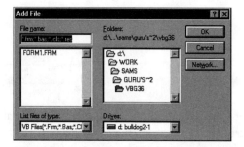

This is not permanent, however, until you save the project. To cancel out of the operation, click Cancel. If you want to remove the component any time after you add the component, choose File | Remove File. A confirmation box does not appear for you to verify this operation; the component simply is removed.

> Remember that adding or removing a component is not permanent until you actually save the project.

If you try to remove a new component that has not been saved, a save changes dialog box appears, as shown in Figure 35.6.

Figure 35.6.
The save changes dialog box.

If you click Yes, the Save File As dialog box appears. If you click No, the component is removed and all changes that have been added to this component are lost. If you click Cancel, the operation is canceled and you are returned to the Visual Basic development environment.

Adding or Removing Controls

The controls that can be added to the projects are another very important factor of a Visual Basic project. To add or remove a control to or from a project, you can choose Tools | Custom Controls. This opens the Custom Controls dialog box, shown in Figure 35.7, where you can select or unselect available custom controls.

Figure 35.7.
The Custom Controls dialog box.

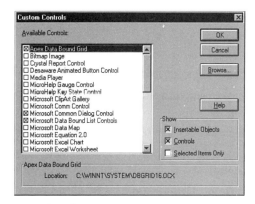

If you do not see the control in the alphabetically ordered list, click the Browse button. This opens the Add Custom Control dialog box, where you can locate the control you want to reference (see Figure 35.8).

Figure 35.8.
The Add Custom Control dialog box.

The only available custom controls that Visual Basic can load are OCXs or VBXs. After you select the control you want, click OK. This makes your new custom control available in the Custom Controls dialog box. To make the custom control available after you select it, click OK. If you want to go back to previously selected items, click the Cancel button.

Available OCXs with 16-Bit Visual Basic

Table 35.1 shows you which OCXs are available with 16-bit Visual Basic and the 32-bit counterpart name.

Table 35.1. OCXs available in 16-bit and 32-bit Visual Basic environments.

OCX name	16-bit filename	32-bit filename
Apex Data Bound Control	DBGRID16.OCX	DBGRID32.OCX
Crystal Report Control	CRYSTL16.OCX	CRYSTL32.OCX
Desaware Animated Button Control	ANIBTN16.OCX	ANIBTN32.OCX
MicroHelp Gauge Control	GAUGE16.OCX	GAUGE32.OCX
MicroHelp Key State Control	KEYSTA16.OCX	KEYSTA32.OCX
Microsoft Comm Control	MSCOMM16.OCX	MSCOMM32.OCX
Microsoft Common Dialog Control	COMDLG16.OCX	COMDLG32.OCX
Microsoft Data Bound List Controls	DBLIST16.OCX	DBLIST32.OCX
Microsoft Grid Control	GRID16.OCX	GRID132.OCX
Microsoft MAPI Control	MSMAPI16.OCX	MSMAPI32.OCX
Microsoft Masked Edit Control	MSMASK16.OCX	MSMASK32.OCX

OCX name	16-bit filename	32-bit filename
Microsoft MultiMedia Control	MCI16.OCX	MCI32.OCX
Microsoft Outline Control	MSOUTL16.OCX	MSOUTL32.OCX
Microsoft PictureClip Control	PICCLP16.OCX	PICCLP32.OCX
OutRider SpinButton Control	SPIN16.OCX	SPIN32.OCX
Pinnacle-BPS Graph Control	GRAPH16.OCX	GRAPH32.OCX
Sheridan 3D Control	THREED16.OCX	THREED32.OCX
Sheridan Tabbed Dialog Control	TABCTL16.OCX	TABCTL32.OCX

You cannot load any 32-bit custom controls in the 16-bit environment.

You can use any of your old VBXs or 16-bit DLLs without any problems in 16-bit Visual Basic 4.0 projects.

Adding or Removing References

To add or remove a reference to or from a DLL, OLB, OCA, TLB, or EXE, you need to choose Tools | References. This opens the References dialog box, which enables you to add or remove references (see Figure 35.9).

To add a reference to any of the unselected references in the list of references, double-click on that reference. To remove the reference from an already selected reference, double-click the selected reference. If you need to add a reference that is not already in the list, click the Browse button. This opens the Add Reference dialog box, where you can locate the file you want to reference (see Figure 35.10).

After you locate the file, click on the file and then click OK. To cancel the adding of a reference, click the Cancel button. To view the classes or objects for this new referenced file, open the Object Browser by choosing View | Object Browser. You can use the Object Browser to view all currently loaded libraries and projects (see Figure 35.11).

Figure 35.9.
*The References
dialog box.*

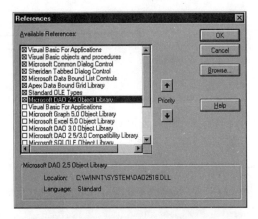

Figure 35.10.
*The Add Reference
dialog box.*

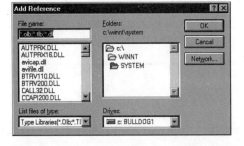

Figure 35.11.
*The Object Browser
dialog box.*

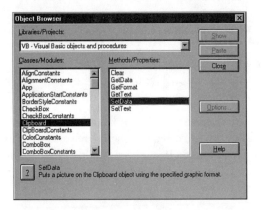

To view the methods and properties available to classes and modules, select the library or method
you want to view from the Libraries/Projects combo box. Then you must select the corresponding class and module from the Classes/Modules drop-down listbox. Based on your selections,
the available Methods/Properties listbox displays various names. This helps you find out what
you can and cannot do with certain methods and properties without having to access online help
or just randomly try things.

Things to Keep in Mind When Developing 16-Bit Projects

You need to be aware of three things when you start to develop in the 16-bit Visual Basic environment.

First, when you are developing 16-bit projects instead of 32-bit, you need to know that the 16-bit environment uses the ANSI character set, whereas the 32-bit environment uses the Unicode character set. The major difference is that the ANSI character set is made up of a 256-character set, whereas the Unicode set is made up of 65,535 characters (some are left empty for future use).

Second, when you use `SaveSetting`, `GettingSetting`, `SaveAllSettings`, and `DeleteSetting` with 16-bit Visual Basic 4.0, these commands are going to use INI files, whereas if you use these same calls in the 32-bit environment, you are going against the Registry.

The third thing is that because the 16-bit environment presently can run on all Windows environments, starting with Windows 3.*x*, it is important to remember that 16-bit Visual Basic cannot work with long filenames at all. This is true whether you are using code or trying to save a project or its components.

Summary

This chapter shows you what you need to be aware of when you get ready to develop in the 16-bit Visual Basic environment. You learned about the differences between Visual Basic 3.0 and 16-bit Visual Basic 4.0. You also learned how to add and remove controls and references, as well as certain things to watch out for when you develop 16-bit projects.

Porting Visual Basic 3.0 to Visual Basic 4.0

by Dwayne R. Gifford

CHAPTER

36

When a new program comes out, one of the most important and least documented questions usually is how to upgrade your data from previous versions of that program.

This chapter tells you how to port previous versions of Visual Basic (VB) into the newest version of Visual Basic.

Porting to a VB 4.0 16-Bit Application

To port an application that was built in Visual Basic 3 or Visual Basic 2.0 to a VB 4.0 16- or 32-bit environment, you will need to follow the same steps. To convert to a Visual Basic 16-bit application, follow these steps:

1. Make a copy of the project, just in case you need to back out.

2. Open the environment into which you want to convert the project.

3. Open the project by choosing File | Open Project. Select the project from the Open Project dialog box that appears. After selecting the project, click OK.

4. The Custom Control Upgrade dialog box appears, showing you a list of VBXs that have corresponding OCXs available (see Figure 36.1).

   Here, you can choose Yes, No, or Help.

Figure 36.1.
The Custom Control Upgrade dialog box.

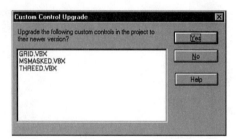

5. If you click Yes, the corresponding OCXs are loaded into the Custom Controls dialog box instead of the VBXs. If you click No, you leave the application as is and load the corresponding VBX for the project. You can click the Help button to see information about the Custom Control Upgrade dialog box.

   If Visual Basic is unable to load any of the controls, it displays a message telling you that it can't load the control you specified (see Figure 36.2).

6. You can click Yes to continue loading the project or No to cancel loading the project. If you click No, you are placed in the environment with all the modules it already had loaded. You then can close the environment and try to figure out what went wrong. Then, you can try again, or click Yes to continue to load the project. By clicking Yes the project loads the old control instead of its new one.

Figure 36.2.
A message informing you that Visual Basic can't load the specified control.

> If a control cannot be loaded in the 16-bit environment, it usually is because the control was not installed properly. Reinstall the control and then try the porting process again.
>
> You cannot load a 16-bit control into a 32-bit environment because the 32-bit environment can use only 32-bit custom controls.

7. After all the controls are loaded, Figure 36.3 will be opened. Here, you can choose OK or OK for All. So, no matter what, you need to upgrade the files to the new version. You can click OK to see each file as it is upgraded, or you can click OK for All to just upgrade all files at once. If an error occurs while you are converting or loading the file to the new program, the convert file dialog box appears, as shown in Figure 36.4.

Figure 36.3.
The convert file from previous version dialog box.

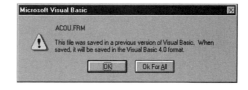

Figure 36.4.
The errors during file conversion dialog box.

8. Here, you are informed that an error has occurred and where you can find the log file and the name of the log file. To acknowledge the error, click OK. The process carries on, and if any further errors occur, the same dialog box appears, displaying a new log filename to which you can refer. To find out what the problem was with the loading of the file, you will need to refer to the log file.

> If a control is not loaded correctly, it is loaded as a Picture Box control.

After all the files are loaded, Figure 36.5 appears.

Figure 36.5.
The Reference Microsoft
DAO 2.5 Object Library
dialog box.

9. In this dialog box, you can choose whether to load the reference to DAO (Data Access Objects) 2.5. If you know that you will be referencing database objects in the project, click the Add button. If you know that your program does not need DAO 2.5 for anything, click Don't Add. If you are not sure, click the Don't Add button. Now when you try to compile, an error will occur. If the error occurs, you will need to add the reference manually. To add this reference, choose Tools | References and then click on Microsoft DOA 2.5 Object Library for 16-bit projects or Microsoft DAO 3.0 Object Library for 32-bit projects. Then click the OK button.

10. After you tell the project whether to reference DAO 2.5 and the project finishes loading, the last step in the conversion is to choose File | Save Project to upgrade the project to 16-bit Visual Basic 4.0. Or, you can choose File | Save Project As, which displays the dialog box shown in Figure 36.6. This dialog box prompts you for each file in the project.

Figure 36.6.
The save file as
dialog box.

11. You have four options in this dialog box: Yes, No, No to All, and Cancel. To update the file to 16-bit Visual Basic 4.0, click Yes. To not save the current file, click No. To not save any other files still to be saved, click No to All. If you want to cancel the process at any time, click the Cancel button to return to the environment.

If you try to close the environment without saving the project first, the save changes dialog box appears, prompting you to save your changes. After you save the project to the Visual Basic 4.0 16-bit application, you will never need to go through this process again for the current project.

After all the files are saved, you need to save the old format and naming convention .MAK file. I suggest leaving the file with the same name but changing the extension to .VBP for *Visual Basic Project*; this way, you will be using the new naming convention.

Some 32-Bit Issues

You need to be aware of a few things when you are porting over to the 32-bit environment.

First, all 16-bit APIs must be redeclared to their 32-bit equivalent or you will be unable to run the ported project. Usually, this means that you must change the name and then change all the Integer parameters to be Long parameter types. For more information on the available 32-bit APIs and the declarations for these APIs, refer to the API Text Viewer that is shipped with Visual Basic 4.0. To open this program, run the file apilod32.EXE, located in the winapi directory of your Visual Basic 32 install, or click the API TEXT VIEWER icon located in the 32 Visual Basic program group. This opens the API Viewer, as shown in Figure 36.7, which enables you to open any of the available API text files for viewing.

Figure 36.7.
The API Viewer.

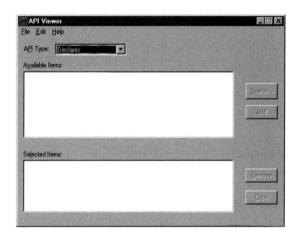

If the file you are opening is a text file, and it is the first time you are opening this text file during this session, you are prompted to convert the text file into a database file for searching purposes. If you click Yes, an Access 95 database is built based on the text file you just opened. Do not worry about a backup because the viewer does not touch the original file. After you open the file, you can select as many APIs at a time as you want. To select an API, double-click the name from the Available Items listbox or select the name and then click the Add button. After you add an API to the Selected Items listbox, you can click the Copy button. This copies the declaration required for this API to the Clipboard. Figure 36.8 shows you what the Viewer looks like when it has multiple APIs in the Selected Items listbox.

Figure 36.8.
*The Text API Viewer
with selected APIs.*

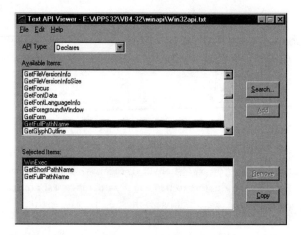

After you have selected all the APIs you want to use, click the Copy button to copy the items to the Clipboard. Then paste the copied information into the module of Visual Basic. For more information on APIs, refer to Chapter 6, "Using the Win95/Win32 API."

Make sure that all the equivalent OCXs for the presently used VBXs are installed and registered. You must do this, or you will not be able to port the project over to 32-bit Visual Basic.

A workaround is available to convert the project if you do not have all the OCXs required for conversion, but it is a bit awkward. First, load the project into 16-bit Visual Basic 4.0 if you have it available. This enables you to change all the old VBXs over to other OCXs that will function in a similar fashion for you. You then will be able to convert the project over to the 32-bit environment. This is not the best answer, but it works if you cannot find the equivalent OCXs for the current VBXs.

Summary

This chapter gives you an idea of the steps required to convert a project that was saved in an earlier version of Visual Basic to either the 16-bit or the 32-bit of Visual Basic 4.0.

Cross-Platform Development

by Dwayne R. Gifford

CHAPTER 37

The last few chapters have discussed converting code from Visual Basic 3.0 to Visual Basic 4.0, based upon whether you wanted to create 32-bit applications or 16-bit applications. This chapter focuses on new application development. It is specifically designed to help the developers and project managers consider the implications of cross-platform development with Visual Basic 4.0.

Cross-platform development is defined as the methods undertaken to write programs that can run on more than one platform. In this context, *platforms* refer to different operating systems, specifically Windows 3.*x*, Windows 95, and Windows NT. (In other contexts, *cross-platform development* can imply different hardware as well, such as writing a C program that can be compiled either on a mainframe, mini-computer, or PC workstation.) If you plan on marketing your program, cross-platform development can increase your market by ensuring that your program runs on multiple platforms. In other contexts, people choose to develop for multiple platforms just to give their users products that perform better or otherwise take advantage of operating system features.

When code can be transferred from one platform to another by using a compiler specific to that platform, the code is said to be *portable*. Applications can achieve different levels of portability, based roughly on how much work it will take to get the program to compile on each platform. This chapter defines levels of portability relevant to Visual Basic 4.0 and the Windows operating systems, and helps the project manager and programmer decide upon a level of portability that may best suit a particular project.

Finally, this chapter offers a set of development guidelines specific to concerns for portability. These include analysis guidelines, development practices, and testing considerations.

Examining Portability

You can make your application portable across different platforms in many ways. The amount of time you want to spend creating a portable application will determine the completeness of the portability.

Much the same as any area of programming, the more features that need to be in the final product, the more time will need to be spent creating the product. For example, in Visual Basic, you can very quickly make a database application using the Data Form designer. In less than two minutes, you can build a complete, functioning editing form for your database. However, if you desire better and different features than are provided by the Data Form wizard, you'll need to spend some time (more than two minutes) adding in the desired features.

Similarly, creating an application that simply runs in all Windows environments is very easy. Creating an application that uses the specific features of each version of Windows takes a little more effort.

The following sections discuss levels of portability relevant to Windows platforms. Three levels of portability are considered: strict compatibility, complete portability, and partial portability.

Strict Compatibility: Using the Same .EXE

This is not really portability as much as it is compatibility. Because all versions of Windows are backward-compatible (or nearly so), it follows that compiling for the lowest common denominator will produce an application that runs on all platforms. Thus, you can make a 16-bit version of your program, and it will run on Windows 3.x, Windows NT 3.x, and Windows 95. The files you would distribute with your application would be the 16-bit versions of the OCXs that your application uses.

Unfortunately, this solution is far from ideal. In order for 32-bit operating systems to run 16-bit applications, the applications go through a "thunking" process to make your application believe that it is making 16-bit calls to the Windows API rather than 32-bit calls. In many cases, the result is that the application runs more slowly on the 32-bit platform than on the 16-bit platform.

Besides performance considerations, another reason this is undesirable is that the user interface is only as advanced as Windows 3.1x. Because Windows 3.1x is the final version of 16-bit Windows, no features of later versions have been implemented for 16-bit platforms.

It's also worth noting that you could have done this in Visual Basic 3.0; choosing this approach ignores all of the cool 32-bit features found in VB4.

Complete Portability: Same Code

This is the portability that Microsoft advertises, and it is really pretty good. In fact, it's the highest level of portability discussed here. You'll need to own the Professional or Enterprise Edition of Visual Basic, because the Standard Edition does not compile for the 16-bit environment. You'll also need to conform to some limitations in the design of your application, which are discussed later in this chapter.

Once you are ready to make two versions of your code, you'll simply run 16-bit VB to make one executable, and 32-bit VB to make another executable. Voila—a portable application. Well, it's almost that easy; you may have to mark certain lines of your code as being specific to either the 16-bit or 32-bit environment. Overall, the portability process is quite simple in its basic form. You'll have a 32-bit application to distribute for everyone on the newer operating systems, while not forcing the 16-bit users to have to upgrade just to run your application.

Because the code must be portable, your application will not be able to have any platform-specific features. For example, you won't be able to take advantage of the briefcase replication services in Window 95, because this service does not exist on Windows 3.x or Windows NT 3.x. If platform-specific features are a requirement for your application, it is necessary to look at another degree of portability.

Partial Portability

Achieving a high level of portability does not mean that all of your users will be happy. (More likely, your manager will be happy because you didn't have to spend much time to make an application operate on three separate platforms.)

One reason your users might not be happy is that your application might not look very integrated into the platform. Specifically, your Windows 95 users might notice that the application lacks some of the neat features available in other Windows 95 applications, such as the way folders can be viewed in four different styles, or that the Tree View control doesn't look as slick as the one that Explorer has.

The reason that your application cannot have these controls is that they are available only in the 32-bit environment, and there is no direct equivalent for 16-bit platforms. Thus, you could not compile your application to run on Windows 3.*x* platforms.

If it is important to provide features in your program unique to the target platform, while maintaining the capability to compile the program across different platforms, you'll need to consider *partial portability*. Partial portability implies that while the majority of files are common across all platforms, some files are unique to each platform. In terms of Visual Basic, you would maintain a .VBP project file for each platform, but most of the entries in these project files would point to common files.

In many cases, the design will specify for one or more primary forms to include unique elements, while the lesser-used dialog boxes will be satisfactory using common controls. The .BAS modules will likely be common. An example of such a program is the Partially Portable program, included on the CD-ROM that comes with this book. This program has two versions: 16-bit and 32-bit. The 32-bit version uses custom controls available in Windows 95 and Windows NT versions 3.51 and higher. PP16.VBP is the project for 16-bit windows, and PP32 is the project for 32-bit windows.

The program is small but is intended to demonstrate that partial portability can be achieved without a great deal of recoding. By grouping the majority of the code into common .BAS modules, much of the work of creating a separate, duplicate form is reduced. In addition, the programs will give you some idea of how applications will look different under different environments. The following figures help demonstrate this point.

Figure 37.1 shows how the sample 32-bit version of the program looks in the Windows 95 environment.

Figure 37.1.
PP32 running in Windows 95.

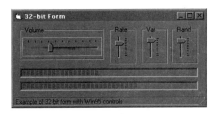

Figure 37.2 shows how the 16-bit version of the program looks under Windows 95. While the controls have less of a high-tech look, the functionality is still obviously identical to the 32-bit version.

Figure 37.2.
PP16 running in Windows 95.

Figure 37.3 shows the 32-bit version under Windows NT 3.51. All of the Windows 95 custom controls function in NT 3.51.

Figure 37.3.
PP32 running in Windows NT 3.51.

Finally, Figure 37.4 shows the 16-bit version under NT 3.51. Since Windows 3.*x* and Windows NT share a very similar interface, you can expect that the program will appear nearly identical on the 16-bit Windows 3.*x* platform.

Figure 37.4.
PP16 running in Windows NT 3.51.

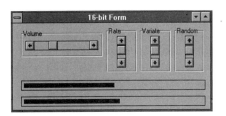

The code to develop this program is included on the CD-ROM that comes with this book. The names of the directories indicate the portability of the files within, as indicated in Table 37.1.

Table 37.1. Files used in the Partially Portable program.

\Partially Portable Program	pp16.vbp	16-bit	The 16-bit VB project file.
\Partially Portable Program	pp32.vbp	32-bit	The 32-bit VB project file.
\Partially Portable Program	PP16.exe		The 16-bit executable.
\Partially Portable Program	pp32.exe		The 32-bit executable.
\Partially Portable Program\ 16-bit specific forms	Gauge16.Frm		Primary form for the 16-bit project.
\Partially Portable Program\ 32-bit specific forms	Gauge32.frm		Primary form for the 32-bit project.
\Partially Portable Program\ for 32-bit specific forms	Gauge32.frx		Binary form file the 32-bit project. .FRX files are created automatically as needed.
\Partially Portable Program\ screen Forms Common	Welcome.frm	Common	The "splash" introducing the partially portable program.
\Partially Portable Program\ Code Common	Main.bas		The common code.

Target Operating Systems

To evaluate the task of writing portable code, it's important to understand the general differences between Windows 3.*x*, Windows 95, and Windows NT 3.51.

Windows 3.*x* is a 16-bit platform. Windows 95 and Windows NT 3.51 (and higher) are both 32-bit platforms. The 32-bit platforms offer greater functionality than do their 16-bit predecessors. In addition to the architectural differences between the operating systems, there is also a difference in the graphical user interface (GUI).

The latest version of the 16-bit Windows 3.*x* platform is Windows for Workgroups 3.11, introduced in 1993. This platform uses an interface that is quite similar to the original Windows 3.0 interface that arrived in 1990.

Windows NT has a very similar interface to Windows for Workgroups 3.11. Windows NT, however, is a high-end operating system, capable of hosting sophisticated services such as SQL Server, advanced file and print sharing services, as well as Internet and other communications services. In addition, there are different versions of Windows NT for different processors.

Windows 95 is the 32-bit upgrade for users of Windows for Workgroups 3.11. It sports a greatly advanced user interface that is the result of several years of research by Microsoft.

GUI Differences

The Graphical User Interface (GUI) in each version of Windows provides a number of built-in controls with the operating system. For example, each version has a built-in listbox, text box, and a number of other controls. You don't have to provide OCX files to supply these controls; they are built into Windows. The GUI for Windows 3.*x* and Windows NT 3.*x* are nearly identical. The same controls are available for each operating system; these controls are listed in Table 37.2.

Windows 95 (and future versions of Windows) are based upon a significantly advanced interface. All of the controls built into prior versions of Windows are supported. In addition, a number of new controls are built-in, as well. Table 37.2 lists these controls, as well as controls with similar functionality in the 16-bit platform. Note that all of the Windows 95 controls will also function on Windows NT 3.51 or higher.

Table 37.2. Windows 95 controls.

Table	Class Name	Description	Similar 16-bit Controls
Table	ImageList	A helper control that acts as a storehouse for bitmap images. These images can then be applied to other controls.	None, but the PLIST control can be coded for similar functionality.
Table	ListView	A list that can display items in one of four different views. The best example of a ListView object is the file display in the Windows 95 Explorer.	None
Table	ProgressBar	Used to display the progress of a potentially long task; can also function as a "gas gauge" to display a nonspecific visual measurement of quantity.	Some third-party controls implement this functionality.

continues

Table 37.2. continued

Table	Class Name	Description	Similar 16-bit Controls
Table	RichTextBox	Similar to the existing TextBox control, the RichTextBox control allows formatting of individual characters in the box. The RichTextBox allows retrieval of data in both ASCII and Rich Text Format.	Some third-party controls implement this functionality.
Table	Slider	A slider with optional tick marks. This is often used in multimedia applications as a volume control. It can be used in any situation where nonspecific visual settings of quantity are desired.	The horizontal scrollbar is typically used for this functionality.
Table	StatusBar	A control that provides a window with up to 16 panel objects. These panels are usually used to display status information at the bottom of the screen.	Individual panel controls are usually used for this functionality.
Table	TabStrip	Creates a visual folder containing pages with index tabs. This metaphor has become quite popular in graphical user interfaces.	Many tab controls are available, including SSTab, which comes with VB.
Table	ToolBar	Implements a collection of buttons, usually used as an application toolbar.	A fixed toolbar can be implemented programmatically, or third-party controls are available.
Table	TreeView	Creates a visual tree representing a hierarchical structure via branches and nodes.	The Microsoft Outline control has similar functionality.

If you intend to design a form that will run across all platforms, it is important to avoid using operating-system specific controls.

Operating System Services

Besides exploiting features of the GUI, there are other reasons you might wish to build a specific version for a particular operating system. There might be a particular feature you would like to take advantage of in an operating system. For example, you might want to make use of the briefcase replication services if the user happens to be running Windows 95, but not if the user is running Windows NT 3.51.

Specific Development Guidelines

When you are developing new applications, there are several considerations to make regarding portability.

Analysis Considerations

Following is a list of tips you should keep in mind while designing a new application:

- *Knowledge of target platforms.* Be sure to know all about the possible target platforms. Know which services each offers, and what the differences are between the graphical user interfaces.

- *Consider available services.* Consider the available services when you are analyzing user requirements. Perhaps the existence of a service such as replication would replace a great deal of coding.

- *Consider separate utilities.* If a particular portion of the program needs access to services that are not available on all platforms, consider whether or not that portion of the program is integral to the application, or if it could be developed as a separate utility and run only on a particular platform.

- *Security implications.* Because different operating systems handle security differently, take care to understand how security might work on each different platform.

Development Considerations

Following aresome development considerations you should keep in mind:

- *Use compiler directives.* VB 4 has a number of compiler directives to determine which code is relevant on each platform. When there is a portion of the code that will be relevant only in the 16-bit environment, use a statement as follows:

```
#If Win16 Then
    ' Place 16-bit statements here
#ElseIf Win32 Then
    '. Place exclusively 32-bit Windows statements here.
#Else
    '. Place other platform statements here.
#End If
```

■ *Group common code.* When different forms are used for different platforms, try to consolidate as much common code as possible into .BAS modules. Leave the logic that is specific to a particular form in the .FRM file. Typically, you will want to move initialization logic such as populating a listbox out to .BAS files. Control-specific initialization can either stay inside the form and be activated by events, or else they can be encapsulated in `#If...#End If` compiler directives.

■ *Note database ramifications.* The 16-bit version of VB uses the Jet 2.5 library, whereas the 32-bit VB uses the Jet 3.0 library. If you need to have databases accessed by both platforms, you'll need to use the Jet 2.5 database. The Jet 2.5 engine is not capable of reading databases created with Jet 3.0. This also affects the availability of features found only in the Jet 3.0 engine, such as database replication.

■ *Consider file system differences.* Be aware of filename length restrictions in 16-bit Windows. Equally important is to note the much looser restrictions in 32-bit Windows. It is no longer valid to assume that all filenames have up to eight characters, followed by a period, and then an extension of up to three characters.

Testing Considerations

It might be wise to invest in an automated testing tool, such as Microsoft Test. Running the same test script across all supported platforms will help to identify any inconsistencies or incompatibilities that might be unique to one particular platform.

Documentation

As mightbe evident from the pictures of the sample application, your application will have a different look and feel, depending upon the target platform. User documentation should comment on how the application can differ depending upon the platform.

Summary

Portability can take different forms, so when someone asks you to write a portable application, make sure you know what you're getting yourself into! Consider the target operating systems, understanding both the differences in architecture as well as the differences in user interfaces.

If you do have to develop partially portable programs, try to maximize the amount of common code, so that you minimize any duplication of effort.

Also, remember to thoroughly test portable applications. The subtle differences between operating systems may cause your application to behave differently on different platforms.

SYMBOLS

INDEX

Add to Your Sams Library Today with the Best Books for Programming, Operating Systems, and New Technologies

The easiest way to order is to pick up the phone and call

1-800-428-5331

between 9:00 a.m. and 5:00 p.m. EST.

For faster service please have your credit card available.

ISBN	Quantity	Description of Item	Unit Cost	Total Cost
0-672-30791-X		Peter Norton's Complete Guide to Windows 95	$39.99	
0-672-30837-1		Visual Basic 4 Unleashed (Book/CD)	$45.00	
0-672-30602-6		Programming Windows 95 Unleashed (Book/CD)	$49.99	
0-672-30796-0		Visual Basic 4 Performance Tuning and Optimization (Book/CD)	$49.99	
0-672-30779-0		Real-World Programming with Visual Basic 4, 2E (Book/CD)	$45.00	
0-57521-041-X		The Internet Unleashed 1996 (Book/CD)	$49.99	
0-672-30737-5		The World Wide Web Unleashed, 2E	$39.99	
1-57521-064-9		Teach Yourself Web Publishing with HTML 3.0 in a Week, 2E	$29.99	
0-672-30609-3		Teach Yourself ODBC Programming in 21 Days	$29.99	
1-57521-005-3		Teach Yourself More Web Publishing with HTML in a Week	$29.99	
❏ 3 ½" Disk		Shipping and Handling: See information below.		
❏ 5 ¼" Disk		TOTAL		

Shipping and Handling: $4.00 for the first book, and $1.75 for each additional book. Floppy disk: add $1.75 for shipping and handling. If you need to have it NOW, we can ship product to you in 24 hours for an additional charge of approximately $18.00, and you will receive your item overnight or in two days. Overseas shipping and handling adds $2.00 per book and $8.00 for up to three disks. Prices subject to change. Call for availability and pricing information on latest editions.

201 W. 103rd Street, Indianapolis, Indiana 46290

1-800-428-5331 — Orders   1-800-835-3202 — FAX   1-800-858-7674 — Customer Service

Book ISBN 0-672-30929-7

Special VBNet Upgrade Offer!

Get your app on the Web with VBnet 2.0 for only $129!

(Over 30% Savings! Regular Price $197)

Visual Basic Application ➡ Internet Application

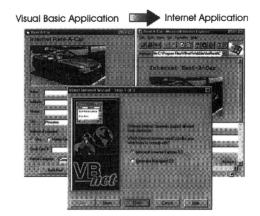

Get running on the Web!

Got your Visual Basic Form on the Web with VBnet™ 1.0? Now you can leverage your Visual Basic skills to develop database-aware client/server applications for the Internet. With VBnet 2.0, the new add-in for Visual Basic 4.0 from TVObjects™ Corporation, VB programs are converted quickly and easily to Web-ready applications. No need to spend time learning Internet languages or protocols—the VBnet Internet Wizard guides you step-by-step through the generation process.

Client/Server Productivity for the Web

VBnet supports Web ODBC database access, HTML 3.0, custom controls, and works with Microsoft Internet Explorer and NetScape Navigator and generates ActiveX controls, VBScript and JavaScript-enabled Web pages.

VBnet 2.0 also includes

- a FREE VBScript Syntax Checker!
- Comprehensive reporting
- Support for Internet standard image formats

Subscribe now and save!

Call for details about our new VBnet Subscription Plan. Subscribers will receive for the year: Unlimited Technical Support; 3 VBnet releases (including at least one major release), TVObjects Quarterly Customer Newsletter, Subscriber-Only Promotional Offers.

Yes!

I am interested in saving *over 30%*!
Please contact me.

Name:_____

Company:_____

Phone:_____

Fax:_____

E-Mail Address:_____

The Enterprise Broadcasting Company™
29 Emmons Drive • Princeton, NJ 08540
Phone: 609-514-1444 • Fax: 609-514-1004

Fax this form to
609-514-1004
or call **1-800-85VBNET**

Limited Time Offer!
Prices subject to change.

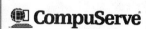

CD INSTALL

What's on the Disc

The companion CD-ROM contains all the source code and project files developed by the authors, plus an assortment of evaluation versions of third-party tools. The disc is designed to be explored using a browser program. Using the browser, you can view information concerning products and companies and install programs with a single click of the mouse. To install the browser, here's what to do:

Windows 3.1/NT Installation Instructions

1. Insert the CD-ROM disc into your CD-ROM drive.
2. From File Manager or Program Manager, choose Run from the File menu.
3. Type `<drive>\setup` and press Enter, where `<drive>` corresponds to the drive letter of your CD-ROM. For example, if your CD-ROM is drive D:, type `D:\SETUP` and press Enter.
4. Installation creates a program manager group named VB4 Tricks. To browse the CD-ROM, double-click on the Guide to the CD-ROM icon inside this program manager group.

Windows 95 Installation Instructions

1. Insert the CD-ROM disc into your CD-ROM drive.
2. From the Windows 95 desktop, double-click on the My Computer icon.
3. Double-click on the icon representing your CD-ROM drive.
4. Double-click on the icon titled Setup.exe to run the installation program.
5. Installation creates a program group named VB4 Tricks. To browse the CD-ROM, press the Start button and select Programs. Then choose VB4 Tricks, followed by Guide to the CD-ROM to run the browser program.

The browser program requires at least 256 colors. For best results, set your monitor to display between 256 and 64,000 colors. A screen resolution of 640×480 pixels is also recommended. If necessary, adjust your monitor settings before using the CD-ROM.